Frommer's®

Northern Italy

with Venice, Milan & the Lakes

5th Edition

by John Moretti

WILEY

Wiley Publishing, Inc.

Published by:

WILEY PUBLISHING, INC.

111 River St.
Hoboken, NJ 07030-5774

ISBN 978-0-470-49732-6

Editor: Jennifer Polland
Production Editor: Heather Wilcox
Cartographer: Guy Ruggiero
Photo Editor: Richard Fox
Production by Wiley Indianapolis Composition Services

Front cover photo: Mountain village of St Magdalena, Le Odle mountains, Val di Funes, South Tirol, Alto Adige Dolomites, Italy © Rainer Jahns/Alamy Images
Back cover photo: Grand Canal and Santa Maria della Salute overlook Venice's Grand Canal at twilight, Venice © Guido Cozzi/Atlantide Phototravel/Corbis

For information on our other products and services or to obtain technical support, please contact our Customer Care Department within the U.S. at 877/762-2974, outside the U.S. at 317/572-3993 or fax 317/572-4002.

Wiley also publishes its books in a variety of electronic formats. Some content that appears in print may not be available in electronic formats.

Manufactured in the United States of America

5 4 3 2 1

CONTENTS

4 SUGGESTED ITINERARIES IN NORTHERN ITALY   80

5 VENICE   91

6 THE VENETO   174

7 TRENTINO–ALTO ADIGE: THE DOLOMITES & SOUTH TIROL — 223

8 FRIULI-VENEZIA GIULIA — 255

9 MILAN & LOMBARDY — 271

10 THE LAKES — 321

11 PIEDMONT & THE VALLE D'AOSTA — 348

12 LIGURIA & THE ITALIAN RIVIERA 384

13 FAST FACTS 435

14 USEFUL TERMS 441

INDEX 454

LIST OF MAPS

ABOUT THE AUTHOR

John Moretti is a freelance writer whose musings about Italy have appeared in the *International Herald Tribune, The Independent on Sunday,* and the *New York Sun,* among others. He is the author of several travel guides and a book for aspiring expatriates, *Living Abroad in Italy.* His career highlights include interviewing Giorgio Armani for A&E Biography, producing a documentary on Italian soccer for Australian television, singing on tour with a Franciscan monk and his evangelical heavy-metal band, and following his favorite sporting event, the Tour de France. He grew up outside Boston and is a graduate of Middlebury College.

HOW TO CONTACT US

In researching this book, we discovered many wonderful places—hotels, restaurants, shops, and more. We're sure you'll find others. Please tell us about them, so we can share the information with your fellow travelers in upcoming editions. If you were disappointed with a recommendation, we'd love to know that, too. Please write to:

Frommer's Northern Italy, 5th Edition
Wiley Publishing, Inc. • 111 River St. • Hoboken, NJ 07030-5774

AN ADDITIONAL NOTE

Please be advised that travel information is subject to change at any time—and this is especially true of prices. We therefore suggest that you write or call ahead for confirmation when making your travel plans. The authors, editors, and publisher cannot be held responsible for the experiences of readers while traveling. Your safety is important to us, however, so we encourage you to stay alert and be aware of your surroundings. Keep a close eye on cameras, purses, and wallets, all favorite targets of thieves and pickpockets.

FROMMER'S STAR RATINGS, ICONS & ABBREVIATIONS

Every hotel, restaurant, and attraction listing in this guide has been ranked for quality, value, service, amenities, and special features using a **star-rating system.** In country, state, and regional guides, we also rate towns and regions to help you narrow down your choices and budget your time accordingly. Hotels and restaurants are rated on a scale of zero (recommended) to three stars (exceptional). Attractions, shopping, nightlife, towns, and regions are rated according to the following scale: zero stars (recommended), one star (highly recommended), two stars (very highly recommended), and three stars (must-see).

In addition to the star-rating system, we also use **seven feature icons** that point you to the great deals, in-the-know advice and unique experiences that separate travelers from tourists. Throughout the book, look for:

(Finds)	Special finds—those places only insiders know about
(Fun Facts)	Fun facts—details that make travelers more informed and their trips more fun
(Kids)	Best bets for kids, and advice for the whole family
(Moments)	Special moments—those experiences that memories are made of
(Overrated)	Places or experiences not worth your time or money
(Tips)	Insider tips—great ways to save time and money
(Value)	Great values—where to get the best deals

The following **abbreviations** are used for credit cards:

AE American Express	**DISC** Discover	**V** Visa
DC Diners Club	**MC** MasterCard	

TRAVEL RESOURCES AT FROMMERS.COM

Frommer's travel resources don't end with this guide. Frommer's website, **www.frommers.com**, has travel information on more than 4,000 destinations. We update features regularly, giving you access to the most current trip-planning information and the best airfare, lodging, and car-rental bargains. You can also listen to podcasts, connect with other Frommers.com members through our active-reader forums, share your travel photos, read blogs from guidebook editors and fellow travelers, and much more.

The Best of Northern Italy

Northern Italy's riches are vast, varied, and yours to discover, from art-packed museums and mosaic-filled cathedrals to Roman ruins and hill towns amid vineyards that produce some of Europe's best wines. You can dine at refined restaurants that casually flaunt their Michelin star ratings, or chow down with the town priest and police chief at *osterie* (small local eateries) that have spent generations perfecting traditional recipes. You can spend the night in a sumptuous Renaissance villa on Lake Como in the Alpine foothills where Napoleon once stayed (the Villa d'Este), or in a converted 17th-century Venetian *palazzo* where the room opens directly onto the Grand Canal. Here's a short list of the best of what northern Italy has to offer.

1 THE BEST TRAVEL EXPERIENCES

- **Taking a Gondola Ride in Venice:** Yes, it looks hokey. Yes, it's way overpriced. But when it comes down to it, there's nothing quite so romantic after a long Venetian dinner as a ride on one of these long black skiffs. Settle back into the plush seats with that special someone and a bottle of wine, and slide through the waters of Venice's back canals guided by the expert oar of a gondolier. See p. 100.
- **Spending a Day Among the Islands of the Venetian Lagoon:** Venice's ferry system extends outside the city proper to a series of other inhabited islands in the lagoon. First stop, Murano, a village where the famed local glass-blowing industry began and where its largest factories and best artisans still reside. Not only can you tour a glass factory (complete with a hard sell in the display room at the end), but you'll discover a pair of lovely churches, one hung with paintings by Giovanni Bellini, Veronese, and Tintoretto, the other a Byzantine-Romanesque masterpiece of decoration. The isle of Burano is a colorful fishing

village with an ancient lace-making tradition and houses in a variety of supersaturated hues. Nearby, lonely Torcello may have been one of the first lagoon islands settled, but it's long been almost abandoned, home to a straggly vineyard, reed-banked canals, the fine Cipriani restaurant, and a stunning Byzantine cathedral swathed in mosaics (see "The Best Churches," below). Time it right, and you'll be riding the last ferry back from Torcello into Venice proper as the sun sets and lights up the lagoon waters. See p. 172.
- **Cruising the Brenta Canal:** The lazy Brenta Canal, lacing its way into the Veneto from Venice's lagoon, has long been the Hamptons of Venice, where the city's nobility and merchant princes have kept summer villas. From the massive, palatial Villa Pisani, with its elaborate gardens, to the Villa Foscari, designed by Palladio himself, most of these villas span the 16th to 19th centuries and are open to visitors. In the past few years, a few have even been opened as elegant hotels. There are two ways to

tour the Brenta: on a leisurely full-day cruise between Padua and Venice, stopping to tour several villas along the way with an optional fish lunch; or by driving yourself along the banks, which allows you to pop into the villas you are most interested in—plus you can pull over at any grassy embankment for a picnic lunch on the canal. See p. 187.

- **Driving the Great Dolomite Road:** From the Adige Valley outside Bolzano (Bozen in German) across to the ski resort of Cortina d'Ampezzo runs 110km (68 miles) of twisting, winding, switch-backed highway, called the Great Dolomite Road, which wends its way around some of the most dramatic mountain scenery in Italy. The Dolomiti are craggier and sheerer than the Alps, and as this road crawls around the peaks and climbs over the passes, one breathtaking panorama after another opens before you, undulating to the distant Po plains to the south and to the mighty Swiss Alps to the north. See p. 248.

- **Riding the Cable Cars over Mont Blanc:** There are not many more dramatic trips in Europe than this one, where a series of cable cars and gondolas rise from Courmayeur in the Valle d'Aosta to the 3,300m (10,824-ft.) Punta Helbronner, from which the icy vistas spread over Mont Blanc's flank in one direction and across to Monte Cervina (the Matterhorn) in the other. It is here that the true thrill ride begins as you clamber into a four-seat enclosed gondola that dangles from a trio of stout cables some 2.4km (1½ miles)

above the deep fissures of the Vallée Blanche glacier. It takes half an hour to cross to Aiguille du Midi on French soil—the longest cable car ride in the world not supported by pylons. From here, you can take a jaunt down into France's charming Chamonix if you'd like, or turn around to head back into Italian territory, perhaps stopping at the Alpine Garden two-thirds of the way back to Courmayeur to sun yourself and admire the wildflowers. See p. 381.

- **Hiking the Cinque Terre:** At the southern end of the Italian Riviera lies a string of former pirate coves called the Cinque Terre. These five fishing villages are linked by a local train line and a meandering trail that clambers over headlands, plunges amid olive groves and vineyards, and skirts cliff edges above the glittering Ligurian Sea and hidden scraps of beach. The villages also share an excellent communal white wine. Though tourists are discovering this magical corner of Italy, there are as yet no big resort hotels or overdevelopment, just *trattorie* on the tiny harbors and houses and apartments converted into small family hotels and short-term rental units. It takes a full, long day to hike from one end to the other, or you can simply walk the stretches you prefer (conveniently, the trails get progressively easier from north to south) and use the train to connect to the other towns. Pause as you like in the *osterie* and bars of each town to sample the dry Cinque Terre white wine and refresh yourself for the next stretch. See p. 426.

2 THE BEST MUSEUMS

- **Galleria dell'Accademia** (Venice): The single most important gallery of Venetian painting and one of Italy's top museums was founded in 1750 and gorgeously installed in this trio of

Renaissance buildings by Napoleon himself in 1807. (Napoleon swelled the collections with altarpieces confiscated from churches and monasteries he suppressed.) The works, spanning the 13th through 18th centuries, include masterpieces by all the local northern Italian greats—the Bellini clan, Paolo Veneziano, Carpaccio, Giorgione, Mantegna, Piero della Francesca, Lorenzo Lotto, Palma il Vecchio, Paolo Veronese, Titian, Tintoretto, Tiepolo, and Canaletto. See p. 151.

- **Collezione Peggy Guggenheim** (Venice): The Guggenheim family was among the 20th century's greatest art patrons. Peggy not only amassed a stunning collection of modern art; she even married Max Ernst. Her half-finished 18th-century *palazzo* on the Grand Canal is now installed with her collections, including works by Picasso, Pollock (an artist Peggy "discovered"), Magritte, Dalí, Miró, Brancusi, Kandinsky, and Marini. See p. 150.

- **South Tyrol Museum of Archaeology** (Bolzano): Bolzano's major sight is a high-tech, modern museum crafted around one of the most important archaeological finds of the past 50 years. When hikers first discovered the body of Ötzi high in the Alps at the Austrian border, everyone thought he was a mountaineer who had succumbed to the elements. He turned out to be a 5,300-year-old hunter whose body, clothing, and tools had been preserved intact by the ice in which he was frozen. The Ice Man has done more to give us glimpses into daily life in the Stone Age than any other find, and the museum excels at relaying all that scientists are still learning from him. See p. 234.

- **Pinacoteca di Brera** (Milan): One of Italy's finest collections of art, from

medieval to modern, is housed in a 17th-century Milanese *palazzo*. Venice's Accademia may have a richer collection of Venetian art, but the Brera has a broader collection of masterpieces from across northern and central Italy. As with the Accademia, the Brera started as a warehouse for artworks Napoleon looted from churches, monasteries, and private collections. There are masterpieces from Mantegna, Raphael, Piero della Francesca, the Bellinis, Signorelli, Titian, Tintoretto, Reni, Caravaggio, Tiepolo, and Canaletto, and great works by 20th-century geniuses such as Umberto Boccioni, Gino Severini, Giorgio Morandi, and Giorgio de Chirico. They even throw in some works by Rembrandt, Goya, and Reynolds. See p. 282.

- **Museo Egizio & Galleria Sabauda** (Turin): The world's first real museum of Egyptian artifacts remains one of the most important outside Cairo and London's British Museum. The history between Italy and Egypt dates back to Julius Caesar and Cleopatra, though this collection of 30,000 pieces was largely amassed by the Piedmont Savoy kings. The exhibits range from a papyrus *Book of the Dead* to a full 15th-century-B.C. temple to fascinating objects from everyday life. But Egypt isn't all; upstairs the Galleria Sabauda displays the Savoys' amazing collection of Flemish and Dutch paintings by Van Dyck, van Eyck, Rembrandt, Hans Memling, and Van der Weyden. See p. 356.

3 THE BEST CHURCHES

- **Basilica di San Marco** (Venice): No church in Europe is more lavishly decorated, more exquisitely mosaic-covered, more glittering with gold than Venice's

San Marco. Built in the 11th century, the church has as its guiding architectural and decorative principles Byzantine style, but more than 7 centuries of expansion and decoration have left behind Romanesque and Gothic touches as well. The interior is encrusted with more than 3,700 sq. m (39,826 sq. ft.) of gold-backed mosaics crafted between the 12th and 17th centuries, some based on cartoons by Tintoretto, Veronese, and Titian. The uneven floor is a mosaic of marble chips in swirling patterns, the Pala d'Oro altarpiece a gem-studded golden trophy from Constantinople. Stairs lead up to a view over the piazza from atop the atrium, where visitors get to see up close both the mosaics and the original *Triumphal Quadriga,* four massive bronze horses probably cast in the 2nd century A.D. See p. 142.

- **Santa Maria Gloriosa dei Frari** (Venice): "I Frari" is named for the Franciscan "brothers" who founded this Gothic giant in 1250. It was rebuilt between 1330 and 1453, which made it one of the most art-bedecked churches in Venice, filled with works of art by Donatello, Titian, Giovanni Bellini, and Canova. See p. 157.

- **Cattedrale di Torcello** (Torcello, Venice): Venice's oldest church is pretty much all that remains of one of the lagoon's earliest settlements on the all-but-abandoned island of Torcello, north of what is now the city of Venice. Santa Maria Assunta was begun in the 7th century, its interior slathered with glittering gold-backed Byzantine mosaics in the 11th and 12th centuries, precursors to those that would later decorate Venice's San Marco. The inside of the entrance wall is filled with a massive *Last Judgment.* This was a common device in medieval churches: placing above the door from which parishioners would exit a scene depicting both the heavenly rewards that await the faithful and the horribly inventive, gruesome punishments for the damned in hell—sort of a final sermon at the end of the

service to remind everyone what was at stake and to keep them holy until the next Sunday. The bell tower offers a pretty panorama over the sparsely populated island and surrounding lagoon. See p. 173.

- **Basilica di Sant'Antonio** (Padua): Think of all the people of Italian descent you know, or have heard of, named Tony. You're starting to get an idea of how popular the 13th-century, Portuguese-born St. Anthony is among Italians. The patron of the lost lived in Padua, and when he died in 1231, the citizenry quickly canonized the man and began building this huge church to honor his remains. It was finished in a remarkably short 76 years. The style in 13th-century Veneto was still largely Byzantine, so the brick basilica is topped by an octet of domes and twin minaret-style bell towers. Donatello, whose *Gattamelata* (the first large equestrian bronze cast since ancient Roman times) sits out front, even crafted the high altar, but that is virtually ignored by the flocks of faithful in favor of a chapel off the left aisle. This is where a constant stream of supplicants files past the saint's tomb to press their palms against it and leave flowers, small gifts, pictures, and written prayers asking him to help them find everything from lost health to lost love to lost children (some even pray for material objects, but rarely). Il Santo's robes are also preserved here, as are the silver-tongued preacher's miraculously preserved jawbone, vocal chords, and tongue, all kept in a chapel behind the high altar. See p. 181.

- **Basilica San Zeno Maggiore** (Verona): Verona is home to perhaps the greatest Romanesque basilica in all of northern Italy, a stunning example of the early medieval sculptor's art. Between the 9th and 12th centuries, architects raised the church, created the massive rose window in the facade, and hired artists who revived the ancient art of casting in bronze to create magnificent doors set with 48 wonderfully minimalist panels telling stories from the Bible as well as the life of St. Zeno. The stone reliefs flanking them date to the 12th century. The 12th- to 14th-century frescoes inside lead up to Andrea Mantegna's 15th-century altarpiece. See p. 215.

- **Basilica** (Aquileia): Tiny Aquileia was a major town in Roman times and built a church in A.D. 313 just as soon as Constantine the Great declared the religion legal in the empire. The town was a hotbed of early Christianity, hosting a theological conference in 381 attended by the likes of Jerome and Ambrose. Though the church was rebuilt and frescoed in the 11th and 12th centuries, the original flooring has been uncovered and is now on display, a marvelous and precious mosaic of complicated paleo-Christian and pagan iconography. A crypt retains more mosaics from the 4th century, plus even earlier ones from a pagan house dating to the early 1st century A.D. See p. 265.

- **Tempietto Longobardo** (Cividale): This fantastic 8th-century church hollowed out of the cliff face over Cividale's mighty gorge gives us a precious glimpse into true Lombard style, before the High Middle Ages began to mix and mingle the cultural groups of northern Italy. Flanking the entryway are statues and decorations carved directly out of the native limestone in an early Lombard Romanesque style. See p. 270.

- **Duomo** (Milan): The greatest Gothic cathedral south of the Alps, a massive pile of pinnacles and buttresses, was begun in the 14th century and took 500 years to complete—but it remained true to its original, Gothic styling. It's the fourth-largest church in the world, its cavernous interior peppered with statues and monuments. The highlight, though, is the chance to climb up onto the eaves, weave your way through the statue-peaked buttresses, and clamber up onto the very rooftop to gaze out across the hazy city and beyond to the Alps rising from the lakes north of the Lombard plain. See p. 281.

- **Certosa** (Pavia, outside Milan): Though Milan's Sforza family completed this Carthusian monastery, called a charterhouse, it's really the late-14th-century brainchild of the Visconti clan. The massive building, rich with Lombardesque decorations and sculptures, was commissioned by Gian Galeazzo in 1396 as thanks that his second wife was delivered from illness and bore him heirs. It became the repository of funerary monuments to Milan's greatest rulers and despots. Though Ludovico il Moro and his wife, Beatrice d'Este, boast the finest monument, neither is buried here. Indeed, the repository was never meant to be in Pavia in the first place; cash-poor Santa Maria della Grazie in Milan—the one with Leonardo's *The Last Supper* and the home of Beatrice's remains—sold it to the charterhouse. This is still a working monastery, now hosting a Cistercian community, and you can tour an example of the little houses they occupy (a far cry from the cramped cells one pictures monks enduring) and purchase their own beauty products and liqueurs. See p. 306.

- **Cappella Colleoni** (Bergamo): The mercenary commander Bartolomeo Colleoni, a son of Bergamo, fought so gloriously on behalf of Venice that he was actually given the generalship over the entire Venetian army (unheard of in such a suspicious republic formed of interlocking check-and-balance branches of power). They commissioned Verrocchio to erect a statue in his honor in Venice and gave Colleoni control of his hometown. He was foresighted enough to commission his own tomb, which was created in the late 15th century as a separate chapel in Bergamo's cathedral. Colleoni invited one of the great sculptors decorating the magnificent charterhouse at Pavia to carve on his tomb a complex series of panels and statues whose symbolisms interweave in medieval style grafted onto Renaissance architecture. In the 18th century, Tiepolo was brought in to fresco the ceiling. See p. 312.

- **Basilica di Superga** (Turin): Turin got a taste of the extravagant southern Italian baroque in the early 18th century when Sicilian architect Juvarra set up shop in town. After the Virgin saved the city from French troops, the Savoys dutifully erected a church in her honor and hired Juvarra for the job. He married early neoclassical ideals of proportion with the theatricality of the baroque to build this magnificent balcony overlooking the Alps in the hills above Turin. Vittorio Amadeo II liked his results so much he decided to turn it into the Royal Tomb, wedging monuments to various Savoys into the chapels and the underground Crypt of Kings. See p. 358.

- **Sacra di San Michele** (outside Turin): Its stony bulk, elaborate carvings, and endless staircases, all towering over the valley from a Monte Pirchiriano perch, give this abbey a movie-set air more appropriate to a Tibetan monastery than to a Christian abbey. The gravity-defying way it hangs halfway off the cliff face is all the more remarkable when you consider that the engineering is purely medieval—started in 983 and rebuilt in the 1100s. Before the Savoys were the bigwig kings they became, their early members were buried here, in rock-carved chapels under the partly frescoed main church interior; today free concerts are held here April through September, with a range of offerings from Gregorian chants and Celtic music to classical pieces and gospel hymns. See p. 363.

4 THE BEST ARTISTIC MASTERPIECES

- **Tintoretto's Scuola Grande di San Rocco** (Venice): When the Scuola di San Rocco (a sort of gentlemen's club/ lay fraternity) held an art competition in 1564, the Renaissance master Tintoretto pulled a fast one on his rivals. Instead of preparing a sketch for the judges like everyone else, he went ahead and finished a painting, secretly installing it in the ceiling of the Sala dell'Albergo off the second-floor hall. The judges were suitably impressed, and Tintoretto got the job. Over the next 23 years, the artist filled the *scuola*'s two floors with dozens of works. The *Rest on the Flight into Egypt* on the ground floor is superb, but his masterpiece hangs in that tiny Sala dell'Albergo, a huge *Crucifixion* that wraps around the walls and ranks among the greatest and most moving works in the history of Venetian art. The San Rocco baroque orchestra holds excellent regular chamber concerts in this fantastic setting; for info, contact © 041-962-999 or www.musicinvenice. com. See p. 151.

- **Veronese's *Feast in the House of Levi,* Accademia** (Venice): Paolo Veronese was a master of human detail, often peopling his large canvases with a rogues' gallery of characters. When Veronese unveiled his *Last Supper,* puritanical church bigwigs nearly had a conniption. They threatened him with charges of blasphemy for portraying this holiest of moments as a rousing, drunken banquet that more resembled paintings of Roman orgies than the Last Supper. Veronese quickly retitled the work *Feast in the House of Levi,* a less holy subject at which Jesus and the Apostles were also present, and the mollified censors let it pass. See p. 151.

- **Giotto's Scrovegni Chapel** (Padua): Padua's biggest sight by far is one of the two towering fresco cycles created by Giotto (the other one is in Assisi), the artist who did more than any other to lift painting from its static Byzantine stupor and set it on the naturalistic, expressive, dynamic Gothic road toward the Renaissance. From 1303 to 1306, Giotto covered the walls of this private chapel with a range of emotion, using foreshortening, modeled figures, and saturated colors, revolutionizing the concept of art and kicking off the modern era in painting. The chapel, as a whole, is breathtaking, depicting scenes from the life of Mary and Jesus in 38 panels. See p. 183.

- **Leonardo da Vinci's *The Last Supper,* Santa Maria delle Grazie** (Milan): This tempera fresco looks somehow more like a snapshot of a real dinner table than the staged holy event that Last Suppers usually appear to be—instead of a hovering halo, Jesus' holy nimbus is suggested by the window behind his head. Leonardo was as much a scientist and inventor as he was painter, and unfortunately for us, he was wont to try new painting techniques directly on his major commissions rather than testing them fully first. When painting one fresco in Florence, he used wax in the pigments, but when it was drying too slowly, he put heaters along the wall, and the whole thing simply melted. Whatever chemistry he was experimenting with in Milan when Ludovico il Moro hired him to decorate the refectory (dining hall) of Santa Maria della Grazie with a Last Supper, it didn't work properly. The fresco began deteriorating almost as soon as he finished painting it, and it had to be touched up

and painted over several times in the succeeding centuries. It also didn't help when Napoleon's troops moved in and used the wall for target practice, or when Allied World War II bombs tore the roof off the building, miraculously not damaging the fresco but still leaving it open to the elements for 3 years. A lengthy restoration has stripped away the centuries of grime and overpainting, so what we see now is more or less pure Leonardo, even if the result is extremely patchy and looks rather faded. See p. 283.

- **Michelangelo's *Rondanini Pietà,* Castello Sforzesco** (Milan): During a lifetime in which he became the foremost artist of his age, acknowledged as a genius in painting, fresco, architecture, and engineering, Michelangelo never lost his love for marble and chisel. At age 89, he was working yet again on one of his favorite subjects, this *Pietà.* It may be unfinished—in fact, Michelangelo was in the midst of changing it wholesale, reordering the figures and twisting the composition around—but this tall, languid representation of Mary and Nicodemus bearing the body of Christ remains one of Michelangelo's most remarkable works. At the end of his life, Michelangelo had grown so advanced in his thinking and artistic aesthetics that this remarkable, minimalist work (the sculptor had early on developed a rough style dubbed *non-finito,* or "unfinished") looks eerily as if it were chiseled in the 1950s rather than the 1560s. Michelangelo was in his Roman studio chiseling away on the statue when, on February 12, 1564, he was struck with a fever and took to bed. He died 6 days later. See p. 281.

- **Mantegna's *Dead Christ,* Pinacoteca di Brera** (Milan): This masterpiece of the Brera's collection displays not only Mantegna's skill at modeling and keen eye for texture and tone, but also his utter mastery of perspective and how he used it to create the illusion of depth. In this case, we look at Jesus laid out on a slab from his feet end, the entire body foreshortened to squeeze into a relatively narrow strip of canvas. Like many great geniuses in the arts, Mantegna actually warped reality and used his tools (in this case, perspective and foreshortening) in an odd way to create his image. Most art teachers would tell you that the rules of perspective would call for the bits at the "near end" (in this case, the feet) to be large and those at the far end (that is to say, the head) to be small to achieve the proper effect, but Mantegna turned it around. At first glance, the work seems wonderfully wrought and perfectly foreshortened. But after staring a few moments, you realize the head is grotesquely large and the feet tiny. Mantegna has given us perfect foreshortening by turning perspective on its end. See p. 282.

5 THE BEST CASTLES

- **Museo Castelvecchio** (Verona): Most people do the Romeo-and-Juliet trail, peak at the ancient Arena, and then call it a day in Verona. Unfortunately, few make it to the stunning castle on the river. This 14th-century stronghold, complete with its own fortified bridge across the river, was built by "Big Dog" Cangrande II Scaligeri. It was so mighty that it survived the centuries intact until the Nazis bombed it in World War II. Though there are collections of local wood sculptures and canvases by Tintoretto, Tiepolo, Veronese, Bellini, and local boy Pisanello, the true treat here is just wandering the maze of halls, passageways, stony staircases, and ramparts to relive the bad old days of the Middle Ages. See p. 212.

- **Castello Sabbionara** (Avio): This bellicose castle was a true fortress and makes no bones about it. Built in the 11th century and enlarged in the 13th century, it helped define and hold the line between the constantly warring neighboring powers of Venice and Austria. It switched hands several times, and in the 13th century the Guard's Room was frescoed with marvelous scenes of battles fought here. See p. 230.

- **Castello di Buonconsiglio** (Trent): Serious history went down in Trent's Castle of Good Council. The name might not be apt, however, because the famous Council of Trent (p. 226)—many sessions of which were held here—effectively put up the wall between the Vatican and the burgeoning Protestant movement that ended up being the cause (or at least excuse) for many European wars and numerous unjust politico-social systems, from the 16th century all the way to the recent unrest in Northern Ireland. Much later, leaders of the *Irrendentisti* (a World War I–era movement to return the then-Austrian South Tirol region to Italy) were imprisoned here, including the popular Cesare Battisti, who was executed in the yard. The castle is vast, built around the core 13th-century Castelvecchio and 15th-century palace of Trent's bishop-prince. The highlight is the *Cycle of the Months* fresco painted around 1400 and laden with late medieval symbolism. See p. 225.

- **Castel Roncolo** (Bolzano): This 13th-century castle sits atop a small cliff upriver from the town and looks like the most livable medieval castle you can imagine: cozy, with views of the vineyards. The central courtyard is hung with staircases and open wood balconies running along the upper stories, while many rooms retain all sorts of wonderfully crude medieval frescoes, including a lovely set that tells the story of Tristan and Isolde, a popular romantic tale from the Middle Ages. See p. 235.

- **Castel Tirolo** (outside Merano): The entire Tirol, covering this region of Italy and much of western Austria, was once ruled from this medieval fortress perched dramatically on an outcropping 4.8km (3 miles) outside Merano. You must walk a long and narrow path to get here, where there's a gorgeously frescoed Romanesque chapel and a new museum on Tirolean history and culture. See p. 241.

- **Castello di San Giusto** (Trieste): Built between 1470 and 1630 and pleasingly castlelike, this gem has mighty ramparts to walk for city vistas, modest collections of armor and furnishings to peruse, and outdoor concerts and films presented in the huge courtyard in summer. See p. 258.

- **Castello di Miramare** (near Trieste): The "Castle Admiring the Sea" rises in gleaming white fairy-tale splendor along the coastline. Built in the 1850s, it was doomed to host ill-fated potentates ever since. Its original owner, Austrian Archduke Maximilian, was sent to Mexico to be emperor and ended up shot. Archduke Ferdinand spent the night here before going off to Sarajevo to be shot (which kicked off World War I). Other dukes and ladies have met bitter ends after sojourning here, which is perhaps why it is now public property and no longer a royal guesthouse. They do nice concerts here, plus sound-and-light shows telling the sad tale of the castle's builder, Maximilian. See p. 260.

- **Castello Scaligero** (Sirmione): This mighty midget is not spectacular as far as castles go, but—if you can apply this phrase to a fortress—it's cute as a button. Unimportant in most respects, it *is* darn picturesque, guarding the entrance to town with somber 13th-century stone turrets and surrounded by its little moat complete with drawbridges. See p. 322.

- **Castello di Fenis** (**Castle of Fenis;** outside Aosta): The Challant viscounts controlled the Aosta Valley from this stronghold throughout the Middle Ages. The frescoed figures strolling about the balconies of its central courtyard spout cartoon balloonlike scrolls of speech that are a treasure-trove for linguists unlocking the origins of the local dialect, which is founded largely in a medieval variant on French. The furnishings, though all genuine castle antiques, were culled from sources throughout this area, Switzerland, and France to give the place that medieval lived-in look. See p. 376.

6 THE BEST VILLAS & PALAZZI

- **Palazzo Ducale** (Venice): The Gothic *palazzo* from which the Venetian Republic was ruled for centuries offers two incredible experiences. One is simply to wander the gorgeous rooms and halls, which are decorated with frescoes and paintings (including the world's largest oil canvas) by all the Venetian School greats, from Titian, Tintoretto, and Veronese on down. The placards in each room are marvelously informative, not only about the art but also about the function of each room and its role in government or daily Venetian life. But to discover what really made the Byzantine Venetian political machine tick, take the Secret Itineraries tour, which lets you slip behind the camouflaged doors and enter the hidden world of the palace-within-the-palace, the chambers in which the real governing took place, all wedged into the massive space between the inner and outer walls of the *palazzo*. See the chamber where the powerful Council of Ten met, the tiny office where the doge's secretary kept track of all the machinations going on in high society, the tribunal where three judges condemned the guilty and hanged them from the rafters, and the cramped "leads" cells under the roof from which Casanova famously escaped. Then saunter across the storied Bridge of Sighs to explore the dank, dungeonlike prisons across the canal where lesser criminals served out their miserable terms—lagoon floods and all. See p. 146.

- **Ca' d'Oro** (Venice): Though no longer graced with the decorative facade that earned Venice's most beautiful *palazzo* its name House of Gold, the 15th-century Ca d'Oro remains one of the most gorgeous palaces in Venice, outside (see the main facade from the Grand Canal) and in. The gallery of art, donated—along with the palace—to the state by Baron Giorgio Franchetti in 1916, includes paintings by Van Dyck, Giorgione, Titian, and Mantegna. There's also a small ceramics museum and fantastic canal views. See p. 158.

- **Ca' Rezzonico** (Venice): Even though Venice was, in fact, well past its heyday in the 18th century and technically in decline, this is nonetheless the era in which the city expressed its own unique character fully, the age of Casanova and costume balls, all the things we picture when we think of Venice. To this end, the Rezzonico, built in 1667 by the same architect who crafted the baroque Santa Maria della Salute and topped with an extra story in 1745 (and once owned by poet Robert Browning), was turned into a museum of the 18th century. The powers that be wanted the "museum" moniker to be taken lightly;

in reality what the city has done is outfit this gracious *palazzo* as an actual house from the era as closely as possible, using pieces culled from across the city. Adding to the 200-year time warp are a series of scenes from daily Venetian life painted by Pietro Longhi, plus several carnival frescoes that Giandomenico Tiepolo (son of the more famous Giovanni Battista Tiepolo) originally painted for his own house. See p. 154.

- **Villa Pisani** (Stra, Brenta Canal): Tiepolo frescoed the ballroom for this massive 18th-century villa built for the family of a Venetian doge, though Napoleon bought it in 1807. Its most notorious moment, though, came in 1934, when two European leaders met here for their very first summit: Benito Mussolini and Adolf Hitler. The rooms are sumptuous, and the gardens are extensive and include a quirky hedge maze. See p. 187.

- **Villa Barbaro** (outside Asolo): Though the villas right around Vicenza get more visitors, this 1560 Palladio-designed masterpiece outside Asolo is perhaps the most gorgeous to visit. That's because it matches the perfect Palladian architecture with stunning frescoes by Veronese, which carpet almost every inch of wall and ceiling inside. And to think it's still actually in private hands (with owners gracious enough to allow visitors in)! See p. 195.

- **Villa Rotonda** (outside Vicenza): If you've seen Monticello, the architecture of Washington, D.C., or Inigo Jones's buildings, you'll be prepared for La Rotonda—it was the model for them all. UNESCO has placed this pinnacle of Palladio's architectural theories, a towering monument of human achievement and ingenuity, on the same World Heritage List as the Pyramids. This is Palladio's strict neoclassical take on the Renaissance in all its textbook glory, an ancient temple rewritten as a home and softened by Renaissance geometry of line. It was also one of his last, started in 1567, but largely executed by a faithful follower after the master's death. See p. 203.

- **Villa Valmarana** (outside Vicenza): Mattoni's 17th-century Palladian-style villa is nicknamed *ai Nani*, or "of the dwarves," because its walls are patrolled by an army of stone dwarves. The architecture isn't all that remarkable, but the 18th-century frescoes inside by Giambattista and Giandomenico Tiepolo certainly are. See p. 203.
- **Palazzo Patriarcale** (Udine): Until 1734, it was the bishops who ruled Udine as patriarchs, and the final patriarch had the foresight to invite Tiepolo to Udine to decorate their palace with scenes from the Old Testament that double as early-18th-century fashion shows. There's also a fine collection of locally carved wood sculptures spanning the 13th to 18th centuries. See p. 267.
- **Palazzo Te** (Mantua): Raphael's protégé Giulio Romano, hounded from Rome over a scandalous series of erotic engravings, was let loose to fill libidinous Federico Gonzaga's Mannerist pleasure palace with racy frescoes. The place was built to look as if it were crumbling, from arch keystones to the illusionist frescoes in the Room of Giants. See p. 318.
- **Il Vittoriale** (Gardone, Lake Garda): Gabriele D'Annunzio was a Romantic ideal made of flesh, an Italian Hemingway-meets-Shelley, an adventurer, soldier, and poet who napped on a funeral bier covered in leopard skins; who carried on a torrid affair with the greatest actress of his age, Eleonora Duse; and who crafted every iota of his villa in meticulous Victorian detail. It's said that Mussolini himself gave D'Annunzio the property—either to honor his vociferous support of Fascism or simply to shut him up before he said something to get them all into trouble. D'Annunzio

was a bit of a hothead and not much of a team player. In 1918, he flew to Vienna just to drop leaflets on it and prove, to what he saw as the wimpy Italian military command, that he could penetrate that far. When the Adriatic town of Fiume, previously promised to Italy, ended up in Yugoslav hands, he led his own army to occupy the town and claim it—much to the chagrin of the Italian commanders, who had to talk him into giving it up and coming home (this is the "victory" after which the villa is named). With a whole villa to keep him occupied, D'Annunzio proceeded to remake it to his own image. The very route guests take upon entering is a subtle and intricate play on the structure of Dante's *Divine Comedy*. The sheer volume of bric-a-brac is enough to drive a maid with a feather duster nuts, but is redeemed by the fantastic anecdote or quirky explanation behind each one (hope for a chatty guide with a good command of English). Nestled in the extravagant gardens are a structure built as a ship, the actual boat D'Annunzio commanded during the Great War, his biplane, and his heroic hilltop tomb. See p. 325.

- **Palazzo Reale** (**Royal Palace;** Turin): This was where the Savoy kings hung their crowns in all the sumptuous, overwrought, gilded glory that the 17th and 18th centuries could offer. From Gobelin tapestries to Oriental vases, from the royal armory to the elegant gardens laid out by master landscape architect Le Nôtre (who did the Versailles gardens and those of the Tuileries in Paris), this palace drips with royal frippery. See p. 357.
- **Palazzina di Caccia di Stupinigi** (outside Turin): Sicilian baroque genius Juvarra laid out this extravagant and palatial hunting lodge for the Savoys in 1729. To fill the numerous frescoed rooms and vast halls of its giant, sinuous X-shape, local authorities have collected

furnishings, paintings, and other decorative elements from dozens of Savoy palaces to create here a sort of museum of 18th- and 19th-century interior decor. Napoleon liked it so much that he set up housekeeping here for a time when he first conquered the region before pressing on. (***Note:*** The lodge is closed for restoration, likely through 2010.) See p. 358.

- **Galleria Nazionale di Palazzo Spinola** (Genoa): The Spinola provides its collection of canvases (by Antonello da Messina, Guido Reni, Luca Giordano, Van Dyck, and Strozzi), with a stellar backdrop consisting of a Genovese palace of which the merchant/banking Spinola family lavishly frescoed and decorated each room. See p. 393.

7 THE BEST FESTIVALS

- **Carnevale** (Venice): Every spring Venice brings back the 18th century in all its silk and brocade, pouf-sleeved, men-wearing-colored-hose, Casanova, ballroom-dancing glory. In most Catholic countries, the week before Lent begins has long been a time to let down your hair and party. It all culminates in Shrove Tuesday, the day of feasting before Ash Wednesday kicks off the sober Lenten period. This bash has earned the day the nickname Fat Tuesday—called *Martedì Grasso* in Italian, but better known by its French name, Mardi Gras. Venice ranks with Rio and New Orleans as host of one of the most elaborate and famous Carnival celebrations anywhere. Rather than a Bacchanalian bash, Venice goes the genteel route, with concerts and masked costume balls filling performance spaces, churches, and frescoed palaces. Ten days leading up to Shrove Tuesday. See p. 162 and 164.
- **Venice International Film Festival:** This is one of the movie business's premier festivals, ranking just below Cannes in importance. The best films made over the past year from around the world are screened for audiences and judges at the Palazzo del Cinema, other movie houses, and sometimes even open-air piazzas. Unlike, say, the Oscars, which celebrates

highly promoted Hollywood products, this is a chance for all movies—from would-be blockbusters to low-budget, unknown indies—to catch the attention of critics and distributors. Late August/early September. See p. 162.
- **Biennale d'Arte** (Venice): One of the most important art festivals in the world is hosted every 2 years by the city of Venice. Contemporary artists (both celebrated modern masters and talented unknowns), critics, and art aficionados from around the world fill the hotels to attend shows and peruse the works displayed in the gardens and Arsenale warehouses at the far end of the Castello district. June to early November, odd years. See p. 162.
- **Regata Storica** (Venice): Every Venetian must have an 18th-century outfit mothballed in a closet to break out for yearly fetes such as Carnevale and, of course, this "historical regatta"—less of a race than merely a parade of gorgeously bedecked gondolas and other boats laden with costumed gentry for a day cruising the Grand Canal. First Sunday in September. See p. 163.
- **Partita a Scacchi** (Marostica): A living chess match may be a throwaway gag to Mel Brooks or a special-effect sequence in a Harry Potter film, but it's the highlight of Marostica's calendar. This pretty

little medieval hamlet, which barely fills the bottom third of the ring made by its ancient wall clambering up the hillside, would probably be overlooked if it weren't for the biennial festival that turns the checkerboard main piazza in front of the castle into a weird piece of yesteryear. After a parade of costumed gentlefolk and medieval-style entertainers (jugglers, fire-eaters, clowns), people dressed as chess pieces fill the piazza's board, the players sit atop a stage ready to call out their moves, and the match begins. Actually, it's technically not chess as we know it but rather a medieval variant, and it's not a proper match, since they're, in fact, re-creating, move for move, a game played in the 15th century between two noblemen vying for the hand of a fair lady. Still, it's all great fun. Marostica has only a handful of hotels, so book a few months in advance. Second Sunday in September, even years. See p. 199.

- **Concerti in Villa** (Vicenza): The Veneto region around Vicenza opens up its villas or their grounds for a series of summertime concerts and performances. From famous masterpieces like Palladio's La Rotonda to little-known Renaissance villas, the settings are memorable and the music is sweet. June and July. See p. 200.

- **Opera in Arena** (Verona): La Scala and La Fenice may be more famous, but few opera stages in Italy have a more natural dramatic setting than Verona's ancient Roman amphitheater. Every season they put on *Aïda* as they have since 1913, surrounded by other operatic masterpieces by Giuseppe Verdi. For a huge 2,000-year-old sports stadium open to the sky, the Arena enjoys surprisingly good acoustics. Late June through August. See p. 211.

- **Festival Shakespeariano** (Verona): Verona mixes its two powerhouse attractions—ancient Roman heritage and Shakespearean fame—in a theater festival of Shakespeare's plays (along with ballets and concerts, from classical to jazz) put on in the garden-set ruins of the Teatro Romano ancient theater. See p. 208.

- **Palio** (Asti): Medieval pageantry precedes a breakneck horse race on the piazza. The 2 weeks leading up to it are known as the **Douja d'Or,** a grape-and-wine festival and trade fair. Rival town **Alba** spoofs the event with a race of their own—riding asses—in their **Palio degli Asini** on the first Sunday in October. Third Sunday in October. See p. 365.

- **Sanremo Festival** (San Remo): It's the Grammy Awards meets Sundance meets *American Idol.* Since 1950, Sanremo has been Italy's beloved festival of pop music, where faded Italian stars get to strut their stuff, major international rock stars and artists are invited to perform, and scruffy teenage musicians from across Italy get the chance to play that carefully crafted song they just know would be a number-one hit if only they could sign a record contract (and many do). If you want to hear what will be belting out of boom boxes and Fiat speakers this summer at Italy's beaches and pumping in the discos, listen to the winning performances here. Late February or early March. See p. 402.

- **Sagra del Pesce** (Camogli): Take the world's largest frying pan (3.6m/12 ft. across) and place it on the wide, waterfront promenade of this tiny Riviera fishing town. Fill the pan with sizzling sardines and the town with hungry folks ready to party. There you have a *sagra,* or celebration of food—in this case, seafood, the town's traditional economic lynchpin. Second Sunday in May. See p. 412.

8 THE BEST LUXURY HOTELS

- **Hotel Gritti Palace** (Venice): The grandest hotel on the Grand Canal has hosted the crème de la crème of whoever visits Venice since Doge Andrea Gritti built the palace in the 16th century. Charles de Gaulle, Winston Churchill, Truman Capote, John Ruskin, Henry Ford, Mick Jagger, Giorgio Armani, Robert De Niro, Charlie Chaplin . . . the list goes on. This place is luxury everything: hand-painted and inlaid antiques, 18th-century stuccoed ceilings, cutting-edge designer entertainment centers, and, of course, balconies overlooking the Grand Canal (well, from the top-notch rooms, at least—everyone else gets to enjoy the water from the restaurant or piano bar, or can overlook a side canal). See p. 112.

- **Hotel Danieli** (Venice): Venice's *bacino* (the bay into which the Grand Canal spills) is lined with luxury hotels, but none beats the Danieli, a 14th-century doge's palace of pink plaster and elaborate marble windowsills that's been a hotel since 1822. The centerpiece is a four-story, sky-lit, enclosed courtyard of Byzantine-Gothic arches, open stairwells, balustrades, and verdant potted plants, off of which sit luxurious salons. It's worth popping your head in just to see it, even if you don't stay here. The rooms vary, but no matter what, insist upon a lagoon view—and try to stay in the original wing or, failing that, the larger rooms of the 19th-century *palazzo* next door (by all means, avoid the bland, albeit cushy, 1940s wing). See p. 116.

- **Hotel Cipriani** (Venice): This is the last independent, locally owned luxury hotel in Venice, and quite possibly the best. It sits in splendid isolation at the tip of Giudecca, the only large island of central Venice not connected by a bridge (rather, it's a 10-min. boat ride to Piazza San Marco). Giuseppe Cipriani, the Venetian impresario behind Harry's Bar and the Locanda Cipriani on Torcello, where Ernest Hemingway loved to hang out (Cipriani even made it into a Papa story), crafted this retreat out of several Renaissance *palazzi* in 1959, offering stylish accommodations, discreet service, and modern comfort. See p. 126.

- **Hotel Excelsior** (Venice): The Lido might never have been developed as a bathing resort if not for the prescience of Nicolò Spada, who created the Excelsior's Moorish-style central structure in 1907. As one of Venice's only custom-built luxury hotels, it didn't have to abide by all the historical considerations converted *palazzi* now have to take into account, so its architectural plans allowed for more spacious accommodations than those found in most Venetian hotels. Rooms overlook either the Adriatic (there's a private beach across the road) or the small, lush, Moorish garden. It also sports all the resort-type amenities: pool, fitness center, golf and tennis, and sauna. See p. 127.

- **Villa Margherita** (Mira Porte, Brenta): This villa's role as a guesthouse hasn't changed much since it was built in the 17th century by Venice's Contarini family. It still looks much like a country-villa home (if your family happened to be Venetian and fabulously wealthy), with rooms overlooking the gardens, a restaurant across the street along the canal, and a similar sister property nearby with a swimming pool. See p. 189.

- **Hotel Villa Cipriani** (Asolo): In 1962, Giuseppe Cipriani branched out from his premium-grade Venice mini-empire to turn this 16th-century villa into a well-appointed hotel. Once the home of poets Robert and Elizabeth Barrett

Browning, it enjoys a dreamlike setting: the medieval hill town of Asolo, famed for its vistas over the Veneto. See p. 194.

- **Hotel Greif** (Bolzano): Boutique hotels have officially arrived in Italy—though so far only the Greif seems to have heard. The Staffler family has owned this 500-year-old hotel on the main square of Bolzano—the Dolomiti's liveliest town—since 1796. But in 1999 and 2000, they decided to overhaul it completely in a minimalist, modern vein of burnished steel and original contemporary art mixed with 19th-century antiques and an Internet-equipped laptop in every room. See p. 235.

- **Four Seasons Hotel Milano** (Milan): In 1993, the Four Seasons opened and rewrote the rules on deluxe hotels in Milan. Seven years were spent restructuring and transforming a 1476 convent, a process that brought many of its Renaissance elements back to light, including a lovely cloister. The rooms are huge by Italian city standards and flush with amenities and small luxuries such as CD stereos and king-size beds. The bi-level suites with frescoed vaulting are particularly nice. See p. 294.

- **Grand Hotel et de Milan** (Milan): How do you define superior service? While resident guest Giuseppe Verdi, who lived for 30 years in the suite now named for him, lay dying in his bed, the hotel spread straw over the streets under his window every day to muffle the sounds of carriage wheels so as not to disturb the maestro's rest. They're constantly upping the luxury quotient here to keep the 1863 hotel looking and feeling its best. This means marble surfaces and lush upholstery, thick curtains, and antique furnishings. Okay, so the opera music trickling lightly from hidden speakers may be overdoing it, but what did you expect from a hotel 3 blocks from La Scala that has played host to divas and tenors for decades? See p. 294.

- **Villa d'Este** (Cernobbio, Lake Como): On short lists of the world's greatest hotels, the Villa d'Este always ranks near the top. There's nothing reproduction or faux about this place. The villa is true Renaissance, the marble precious, the guest book A-list, and the Empire furnishings so genuine they actually date back to Napoleon's tenure when his aide-de-camp owned it. Add to all that several pools (one floating on the lake), a vast park that hides tennis courts, a fitness center that includes squash courts and a virtual driving range, and a trio of restaurants. See p. 334.

- **Grand Hôtel et des Iles Borromées** (Stresa, Lake Maggiore): Ernest Hemingway loved this retreat by the lake so much he set part of *A Farewell to Arms* at the hotel. Shell out 3,200€, and you can stay in the suite named after him (two bedrooms with king-size beds and huge marble bathrooms in each, frescoed ceilings, lake-view terrace). An old lily of the Italian hotel scene, this hotel ranks among Europe's most exclusive hotels. Rooms are sumptuously appointed in a variety of styles, from 19th-century inlaid wood to lavish Empire style to opulent Italianate rooms of lacquered furnishings and Murano chandeliers. See p. 345.

- **Hotel Splendido/Splendido Mare** (Portofino): Portofino is the fishing village chosen by the world's jet-set elite as their own little bit of Italy, its tiny harbor overshadowed by yachts, and the hillside Splendido hotel booked by the top names from Hollywood, European nobility registers, and CEO boardrooms. The villa itself is 19th century, though its foundation is a 16th-century monastery, set amid olive groves a 10-minute walk above the town. Suites come with antique furnishings and cutting-edge entertainment centers. The sister hotel, Splendido Mare, sits right at the harborfront, stays open year-round, and offers dining with a view of the boats. See p. 420.

- **Royal Hotel** (San Remo): With such a small town and such a major pop festival, once a year you'll find a concentration of rock stars here rarely seen outside of a major benefit concert. The rest of the year, almost all of us can enjoy its private beach across the road, its cushy accommodations, its stuccoed bar, and the wonderful pool styled as if it were carved out of rock. See p. 403.

9 THE BEST MODERATELY PRICED HOTELS

- **Pensione Accademia** (Venice): If you ever wanted to live like Katharine Hepburn, here's your chance. Well, not exactly, though her character did live in this 16th-century Villa Maravege (Villa of Wonders) in the 1955 film *Summertime.* It sits in an enviable position, a flower-filled garden at the confluence of two canals emptying into the Grand Canal, and the rooms are done in a tasteful antique style that makes you feel as if you're staying in the home of your wealthy Venetian relative rather than in a hotel. See p. 121.
- **Hotel San Cassiano Ca'Favretto** (Venice): It's one of the cheapest hotels on the Grand Canal—plus the rooms and bar terrace overlook the prettiest stretch of the canal, with the Ca' d'Oro directly across the waters. Even most non–Grand Canal rooms overlook a side canal. All that, and the hotel in the 16th-century villa retains much of its 18th-century ambience (though room decor is vintage 1970s repro antiques). See p. 123.
- **Hotel Majestic Toscanelli** (Padua): The management of the Toscanelli is always reinvesting in this gem of a hotel, three quiet shop- and *osteria*-lined blocks from the central Piazza delle Erbe. The reception is warm and helpful, and the location excellent. See p. 185.
- **Hotel Aurora** (Verona): Situated right on the scenic Piazza delle Erbe, the Aurora enjoys a combination of prime location, low prices, and perfect, simple comfort that keeps guests coming back. See p. 217.
- **Antica Locanda Solferino** (Milan): The most wonderfully eclectic hotel in Milan exudes character. It sits in the heart of the fashionable Brera neighborhood, its quirky amalgam of furnishings fitted into generally spacious rooms. Sig. Gerardo Vitolo leads one of the friendliest managements in town; it's no wonder this delightful place stays booked by regulars, who enjoy its creaky, homey atmosphere. See p. 295.
- **Agnello d'Oro** (Bergamo): Bergamo may not quite be the Alps, but you're high up enough in their foothills that this tall, narrow ocher building with its flower-box windows, patio fountain, and sloping roof looks perfectly appropriate, offering a bit of Italianate Alpine charm smack-dab in the center of the pedestrian medieval quarter. Furnishings are simple and serviceable, but the price and location can't be beat. See p. 313.
- **Du Lac** (Bellagio, Lake Como): Of all the hotels lining Bellagio's little lakefront piazza, the Du Lac is the friendliest by a long shot. For over a century and a half, it has offered comfort and genuine hospitality, from the panoramic dining room and rooftop sun terrace to the simple but fully stocked rooms and the bar tables tucked under the arcades of the sidewalk. The hotel recently added a pool and tennis courts. See p. 336.
- **Verbano** (Stresa, Lake Maggiore): Why shell out hundreds of dollars for a hotel

by the lake when you can have one *on* the lake for half the price? The dusty rose villa of the Verbano sits at the tip of Isola dei Pescatori, an island of colorful fishermen's houses in the midst of Lake Maggiore, with views over the landscaped Isola Bella, the lake, and the Alps beyond from most rooms and also from the gravelly terrace, where they serve excellent meals. See p. 346.

10 THE BEST BUDGET GEMS

- **Hotel La Residenza** (Venice): Just off the highly fashionable Riva degli Schiavoni sits one of the great remaining cheap *pensioni* in Italy, a 15th-century *palazzo* converted into an inexpensive hotel. Hotels this cheap are hard to come by anywhere in Venice, let alone in such a prime location, and none have such remarkable decor and faded style. Its 15 rooms occupy the *piano nobile,* the high-ceilinged "noble floor" where the wealthy family once lived, so it sports 18th-century stuccoes over Venetian-style furnishings, 17th-century oil paintings, and Murano chandeliers. See p. 119.

- **Foresteria Valdese** (**Palazzo Cavagnis;** Venice): If La Residenza (see above) is full, you may luck into even more decaying style (18th-c. frescoes decorate the ceilings in several rooms) for less money at this 16th-century *palazzo* run as a sort of hostel by the Waldesian and Methodist Church. The drawbacks are that it's a sort of hostel-type arrangement—many, but not all, of the accommodations are shared rooms—and the rooms lack amenities such as telephones and air-conditioning. The location isn't quite as sweet as that of La Residenza, but the rooms do have balconies over a lovely small side canal. See p. 118.

- **Hotel Galleria** (Venice): This place is remarkable: a 17th-century *palazzo* with double rooms for under 110€, a half-dozen of which open directly onto the Grand Canal, and it's next door to one of Venice's top sights, the Accademia Gallery. All that and you get breakfast (including freshly baked bread) in bed. See p. 121.

- **Pensione Guerrato** (Venice): This charming *pensione* is run by a pair of brothers-in-law in a converted 13th-century convent near the daily Rialto market. The furnishings are mismatched but lovely, a mix of antiques culled from markets over the years, and the breakfast is excellent. They also rent two great apartments at excellent prices near San Marco. See p. 122.

- **Hotel Bernardi-Semenzato** (Venice): The friendly Pepoli family runs this well-maintained *palazzo* hidden a block off the main drag about halfway between the train station and San Marco. It's surrounded by *osterie* and good restaurants patronized by locals, and the modernized rooms retain rough wood-beam ceilings and antique-style furnishings. They also rent simple but spacious rooms in two annexes nearby that make you feel as if you're staying in your own Venetian apartment; one room has a fireplace, another overlooks a pair of side canals. See p. 125.

- **Due Mori** (Vicenza): Just off the central Piazza dei Signori lies this simple, no-frills but comfortable hotel, the oldest in Vicenza, packed with genuine 19th-century antiques and a friendly reception. See p. 204.

- **Grifone** (Sirmione, Lake Garda): Would you believe a vine-covered hotel where the simple rooms enjoy views of the lake and access to a small beach for under 80€ a person? Well, that's on offer at this gem of an inn around the corner from the little medieval castle. Book early. See p. 323.

- **Fasce** (Santa Margherita Ligure): This little hotel a few blocks up from the harbor is now in its third generation of family management, which includes the incredibly helpful British-born Jane at the front desk. Not only are the bright

guest rooms spacious and comfortable, and the surroundings a lovely profusion of plants and flowers, but they pile on the extras, from free bicycles to Cinque Terre packets for guests who stay at least 3 nights (including a train ticket a day and all the info you need to explore the coast). See p. 416.

11 THE BEST COUNTRYSIDE RETREATS

- **Cavallino d'Oro/Goldenes Rössl** (Kastelruth/Castelrotto, near Bozen): The village is a full-bore Tirolean mountain hamlet straight out of the Middle Ages, and this rambling hotel has sat at the cobblestone center of town since the 1400s, its swinging shingle emblazoned with its Golden Horse moniker. It includes the corner bar where the locals hang out for lunch and a genuine, preserved 18th-century *Stuben* (beer nook) in the restaurant at back. It's a nice mix of new and old: The lounge has a widescreen TV with 300 digital channels set next to a picture window of the Alps; the rooms offer modern comforts amid hand-painted wood furnishings and four-poster beds. Best of all, the Urthaler family couldn't be more welcoming, and they happen to be Frommer's fans. See p. 237.

- **Hotel Castello Schloss Labers** (outside Merano): The road from town wends its way through vine-clad hills to the Stapf-Neubert family's 11th-century, countryside castle—a hotel since 1885. The cozy hunting salons cluster around a magnificent central staircase that leads up to the eclectic collection of rooms tucked into towers, eaves, and high-ceilinged rooms. A statue-studded garden out back offers views across the valley to the surrounding peaks, and they also have a heated pool, tennis courts, and a Tirolean restaurant. See p. 243.

- **Villa Fiordaliso** (Gardone Riviera, Lake Garda): This Liberty-style villa was built in 1903 and immediately started attracting formidable owners, including poet Gabriele d'Annunzio and, later, Claretta Petacci, Mussolini's mistress (this is where they spent their final weeks in semi-hiding at the end of World War II before being hunted down and killed). Things have calmed down considerably since then, the villa transformed in 1990 into one of the most popular high-end restaurants in the lake region (it even has a Michelin star now), with seven elegant guest rooms upstairs. See p. 326.

- **Villa La Meridiana/Az. Agrituristica Reine** (near Alba): An *agriturismo* is a working farm whose family opens their home and hospitality to guests. The Pionzo family runs this gracious *agriturismo* above the Piedmont wine town of Alba, with rooms in the main house and others converted from the former stalls, almost all overlooking the vineyards that produce their Barbera wine, the surrounding village-capped hills, and the peaks of the Alps in the distance. The ample breakfast may include apricot preserves from their own orchard and sheep's milk cheese from the neighbors. See p. 369.

- **La Cascina del Monastero** (outside La Morra): The di Grasso family runs an *agriturismo* similar to Villa La Meridiana (see above); it's another vineyard and fruit orchard farm outside a Piemontese village with large guest rooms and apartments filled with comfortable rustic furnishings and exposed wood beams. This place would be worth staying at if only for the sumptuous breakfast spread, the only drawback being that you may have to cancel lunch plans and return to your room for a nap. See p. 372.

- **Milleluci** (outside Aosta): Four matrilineal generations of hoteliers have turned this family farm into one of the coziest, friendliest hotels in the whole of the Valle d'Aosta. A fire crackles in the large lounge downstairs, and the rooms are done in woodsy Alpine style with canopy beds in suites, traditional wood furnishings, and hand-hewn ceilings. In true country tradition, the breakfast here is overwhelming, with freshly baked pies, cakes, and breads every morning accompanied by farm-fresh cheese, milk, and preserves. Unlike most countryside retreats, the Milleluci sports plenty of facilities a four-star hotel would be jealous of: a heated outdoor pool, tennis courts, exercise facilities, hot tub, and sauna. See p. 379.

- **La Grange** (Courmayeur-Entrèves): Entrèves may not properly be countryside, but this tiny collection of Alpine chalets below the Mont Blanc cable-car station is so small it barely qualifies as a village, and the atmosphere is fully rustic. The Berthold family converted this hotel from a barn by fitting the rooms with a mix of antiques and sturdy country furnishings. It makes a refreshing (and far less expensive) alternative to the resort hotels of Courmayeur just down the road. See p. 382.

12 THE BEST RESTAURANTS

- **Do Forni** (Venice): Though the menu is vast, they seem to devote equal attention to every single dish, making this one of the best restaurants in Venice (though also the most eyebrow-raisingly expensive). The bulk of the place is done in a vaguely rustic style, but the best room is the front one, fitted out like a car from the luxurious Orient Express. See p. 132.

- **La Cusina** (Venice): One of the few hotel dining rooms worth singling out. In warm weather, this becomes one of the most romantic dinner settings in town, the tables set on terraces that hang over the Grand Canal. The location alone makes it worth booking ahead, but happily the cooking is as delicious as the view is stunning, offering an inventive take on Italian cuisine based on Venetian and Veneto traditions and using the freshest ingredients. See p. 132.

- **Le Bistrot de Venise** (Venice): The menu at this upscale bistro is split three ways to satisfy your appetite (or at least, make your choice harder): Venetian/Italian, French, and ancient local recipes culled from historic cookbooks and documents. They attract hip artistic types by turning the back room into a coffeehouse-style performance space most nights, hosting poets, acoustic musicians, art exhibits, and cabarets. See p. 133.

- **Al Covo** (Venice): Texan Diane Rankin makes the pastries and chats with guests while husband-chef Cesare Benelli watches over the kitchen at this always-popular restaurant that mixes a warm welcome and excellent fresh seafood dishes with relatively reasonable prices (especially on the quality wine list). See p. 136.

- **Trattoria Milanese** (Milan): In a city with many fine restaurants whose stars rise and fall almost as soon as they make it onto the map, La Milanese is a stalwart survivor, a traditional trattoria that has never stopped offering typical Milanese dishes, smart service, and moderate prices, a formula that has kept it successful for over 70 years now. See p. 301.
- **Antica Hosteria del Vino Buono** (Bergamo): This cozy restaurant is spread over two floors of a corner *palazzo* on the market square. The food is mountain-style, rib-sticking good, heavy on the game meats and thick polenta accompanied by hearty red wines. See p. 314.
- **Ochina Bianca** (Mantua): Mantuan cooking is somewhat more complex than most northern Italian cuisines, and the Venturinis put their own innovative spin on it at the "White Goose," marrying local ingredients with fresh fish from the Mincio and game in this elegant restaurant. See p. 320.
- **C'era Una Volta** (Turin): That you have to ring the bell and climb to the first floor gives this place a clubby air, but owner Piero Prete will instantly make you feel like a longtime member as he greets you warmly and comes back around to help you select your wine. The cooking is traditional Torinese, excellently prepared. See p. 361.
- **Lalibera** (Alba): Franco and Manuele reign over this stylish dining room on an alley off a pedestrian shopping street, with Marco in the kitchen crafting excellent variants on Piemontese cuisine by using only the freshest of ingredients, all locally produced, from the cheese to the fruit to the meats. See p. 370.

13 THE BEST COUNTRYSIDE EATERIES

- **Al Camin** (outside Cortina d'Ampezzo): This barnlike structure lies along the rushing Run Brigantine mountain stream, 10 minutes outside town, serving hearty Alpine food in a woodsy dining room around a stone fireplace. Some regional specialties that are hard to find elsewhere these days are staples on Al Camin's seasonal menus. See p. 253.
- **L'Osteria del Vignaiolo** (La Morra): This place is sophisticated rustic, with simple rooms with pale-gold walls expanding to tables outside in summer. It's set amid the vineyards that produce its excellent wines and provide the excellent views. The cooking, in the hands of chef Luciano Marengo, samples from the varied bounty of Piemontese regional cuisines, accompanied by choice cheese platters and, of course, some of the best fine wines in Italy. See p. 373.
- **La Maison de Filippo** (Entrèves): This is the never-ending meal to beat all feasts. I honestly tried to keep track of the courses, but after the seventh appetizer, I had to give it up. But it's not just quantity (two words: pace yourself): The food actually manages to be fantastic as well, and it's served in an archetypal rustic-countryside dining room of low wood ceilings and open kitchens. Sometimes there's even a dog under the table. Book here and then plan to spend much of the next day merely digesting. See p. 383.

14 THE BEST DOWN-HOME *TRATTORIE* & *OSTERIE*

- **Vino Vino** (Venice): Antico Martini is a pricey but good restaurant near La Fenice opera house; Vino Vino is its worst-kept secret, an inexpensive *osteria* branch that serves simple but tasty dishes that come out of the same kitchen. You choose from the daily chalkboard menu, stake out a table, and then carry your meal to it along with a wine from their excellent and extensive shared wine cellar. See p. 135.

- **Ai Tre Spiedi** (Venice): Although this place recently changed ownership and isn't the hidden gem it once was, you'll still find a great Venetian meal at reasonably low prices—not the cheapest in town, but some of the best value for your money. The owners are jolly, and the food is excellent, including the fish (which is often dicey at the more inexpensive places in Venice). See p. 135.

- **Cantina do Mori** (Venice): Notwithstanding the change in management (and a slight price hike), the Cantina do Mori has remained one of the best *bacari* in Venice, a wine bar that serves exquisite *cicchetti* (tapaslike snacks) to a crowd of regulars nightly under the low-beam ceilings that seem unchanged since the joint opened in 1462. After all, this is the place where even Casanova supposedly came to tipple between affairs. See p. 140.

- **Toni del Spin** (Treviso): Seventy years of satisfying Trevisani diners has imparted a patina of reliability to this down-home trattoria of crisscrossing beams, swirling fans, and chalkboard menus. The choices are limited, but each dish is excellent, mixing local traditions with experimental cooking and some international dishes. The wine list is stellar—they also run the wine shop across the street. See p. 192.

- **La Taverna di Via Stella** (Verona): The Vantini brothers and their buddies run this newish, laid-back *osteria* that feels as if it's been around for centuries. Here the local volunteer fire squad shows up to hang out in uniform and hit on girls, and office workers troop in to unwind over traditional Veronese dishes and wine (of their some 180 bottles, 10 varieties are opened nightly so that you can sample by the glass). See p. 220.

- **Osteria del Duca** (Verona): The ladies bustling around this old fave of a trattoria know to double-check with foreign visitors who have inadvertently ordered one of the many traditional Veronese dishes made of horse or donkey meat. The setting is romantic in true Verona style: It's on the ground floor of a medieval *palazzo* that most likely belonged to the historical Montecchi family, immortalized by Shakespeare as the Montagues, whose son Romeo fell in love with Juliet of the enemy Capulet clan. See p. 220.

- **Vineria Cozzi** (Bergamo): Leonardo Vigorelli's wine bar is the turnstile around which Bergamo's upper city spins, a requisite stop for locals and visitors alike who enjoy his hospitality, good wine selection, and yummy panini, meat and cheese platters, and simple dishes. See p. 315.

Northern Italy in Depth

Of all the great things that northern Italy has to offer, the best is its geographical diversity. There are days when you can ski the Alps in the morning and sunbathe on the Riviera in the afternoon. It seems like it doesn't get much better than that.

But it does get better. On your way, you can stop off in the valleys of Piedmont and sample some of the world's most prestigious wines and enjoy precious truffles. Farther east in Milan, shopaholics can revel in a fashionista's heaven on earth, while art historians can make the pilgrimage to Caravaggio's home just up the road. Medieval buffs marvel at the castles that outnumber towns in the Tirolean upper Adige, where Italian is a foreign tongue and the *lingua francas* are ancient dialects of French and German. Pass down through Italy's majestic lakes and vaunted Dolomite resorts, feel Shakespeare's presence at the home of Romeo and Juliet in Verona, stop off to see a Giotto masterpiece, and eat your way through the Po River valley to Venice, one of the most romantic cities in the world. On the south side of the valley, the spectrum ranges from the dreamy canals and Byzantine mosaics of Venice to Cremona, the birthplace of the Stradivarius violin, to fishing villages and chic resorts along the Ligurian Riviera.

This small and wealthy corner of the world offers a selection of everything that makes medieval Italy seductive, from the grand old port cities of Genoa and Trieste to the graceful, art-rich cities of the Veneto. But northern Italy also represents the sleek, modern Italy that is associated with A-list names like Armani, Alfa Romeo, and Alessio. A mastery of design and fashion are only a logical outgrowth of an efficient culture that once used state-of-the-art canals—sketched out by Leonardo Da Vinci—to transport marble to construction projects like the Duomo in Milan, which is now the fourth-largest cathedral in Christendom.

From the iconic architecture of Andrea Palladio to Milan's elegant fashion designs, the history of northern Italy is the story of the visibly irresistible. This chapter will help make sense of the events behind it all, and hopefully shed some light on the northern Italian persona that made this legacy possible.

1 NORTHERN ITALY TODAY

Any chapter that takes the pulse of a certain region would logically begin in the most important city, but in the case of northern Italy, there is no such place, and any attempt to coin one of the cities as the region's "capital" would be to ignore centuries of vastly different histories. Genoa is the principal port and has been a leading maritime power since the beginning of the second millennium. Turin was briefly the capital of a newly unified Italy, in the late 1800s, the home to its erstwhile royal family and the country's car-making Goliath, to boot. Milan is Italy's financial capital, home to most of the nation's media, and it has a stronghold on its design and fashion. Venice is unarguably the mecca for tourists, and places like Trieste and Bolzano had little shared history with the rest of Italy before World War I anyway. That is as good a starting point as any to a look at

Learn Your Stripes: Northern Italian Soccer Teams

It's amazing that a black-and-white-striped soccer (known as football in Italy) jersey can mean the world to a European and nothing at all to a typical North American: "Maybe he's a fan of the referee?" Before you depart for northern Italy, you should memorize the colors of at least the big three: Inter, Juventus, and A.C. Milan.

A.C. Milan: A.C. Milan launched its owner, Silvio Berlusconi, to fame on a national level and eventually into the prime minister's chair as well. Founded in 1899 by English expats as a "football and cricket club" (hence Milan, not Milano), the *rossoneri* saw their Golden Years right after Berlusconi bought the club in 1986 and signed Dutch superstars Ruud Gullit, Frank Rijkaard, and Marco Van Basten. The team wears red-and-black jerseys.

Internazionale (aka Inter): The national champions in 2006, 2007, 2008, 2009, and hopefully 2010 as well, Inter wears black-and-blue stripes—in Italian, the *nerazzurri*. The Milanese club split off from cross-town rivals A.C. Milan in 1908 because of the latter's preference for granting playing time only to Italians. As it had a number of players from nearby Switzerland on its roster, it deemed itself an "international" club, and the name was born. It is the only club to have spent its entire history in the top league, Serie A.

Juventus: The fan base for the Agnelli family's personal soccer team, founded in 1897, is hardly confined to Turin. The *bianconeri* have long been popular in Sicily and the rest of the south, where most of the labor came from for the Agnelli's automaking factories. Something akin to the New York Yankees, the fellows in black-and-white stripes have won more national championships than any other club and are either unconditionally loved or passionately hated across the country. As a Red Sox fan and *interista,* I think black-and-white stripes are a fashion faux pas in general.

what makes up the northern Italian body politic and psyche—if such a thing exists.

Northern Italians have always been an efficient and innovative people when it comes to industry, designing canals and locks to bring marble to construction projects, perfecting manufacturing methods and inventing various machines—not to mention the generation of electricity by Alessandro Volta.

This ingenuity has led Italy—and northern Italy, in particular—to economic success. Today Italy ranks as the world's tenth-largest economy, and northern Italy's GDP per capita is about 25% higher than the European Union average. This industrial base runs the gamut from manufacturing giants such as Turin-based **Fiat** (the world's 6th-largest carmaker after its 2009 acquisition of Chrysler) and Trieste-based insurer **Assicurazioni Generali** (the 47th-largest company in the world) to midsize family businesses that make up the lion's share of Italian productivity, to little mom-and-pop shops. Thankfully, this last group, small locally owned businesses, is the bread-and-butter of the economy. Lombardy is famous for manufacturers of this scale—things like bicycle frames and household goods come to mind—while the northeast is generally known for its furniture makers and increasingly for its import businesses, buying things like shoes made in Eastern Europe.

As home to so many entrepreneurs, northern Italy has an unsurprising appetite for politicians who offer hope for laissez-faire capitalism in a socialist country. In the 1990s, one of their own, a cruise ship crooner turned real estate investor turned media mogul, came to the forefront of Italian politics and has refused to go away since. **Silvio Berlusconi,** who hails from just outside Milan, is the country's wealthiest man and often its prime minister, too. (Berlusconi has served as Italy's prime minister three separate times: from 1994 to 1995, from 2001 to 2006, and currently since 2008.) He presides over *Il Popolo della Libertà* (The People of Freedom), a right-wing coalition that, while not universally popular in the north, certainly has its roots in northern populism. In fact, the third-biggest party in Berlusconi's People of Freedom coalition is the Northern League.

Since 2008, Berlusconi has served as Italy's prime minister, though, like his previous terms in this position, his current term has been riddled with gaffes and accusations of corruption. The scandals surrounding the 73-year-old's business dealings and conflicts of interest gave way to scandals surrounding his private life—in particular, a penchant for partying with 18-year-old girls at his Sardinian villa. He has also attracted attention with his public gaffes, like calling U.S. President Barack Obama "tan." While liberal northerners like to think it is the pro-unity south that put Berlusconi into power, the 2009 rallies in northern cities that implore him to continue indicate that Berlusconi has supporters in northern Italy as well. Considering the political hurdles Berlusconi has cleared in the past (see "Democracy at Last," later in this chapter), it is unlikely these peccadillos will loosen his grip on power.

2 LOOKING BACK AT NORTHERN ITALY

PREHISTORY & EARLY SETTLERS

Findings in caves around Isneria in the Abruzzi suggest that humans settled in Italy about a million years ago. Neanderthal man made a brief appearance, and Cro-Magnon, who knew how to fish and domesticate animals, showed up about 18,000 years ago.

Though prehistoric early cultural groups such as the Ligurians (Neolithic rulers of northwestern Italy—not just Liguria, but Piedmont and Lombardy as well—in 2400–1800 B.C.), Remedello (Copper Age folks centered on Brescia in 1800–1600 B.C.), Veneti (Bronze Age Illyrians settling the Veneto region around 1000 B.C.), and Villanovans (an influential Iron Age people of 1000–800 B.C. from the area around Bologna) inhabited parts of northern Italy, most of the peninsula's early action took place in central and southern Italy. Magna Graecia (Greater Greece) controlled Sicily and southern Italy all the way up to Naples. The Etruscans, probably a people who emigrated from Asia Minor between the 12th and 8th centuries B.C., settled into central Italy, ruling Tuscany, Umbria, and, as the Tarquin dynasty, acting as kings of a small Latin village, atop hills at a bend in the Tiber River, called Rome.

THE RISE OF ROME

Leaving aside the famous legend of a she-wolf nursing the abandoned twins Romulus and Remus (the former kills his brother and founds a village called Rome) and Virgil's *Aeneid* (Aeneas of Troy flees the burning city at the end of the Trojan War,

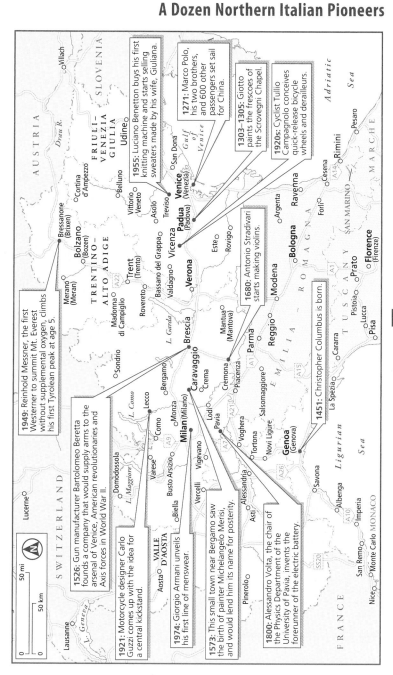

1949: Reinhold Messner, the first Westerner to summit Mt. Everest without supplemental oxygen, climbs his first Tyrolean peak at age 5.

1955: Luciano Benetton buys his first knitting machine and starts selling sweaters made by his wife, Giuliana.

1271: Marco Polo, his two brothers, and 600 other passengers set sail for China.

1303–1305: Giotto paints the frescoes of the Scrovegni Chapel.

1920s: Cyclist Tullio Campagnolo conceives quick-release bicycle wheels and derailleurs.

1680: Antonio Stradivari starts making violins.

1526: Gun manufacturer Bartolomeo Beretta founds a company that would supply arms to the arsenal of Venice, American revolutionaries and Axis forces in World War II.

1921: Motorcycle designer Carlo Guzzi comes up with the idea for a central kickstand.

1974: Giorgio Armani unveils his first line of menswear.

1573: This small town near Bergamo saw the birth of painter Michelangelo Merisi, and would lend him its name for posterity.

1800: Alessandro Volta, the chair of the Physics Department of the University of Pavia, invents the forerunner of the electric battery.

1451: Christopher Columbus is born.

makes his way to Romulus's little village, and turns it into an ancient superpower), Rome probably began as a collection of Latin and Sabine villages in the Tiber Valley. It was originally a kingdom ruled by the Etruscan Tarquin dynasty. In 509 B.C., the last Tarquin king raped the daughter of a powerful Roman. After the girl committed suicide, infuriated Romans ejected the king and established a republic ruled by two consuls (chosen from among the patrician elite) whose power was balanced by tribunes elected from among the plebian masses.

The young Roman Republic sent its military throughout the peninsula and, by 279 B.C., ruled all of Italy. Rome's armies trampled Grecian colonies throughout the Mediterranean and, after a series of brutal wars, defeated Carthage (present-day Tunisia), a rival sea power and once Rome's archenemy. By 146 B.C., Rome controlled not only all of the Italian peninsula and Sicily, but also North Africa, Spain, Sardinia, Greece, and Macedonia.

Still, Rome wanted more. It invaded Gaulish lands to the north and added what we now call France and Belgium to its realm. Rome even crossed the English Channel and conquered Britain all the way up to the Scottish Lowlands (Hadrian's Wall still stands as a testament to how far north the Roman army got). However, so much military success so distant from

Rome itself resulted in a severely weakened home front. With war booty filling the coffers, Rome ended taxation on its citizens. So much grain poured in from North Africa that the Roman farmer couldn't find a market for his wheat and simply stopped growing it. The booty had an additional price tag: corruption. Senators advanced their own lots rather than the provinces ostensibly under their care. Plebeians clamored for a bigger share, and the slaves revolted repeatedly. More reforms appeased the plebes, while the slaves were put down with horrific barbarity (one famous slave revolt, led by Spartacus, was stopped by capturing the slave army and crucifying it on crosses that lined both sides of the Via Appia from Rome and stretched for miles upon miles).

HAIL CAESAR!

At the end of the 2nd century B.C., the Republic, sped along by a corrupt Senate, was corroding into near-collapse. Julius Caesar—successful general, skilled orator, and shrewd politician—stepped in to help maintain control over Rome's vast territories, but from the day Caesar declared himself "dictator for life," Rome, as a republic, was finished. After sharing governmental power with others in a series of Triumvirates, Caesar became the sole consul in 44 B.C.

DATELINE

- **Prehistory** Neanderthal humans roam Italy; around 10,000 B.C., Cro-Magnon shows up.
- **1200** B.C. Etruscans begin to emigrate from Asia Minor, settling in Tuscany.
- **800** B.C. Greeks colonize Sicily and the peninsula's boot (collectively "Magna Graecia").
- **753** B.C. Romulus, says legend, founds Rome. In fact,

Rome grows out of a strategically located shepherd village.

- **700** B.C. Etruscans rise in power—peaking in the 6th century B.C.—and make Rome their capital.
- **509** B.C. Republic of Rome is founded; power is shared by two consuls.
- **494–450** B.C. Office of the Tribune is established to defend plebeian rights. The Twelve Tablets stating basic

rights are carved, the foundation of Roman law.

- **279** B.C. Romans now rule the entire Italian peninsula.
- **146** B.C. Rome defeats Tunisian power in Carthage; the Republic now controls Sicily, North Africa, Spain, Sardinia, Greece, and Macedonia.
- **100** B.C. Julius Caesar is born.
- **60** B.C. Caesar, Pompey, and Crassus share power in the First Triumvirate.

Caesar rose in popular influence partly by endearing himself to the lower classes through a lifelong fight against the corrupt Senate. As his power crested, he forced many immoral senators to flee Rome, introduced social reforms, inaugurated the first of many new public building programs in the center of Rome (still visible as the Forum of Caesar), and added Gaul (France) to the dying Republic. But Caesar's emphasis on the plebeians and their concerns (as well as his own thirst for power) did little to endear him to the old guard of patricians and senators. On March 15, 44 B.C., Caesar strolled out of the Baths of Pompey to meet Brutus, Cassius, and other "friends" who lay in wait with daggers hidden beneath their togas.

Caesar left everything to his nephew and heir, the 18-year-old Octavian. From the increasingly irrelevant Senate, Octavian eventually received the title Augustus, and from the people, lifetime tribuneship. And so Octavian became Emperor Augustus, sole ruler of Rome and most of the Western world.

THE EMPIRE

Augustus's long reign ushered in Pax Romana, 200 years of peace under Roman rule. The new emperor, who preferred to be called "First Citizen," reorganized the military and the provincial governments and reinstituted constitutional rule. Succeeding emperors weren't so virtuous: deranged Tiberius and Caligula; henpecked Claudius I; and Nero, who in A.D. 64 persecuted the Christians of Rome with a viciousness easily equal to the earlier slave repressions. Several of the military commanders who became emperors were exceptions to the tyrant mold. Late in the 1st century, Trajan expanded the empire's eastern boundaries and constructed great public works, including a vast series of markets.

At this peak, Rome knew amenities not to be enjoyed again in Europe until the 18th century. Citizens were privileged to have police protection, fire fighting, libraries, sanitation, huge public baths (such as the Caracalla by the Appian Way), and even central heating and running water—if they could afford them.

The empire's decline began around A.D. 200. After sacking the city several times, Goths and other Germanic tribes set up their own leaders as emperors and were more interested in the spoils of an empire than in actually running one. And while Gibbon's famous opus *The Decline and Fall of the Roman Empire* takes up an entire bookshelf to explain Rome's downfall, in the end it all boils down to the fact that the empire had become just too big to manage.

After embracing Christianity in his famous 313 Edict of Milan, Emperor Constantine I tried to resolve the problem by

---

- **51** B.C. Caesar triumphs over Gaul (France).
- **44** B.C. March 15, Caesar is assassinated, leaving all to his nephew and heir, Octavian.
- **27** B.C. Octavian, now Augustus, is declared emperor, beginning the Roman Empire and 200 years of peace and prosperity.
- A.D. **29 (or 33)** Jesus is crucified in Roman province of Judea.

- **64–100** Nero persecutes Christians; a succession of military commanders restores order; Trajan expands the empire.
- **200** Goths invade from the north; the empire begins to decline.
- **313** With the Edict of Milan, Emperor Constantine I grants Christians freedom of religion. By 324, it is declared the official religion. Constantine also establishes

Constantinople as the eastern capital, splitting the empire in half.
- **410–76** Waves of northern barbarian tribes continue to overrun Italy and sack Rome itself, eventually setting up their own puppet "emperors."
- **476** Last emperor deposed; the empire falls; the Dark Ages begin.
- **590–604** Church asserts political control as Pope

continues

moving the capital of the empire from Rome to the city of Byzantium (later renamed Constantinople and today known as Istanbul). The Roman Empire was irrevocably split in half: a western Roman Empire comprising most of Europe and North Africa, and an eastern Roman Empire filling southeast Europe and the Near East.

CURTAIN GOING DOWN: THE DARK AGES

In 476, the last emperor (ironically, named Romulus) fell from power and the Roman Empire collapsed. It would be 1,500 years before Italy was once again united as a single nation. As the 6th century opened, Italy was in chaos. Waves of barbarians from the north poured in while provincial nobles engaged in petty bickering, and Rome became the personal fiefdom of the papacy. The Goths continued to rule the "Western Roman Empire" nominally from Ravenna but were soon driven out by Constantinople. It was the Roman Catholic Church, beginning with Pope Gregory I "the Great" late in the 6th century, that finally provided some stability. In 731, Pope Gregory II renounced Rome's nominal dependence on Constantinople and reoriented the Roman Catholic Church firmly toward Europe—in the process, finalizing the empire's division into east and west.

During the Dark Ages, some inhabitants of the Veneto flatlands, seeking some degree of safety from the barbarian hordes, slowly moved out onto the islets of the north Adriatic's wide, marshy lagoon. The villages they founded eventually grew into the fairy-tale city of Venice. In 564, another Germanic tribe, called the Lombards, clambered over the Alps and swept through much of Italy, conquering a good two-thirds of the peninsula ruled from their base at Pavia. By 599, Pope Gregory I "the Great" had begun flexing the secular power of the papacy (beginning a policy that would eventually set the pope at the head of Europe's power structure), negotiating a peace between Constantinople and Italy's new Lombard rulers.

The Lombards weren't satisfied, though, and by 752 had conquered Ravenna itself. The pope cast around for a new ally against the Lombards and settled on the powerful king of another Barbarian tribe, Pepin the Short of the Franks. In 754, Pepin invaded Italy and thrashed the Lombards; 20 years later, his famous son, Charlemagne, followed suit. Not satisfied with merely the Lombard crown, the French king continued to Rome and convinced the pope to crown him as a new emperor, the so-called Holy Roman Emperor, on Christmas Day in the year 800. This new imperial office would become the plum of western European monarchies for nearly a millennium and further helped cement the relationship

Gregory I "the Great" brings some stability to the peninsula.

■ **774–800** Frankish king Charlemagne invades Italy and is crowned emperor by Pope Leo III. Upon his death, Italy dissolves into a series of small warring kingdoms.

■ **962** Holy Roman Empire founded under Otto I, king of Saxony; serves as the temporal arm of the church's spiritual power.

■ **11th century** Normans conquer southern Italy and introduce feudalism. The first Crusades are launched.

■ **1309–77** Papacy abandons Rome for Avignon, France.

■ **1350** The Black Death decimates Europe, reducing Italy's population by a third.

■ **1450** City-states hold power; Venice controls much of the eastern Mediterranean. The Humanist movement rediscovers the art and

philosophy of ancient Greece and gives rise to the artistic Renaissance.

■ **ca. 1500** Peak of the High Renaissance; Italian artists working at the turn of the 15th century include Leonardo da Vinci, Michelangelo, Raphael, Botticelli, Giovanni Bellini, Mantegna, and Titian.

■ **1519–27** Carlos I Habsburg of Spain is crowned Holy Roman Emperor as Charles V in 1519. He wages war

Habsburgs

Though the Habsburgs were never Italian, their imperial shenanigans frequently impacted northern Italy as they played out their power struggles with France on Italian battlefields, using Italian territories and duchies as pieces in a giant, prolonged, and often bloody chess match. The Habsburg name confuses some, though. It began with the 13th-century rulers of Swabia, in southern Germany. The family's main man in the early 16th century was Carlos of Ghent, who became king of Spain and, in 1519, changed his name to Holy Roman Emperor Charles V. When he abdicated in 1556, he left the Spanish crown to his heirs—the Spanish Habsburgs—but left the family's Austrian/Bavarian lands, as well as the imperial title, to little brother Ferdinand I, whose heirs kept the title and the Austro-Hungarian dynasty for centuries.

between the papacy and the secular titular head of western Europe.

During the Middle Ages, northern Italy fragmented into a collection of city-states. The Lombards had to be content with a reduced duchy filling the Po Valley south of the Alps and Italy's large lakes, wedged between the eastern territory of the Republic of Venice and the western Duchy of Savoy in Piedmont, as well as the coastal territory ruled by the maritime Republic of Genoa. Plenty of principalities, duchies, republics, and smaller city-states filled in the cracks, with Austrian Habsburg rulers snaking their influence down the Adige River valley into the Dolomites, as well as across the eastern Alps to the coastline curving around the

Northern Adriatic, founding the port of Trieste. This put them in constant conflict with the territories of Venice, and the line dividing the realms of Venice's Republican doges and Austria's Habsburg emperors continued to shift, expand, and retreat well into the 20th century.

Meanwhile, the papacy's temporal power—the Papal States—slowly but inexorably shrank, eventually encompassing only Rome and portions of central Italy's provinces. Its political concerns turned to arguing with the German and Austrian emperors over the office of Holy Roman Emperor, which became increasingly irrelevant to daily affairs as the Renaissance dawned.

against the French, and the pope scurries back and forth in support of one side then the next as their wars in Italy played out largely in Italy over Italian territories. In 1527, Charles V marches into Rome and sacks the city, while Pope Clement VII escapes. Charles occupies nearly all of northern Italy, divvying it up among his followers.

- **1535** Francesco II Sforza of Milan dies, leaving the Duchy in Spanish Habsburg hands.
- **1545–63** Council of Trent takes a hard line against the reformist Protestant movements sweeping Europe north of the Alps, launching the Counter-Reformation and, as an unexpected consequence, ultimately reducing the pope's power as a secular ruler of Europe to

merely a prince of central Italy.
- **17th–18th centuries** Italy's darkest hour: Brigands control the countryside, the Austrians and Spanish everything else. By the mid–18th century, wealthy northern Europeans begin taking the Grand Tour, journeying to Italy to study ancient architecture and Italian old masters (as well as taking

continues

In the mid–14th century, the Black Death ravaged Europe, killing a third of Italy's population. Despite such setbacks, northern Italian cities grew wealthy from Crusade booty, trade with one another and with the Middle East, and banking. These wealthy principalities and pseudo-republics ruled by the merchant elite flexed their muscles in the absence of a strong central authority.

CURTAIN GOING UP: THE RENAISSANCE

The Renaissance peaked in the 15th century as northern cities bullied their way to city-state status. Even while warring constantly with one another to extend their territories, such ruling families as the Medicis in Florence, the Estes in Ferrara, and the Sforzas and Gonzagas in Milan grew incredibly rich and powerful.

The princes, popes, and merchant princes who ruled Italy's city-states, spurred on by the Humanist philosophical movement, collectively bankrolled the explosion of poetic and artistic expression we now call the Renaissance (see "Northern Italy's Art & Architecture" section, below). But with no clear political authority or unified military, Italy was easy pickings, and by the mid–16th century, Spain, courtesy of Charles V, occupied nearly all of the country.

THE SECOND FALL

From the mid–16th century until the end of the 18th century, Italy suffered economic depression and foreign domination. As emphasis on world trade shifted away from the Mediterranean, Italy's influence diminished. Within Italy itself, Spanish Bourbons controlled the kingdoms of the south, the pope the center, and Austria and France fought over rule of the north, using Italy's realms—from the large Lombard duchy of Milan to tiny principalities like Mantua—as pawns in their power struggles. The only notable free state was the mighty Republic of Venice (though the extent of its landlubbing provinces in the Veneto, Dolomites [Dolomiti], and Friuli slowly shrank). These foreign overlords kept raising taxes, farming declined, the birthrate sank, and bandits proliferated. The 18th century is viewed as Italy's nadir. In fact, only Europe's eager ear for Italian music and eye for art and architecture kept the Italian profile haughty and its cultural patrimony resplendent.

It was the late-18th-century French Revolution and the arrival of Napoleon that lit Italy's nationalistic fire, although it would be the mid–19th century before the Risorgimento movement and a new king could spread the flame.

advantage of the sunny clime and low-cost living). Italy's tourism industry has begun.
- **1784** The French Revolution sparks Italian nationalism.
- **1796–1814** Napoleon sweeps through Italy, installing friends and relatives as rulers.
- **1814** Napoleon is defeated at Waterloo.
- **1830** Beginning of the Risorgimento political movement in Turin and Genoa, which will culminate in Italian nationalism, accompanied by a new Renaissance of literature and music.
- **1861** Kingdom of Italy is created under Vittorio Emanuele II, Savoy king of Piedmont (Piemonte), and united through the military campaign of General Garibaldi. Turin serves briefly as interim capital.
- **1870** Rome, last papal stronghold, falls to Garibaldi. Italy becomes a country; Rome is its capital.
- **Late 19th century** Mass emigration to America and other foreign shores, though mostly from the impoverished, agricultural south.
- **1915** Italy enters World War I on Allied side.
- **1922** Mussolini marches on Rome and puts his Fascist Blackshirts in charge of the

THE SECOND RISE: THE 19TH CENTURY

Italians initially gave Napoleon an exultant *benvenuto!* when he swept through the peninsula and swept out Italy's 18th-century political disasters (along with the Austrian army). But Napoleon, in the end, neither united Italy nor provided it with self-government—he merely set up his own friends and relatives as new princes and dukes. Many Italians, however, were fired up by the Napoleonic revolutionary rhetoric. The Risorgimento (resurgence) nationalist movement—an odd amalgam of radicals, moderate liberals, and Roman Catholic conservatives—struggled for 30 years to create a single, united Italy under a constitutional monarchy.

You'll find Risorgimento heroes' names recalled in streets and *piazze* throughout Italy: Giuseppe Mazzini provided the intellectual rigor for the movement, the political genius of noble-born Camillo Cavour engineered the underpinnings of the new nation (he served as its second prime minister), and General Giuseppe Garibaldi and his "Red Shirt" soldiers did the legwork by conquering reluctant or foreign-controlled territories. In 1861, Vittorio Emanuele II of the southern French House of Savoy, previously king only of Piedmont and Liguria, became the first king of Italy. By 1871, Garibaldi finally defeated the papal holdout of Rome, and the great city once again became capital of a unified Italy.

FINALLY, A NATION UNITED

A united nation? On paper, yes, but the old sectional differences remained. While there was rapid industrialization in the north, the south labored under the repressive neo-feudal agricultural ways of the late 19th century, creating a north-south division and mutual mistrust that still pervades Italian society. The north views the south as indolent, a welfare state sucking dry the money made in the industrial north; the south sees the north as elitist and arrogant, constantly proposing or enacting laws to keep the south economically depressed. Many southerners escaped economic hardship and political powerlessness by emigrating to the industrialized north, or to greener pastures abroad in the U.S., South America, or northern Europe.

Italy entered World War I on the Allied side in exchange for territorial demands, and to vanquish that old foe Austria. In the end, the Austro-Hungarian Empire was defeated, but at the Paris Peace Conference, Italy was granted much less territory than had been promised (though it did receive Trieste), which compounded the country's problems. As southerners

country, declaring himself prime minister.

- **1935** Mussolini defeats and annexes Ethiopia.
- **1939** Italy enters the war by signing an alliance with Nazi Germany.
- **1943** Italy switches sides as Allied troops push Nazis north up peninsula; by 1945, Mussolini and mistress executed by partisans, strung up at a Milan gas station,

and pelted with stones by the crowds.

- **1946** A national referendum narrowly establishes the Republic of Italy.
- **1950–93** Fifty changes of government were seen, along with the "economic miracle" that has made Italy the world's fifth-leading economy.
- **1993–97** Series of disasters rocks Italy's cultural roots:

1993 Mafia bombing of Florence's Uffizi Galleries; January 1996 fire at Venice's La Fenice opera house; April 1997 conflagration in Turin's cathedral; and September 1997 earthquakes in Umbria, which destroyed priceless frescoes in Assisi.

- **1993–2000** Italy's Christian Democrat–controlled government dissolves amid corruption allegations. Silvio

continues

abandoned the country in droves, the economy stagnated, and what remained of Italy's world importance seemed to be fading rapidly, along came Benito Mussolini, promising to restore national pride and bring order out of the chaos.

FASCISM REIGNS

Mussolini marched on Rome in 1922, forced the king to make him premier, nicknamed himself Il Duce (the Duke), and quickly repressed all other political factions. He put his Fascist "Blackshirts" in charge of the entire country: schools, the press, industry, and labor. Seeking, as Italian despot-hopefuls throughout history have done, to endear himself to the general populace, Mussolini instituted a vast public-works program, most of which eventually failed. Mussolini fancied himself a second Caesar and spent some time excavating the archaeological remains of ancient Rome—not always with the most stringent scientific methods—to help glorify his reign and lend it authority. The Great Depression of the 1930s made life considerably more difficult for Italians, and, to divert attention from his shortcomings as a ruler, Mussolini turned to foreign adventures, defeating and annexing Ethiopia in 1935.

Mussolini entered Italy into World War II as an Axis ally of the Nazis, but the Italian heart was not really in the war, and most Italians had little wish to pursue Hitler's anti-Semitic policies. Armed partisan resistance to the official government forces and to the Nazis remained strong. By 1945, the Italian people had had enough. They rose against Mussolini and the Axis, and the Fascists were disbanded. King Victor Emmanuel III, who had collaborated with the Fascists without much enthusiasm during the past 2 decades, appointed a new premier. At the end of the war, Mussolini and his mistress were pictured in the world press hanging by their heels at a Milanese gas station after being shot by partisans.

DEMOCRACY AT LAST

After the war, Italians narrowly voted to become a republic, and in 1946, a new republican constitution went into effect. Various permutations of the center-right Christian Democrat party ruled in a succession of more than 50 governments until 1993, when the entire government dissolved in a flurry of corruption and graft. The country's leaders were prosecuted (and many jailed) by what became known as the "Clean Hands" judges of Milan. The two main parties, the Christian Democrats and the Communists, both splintered in the aftermath, giving rise to some 16 major political parties and countless minor ones.

Berlusconi's right-wing coalition holds power for a few months, followed by center–left wing coalitions that introduce the most stable governments in decades under prime ministers Romano Prodi, Massimo d'Alema, and Giuliano Amato.

- **2001** The first cases of BSE (mad cow disease) in Italy are confirmed; beef consumption plummets over

70%, and the government temporarily bans many kinds of steak on the bone. Media magnate (and the world's 29th-richest man) Silvio Berlusconi—briefly prime minister in 1993, but brought down by professional and political scandals—gains control, once again, of the Italian government as part of a center-right coalition including the neo-Fascist Alleanza Nazionale party

and the racist and separatist Lega del Nord, which wants to make northern Italy a new country called "Padania" with Milan as its capital (leaving Rome to govern the shrunken "Italy" of the south).

- **2002** January 1: Italy, along with most of western Europe, adopts the euro as its currency. January 2: Prices on everything skyrocket.

The parties formed various coalitions, leading to such strange political bedfellows as the Forza Italia alliance, headed by media mogul Silvio Berlusconi, which filled the national power vacuum during 1994. It included both the nationalist Alleanza Nazionale party (the modern incarnation of the Fascist party) and the Lega del Nord, the separatist "Northern League" (originally the "Lombard League"), which wanted to split Italy in half, making Milan capital of a new country in the north called "Padania" and leaving Rome to govern the poor south. In 2000, though, the Lega changed its tune to become more palatable and call for devolution, a decentralized government with more power going to individual regions.

In 1994, the center-left Olive Tree coalition swept the national elections and Italy enjoyed a novelty: 3 years of stable rule under the government of Prime Minister Romano Prodi, replaced by a center-left government of Massimo D'Alema. Interestingly, given the stereotype among fellow Europeans of Italy as a nation prone to graft and political chaos, Prodi—an economist before becoming prime minister and the man who reined in Italy's debt to qualify the country for the European Union—was later named to head the European Commission to restore its status after a humiliating scandal.

By 2001, Berlusconi had fought off the dozens of legal charges of corruption (though courts in Spain, trying him for corporate crimes relating to his business relations in Iberia, found him guilty), and in April of that year, he and his right-wing Forza Italia partners came back into power, just in time to shepherd Italy through the switch from the lira to the euro in 2002 (originally a left-wing initiative). Berlusconi continued to consolidate power through 2002 and 2003, introducing ever more legislation to protect himself and his interests from criminal investigations, as well as laws that would allow his private media company to control even more of the country's communications industry (through the trio of state-run RAI channels and his own Mediaset network, he already controls the six most popular of Italy's seven broadcast channels). It is hard to say whether it was Berlusconi's legal troubles or his unpopular decision to support the United States' invasion and occupation of Iraq that turned the tide against him. Whatever the cause, the result in the 2006 elections was a loss to Romano Prodi by a slim margin of votes, though the triumphant return of the "Professor" was short-lived. Berlusconi, aka "The Knight," came galloping back to power in the elections of 2008. He is currently serving as Italy's prime minister again, and though his current term has

- **2003** Prime Minster Berlusconi, who, through private media holdings and his government post, controls 98% of Italian television (not to mention the country's largest publishing empire), and who, in late 2002, fired his foreign minister and declared that he himself would run that office, forces through legislation to protect himself from being prosecuted for any crimes while in office—conveniently, just as one of the many bribery cases that have been brought against him was about to come to a conclusion.
- **2006** Italy's highest appeals court confirms Romano Prodi's razor-thin victory over Berlusconi in national elections, sending the one-time professor and European Commission President back to Palazzo Chigi.
- **2008** The People of Freedom (*Il Popolo della Libertà*, PdL) party is founded when Forza Italia is merged with National Alliance. As the leader of this center-right political party, Berlusconi is once again elected Prime Minister in the 2008 general elections.

been surrounded by personal scandal, he still seems to have strong supporters.

Politically, some things never change in Italy. The same mistrust among factions continues: Cities are still paranoid about their individuality and their rights, and the division between north and south is as sharp as ever. The Mafia had, by the late 19th century, become a kind of shadow government in the south, and to this day it controls a staggering number of politicians (including senators and even prime ministers), national officials, and judges, providing one scandal after another.

The outsider looks and wonders how the country keeps going amid the political chaos, Byzantine bureaucracy, and deep regional differences. The Italian just shrugs and rolls his eyes. Italians have always excelled at getting by under difficult circumstances and making the most of any situation. If nothing else, they're masters at survival.

3 NORTHERN ITALY'S ART & ARCHITECTURE

ART

When you mention art in Italy, most people's thoughts fly first to the Renaissance—to Giotto, Donatello, Michelangelo, Raphael, and Leonardo. But Italy's artistic heritage actually goes back at least 2,500 years.

Classical Art: Greeks, Etruscans & Romans (5th c. B.C.–5th c. A.D.)

Today all, or almost all, design roads lead to Milan. In the beginning, though, all roads led from Athens. What the **Greeks** identified early on that captured the hearts and minds of so many was the classical rendering of form. To the ancients, *classic* or *classical* simply meant perfection—of proportion, balance, harmony, and form. To the Greeks, man was the measure of perfection, an attitude lost in the Middle Ages and not rediscovered until the dawn of the Renaissance.

Although those early tourists to the Italian peninsula, the **Etruscans,** arrived with their own styles, by the 6th century B.C., they were borrowing heavily from the Greeks in their sculpture (and importing thousands of Attic painted vases). The **Romans,** in turn, copied heavily from the Greeks, often ad nauseam as they cranked out countless facsimiles of Greek sculptures to decorate Roman patrician homes and gardens. Bronze portraiture, a technique with Greek and Etruscan roots, was polished to photographic perfection.

Although painting got rather short shrift in ancient Rome (it was used primarily for decorative purposes), bucolic frescoes, the technique of painting on wet plaster, adorned the walls of the wealthy in Rome, though nothing significant survives in the north of Italy. Mosaics were rather better done and survived the ages more intact; you can see some of the best Roman mosaic flooring at the excavations of Aquileia in the Friuli.

Byzantine & Romanesque (5th–13th c.)

Artistic expression in the Dark Ages and early medieval Italy was largely church related. Mass was recited in Latin, so to help explain the most important lessons to the illiterate masses, biblical bas-reliefs around the churches' main doors, as well as wall paintings and altarpieces inside, told key tales to inspire faith in God and fear of sin (Last Judgments were favorites). Otherwise, decoration was spare, and what little existed was often destroyed, replaced, or covered over the centuries as tastes changed and cathedrals were remodeled.

The Byzantine style of painting and mosaic was very stylized and static, an iconographic tradition imported from the remnant eastern half of the Roman Empire centered at Byzantium (its major political outposts in Italy were Ravenna and Venice). Faces (and eyes) were almond-shaped with pointy little chins, noses long with a spoonlike depression at the top, and folds in robes (always Virgin Mary blue over red) represented by stylized cross-hatching in gold leaf.

Romanesque sculpture was somewhat more fluid, but still far from naturalistic, usually idiosyncratic and often wonderfully childlike in its narrative simplicity, frequently freely mixing biblical scenes with the myths and motifs from local pagan traditions that were being slowly incorporated into early medieval Christianity.

Romanesque art was seen as crude by most later periods and usually replaced or destroyed over the centuries; it survives mostly in scraps, innumerable column capitals and tympanums or carvings set above church doors all across Italy. Some of the best major examples of this era in northern Italy include the astounding mosaics decorating San Marco cathedral in Venice, a late Byzantine church of domes and a glittering array of mosaics. (However, while the overall effect is indeed Byzantine, many of the mosaics are from various later dates.) **Verona's San Zeno Maggiore** sports 48 relief panels on the bronze doors, one of the most important pieces of Romanesque sculpture in Italy, cast between the 9th and 11th centuries and flanked by strips of 12th-century stone reliefs. **Aosta's Collegiata dei Santi Pietro e Orso,** on the edge of town, preserves part of an 11th-century fresco cycle and 40 remarkable 12th-century carved column capitals in the cloisters.

International Gothic (Late 13th to Early 15th c.)

Late medieval Italian art continued to be largely ecclesiastical. Church facades and pulpits were festooned with statues and carvings. In both Gothic painting and sculpture, figures tended to be more natural than in the Romanesque (and the colors in painting more varied and rich), but highly stylized and rhythmic, the figures' features and gestures exaggerated for symbolic or emotional emphasis. In painting especially, late Gothic artists, such as Giotto, started introducing greater realism, a sense of depth, and more realistic emotion into their art, sowing the seeds of the Renaissance.

Without a doubt, **Giotto** (1266–1337) was the greatest Gothic artist, the man who lifted painting from its Byzantine funk and set it on the road to the realism and perspective of the Renaissance. His most renowned work is the fresco cycle of Assisi's Basilica di San Francesco, but arguably better (and more certain of its authorship) is Padua's (Padova's) outstanding **Scrovegni (Arena) Chapel.** The bulk of great Gothic art resides in Tuscany and Umbria, but Verona was blessed to have **Antonio Pisanello** (1395–1455), whose frescoes survive in Sant'Anastasia and San Fermo, and in Mantua (Mantova) at the Palazzo Ducale.

Renaissance & Mannerism (Early 15th to Mid–17th c.)

From the 14th to 16th centuries, the popularity of the Humanist movement in philosophy prompted princes and powerful prelates to patronize a generation of innovative young artists. These painters, sculptors, and architects were experimenting with new modes in art and breaking with static medieval traditions to pursue a greater degree of expressiveness and naturalism, using such techniques as linear perspective (actually pioneered by architect Brunelleschi and sculptors Donatello and Ghiberti). The term *Renaissance,* or "rebirth," was only later applied to this period in Florence, from which the movement spread to the rest of Italy and Europe.

Eventually, the High Renaissance began to stagnate, producing vapid works of technical perfection but little substance. Several artists sought ways out of the downward spiral. Mannerism was the most interesting attempt, a movement that found its muse in the extreme torsion of Michelangelo's figures—in sculpture and painting—and his unusual use of oranges, greens, and other nontraditional colors, most especially in the Sistine Chapel ceiling. In sculpture, Mannerism produced twisting figures in exaggerated *contraposto* positioning.

This list of Renaissance giants merely scratches the surface of the masters Italy gave rise to in the 15th and 16th centuries.

Donatello (Donato Bardi; ca. 1386–1466) was the first full-fledged Renaissance sculptor, with a patented *schiacciato* technique of warping low relief surfaces and etching backgrounds in perspective to create a sense of deep space. His bronze and marble figures are some of the most expressive and psychologically probing of the Renaissance. Among his many innovations, this unassuming artist cast the first equestrian bronze since antiquity, the *Gattamelata* in Padua.

Leonardo da Vinci (1452–1519) was the original "Renaissance Man," dabbling his genius in a bit of everything, from art to philosophy to science (on paper, he even designed machine guns and rudimentary helicopters). Little of his remarkable painting survives, however, as he often experimented with new pigment mixes that proved to lack the staying power of traditional materials. Leonardo invented such painterly effects as the fine haze of *sfumato,* "a moisture-laden atmosphere that delicately veils . . . forms." Unfortunately, the best example of this effect, his fresco of *The Last Supper* in Milan (1495–97), is sadly deteriorated, and even the ongoing multidecade restoration is saving but a shadow of the fresco's glory. See his *Portrait of a Musician* in

Milan's Pinacoteca Ambrosiana for a better-preserved example.

Michelangelo Buonarotti (1475–1564), heavyweight contender for world's greatest artist ever, was a genius in sculpture, painting, architecture, and poetry. He marked the apogee of the Renaissance. A complex and difficult man—intensely jealous, probably manic-depressive, and certainly homosexual—Michelangelo enjoyed great fame in a life plagued by a series of never-ending projects commissioned by Pope Julius II, including Rome's Sistine Chapel frescoes. Michelangelo worshiped the male nude as the ultimate form and twisted the bodies of his figures (torsion) in different, often contradictory directions *(contraposto)* to bring out their musculature. When forced against his will to paint the Sistine Chapel, he broke almost all the rules and sent painting headlong in an entirely new direction—the Mannerist movement—marked by nonprimary colors, Impressionistic shapes of light, and twisting muscular figures. While you'll have to go to Florence and Rome to see his greatest works, including the *David,* you can admire his final work (for free, no less) in Milan, an oddly modern, elongated *Pietà* he was still working on when he died at age 89.

Raphael (Raffaello Sanzio; 1483–1520) is rightfully considered one of Western art's greatest draftsmen. Raphael produced a body of work in his 37 short years that ignited European painters for generations to come. So it's only fitting that his only significant work in northern Italy, kept in Milan's Pinacoteca Ambrosiana, is a sketch, one for the *School of Athens,* the fresco of which graces the papal apartments of the Vatican, at once a celebration of Renaissance artistic precepts, the classical philosophers whose rediscovery spurred on the Renaissance, and Raphael's contemporaries (the various "philosophers" are actually portraits of Leonardo, Bramante, and Raphael himself—Michelangelo is not in the sketch but was added in the painting).

Fun Facts   What's in a Name?

Many Italian artists came to be known by nicknames—usually based on the town from which they came—which are the names that we call them today. "Tintoretto" was called that because of his love of color (*tinto* in Italian). Leonardo had no official last name (he was the bastard son of a serving wench and her boss, a minor noble and landowner in the small town of Vinci), so everyone just called him "Leonardo from Vinci." Some also had silly nicknames, like Sandro Filipepi, better known to his buds as "Little Barrels"—or, in Italian, Botticelli.

All of the above artists hailed from central Italy. Now we get to some homegrown northern Italian talents. Though his father, **Jacopo** (1400–71), and brother, **Gentile** (1429–1507), were also fine practitioners of the family business (Jacopo really more from a Gothic vein, a student of Gentile da Fabriano and rival to Pisanello), it was **Giovanni Bellini** (1430–1516) who towered above them all with his painterly talent, limpid colors, sculptured forms, and complex compositions. Both he and his brother are best represented by works in Venice's Accademia and Palazzo Ducale, as well as Milan's Pinacoteca di Brera. Giovanni Bellini's style and talent reverberated through Venetian art for generations; he himself taught the likes of Titian, Giorgione, Sebastiano del Piombo, and Palma il Vecchio.

Gentile and Giovanni had a sister, too, and, as it happened, she married a young painter named **Andrea Mantegna** (1431–1506). Mantegna excelled at three of the main tenets of Renaissance art: He was an early perfector of perspective (which he could warp masterfully), he was a keen observer of anatomy (which he modeled with sculptural exactitude), and he made careful studies of ancient architecture (the proportions and details of which he incorporated into his paintings). You'll find Mantegna's paintings throughout the region, from his early *Madonna and Child with Saints* altarpiece for Verona's San Zeno, to his work as court painter to the

Gonzagas in Mantua (the Palazzo Ducale's *Camera degli Sposi*), to his unparalleled *Dead Christ,* considered the masterpiece of Milan's Pinacoteca di Brera (no small honor, considering the heavyweights inhabiting the premier art gallery in northern Italy).

Titian (Tiziano Vecellio; 1485–1576) was the father of the Venetian High Renaissance, who imparted to the school his love of color and tonality and exploration of the effects of light on darkened scenes. In Venice, you'll find his works everywhere, from canvases in the Accademia collections to altarpieces decorating churches, such as the Frari, to his early and famous *Battle* scene (1513) in the Palazzo Ducale's Sala del Maggior Consiglio.

After Titian, 16th-century Venetian art was dominated by two powerful talents, Paolo Veronese and **Tintoretto** (Jacopo Robusti; 1518–94). Tintoretto was something of a Venetian Mannerist, using a rapid, loose brushwork and a slightly somber, shadow-filled take on the tones of Titian's palette that together imparted a realism and vitality to his painting. Venice's Accademia has some works, of course, but his crowning glory is the Scuola Grande di San Rocco in Venice, for which he painted well over a dozen large-scale canvases. He also holds the honor of having produced (with the help of son Domenico) the largest oil painting in the world (6.9×24m/23×79 ft.), the *Paradise* decorating the end wall of the Sala del

Maggior Consiglio in the Palazzo Ducale in Mantua.

Verona-born **Paolo Veronese** (Paolo Caliari; 1528–88) had a much brighter, tighter style, and he loved crowding his canvases with hordes of extras straight out of 16th-century central casting. In fact, his broad inclusion of earthy details ran him afoul of the Counter-Reformation spirit of the times, and he avoided incurring the church's wrath over the crowd of serving wenches and slave boys populating a *Last Supper* he painted only by hastily retitling it *Feast in the House of Levi* (now in Venice's Accademia). The church of San Sebastiano boasts his ceiling frescoes, but it's Venice's Palazzo Ducale that bookends the career of Veronese (containing both his earliest paintings and one of his final ones). His earliest Venetian commissions (1553) were for paintings in the chambers where two groups in the highest echelons of Venice's ruling body met, the Sala del Consiglio dei Dieci and the Sala dei Tre Capi del Consiglio. One of his final works (finished by his studio) was the huge *Apotheosis of Venice* decorating the ceiling of the Sala del Maggior Consiglio. Veronese would be the main artist to inspire Tiepolo and others in Venice's next generation of baroque artists.

Baroque & Rococo (Late 16th to 18th c.)

The baroque is a more theatrical and decorative take on the Renaissance, mixing a kind of super-realism based on the peasant models and chiaroscuro (harsh light and exaggeratedly dark shadows) of Caravaggio with compositional complexity and explosions of dynamic fury, movement, color, and figures. Rococo is this later baroque art gone awry, frothy and chaotic.

The baroque period produced many fine artists, but only a few true geniuses, and most of them (including Caravaggio and Bernini) worked in Rome and the south. **Giovanni Battista Tiepolo** (1696–1770) was, by a long shot, the best rococo

artist there was, influenced by not only his Venetian late-Renaissance predecessors but also the Roman and Neapolitan baroque. His specialty was painting ceiling frescoes (and canvases meant to be placed in a ceiling) that opened up the space into frothy, cloud-filled heavens of light, angels, and pale, sunrise colors. Though he painted many works for Veneto villas, including the sumptuous Villa Valmarana and Villa Pisani, he also spent much of his time traveling throughout Europe on long commissions (his work in Würzburg, Germany, enjoys distinction as the largest ceiling fresco in the world). His son, **Giovanni Domenico Tiepolo** (1727–1804), carried on the family tradition in a Venice increasingly ruled by genre masters like **Antonio Canaletto** (1697–1738), whose ultrarealistic scenes of Venetian canals and palaces were snapped up by the collectors from across the Alps who began sniffing around Italy on their Grand Tour.

Late 18th Century to Today

After carrying the artistic church of innovation for over a millennium, Italy ran out of steam with the baroque, leaving countries such as France to develop the heights of neoclassicism (though Italy produced a few fine neoclassical sculptures) and late-19th-century Impressionism (Italians had their own version, called the Macchiaioli). Italy has not played an important role in late-19th/20th-century art, though it has produced a few great artists, all of whose works grace the excellent Pinacoteca di Brera, the Palazzo Reale, and the modern art gallery adjoining the Duomo, the Museo Civico d'Arte Contemporanea, all in Milan.

Antonio Canova (1757–1822) was Italy's top neoclassical sculptor, popular for his mythological figures and Bonaparte portraits (he even did both Napoleon and his sister Pauline as nudes); in addition to the Brera in Milan, you'll find his work in Venice's Museo Correr. **Giovanni Fattori**

(1825–1908) was the best of the Macchi-aioli, fond of battle scenes and landscapes populated by the Maremma's long-horned white cattle.

A sickly boy and only moderately successful in his short lifetime, **Amadeo Modigliani** (1884–1920) helped reinvent the portrait in painting and sculpture after he moved to Paris in 1906. He is famed for his elongated, mysterious heads and rapidly painted nudes. Check them out at Milan's Pinacoteca di Brera. **Giorgio de Chirico** (1888–1978) was the founder of freaky *metafisica,* "metaphysical painting," a forerunner of surrealism wherein figures and objects are stripped of their usual meaning through odd juxtapositions, warped perspective and reality, unnatural shadows, and other bizarre effects, as well as a general spatial emptiness. **Giorgio Morandi** (1890–1964) was influenced by *metafisica* in his eerily minimalist, highly modeled, quasi-monochrome still lifes. His paintings also decorate Turin's Galleria d'Arte Moderna.

Italian artists living in 1909 Paris made a spirited attempt to take the artistic initiative back into Italian hands, but what the **Futurist** movement's **Umberto Boccioni** (1882–1916) came up with was largely cubism with an element of movement added in. **Gino Severini** (1883–1966) contributed a sophisticated take on color, which rubbed off on the core cubists as well. Both are represented at Milan's Pinacoteca di Brera and the Palazzo Reale.

ARCHITECTURE

While each architectural era has its distinctive features, there are some elements, general floor plans, and terms common to many. Also, some features may appear near the end of one era and continue through several later ones.

From the Romanesque period on, most churches consist of either a single, wide aisle or a wide central nave flanked by two narrow aisles. The aisles are separated from the nave by a row of columns, or by square stacks of masonry called piers, usually connected by arches.

This main nave/aisle assemblage is usually crossed by a perpendicular corridor called a transept near the far, east end of the church so that the floor plan looks like a Latin Cross (shaped like a crucifix). The shorter, east arm of the nave is the holiest area, called the chancel; it often houses the stalls of the choir and the altar. If the far end of the chancel is rounded off, we call it an apse. An ambulatory is a curving corridor outside the altar and choir area, separating it from the ring of smaller chapels radiating off the chancel and apse.

Some churches, especially after the Renaissance, when mathematical proportion became important, were built on a Greek cross plan, each axis the same length. By the baroque period, funky shapes became popular, with churches built in the round, or as ellipses, and so forth.

It's worth pointing out that very few buildings (especially churches) were built in only one particular style. These massive, expensive structures often took centuries to complete, during which time tastes would change and plans would be altered.

Ancient Rome (1st c. B.C.–4th c. A.D.)

The Romans made use of certain Greek innovations, particularly architectural ideas. The first to be adopted was post-and-lintel construction—essentially, a weight-bearing frame, like a door. Later came adaptation of Greek columns for supporting buildings, following the classical orders of Doric column capitals (the plain ones) on the ground floor, Ionic capitals (with the scrolls on either end) on the next level, and Corinthian capitals (flowering with acanthus leaves) on the top.

Romans thrived on huge complex problems for which they could produce organized, well-crafted solutions. Roman builders became inventive engineers, developing hoisting mechanisms and a specially trained workforce. They designed towns, built civic centers, raised grand temples and public baths, and developed the basilica, a rectangle supported by arches atop columns along both sides of the interior and with an apse at one or both ends. Basilicas were used for courts of justice, banking, and other commercial structures. The design was repeated all over the Roman world, beginning around the 1st century A.D. Later, early Christians adapted the architectural style for the first grand churches, still called basilicas.

Although marble is traditionally associated with Roman architecture, Roman engineers could also do wonders with bricks or even prosaic concrete. Their urban planning still stamps the street layouts of cities from **Aosta** (which preserves a gate and theater stage) to **Brescia** (with an ancient temple and theater remaining in the city center) to **Verona** (which preserves a magnificent ancient amphitheater still used for performances).

Romanesque (A.D. 800–1300)

The Romanesque took its inspiration and rounded arches from ancient Rome (hence the name). Romanesque architects concentrated on building large churches with wide aisles to fit the ranks of people who came not only to hear the priests say Mass but mainly to worship at the altars of various saints. To support the weight of all that masonry, though, the walls had to be thick and solid (meaning they could be pierced only by few and rather small windows) resting on huge piers, giving Romanesque churches a dark, somber, mysterious, and often oppressive feeling.

The most identifiable Romanesque feature is rounded arches. These load-bearing architectural devices allowed the architects to open up wide naves and spaces, channeling all the weight of the stone walls and ceiling across the curve of the arch and down into the ground via the columns or pilasters. The style also made use of blind arcades, decorative bands of "filled-in" arches, the columns engaged in the wall

and the arches' curves on top protruding mere inches. Set into each arch's curve is often a lozenge, a diamond-shaped decoration, typically inlaid with colored marbles.

The **Basilica of Sant'Ambrogio in Milan** (11th–12th c.) is festooned with the tiered loggias and arcades that would become hallmarks of the Lombard Romanesque.

Gothic (Late 12th to Early 15th c.)

By the late 12th century, engineering developments—most significantly the pointed arch, which could bear a much heavier load than a rounded one—freed architects from the heavy, thick walls of Romanesque structures and allowed ceilings to soar, walls to thin, and windows to proliferate.

Instead of dark, somber, relatively unadorned Romanesque interiors that forced the eyes of the faithful toward the altar and its priest droning on in unintelligible Latin, the Gothic churchgoer's gaze was drawn up to high ceilings filled with light, a window unto heaven. The priests still gibbered in a dead language, but now peasants could "read" the Gothic comic books of colorful frescoes lining the walls and panels in stained-glass windows.

In addition to those pointy arches, another Gothic innovation was the famous flying buttress. These free-standing exterior pillars connected by graceful, thin arms of stone help channel the weight of the building and its roof out and down into the ground. To help counter the cross-forces involved in this engineering sleight of hand, the piers of buttresses were often topped by heavy pinnacles or statues. Inside, the general pointiness continued with cross-vaults: The square patch of ceiling between four columns, instead of being flat, would arch up to a point in the center, creating four sail shapes, sort of like the underside of a pyramid with bulging faces. The X separating these four "sails"

Andrea Palladio—Father of Neoclassicism

Order, balance, elegance, harmony with the landscape, and a human scale are all apparent in the creations of architect **Andrea Palladio** (1508–80). Palladio was working as a stonemason and sculptor when, at 30, inspired by the design of ancient buildings he studied on trips to Rome, he turned his hand to architecture and applied the principles of classical proportion to Renaissance ideals of grace, symmetry, and functionality. Vicenza, the little city near Venice where Palladio lived as a boy and where he returned in his prime, is graced with many Palladian *palazzi* and a church as well as his Teatro Olimpico. In Venice he designed the churches of San Giorgio Maggiore and Redentore.

Palladio is best known, though, for the villas he built on the flat plains of the Veneto for Venetian nobles yearning to escape the cramped city. Nineteen of these villas still stand, including what may be his finest, **La Rotunda,** outside Vicenza. The design of this and Palladio's other villas—square, perfectly proportioned, elegant yet functional—may strike a note of familiarity with American and British visitors: Palladio influenced generations of architects who followed his lead when they designed neoclassical plantation houses in the American South and country estates in England, his "Palladian" style informing everything from British architecture to Thomas Jefferson's Monticello.

Other Palladio masterpieces include Vicenza's Palazzo della Ragione and Palazzo Valmarana (1566), and, in the Veneto countryside around Vicenza, the Villa Babaro and Villa Foscari. His final work is the Teatro Olimpico, in Vicenza (1580), an attempt to reconstruct a Roman theater stage backdrop as described in ancient writings. He also designed the Venetian churches San Giorgio Maggiore (1565–1610) and Il Redentore.

was often reinforced with ridges called ribbing. As the Gothic style progressed, four-sided cross-vaults became six-, eight-, or multisided as architects played with the angles they could make. In addition, tracery—delicate, lacy spider webs of carved-stone curlicues—graced the pointy end of windows and just about any acute angle throughout the architecture.

The true, French-style Gothic flourished only in northern Italy, and the best example is **Milan's massive cathedral (Duomo),** a festival of pinnacles, buttresses, and pointy arches begun in the late 14th century. **Venice's I Frari** is a bit airier and boxier; **Padua's Basilica di Sant'Antonio** is largely Gothic, though its Romanesque facade and Byzantine domes

throw you off. In palace architecture, the Venetians developed a distinctive style of insetting lacy, lithe, pointed marble windows with an Eastern flair into pale pastel plaster walls. This is seen in countless palaces across **Venice,** especially in its most lavish: **Ca' d'Oro, Ca' Foscari,** and the model against which all were measured, the **Palazzo Ducale** itself.

Renaissance (15th–17th c.)

As in painting, Renaissance architectural rules stressed proportion, order, classical inspiration, and mathematical precision to create unified, balanced structures. It was probably a Florentine architect, Filippo Brunelleschi, in the early 1400s, who first truly grasped the concept of "perspective" and provided artists with ground rules for creating the illusion of three dimensions on a flat surface.

The early Renaissance was truly codified by central Italian architects working in Florence and Rome, though influential early Florentine theorist **Leon Battista Alberti** (1404–72) built structures across Italy, including Sant'Andrea in Mantua. Urbino-born **Donato Bramante** (1444–1514), who would find fame in Rome building St. Peter's, got his start in Milan by converting the older church of San Satiro and rebuilding the altar end of Santa Maria delle Grazie.

The undisputed master of the High Renaissance was **Andrea Palladio** (1508–80), from the Veneto, who worked in a much more strictly classical mode of columns, porticoes, pediments, and other ancient temple–inspired features (see the "Andrea Palladio—Father of Neoclassicism" box, below). In Venice, **Jacopo Sansovino** (1486–1570) reigned supreme, his loggia and Libreria Sansoviniana lining St. Mark's Square becoming a cornerstone of the High Renaissance, to be copied and repeated in such far-flung architectural endeavors as the cast-iron facades in New York's SoHo district.

Raphael protégé **Giulio Romano** (1492–1546) designed Mantua's impressive **Palazzo Te; Galeazzo Alessi** (1512–72) was the premier architect of Genoa's famed palaces, many of which are now museums.

Baroque & Rococo (17th–18th c.)

More than any other movement, the **baroque** aimed toward a seamless meshing of architecture and art. The stuccoes, sculptures, and paintings were all carefully designed to complement each other—and the space itself—to create a unified whole. This whole was both aesthetic and narrative, the various art forms all working together to tell a single biblical story (or often to subtly relate the deeds of the commissioning patron to great historic or biblical events).

In the baroque, classical architecture exchanges its crisp angles and ruler-straight lines for curves of complex geometry and an interplay of concave and convex. The overall effect is to lighten the appearance of structures and add movement of line and vibrancy to the static look of the classical Renaissance.

Unlike the sometimes severe and austere designs of the Renaissance, the baroque was playful. Architects festooned structures and encrusted interiors with an excess of decorations intended to liven things up—lots of ornate stuccowork, pouty cherubs, airy frescoes, heavy gilding, twisting columns, multicolored marbles, and general frippery.

The baroque was also a movement of multiplying forms. The baroque asked, why make do with one column when you can stack a half-dozen partial columns on top of each other, slightly offset, until the effect is like looking at a single column though a fractured kaleidoscope? The baroque loved to pile up its forms and elements to create a rich, busy effect, breaking a pediment curve into segments so each would protrude farther out than the last, or building up an architectural feature by stacking short sections of concave walls, each one curving to a different arc.

Rococo is the baroque gone awry into the grotesque, excessively complex and dripping with decorative tidbits.

The baroque flourished across Italy, but frankly, little of it was truly inspired architecture. You'll find good examples in Venice's Santa Maria della Salute, and especially in Turin, from the Castellamonte-designed Piazza San Carlo to the great works of Guarino Guarini (San Lorenzo, Palazzo Carignano, the San Sidone chapel for the Holy Shroud in the cathedral) and Filippo Juvarra (Basilica di Superga, Palazzina di Stupinigi).

Neoclassical to Modern (18th–21st c.)

By the middle of the 18th century, as a backlash against the excesses of the baroque and rococo, architects, inspired by the rediscovery of Pompeii and other ancient sites, began turning to the austere simplicity and grandeur of the classical age and inaugurated a **neoclassical** style. The classical ideals of mathematical proportion and symmetry, first rediscovered during the Renaissance, are the hallmark of every classically styled era—a reinterpretation of ancient temples into buildings and massive colonnaded porticos. Northern Italy's two famed opera houses are both excellent neoclassical exercises: Milan's La Scala and Venice's La Fenice. To see perhaps the best example of the chilliness the neoclassical style often entailed, pop into Padua's Caffè Pedrocchi for a cappuccino (interestingly, the architect, Giuseppe Japelli—who also worked in rococo and Palladian idioms—drew inspiration not just from classical Greece/Rome but also ancient Egypt).

Italy's take on the early-20th-century Art Nouveau movements was called **Liberty.** Like all Art Nouveau, decorators rebelling against the era of mass production stressed a craft of uniqueness, creating asymmetrical, curvaceous designs based on organic inspiration (plants and flowers) and using wrought iron, stained glass, tile, and hand-painted wallpaper.

The **Industrial Age** of the late 19th/early 20th centuries brought with it the first genteel shopping malls of glass and steel girders, such as the famed Galleria in Milan. Mussolini made a spirited attempt to bring back ancient Rome in what can only be called **Fascist** architecture: Deco meets Caesar. Monumentally imposing and chillingly stark white marble structures are surrounded by classical-style statues. Fascist architecture still infests all corners of Italy, though most of the right-wing reliefs and the repeated engravings of "DVCE"—Mussolini's nickname for himself—have long since been chipped out. One of the best, easily accessible, oft-overlooked examples is Milan's massive train station (so if you're stuck with a long wait, wander outside to squint up at the weird Deco gargoyles and call your layover sightseeing).

Fitting into no style is Turin's truly odd **Mole Antonellina** (1863–97), designed as a synagogue but later put to various uses (currently, it is a film museum). Its squat brick base is topped by a steep cone supporting several layers of Greek temples piled one atop the other at right angles, capped off in turn by a needlelike spire at 166m (544 ft.).

Since then, Italy has mostly poured concrete and glass skyscrapers like the rest of us, though a few architects in the medium have stood out. The mid–20th century was dominated by **Pier Luigi Nervi** (1891–1979) and his reinforced concrete buildings, including Turin's Exposition Hall (1949). Italy's greatest living architect, Pritzker Prize–winning **Renzo Piano** (b. 1937), lives in Paris, and most of his great commissions, including the Pompidou, are outside of Italy.

---

4 NORTHERN ITALY IN POPULAR CULTURE

LITERATURE

NONFICTION The best way to understand Italy's recent history is to read **Paul Ginsborg**'s seminal work, *A History of Contemporary Italy: Society and Politics, 1943–1988* (Palgrave Macmillan, 2003). Don't be put off by the academic sound of the title. It is extremely readable, comical at times, and probably the most oft-quoted history of modern Italy in the English-speaking world. A lot of ink has been spilled on modern Italian culture;

none of it allows the same insight as Ginsborg's history.

Giacomo Casanova was a native Venetian and a renowned writer and adventurer famous for his romantic exploits. Although he wrote mostly in French and the most entertaining chapters of his life as a philanderer generally took place in faraway cities, he did dedicate some space to Venice in his memoirs, *History of My Life,* written in several volumes, and a read through his exploits gives you a good idea of what life was like—or, at least, life among the very wealthy—in 18th-century Venice.

Few other countries have suffered or enjoyed this foreign examination of its national character and culture. The letters and poems of Romantic writers **Percy Bysse Shelly** and **John Keats,** and the travel writings of **D. H. Lawrence** and **H. V. Morton** include notable observations of northern Italy, which are almost universally flattering. In recent years, that torch has been passed to **Tim Parks,** a British expatriate who has lived in Verona with his Italian wife since 1981. His observations through the 1990s are documented in *Italian Neighbours* (William Heinemann Ltd, 1992) and *An Italian Education* (Harper Perennial, 1996), which, mercifully, lacks the wide-eyed romantic view taken by so many others.

Of course, the best way to avoid that naïveté is to read the Italians themselves—when their texts are available in English. **Luigi Barzini**'s *The Italians* (Touchstone, 1996) is a great place to start, but for an insider's view on today's Italy, check out **Alexander Stille**'s *The Sack of Rome: How a Beautiful Country with a Fabled History and a Storied Culture was Taken Over by a Man Named Silvio Berlusconi* (Penguin Press HC, 2006). **Gian Antonio Stella** and **Sergio Rizzo** wrote a definitive work on modern Italian politics, *The Caste: How Italian Politicians Have Become Untouchable* (Rome: Saggi Italiani, 2007).

FICTION Northern Italy is the birthplace of many of the country's novelists and poets, from **Alessandro Manzoni, Italo Calvino, Carlo Levi,** and **Primo Levi** to the modern minds of **Dario Fo** and **Umberto Eco,** even if few of them wrote about their home.

The one great exception is Manzoni, who often wrote of northern Italy. His novel *The Betrothed* (*I Promessi Sposi,* in Italian), first published in 1827, is the quintessential northern Italian novel and is still considered the greatest work of fiction in modern Italian history. It is a love story about a young couple whom the local priest refused to marry, and their respective trials. For the student of northern Italy, it is a vivid account of the years of famine and plague in Milan, and the days when the Spanish nobility terrorized the northern tier. Wandering around the lakes region, especially, you'll miss the significance of the names of hotels, boats, and more without having read this masterpiece.

Perhaps the most famous work of fiction to be set in northern Italy is **William Shakespeare**'s iconic play *Romeo and Juliet,* which takes place in Verona. Shakespeare had a penchant for northern Italy and depicted the northern Italian bourgeoisie in several other plays which were set in the region: *The Merchant of Venice* naturally takes place in Venice, and *Othello* takes place partly in Venice.

Beyond Shakespeare, perhaps the most famous Venetian scenery is found in **Thomas Mann**'s novella *Death in Venice* (1912), which portrays a tourist on the Lido and his obsession with a young Polish boy. The story describes Venice's beaches and canals in detail; Mann said he came up with the idea for the plot while on vacation in Venice. **Ernest Hemingway,** by contrast, was driving an ambulance through war zones and convalescing from an injury in a Milan hospital when he pictured the backdrop for *A Farewell to Arms* (1929), his semi-autobiographical novel about an American ambulance driver serving in Italy during World War I.

FILM

It's hard to find a more impressive movie backdrop than Venice, which is why it pops up in everything from Shakespeare to James Bond.

Michael Radford's 2004 take on *The Merchant of Venice* brings 16th-century Venice into vivid color. There are also several silver-screen productions of *Othello;* the best-known version is probably Orson Welles's 1955 production in which he plays the title role of Othello.

There are a number of James Bond films which feature Venice and northern Italy. The very best Bond scene in Venice is a toss-up between the boat chase in *Moonraker* (1979) and a scene from *Casino Royale* (2006) in which an entire Venetian palazzo sinks into the lagoon. The most recent James Bond film, *Quantum of Solace* (2008), also features northern Italy, with a car chase scene set against the dramatic backdrop of Lake Garda.

One of the most famous films set in Venice is Luchino Visconti's 1971 adaptation of Thomas Mann's *Death in Venice,* called *Morte a Venezia* in Italian. Perhaps the most haunting scene in that film takes place on the sandy beaches of the Lido, when the main character, played by Dirk Bogarde, dies while sitting in a white suit on a beach chair. The characters in that story were not Italian, and the film has little to do with Italy other than that the tourists were vacationing there, but the northern Italian scenery is still breathtaking.

Visconti also directed the 1960 classic film *Rocco and His Brothers* (*Rocco e I Suoi Fratelli,* in Italian). Unlike *Death in Venice,* this film is a true northern Italian tale that depicts a family from the south trying to set down roots in job-rich northern Italy; this film stands out among several perfunctory films on that touchy subject. Similarly, a film that portrays the economic differences between northern and southern Italy is *Bread and Chocolate* (1973); this film presents a comical take on a southern Italian immigrant's attempt to become a member of Swiss society. (While this story technically unfolds in Switzerland just over the border from Lombardy, it has come to symbolize the plight of the southern immigrant moving from Puglia and Naples to Milan, Turin, and the Italian-speaking Swiss canton of Ticino.)

One of the best modern films featuring northern Italy is Silvio Soldini's *Bread and Tulips* (*Pane e Tulipani,* in Italian; 2000), about a middle-aged woman named Rosalba's spiritual rebirth in Venice. The familiar sound of that title is not accidental—like the character in *Bread and Chocolate,* Rosalba ventures to the north, where she finds opportunity. The beginning of the movie is set in the most recognizable of modern Italian landmarks: an Autogrill service station. When the tour bus carrying Rosalba's chauvinistic husband pulls out of the parking lot without her, she embarks on a trip that, instead of taking her home to her native Ancona, brings her north to Venice, where she finds a job as an assistant florist and a respite from her unbearable life.

MUSIC

In the 14th century, Italy's music swept Europe. The country was an innovator in medieval music—**St. Ambrose,** bishop of Milan in the 4th century, introduced to the church the custom of singing liturgical chants. In the 12th century, **Guido d'Arezzo** developed the basis of the musical notation that we use today. Blind **Francesco Landini** introduced sophisticated, varied rhythms. And in the mid–16th century, the first violin appeared. Cremona artisans became the international standard-bearers of fine instrument craftsmanship, and local son **Stradivari,** who learned his craft under the great master **Amati,** achieved a standard in violin design never improved upon.

Poets, who wanted a closer relationship between word and music, got their wish by the late 16th century. Until then, music had been but an incidental element in various entertainments, but a group in Florence wanted to adapt Greek drama, which they believed had been sung throughout, to a new kind of "musical drama." It came to be called "opera," a new form that caught on fast. The first great composer of opera was **Monteverdi,** of *Orfeo* fame, who's enjoying a new popularity today. Monteverdi managed to "translate human suffering into sound," lighting the way for succeeding generations of Italian composers.

Since Venice opened the first public opera house in 1637, it has continued to promote both operatic composers and productions. Venice's preeminent composer in the early 18th century was **Antonio Vivaldi,** who wrote more than 40 operas. The prolific **Scarlatti** (known mainly for his instrumental music) was also a composer of opera, turning out more than 100 in an exuberant rococo style. It's also possible that Scarlatti played some of his music on **Bartolomeo Cristofori**'s 1709 invention, the *pianoforte,* forerunner of the modern piano.

Italy has produced many fine composers, but **Giuseppe Verdi** was the unquestioned operatic master of the 19th century. Verdi, son of an innkeeper, understood dramatic form and wrote exquisite melodies, and his musicianship was unsurpassed. He achieved success early on with his third opera, *Nabucco,* a huge hit, and then turned out *Rigoletto, Il Trovatore, Un Ballo in Maschera,* and *Aïda*—works that remain popular today. His powers continued unchecked as he grew older, maturing musically with such works as *Don Carlo* and his great *Otello* (written when the master was 73). At 80, he astonished the musical world with *Falstaff,* a masterpiece in *opera buffa* form, unlike anything he'd composed before.

Opera buffa was Italy's most popular operatic form in the early 19th century, works of comedy with more surface than depth in which, unlike grand opera, individual musical numbers alternate with spoken dialogue. Opera buffa had its origins in the wisecracking comedians who had long entertained at fairs. **Rossini**'s charming *The Barber of Seville* and **Donizetti**'s *Daughter of the Regiment* are examples of the form.

Rossini and Donizetti were also significant contributors to grand opera in the early and mid–19th century. **Puccini** came along a bit later, and his lyrical *La Bohème, Tosca,* and *Madama Butterfly* continue to please crowds. Well known to today's international audiences is American-born (with Italian parentage) **Gian-Carlo Menotti,** who died in 2007. He spent much of his life in Italy, composed *Amahl and the Night Visitors,* and created the huge Festival of Two Worlds music extravaganza in Spoleto, one of the world's top festivals for classical and instrumental music.

5 EATING & DRINKING IN NORTHERN ITALY

For Italians, eating is not just something to do for sustenance three times a day. Food is an essential ingredient of the Italian spirit, practically an art form in a culture that knows a lot about art. Even when Italy was a poor nation, it was said that poor Italians ate better than rich Germans or English or Americans.

Italians pay careful attention to the basics in both shopping and preparation. They know, for instance, which region produces the best onions or choicest peppers and when is the prime time of year to order porcini mushrooms, asparagus, truffles, or wild boar. If they're dining out, Italians expect the same care and pride they put into home cooking—and they get it. There are a lot of wonderful places to eat in Italy, from fancy *ristoranti* to more humble, homey *trattorie* and neighborhood joints called *osterie*.

MEALS

Prima colazione (breakfast) is treated lightly—a cappuccino and *cornetto* (croissant with a light sugar glaze) at the corner bar. There are exceptions: Many hotels, tired of hearing foreign guests grouse about the paltry morning offerings of this *"continentale"* breakfast, have taken to serving sumptuous buffets like those offered in the United States and north of the Alps, complete with ham, cheese, and sometimes eggs.

At the big meal of the day—be it *pranzo* (lunch) or *cena* (dinner)—portions on a plate may be smaller than visitors are accustomed to, but a traditional meal gets you four full courses: *antipasto,* primo, secondo, and *contorno.* The **antipasto** (appetizer) is often a platter of *salumi* (cold cuts), *bruschette,* or *crostini* (toasted or grilled bread topped with pâté or tomatoes) and/or vegetables prepared in oil or vinegar, or perhaps prosciutto and melon. Next is the **primo** (first course), which may be a *zuppa* or *miestra* (soup), pasta, *risotto* (arborio rice boiled to be thick and sticky, usually studded with some vegetables), or *polenta* (a cornmeal mush, often mixed with mushrooms or a dollop of meat ragù). The **secondo** (second course) is usually meat, fish, seafood, chicken, or game. To accompany it, you order a **contorno** (side dish) of vegetables or a salad. Traditionally, you won't find a pile of veggies next to your meat on the plate as in most American restaurants; however, a recent trend in Italian restaurants (especially ones that indulge in a more creative menu) is to include a side dish carefully chosen to complement your main course. At the end of the meal, dig into a **dolce** (dessert)—fruit, gelato (ice cream), tiramisu (sweetened, creamy mascarpone cheese atop espresso-soaked lady fingers), or *formaggio* (cheese) are traditionally offered.

Meals are usually accompanied by **wine** and a bottle of mineral water (*con gas* or *senza gas*/fizzy or still), and followed by an espresso. (One sure way to alienate an Italian waiter is to order cappuccino after dinner—it's usually drunk only in the morning.) Espresso is often followed by **grappa,** a fiery *digestivo* liqueur made from what's left over after the winemaking process.

RESTAURANTS

Traditionally, a **ristorante** (restaurant) is a bit formal and more expensive than a family-run **trattoria** or **osteria,** but the names are used almost interchangeably these days (trendy, expensive eateries often call themselves *osterie,* and little local joints may aggrandize themselves with the term *ristorante*).

To save money and grab a meal with Italians on their lunch break, pop in to a **tavola calda** (literally "hot table"), a kind of tiny cafeteria where a selection of prepared hot dishes is sold by weight. A **rosticceria** is a *tavola calda* with roasting chickens in the window. Increasingly, trendy **enoteche** (wine bars) usually offer ample platters of cheese and mixed *salumi* (cured meats) such as salami, prosciutto (salt-cured ham hock), *lardo* (salt-cured pork fat aged on marble slabs), and *mortadella* (bologna); most also offer a hot dish or two.

Any **bar** (a combo bar and cafe, where you go for your morning cappuccino, after-school ice cream, and evening aperitif) will also sell *panini* (sandwiches on a roll), *tramezzini* (giant tea sandwiches on sliced bread with the crusts cut off), and *piadine* (flatbread sandwiches).

PASTA

Aside from pizza, pasta is probably Italy's best-known export. It comes in two basic forms: **pastasciutta** (dry pasta), the kind most of us buy at the grocery store, and

Coffee All Day Long

Italians drink **caffè** (coffee) throughout the day, but only a little at a time and often while standing in a bar—remember that a "bar" in Italy is the place to go for your daily caffeine buzz. There's usually liquor available too, but it's the caffè that draws the customers.

Five types of coffee are popular in Italy. Plain old **caffè** is straight espresso in a demitasse, saturated with sugar and downed in one gulp. Espresso from a machine (as opposed to that made in the stove-top kettles most Italians use at home) is prepared by forcing steam through the tightly packed grounds, and despite popular perception, it actually contains less caffeine than typical American drip coffee; it's the rich taste that makes espresso seem so strong. **Cappuccino** is espresso mixed with hot milk and an overlay of foamy steamed milk, usually sipped for breakfast with a pastry and never as an after-dinner drink. "Stained" **caffè macchiato** is espresso with a wee drop of steamed milk, while **latte macchiato** is the reverse, a glass of hot milk "stained" with a shot of espresso. **Caffè coretto** is espresso "corrected" with a shot of liquor. **Caffè hag** is decaf. Most Italians hold in disdain the murky watered-down coffee that percolates in offices and kitchens across America, so if you want a big mug like the stuff at home, you'll have to order **caffè americano.**

pasta fresca (fresh pasta) or *pasta fatto a mano* (handmade), the kind that most self-respecting establishments in Italy, even those of the most humble ilk, will probably serve.

Pastasciutta comes in long strands, including *spaghetti, linguine,* and *trenette;* and in tubular *maccheroni* (macaroni) forms such as *penne* (pointed pasta quills) or *rigatoni* (fluted tubes), to name only a few. Pasta fresca is made in broad sheets and then cut into shapes used in lasagna, cannelloni, and the stuffed pastas tortelloni and ravioli, or into noodles ranging from wide pappardelle to narrow fettuccine. If you sense that this isn't even a dent in the world of pasta, you're right: There are more than 600 pasta shapes in Italy.

ITALY'S REGIONAL CUISINES

Each Italian region has had thousands of years to develop its own culinary practices—and its own distinctive wines—and each still proudly sticks by its native dishes. What most Americans think of as Italian dishes is what Italian emigrants brought with them to the U.S., but the majority of those came from southern Italy, which is why when we think "Italian," we think of olive oil, pasta with tomato sauce, garlic, and pizza. Generally, though, northern Italian cooking uses a lot more cream and butter in sauces, in addition to tomatoes. Also, pasta is not necessarily the first course of choice up north, often substituted by risotto or polenta.

VENICE & THE VENETO Venice gained fame and fortune as the spice market of the world beginning in the 12th century (when Marco Polo visited the Orient), which may help account for the amazing ways local chefs dress up the scampi, crab, squid, and other creatures they pluck from the Adriatic. The Venetians also have raised that humble combination of liver and onions *(fegato alla veneziana)* to an irresistible level of haute cuisine, and have done the same with *risi e bisi* (rice and peas).

THE DOLOMITES Dolomiti food is mountain food: rib-sticking and hearty, largely influenced by Austrian cuisine. Look for *speck* ham, *canederli* bread dumplings in thick broths, Wiener schnitzel, and *grostl* (hash made of veal, onions, and potatoes).

THE FRIULI Alpine cuisine runs from the Tirolese influences of the Dolomites to Venetian specialties to Slovenian cuisine. They toss sauerkraut in their minestrone and call it *jota,* and serve up platters of everything from San Daniele prosciutto (the most delicate, expensive, and delicious in all of Italy) to *brovada* (a peasant dish of sausage, turnips, and grape skins).

LOMBARDY Like other northern regions, Lombardy favors butter over olive oil and seems not to be overly concerned with cholesterol. A specialty is *osso buco,* sliced veal sautéed with the bone and marrow. A fine starter for any meal is the region's vegetable soup with rice and bacon, *minestrone alla milanese,* or a risotto made from arborio rice that grows on the region's low-lying plains and is often served in place of pasta. *Panettone,* the region's most popular dessert, is a local version of fruit cake that arrived from Vienna courtesy of Lombardy's 19th-century Austrian rulers. Austria also exported to Lombardy the breaded veal scallop of Wiener schnitzel, in Italy called *cotoletta alla Milanese.* Remember, too, that Lombardy is blessed with the Italian lakes, and trout and perch find their way into ravioli and other pasta dishes as well as simply sautéed as a secondo.

PIEDMONT & VALLE D'AOSTA As befits these regions of cold winters, meat roasts and hearty soups are served, often accompanied by thick slabs of polenta. Piedmont is blessed with strong-flavored white truffles (the lovely town of Alba is Italy's truffle center), and they're used in a favorite local dish, *fonduta,* a fonduelike

cheese dip mixed with milk and eggs. Piedmont is also home to Gorgonzola cheese.

LIGURIA This is the homeland of the seafarers of Genoa, who brought back from the New World many cooking ingredients now taken for granted. What, for instance, would Italian cooking be without tomatoes, potatoes, or peppers? The sea-skirted region is also famous for its seafood, including a shellfish soup called *zuppa di datteri,* and for pesto, a pasta sauce of ground basil, pine nuts, and olive oil. To the world of bread, Liguria has contributed focaccia—flat, delicious, and often topped with herbs or, when eaten as a snack, with cheese and vegetables.

WINE

Italy, with the right kind of terrain and the perfect amounts of sun and rainfall, happens to be ideal for growing grapes. Centuries ago, the Etruscans had a hearty wine industry, and the ancient Greeks bolstered it by transplanting their vine cuttings to Italy's southlands. And it was Italy, under the Romans, that first introduced the vine and its possibilities to France and Germany. Today Italy exports more wine to the rest of the world than any other country does. But there's plenty left at home from which to choose; more than 2,000 wines are produced in Italy.

Each region has different growing conditions, and so each has its own special wines. **Piedmont** is the north's premier wine region, known for its heavy reds, including Barolo, Barbaresco, Barbera, and Grignolino, as well as sparkling white Asti Spumanti. With these vineyards so close at hand, coastal **Liguria** hasn't developed many notable wines of its own, save the white of Cinque Terre. The **Veneto** specializes in Valpolicella and Bardolino reds and, among whites, pinot grigio and Soave. The **Trentino** adds Tirolese varieties such as Traminer to cabernet, local wines such as Vernatsch, and pinot grigio, bianco, and nero. The **Friuli** masters the

Italian Wine Classifications

In 1963, Italy's wine was codified into two classifications: table wine and DOC. **DOC** *(Denominazione di Origine Controllata)* wines are merely those a government board guarantees have come from an official wine-producing area and meet the standard for carrying a certain name on the label. A **vino di tavola (table wine)** classification merely means a bottle doesn't fit the preestablished standards and is no reflection of the wine's quality (see below).

In 1980, a new category was added. **DOCG** (the *G* stands for *Garantita*—guaranteed) is granted to wines with a certain subjective high quality. Traditionally, DOCG labels were merely the highest-profile wines that lobbied for the status (getting DOC and especially DOCG vastly improves reputations and, therefore, sales, though the costs of annually putting the wine up for testing are high).

When the appellation was introduced, only five prestigious wines qualified as DOCG: Brunello, Barolo, Barbaresco, Chianti, and Vino Nobile di Montepulciano. Today, there are dozens.

The wines have a few extra hoops to jump through to retain their *Garantita* status. The vineyards need to practice specific growing methods and cannot exceed a certain yield of fruit every year. The wines are subject to chemical analysis by government agencies. And to qualify in the first place, a wine must have held DOC status for at least 5 years.

Though **vino di tavola** usually connotes a humble, simple, quaffable house wine from some indeterminate local producer (perhaps a local farmer's cooperative or even the restaurant owner's brother-in-law), in the 1980s and 1990s, this "table wine" classification was also co-opted by wine estates that wanted to experiment with grape mixtures and tinker with foreign varietals to create nontraditional but mighty wines. The problem is that these could never be called DOC or DOCG, which by law must follow strict formula guidelines. When many respectable producers started mixing varietals with French grapes, such as merlot, cabernet, and chardonnay, to produce wines that, though complex and of high quality, don't fall into the conservative DOC/DOCG system, such a wine could then, by law, only be called a "lowly" *vino di tavola.*

These highbred "table wines" became known melodramatically as **supervini.** There's no guarantee of quality with these experimental wines, but most self-respecting producers would never have put on the market a failure or something undrinkable.

In 1992, a new classification called **IGT** *(Indicazione Geografica Tipica)* was established, indicating that the wine is "typical of a geographic place." This class

pinot grapes and cabernets as well, though local traditional wines Tocai, Verduzzo, and Malvasia are more unusual. **Lombardy** is not particularly known for its wines, though the area around Bergamo produces perfectly fine merlot, cabernet, pinot bianco, and pinto grigio, in addition to local Valcalepio; west of Brescia, they bottle an excellent sparkling dry white wine called Franciacorta that, while not as famous as Asti, was the first to gain has been used both to cover some regional wines that are quite good yet are not famous enough (or lack a PR budget that's big enough) to go for DOC/DOCG status and also as a home for those *supervini*—a "geographic place" can be as small as one vineyard, so that vineyard's *supervino* can be called an IGT.

For that matter, there's no real guarantee that what you're drinking in a DOCG wine is exactly what it's supposed to be. The practice of misrepresenting on the label the contents in a bottle of wine is as old as the labels themselves, which dates to the Romans. Take the most recent high-profile case, the so-called Brunellopoli scandal (a nod to the "Tangentopoli" political bribing scandal of the 1980s).

In 2008, Italian investigators began looking into reports that some producers of the famed Tuscan wine were sneaking in varietals other than the Sangiovese required by law—most shockingly, that some grapes were actually trucked up from Southern regions where land and therefore grapes are generally cheaper. This investigation had all the trimmings and trappings of a high-profile murder case, with police cordoning off wine cellars and carting off thousands of bottles of evidence from the crime scene. (Keep in mind that this sort of chicanery is not limited to Italy. In 1994, a number of California growers paid millions in fines for taking cheap grapes and laying a thin layer of Zinfandel on top and selling it as zin. The Franzia brothers referred to this process as "blessing the load.")

Such hallowed names as Antinori, Banfi, and Frescobaldi churned up their PR machines when their estates were implicated but at the same time hatched plans to sell the wines under a different name to bring in at least some sort of revenue. About this time, the U.S. announced a plan for an import embargo on any bottle that could not be guaranteed as 100% Sangiovese. Ironically, some suggested that the reason other varietals were being used in the first place was to cater to more tender American tastes. In the end, only a few bottles of Banfi were deemed to have some suspect characteristics, and no producer was actually convicted of fraud and sent to jail for the recommended 6 years.

The practical upshot of all this: DOC and DOCG wines represent the best of traditional wine formulas. IGT wines are unique wines from even smaller specific areas or single vintners and make up one of the fastest-growing categories among the better wines. *Vino da tavola* is now just used for what it was originally intended to mean: simple, hearty, tasty table wines that go well with any meal but probably won't send wine snobs into ecstasies of flowery poetic description.

DOCG status (see "Italian Wine Classifications," below).

Grappa, made from the skins, seeds, vines, and other remnants at the bottom of the pressing barrel, is a fiery *digestivo* drunk at the end of a meal to help you "digest" those large Italian repasts.

An *amaro* is a bitter liqueur drunk in midafternoon or before or after a meal.

Planning Your Trip to Northern Italy

With such a long laundry list of historical treasures, epicurean pleasures, and equally tempting outdoor resorts, the hardest part of planning a trip to northern Italy will be deciding where to spend your time. Fortunately, much of what you will want to see and do can be dictated by the seasons, and anyway, with such short distances between the cities, a change of heart might be only a 2-hour train ride away.

Getting around northern Italy is a breeze (minus the city and highway traffic and the occasional jam-packed train), and getting to and from the region couldn't be easier with a nice selection of local airports and a very busy international airport in Milan.

In fact, it is so easy to travel to northern Italy that the greatest hindrance might be that the region is so very busy. You'll have to plan far ahead to get a nice hotel room in Milan—especially during the spring and fall fashion weeks and the design trade show in April. Self-catered chalets in the Alps and the Dolomites fill up many months prior to the weeks around New Year's Eve, and the choicest spots on the Riviera and Cinque Terre are snapped up before it starts getting hot. As for Venice, it's a general mob scene in any month not containing an *R* and during any of its spectacular festivals. The secret is to plan your trip months in advance, or at least secure accommodations and tickets to museums and concerts in advance.

Other than that, if you do your homework on special events, pick the right place for the right season, and pack for a variety of climates, preparing for a trip to northern Italy should be pleasant and uncomplicated.

For additional help and for more on-the-ground resources in northern Italy, please turn to "Fast Facts," on p. 435.

1 WHEN TO GO

The best time to visit northern Italy really depends on what you're planning to do. Skiers will find the best snow in the Dolomites in February and March, whereas sun worshippers will find the best sun and people-watching on the Riviera in the height of summer. Wine enthusiasts will find grapes on the vine in late summer and early fall, and might even take part in an early October harvest.

In a general sense, **April** to **June** and **September** and **October** are the most pleasant months for touring Italy—temperatures are usually mild and the hordes of tourists not so intense. But starting in mid-June, the summer rush really picks up, and from July to mid-September, the country teems with visitors. (It should also be noted that the post-summer cooling rains come to northern Italy almost like clockwork on Sept. 1 and can last a week or two.)

August (with July a close runner-up) is the worst month to visit any Italian city. Not only does it get uncomfortably hot, muggy, and crowded with foreigners, but the entire country goes on vacation from at least August 15 to the end of the month—

and a good percentage of Italians take off the entire month, leaving the urban centers to the tourists. Venice in July and August is a swarming and sweltering Disneyland. Elsewhere, many hotels, restaurants, and shops are closed in mid-August—except along the coast and on the islands, which is where most Italians head.

From **late October to Easter,** most tourist sights have shorter winter hours or close for renovation periods, many hotels and restaurants take a month or two off between November and February, beach destinations become padlocked ghost towns, and it can get much colder than you'd expect (it may even snow). The crowds thin remarkably, especially in Venice.

In **mountain towns and ski resorts,** high season is from mid-December through mid-March; low season is June, when many hotels are closed (which is a shame, for there's great hiking in the mountains during June's warm days).

High season on most airlines' routes to Milan usually stretches from June to the end of September, plus Christmas/New Year's week. This is the most expensive and most crowded time to travel. **Shoulder season** is from the Easter season (usually late Mar or Apr) to May, late September to October, and December 15 to 24. **Low season** is generally January 6 to mid-March, November 1 to December 14, and December 25 to March 31.

WEATHER

It's hot all over Italy in **summer,** especially inland. The high temperatures begin in May (sometimes later for the Alps), often lasting until some time in late September. July and August can be impossible, which explains why life in the cities slows down considerably (and life in the coastline resorts comes alive). Few budget hotels have air-conditioning (and just a handful of hotels in all of Italy have discovered mosquito screens, so when you open the windows for some respite from the heat, you tend to invite dozens of tiny bloodsuckers

in as well). In Venice, the November rains kick off *acqua alte,* when the lagoon backs up a few times each month, flooding the central city with .6 to 1.8m (2–6 ft.) of water (no joke). That may sound like an invitation to stay away, but I think it's one of the most remarkable times to be there. Bring rubber boots.

Winters in the north of Italy are cold with rain and snow, and December through February can often be unpleasant unless you're skiing in Cortina or enjoy a snow-sprinkled city. Nights can be cold, and hotels' heating systems can be frustrating sometimes. Purpose-built, modernized hotels in their own buildings often have independent heating/cooling systems you (or they) can control, but in older hotels and in small ones that take up only part of a building, the heat can often be turned on for the winter only on a pre-established date dictated by the local government, and left on only during certain hours of the day (just one of the many lovely laws still hanging on from the Fascist era).

For the most part, it's drier in Italy than in North America. Since the humidity is lower, high temperatures don't seem as bad; exceptions are cities known for their humidity factor, such as Venice. It's important to remember that this is not a country as smitten by the notion of air-conditioning and central heating as the United States. And remember that the inexpensive hotels we list in this book are often the very places that will remind you of the pros and cons of ancient stone palazzi built with 1m-thick (3-ft.) walls. Don't expect the comfort of the Ritz at cheaper inns.

HOLIDAYS

Offices and shops in Italy are closed on the following dates: **January 1** (New Year's Day), **January 6** (Epiphany, usually called *La Befana,* after Italy's Christmas Witch, who used to bring the presents until Hollywood's version of Santa Claus moved the gift giving to Dec 25 by popular kiddie

Hot Tickets

For major events where tickets should be procured well before arriving on the spot, check out **Box Office** at ✆ **055-210-804** or www.boxol.it. They will deliver tickets only to an Italian address, but you can buy ahead of time and pick them up at the booth when you arrive.

demand, though a few presents are always held over for *La Befana*), **Easter Sunday, Easter Monday, April 25** (Liberation Day), **May 1** (Labor Day), **August 15** (Assumption of the Virgin—much of Italy takes its summer vacation **Aug 15–30**), **November 1** (All Saints' Day), **December 8** (Feast of the Immaculate Conception), **December 25** (Christmas Day), and **December 26** (Santo Stefano); most Italians' **Christmas**

holidays last from December 24 though January 6.

Closings are also observed in the following cities on feast days honoring patron saints: Venice, **April 25** (St. Mark); Genoa and Turin, **June 24** (St. John the Baptist); Bologna, **October 4** (St. Petronio); Trieste, **November 3** (San Giusto); and Milan, **December 7** (St. Ambrose).

CALENDAR OF EVENTS

For more details on each event below, contact the **tourist office** of the city or town where the festival is held (see the individual chapters).

For an exhaustive list of events beyond those listed here, check http://events.frommers.com, where you'll find a searchable, up-to-the-minute roster of what's happening in cities all over the world.

JANUARY

Epiphany celebrations, nationwide. All cities, towns, and villages in Italy stage Roman Catholic Epiphany observances and Christmas fairs. From Christmas to January 6.

Festival of Italian Popular Song, San Remo (Italian Riviera). A 3-day festival where major artists and up-and-comers perform the latest Italian pop songs and launch the newest hits. Late January.

Foire de Saint Ours, Aosta, Valle d'Aosta. Observing a tradition that has existed for 10 centuries, artisans from the mountain valleys come together to display their wares—often made of wood, lace, wool, or wrought iron—created during the long winter months. Late January.

FEBRUARY

Carnevale (Carnival), Venice. Venice's Carnival evokes the final theatrical 18th-century days of the Venetian Republic. Historical presentations, elaborate costumes, and music of all types in every piazza cap the festivities. The balls are by invitation, but the cultural events, piazza performances, and fireworks (Shrove Tuesday) are open to everyone. See chapter 5 for more information. From two Fridays before Shrove Tuesday to Shrove Tuesday.

APRIL

Good Friday and Easter Week observances, nationwide. Processions and age-old ceremonies—some from pagan days, some from the Middle Ages—are staged. Beginning on the Thursday or

Friday before Easter Sunday, usually in April.

MAY

Voga Longa, Venice. This 30km (19-mile) rowing "race" from San Marco to Burano and back again has been enthusiastically embraced since its inception in 1975, following the city's effort to keep alive the centuries-old heritage of the regatta. The event is colorful, and every local seems to have a relative or next-door neighbor competing. For details, call ✆ **041-521-0544.** A Sunday in mid-May.

JUNE & EVENTS THAT LAST THROUGHOUT THE SUMMER

Regatta of the Great Maritime Republics. Every year, the four medieval maritime republics of Italy celebrate their glorious past with a boat race that rotates among Venice, Amalfi, Genoa, and Pisa. Call the tourist offices for details.

Biennale d'Arte, Venice. This is Europe's most prestigious—and controversial—International Exposition of Modern Art, taking place in odd-numbered years only. More than 50 nations take part, with art displayed in permanent pavilions in the Public Gardens and elsewhere about town. Many great modern artists have been discovered at this world-famous show. Contact the board at ✆ **041-521-8711** (www.labiennale.org) for more information. June to October.

Shakespearean Festival, Verona. Ballet, drama, and jazz performances are included in this festival of the Bard, with a few performances in English. June to September.

JULY

Arena di Verona (Outdoor Opera Season in Verona), Verona. Culture buffs flock to the open-air, 20,000-seat Roman amphitheater, one of the world's best preserved. The season lasts from early July to August for awesome productions of *Aïda* and others.

Festa del Redentore (Feast of the Redeemer), Venice. This celebration marking the July 1576 lifting of a plague that had gripped the city is centered around the Palladio-designed Chiesa del Redentore on the island of Giudecca. A bridge of boats across the Giudecca Canal links the church with the banks of Le Zattere in Dorsoduro, and hundreds of boats of all shapes and sizes fill the Giudecca. It's one big floating *festa* until night descends and an awesome half-hour *spettacolo* of fireworks fills the sky. Third Saturday and Sunday in July.

AUGUST

Rossini Opera Festival, Pesaro. The world's top bel canto specialists perform Rossini's operas and choral works at this popular festival on the Italian Adriatic Riviera. Mid-August to late September.

Venice International Film Festival. Ranking after Cannes, this film festival brings together stars, directors, producers, and filmmakers from all over the world. Films are shown day and night to an international jury and to the

---

ⓘ **Tips** **Dog Days of August**

Try to avoid traveling to Italy in August, as this is when most Italians take their **ferie** (vacations) and many shops and restaurants in the cities will be closed. Also keep in mind that many of the lodgings that will be open in August do not have air-conditioning.

public, at the Palazzo del Cinema, on the Lido, and other venues. Contact the tourist office or the Venice Film Festival (© **041-272-6501** or 041-524-1320; www.labiennale.org). Two weeks in late August to early September.

Regata Storica, Grand Canal, Venice. Just about every seaworthy gondola, richly decorated for the occasion and piloted by *gondolieri* in colorful livery, participates in the opening cavalcade. The aquatic parade is followed by three regattas that proceed along the Grand Canal. You can buy grandstand tickets through the tourist office or arrive early and pull up along a piece of embankment near the Rialto Bridge for the best seats in town. First Sunday in September.

Giostra del Saracino (Joust of the Saracen), Arezzo. A colorful procession in full historical regalia precedes the 13th-century-style tilting contest, with knights in armor in the town's main piazza. First Sunday in September.

Partita a Scacchi con Personnagi Viventi (Living Chess Game), Marostica. This chess game is played in the town square by living pawns in period costume. The second Saturday and Sunday of September during even-numbered years.

Sagra del Tartufo, Alba, Piedmont. The truffle is the honoree of this festival

in Alba, the truffle capital of Italy, with contests, truffle-hound competitions, and tastings of this ugly but precious and delectable (and expensive) fungus. Two weeks in mid-October.

Maratona (Marathon), Venice. The marathon starts at Villa Pisani on the mainland, runs alongside the Brenta Canal, and ends along the Zattere for a finish at the Basilica di Santa Maria della Salute on the tip of Dorsoduro. For details, call © **041-950-644.** Usually the last Sunday of October.

Festa della Salute, Venice. For this festival, a pontoon bridge is erected across the Grand Canal to connect the churches of La Salute and Santa Maria del Giglio, commemorating another delivery from a plague in 1630 that wiped out a third of the lagoon's population; it's the only day La Salute opens its massive front doors (a secondary entrance is otherwise used). November 21.

La Scala Opera Season, Teatro alla Scala, Milan. At the most famous opera house of them all, the season opens on December 7, the feast day of Milan's patron St. Ambrogio, and runs into July. Though it's close to impossible to get opening-night tickets, it's worth a try; call © **02-860-787** or 02-860-775 for the box office, 02-7200-3744 for a listing of performances (www.teatroallascala.org).

2 ENTRY REQUIREMENTS

PASSPORTS

Anyone traveling to Italy from outside the 15 Schengen agreement countries (which essentially comprises all of western Europe except the U.K. and Ireland) will need a

passport to enter. You technically do not need a passport to travel between these countries, although you are required to present one to authorities upon request, as they are commonly looking for fugitives from justice or illegal immigrants. You are required to present a passport at hotel desks in Italy for the same reason. Citizens of the United States, Canada, the U.K., Australia, and New Zealand are allowed to stay in Italy for 90 days; after that period, they are required to have a residence visa.

For information on how to get a passport, go to "Passports" in the chapter 13, "Fast Facts."

VISAS

U.S., Canadian, U.K., Irish, Australian, and New Zealand citizens with a **valid passport** don't need a visa to enter Italy if they don't expect to stay more than 90 days and don't expect to work there. If, after entering Italy, you find you want to stay more than 90 days, you can apply for a permit for an extra 90 days, which, as a rule, is granted immediately. Go to the nearest *questura* (police headquarters) or your home country's consulate.

For more information on visas to visit or stay in Italy, go to the Foreign Ministry's English-language page at **www.esteri. it/visti/index_eng.asp**.

CUSTOMS

What You Can Bring into Italy

Foreign visitors can bring along most items for personal use duty-free, including merchandise up to $800, such as fishing tackle, a pair of skis, two tennis rackets, a baby carriage, two hand cameras with 10 rolls of film or a digital camera, computer, CD player with 10 CDs, tape recorder, binoculars, personal jewelry, portable radio set (subject to a small license fee), and 400 cigarettes and a quantity of cigars or pipe tobacco not exceeding 500 grams (1.1 lb.). There are strict limits on importing alcoholic beverages. However, for alcohol bought tax-paid, limits are much more liberal than in other countries of the European Union.

If you are planning to mail items to Italy, you can mail only merchandise costing up to $200. That means that if you are having your laptop or your skis shipped to you, make sure they do not appear to be straight from the shop. Otherwise, you could face either providing a receipt that you may have discarded years ago, or paying the 20 percent **Value Added Tax (IVA)**.

What You Can Take Home from Italy

For information on what you're allowed to bring home, contact one of the following agencies:

U.S. Citizens: U.S. Customs & Border Protection (CBP), 1300 Pennsylvania Ave., NW, Washington, DC 20229 (✆ **877/ 287-8667;** www.cbp.gov).

Canadian Citizens: Canada Border Services Agency (✆ **800/461-9999** in Canada, or 204/983-3500; www.cbsa-asfc. gc.ca).

U.K. Citizens: HM Customs & Excise, at ✆ **0845/010-9000** (from outside the U.K., 020/8929-0152), or consult their website at www.hmce.gov.uk.

Australian Citizens: Australian Customs Service, at ✆ **1300/363-263,** or log on to www.customs.gov.au.

New Zealand Citizens: New Zealand Customs, the Customhouse, 17–21 Whitmore St., Box 2218, Wellington (✆ **04/ 473-6099** or 0800/428-786; www.customs. govt.nz).

MEDICAL REQUIREMENTS

There are no special medical requirements for entering Italy. For more information on staying healthy while over there, please see "Health" later in this chapter.

GETTING TO NORTHERN ITALY

By Plane

If you're flying across an ocean, you'll most likely fly into Milan's **Malpensa Airport** (**MXP;** ✆ **02-2680-0613;** www.sea-aeroportimilano.it), 45km (28 miles) from downtown—closer to Como than to Milan itself.

From **Malpensa,** a 40-minute express train heads half-hourly to Cadorna train station in western Milan rather than to the larger and more central Stazione Centrale from which most trains onward to Tuscany will leave (you'll have to take the Metro to get there). The Malpensa Express train costs 11€. To grab a bus instead, which will take you directly to the central downtown rail station, take the **Malpensa Shuttle** (✆ **02-5858-3185**) for 7€, which leaves two or three times per hour for the 50-minute ride to the east side of Milan's Stazione Centrale. A taxi to the city center runs about 70€.

For flights to Milan from within Europe, you might also fly into **Linate Airport** (**LIN;** ✆ **02-7485-2200;** www.sea-aeroportimilano.it), about 8km (5 miles) southeast of the city, a much more convenient option. From **Linate, STAM buses** (✆ **02-717-100**) make the 20-minute trip to Milan's Stazione Centrale every 20 to 30 minutes daily from 7am to 11pm, and cost 2€. The slightly slower city bus no. 73 leaves hourly for the S. Babila Metro stop downtown (1€ for a regular bus ticket bought from any newsagent inside the airport, but not onboard).

From Milan's Stazione Centrale, you can get trains to Florence (see "Getting There," in chapter 5).

Flying Directly to Genoa, Bergamo, or Venice

Budget carriers within Europe fly to a number of northern Italian cities; three of the most popular are Genoa's **Cristoforo Colombo Airport** (www.airport.genova.it), Bergamo's **Orio al Serio** (www.sacbo.it), and Venice's **Marco Polo Airport** (www.veniceairport.it).

In Venice, **ATVO** buses (www.atvo.it) run every 30 minutes between Piazzale Roma and the airport for 3€, and also run to the busy train station in nearby Mestre on a more frequent basis. Bergamo's airport is easily reached from Milan with a shuttle that leaves every 30 minutes from the main station, Stazione Centrale, which takes about an hour door-to-door and costs about 9€ one-way. Genoa's airport is very close to the downtown, taking 20 minutes on the bus (4€) that runs to the Stazione Principe.

By Car

If you're planning to drive to northern Italy, you'll likely need to rent a car. You'll get the **best rental rate** if you book your car from home instead of renting direct in Italy—in fact, if you decide to rent once you're over there, it's worth it to call home to have someone arrange it all from there. You must be 25 or older to rent from most agencies (although some accept ages 21 and up).

The legalities and contractual obligations of renting a car in Italy (where accident and theft rates are very high) are more complicated than those in almost any other country in Europe. You must have nerves of steel, a sense of humor, a valid driver's license or International Driver's Permit (with photo), and a valid passport; and you must be 25 or over (some places accept 21). Payment and paperwork are much easier if you present a valid credit card with your completed rental contract (many companies won't even consider a non–credit card payment). If that isn't possible, you'll likely be required to pay a substantial deposit, sometimes in cash. Insurance on all vehicles is compulsory, though what kind and how much is up to you and your credit card company: Ask the right questions and check with your credit card company before leaving home.

Note: If you're planning to rent a car in Italy during high season, you really should book well in advance: It's not at all unusual to arrive at the airport in Milan in June and July to find that every last agent is all out of cars, perhaps for a week.

When offered the choice between a compact car and a larger one, always choose the smaller car (unless you have a large group)—you'll need it for maneuvering the winding, steeply graded Italian roads and the impossibly narrow alleyways of towns and cities. Likewise, if you can drive a stick shift, order one; it'll help you better navigate the hilly terrain. It's also a good idea to opt for the **Collision Damage Wavier (CDW).** Although the 19% IVA value-added tax is unavoidable, you can do away with the government airport pickup tax of 10% by picking up your car at an office in town.

See p. 440 in "Fast Facts" for a list of rental-car companies in northern Italy.

The main *autostrada,* or super highway, that runs the length of the Po valley from Turin to Trieste is the A4. From Milan, you'll need to follow the signs for the *tangenziale,* or beltway, that will eventually lead to an exit to whatever highway you choose. Getting onto the *tangenziale,* however, can be tricky. Insist on specific, detailed directions from the car rental agencies and make use of a co-pilot; otherwise, just do it the Italian way and feel your way onto it by intuition. If you're calm and patient, seemingly ridiculous road signs really do make sense.

Northern Italy is rather compact. Genoa to Milan, for example, is 129km (80 miles) on a highway where people regularly drive in excess of 129kmph (80mph). Milan to Verona is about 161km (100 miles), and Verona to Venice is another 121km (75 miles). Coast to coast, then, is only 4 hours, even at North American driving speeds—that is when there is not traffic. In reality, this is the most traveled highway in all of Europe, so the going can get slow, especially on Friday afternoons and Sunday nights, and rush hour around the cities is epic. Plan to travel mid-week and midday, if possible. See **www.autostrade.it** for live traffic updates.

Tolls can also get expensive, costing about 1€ for every 19km (12 miles), which means that it would cost about 20€ for a trip from Genoa to Venice. Add in the gasoline and the car rental, and it's cheaper to take the train from city to city even with two people.

For more information on driving in Italy, from road rules to gasoline, see "Getting Around," below.

By Train

Traveling to northern Italy by train is the best option if you're looking to visit the major sites without the hassle of renting and driving a car. Most towns in northern Italy have their own train stations; the major train hubs are in Genoa, Turin, and Milan.

Along the major east-west train line in northern Italy, the distance from Turin to Milan is about an hour and 20 minutes; the trips costs 23€ (second class) on the Eurostar high-speed train. Milan to Verona is the same price (train travel in Italy is priced per kilometer, with different rates for the speed of the train and the class). Verona and Padua are 40 minutes apart by train, and the trip costs 13€. The train continues east to Venice; from Padua, it will take 20 minutes to get to Venice and will cost 12€. The fastest way to continue on to Trieste from Venice is on the international **Cisalpino** train (www.raileurope.com), which costs 14€ and takes about an hour and a half.

The major north-south train lines in northern Italy are Milan-Genoa (1½ hr. and 15€ on the midspeed Intercity train) and Trento-Verona (1 hr. and 5€ on the infrequent, high-speed trains to and from Austria). Otherwise, apart from the main artery that runs from Milan to Rome and quicker lines along the coasts, north-south routes around here can be pretty slow going because they rely on the regional trains that stop at every minor hamlet in the valleys.

For more information about train travel in Italy, see "Getting Around," below.

GETTING AROUND
By Car

Much of northern Italy is accessible by public transportation, but to explore remote vineyards, ski resorts, and smaller towns on the lakes, a car will be very useful. In fact, one of the most common and convenient ways to take a tour of this area is to fly or take a train into, say, Milan, see the city, and then pick up a rental car to wend your way through whichever bit takes your fancy before ending up in Genoa, Venice, or Bologna (or Florence or Rome to the south), where you can drop off the car and fly home.

That said, driving in Italy is also notoriously nerve-racking—for both the winding roads and the Italian penchant for driving a Fiat like a Ferrari. Both rental-car and gas prices are as high as they get in all of Europe. Before leaving home, you can apply for an **International Driver's Permit** from the American Automobile Association (AAA; ℂ **800/222-1134** or 407/444-4300; www.aaa.com). In Canada, the permit is available from the Canadian Automobile Association (CAA; ℂ **613/247-0117;** www.caa.ca). In the U.K., contact the British Automobile Association (AA; ℂ **0800/26-20-50;** www.theaa.com). Technically, you need this permit, your actual driver's license, and an Italian translation of the latter (also available

from AAA and CAA) to drive in Italy, though in practice your license itself often suffices. (Take all three along, to be safe.)

Italy's equivalent of AAA is the **Automobile Club d'Italia (ACI),** a branch of the Touring Club Italiano. They're the people who respond when you place an emergency call to ℂ **803-116** for road breakdowns, though they do charge for this service if you're not a member. If you wish, you may join at the border as you're driving into Italy or at one of the club's regional offices (in Milan, Viale Scarca 336, ℂ **02-661-271**). You can also join online at **www.aci.it**.

DRIVING RULES Italian drivers aren't maniacs; they only appear to be. Actually, they tend to be very safe and alert drivers—if much more aggressive than Americans are used to. If someone races up behind you and flashes his lights, that's the signal for you to slow down so he can pass you quickly and safely. Stay in the right lane on highways; the left is only for passing and for cars with large engines and the pedal to the metal. If you see someone in your rearview mirror speeding up with his hazard lights blinking, get out of the way because it means his Mercedes is opened up full throttle. On a two-lane road, the idiot passing someone in the opposing traffic who has swerved into your lane expects you to veer obligingly over into the shoulder so three lanes of traffic can fit—he would do the same for you. (Plus, the alternative is not pretty.)

Autostrade are superhighways, denoted by green signs and a number prefaced with an *A,* like the A1 from Rome to Florence. A few aren't numbered and are simply called *raccordo,* a connecting road between two cities (such as Florence-Siena and Florence-Pisa). On longer stretches, *autostrade* often become toll roads. **Strade Statale** are state roads, usually two lanes wide, indicated by blue signs. Their route numbers are prefaced with an *SS* or an *S,* as in the SS222 from Florence to Siena.

On signs, however, these official route numbers are used infrequently. Usually, you'll just see blue signs listing destinations by name with arrows pointing off in the appropriate directions. Even if it's just a few kilometers down on the road, often the town you're looking for won't be mentioned on the sign at the appropriate turnoff. It's impossible to predict which of all the towns that lie along a road will be the ones chosen to list on a particular sign. Sometimes the sign gives only the first minuscule village that lies past the turnoff, at other times it lists the first major town down that road, and some signs mention only the major city the road eventually leads to, even if it's hundreds of kilometers away. It pays to study the map before coming to an intersection.

The **speed limit** on roads in built-up areas around towns and cities is 50kmph (31 mph). On rural roads and the highway, it's 110kmph (68 mph), except on weekends, when it's upped to 130kmph (81 mph). Italians have an astounding disregard for these limits, mostly because the limits are enforced only if the offense is egregious. However, police can ticket you and collect the fine on the spot. The blood-alcohol limit in Italy is 0.05%, often achieved with just two drinks, but this, too, is not enforced as often as it is in northern Europe or North America. Clearly drunk drivers, however, can expect to be arrested.

As far as *parcheggio* (parking) is concerned, on streets, white lines indicate free public spaces and blue lines indicate pay public spaces. Meters don't line the sidewalk; rather, there's one machine on the block where you punch in how long you want to park. The machine spits out a ticket that you leave on your dashboard. Sometimes streets will have an attendant who'll come around and give you your time ticket (pay him or her when you get ready to leave). If you park in an area marked PARCHEGGIO DISCO ORARIO, root

around in your rental car's glove compartment for a cardboard parking disc (or buy one at a gas station). With this device, you dial up the hour of your arrival (it's the honor system) and display it on your dashboard. You're allowed *un ora* (1 hr.) or *due ore* (2 hr.), according to the sign. **Parking lots** have ticket dispensers, but booths are not usually manned as you exit. Take your ticket with you when you park; when you return to the lot to get your car and leave, first visit the office or automated payment machine to exchange your ticket for a paid receipt that you then use to get through the automated exit.

ROAD SIGNS Here's a brief rundown of the road signs you'll most frequently encounter. A **speed limit** sign is a black number inside a red circle on a white background. The **end of a speed zone** is just black and white, with a black slash through the number. A red circle with a white background, a black arrow pointing down, and a red arrow pointing up means **yield to oncoming traffic,** while a point-down red-and-white triangle means **yield ahead.** In town, a simple white circle with a red border, or the words *zona pedonale* or *zona traffico limitato,* denotes a **pedestrian zone** (you can drive through only to drop off baggage at your hotel); a white arrow on a blue background is used for Italy's many **one-way streets;** a mostly red circle with a horizontal white slash means **do not enter.** Any image in black on a white background surrounded by a red circle means that image is **not allowed** (for instance, if the image is two cars next to each other, it means no passing; a motorcycle means no Harleys permitted, and so on). A circular sign in blue with a red circle-slash means **no parking.**

GASOLINE *Benzina* (gas or petrol) is even more expensive in Italy than in the rest of Europe. Even a small rental car can guzzle about 60€ for a fill-up. There are many pull-in gas stations along major roads and on the outskirts of town, as well as 24-hour rest stops along the *autostrada* highways, but in towns most stations are small sidewalk gas stands where you parallel park to fill up. Almost all stations are closed for *riposo* and on Sundays, but the majority of them now have a pump fitted with a machine that accepts bills so you can self-service your tank at 3am. Unleaded gas is *senza piombo.*

By Train

Italy has one of the best train systems in Europe, especially the northern half, and even traveling on a regional level you'll find many destinations connected. Most lines are administered by the state-run **Ferrovie dello Stato,** or **FS** (*©* **892-021** for national train info, or 199-166-177 to buy tickets; www.trenitalia.com), but servicing the Casentino and western Valdichiana in Tuscany is a private line called **LFI,** and northern Umbria is serviced by the private **FCU.** About the only difference you'll notice is that these private lines don't honor special discount cards or passes (see "Special Passes & Discounts," below).

Italian trains are about as clean and comfortable as commuter trains in the United States, which is to say, it really depends. Though increasingly trains are of the boring straight-through commuter variety, on long-haul runs especially you'll still be blessed with those old-fashioned cars made up of *couchette* compartments that seat only six or occasionally eight. First class (*prima classe*) is usually only a shade better than second class (*seconda classe*), with four to six seats per *couchette* instead of six to eight. The only real benefits of first class comes if (a) you're traveling overnight, in which case four berths per compartment are a lot more comfortable than six or (b) the train is overcrowded, and first-class gives you much more breathing space and legroom.

Few visitors are prepared for how **crowded** Italian trains can sometimes get,

though you can count your blessings that, with the increase in automobile travel, they're not as crowded as they were in times gone by. An Italian train is full only when the corridors are packed solid and there are more than eight people sitting on their luggage in the little vestibules by the doors. Overcrowding is often a problem on Friday evenings, weekends, and holidays, especially in and out of big cities, or just after a strike. In summer the crowding escalates, and any train going toward a beach in August all but bulges like an overstuffed sausage.

Italian trains come in six varieties based on how often they stop. The **Eurostar (ES)** is the "pendulum" train that zips back and forth between Naples and Milan, stopping at Rome, Florence, and Bologna along the way, and there is also one that crosses northern Italy (described earlier). It's the fastest but most expensive option (first class only, a meal included); it has its own ticket window at the stations and *requires* a seat reservation. Other **Eurostar/Eurocity** (**ES/EC, EN** if it runs overnight) trains connect Italian cities with cities outside the country; these are the speediest of the standard trains, offering both first and second class and always requiring a supplement (except for Eurail passholders, though the conductors won't always believe you on this one); **Intercity (IC)** trains are similar to Eurocity trains in that they offer both first and second class and require a supplement, but they never cross an international border.

Of the regular trains that don't require supplements—often called *Regionale* (R) if they stay within a region (Tuscany) or *Interregionale* (IR) if they don't (Tuscany to Umbria)—the **Espresso** stops at all the major and most of the secondary stations, the **Diretto** stops at virtually every station, and the snail-paced **Locale** (sometimes laughingly called *accelerato*) frequently stops between stations in the middle of the countryside for no apparent reason.

When buying a **regular ticket,** ask for either *andata* (one-way) or *andata e ritorno* (round-trip). If the train you plan to take is an ES/EC or IC, ask for the ticket *con supplemento rapido* (with speed supplement) to avoid on-train penalty charges. On a trip under 200km (124 miles), your ticket is good to leave within the next 6 hours; over 200km, you have a full day. (This code isn't rigorously upheld by conductors, but don't push your luck.) On round-trip journeys of less than 250km (155 miles), the return ticket is valid only for 3 days. This distance-time correlation continues, with an extra day added to your limit for each 200km above 250km (the maximum is 6 days). If you board a regular train without a ticket (or board an IC/EC without the supplement), you'll have to pay a hefty "tax" on top of the ticket or supplement, which the conductor will sell you. Most conductors also get extremely crabby if you forget to **stamp your ticket in the little yellow box** on the platform before boarding the train.

Schedules for all lines running through a given station are printed on posters tacked up on the station wall. *Binario (bin)* means "track." You can also get official schedules (and more train information, some even in English) on the Web at **www.ferroviedellostato.it**.

Stations tend to be well run, with luggage storage facilities at all but the smallest and usually a good bar attached that serves surprisingly palatable food. If you pull into a dinky town with a shed-size or nonexistent station, find the nearest bar or *tabacchi,* and the man behind the counter will most likely sell you tickets.

SPECIAL PASSES & DISCOUNTS To buy the **Eurail Italy Pass,** available only outside Italy and priced in U.S. dollars, contact **Rail Europe** (www.raileurope. com). You have 2 months in which to use the train a set number of days; the base number of days is 3, and you can add up to 7 more. For adults, the first-class pass

costs $239, second class is $211. Additional days cost roughly $30 more for first class, $25 for second class. For youth tickets (25 and under), a 3-day pass is $171 and additional days about $20 each. Saver passes are available for groups of two to five people traveling together at all times, extending a discount of about $20 off an adult pass.

There are also Italy-Greece, Italy-Spain, and Italy-France combinations, in addition to a **rail-and-drive** pass. This is valid for 2 months, during which you can use 3 rail days and 2 car days (and add more car or rail days cheaply). Prices start at $398 for second-class tickets and an economy car. Fares vary depending on type of car.

When it comes to regular tickets, if you're **under 26,** you can buy at any Italian train station a 40€ **Carta Verde (Green Card)** that gets you a 10% discount for domestic trips and 25% on international connections on all FS tickets for 1 year. Present it each time you go to buy a ticket. A similar deal is available for anyone **over 75** with the **Carta d'Argento (Silver Card):** 15% off domestic and 25% off international, for 30€. Children 11 and under always ride half-price (and can get the passes mentioned above at half-price), and kids under 4 ride free.

By Bus

Although trains are quicker and easier, you can get just about anywhere through a network of dozens of local, provincial, and regional bus lines (see below), but in northern Italy you'll mainly be using buses in the cities where there is no subway or, in the case of Venice, boat, available. **Schedules** in cities are posted in a little box on the pole of the large orange or yellow signs that demarcate the stops. Keep in mind that in smaller towns buses exist mainly to shuttle workers and schoolchildren, so the most runs are on weekdays, early in the morning, and usually again around lunchtime.

A town's **bus stop** is usually either the main piazza or, more often, a large square on the edge of town or the bend in the road just outside the main city gate. You should always try to find the local ticket vendor—if there's no office, it's invariably the nearest newsstand or *tabacchi* (signaled by a sign with a white T), or occasionally a bar—but you can usually also buy tickets on the bus. You can also flag a bus down as it passes on a country road, but try to find an official stop (a small sign tacked onto a telephone pole). Tell the driver where you're going and ask him courteously if he'll let you know when you need to get off. When he says *"E la prossima fermata,"* that means yours is the next stop. *"Posso scendere?"* (*Poh*-so *shen*-dairay?) is "May I please get off?"

NORTHERN ITALY BUS LINES   Unlike in central Italy and even the South, buses in northern Italy have limited appeal, as nearly every town is easily reached by train. Popular destinations for buses include hard-to-reach ski areas in the Alps and Dolomites, isolated towns in the Veneto, the Lakes Region (although it is a much prettier ride by boat), and beach resorts along the Ligurian coast.

Austostradale, with an office in Piazza Castello, Milan (✆ **166-845-010;** www. autostradale.it), offers regular service to Aosta and to the Dolomite ski resorts of Madonna del Campiglio and Cortina d'Ampezzo. To move around the Dolomites, you can catch a bus from the unfortunately acronymed **SAD** company (✆ **0472-801-075;** www.sad.it). To get to the Alpine resorts from Aosta, look for **SAVDA** buses (✆ **0165-841-397**).

The Lakes Region is also best navigated by bus if you find the ferry schedule inconvenient. For towns on Lake Garda, contact **SAIA** (✆ **030-223-761**) in Brescia or **APT** (✆ **045-800-4129**) in Verona. For Lake Como, look for the blue **SPT** buses (✆ **031-304-744**) in the center of any of the towns.

There is no shortage of local trains along the Ligurian coast (in fact, most trains stop in every small town, like it or not), but still a handful of companies operate bus service to popular destinations. One of them is **Riviera Trasporti** (✆ **0184-592-706;** www.rivieratrasporti. it), which connects towns along the northern coast: San Remo, Imperia, Bordighera, and Ventimiglia.

In the Veneto, neither Bassano del Grappa nor Asolo is reachable by train. To get to Bassano, and then on to Asolo, you'll need to catch a **FTV** bus (✆ **0424-30-850;** www.ftv.vi.it) in Vicenza.

4 MONEY & COSTS

Frommer's lists exact prices in the local currency. The currency conversions quoted above were correct at press time. However, rates fluctuate, so before departing, consult a currency exchange website, such as **www.oanda.com/convert/classic,** to check up-to-the-minute rates.

Like many other European countries, Italy uses the euro as its currency. Euro coins are issued in denominations of .01€, .02€, .05€, .10€, .20€, and .50€, as well as 1€ and 2€; bills come in denominations of 5€, 10€, 20€, 50€, 100€, 200€, and 500€.

The aggressive evolution of international computerized banking and consolidated ATM networks has led to the triumph of plastic throughout the Italian peninsula—even if cold cash is still the most trusted currency, especially in smaller towns or cheaper mom-and-pop joints, where credit cards may not be accepted. Traveler's checks, while still the safest way

€	US$	Can$	UK£	Aus$	NZ$
1	$1.40	C$1.52	£0.86	A$1.72	NZ$2.16

to carry money, are going the way of the dinosaur.

You'll get the best rate if you **exchange money** at a bank or one of its ATMs. The rates at "Cambio/change/wechsel" exchange booths are invariably less favorable but still a good deal better than what you'd get exchanging money at a hotel or shop (a last-resort tactic only). The bill-to-bill changers you'll see in some touristy places exist solely to rip you off.

ATMS

The easiest and best way to get cash away from home is from an ATM (automated teller machine), referred to in Italy as a "Bancomat." ATMs are very prevalent in the cities of northern Italy and are not as common in smaller towns and villages. While every town usually has one, it's good practice to fuel up on cash in urban centers, ideally during business hours. (International circuits seem to go off-line on occasion late at night and on weekends.) The **Cirrus** (© **800/424-7787;** www.mastercard.com) and **PLUS** (© **800/843-7587;** www.visa.com) networks span the globe. Go to your bank card's website to find ATM locations in northern Italy.

Be sure to check with your bank that your card is valid for international withdrawal and that you have a four-digit PIN. (Most ATMs in Italy will not accept any other number of digits.) Also, be sure you know your daily withdrawal limit before you depart. *Note:* Many banks impose a fee every time you use a card at another bank's ATM, and that fee can be higher for international transactions (up to $5 or more) than for domestic ones (where they're rarely more than $2). In addition, the bank from which you withdraw cash may charge its own fee, although this is

not common practice in Italy. For international withdrawal fees, ask your bank.

If at the ATM you get a message saying your card isn't valid for international transactions, don't panic: It's most likely the bank just can't make the phone connection to check it (occasionally this can be a citywide epidemic) or else simply doesn't have the cash. Try another ATM or another town.

CREDIT CARDS

Credit cards are widely accepted in northern Italy these days, especially in hotels and larger establishments. However, it is always a good idea to carry some cash, since some small businesses may accept only cash or may claim that their credit card machine is broken to avoid paying fees to the credit card companies.

Visa and **MasterCard** are almost universally accepted at hotels, plus most restaurants and shops; the majority of them also accept **American Express. Diners Club** is gaining some ground. *Note:* It is an unfortunately common practice among many restaurants in Italy to claim that the credit card machine is down when, in fact, it is more often the case that the owner simply doesn't want to pay the merchant fees. On more than one occasion I've insisted that they try it just in case, as I had no cash, and—surprise—it's been instantly fixed! The best way to avoid this chicanery is to inform the waitstaff up front that you intend to use a credit card. If they tell you it's broken, you have the option of finding a restaurant where the machine "works."

Chip and PIN represent a change in the way that credit and debit cards are used. The program is designed to cut down on the fraudulent use of credit cards. More and

What Things Cost in Venice

Vaporetto ticket (from the train station to San Marco)	6.50€
Double room at the Hotel Cipriani (very expensive)	1,200.00€
Double room at Antica Locanda Sturion (moderate)	250.00€
Double room at Hotel Bernardi-Semenzato (inexpensive)	80.00€
Continental breakfast (cappuccino and croissant standing at a bar)	3.00€
Lunch for one at Cantina Do Mori (inexpensive)	8.00€
Dinner for one, with table wine, at Do Forni (expensive)	70.00€
Dinner for one, with table wine, at Ai Tre Spiedi (moderate)	45.00€
Dinner for one, with table wine, at Da Remigo (inexpensive)	30.00€
Glass of wine	2.00€–7.00€
Coca-Cola (standing/sitting in a bar)	2.00€/3.50€
Cup of espresso (standing/sitting in a bar)	0.75€/1.00€
Admission to the Accademia	10.00€

more banks—especially in Europe—are issuing customers chip and PIN versions of their debit or credit cards. In the future, more and more vendors will be asking for a four-digit PIN, which will be entered into a keypad near the cash register. For now, traditional "swipe" cards are commonly accepted in northern Italy even though they are being phased out elsewhere, and chip cards are also commonly accepted.

Finally, be sure to let your bank know that you'll be traveling abroad to avoid having your card blocked after a few days of big purchases far from home. Note that many banks now assess a 1% to 3% "transaction fee" on **all** charges you incur abroad (whether you're using the local currency or your native currency).

5 HEALTH

STAYING HEALTHY

There are no special health risks you'll encounter in Italy. The tap water is safe—excellent, even—and medical resources are high quality.

General Availability of Healthcare

With Italy's partially socialized medicine, you can usually stop by any hospital emergency room with an ailment, get swift and courteous service, receive a diagnosis and a prescription, and be sent on your way with a wave and a smile—without filling out a single sheet of paperwork. However, the benefits of Italy's partially socialized medicine really apply only to Italians, so

foreigners should be prepared to pay medical bills up front.

Pharmacies offer essentially the same range of generic drugs available in the United States, plus a lot of them that haven't been approved yet by the U.S. Food and Drug Administration. Pharmacies are also the only place you'll find simple stuff such as aspirin and run-of-the-mill cold medicines: You won't find Tylenol at any old corner store (even if there were such a thing as a corner store).

Strangely, though, I have found it very hard to locate decongestants in Italy the way you can in other countries. If you regularly suffer from a stuffy nose, it is best to pack a good supply of Sudafed with you before you leave.

WHAT TO DO IF YOU GET SICK AWAY FROM HOME

For travel abroad, you may have to pay all medical costs up front and be reimbursed later. Before leaving home, find out what medical services your **health insurance** covers. Your health insurance in your home country may not cover any extended treatment abroad. However, even if you don't have insurance, you will be seen and treated in an emergency room, just as you would at home.

Northern Italy has good **hospitals** (see p. 436 in chapter 13), and Italy's public health care system is generally well regarded.

Pharmacies in Italy are ubiquitous (look for the green cross) and they serve almost like mini-clinics, where pharmacists diagnose and treat minor ailments, like flu symptoms and general aches and pains,

with over-the-counter drugs. In Italy, most over-the-counter drugs are available in either generic form or a local brand. You may want to pack a simple decongestant, which is oddly rare in Italy. Pack prescription medications in your carry-on luggage, and carry them in their original containers, with pharmacy labels—otherwise, they won't make it through airport security. Carry the generic name of prescription medicines, in case a local pharmacist is unfamiliar with the brand name.

Pharmacies in Venice, Milan, and several other towns in northern Italy often take turns doing the night shift. Normally there is a list posted at the entrance of each pharmacy, telling customers which pharmacy is open which night of the week.

If you experience an emergency, dial 🕿 **113**, Italy's general emergency number. For an ambulance, call 🕿 **118.** We list additional emergency numbers in "Fast Facts," p. 436.

6 SAFETY

Italy is a remarkably safe country, and in my opinion, northern Italy is one of the safest regions on Earth. The worst threats you'll likely face are the pickpockets that sometimes frequent touristy areas and public buses; just keep your valuables in an under-the-clothes money belt there and you should be fine. There are, of course, thieves in northern Italy, as there are everywhere, so be smart; don't leave anything valuable in your rental car overnight, and leave nothing visible in it at any time to avoid tempting a would-be thief. I have had a car full of valuables, including my passport, stolen on a respectable street in Milan, so it does happen. The fact that there is so little overt crime in Italy, though, is a good thing, as police enforcement is notoriously lax. If you do happen to be robbed, you can fill out paperwork at the nearest police station, but this is

mostly for insurance purposes—don't expect them to actually hunt down the perpetrator or find your lost valuables.

In general, avoid public parks at night and public squares in the wee hours of the morning. The square in front of Milan's main train station is pretty dodgy at any hour. Travelers—especially young women—should avoid the port area of Genoa after dark. Other than that, there is a remarkable sense of security in this wealthy corner of the world.

Unfortunately, a level of racism still exists in Italy, and recent immigrants from Africa are often discriminated against and are occasionally accused of committing the few crimes that do exist in northern Italy—even if the accusations are unwarranted. As a result, people of African descent may meet some skeptical looks in the northeast especially, unless they clearly appear to be well-heeled Westerners. Late at night, however, if there is trouble around, police will probably not make any distinction at all.

7 SPECIALIZED TRAVEL RESOURCES

In addition to the destination-specific resources listed below, please visit Frommers.com for additional specialized travel resources.

GAY & LESBIAN TRAVELERS

Italy as a whole, and northern Italy in particular, is gay-friendly. Homosexuality is legal, and the age of consent is 16. Luckily, Italians are already more affectionate and physical than Americans in their general friendships, and even straight men occasionally walk down the street with their arms around each other—however, kissing anywhere other than on the cheeks at greetings and goodbyes will certainly draw attention. As you might expect, smaller towns tend to be less permissive and accepting than cities. Milan has the largest and most visible homosexual population, and during fashion week especially, gay travelers will feel particularly at home.

Italy's national association and support network for gays and lesbians is **ARCI-Gay/ARCI-Lesbica.** The national website is **www.arcigay.it**, and every city has a local office. In **Venice,** it is found at San Polo 2003 (© **340-593-8934**); in **Trieste,** Via Pondares 8 (© **040-630-606**); in **Verona,** Via Gela 9 (© **045-810-6253**); in **Milan,** Via Bezzecca 3 (© **02-54-12-22-25;** www.arcigaymilano.org); in **Genoa,** Corso Torino 46/1 (© **010-565971;** http://nuke.arcigaygenova.it); and in **Turin,** Via Fratelli Faa di Bruno 2 (© **011-19-70-31-45;** www.arcigaytorino.it).

TRAVELERS WITH DISABILITIES

In Italy, a few of the top museums and churches have installed ramps at the entrances, and a few hotels have converted first-floor rooms into accessible units by widening the doors and bathrooms. Other than that, don't expect to find much of northern Italy—or really any part of Italy—easy to tackle. Builders in the Middle Ages and the Renaissance didn't have wheelchairs or mobility impairments in mind when they built narrow doorways and spiral staircases, and preservation laws keep modern Italians from being able to do much about this. Buses and trains can cause problems as well, with high, narrow doors and steep steps at entrances. There are, however, seats reserved on public transportation for travelers with disabilities.

One organization that helps travelers with disabilities in Tuscany is **Accessible Italy** (© **378-0549-9411;** www.accessible italy.com). It provides travelers with information about accessible tourist sites and places to rent wheelchairs, as well as offering organized "Accessible Tours" around Italy. Additionally, this nonprofit organization invests its proceeds in Italy's infrastructure, to make the country more accessible.

FAMILY TRAVEL

Italy is a family-oriented society, and kids have free rein just about anywhere they go. A crying baby at a dinner table is greeted with a knowing smile rather than with a stern look. Children under a certain age almost always receive discounts, and maybe a special treat from the waiter, but the availability of such North American accoutrements as child seats for cars and dinner tables are more the exception to the rule than the norm.

WOMEN TRAVELERS

Women feel remarkably welcome in Italy—sometimes a bit too welcome, actually. It seems every young Italian male is out to prove himself the most irresistible lover on the planet; remember, this is the land of Romeo and Casanova, so they have a lot to live up to. And with most every Italian woman playing the especially hard-to-get Juliet, well, you see what's coming next for attractive foreign women.

It should be noted that, culturally, northern Italy feels a lot more like its Austrian and Swiss neighbors in the sense that the divide between the sexes is not quite as deep, a lot more egalitarian and perhaps less chivalrous than, say, Sicily, but naturally attractive women everywhere will, er, attract attention.

Note that much of the attention is kept to verbal flirtation and that occasional inappropriate touching deserves a slap in the face. These men want to conquer you with their charm, not their muscles. Rape is much rarer in Italy than in the United States—but it does happen, mostly by non-Italian men, if you believe the newspapers. Use common sense: Don't walk through poorly lit city parks alone late at night, especially in Milan, Turin, and Genoa.

MULTICULTURAL TRAVELERS

Italy for centuries was and, to a large degree, still is a homogenous culture. Add to that the fact that issues of race here are discussed so frankly and openly—there's apparently no taboo to saying, in a loud voice, "That black guy over there. . . ." Moreover, the reality is that most people of African descent in Italy are working as street vendors, not bankers. All this may make travelers with darker skin feel—correctly at times—as if they're being singled out.

Pockets of outright racism do exist in Italy, especially in the Veneto and the Northeast in general. There African and South Asian workers fill the need for low-paid labor and, according to outfits like the Northern League, are generally responsible

for any crime that might occur in the streets. Skinhead violence is extremely rare, but you might expect the occasional slur from a soccer hooligan and maybe some sideways glances from a few provincial old men.

SENIOR TRAVEL

Italy is a multigenerational culture that doesn't tend to marginalize its seniors, and older people are treated with a great deal of respect and deference throughout Italy. But there are few specific programs, associations, or concessions made for them. The one exception is on admission prices for museums and sights, where those ages 60 or 65 and older will often get in at a reduced rate or even free. There are also special train passes and reductions on bus tickets and the like in various towns (see "Getting Around," earlier in this chapter). As a senior in Italy, you're *un anziano* (*una anziana* if you're a woman), or "ancient one"—consider it a term of respect and let people know you're one if you think a discount may be in order.

STUDENT TRAVELERS

The **International Student Travel Confederation** (**ISTC;** www.istc.org) was formed in 1949 to make travel around the world more affordable for students. Check out its website for comprehensive travel services information and details on how to get an **International Student Identity Card (ISIC),** which qualifies students for substantial savings on rail passes, plane tickets, entrance fees, and more. It also provides students with basic health and life insurance and a 24-hour help line. The card is valid for a maximum of 18 months. You can apply for the card online or in person at **STA Travel** (*©* **800/781-4040** in North America; www.statravel.com), the biggest student travel agency in the world; check out the website to locate STA Travel offices worldwide. If you're no longer a student but are still under 26, you can get an **International Youth Travel**

Card (IYTC) from the same agency, which entitles you to some discounts. Travel CUTS (℡ 800/592-2887; www.travelcuts.com) offers similar services for both Canadians and U.S. residents. Irish students may prefer to turn to USIT (℡ 01/602-1904; www.usit.ie), an Ireland-based specialist in student, youth, and independent travel.

In northern Italy, students will find many university cities that offer ample student discounts and inexpensive youth hostels. Padua is home to one of Italy's oldest universities, founded in 1222, and today it is still a thriving student city with a young university population that keeps the city's piazzas and cafes alive.

SINGLE TRAVELERS

On package vacations, single travelers are often hit with a "single supplement" to the base price. To avoid it, you can agree to room with other single travelers or find a compatible roommate before you go, from one of the many roommate-locator agencies. This is also a good way to avoid the relatively high cost of a double room–single use, as opposed to splitting a double.

8 SUSTAINABLE TOURISM

Environmentalism in Italy has always been an area of stark contrasts. Italians conserve fuel and energy like most Europeans do, they go to great lengths to limit air pollution, and their shopping habits of consuming locally grown vegetables and bringing a bag to the store would put a smile on just about any environmentalist's face. Meanwhile, local entities' recycling efforts are dubious (investigative journalism reveals that most of the recyclables and trash in Rome, for example, ended up in the same place anyway), and, incredibly, sewage treatment plants have only begun to spring up around Milan in the past decade or so. Previously, it simply was flushed into the rivers.

That aside, the tourism industry here leads the charge in protecting the resources of a country where visitor spending accounts for a whole lot of the nation's income. Northern Italy has taken several measures to ensure sustainable tourism. Many hotels in Milan and other northern Italian cities, as well as higher-end *agriturismi* in the countryside, have implemented green practices, like encouraging patrons to reuse towels rather than throw them immediately in the wash. Organic agriculture is widespread, especially on smaller farms around northern Italy that host visitors, so when you eat in a restaurant in this region, chances are that the food didn't travel very far to get to your table. (The insistence on bottled water, however, is one blemish on an otherwise good record.)

Towns and provinces push for more intercity cycling paths to connect tourist sites, and many cities, like Milan, have implemented a bike-sharing program, which, for a nominal fee, allows people to ride bicycles around town for short increments of time (usually 30 min.). You pick up a bike in one of the many racks around town and leave it at another. Milan has also managed to cut down on traffic by instituting a fee for cars to enter the city center during the day from Monday to Friday. Venice, on the other hand, has no car traffic, since the only means of transportation in the city is boat. This water traffic—as well as a history of poor sewage systems that fed right into the canals—has contributed to high levels of pollution in the city's water. However, Venice has recently taken measures to improve its water quality by installing more septic tanks and controlling sewage flow, and by improving standards of water treatment.

General Resources for Green Travel

The following websites provide valuable wide-ranging information on sustainable travel. For a list of even more sustainable resources, as well as tips and explanations on how to travel greener, visit www.frommers.com/planning.

- **Responsible Travel** (www.responsibletravel.com) is a great source of sustainable travel ideas; the site is run by a spokesperson for ethical tourism in the travel industry. **Sustainable Travel International** (www.sustainabletravelinternational.org) promotes ethical tourism practices, and manages an extensive directory of sustainable properties and tour operators around the world.

- In the U.K., **Tourism Concern** (www.tourismconcern.org.uk) works to reduce social and environmental problems connected to tourism. The **Association of Independent Tour Operators** (AITO; www.aito.co.uk) is a group of specialist operators leading the field in making holidays sustainable.

- In Canada, **www.greenlivingonline.com** offers extensive content on how to travel sustainably, including a travel and transport section, and profiles of the best green shops and services in Toronto, Vancouver, and Calgary.

- In Australia, the national body which sets guidelines and standards for eco-tourism is **Ecotourism Australia** (www.ecotourism.org.au). **The Green Directory** (www.thegreendirectory.com.au), **Green Pages** (www.thegreenpages.com.au), and **Eco Directory** (www.ecodirectory.com.au) offer sustainable travel tips and directories of green businesses.

- **Carbonfund** (www.carbonfund.org), **TerraPass** (www.terrapass.org), and **Carbon Neutral** (www.carbonneutral.org) provide info on "carbon offsetting," or offsetting the greenhouse gas emitted during flights.

- **Greenhotels** (www.greenhotels.com) recommends green-rated member hotels around the world that fulfill the company's stringent environmental requirements. **Environmentally Friendly Hotels** (www.environmentallyfriendlyhotels.com) offers more green accommodation ratings. The **Hotel Association of Canada** (www.hacgreenhotels.com) has a Green Key Eco-Rating Program, which audits the environmental performance of Canadian hotels, motels, and resorts.

- **Sustain Lane** (www.sustainlane.com) lists sustainable eating and drinking choices around the U.S.; also visit **www.eatwellguide.org** for tips on eating sustainably in the U.S. and Canada.

- For information on animal-friendly issues throughout the world, visit **Tread Lightly** (www.treadlightly.org). For information about the ethics of swimming with dolphins, visit the **Whale and Dolphin Conservation Society** (www.wdcs.org).

- **Volunteer International** (www.volunteerinternational.org) has a list of questions to help you determine the intentions and the nature of a volunteer program. For general info on volunteer travel, visit **www.volunteerabroad.org** and **www.idealist.org**.

Public transportation is generally reliable, and trains provide an excellent way of getting around northern Italy. Buses can also take you around the countryside. However, there is no escaping the fact that most often a family with luggage will need a car to get around the remote areas of the northern Italian countryside.

Overall, as a nation that needs to import the great majority of its energy from far away, and with 60 million people living in relative proximity, Italians have always been a culture to live and consume at a sustainable rate and a very human scale.

You can do your part by reusing towels, taking public transportation whenever possible, discarding trash and recyclables in the appropriate white and blue bins around the region, and eating locally grown produce. And don't shy away from Italy's tap water; it's very good.

9 SPECIAL-INTEREST TRIPS & ESCORTED GENERAL-INTEREST TOURS

SPECIAL-INTEREST TRIPS
Academic Trips & Language Classes

A number of organizations offer intensive Italian language courses for adults in northern Italy, especially in Venice and Milan. A good budget option that attracts a variety of ages is the **Venice Institute** (www.istitutovenezia.com), which holds week-long courses in Venice and Trieste starting at 160€ for the week. (One of the other great values of the experience is staying at the secluded Palladian cloisters on the Giudecca for about 35€ per night for a single.) There are language courses for every ability level, and the instructors are certified in Italian as a second language.

Milan is a venue for Italian classes, because many employees of foreign countries relocate here without much of a background in the language. **The International House of Milan** (www.ihmilano.com) is well known in these circles, as it specializes in key sectors; for example, there is a 2-week program devoted to the language of the fashion and design industry, which costs 530€. A slightly more affordable option is the **Scuola Leonardo da Vinci** (www.scuolaleonardo.com), where a general 2-week course is available for 300€. It also has more specialized courses for food and gastronomy, and other subjects; prices and required fluency levels increase with specialization.

Adventure & Wellness Trips
Bike Tours

In many ways, northern Italy is the birthplace of cycling, or at least home to many of the biggest names in the industry. Bianchi, Campagnolo, De Rosa, and Pinarello are all headquartered in Lombardy or the Veneto, regions that also host the most exciting stages of the Giro d'Italia, which ends in Milan.

Organizing your own bike tour is easy if you rely on a few resources. Arm yourself with a good map and make use of the resources of the **Club Alpino Italiano,** 7 Via E. Fonseca Pimental, Milan 20127 (© **02-2614-1378;** fax 02-2614-1395; www.cai.it). You can rent a bike by the week or longer at outlets in most cities.

Several operators specialize in setting up itineraries and making some of the arrangements for you or in leading fully guided tours. **Ciclismo Classico** ★★ (© **800/866-7314** in the U.S., or 781/646-3377; fax 781/641-1512; www.ciclismoclassico.com) is one of the best operators and has been leading bike and walking tours in Italy since 1988. A week-long tour of Piedmont runs about 4,500€ per person, staying at premier accommodations. April through November, the outfit runs several guided tours through the Alps, Dolomites, and Fruili, and a pair of trips out of Venice. Six- to 15-day trips usually include Italian-language and cooking lessons, along with wine tasting and cultural itineraries. Groups average 10 to 18 people, with all ages and ability levels welcome.

Experience Plus (℅ **800/685-4565** in the U.S., or 970/484-8489; www.experienceplus.com) offers both guided and self-guided biking and walking tours through northern Italy lasting 8 or 9 days.

Walking Tours

If you don't feel the need to cover so much territory, you can appreciate even more of the countryside by walking or hiking (called *trekking* in Italian). Italy's resource for everything from countryside ambles to serious mountain trekking is the **Club Alpino Italiano,** 7 Via E. Fonseca Pimental, Milan 20127 (℅ **02-2614-1378;** fax 02-2614-1395; www.cai.it).

Many outfits run walking tours in northern Italy. Besides **Ciclismo Classico** (see above), you might want to try **Butterfield & Robinson,** 70 Bond St., Ste. 300, Toronto, ON M5B 1X3 (℅ **800/678-1147** or 416/864-1354; fax 416/864-0541; www.butterfield.com); or **Country Walkers** ★ (℅ **800/464-9255** in the U.S., or 802/244-1387; www.countrywalkers.com), which has a rather refined, romantic outlook on walking and offers several northern Italy tours, including tours in Cinque Terre and the lakes region.

For walking tours in Venice, one of the better resources is **Context Travel** (℅ **215/609-4888;** www.contexttravel.com), which offers tours and seminars led by graduate students and other experts in their respective fields on everything from Renaissance art to ceramics to cuisine.

Food & Wine Trips

Just as it's not hard to find a cooking class in Italy (most top-flight hotels will show you how to make a classic northern Italian dish and pair it with the right wine for some extra money), nearly every organized tour will have a strong culinary component. For example, check out **Discover Friuli** (www.discoverfriuli.com), which combines language courses, cooking classes, and wine tours in a single program.

Wine tours in Italy are often a trade unto themselves. Most tourist boards will have a selection of guided tours of the vineyards in their province (mentioned in the individual chapters). Friuli is heavily promoting itself as a wine destination and has even unveiled a fleet of **yellow Vespas** (www.collioinvespa.it) as part of the promotion. These Vespas can be rented at various tour agencies in the region, such as **Key Tre Viaggi** (www.keytreviaggi.it), which offers a Vespa tour with a self-guided itinerary, private tours of vineyards, and a 2-night package in an *agriturismo* starting at 192€ per person.

There are also tour companies which concentrate solely on wine. **Cellar Tours** (www.cellartours.com), one of the better-known, high-end wine tour operators, will chauffer you in a Mercedes to the most prestigious vineyards in Piedmont, Friuli, and the Veneto, and put you up in five-star accommodations; their tours cost 375€ to 1,000€ per person, per day, depending on the trip. Sara Cossiga is an art historian, journalist, tour guide, and sommelier who offers wine-focused tours of Venice and the Veneto; contact **Venice & Veneto Gourmet** (www.veneceveneto gourmet.com) for more information.

Cooking Schools

Italy's best-known cooking schools seem to be in Tuscany—but northern Italy still has its share of cooking classes and excellent cuisine. **LINGUA IT** (℅ **045-597-975;** www.linguait.it) is an Italian-language school in Verona which offers a course on the food and wine of the region. In **Genoa, A Door to Italy** (℅ **010-246-5870;** www.adoortoitaly.com) offers 1-week and 2-week classes (for about 200€ per week), ranging from the basics of making pasta to preparing more elaborate Ligurian dishes.

Generally, small group classes at a local inn are more memorable culinary experiences. The **Acquolina Venezia** bed and breakfast (© **041-526-2336;** www. acquolinavenezia.com) in Venice offers interesting and intimate cooking courses; take the boat out to Lido from San Marco and join Marika Seguso in her kitchen for a 4-hour course. First-timers learn how to prepare Venetian seafood dishes as well as innovative vegetable sides and classic desserts.

Some hotels also offer cooking classes. The **Four Seasons** (© **02-77088;** www.four seasons.com) in **Milan** recently launched its own cooking classes; half-day classes cost 90€ for guests, starting with a discussion of the daily menu with the hotel chefs and ending with a four-course lunch.

ESCORTED GENERAL-INTEREST TOURS

From the priciest pampered tours to the most inexpensive bare-bones trips, you'll find no shortage of tour operators who offer tours to northern Italy. Many travelers opt for escorted tours because they let you sit back and enjoy the trip without having to drive or worry about details. They take you to the maximum number of sights in the minimum amount of time with the least amount of hassle. They're particularly convenient for people with limited mobility, and they can be a great way to make new friends. On the downside, you'll have little opportunity for serendipitous interactions with locals. While these escorted trips are hassle-free and often cost-efficient, there really is no substitute for exploring the back roads of northern Italy in small numbers, making spur-of-the-moment decisions and finding unexpected gems.

Some tour operators who offer downright cheap deals to northern Italy are **Globus Escorted Tours** (© **866/755-8581;** www.globusjourneys.com), **Insight Vacations** (© **866/680-1241;** www.insight vacations.com), and **Trafalgar Tours** (© **866/544-4434;** www.trafalgar.com). It's hard to book your own hotels, transportation, and food for anything near the prices offered by these companies, but you likely won't stay or eat at top-notch establishments.

One higher-quality—and more expensive—tour operator is **Go Ahead Tours** (© **800/590-1170;** www.goaheadtours. com). They offer refined trips that focus heavily on food and wine rather than just the standard tourist sites. For example, they offer an 11-day tour called "Venice, Como & the Italian Riviera."

For more information on escorted general-interest tours, including questions to ask before booking your trip, see www. frommers.com/planning.

10 STAYING CONNECTED

If you want to be in touch, it is a good idea to rent a cellphone on your visit to northern Italy. Pay phones have not entirely gone by the wayside, but these days there are very few pay phones in Italy—a place where there are far more cellular numbers than land line numbers.

Alternatively, you can buy phone cards with special fixed rates to the United States, Canada, Australia, and other countries (*una carta telefonica prepagata per chiamare gli Stati Uniti, Canada . . .*). The rates on these phone cards are heavily discounted from what you would pay from a land line and far less expensive than calling abroad from a cellphone. Newsstands and tobacconists in cities carry these cards.

TELEPHONES
To call northern Italy:

1. Dial the international access code: 011 from the U.S.; 00 from the U.K., Ireland, or New Zealand; or 0011 from Australia.
2. Dial the country code 39.
3. Dial the city code (for Milan: 02) and then the number. (Do not drop the initial 0 as you might in other European countries.) Even when calling within Italy, you always need to dial the city code first.

To make international calls: To make international calls from Italy, first dial 00 and then the country code (U.S. or Canada 1, U.K. 44, Ireland 353, Australia 61, New Zealand 64). Next, dial the area code and number. For example, if you wanted to call the British Embassy in Washington, D.C., you would dial 00-1-202-588-7800.

For directory assistance: Each cellphone carrier has its own directory assistance number, which is listed automatically in the address book of your SIM card. For Telecom Italia, and its mobile carrier, TIM, the directory assistance number is ℂ **412.**

For operator assistance: For operator assistance in making either a domestic or an international call from a Telecom Italia land line, call ℂ **170.**

Toll-free numbers: Numbers in Italy beginning with 800 or 877, and a few others beginning with 8, are toll-free, but calling a 1-800 number in the States from Italy is not toll-free. In fact, it costs the same as an overseas call.

CELLPHONES

The three letters that define much of the world's wireless capabilities are **GSM** (Global System for Mobile Communications), a big seamless network that makes for easy cross-border cellphone use throughout Europe and dozens of other countries worldwide. GSM phones function with a removable plastic SIM card, encoded with

your phone number and account information. If your cellphone is on a GSM system and you have a world-capable multiband phone such as many Sony Ericsson, Motorola, or Samsung models, you can make and receive calls across civilized areas around much of the globe, including Italy. Just call your wireless operator and ask for "international roaming" to be activated on your account. Unfortunately, per-minute charges can be high—usually $1 to $1.50 in Italy. Coverage with major carriers is excellent in northern Italy cities, like Milan, but can be spotty sometimes in the region's less populated countryside.

For many, **renting** a phone is a good idea. While you can rent a phone from any number of overseas sites, including kiosks at airports and at car-rental agencies, we suggest renting the phone before you leave home. There are a number of places in Milan where you can rent cellphones, but it is generally expensive.

Buying a phone can be economically attractive, as Italy has relatively cheap prepaid phone programs. Once you arrive at your destination, stop by a local cellphone shop and get the cheapest package; you'll pay less than $100 for a phone and a starter calling card. The best deals will probably be in Milan. The city's principal train station, Stazione Centrale, has several cellular stores in the lower-level shopping center. Local calls may be as low as 10¢ per minute, and incoming calls are free.

INTERNET & E-MAIL

More and more hotels, resorts, airports, cafes, and retailers are going **Wi-Fi** (wireless fidelity), becoming "hotspots" that offer free high-speed Wi-Fi access or charge a small fee for usage. Most hotels and lots of wine bars and Irish pubs in Milan have wireless Internet access, as do many hotels throughout northern Italy. In Milan, a reliable cafe to go to for wireless Internet access is **Bar Magenta,** on Carducci 13 at Corso Magenta (ℂ **02-805-3808**).

Most major airports have **Internet kiosks** that provide basic Web access for a per-minute fee that's usually higher than cybercafe prices. Both of Milan's airports offer wireless Internet access; see www.sea-aeroportimilano.it for more information.

If you are bringing your own computer, keep in mind that the outlets are 220V in Italy, and you will need an adapter for a U.K. or North American plug—the same one used for France and most of the rest of the Continent.

If you're not traveling with your own computer, you'll generally find small Internet cafes scattered around high-density tourist locales throughout northern Italy. A reliable Internet cafe in Milan is **Grazia Internet Café,** Piazza Duca d'Aosta 14 (𝒞 **02-670-0543**), a large computer lab just outside Milan's Stazione Centrale. In Venice, one of the bigger Internet cafes is **Venetian Navigator** (Casselleria 5300; 𝒞 **041-277-1056;** www.venetiannavigator. com), which is between San Marco and the Grand Canal.

11 TIPS ON ACCOMMODATIONS

Italy ceased to be the country of the cheap *pensione* a long time ago. In fact, it takes some searching these days to find a hotel room with a shared bathroom.

Hotels are **rated** by regional boards on a system of one to five stars. Prices aren't directly tied to the star system, but for the most part, the more stars a hotel has, the more expensive it'll be—but a four-star in a small town may be cheaper than a two-star in Venice. The number of stars awarded a hotel is based strictly on the amenities offered and not how clean, comfortable, or friendly a place is, or whether it's a good value for the money overall.

A few of the four- and five-star hotels have their own private **garages,** but most city inns have an agreement with a local garage. In many small towns, a garage is unnecessary because public parking, both free and pay, is widely available and never too far from your hotel. Parking costs and procedures are indicated under each hotel, and the rates quoted are per day (overnight). It should go without saying that there are no garages in Venice, as there are no cars.

The **high season** throughout most of northern Italy runs from Easter to early September or October—peaking June

through August—and from December 24 to January 6. You can almost always bargain for a cheaper rate if you're traveling in the shoulder season (early spring and late fall) or winter off season (not including Christmas). In these reviews, I usually quote a range of prices. If there is one figure only, that represents the maximum. Prices vary so wildly, depending entirely on availability, that sometimes the only dependable figure is the highest the hotel is allowed to charge. The moral of the story: If it seems like availability is high, you should be getting a discount.

Supposedly, Italian hotels must quote the price for **breakfast** separately from the room and can't force it on you if you don't want it. However, most hotels include breakfast automatically in the room rate, hoping you won't notice, and many also argue that breakfast is required at their hotel. I've tried to include the separate per-person breakfast price for each hotel. With very few exceptions, Italian hotel breakfasts tend to consist of a *brioche,* or croissant (called a *cornetto* anywhere south of Bologna), and coffee, occasionally with juice and fresh fruit as well. It's rarely worth the 3€ to 15€ charged for it, since you can get the same breakfast—and freshly made instead of packaged—for around 2€ at the bar down the block. Ask for your room quote with a *prezzo senza colazione* (pretz-zoh sen-zah coal-lat-zee-oh-nay), or price without breakfast.

AGRITURISMO (STAYING ON A FARM)

The *agriturismo* movement is gaining ground in Italy. Though Tuscany is at the forefront of this movement, northern Italy also highlights this rural movement. *Agriturismi* are working farms or agricultural estates that offer accommodations to visitors who want to stay out in the countryside. An operation can call itself *agriturismo* only if (a) it offers fewer than 30 beds total, and (b) the agricultural component of the property brings in a larger economic share of profits than the hospitality part—in other words, the property has to remain a farm and not become just a rural hotel. That's why you'll almost always be offered homemade sausages, home-pressed olive oil, and so on, either because they've been doing it that way for years or because these country barons essentially have been required to become farmers by law.

Agriturismi are generally a crapshoot. The types of accommodations can vary dramatically. Most, though, are mini apartments, usually rented out with a minimum stay of 3 days or a week. Sometimes you're invited to eat big country dinners at the table with the family; other times you cook for yourself. Rates can vary from 60€ for two per day to 250€ and beyond—as much as a board-rated four-star hotel in town. I've reviewed a few choice *agriturismi* throughout this book, but there are hundreds more.

If you feel handy enough with Italian, you can avail yourself of the three independent national organizations that together represent all *agriturismi* (or, at least, all the reputable ones).

Go to the website of **Terranostra** (www.terranostra.it) and click on *"La tua*

vacanza," then *"Ricerche."* This will bring up a map of Italy. Mouse over each region, and you'll find a list of local *agriturismi;* for example, in Lombardia, you'll find over 100 choices. They are arranged, unfortunately, alphabetically by name of the actual property (not by, say, town, which would make selecting one so much easier), with price categories of *basso* (low), *medio* (medium), and *alto* (high). Click on the property name, and you'll get a review with pictures and symbols (in Italian, but understandable enough), plus contact info and a link to the place's own website, if available.

At the site of **Turismo Verde** (www.turismoverde.it), click on *"Scegli il tuo Agriturismo,"* and choose from a list of regions and then provinces (for example, click on Liguria and then La Spezia for something in or near Cinque Terre); this will give you a list of local *agriturismi.* Another useful website is **Agriturist** (www.agriturist.it), which is easy to navigate and offers its text in English. You can find hundreds upon hundreds of individual properties via a search engine.

In the States, a few agencies will help you track down a perfect *agriturismo* in Italy; Ralph Levey's **Italy Farm Holidays,** 547 Martling Ave., Tarrytown, NY 10591 (© **914/631-7880;** fax 914/631-8831; www.italyfarmholidays.com), represents a few northern Italian properties and can help you book a stay there. For apartment, farmhouse, or cottage stays of 2 weeks or more, **Idyll Untours** (© **888-868-6871;** www.untours.com) provides exceptional vacation rentals for a reasonable price—which includes air/ground transportation, cooking facilities, and on-call support from a local resident. Best of all: Untours—named the "Most Generous Company in America" by Newman's Own—donates most profits to provide low-interest loans to underprivileged entrepreneurs around the world (see website for details).

House-Swapping

House-swapping is becoming a more popular and viable means of travel; you stay in their place, they stay in yours, and you both get a more authentic and personal view of a destination, the opposite of the escapist retreat many hotels offer. Try **HomeLink International** (http://homelink.org), the largest and oldest home-swapping organization, founded in 1952, with more than 11,000 listings worldwide ($115 yearly membership). **InterVac.com** ($100 for over 10,000 listings) is also reliable. **Craigslist.org** also has an extensive list of housing swap options in Italy, as many Italians are eager to find a cheap vacation alternative in American cities.

VILLA RENTALS

Each summer, thousands of visitors rent an old farmhouse, or "villa," a marketing term used to inspire romantic images of manicured gardens, a Renaissance mansion, and chianti martinis, but in reality this term guarantees no more than four walls and most of a roof.

Actually, finding your countryside Eden isn't that simple, and if you want to ensure a romantic and memorable experience, brace yourself for a lot of research and legwork. Occasionally, you can go through the property owners themselves, but the vast majority of villas are rented out via agencies (see below).

Shop around for a trustworthy agent or representative. Often several outfits will list the same property but charge radically different prices. At some, you sign away any right to refunds if the place doesn't live up to your expectations. Make sure the agency is willing to work with you to find the right property. Try to work with someone who has personally visited the properties you're considering, and always ask to see lots of photos: Get the exterior from several angles to make sure the railroad doesn't pass by the back door, as well as pictures of the bedrooms, kitchen, and bathrooms, and photos of the views out each side of the house.

If you're traveling with other couples, ask to see a floor plan to make sure access to the bathroom isn't through one couple's bedroom. Find out if this is the only villa on the property—some people who rent the villa for the isolation find themselves living in a small enclave of foreigners all sharing the same small pool. Ask whether the villa is purely a rental unit or if, say, the owning family lives there during winter but lets it out during summer. Renting a lived-in place offers pretty good insurance that the lights, plumbing, heat, and so on will all be working.

One of the best agencies to call is **Rent-villas.com** (formerly Rentals in Italy), 700 E. Main St., Ventura, CA 93001 (© **800/726-6702** or 805/641-1650; fax 805/641-1630; www.rentvillas.com). Its agents are very helpful in tracking down the perfect place to suit your needs. A U.K. agency—and one of the best all-around agents in Britain—is **International Chapters,** a division of Abercrombie & Kent, Sloane Square House, Holbein Place, London SW1W 8NS (© **08450/700-618**). Marjorie Shaw's **Insider's Italy,** 41 Schermerhorn St., Brooklyn, NY 11201 (© **718/855-3878;** fax 718/855-3687; www.insiders italy.com), is a small, upscale outfit run by a very personable agent who's thoroughly familiar with all of her properties and with Italy in general.

The **Parker Company Ltd.,** Seaport Landing, 152 Lynnway, Lynn, MA 01902 (© **800/280-2811** or 781/596-8282; fax

781/596-3125; www.theparkercompany. com), handles overseas villa rentals and offers several properties in northern Italy.

For some of the top properties, call the local representative of the Cottages to Castles group. In the United Kingdom, contact **Cottages to Castles,** Tuscany House, 10 Tonbridge Rd., Maidstone, Kent ME16 8RP (© **1622/775-217;** www.cottagesto castles.com).

One of the most reasonably priced agencies is **Villas and Apartments Abroad, Ltd.,** 370 Lexington Ave., Ste. 1401, New York, NY 10017 (© **212/897-5045;** fax 212/897-5039; www.vaanyc. com). **Homeabroad.com,** 22 Railroad St., Great Barrington, MA 02130 (© **413/528-6610;** www.homeabroad.com), handles hundreds of rather upscale properties. A popular but *very* pricey agency is **Villas International,** 4340 Redwood Hwy., Ste. D309, San Rafael, CA 94903 (© **800/221-2260** or 415/499-9490; fax 415/499-9491; www.villasintl.com).

Suggested Itineraries in Northern Italy

Northern Italy is an ideal getaway for people with varied interests, or for those who simply can't make up their minds. There is something for everyone here: sun and sea for beach lovers, Alpine peaks for adventurers, exquisite restaurants and art collections for the urbanite, rustic vineyard living for the farmer-at-heart. Romeo and Juliet's Verona is second only to the canals of Venice in amorous appeal, though smitten couples will find romantic settings at every turn. Two of the following itineraries are designed around the most popular themes of any northern Italian vacation: a wine-and-dining tour for gourmet romantics, and a week in the snowy peaks for skiers and snowboarders. Then there are two itineraries that attempt to capture the best of the area's myriad attractions in 1-week and 2-week tours, respectively. (In general, these itineraries pack in

as much as possible; if you'd like to stay in one place for more time, trim out the fat using the star icon—★—as your guide.) All the routes begin in Milan, as Malpensa airport is the most common gateway to northern Italy, though tours could just as easily start at any of the area's many smaller airports that cater to European budget carriers. Remember that traveling from one end of the region to the other can be done in a single afternoon, if you follow the Po River plain. For train riders, this means becoming very familiar with the Milan-Venice high-speed link (and the spurs to Genoa and Turin), and for drivers, Autostrada A4. While it's tempting to try alternate local roads, the A4 is Italy's most traveled highway for good reason—it saves a huge amount of time and goes almost everywhere you want to be.

1 THE REGIONS IN BRIEF

VENICE & THE VENETO

The Po River created the vast flood plain of the **Veneto** under the brow of pre-Venetian Alps to the north and the Dolomites in the west. What draws visitors to these agricultural flatlands are the art treasures of **Padua (Padova),** the Renaissance villas of Palladio in **Vicenza,** the ancient Roman and pseudo-Shakespearean sights of **Verona,** and—rising on pilings from a lagoon on the Adriatic coast—that most serene city of canals and year-round carnival, **Venice (Venezia).**

THE FRIULI-VENEZIA GIULIA

This forgotten northeast corner of Italy marks the border with Slovenia, a region of tame Alps, rolling hills, and Adriatic beaches. Its culture lies at the crossroads of Italy, Yugoslavia, and Austria—the Adriatic city of **Trieste** was once the main port for Vienna and the Habsburgs, and has the coffeehouses to prove it. The influence of the old, neighboring sea power Venice is still strong in its staunch ally of **Udine,** while nearby **Cividale dei**

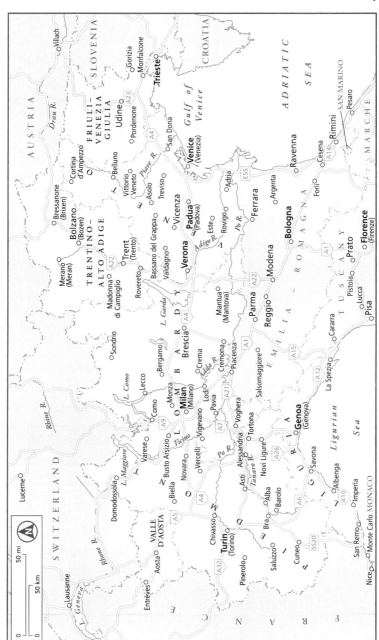

Friuli preserves remnants of cultures from the Celts through the Lombards, with coastal **Aquileia** weighing in with Roman ruins and mosaics.

THE DOLOMITES & SOUTH TIROL

The **Dolomites,** bordering Austria, cap the eastern stretches of the **South Tirol** region with sharp pinnacles straight out of a fairy tale, while the peaks of the Alps crown the west. This region comprises legendary resorts such as **Cortina d'Ampezzo** and **Merano,** as well as cities such as **Trent (Trento)** and **Bolzano**—home to a fascinating international scientific treasure, the prehistoric Ice Man—that lie at the crossroads of the German and Italian worlds.

MILAN & LOMBARDY

Lombardy **(Lombardia)** is Italy's wealthiest province, an industrial, financial, and agricultural powerhouse named for the Lombards, a Germanic people who migrated south over the Alps in the early Dark Ages (they were part of the barbarian hordes that overran the Roman Empire). Beyond its Po Valley factories and cities, the scenic diversity of this prosperous region ranges from legendary lakes like **Como, Garda,** and **Maggiore** backed by Alpine peaks to the fertile plains of the Po River. The region's capital, **Milan (Milano)**—hotbed of high fashion, high finance, and avant-garde design—is a city of great art and architecture (Leonardo's *The Last Supper* is but the beginning), and the region's Renaissance past is still much in evidence in mountain town **Bergamo,** merchant city **Mantua (Mantova),** musical **Cremona** (where Stradivarius once crafted his violins), and the other cities of the Lombard plains.

PIEDMONT & THE VALLE D'AOSTA

Piedmont **(Piemonte)** means "foot of the mountains," and the Alps are in sight from almost every parcel of Italy's northernmost province, which borders Switzerland and France. The flat plains of the Po River rise into rolling hills clad with orchards and vineyards. North of **Turin**—the historic baroque capital of the region and, with its wealth of auto factories, a cornerstone of Italy's "economic miracle"—the plains meet the Alps head-on in the **Valle d'Aosta,** with its craggy mountains, rugged mountain folk, and year-round skiing at resorts such as **Courmayeur** and **Entrèves** in the shadow of **Mont Blanc.**

LIGURIA: THE ITALIAN RIVIERA

The Italian Riviera follows the Ligurian Sea along a narrow coastal band backed by mountains. At the center of the rocky coast of **Liguria** is **Genoa (Genova),** the country's first port and still its most important—a fascinating city that greets visitors with a remarkable assemblage of Renaissance art and architecture. Some of Italy's most famous seaside retreats flank Genoa on either side, from the tony resort of **San Remo** on France's doorstep all the way down to the picturesque string of fishing villages known as the **Cinque Terre** that line the coast just above Tuscany.

---

2 NORTHERN ITALY FOR GOURMANDS

This 10-day loop includes the area's top winegrowing regions and a sampling of the various local cuisines. Eat and drink your way through the birthplace of chocolate; the home of Italy's finest truffles; the regions that produce Barolo, Amarone, and Soave; and the restaurants that have perfected the recipes for polenta, risotto, and tortelli. There is so much here for gourmands, in fact, that many tasty dishes found on the area's outskirts had to be skipped: the pesto of Genoa and the fondue of the Alps, for example—but it's hard for those simple meals to stack up to the culinary grandeur of northern Italy's heartland.

Day ❶: Arrive in Milan

Though it's the capital of northern Italy in many senses, and no slouch on the culinary scene, Milan is not hailed for its cuisine in the same way that many other cities around the region are. Instead, the city is best known for its shopping, its culture, and its lively nightlife. Be sure to check out the Pinacoteca di Brera and, of course, the Duomo, before hitting the clothing stores downtown and the cocktail bars of Brera. If you haven't yet reserved tickets to see Leonardo da Vinci's *The Last Supper* (p. 283) or a performance at **La Scala** (p. 304), this would be a good time to do so in person and save those unforgettable experiences for your last day here. Chances are slim that you will get in to see Leonardo's masterpiece unannounced. For dinner, stop by the **Trattoria Milanese** (p. 301) for the city's famous cutlet and risotto. (*Note:* It is a universal opinion in Italy that landlocked Milan actually has some of the country's best seafood, because the high prices fetch the best fresh fish. Just don't order it on Mon, the day after the fish market is closed.)

Day ❷: Turin ★

The 2006 Winter Olympics cast a spotlight on Turin's excellent restaurants. This is the capital of a region (Piedmont) with perhaps more claims to both oenological and gastronomic fame than any other in Italy. **C'era Una Volta** and **Ristorante Tre Galline** (p. 361 and 362) are two of the most popular eateries, but there are dozens of superb ones from which to choose. Even if you are not a tourist-office kind of traveler, by all means, at least stop by the booth in the Porta Nuova train station to pick up a brochure on the latest culinary happenings. The city commonly hosts citywide tastings, where restaurants offer special deals and sampling menus. The tourist office also hands out discount passes to such food boutiques as chocolate stores. (Did you know that the Torinese invented chocolate, before passing the tradition on to the neighboring Swiss?)

Day ❸: Barolo & Barbaresco ★

Anyone serious about Italian wines will already be familiar with these blockbuster names, famous for their precious and delicate reds. Bear in mind that the estates around here are not as welcoming to the general public as those in, say, Chianti, but a simple drive around the vineyards and a stop in the area's many wine bars is enough to quench any oenophile's thirst. (See chapter 11.)

Days ❹ & ❺: Brà, Alba & Asti ★★

In any other kind of tour, this triangle of medieval towns might be given a skip, but a gourmand's itinerary of northern Italy without the Langhe, as the area is known, would be like a religious pilgrimage without St. Peter's Basilica. Asti's Moscato grapes produce the country's best-known *spumante*, while Alba is ground zero for the legendary white truffle. Not coincidentally, the headquarters for the world's best-known culinary fraternity is based here, in Brà. **Slow Food**—with a culinary school in the city and chapters in Europe, in North America, and across the globe—promotes a doctrine of careful attention to local, quality food. In odd-numbered years in Brà, it hosts Salone del Gusto, a sort of culinary trade fair with seminars and tasting booths, while in even years, the organization holds an international cheese conference, with more varieties than you could sniff in an entire weekend. Check its website (www.slowfood.com) for dates. (See chapter 11.)

Day ⑥: Cremona & Mantua ★★

Hopefully, you've eaten only small, delicate dishes of mushrooms and truffles until this point (however unlikely that is) and have kept an appetite for a great dinner in Mantua. Skip breakfast in Asti and save time in the morning for side trips to Tortona and/or Pavia to pick up a few inexpensive bottles of Oltrepo' Tortonese and Oltrepo' Pavese, respectively. Stop off in Cremona to see the hometown of **Stradivarius violins** and try some of the area's famous pumpkin-stuffed tortellini. Chances are, you'll like it so much you'll want to order the same thing in Mantua, about an hour away. It is also a specialty there, along with its excellent risotto. Tour

the city's marvelous **Palazzo Ducale** (p. 146) and its works by Titian, and then move on to dinner at either the **Leoncino Rosso** (p. 320) or the **Ochina Bianca** (p. 320). Mantua has some of the best dining around for such an unheralded city, and its lovely, quiet streets make for a great postprandial stroll. Either spend the night here or make the brief trip north to Verona for a nightcap at the **Bottega del Vino** (p. 219), boasting one of the most highly respected wine cellars in all of Italy.

Day ⑦: Verona & Its Neighboring Vineyards ★★★

The vineyards just north of the city are the home to the whites of Soave and the reds of Valpolicello, including the savored

Amarone. The area is so serious about its privacy and guarding its secrets that it doesn't have much tourist infrastructure to speak of. The best place to enjoy the wines is back in the *trattorie* of Verona, either the **Osteria del Duca** (p. 220) or the **Taverna di Via Stella** (p. 220), or in one of the bars on Piazza delle Erbe, perhaps a well-deserved return trip to the legendary **Bottega del Vino** (p. 219). Even the little touristy restaurants next to the Arena are a memorable experience, especially if there is an opera there that night.

Days ❽ & ❾: Venice ★★

It's easy to get a lousy dinner in Venice, but almost as easy to get a fantastic one. See "The Best Restaurants," in chapter 1, for a partial listing, or "Where to Dine," on p. 128. This is your chance for some of the region's freshest seafood and the city's trademark *seppioline* (cuttlefish, whose black ink colors the spaghetti or risotto). It

would be uncouth not to start off in some tiny bar for a glass of the northern Veneto's *prosecco* (sparkling white wine) or, better, a *spritz* of white wine and soda water, or the bitter Aperol. Between meals and aperitifs, there should be enough time to see some of the city's famed palaces and take a spin on a **gondola** at night. Don't forget the requisite bottle of *prosecco!*

Day ❿: Bergamo ★ & Milan

You can't leave northern Italy without having polenta from Bergamo, and there's no better place to do it than at the **Antica Hosteria del Vino Buono** (p. 314). As the name suggests, they have some pretty good wine there, too, not least of which is the locally grown **Franciacorta.** Milan is a short drive away, so you'll have time in the afternoon to get that pair of leather pants you had your eye on, or to see the aptly named *The Last Supper* before your flight home.

---

3 NORTHERN ITALY IN THE SNOW

The northern border of Italy is a long stretch of snowcapped peaks, teeming with outdoor enthusiasts and offering spectacular Alpine scenery—not to mention some great cheese-loaded food. Most Italians prefer to spend a week in one resort, and indeed most hotels tend to rent out rooms by the week. But it is certainly possible to visit several winter wonderlands in a single trip if you find those hotels that offer a 2- or 3-night stay, and book them well ahead of time. (It's best to try later in the winter, when the snow is better anyway.) This 10-day loop hits the top spots for skiing, snowboarding, and generally soaking in the mountain atmosphere. You will need to rent a car, and if you pick it up and return it at Malpensa airport instead of in Milan, you will save time. *A final caution:* Some mountain roads close after a very heavy snowstorm. In any case, you are required to have tire chains, so book them well ahead of time, with your car.

Day ❶: Turin & Aosta ★

As the 2006 Olympic Games showed, Turin is a natural gateway to the Alps and a stunning city in the wintertime. Most important, it's just over an hour's drive from Malpensa airport. Winter sports enthusiasts can check out the multimillion-dollar sports complexes where the ice hockey and skating events were held, but

be sure to have an introductory cappuccino at one of the city's centuries-old cafes. Linger over lunch, explore the haunts of Italy's former royalty, and stay until sunset; the city also has an impressive artists' lights exhibition, which hangs over each of the major thoroughfares in winter months. It is truly a memorable scene. From Turin, it is only about an hour's drive to Aosta, at the foothills to the Alps and a great place to stay for the night before skiing. (See chapter 11.)

Days ❷, ❸ & ❹: Mont Blanc & Cervinia (The Matterhorn) ★★★

Mont Blanc (Monte Bianco to your hosts) is the pinnacle of the Alps in every sense. It is international, boasting the convergence of France, Italy, and Switzerland; it has great Alpine food and culture at every turn; and it is the highest point in Europe. From **Courmayeur,** take the tramway to the top, or **Punta Helbronner,** and ski/snowboard down the heavenly Vallée Blanche glacier into Chamonix, France. There are buses there for the return trip to Italy, through the tunnel. Guides can take you backcountry skiing just about anywhere you like (weather, crevasses, and avalanche danger permitting). Set aside 1 day to visit nearby Cervinia and the Matterhorn, which is less challenging but just as scenic. Take the cable cars up to Plateau Rosa and wind your way down the slopes to Zermatt, Switzerland, for lunch. At the end of the ski day, don't waste too much time in **Breuil,** which is not nearly as cozy and quaint as Courmayeur, and make tracks for Milan for some much better nightlife. (See chapter 11.)

Day ❺: Milan, Verona & Trento ★

This is your big driving day to get to the "other" Alps, the Dolomites, and Autostrada A4 is far and away the fastest way to go. Take a break from the outdoors, do some shopping in Milan in the morning, and then head out toward Verona for a late lunch and a walk around the home of Romeo and Juliet (see chapter 6). In winter, it will be at its most authentic and almost completely devoid of other tourists. The late afternoon, when the sunset starts to reflect off the craggy Dolomite peaks, is the best time to take the scenic A22 highway to Trento (see chapter 7). The city is a captivating entrance to this German-speaking part of Italy, especially

under a snowfall, and an excellent place to have dinner and spend the evening.

Day ❻: Bolzano, Merano & the Great Dolomite Road ★★★

Visit Ötzi, the 5,300-year-old **"Ice Man"** found frozen in the Alps in the 1990s, who now makes his home in the **South Tyrol Museum of Archaeology** in Bolzano (p. 234). Just 27km (17 miles) away is the magical town of Merano, where snow-scene lovers should take the **Winter Walk** (p. 241) along the Passer River toward the splendid **castle of the counts of Tirol** (p. 241). Before sunset, start making your way over to Cortina d'Ampezzo along the Great Dolomite Road for perhaps the most spectacular mountain drive in Italy. (Remember that this road might be closed after a mighty snowfall, so be prepared to nix Cortina, if necessary, and spend an extra day or two skiing Madonna del Campiglio.)

Days ❼ & ❽: Cortina d'Ampezzo ★★

Keeping to the Winter Olympics theme started in Turin, enjoy one of the older versions in Cortina, which hosted the games in 1956 (see chapter 7). Those tired of skiing can always go ice-skating at the old **Olympic rinks,** but the slopes are spectacular and have the scenery to match. The town itself is a little pricey at night, but the romantic setting is unmatched anywhere else in the mountains. After making your last turns on the slopes on the second day, head back toward Bolzano and then Trento on the Great Dolomite Road. (If it has closed after a storm, your best option is to take the A22 to Venice.)

Days ❾ & ❿: Back to Malpensa, via Valtellina & Lake Como ★

It is not a long drive along the S42 to Ponte di Legno and its nationally known sled-dog school. Continue on the S42 and turn onto the S39 toward the ski resort of Aprica. From there, the S38 highway leads along the Valtellina valley, where restaurants in the wintertime are almost always serving the inimitable *pizzoccheri* of northern Lombardy: buckwheat pasta mixed with melted taleggio cheese, potatoes, and garlic, a must-have on any ski trip to northern Italy. Soon you'll reach the northern tip of Lake Como, a peaceful oasis in winter just north of Malpensa airport. (See chapter 10.)

4 NORTHERN ITALY IN 1 WEEK

This brief, 1-week loop brings you to northern Italy's must-see destinations, starting in Milan, northern Italy's major gateway, and winding up in Venice, before a 3-hour train ride back to the Lombard capital. It follows a very simple route that could easily be taken by train.

Day ❶: Arrive in Milan ★

Most of this large city's major sites are confined to the area around the Duomo, in the epicenter, a good place to start any tour. The two top attractions, however, seeing a performance at **La Scala** opera house and viewing Leonardo da Vinci's *The Last Supper,* will require advance reservations. This is one of the few cities in the entire country with a reputation for nightlife, so if you are looking for chic bars and active nights past 11pm, best to get it done here. Also, if you're here during Fashion Week or during another major trade fair, be sure to reserve your hotel in advance. (See chapter 9.)

Day ❷: Lake Como ★★

With a daylong boat pass, spend the day crisscrossing the lake, from **Como** and nearby **Cernobbio,** home of the famed **Villa d'Este,** up and over to **Bellagio,** one of the most captivating lake towns in the country. Skip over to the western shore to hike up in the scenic hills above **Menaggio.** On the opposite shore is **Varenna,** an excellent place to have lunch or dinner, especially at the **Vecchia Varenna** (p. 341). This is also the side of the lake that has train tracks leading to Milan, and—even better—straight to Bergamo via **Lecco.** (See chapter 10.)

Day ❸: Bergamo, Brescia & Verona ★

Spend the morning exploring Bergamo's Old City, around the stunning **Piazza Vecchia** and **Piazza del Duomo** (see chapter 9). After a polenta lunch, make a quick stop to see the **Loggia** in Brescia (p. 308) and the city's excellent collection of paintings in the **Pinacoteca Tosio-Matinengo** (p. 308) before heading to Verona for the rest of the afternoon. (Bergamo to Brescia, and Brescia to Verona, are each only 45-min. train rides.) In Verona, don't miss the slightly hokey but nevertheless magical **House of Juliet** (p. 211) and, if you're there at the right time, an opera inside the city's Roman **Arena** (p. 211). (You'll need to reserve ahead for tickets and bring some *very* nice clothes.) The performance will be one you'll remember for a lifetime.

Day ❹: Vicenza & Padua ★★

Here are two gems shamefully overlooked by Venice-bound travelers, separated by a 30-minute train ride. After a coffee in Verona's **Piazza delle Erbe** (p. 213), head for Vicenza. Just walking around the city is inspiring enough, as it is a UNESCO World Heritage Site, but take time to see the **Teatro Olimpico** (p. 202) and, if it is open, the **Basilica Palladiana** (p. 201). Two great side trips would be to see the massive outdoor chessboard in Marostica, accessible by a 40-minute bus ride, or, if you are driving, by all means check out the **Villa Rotonda** (p. 203), on the outskirts of the city. The highlight of the day, however, will probably be the **Scrovegni Chapel** (p. 183), in Padua, and its frescoes by Giotto. *Note:* Padua is so close to Venice that budget travelers might plan to book a hotel here, as it will cost a fraction of a night on the lagoon.

Days ⑤ & ⑥: Venice ★★★

You'll need at least 2 nights in Venice and will wish you had the time and money for 10 more, especially if you come in the off season when the atmosphere is so much more pleasant. (In fact, if you come in July

or early Aug, the crowds can really be suffocating. Booking a hotel in advance will be essential.) By all means, try to time your visit with one of the city's many festivals, especially the **Regata Storica** (p. 163). Pick and choose your days' itinerary from chapter 5, but be sure to spend some daytime hours in lesser-visited quarters, such as **Cannaregio** and the **Jewish Ghetto** (p. 158 and 159). But don't snub the gondola ride as too touristy; grab a bottle of *prosecco* and float through the canals at night.

Day ⑦: Last Day in Milan

It's only a 3-hour train ride back to Milan, so you should have lots of time to do the things you missed on the first day. If you've already seen the Scala, why not go for the other end of the cultural spectrum and catch a game at Italy's most revered soccer stadium, **San Siro?** Or if shopping is your priority, don't miss the frequent outdoor markets, listed on p. 281.

5 NORTHERN ITALY IN 2 WEEKS

Start with the first 6 days of the previous tour, and then, if you have another week to spend, rent a car in Venice and return westward, dropping it off in Milan. (It will be cheaper than renting it at the beginning and paying an extra week.) With the car, you can check out all the harder-to-reach spots along the way. These include remote roads in the Dolomites and the vineyards near Turin.

Day ❼: Treviso, Bassano del Grappa & Cortina d'Ampezzo

This is a day of driving, with some spectacular scenery as the trip progresses. Stop in Treviso to see its lively **fish market** (p. 189) in the morning and work up an appetite for lunch at an inimitable **Toni del Spin** (p. 192). Continue northeast through the region that produces *prosecco,* Italy's answer to champagne, toward Asolo and Bassano del Grappa, for a great mixture of country life and impressive architecture. Approach Cortina d'Ampezzo in the evening, as the last rays of sun hit off the Dolomites and Cortina's fashionable restaurants and cafes come to life.

Day ❽: Bolzano & Trento

Take a morning drive through one of the most beautiful roads in Italy, the **Great Dolomite Road** (p. 248), which leads through the snowcapped peaks to Bolzano. At the city's archaeological museum, meet Ötzi, the 5,300-year-old **"Ice Man"** (p. 234) found frozen in these mountains in the 1990s. After lunch, take a side trip to Merano to stretch your legs on a nice walk along its river, and then continue south to Trento for the night. See where the Council of Trent congregated at the **Castello di Buonconsiglio** (p. 225), and have an unforgettable meal at the **Scrigno del Duomo** (p. 230).

Day ❾: Lake Garda & Cremona ★

In the morning, drive down the lake's more interesting western shore and join the windsurfers at **Riva del Garda** (p. 328), see Mussolini's old haunts in **Salo** (p. 321), and enjoy the captivating old city of **Sirmione** (p. 321). Then hop on the A4 highway to Brescia and turn south on the A7 to Cremona. See where **Stradivarius violins** were crafted and be sure to try some of the pumpkin-filled tortellini, one of the best pasta dishes in northern Italy.

Days ❿ & ⓫: Cinque Terre & Portofino ★★

The best way to approach the Cinque Terre from Cremona is to curve onto the A1 to Parma, and from there the A15 to La Spezia. After a morning on the highway, you'll be eager to leave your car behind in either Riomaggiore or Manarola and take a walk along the spectacular Via dell'Amore from village to village. (Again, book a hotel ahead of time in high season, as this place has become very popular among American tourists.) Although the extremely windy road between towns is scenic, it is time-consuming and can be downright nauseating. Instead, the next day, hop on the A12 highway for the much shorter route to Portofino, and enjoy a peaceful sunset on the port and perhaps a boat trip along the inlets. Budget travelers might wish to spend the second night in nearby Genoa, as Portofino and even Santa Margherita are very expensive.

Day ⑫: Genoa ★

After a day of dolphin-watching at sea, younger audiences, especially, will love Genoa's **aquarium** (p. 391), Europe's largest, which has a slew of fun activities during the day and even hosts a sleepover for kids in front of the shark tank. While the little ones are being entertained, couples can enjoy a candle-lit seafood dinner in the Old Quarter and perhaps a night of symphony at the Carlo Felice theater.

Day ⑬: Piedmont Wine Country & Turin ★★

South of Alba are the revered vineyards of Barolo and Barbaresco, while just to the east of Alba is the town of Brà, rapidly becoming Italy's culinary capital. After lunch, take a quick drive up to Turin to see all that the city has to offer, especially the facilities that were spruced up for the 2006 Winter Olympics. (See chapter 11.)

Day ⑭: Lake Maggiore & Milan ★

Spend a leisurely day strolling the lakeside promenade in lovely Stresa and on ferries to the Borromean Islands. Fortunately, the lake is not far from Turin and extremely close to Malpensa airport, where you can drop off your car. (See chapter 10.)

Venice

Lord Byron called Venice (Venezia) "a fairy city of the heart." La Serenissima, "The Most Serene," is an improbable cityscape of stone palaces that seem to float on water, a place where cats nap on Oriental marble windowsills set in colorful plaster walls. Candy-striped pylons stand sentry outside the tiny stone docks of *palazzi* whose front steps descend into the gently lapping waters of the canals that lace the city.

In Venice, cars are banned—every form of transportation floats, from water taxis and *vaporetti* (the public "bus" ferries) to ambulance speedboats and garbage scows. Venice is a place where locals stop at the *bacaro* (wine bar) to take *un ombra* (literally "a little bit of shade," in practice, a glass of wine) and munch on *cicchetti* (tapaslike snacks) or linger over exquisite restaurant seafood dinners.

It is also a city of great art and grand old masters. Venetian painting featured early masters such as the Bellini clan—Jacopo from the 1420s, sons Giovanni and Gentile from the 1460s. By the early 1500s, Venice had taken the Renaissance torch from Florence and made it its own, lending the movement the new color and lighting schemes of such giants as Giorgione, Tiziano (Titian), Paolo Veronese, and Tintoretto.

So much for Venice the Serenissima. There's also Venice the insanely popular and overcrowded. Certainly, the tourists can seem inescapable, and prices can be double or triple here what they are elsewhere in Italy.

But visitors flock to this canalled wonder for very good reason: Venice is extraordinary, it is magical, and it is worth every cent. Its existence defies logic, but underneath its otherworldly beauty and sometimes-stifling tourism, Venice is a living, breathing, singular city that seems almost too exquisite to be genuine, too fragile to survive the never-ending stream of visitors who have been making the pilgrimage here for 1,500 years.

As barbarian hordes washed back and forth across the Alps during the decline of the Roman Empire (starting in the 4th c.), inhabitants of the Veneto flatlands grew tired of being routinely sacked and pillaged along the way. By the 6th century, many had begun moving out onto the mud-flat islands of the marshy lagoon, created by what was in ancient times the Po River delta, to take up fishermen's lines or trading ships. When they saw that one barbarian horde, the Lombards, had stayed to settle the upper Po valley (still called Lombardy), these Veneti decided to remain on their new island homes and ally themselves instead with the eastern remnant of the old Roman Empire, Byzantium.

Oddly, what we now consider central Venice was the last area settled. After Attila the Hun rampaged through, citizens of the Roman town of Altino moved out onto Torcello and founded a tidy commercial empire under the control of the Byzantine emperor—ironic, since Torcello's star has long since fallen and it is now the least built-up of all of greater Venice's major inhabited islands. Townsfolk from Oderzo moved to Malamocco and made it the lagoon's political capital (the original site is now underwater, and the Malamocco that survives nearby is a fishing village on the southern stretch of the Lido, near the golf course). After barely defeating Charlemagne's son Pepin there in 810, the capital was moved to the more protected Rialto islands—now central Venice.

Greater Venice's oldest surviving structure is the cathedral on Torcello, founded in 639, but today's site is largely from the 9th and 10th centuries. In fact, sparsely populated Torcello is one of the best glimpses into what early Venice must have looked like—scattered buildings and canals banked by waving rushes and reeds, everything outlined by the dotted lines of wooden piles hammered down into the mud. This construction is what underlies all those stone *palazzi* of central Venice: a framework foundation of sunken tree trunks, hammered down into the *caranto* (a solid clay layer under the surface of mud and sand) and preserved in the anaerobic atmosphere of their muddy tomb, overlain with Istrian stone.

As its power began to peak in the early 13th century, Venice led the fourth and most successful Crusade, capturing Constantinople itself. It went on to conquer territories across what are today Turkey, the Greek Isles, and Crete—and eventually became the capital of Italy's inland provinces, now the Veneto, Trentino, and Friuli. By 1300, it was one of the largest cities and the leading maritime republic of Europe and the Mediterranean. Although the Black Death carried off over half the population from 1347 to 1350, Venice bounced back and remained a maritime power until the 18th century, when trade through the new American colonies would increasingly steal much of the city's thunder.

By the end of the 18th century, Venice had run out of steam commercially, not to mention militarily, after centuries spent fighting the Turks (who slowly regained most of Venice's Aegean and Greek territories). By the time Napoleon came along in 1797, the Venetian Republic offered little resistance. Napoleon gave control of Venice to Austria, under whose rule it remained for almost 70 years. Daniele Manin did stage an unsuccessful minirevolution in 1848 and 1849, during which Venice was privileged to become the first city attacked from the air—by a fleet of hot-air balloons armed with long-fused time bombs. The Risorgimento (unification) movement and its king, Vittorio Emanuele II, defeated the Austrians, gained control of the Veneto, and made it a part of the newly minted state of Italy in 1866.

In its position at the crossroads of the Byzantine and Roman—later Eastern and Western—worlds, Venice, over many centuries, acquired a unique amalgamated heritage of art, architecture, and culture. And although hordes of traders and merchants no longer pass through as they once did, Venice nonetheless continues to find itself at a crossroads: an intersection in time between the uncontested period of maritime power that built it and the modern world that keeps it ever-so-gingerly afloat.

It is a great disservice to allot Venice the average stay of 2 nights and 3 days (it sometimes takes the better part of a day just to find your hotel). If you can, stay at least 3 nights and preferably longer—Venice has the potential to be the highlight of your travels through Italy.

Leave your heels and excess luggage at home, and make sure to toss the map and this guide in your daypack for at least an afternoon, turn left when the signs to the sights point right, and get lost in the back *calli* (streets) and uncrowded *campi* (squares) where tourists seldom tread, and you will encounter the true, living, breathing, gloriously decaying side of this most serene city.

1 GETTING THERE

BY PLANE You can fly into Venice from North America via Rome or Milan with Alitalia or a number of other airlines, or by connecting through a major European city with European carriers. No-frills carrier **Ryanair** (www.ryanair.com) flies direct from London much more cheaply than the major airlines, as does **easyJet** (www.easyjet.com).

Flights land at the **Aeroporto Marco Polo**, 7km (4¼ miles) north of the city on the mainland (© **041-260-9260**; www.veniceairport.it). There are two bus alternatives: The special **ATVO airport shuttle bus** (© **041-383-672**; www.atvo.it) connects with Piazzale Roma not far from Venice's Santa Lucia train station (and the closest point to Venice's attractions accessible by car or bus). Buses leave for/from the airport about every 30 minutes, cost 3€, and make the trip in about 20 minutes. The slightly less expensive, twice-hourly local public **ACTV bus no. 5** (© **041-541-5180**) costs 1.50€ and takes 30 to 45 minutes. Buy tickets for either at the newsstand just inside the terminal from the signposted bus stop. With either bus, you'll have to walk to/from the final stop at Piazzale Roma to the nearby *vaporetto* (water bus) stop for the final connection to your hotel. It's rare to see porters around who'll help with luggage, so pack light.

A **land taxi** from the airport to the Piazzale Roma (where you get the *vaporetto*) will run about 35€.

The most fashionable and traditional way to arrive in Piazza San Marco is by sea. For 13€, the **Cooperative San Marco/Alilaguna** (© **041-240-1701**; www.alilaguna.it) operates a large *motoscafo* (shuttle boat) service from the airport with stops at Murano and the Lido before arriving after about 1 hour in Piazza San Marco. Call for the daily schedule of a dozen or so trips from about 6am to midnight; the schedule changes with the season and is coordinated with the principal arrival/departure of the major airlines (most hotels have the schedule). If your hotel isn't in the Piazza San Marco area, you'll have to make a connection at the *vaporetto* launches (your hotel can help you with the specifics if you booked before you left home).

A **private water taxi** (20–30 min. to/from the airport) is convenient but costly—a legal minimum of 60€, but usually closer to 85€, for two to four passengers with few bags. It's worth considering if you're pressed for time, have an early flight, are carrying a lot of luggage (a Venice no-no), or can split the cost with a friend or two. It may be able to drop you off at the front (or side) door of your hotel or as close as it can maneuver given your hotel's location (check with the hotel before arriving). Your taxi captain should be able to tell you before boarding just how close he can get you. Try the **Corsorzio Motoscafi Venezia** (© **041-522-2303**; www.motoscafivenezia.it) water taxis.

BY TRAIN Trains from Rome (4½–7 hr.), Milan (2½–3½ hr.), Florence (3 hr.), and all over Europe arrive at the **Stazione Venezia–Santa Lucia** (© **041-721-253**; www.ferroviedellostato.it). To get there, all must pass through (though not necessarily stop at) a station marked Venezia-Mestre. Don't be confused: Mestre is a charmless industrial city that's the last stop on the mainland. Occasionally trains end in Mestre, in which case you have to catch one of the frequent 10-minute shuttles connecting with Venice; it's inconvenient, so when you book your ticket, confirm that the final destination is Venezia–Stazione Santa Lucia.

Between the station's large front doors is a small, understaffed **tourist office** (© **041-529-8727**), with lines that can be discouraging and a strict "one person allowed in at a time" policy that is dictated by the office's miniscule size. It's open daily 8am to 6pm. Next door there is an office that will help you find a hotel; it's open 8am–9pm. The railway info office, marked with a lowercase *i,* is also in the station's main hall, staffed daily from 7am to 9pm.

On exiting, you'll find the Grand Canal immediately in front of you, a sight that makes for a heart-stopping first impression. You'll find the docks for a number of *vaporetto* lines (the city's public ferries or "water buses") to your left and right. Head to the booths to your left, near the bridge, to catch either of the two lines plying the Canal Grande: the no. 82 express, which stops only at the station, San Marcuola, Rialto Bridge, San Tomà, San Samuele, and Accademia before hitting San Marco (26 min. total); and the misnamed no. 1 *accelerato,* which is actually the local, making 14 stops between the station and San Marco (a 31-min. trip). Both leave every 10 minutes or so, but every other no. 82 stops short at Rialto, meaning you'll have to disembark and hop on the next no. 1 or 82 that comes along to continue to San Marco.

Note: The no. 82 goes in two directions from the train station: left down the Canal Grande toward San Marco—which is the (relatively) fast and scenic way—and right, which also eventually gets you to San Marco (at the San Zaccaria stop) but takes more than twice as long because it goes the long way around Dorsoduro (and serves mainly commuters). Make sure the no. 82 you get on is headed to San Marco.

BY BUS　　Though rail travel is more convenient and commonplace, Venice is serviced by long-distance buses from all over mainland Italy and some international cities. The final destination is Piazzale Roma, where you'll need to pick up *vaporetto* no. 82 or no. 1 (as described under "By Train," above) to connect you with stops in the heart of Venice and along the Grand Canal.

BY CAR　　The only wheels you'll see in Venice are those attached to luggage. Venice is a city of canals and narrow alleys. **No cars are allowed**—even the police and ambulance services use boats. Arriving in Venice by car is problematic and expensive—and down-right exasperating if it's high season and the parking facilities are full (they often are). You can drive across the Ponte della Libertà from Mestre to Venice, but you can go no farther than Piazzale Roma at the Venice end, where many garages eagerly await your euro. Do some research before choosing a garage—the rates vary widely, from 4.50€ for every 2-hour period with no day rate at the communal **ASM garage** (✆ 041-272-7304; www.asmvenezia.it) to 30€ per day at private outfits like **Garage San Marco** (✆ 041-523-2213; www.garagesanmarco.it), in Piazzale Roma. If you have reservations at a hotel, check before arriving: Most of them offer discount coupons for some of the parking facilities; just ask the hotel in which garage you need to park and pay for parking upon leaving the garage.

Vaporetto line nos. 1 and 82, described under "By Train," above, both stop at Piazzale Roma before continuing down the Canal Grande to the train station and, eventually, Piazza San Marco.

2 ORIENTATION

VISITOR INFORMATION

TOURIST OFFICES　　There's a small office in the train station (see "By Train," above), but the main office is located right when you get off the *vaporetto* at the San Marco stop,

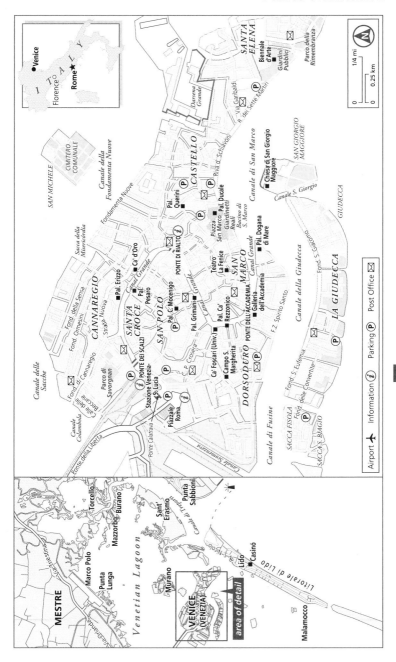

Airport ✈ Information ⓘ Parking Ⓟ Post Office ⊠

Venice by the Numbers

Central Venice is divided by Venice's longest (4km/2¹/₂ miles) and widest (30–70m/98–230 ft.) waterway, the Grand Canal. Its 118 islands are separated by approximately 170 canals and connected by some 430 footbridges, mostly stone with iron balustrades added in the 19th century.

Only four bridges cross the Grand Canal: the **Ponte degli Scalzi,** just outside and to the left of the train station; the elegant white marble **Ponte Rialto** (by far the most recognizable bridge and, for centuries, the only one), connecting the districts of San Marco and San Polo; the wooden **Ponte Accademia,** connecting the Campo Santo Stefano area of the San Marco neighborhood with the Accademia museum across the way in Dorsoduro; and, since late 2008, the futuristic **Ponte della Costituzione** (also known as the Calatrava bridge, after famed Spanish architect Santiago Calatrava, who designed it), which you will see around the corner to your right when you exit the train station.

in a stone pavilion wedged between the small green park on the Grand Canal called the Giardinetti Reali and the famous Harry's Bar. It's called the **Venice Pavilion/Palazzina dei Santi** (© **041-529-8710** or 041-522-5150; www.turismovenezia.it; *vaporetto:* San Marco) and is, frankly, often more interested in running its gift shop than in helping tourists. It's open daily from 10am to 6pm. They've kept open the old (and just as indifferent) office under the arcade at the west end of Piazza San Marco at no. 71F, on the left of the tunnel-like street leading to Calle dell'Ascensione (© **041-529-8740;** *vaporetto:* San Marco). It's open Monday to Friday 9am to 3:30pm. During peak season, a small info booth with erratic hours operates in the arrivals hall at the Marco Polo Airport.

The tourist office's *LEO Bussola* brochure is useful for museum hours and events, but their map helps you find only *vaporetto* lines and stops (it's well worth buying a street map at a news kiosk; see "Getting Around," below). More useful is the info-packed monthly *Un Ospite di Venezia* (www.unospitedivenezia.it); most hotels have a handful of copies. Also keep an eye out for the ubiquitous posters around town with exhibit and concert schedules. The classical concerts held mostly in churches are touristy but fun and are advertised by an army of costumed touts handing out leaflets on highly trafficked streets.

WEBSITES The city's official tourist-board site is **www.turismovenezia.it**; the official site of the city government (also full of good resources) is **www.comune.venezia.it**. A couple of good privately maintained sites are **Meeting Venice** (**www.meetingvenice.it**) and **Doge of Venice** (**www.doge.it**).

CITY LAYOUT

Keep in mind as you wander seemingly hopelessly among the *calli* (streets) and *campi* (squares) that the city wasn't built to make sense to those on foot but rather to those plying its canals. No matter how good your map and sense of direction, time after time you'll get lost. Just view it as an opportunity to stumble across Venice's most intriguing corners and vignettes.

Venice lies 4km (2½ miles) from terra firma, connected to the mainland burg of Mestre by the Ponte della Libertà, which leads to Piazzale Roma. Snaking through the city like an inverted *S* is the **Canal Grande (Grand Canal),** the wide main artery of aquatic Venice.

The city is divided into six *sestieri* ("sixths," or districts or wards). **Cannaregio** stretches north and east, from the train station to the Jewish Ghetto and on to the vicinity of the Ca' d'Oro north of the Rialto Bridge. To the east beyond Cannaregio (and skirting the area north and east of Piazza San Marco) is **Castello,** whose ritzy canal-side esplanade, Riva degli Schiavoni, is lined with deluxe accommodations. The central **San Marco** shares this side of the Grand Canal with Castello and Cannaregio, anchored by the magnificent Piazza San Marco and St. Mark's Basilica to the south and the Rialto Bridge to the north; it's the city's commercial, religious, and political heart. On the other side of the Grand Canal, **San Polo** is north of the Rialto Bridge, stretching west to just beyond Campo dei Frari and Campo San Rocco. The residential **Santa Croce** is next, moving north and west, stretching all the way to Piazzale Roma. Finally, the residential **Dorsoduro** is on the opposite side of the Accademia Bridge from San Marco. It's the largest *sestiere* and something of an artists' haven, though escalating rents make it hardly bohemian these days.

Venice shares its lagoon with several other islands. Opposite Piazza San Marco and Dorsoduro is **La Giudecca,** a tranquil working-class place with mostly residential neighborhoods. The **Lido di Venezia** is the city's sandy beach; it's a popular summer destination and holds a concentration of seasonal hotels.

Murano, Burano, and **Torcello** are popular destinations northeast of the city and easily accessible by public transport *vaporetto.* Since the 13th century, Murano has exported its glass products worldwide; it's an interesting half-day trip for those with the time, but you can do just as well in "downtown" Venice's myriad glass stores. Colorful fishing village–style Burano was and still is equally famous for its lace, an art now practiced by so few island women that its prices are generally unaffordable. Torcello is the most remote and least populated. The 40-minute boat ride is worthwhile for history and art buffs, who'll be awestruck by the Byzantine mosaics of the cathedral (some of Europe's finest outside Ravenna), whose foundation dates to the 7th century, making this the oldest Venetian monument in existence. **San Michele** is the cemetery island where such celebrities as Stravinsky and Diaghilev are buried.

Finally, the industrial city of **Mestre,** on the mainland, is the gateway to Venice and holds no reason for exploration. In a pinch, its host of inexpensive hotels is worth consideration when Venice's hotels are full, but that's about all.

VENICE

5

ORIENTATION

The Scope of Venice

Central Venice refers to the built-up block of islands in the lagoon's center, including St. Mark's, the train station, and everything else in the six main *sestieri* that make up the bulk of the tourist city. Greater Venice includes all the inhabited islands of the lagoon—central Venice plus Murano, Burano, Torcello, and the Lido. The Lagoon comprises everything, from the city to the mud flats to the fish farms to the dozens of abandoned or uninhabited islets.

A Note on Addresses

Within each *sestiere* is a most original system of numbering the *palazzi*, using one continuous string of 6,000 or so numbers. The format for addresses in this chapter is the official mailing address: the *sestiere* name followed by the building number in that district, followed by the name of the street or *campo* on which you'll find that address—for example, San Marco 1471 (Salizzada San Moisè) means the mailing address is San Marco 1471, and you'll find it in the San Marco district on Salizzada San Moisè. Be aware that San Marco 1471 may not necessarily be found close to San Marco 1475 and that many buildings aren't numbered at all.

NEIGHBORHOODS IN BRIEF

Based on a tradition dating from the 12th century, for tax-related purposes, the city has officially been divided into six *sestieri* (literally, "sixths," or wards) that have basically been the same since 1711. The Canalazzo or Canale Grande (Grand Canal) neatly divides them into three on each bank.

San Marco The central *sestiere* is anchored by the Piazza San Marco and the Basilica di San Marco to the south and the Rialto Bridge to the north. This is the most visited (and, as a result, the most expensive) of the *sestieri*. It's the commercial, religious, and political heart of the city and has been for more than a millennium. It is also its musical heart, home to the legendary La Fenice Opera House; devastated by a fire in 1996, it was reopened in 2005 after an extensive restoration. Although you'll find glimpses and snippets of the real Venice here, ever-rising rents have nudged resident Venetians to look for housing in the outer neighborhoods: You'll be hard-pressed to find a grocery store or dry cleaner here. But if you're looking for Murano glass trinkets and mediocre restaurants, you'll find an embarrassment of choices. This area is a mecca of first-class hotels—but with direction from Frommer's, you can stay here in the heart of Venice without going broke.

Cannaregio Sharing the same side of the Grand Canal with San Marco, Cannaregio stretches north and east from the train station to include the Jewish Ghetto and into the canal-hugging vicinity of the Ca' d'Oro and the Rialto Bridge. Its outer reaches are quiet, unspoiled, and residential ("*What* high-season tourist crowds?" you may wonder); one-third of Venice's ever-shrinking population of 65,000 is said to live here. Most of the city's one-star hotels are clustered about the train station—not a dangerous neighborhood but not one known for its charm, either. The gloss and dross of the tourist shop–lined Lista di Spagna strip continues as it morphs into the Strada Nuova in the direction of the Rialto Bridge.

Castello This quarter, whose tony Riva degli Schiavoni follows the Bacino di San Marco (St. Mark's Basin), is lined with first-class and deluxe hotels. It begins just east of Piazza San Marco, skirting Venice's most congested area to absorb some of the crowds and better hotels and restaurants. But if you head farther east in the direction of the Arsenale or inland away from the *bacino,* the people traffic thins out, despite the presence of such major sights as Campo SS. Giovanni e Paolo and the Scuola di San Giorgio.

San Polo This mixed-bag *sestiere* of residential corners and tourist sights stretches northwest of the Rialto Bridge to the principal church of Santa Maria dei Frari and the Scuola di San Rocco. The hub of activity at the foot of the bridge is greatly due to the Rialto market that has taken place here for centuries— some of the city's best restaurants have flourished here for generations, along-side some of its worst tourist traps. The spacious Campo San Polo is the main piazza of Venice's smallest *sestiere.*

Santa Croce North and northwest of the San Polo district and across the Grand Canal from the train station, Santa Croce stretches all the way to Piazzale Roma. Its eastern section is generally one of the least-visited areas of Venice—making it all the more desirable for curious visitors. Less lively than San Polo, it is as authentic and feels light-years away from San Marco. The quiet and lovely Campo San Giacomo dell'Orio is considered to be its heart.

Dorsoduro You'll find the residential area of Dorsoduro on the opposite side of the Accademia Bridge from San Marco. Known for the Accademia and Peggy Guggenheim museums, it is the largest of the *sestieri* and has been known as an artists' haven (hence the tireless comparison with New York's Greenwich Village—a far cry) until recent escalations of rents forced much of the community to relocate elsewhere. Good neighborhood restaurants, a charming gondola boatyard, the lively Campo Santa Margherita, and the sunny quay called le Zattere (a favorite promenade and gelato stop) all add to the character and color that make this one of the city's most-visited areas.

La Giudecca Located opposite the Piazza San Marco and Dorsoduro, La Giudecca is a tranquil working-class residential area where you'll find a youth hostel and a handful of hotels (including the deluxe Cipriani, one of Europe's finest).

Lido di Venezia This slim, 11km-long (6¾-mile) area is the city's beach; separating the lagoon from the open sea and permitting car traffic, its concentration of seasonal hotels (its landmark hotels serving as home base for the annual Venice Film Festival) makes it a popular summer destination, but it is also quite residential.

VENICE

5

ORIENTATION

GETTING AROUND

Aside from on boats, the only way to explore Venice is by walking—and getting lost repeatedly. You'll navigate many twisting streets whose names change constantly and don't appear on any map, and streets that may very well simply end in a blind alley or spill abruptly into a canal. You'll also cross dozens of footbridges. Treat getting bewilder-ingly lost in Venice as part of the fun, and budget more time than you'd think necessary to get wherever you're going.

STREET MAPS & SIGNAGE The free map offered by the tourist office and most hotels has good intentions, but it doesn't even show—much less name or index—all the *calli* (streets) and pathways of Venice. For that, pick up a more detailed map (ask for a

Cruising the Canals

A leisurely cruise along the **Grand Canal** ★★★ from Piazza San Marco to the Ferrovia—or the reverse—is one of Venice's must-dos (p. 150). It's the world's most unusual Main Street, a watery boulevard whose *palazzi* have been converted into condos. Lower water-lapped floors are now deserted, but the higher floors are still coveted by the city's titled families, who have inhabited these glorious residences for centuries; others have become the summertime dream homes of privileged expats, drawn here as irresistibly as the romantic Venetians-by-adoption who preceded them—Richard Wagner, Robert Browning, Lord Byron, and (more recently) Woody Allen.

As much a symbol of Venice as the winged lion, the **gondola** ★★★ is one of Europe's great traditions, incredibly and inexplicably expensive but truly as romantic as it looks (detractors who write it off as too touristy have most likely never tried it). Though it's often quoted in print at differing official rates, expect to pay 80€ for a 40-minute tour (100€ 7pm–8am), with up to six passengers, and 40€ for every additional 20 minutes (50€ at night). That's not a typo: 150€ an hour for an evening cruise. ***Note:*** At these ridiculously inflated prices, there is no need to tip the gondolier. Aim for late afternoon before sundown, when the light does its magic on the canal reflections (and bring a bottle of *prosecco* [a champagne-like wine] and glasses). If the gondola price is too high, ask visitors at your hotel or others lingering about at the gondola stations if they'd like to share it. Before setting off, establish with the gondolier the cost, time, and route explanation (any of the back canals are preferable to the trafficked and often choppy Grand Canal). They're regulated by the **Ente Gondola** (📞 **041-528-5075;** www.gondola venezia.it), so call if you have any questions or complaints.

And what of the serenading gondolier immortalized in film? Frankly, you're better off without. But if warbling is de rigueur for you, here's the scoop. An ensemble of accordion player and tenor is so expensive that it's shared among several gondolas traveling together. A number of travel agents around town book the evening serenades for around 35€ per person. The number of *gondolieri* willing to brave the winter cold and rain is minimal, though some come out of their wintertime hibernation for the Carnevale period.

There are 12 gondola stations around Venice, including Piazzale Roma, the train station, the Rialto Bridge, and Piazza San Marco. There are also a number of smaller stations, with gondoliers standing alongside their sleek 11m (36-ft.) black wonders looking for passengers. They all speak enough English to communicate the necessary details.

pianta della città at news kiosks—especially those at the train station and around San Marco) or most bookstores. The best (and most expensive) is the highly detailed **Touring Club Italiano map,** available in a variety of forms (folding or spiral-bound) and scales. Almost as good, and easier to carry, is the simple and cheap **1:6500 folding map** put out by Storti Edizioni (its cover is white-edged with pink, which fades to blue at the bottom).

Venetian Dialect

If, after a few days in Rome and Florence, you were just getting the hang of correlating your map to the reality of your new surroundings, you can put aside any short-term success upon your arrival in Venezia. Even the Italians (non-Venetian ones) look befuddled when trying to decipher street names and signs (given that you can ever find any).

Venice's colorful thousand-year history as a once-powerful maritime republic has everything to do with its local dialect, which absorbed nuances and vocabulary from far-flung outposts in the East and from the flourishing communities of foreign merchants who, for centuries, lived and traded in Venice. A linguist could gleefully spend a lifetime trying to make some sense of it all. From Venetian dialect we've inherited such words as *gondola* (naturally), *ciao, ghetto, lido,* and *arsenal.*

But for the Venice-bound traveler just trying to make sense of Venetian addresses, the following should give you the basics. (And don't even try to follow a conversation between two *gondolieri!*)

ca' The abbreviated use of the word *casa* is used for the noble *palazzi,* once private residences and now museums, lining the Grand Canal: Ca' d'Oro, Ca' Pesaro, and Ca' Rezzonico. There is only one *palazzo,* the Palazzo Ducale, the former doge's residence. However, as time went on, some great houses gradually began to be called *"palazzi,"* so today you'll also encounter the Palazzo Grassi or the Palazzo Labia.

calle Taken from the Spanish (though pronounced as if Italian, *ca*-lay), this is the most commonplace word for "street," known as *via* or *strada* elsewhere in Italy. There are numerous variations. *Ruga,* from the French word *rue,* once

Still, Venice's confusing layout confounds even the best maps and navigators. You're often better off just stopping every couple of blocks and asking a local to point you in the right direction (always know the name of the *campo*/square or major sight closest to the address you're looking for, and ask about that).

As you wander, look for the ubiquitous yellow signs (well, *usually* yellow) whose destinations and arrows direct you toward five major landmarks: **Ferrovia** (the train station), **Piazzale Roma, Rialto** (the main bridge), **San Marco,** and the **Accademia** (also useful as the only other Grand Canal bridge below the train station).

BY BOAT The various *sestieri* are linked by a comprehensive *vaporetto* (water bus/ferry) system of about a dozen lines operated by the **Azienda del Consorzio Trasporti Veneziano (ACTV),** Calle Fuseri 1810, off the Frezzeria in San Marco (© **041-528-7886** for both offices; www.actv.it). Transit maps are available at the tourist office and most ACTV stations. It's easier to get around on foot; the *vaporetti* principally serve the Grand Canal (and can be crowded in summer), the outskirts, and the outer islands. The crisscross network of small canals is the province of delivery vessels, gondolas, and private boats.

A ticket valid for 1 hour of travel on a *vaporetto* is a steep 6.50€, while the 24-hour ticket, at 18€, is a good buy if you'll be making more than two trips spread out through the day.

meant a *calle* flanked with stores, a designation no longer valid. A *ramo* (literally "branch") is the offshoot of a street and is often used interchangeably with *calle*. *Salizzada* once meant a paved street, implying that all other, less important *calles* were once just dirt-packed alleyways. A *stretto* is a narrow passageway.

campo   Elsewhere in Italy it's *piazza*. In Venice, the only piazza is the Piazza San Marco (and its two bordering *piazzette*); all other squares are *campi* or the diminutive, *campielli*. Translated as "field" or "meadow," these were once small, unpaved grazing spots for the odd chicken or cow. Almost every one of Venice's *campi* carries the name of the church that dominates it (or once did), and most have wells, no longer used, in the center.

canale   There are three wide, principal canals: the Canal Grande (affectionately called "il Canalazzo," the Canal), the Canale della Giudecca, and the Canale di Cannaregio. Each of the other 160-odd smaller canals is called a *rio*. A *rio terrà* is a filled-in canal—wide and straight—now used as a street. A *piscina* is a filled-in basin, now acting as a *campo* or piazza.

fondamenta   Referring to the foundations of the houses lining a canal, this is a walkway along the side of a *rio* (small canal). Promenades along the Grand Canal near the Piazza San Marco and the Rialto are called *riva,* as in the Riva del Vin or Riva del Carbon, where cargo such as wine and coal were once unloaded.

ramo   Literally "branch," a small side street.

sottoportego   An alley that ducks under a building.

Most lines run every 10 to 15 minutes from 7am to midnight, and then hourly until morning; most *vaporetto* docks (the only place you can buy tickets) have timetables posted. Note that not all stations sell tickets after dark; if you haven't bought a pass or extra tickets beforehand, you'll have to settle up with the conductor onboard (you'll have to find him— he won't come looking for you) for an extra .50€ per ticket or risk a stiff fine, no excuses accepted. Also available are 48-hour tickets (28€) and 72-hour tickets (33€). If you're planning to stay in Venice a while, it makes sense to pick up a Venice Card (see "Venice Discounts," on p. 107), with which you can buy 1-hour *vaporetto* tickets for 1€.

Just three bridges spanned the Grand Canal until 2008 when a fourth was added connecting the train station with Piazzale Roma. To fill in the gaps, *traghetti* skiffs (oversize gondolas rowed by two standing *gondolieri*) cross the Grand Canal at eight intermediate points. You'll find a station at the end of any street named Calle del Traghetto on your map and indicated by a yellow sign with the black gondola symbol. The fare is .50€, which you hand to the gondolier when boarding. Most Venetians cross standing up. For the experience, try the Santa Sofia crossing that connects the Ca' d'Oro and the Pescheria fish market, opposite each other on the Grand Canal just north of the Rialto Bridge—the gondoliers expertly dodge water traffic at this point of the canal, where it's the busiest and most heart-stopping.

BY WATER TAXI *Taxi acquei* (water taxis) charge high prices and aren't for visitors watching their euros. The meter starts at a hefty 14.50€ and clicks at 1.80€ per minute. Each bag over 50cm long (20 in.) costs 3€, plus there's an 8€ supplement for service from 10pm to 7am and an 8€ surcharge on Sundays and holidays (these last two charges, however, can't be applied simultaneously). If they have to come get you, tack on another 6€. Those rates cover up to two people; if any more squeeze in, it's another 1.50€ per extra passenger (maximum 20 people). Taking a taxi from the train station to Piazza San Marco or any of the hotels in the area will put you back about 60€ for two people, while there is a fixed 95€ fee to go or come from the airport. Note that only taxi boats with a yellow strip are the official taxis sanctioned by the city.

Six water-taxi stations serve key points in the city: the **Ferrovia, Piazzale Roma,** the **Rialto Bridge, Piazza San Marco,** the **Lido,** and **Marco Polo Airport. Radio Taxi** (*©* **041-522-2303**) will come pick you up anyplace in the city.

BY GONDOLA To come all the way to Venice and not indulge in a gondola ride could be one of your biggest regrets. Yes, it's touristy, and, yes, it's expensive (see the "Cruising the Canals" box, on p. 100), but only those with a heart of stone will be unmoved by the quintessential Venetian experience. Do not initiate your trip, however, until you have agreed upon a price and synchronized watches. Oh, and don't ask them to sing.

(*Fast Facts*) **Venice**

Acqua Alta During the notorious tidal *acqua alta* (high water) floods, the lagoon backwashes into the city, leaving up to 1.5 to 1.8m (5–6 ft.) of water in the lowest-lying streets (Piazza San Marco, as the lowest point in the city, goes first). These floods can start as early as late September or October, usually taking place November to March. As many as 50 a year have been recorded since they first started in the late 1700s. The waters usually recede after just a few hours and are often virtually gone by noon. Walkways are set up around town, but wet feet are a given. The complex system of hydraulic dams being constructed out in the lagoon to cut off these high tides (a controversial project due to its environmental impact, whose progress ebbs and flows depending on who is in government) is well underway but won't be operational for years.

American Express Unfortunately, American Express closed its Venice office in 2009, leaving offices only in Milan and Rome.

Bookstores See p. 166.

Business Hours Standard hours for shops are 9am to 12:30pm and 3 to 7:30pm Monday to Saturday. In winter, shops are closed on Monday morning, while in summer it's usually Saturday afternoon. Most grocers are closed on Wednesday afternoon year-round. In Venice, just about everything is closed on Sunday, though tourist shops in the tourist spots such as the San Marco area are permitted to stay open during high season. Restaurants are required to close at least 1 day a week, called *il giorno di riposo,* though the particular day varies from one trattoria to another. Many are open for Sunday lunch but close for Sunday dinner. Restaurants that specialize in fish and seafood also typically close Monday, when the fish market is closed. Restaurants will close for holidays, translated as *chiuso per ferie,* sometime in July or August, frequently over Christmas, and sometime in January before the Carnevale rush.

Climate May, June, September, and early October are the best months with respect to weather to visit (and the most crowded). July and August are hot—at times, unbearably so. April and late October/early November are hit-or-miss; it can be either glorious or cool, rainy, and damp, and only marginally less crowded. Also see "Acqua Alta," above.

Consulates The nearest **U.S. Consulate** is in Milan at Via Principe Amedeo 2/10 (© **02-290-351**). It's open Monday to Friday 8:30am to 12:30pm and 1:30 to 5:30pm. The **U.K. Consulate** in Venice is on the mainland in Mestre, at Piazzale Donatori di Sangue 2 (© **041-505-5990**); it's open Monday to Friday 10am to 1pm. Like the U.S., **Australia** and **New Zealand** have consulates in Milan, about 3 hours away by train (see chapter 9); all also maintain embassies in Rome. The **Canadian Consulate** closed its office in Milan in 2007; emergencies can be directed to the embassy in Rome (© **06-854-441**).

Crime Be aware of petty crime like pickpocketing on the crowded *vaporetti,* particularly the tourist routes, where passengers are more intent on the passing scenery than on watching their bags. Venice's deserted back streets were once virtually crime-proof; occasional tales of theft are circulating only recently. Generally speaking, it's one of Italy's safest cities.

Drugstores Venice's pharmacies take turns staying open all night. To find out which one is on call in your area, ask at your hotel and check the rotational duty signs posted outside all drugstores.

Emergencies In Venice and throughout Italy, dial © **113** to reach the **police.** Some Italians will recommend that you forgo the police and try the military-trained **Carabinieri** (© **112**). For an **ambulance,** phone © **523-0000.** To report a **fire,** dial © **115,** 041-520-0222, or 041-520-0223. For any **tourism-related complaint** (rip-offs, exceedingly shoddy service, and so on), dial the special agency **Venezia No Problem** toll-free at © **800-355-920.**

Fax From both the main post office and its Piazza San Marco branch (see "Mail," below), you can send faxes to almost any destination, with the odd exception of the United States. For service to the United States, ask at your hotel; most will agree to do it for either a per-page or an estimated-per-minute cost. Or look for SERVIZIO FAX signs in the windows of *cartolerie* (stationery stores).

Holidays Venice's patron saint, San Marco (St. Mark), is honored on April 25. For a list of official state holidays, see the "Holidays" section on p. 53.

Hospitals The **Ospedale Civile Santi Goivanni e Paolo** (© **041-785111**), on Campo Santi Giovanni e Paolo, has English-speaking staff and provides emergency service 24 hours a day (*vaporetto:* San Toma).

Internet Access For checking e-mail, you have many options around the city. Try **Venetian Navigator,** Castello 5300 on Calle Caselleria between San Marco and Campo Santa Maria Formosa (© **041-277-1056;** www.venetiannavigator.com; *vaporetto:* San Marco, Zaccaria, Rialto), daily 10am to 10pm from May through October and until 8:30pm the rest of the year, which charges 4.50€ for 30 minutes and 8€ per hour (6€ per hour with a Rolling Venice card). Venetian Navigator has another Internet point near the Rialto bridge, at San Marco 5239 on Calle Stagneri. Near the train station, you'll find **VeNice Internet Point,** at Lista di Spagna 149 (when you come out of the station, turn left and it'll be on your right before you come to the first campo), which is open daily 9am to 11pm and charges the same fees as Venetian Navigator.

Laundry The laundry service most convenient to San Marco is **Gabriella** (© **041-522-1758**), San Marco 985 on Rio Terrà Colonne (off Calle dei Fabbri), where they wash and dry your clothes for you within an hour or two for 16€ per load. They are open Monday to Friday 9:30am to 12:30pm and 2:30 to 7pm. There is a self-service laundromat at Castello 4826, on Calle Corte Rotta just north of the San Zaccaria church. It costs 5.50€ to wash a large load of laundry and 4.50€ to dry. They are open Monday to Saturday 8:30am to 11pm and Sunday 9:30am to 9:30pm.

Lost & Found The central **Ufficio Oggetti Rinvenuti** (© **041-274-8225**) is in the annex to the City Hall (Municipio), at San Marco 4134, on Calle Piscopia o Loredan, just off Riva del Carbon on the Grand Canal, near the Rialto Bridge (on the same side of the canal as the Rialto *vaporetto* station). Look for *scala* (stairway) C; the lost-and-found office is in the Economato section on the *mezzanino* level, one flight up. The office is ostensibly open only on Monday, Wednesday, and Friday from 9:30am to 12:30pm, but someone is usually available weekdays from 9:30am until the building closes at 1:30pm.

There's also an **Ufficio Oggetti Smarriti** at the airport (© **041-260-9260**). The train station no longer has a lost-and-found, so if you lose something on the train or in the station, definitely talk to the police (they have a small office next to Track 1), but they are likely to direct you to the central Ufficio Oggetti Rinvenuti in the city hall annex.

Luggage Storage The *deposito bagagli* in the train station (© **041-785-531**) is open daily from 6am to 11:50pm and charges 4€ for each bag for the first 5 hours, and then 60¢ for each additional hour through the 12th hour. Then it's 20¢ an hour.

Mail Venice's **Posta Centrale** is at San Marco 5554, 30124 Venezia, on the San Marco side of the Rialto Bridge at Rialto Fontego dei Tedeschi (© **041-271-7111** or 041-528-5813; *vaporetto:* Rialto). This office sells stamps at Window 12 Monday to Saturday 8:30am to 6:30pm (for parcels, 8:10am–1:30pm). If you're at Piazza San Marco and need postal services, walk through Sottoportego San Geminian, the center portal at the opposite end of the piazza from the basilica on Calle Larga dell'Ascensione. Its usual hours are Monday to Friday 8:30am to 2pm and Saturday 8:30am to 1pm. You can buy *francobolli* (stamps) at any *tabacchi* (tobacconists). The limited mailboxes seen around town are red.

Police In an emergency, dial © **112** or **113.**

Taxes & Tipping See "Fast Facts: Northern Italy," p. 435.

Telephone See "Area Codes," in "Fast Facts: Northern Italy," p. 435.

Travel Agencies **Intras City Service,** at Santa Croce 1303b (© **041-275-0783**), is centrally located, as is **Kele e Teo,** on the Mercerie 4930 (© **041-520-8722;** fax 041-520-8913; www.keleteo.com).

Venice Discounts

The **Museum Pass** grants admission to all the city-run museums over a 6-month period. That includes all the museums of St. Mark's Square: Palazzo Ducale, Museo Correr, Museo Archeologico Nazionale, and the Biblioteca Nazionale Marciana—as well as the Museo di Palazzo Mocenigo (Costume Museum), the Ca' Rezzonico, the Ca' Pesaro, the Museo del Vetro (Glass Museum) on Murano, and the Museo di Merletto (Lace Museum) on Burano. (**Note:** *The Lace Museum is closed for renovations until 2010.*) The Museum Pass is available at any of the participating museums and costs 18€ for adults, 12€ for students under 29. There is also a **San Marco Musuem Pass** that lets you into the museums of St. Mark's plus one of the other museums. It costs 13€, and 7.50€ for students.

Venice, so delicate it cannot handle the hordes of visitors it receives every year, has been toying with the idea of charging admission to get into the very city itself. Slightly calmer heads seem to have prevailed, though, and instead we have **Venice Connected** (www.veniceconnected.it), which started in 2009 and gives discounts if you buy tickets through the website before arriving. You can get tickets for everything from transportation to museums, but you must do it for a particular day that is at least 4 days in the future. In return, the city gets, at least in theory, a better idea of how many people will be in town on a given day.

Also, for tourists between the ages of 14 and 29, there is the **Rolling Venice** card, which is something akin to the Venice Connected discounts for students. It's valid for 1 year, costs just 4€, and entitles the bearer to significant (20%–30%) discounts at participating restaurants, and a similar discount on traghetto tickets. Holders of the Rolling Venice card also get discounts in museums, restaurants, stores, language courses, hotels, and bars across the city (it comes with a thick booklet listing everywhere that you're entitled to get discounts). Year-round, you can pick one up at the **Informagiovani Assessorato alla Gioventù,** Corte Contarina 1529, off the Frezzeria west of St. Mark's Square (*✆* **041-274-7645** or 041-274-7650), which is open Monday to Friday 9:30am to 1pm, plus Tuesday and Thursday 3 to 5pm. July to September you can stop by the special Rolling Venice office set up in the train station daily 8am to 8pm; in winter you can get the pass at the Transalpino travel agency just outside the station's front doors and to the right, at the top of the steps; it's open Monday to Friday 8:30am to 12:30pm and 3 to 7pm, and Saturday 8:30am to 12:30pm.

VENICE

5

WHERE TO STAY

3 WHERE TO STAY

Few cities boast as long a high season as that of Venice, beginning with the Easter period. May, June, and September are the best months weather-wise and, therefore, the most crowded. July and August are hot—at times, unbearably so (few of the one- and two-star hotels offer air-conditioning; when they do it usually costs extra). Like everything else,

VENICE

5

WHERE TO STAY

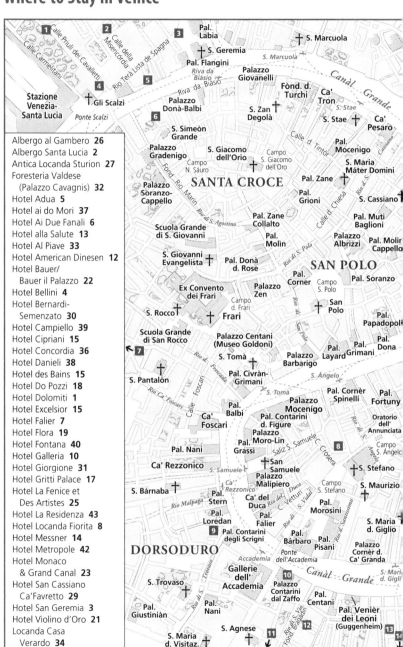

Albergo al Gambero **26**
Albergo Santa Lucia **2**
Antica Locanda Sturion **27**
Foresteria Valdese
  (Palazzo Cavagnis) **32**
Hotel Adua **5**
Hotel ai do Mori **37**
Hotel Ai Due Fanali **6**
Hotel alla Salute **13**
Hotel Al Piave **33**
Hotel American Dinesen **12**
Hotel Bauer/
  Bauer il Palazzo **22**
Hotel Bellini **4**
Hotel Bernardi-
  Semenzato **30**
Hotel Campiello **39**
Hotel Cipriani **15**
Hotel Concordia **36**
Hotel Danieli **38**
Hotel des Bains **15**
Hotel Do Pozzi **18**
Hotel Dolomiti **1**
Hotel Excelsior **15**
Hotel Falier **7**
Hotel Flora **19**
Hotel Fontana **40**
Hotel Galleria **10**
Hotel Giorgione **31**
Hotel Gritti Palace **17**
Hotel La Fenice et
  Des Artistes **25**
Hotel La Residenza **43**
Hotel Locanda Fiorita **8**
Hotel Messner **14**
Hotel Metropole **42**
Hotel Monaco
  & Grand Canal **23**
Hotel San Cassiano
  Ca'Favretto **29**
Hotel San Geremia **3**
Hotel Violino d'Oro **21**
Locanda Casa
  Verardo **34**

VENICE 5 WHERE TO STAY

Locanda Remedio—Hotel
  Colombina **35**
Londra Palace **41**
Luna Hotel Baglioni **24**
Palladio Hotel & Spa **16**
Pensione Accademia **9**
Pensione Guerrato **28**
Pensione La Calcina **11**
Westin Hotel Europa
  & Regina **20**

Family-Friendly Hotels

Albergo ai do Mori (p. 115)   Good news for weary legs: The larger, family-oriented rooms are on the lower floors in this elevator-challenged hotel just around the corner from San Marco. Can-do English-speaking Antonella has a solution for every problem.

Antica Locanda Sturion (p. 122)   Scottish-born Helen or her daughter Nicolette will settle you into any of the spacious rooms, two of which provide the special thrill of a Grand Canal view within sight of the famous Rialto Bridge. *One caveat:* The 69-step hike to the lobby may be a deterrent for little ones or for those who haven't mastered the art of traveling lightly.

Hotel Bernardi-Semenzato (p. 125)   Owner Maria Teresa moonlights as an English teacher. As a mother of three, she's the perfect host for families, who will appreciate the renovated rooms that easily pass as triples or quads.

Pensione Guerrato (p. 122)   Young, euro-conscious families will enjoy the inexpensive rates of this former convent, where an informal and casual atmosphere is nurtured by the upbeat brothers-in-law who run it as if it were their home. Kids should get a kick out of being in the middle of the market's hubbub right on the Grand Canal and within steps of the Rialto Bridge. Spacious rooms are an added plus.

hotels are more expensive here than in any other Italian city, with no apparent upgrade in amenities. The least special of those below are clean and functional; at best, they're charming and thoroughly enjoyable, with the serenade of a passing gondolier thrown in for good measure. Some may even provide you with your best stay in all of Europe.

I strongly suggest that you reserve in advance, even in the off season. If you haven't booked, arrive as early as you can, definitely before noon. The **Hotel Reservations booth** in the train station will book rooms for you, but the lines are long and the staff's patience is often (understandably) thin. For 1€, they'll try to find you a hotel in the price range of your choice; on confirmation from the hotel, they'll accept your deposit by credit card and issue you a voucher, and you pay the balance on your arrival at the hotel. There is a similar hotel reservations booth at the airport, but it charges a bit more.

Another alternative to reserve the same day as your arrival is through the **A.V.A.** (Venetian Hoteliers Association), ℂ **041-522-2264,** or online at www.veneziasi.it. Simply state the price range you want to book, and they'll confirm a hotel while you wait. There are offices at the train station, in Piazzale Roma garages, and in the airport.

Recent state-imposed ordinances resulted in stringent deadlines for the updating of antiquated electrical, plumbing, and sewage systems—costly endeavors. To make up for this, small one- and two-star hotels raised their rates, often applying for an upgrade in category for which they're now potentially eligible. Even more properties stuck TVs on the desks and hair dryers in the bathrooms to garner that extra star so they could inflate their rates during the Jubilee Year 2000. Then, of course, came the euro, and prices jacked up yet again. The good news is that now you'll have accommodations of a better quality; the bad news is that yesteryear's affordable finds are slowly disappearing. The rates below were compiled in late 2009. You can expect an annual increase of anywhere from 2% to 10%, depending on the category, but you might be hit with an increase of as much as 20% if the hotel you pick is one that has been redone recently.

A few peculiarities about Venice hotels have everything to do with the fact that this city built on water does not consistently offer what you might take for granted: elevators, light, and spaciousness. Venice hotels often have tiny bathrooms. The rooms are generally smaller than elsewhere and can be dark, and canal views aren't half as prevalent as we'd like them to be. This doesn't mean that a welcoming family-run hotel in an atmospheric neighborhood can't offer a memorable stay—just don't expect the amenities of the Danieli or Grand Canal vistas.

SEASONAL CONSIDERATIONS   Most hotels observe high- and low-season rates, though many are gradually adopting a single year-round rate, and the high-end-range hotels generally adapt their prices to availability. In the prices listed below, single figures represent rack rates, because the price varies too widely depending on availability; when a range is listed, they represent low- and high-season rates unless otherwise noted. Of course, you will almost always get a deal when reserving through the hotel website ahead of time. Even where it's not indicated in the listings, be sure to ask when you book or when you arrive at a hotel whether off-season prices are in effect. Check the site for special offers. High season in Venice is about March 15 to November 5, with a lull in July and August (when hotel discounts are often offered). Some small hotels close (sometimes without notice or to do renovation work) November or December until Carnevale, opening for about 2 weeks around Christmas and New Year's at high-season rates.

IN SAN MARCO
Very Expensive
Hotel Bauer/Bauer il Palazzo ★   Don't let the modern lobby throw you. This inn, just a few blocks from Piazza San Marco, is one of the top deluxe hotels in town and the only one not owned by a large chain. That means Francesca Bortolotto Possati, the chairman, chief executive, and sole owner of the Bauer Hotel Group, and her attentive staff are more likely to give you personal attention. In 1998, a massive hotel restructuring divided the hotel into two parts: the rather disappointing (especially at these prices) 1950s Hotel Bauer, with its standardized rooms and terrace on a side canal, and the Bauer il Palazzo. This 19th-century palace on the Grand Canal behind the modern wing enjoys views of Santa Maria della Salute across the way. The Palazzo is aiming for boutique-hotel status, with a more intimate reception area, a restaurant opening onto a terrace thrust over the Grand Canal, walk-in closets, and antique Venetian style (genuine 18th-c. wherever possible). The higher the price, the classier the accommodations, with patterned chipped-stone floors, elaborate stuccoed walls and ceilings, engraved mirrors, frescoed bedroom ceilings, and marble bathrooms.

San Marco 1459 (Campo San Moisè), 30124 Venezia. © **041-520-7022.** Fax 041-520-7557. www.bauer venezia.com. 191 units (82 in the Palazzo branch). At Hotel Bauer: 750€ superior; 850€ deluxe double; 1,050€ junior suite; 1,200€ suite. At Bauer Il Palazzo: 950€ double; 1,200€ deluxe suite; 1,500€ double with panoramic view; 1,800€ junior suite with panoramic view; 2,300€ executive suite with panoramic view; 2,600€ Grand Canal suite with panoramic view. Rates include buffet breakfast. AE, DC, MC, V. *Vaporetto:* San Marco–Vallaresso (walk straight up Calle di Ca'Vallaresso then left on Salita San Moisè into the *campo;* the hotel's on the left). **Amenities:** 2 Venetian/Mediterranean restaurants; 2 bars; babysitting; concierge; fitness center; Jacuzzi; room service; sauna; spa; smoke-free rooms; executive-level rooms (the Palazzo suites). *In room:* A/C, TV, VCR (on request in Palazzo), fax (in suites), hair dryer, minibar, Wi-Fi.

Hotel Gritti Palace ★★★ Although there are arguably more chichi hotels along the *bacino* off St. Mark's Square, if you're going for luxury status and the classiest hotel on the Grand Canal, the Gritti has been *it* for decades. It was the 16th-century palace of Doge Andrea Gritti, whose portrait graces one of the antiques-filled lounges, and everyone who is anyone has stayed here over the centuries, from international royalty to captains of industry, literary giants, and rock stars. Rooms have inlaid antique furnishings, gilt mirrors, ornate built-in dressers hand-painted in 18th-century Venetian style, tented curtains over the tall windows, and real box-spring beds set into curtained nooks. Many rooms have connecting doors so that families can share. Three of the suites on the *piano nobile* overlook the Grand Canal from small stone balconies; three more suites overlook the *campo.* Three junior suites open onto a side canal, with walk-in closets and one-and-a-half bathrooms.

San Marco 2467 (Campo del Traghetto/Campo Santa Maria del Giglio), 30124 Venezia. ✆ **041-794-611.** Fax 041-520-0942. www.starwood.com/grittipalace. 91 units. 950€ double deluxe; 1,295€ double with Grand Canal view; 2,300€ junior suite; 2,950€ suite with *campo* (square) view; 4,500€ presidential suite with canal view. AE, DC, MC, V. *Vaporetto:* Santa Maria del Giglio (the hotel is right there). **Amenities:** Venetian/Mediterranean/international restaurant; bar; babysitting; concierge; room service; smoke-free rooms; Wi-Fi; courtesy water taxi (free hourly boat to the Westin Excelsior on the Lido). *In room:* A/C, TV w/pay movies, VCR (in suites), fax (in suites), hair dryer, high-speed Internet, minibar.

Westin Hotel Europa & Regina ★ A recent overhaul of one of Venice's venerable Grand Canal bastions put it back among the city's top hotels. Hidden down a tiny side alley just 2 minutes from Piazza San Marco, this hotel's Tiepolo and Regina wings sport eclectic early-20th-century European furnishings and modern fabrics. The Europa wing is decorated in traditional Venetian style. There's a cozy bar with tables right on the Grand Canal; elegant, airy salons; and professional service. The restaurant is excellent (see the full review on p. 132). Room rates vary greatly with season and view (Canale Grande rooms are priciest). As with any Westin hotel, the best rates are found on their website.

San Marco 2159 (off Via XXII Marzo), 30124 Venezia. ✆ **041-240-0001.** Fax 041-523-1533. www.westin. com. 192 units. 925€ double; 1,230€ double with canal view; 2,158€ suite; 2,250€ suite with partial canal view; 2,775€ suite with canal view or panorama. AE, DC, MC, V. *Vaporetto:* San Marco (head west out of the southwest corner of Piazza San Marco down Saliz San Mose; cross the bridge to continue straight on Calle Larga XXII Marzo; you'll see hotel signs directing you down the alleyways to the left). **Amenities:** Excellent La Cusina restaurant (reviewed later in this chapter); terrace bar on the Grand Canal; babysitting; bikes; children's center; concierge; exercise room; golf course; use of pool at sister hotel on the Lido; room service; sauna; smoke-free rooms; tennis court; watersports equipment/rentals; courtesy water taxi (free hourly boat to the Westin Excelsior on the Lido). *In room:* A/C, TV w/pay movies, fax (on request), hair dryer, Internet, minibar.

Expensive

Hotel Concordia ★ The big selling point here: It's the only hotel in Venice with rooms overlooking St. Mark's (technically, the Piazza San Marco, so what you see are the pinnacles and domes on the side of the cathedral). All rooms are nonsmoking, some of them in 18th-century Venetian period style, done in a floral motif, with ornate little writing desks, gilt mirrors, and Murano chandeliers. Some are done in a slightly scuffed Empire style, with a daybed in the little sitting area. Bathrooms are red marble, and though all rooms are perfectly nice, the Concordia really is all about those precious 15 rooms overlooking the Piazzetta and the Duomo. You have to tackle 27 steps before reaching the reception area and its elevator. If you ask, the hotel will provide you with a coupon for 10% off your bill at the parking garage in Piazzale Roma.

San Marco 367 (Calle Larga San Marco), 30124 Venezia. ☎ **041-520-6866.** Fax 041-520-6775. www.
hotelconcordia.it. 53 units. 490€ double; 540€ junior suite; 620€ suite; extra bed 50€. Rates include buffet
breakfast. AE, DC, MC, V. *Vaporetto:* San Marco-Giardinetti (walk to the right getting off the *vaporetto,* and
then left into Piazza San Marco; cross in front of the basilica and go straight up the Merceria 1 brief block
to take a right on Calle Larga San Marco). **Amenities:** Italian/regional restaurant; bar; babysitting; concierge; room service; smoke-free rooms. *In room:* A/C, TV, hair dryer, minibar, free Wi-Fi.

Hotel Monaco & Grand Canal ★★   You won't get a more choice location: right on
the Grand Canal, across from Harry's Bar, 1 long block from St. Mark's Square; however,
very few of the rooms actually overlook the canal. These tend to be midsize, with ornately
painted headboards and closet doors and nicely done bathrooms with heated towel racks.
Some good news: When they're not booked, the staff can block off the large sitting rooms
of suites to turn them into canal-side doubles. Standard rooms without the view are more
simply furnished but share the same tall ceilings and windows to let in that fine Venetian
light. Several lounges feature windows on the canal, and the bar service, restaurant, and
breakfast move out onto a canal-side terrace in warm weather (in winter, a piano bar
operates in an inner lounge warmed by an open fire).

San Marco 1332 (right at the *vaporetto* stop, at the end of Calle Vallaresso off Salita San Moisè, the main
road leading west out of Piazza San Marco), 30124 Venezia. ☎ **041-520-0211.** Fax 041-520-0501. www.
hotelmonaco.it. 98 units. 530€ double; 610€ superior; 680€ double with canal view; 1,050€ suite with
canal view. Rates include breakfast. AE, DC, MC, V. *Vaporetto:* San Marco-Vallaresso (hotel is right at the
stop). **Amenities:** Venetian/Italian restaurant; bar; babysitting; concierge; room service; smoke-free
rooms; Wi-Fi. *In room:* A/C, TV w/pay movies, hair dryer, Internet, minibar.

Luna Hotel Baglioni ★★   Just off Piazza San Marco on the street leading down to
Harry's Bar, this luxury hotel may be Venice's oldest inn, converted into a hotel from a
convent in the 1200s. "Standard" rooms are situated on dreary airshafts but are otherwise
very nice, midsize with more modish styling and walk-in closets (in some) than that of
the pricier-category rooms. The "deluxe" rooms are richly carpeted, with ornate stucco
around the wall fabrics, Murano chandeliers and sconces, watercolors and prints, and
double sinks with golden fixtures set in the marble bathrooms. Many sprout small balconies with a partial view of the little Royal Gardens at the Grand Canal. Junior suites
are very large, with half-testers and huge bathrooms, though only no. 505 has the views
of the Bacino San Marco (into which the Grand Canal empties). The elegant breakfast
room is covered with remarkable 18th-century frescoes and gilt-edged paintings.

San Marco 1243 (Calle di Ca'Vallaresso), 30124 Venezia. ☎ **041-528-9840.** Fax 041-528-7160. www.
baglionihotels.com. 115 units. 651€ superior double; 687€ superior double with view; 735€ deluxe double; 850€ junior suite; 1,450€ suite; 1,600€ suite with lagoon view; 1,750€ Gran Lagoon suite; 2,050
Giorgione suite on 2 floors. Buffet breakfast 40€. AE, DC, MC, V. *Vaporetto:* San Marco-Vallaresso (it's on
the street leading straight up from the *vaporetto* stop). **Amenities:** Italian/international restaurant; piano
bar (music 2-3 times a week); babysitting; concierge; room service; smoke-free rooms. *In room:* A/C, TV,
VCR (on request in suites), fax (in suites), hair dryer, minibar, free Wi-Fi.

Moderate

Albergo al Gambero ★★   Midway along a main strip connecting Piazza San Marco
and the Rialto Bridge, this was once a budget hotel, but after a full renovation, it now
caters to a slightly better-heeled crowd. Surrounded by striped damasklike bedspreads
and curtains, you can slumber in one of the 14 canal-side rooms (5 have bathrooms,
including no. 203, which also has a small balcony). Rooms on the first two floors have
higher ceilings, though upstairs rooms are more newly renovated. The entire hotel is
nonsmoking. By Venice standards, the budget-level Gambero has all the trappings of a

midscale hotel at moderate prices. Guests receive a 10% discount in the lively ground-floor Bistrot de Venise (p. 133).

San Marco 4687 (on Calle dei Fabbri), 30124 Venezia. © **041-522-4384** or 041-520-1420. Fax 041-520-0431. www.locandaalgambero.com. 30 units. 250€ double; 275€ triple. Rates include continental breakfast. MC, V. *Vaporetto:* Rialto (turn right along canal, cross small footbridge over Rio San Salvador, and turn left onto Calle Bembo, which becomes Calle dei Fabbri; hotel is about 5 blocks ahead on left). **Amenities:** Restaurant (Le Bistrot de Venise, p. 133); bar (in restaurant); concierge; smoke-free rooms. *In room:* A/C, TV, hair dryer, minibar, free Wi-Fi.

Hotel Flora ★ The simple name of this small, charming hotel refers to its greatest attribute: a jewel-like patio garden immediately beyond the welcoming lobby. A delightful place to have breakfast, afternoon tea, or an aperitif, the garden is enclosed by climbing vines and ivy-covered walls, with an antique well, potted flowers, and blooming plants that create a cool green enclave. Seamlessly run by two generations of the highly professional Romanelli family and their friendly staff, the Flora is ideally located on a tony shopping street close to Piazza San Marco. Despite rooms that can vary greatly (in size and furnishings) and small bathrooms, it is forever full of loyal devotees and romance-seekers. On the top floor, room no. 47 looks onto what is allegedly the *palazzo* of Desdemona (of Shakespeare's tragedy *Othello*), with the dome of La Salute church beyond. The hotel added a fitness room in late 2009.

The owners of Hotel Flora also run a hotel in the same area: **Locanda Novecento** (San Marco 2683–2684; © **041-241-3765;** fax 041-521-2145; www.locandanovecento.it), a boutique hotel offering luxury accommodations in nine rooms, each decorated along the theme of "1900." Rooms have the same amenities as the Flora, while the prices are about 40€ higher.

San Marco 2283a (off Calle Larga XXII Marzo, near Campo San Moisè), 30124 Venezia. © **041-520-5844.** Fax 041-522-8217. www.hotelflora.it. 43 units. 260€ double; 320€ superior double; 320€ triple. Rates include buffet breakfast. AE, DC, MC, V. Off-season rates about 20% lower. *Vaporetto:* San Marco–Vallaresso (walk down Calle Vallaresso and turn left onto the V. XXII Marzo; after crossing the San Moisè Bridge and passing the Deutsche Bank, you'll see a sign on left side of street for the hotel, located down a narrow passageway off the V. XXII Marzo). **Amenities:** Bar; babysitting; concierge; small health club; room service. *In room:* A/C, TV, hair dryer, Wi-Fi.

Hotel La Fenice et Des Artistes ★ The hallways are plastered with ornate little mirrors and tons of contemporary paintings and prints, and the location is great—around the corner from La Fenice opera house, halfway between San Marco and the Accademia. It's split into two early-19th-century *palazzi* on either side of a modern lobby entrance grafted into what was once an open courtyard, scraps of which survive off either side of the hall for breakfast alfresco. It's a perfectly nice, elegantly furnished hotel of modest luxury, but unfortunately, the hotel lacks random quality touches, such as a decent air-conditioning system and, in some cases, good beds—some of the mattresses rest on ancient, swaybacked cot springs. The string of homey lounges feel like comfy living rooms, scattered with assorted furnishings, card tables, a TV with VCR, and an Internet point for guest use.

San Marco 1936 (Campiello della Fenice), 30124 Venezia. © **041-523-2333.** Fax 041-520-3721. www. fenicehotels.it. 68 units. 150€–280€ double; 190€–320€ superior double; 180€–320€ triple; 250€–380€ suite. Rates include breakfast. AE, DC, MC, V. *Vaporetto:* Santa Maria del Giglio (walk up into Campo Santa Maria Zobenigo, turn right to cross the footbridge; the road on the other side makes a sharp turn left, and then right to open into the wide Calle Larga/Via XXII Marzo; turn left up Calle delle Veste into Campo San Fantin; turn left to walk around the right flank of Teatro La Fenice; and then make your 1st right down a

Hotel Violino d'Oro ★★ (Value This small boutique hotel at a tiny *campiello* with
a marble fountainhead on the main shopping drag from San Marco to the Accademia
may be relatively new, but the style is ever-popular 18th-century Venetian. The rooms,
bathed in rich colors, are compact but graced with nice touches such as gold decoration
on the marble-top desks, modest stuccoes and Murano chandeliers on the ceilings, very
firm beds, and heated towel racks in the bathrooms. Six doubles even overlook Rio San
Moisè canal, for which you can add 30€ to the price listed below. The low-season rates
are incredible, and even high-season rates are (for Venice) not too bad for this level of
comfort and style. The entire hotel is nonsmoking.

San Marco 2091 (Via XXII Marzo), 30124 Venezia. ℂ **041-277-0841.** Fax 041-277-1001. www.violinodoro.
com. 26 units. 280€ double; 310€ deluxe double; 400€ deluxe double with view; ask about bargain rates
during low season. Rates include buffet breakfast. AE, DC, MC, V. *Vaporetto:* San Marco–Vallaresso (walk
straight up Calle di Ca'Vallaresso, left on Salita San Moisè; cross the wide footbridge, and the hotel is just
across the little *campiello* on the left). **Amenities:** Bar; concierge; room service; smoke-free rooms. *In
room:* A/C, TV, hair dryer, minibar, Wi-Fi.

Locanda Remedio—Hotel Colombina ★ In 2003, the Remedio became the
three-star annex of the four-star **Hotel Colombina** (situated just behind the annex, at
Castello 4416, Calle del Remedio), and it remains, by Venetian standards, a spot offering
unusually large and quiet rooms with fine antiques (and good reproductions) in an
ancient *palazzo* around the corner from one of St. Mark's busiest streets. Most rooms are
on the second floor (no. 27 has lovely ceiling frescoes) off a ballroom-size corridor, and
they feature modernized, if small, bathrooms, and TVs with VCRs (movies in English
are available at the desk).

San Marco 4412 (on Calle del Remedio), 30122 Venezia. ℂ **041-277-0525.** Fax 041-277-6044. www.
hotelcolombina.com. 32 units. 315€ double; 380€ triple. Rates include breakfast. AE, DC, MC, V. *Vaporetto:*
San Marco (exit Piazza San Marco under Torre dell'Orologio and turn right onto Calle Larga San Marco; at
Ristorante All'Angelo, turn left onto Calle va al Ponte dell'Angelo and take 1st right onto Ramo del Anzolo;
cross small footbridge onto Calle del Remedio). **Amenities:** Bar; concierge; smoke-free rooms; Wi-Fi. *In
room:* A/C, TV, hair dryer, minibar.

Inexpensive

Hotel ai do Mori ★ (Value (Kids Antonella, the young hands-on owner/manager,
creates an efficient yet comfortable ambience here. The more accessible lower-floor
rooms (there's no elevator, and the hotel begins on the second floor) are slightly larger
and offer rooftop views, but the top-floor rooms boast views of San Marco's cupolas and
the Torre dell'Orologio, whose two bronze Moors ring the bells every hour (the large
double-paned windows help to ensure quiet). A decade of renovations finished several
years ago brought new tiled bathrooms (with hair dryers and heated towel racks), TVs,
firm mattresses, and air-conditioning. Every room but two has a private bathroom, and
all have wood beams on the ceilings. Room nos. 4 (a small double) and 5 (a triple) share
a bathroom and a small hallway and can be turned into a family suite. Additionally,
Antonella has opened a four-room annex nearby.

San Marco 658 (on Calle Larga San Marco), 30124 Venezia. ℂ **041-520-4817** or 041-528-9293. Fax 041-
520-5328. www.hotelaidomori.com. 11 units. 50€–150€ double; 180€–245€ family suite (up to 5 people).
MC, V. *Vaporetto:* San Marco (exit Piazza San Marco beneath Torre dell'Orologio; turn right at Max Mara
store, and hotel is on left, just before McDonald's). **Amenities:** Bar; concierge; smoke-free rooms; Wi-Fi.
In room: A/C, TV, hair dryer.

VENICE

5

WHERE TO STAY

Hotel Do Pozzi ★ ⟨Finds⟩   Duck off bustling Calle Larga just 150m (492 ft.) from St. Mark's Square, and you'll find a hidden little *campiello* whose namesake "two wells" flanks the round tables where hotel guests take breakfast in warm weather. The quietest rooms overlook this tiny square from flower-fringed windows. All guest rooms are decorated with embroidered fabrics, a few 18th-century Venetian-style pieces, Murano chandeliers, wood floors, and glass mirrors on the closet doors to make the cozy quarters seem roomier. Room nos. 20 and 40 get slivers of Grand Canal views down a short street; no. 47 opens onto the noisy shopping of Calle Larga, but it comes with frescoed ceilings and a small sitting room. Rooms in the seven-room annex, **Dependance Favaro,** around the corner, are largely the same. Guests can receive a 10% discount off meals at the hotel restaurant, Da Raffaele.

San Marco 2373 (off Calle Larga/Via XXII Marzo), 30124 Venezia. ℂ **041-520-7855.** Fax 041-522-9413. www.hoteldopozzi.it. 30 units, plus 6 in Dependance Favaro. 98€–280€ double; 40€–55€ extra bed. AE, DC, MC, V. *Vaporetto:* Santa Maria del Giglio (walk straight up from *vaporetto* stop into Campo Santa Maria Zobenigo, turn right out of the *campo,* and cross the bridge, doglegging slight left and right again onto broad Calle Larga; take the 1st right down a narrow alley to the hotel). **Amenities:** Venetian/Italian restaurant; babysitting; concierge; room service; smoke-free rooms. *In room:* A/C, TV, hair dryer, minibar.

Hotel Locanda Fiorita ★★ ⟨Value⟩   This pretty little hotel is located in a Venetian red *palazzo,* parts of which date from the 1400s, although everything has been renovated in 18th-century Venetian style. The wisteria vine partially covering the facade is at its glorious best in May or June, but the Fiorita is excellent year-round, as much for its simply furnished rooms boasting new bathrooms (now with hair dryers) as for its location on a *campiello* off the grand Campo Santo Stefano. Room nos. 1 and 10 have little terraces beneath the wisteria pergola and overlook the *campiello;* they can't be guaranteed on reserving, so ask when you arrive. Each of the two rooms with shared bathrooms has its own private facilities down the hall. Just a few meters away is **Ca' Morosini** (ℂ **041-241-3800;** fax 041-244-7998; www.camorosini.com), the Fiorita's three-star annex. There you'll find more rooms with views of the *campo.*

San Marco 3457a (on Campiello Novo), 30124 Venezia. ℂ **041-523-4754.** Fax 041-522-8043. www. locandafiorita.com. 16 units. 170€ double. Rates include continental breakfast. AE, DC, MC, V. *Vaporetto:* Sant'Angelo (walk to the tall brick building, and then turn right around its side; cross a small bridge and turn left down Calle del Pestrin; a bit farther down on your left is a small square 3 stairs above street level; hotel is against the back of it). **Amenities:** Babysitting; concierge; room service; smoke-free rooms; Wi-Fi. *In room:* A/C, TV, hair dryer, minibar (annex only).

IN CASTELLO

Very Expensive

Hotel Danieli ★★★   Doge Dandolo built his glorious Venetian Gothic palace three doors down from the Palazzo Ducale in the 14th century, and it's been one of the most sumptuous hotels in Venice since 1822. It vies with the Gritti Palace (which is now in the same family) as the most desirable address in Venice proper and has been host to innumerable kings, celebrities, and other noted guests as far back as Dickens. The tone of this palatial hotel is set by the astounding four-story lobby of balustraded open balconies and stairwells, Venice's Oriental-tinged Gothic arches, and palm fronds. It's ornately decorated throughout, and the rooms vary in decor, size, and style but are all opulently done. Rooms in the original structure have the most atmosphere but are smaller than the accommodations in the 19th-century wing. Either is far preferable to the recently refurbished (in 2008) 1940s wing next door—the rooms are fine there but lack that genteel, vintage touch.

Castello 4196 (Riva degli Schiavoni), 30122 Venezia. ℰ **041-522-6480.** Fax 041-520-0208. http://danieli.
hotelinvenice.com. 231 units. 350€–870€ double; 480€–1,070€ double with lagoon view; 980€–1,510€
junior suite with lagoon view; 1,800€–3,010€ suite with lagoon view; 3,950€ royal suite with lagoon view.
Buffet breakfast 40€. AE, DC, MC, V. *Vaporetto:* San Zaccaria (the hotel's right at the *vaporetto* launch).
Amenities: Roof terrace Italian restaurant; 2 bars (1 w/piano music); babysitting; bikes; children's center;
concierge; exercise room; golf course; use of pool at sister hotel on the Lido; room service; sauna; smoke-
free rooms; tennis court; watersports equipment/rentals. *In room:* A/C, TV w/pay movies, fax (in suite),
hair dryer (in most), minibar, Wi-Fi.

Londra Palace ★   This 19th-century neo-Gothic palace is one of the best values on
the prime real estate of the Riva degli Schiavoni. Tchaikovsky wrote his Fourth Symphony in room no. 108. Accommodations are cushy, with lacquered furniture, and attic
rooms are most romantic. With 100 windows overlooking the San Marco basin, from the
"deluxe" rooms you can enjoy people-watching as well as distant vistas of the lagoon.
Quieter, cheaper "superior" rooms look out on the inner courtyard. The restaurant, Do
Leoni, is one of the best hotel dining rooms in town. The lobby and ground-floor salons
were redesigned by the same architect who does Versace boutiques.

Castello 4171 (Riva degli Schiavoni), 30122 Venezia. ℰ **041-520-0533.** Fax 041-522-5032. www.hotelondra.it.
53 units. 265€–525€ standard double; 365€–625€ deluxe double with lagoon view; 465€–825€ junior
suite; extra bed 100€. Rates include continental breakfast. AE, DC, MC, V. *Vaporetto:* San Zaccaria (on the
canal right at the San Zaccaria *vaporetto* stop). **Amenities:** Excellent Venetian/international restaurant;
bar; babysitting; concierge; golf (on Lido, special rate); room service; tennis (on Lido, special rate). *In
room:* A/C, TV, hair dryer, minibar, Wi-Fi.

Expensive

Hotel Metropole ★★   Vivaldi lived here from 1704 to 1738, when it was the chapter house of La Pietà church next door, and he was its violin and concert master. The
quirky *palazzo* that has evolved from that church building is now a member of the
Romantik hotel association—and aptly so. The owner has tried to outfit his hotel as a
Victorian-style home, packed with quirky collections of curios (fans, purses, bottle openers, crucifixes, cigarette cases), and its public salons are tucked with cozy bars and sitting
niches. Accommodations vary widely in true Romantic style; you may find such details
as Burano glass lamps and Murano chandeliers, inlaid wood furnishings, and Romantic-
era watercolors and prints. Rooms overlook the Bacino San Marco, the side canal where
water taxis pull up, or the courtyard housing the lovely garden restaurant enlivened by
nightly keyboard music. You get free car parking if you let them know you need it before
8pm the day you arrive.

Castello 4149 (Riva degli Schiavoni), 30122 Venezia. ℰ **041-520-5044.** Fax 041-522-3679. www.hotel
metropole.com. 67 units. 500€ double; 750€ junior suite; 1,150€ suite. Buffet breakfast included. Rates
about 30%–40% lower in off season. AE, DC, MC, V. *Vaporetto:* San Zaccaria (walk right along Riva degli
Schiavoni over 2 footbridges; the hotel is next to La Pietà church). **Amenities:** Venetian/Italian restaurant;
bar; babysitting; concierge; room service; smoke-free rooms; Wi-Fi. *In room:* A/C, TV, hair dryer, minibar.

Locanda Casa Verardo ★★ (Finds)   In 2000, Daniela and Francesco took over this
one-star *pensione* and transformed it into a fine three-star hotel (and more than doubled
its size), while still maintaining the feel of a Venetian *palazzo* romantically faded by time.
The wood-paneled lobby is anchored by an ancient stone well. The rooms are done in
chipped-stone floors, Murano chandeliers, and eclectic furnishings, from imposing
armoires and 17th-century reproductions to pseudo Deco and modern functional; three
have small terraces. The best accommodations come with stucco wall decorations and
scraps of old ceiling frescoes—and tops are the six overlooking a little canal. The airy
main hall doubles as a breakfast room.

Castello 4765 (at foot of Ponte Storto), 30122 Venezia. ℰ **041-528-6138** or 041-528-6127. Fax 041-523-2765. www.casaverardo.it. 23 units. 90€–250€ double; 125€–340€ deluxe double; 150€–390€ junior suite for 3–4. Rates include buffet breakfast. Prices much lower in off season; ask when you book. AE, MC, V. *Vaporetto:* San Zaccaria (walk straight ahead on Calle delle Rasse to Campo SS. Filippo e Giacomo; continue straight through the small *campo* to take Calle Chiesa to cross the 1st small bridge, Ponte Storto, to find the hotel on the left). **Amenities:** Bar; babysitting; concierge; room service; smoke-free rooms. *In room:* A/C, TV, hair dryer (on request), minibar, Wi-Fi.

Inexpensive

Foresteria Valdese (Palazzo Cavagnis) ★ ⓥⓐⓛⓤⓔ
Those lucky enough to get a room at this weathered, though elegant, 16th-century *palazzo* will find simple accommodations in a charming *foresteria,* the name given to religious institutions that traditionally provided lodging for pilgrims and guests. Affiliated with Italy's Waldesian and Methodist churches, the *palazzo* often fills the large, recently overhauled dormitory-style rooms with visiting church groups, though everyone is warmly welcomed, and you'll find an international and inter-religious mix here. Most of the plainly furnished rooms in this once-noble residence open onto a balcony overlooking a quiet canal. The 18th-century frescoes that grace the high ceilings in some doubles (including corner room no. 10) and two of the dorms are by the same artist who decorated the Correr Civic Museum—and these rooms will cost you a few euros extra. The reception is open daily from 9am to 1pm and 6 to 8pm. The hotel is nonsmoking. Sheets and towels are provided, but you have to make your own bed.

Castello 5170 (at the end of Calle Lunga Santa Maria Formosa), 30122 Venezia. ℰ **041-528-6797.** Fax 041-241-6238. www.foresteriavenezia.it. 6 units with private bathroom and TV (2–4 beds) often requiring a 2-night stay; 3 dorms (with 8, 11, or 16 beds), all with shared bathroom; 2 mini-apts (sleeping 2, minimum stay often required) with minikitchen and private bathroom. 78€–84€ double; 82€–91€ triple; 114€–126€ quad; 23€–26€ dorm bed. Rates include buffet breakfast. DC, MC, V (but pay 3.5% more to use credit cards). Closed 2 weeks in Nov. *Vaporetto:* Rialto (head southeast to the Campo Santa Maria Formosa; look for the Bar all'Orologio, just where Calle Lunga Santa Maria Formosa begins. The *campo* is just about equidistant from Piazza San Marco and the Rialto Bridge). *In room:* TV (except in dorms), kitchenette (in apts), no phone.

Hotel Al Piave ★★★ ⓥⓐⓛⓤⓔ
The Puppin family's tasteful hotel is a steal: This level of attention, coupled with the sophisticated *buon gusto* in decor and spirit, is rare in this price category. You'll find orthopedic mattresses under ribbon candy–print or floral spreads, immaculate white-lace curtains, stained-glass windows, new bathrooms, and even (in a few rooms) tiny terraces. The family suites—with two bedrooms, minibars, and shared bathrooms—are particularly good deals, as are the small but stylishly rustic apartments with kitchenettes and washing machines (in the two smaller ones). A savvy international crowd has discovered this classy spot, so you'll need to reserve far in advance.

Castello 4838–40 (on Ruga Giuffa), 30122 Venezia. ℰ **041-528-5174.** Fax 041-523-8512. www.hotelal piave.com. 13 units. 120€–175€ double; 145€–225€ superior double; 190€–290€ family suite for 3; 250€–375€ family suite for 4 or 5. Often heavy discounts off season. Rates include continental breakfast. AE, DC, MC, V. Closed Jan 7 to Carnevale. *Vaporetto:* San Zaccaria (walk straight ahead on Calle delle Rasse to small Campo SS. Filippo e Giacomo, take right on Calle San Provolo, and cross over canal to Campo San Provolo; take a left, cross 1st small footbridge, and follow zigzagging street that becomes Ruga Giuffa). **Amenities:** Babysitting; concierge; smoke-free rooms; free Wi-Fi. *In room:* A/C, TV, fridge (family suite), hair dryer, Internet, minibar.

Hotel Campiello ★
At this gem on a tiny *campiello,* the atmosphere is airy and bright, and the relaxed hospitality and quality service are provided by the Bianchini sisters, Monica and Nicoletta. Most rooms are done in authentic 18th-century and Art

Nouveau antiques with inlaid *armadios* (armoirelike cabinets) and bas-reliefs on the headboards. The building's original 15th-century marble-mosaic pavement is still evident, a vestige of the days when the hotel was a convent under the patronage of the nearby San Zaccaria; you'll catch a glimpse of it in the lounge area opening onto a pleasant breakfast room.

Castello 4647 (on Campiello del Vin), 30122 Venezia. © **041-520-5764.** Fax 041-520-5798. www. hcampiello.it. 16 units. 110€–250€ double; 120€–270€ triple; 140€–300€ quad; 170€–350€ suite. Ask about discounts in off season. Rates include buffet breakfast. AE, DC, MC, V. *Vaporetto:* San Zaccaria. **Amenities:** Bar; babysitting; concierge; room service; smoke-free rooms. *In room:* A/C, TV, hair dryer.

Hotel Fontana ★ Three generations of Stainers have been behind the front desk here since 1968 (for the 30 years prior to that, the Fontana was a convent for German nuns), and their warmth seems to pour out of the lobby's leaded-glass windows. The four-story hotel offers a *pensione*-like family atmosphere coupled with a crisp, professional operation. Rooms have lovely antique furnishings but a decided lack of wattage in the overhead lights; the two best on the upper floor have private terraces. The hotel installed an elevator in 2009 that whisks you up to the top for beautiful views of San Zaccaria's 15th-century façade.

Castello 4701 (on Campo San Provolo), 30122 Venezia. © **041-522-0579.** Fax 041-523-1040. www. hotelfontana.it. 15 units. 170€ double; 180€ double with balcony; 220€ triple; 250€ quad. Rates discounted as much as 50% in the off season. Rates include buffet breakfast. AE, DC, MC, V. *Vaporetto:* San Zaccaria (from Riva degli Schiavoni, take any narrow street north to Campiello SS. Filippo e Giacomo; exit this small *campo* from east side, in direction of Campo San Zaccaria, until reaching Campo San Provolo). **Amenities:** Concierge; room service; smoke-free rooms. *In room:* TV, hair dryer (on request).

Hotel La Residenza ★★ Finds Feel like a doge, spend like a pauper. This is an excellent slice of old Venice at a fraction of the usual Venice cost. It's just a block up from the priciest real estate of the Riva degli Schiavoni, but you'd never know it. A few of the rooms at this *pensione*-style small hotel in a 15th-century *palazzo* overlook the very Venetian *campo* out front where kids play soccer and old ladies sit in the sun. Other rooms open onto the surrounding quiet streets. Stuccoes from the 1750s, 17th-century paintings, and a baby grand piano decorate the absolutely fabulous lobby/breakfast room. Half of the rooms still have carpeting, and half feature polished wood floors. All have hand-painted, 18th-century Venetian-style furnishings under Murano chandeliers. There's no elevator (it's 25 steps up to the reception).

Castello 3608 (Campo Bandiera e Moro), 30122 Venezia. © **041-528-5315.** Fax 041-523-8859. www. venicelaresidenza.com. 15 units. 80€–180€ double; 35€ extra bed. Rates include breakfast. AE, MC, V. *Vaporetto:* San Zaccaria (from the *vaporetto*, turn left along Riva degli Schiavoni, cross 3 bridges, and then take your 1st left into the *campo*) or Arsenale (from the *vaporetto* stop, turn left up Riva degli Schiavoni, over 1 bridge, left up Calle del Forno, and left on Calle va in Crosera, which spills into the *campo*). **Amenities:** Concierge; smoke-free rooms; Wi-Fi. *In room:* A/C, TV, hair dryer (on request), minibar.

 Tips Frommer's Discounts

Traveling with Frommer's has its privileges. Many hotels recognize the name and will give readers a Frommer's discount. Just show the book when you check in. Some of the prices listed in the book apply only to the likes of you and me—people who use this book.

Moderate

Hotel alla Salute ★   An airy lobby with beamed ceilings and cool marble floors, a small but lovely terrace garden, and a cozy cocktail bar occupy the ground level of this converted 17th-century *palazzo* on Rio della Fornace. Upstairs the comfortable guest rooms have high ceilings and huge windows (10 with canal views and 4 facing the garden), many of them large enough to accommodate families of four or five at an additional charge. Breakfast is served in the garden in warm weather.

Dorsoduro 222 (on Fondamenta Ca' Balà), 30123 Venezia. (✆ **041-523-5404.** Fax 041-522-2271. www. hotelsalute.com. 56 units, 12 with shower only, some with private bathroom. 160€ double with shared bathroom; 190€ double with private bathroom; 190€ triple with shared bathroom; 220€ triple with private bathroom. Ask about rooms sleeping 4–5 persons. Rates include continental breakfast. MC, V. Often closes in Jan or Feb for upkeep; call ahead. *Vaporetto:* Salute (facing La Salute, turn right and head to 1st small bridge; cross it and walk as straight ahead as possible to next narrow canal, and then turn left, before crossing bridge, onto Fondamenta Ca' Balà). **Amenities:** Bar; concierge; smoke-free rooms; Wi-Fi. *In room:* Hair dryer.

Hotel American Dinesen ★★   Despite its potentially unromantic name (did you travel transatlantic for this?), the Hotel American Dinesen is recommended for both its style and its substance. One of the nicest of Venice's moderate hotels, it has the perfect combination of old-fashioned charm and utility. This three-story hotel located near the Peggy Guggenheim Collection offers a dignified lobby and breakfast room dressed with lovely Oriental carpets and marble floors, polished woods, leaded-glass windows and French doors. The best choices are the larger corner rooms and those overlooking a quiet canal; some have small terraces. Every room is outfitted with traditional Venetian-style furnishings that usually include hand-painted furniture and Murano glass chandeliers. If it's late spring, don't miss a drink on the second-floor terrace beneath a wisteria arbor dripping with plump violet blossoms.

San Vio 628 (on Fond. Bragadin), 30123 Venezia. (✆ **041-520-4733.** Fax 041-520-4048. www.hotelamerican. com. 30 units. 80€–310€ double; 100€–370€ double with canal view; 140€–460€ junior suite. Rates include buffet breakfast. AE, MC, V. *Vaporetto:* Accademia (veer left around the Galleria dell'Accademia museum, taking the 1st left turn, and walk straight ahead until you cross the 1st small footbridge; turn right to follow the Fondamenta Bragadin that runs alongside the Rio di San Vio canal, and the hotel is on your left). **Amenities:** Bar; babysitting; concierge; room service; smoke-free rooms. *In room:* A/C, TV, hair dryer, minibar, free Wi-Fi.

Inexpensive

Hotel Falier ★ (**Value**   Owned by the same fellow who put the lovely Hotel American Dinesen (see above) on Venice's map of moderately priced lodgings, the Falier is his savvy interpretation of less expensive accommodations, particularly worth booking when half-price low-season rates apply. It is a reliable value at this price range, with standard-size rooms (and modern bathrooms) attractively decorated with white lace curtains and flowered bedspreads; some even have wood-beam ceilings. The old-world lobby has potted ferns, Doric columns, and triangle-marble floors. Detractors may feel the need to be closer to Piazza San Marco, when, in truth, the Falier is much closer to the real Venice. It is situated in a lively area lined with stores and bars between the large Campo Santa Margherita, one of the city's most character-filled piazzas, and the much-visited Frari Church.

Dorsoduro 130 (Salizzada San Pantalon), 30135 Venezia. (✆ **041-710-882** or 041-711-005. Fax 041-520-6554. www.hotelfalier.com. 19 units. 80€–190€ double. Rates include continental breakfast. AE, MC, V. *Vaporetto:* Ferrovia. (If you've packed lightly, the walk from the train station is easy, easier yet from the

Piazzale Roma. From the train station, cross the Scalzi Bridge, turn right along the Grand Canal for 45m (148 ft.), and then left toward the Tolentini Church. Continue along the Salizzada San Pantalon in the general direction of Campo Santa Margherita.) **Amenities:** Concierge. *In room:* A/C, TV, hair dryer.

Hotel Galleria ★★ (Value

If you've always dreamed of flinging open your hotel window to find the Grand Canal in front of you, choose this 17th-century *palazzo*. But reserve way in advance—these are the cheapest rooms on the canal and the most charming at these rates, thanks to owners Luciano Benedetti and Stefano Franceschini. They overhauled the hotel in 2004, keeping a sumptuous, 18th-century look in public spaces and giving a cozier look to the new bedrooms. Six guest rooms overlook the canal; others have views that include the Ponte Accademia over an open-air bar/cafe (which can be annoying to anyone hoping to sleep before the bar closes). Breakfast, with oven-fresh bread, is served in your room.

Dorsoduro 878A (at foot of Accademia Bridge), 30123 Venezia. ✆ **041-523-2489.** Fax 041-520-4172. www.hotelgalleria.it. 9 units, 6 with bathroom. 120€ double with shared bathroom; 150€–180€ double with private bathroom; 230€ triple. Rates include continental breakfast. AE, DC, MC, V. *Vaporetto:* Accademia (with Accademia Bridge behind you, hotel is just to your left, next to Totem II Canale gallery). **Amenities:** Babysitting; concierge; room service. *In room:* Hair dryer.

Hotel Messner ★

Hotel Messner and the Hotel alla Salute (see above) are the best choices in the Guggenheim area, at budget-embracing rates. The Messner is a two-part hotel: In the Casa Principale (Main House) are the handsome beamed-ceiling lobby and public rooms of a 14th-century *palazzo* and modernized guest rooms with comfortable modular furnishings and Murano chandeliers (three overlook picturesque Rio della Fornace). The 15th-century *dépendance* (annex), 50m (164 ft.) away, doesn't show quite as much close attention to detail in the decor, but it's perfectly nice and will cost you about 25€ less a night for a double. In summer, you can take breakfast in a small garden.

Dorsoduro 216–217 (on Fondamenta Ca' Balà), 30123 Venezia. ✆ **041-522-7443.** Fax 041-522-7266. www.hotelmessner.it. Main house 13 units; annex 20 units. 120€–150€ double; 150€–170€ triple; 170€–190€ quad. Ask about Frommer's discounts. Rates include continental breakfast. AE, DC, MC, V. Closed Dec 1–27. *Vaporetto:* Salute (follow small canal immediately to right of La Salute; turn right onto 3rd bridge and walk straight until you see the white awning just before reaching Rio della Fornace). **Amenities:** Restaurant (traditional Italian cuisine); bar; babysitting; concierge; room service; smoke-free rooms. *In room:* A/C (main house), TV, hair dryer, Wi-Fi.

Pensione Accademia ★★

This *pensione* is beloved by Venice regulars. You'll have to reserve far in advance to get any room here, let alone one overlooking the breakfast garden, which is snuggled into the confluence of two canals. The 17th-century villa is fitted with period antiques in first-floor "superior" rooms, and the atmosphere is decidedly old-fashioned and elegant (Katharine Hepburn's character lived here in the 1955 classic *Summertime*). Formally and appropriately called the Villa Maravege (Villa of Wonders), it was built as a patrician villa in the 1600s and used as the Russian consulate until the 1930s. Its outdoor landscaping (a flowering patio on the small Rio San Trovaso and a grassy formal rose garden behind) and interior details (original pavement, woodbeam and decoratively painted ceilings) still create the impression that you're a guest in an aristocratic Venetian home from another era.

Dorsoduro 1058 (Fondamenta Bollani, west of the Accademia Bridge), 30123 Venezia. ✆ **041-521-0188** or 041-523-7846. Fax 041-523-9152. www.pensioneaccademia.it. 27 units. 140€–229€ double; 170€–279€ superior double; 200€–315€ junior suite. Rates include breakfast. AE, DC, MC, V. *Vaporetto:* Accademia (step off the *vaporetto* and turn right down Calle Gambara, which doglegs 1st left and then right; it becomes Calle Corfu, which ends at a side canal; walk left for a few meters to cross over the bridge, and then head to the right back up toward the Grand Canal and the hotel). **Amenities:** Bar; babysitting; concierge; room service; Wi-Fi. *In room:* A/C, TV, hair dryer, minibar.

Pensione La Calcina ★   British author John Ruskin holed up here in 1876 when penning *The Stones of Venice* (you can request his room, no. 2, but good luck getting it), and this hotel on the sunny Zattere in the southern Dorsoduro has remained a quasi-sacred preference for writers, artists, and assorted bohemians. Half the unfussy but luminous rooms overlook the Giudecca Canal in the direction of Palladio's 16th-century Redentore. Do your best to avoid the side rooms that overlook a very narrow canal. The outdoor floating terrace and the rooftop terrace are glorious places to begin or end the day. Three suites and two apartments were added in 2002.

Dorsoduro 780 (on Zattere al Gesuati), 30123 Venezia. ✆ **041-520-6466.** Fax 041-522-7045. www.la calcina.com. 28 units. 110€–240€ double without view; 150€–310€ double with Giudecca canal view. Rates include buffet breakfast. AE, DC, MC, V. *Vaporetto:* Zattere (follow le Zattere east; hotel is on water before 1st bridge). **Amenities:** Restaurant; bar; concierge; room service. *In room:* A/C, TV, hair dryer, minibar, Wi-Fi.

IN SAN POLO
Moderate
Antica Locanda Sturion ★★ (Finds)(Kids)   Though there's been a *pensione* on this site since 1290, a recent gutting and rebuilding has made the Sturion into a tastefully moderate hotel managed by the charming Scottish-born Helen and co-owner Flavia. The hotel's reception area is perched four flights (and 69 challenging steps) above the Grand Canal (and, depending on the location of your room, there could be more stairs involved). Unfortunately, only two rooms offer canal views of the Rialto Bridge (as does the delightful breakfast room—is there a better way to start your day?), and these command higher rates; they are big enough for families or groups of three or four. The other rooms have charming views over the Rialto area rooftops. The hotel is tastefully decorated with 18th-century-inspired Venetian furniture, parquet floors, red carpeting, and rich damasklike wallpaper. The hoteliers also have two apartments nearby.

San Polo 679 (on Calle dello Sturion), 30125 Venezia. ✆ **041-523-6243.** Fax 041-522-8378. www.locanda sturion.com. 11 units. 260€ double; 310€ double with Grand Canal view; 325€ triple; 380€ triple with Grand Canal view; 380€ quad; 410€ quad with Grand Canal view. Rates about 40% lower in off season. Rates include buffet breakfast. AE, MC, V. *Vaporetto:* Rialto (from the Rialto stop, cross the bridge, turn left at the other side, and walk along the Grand Canal; Calle dello Sturion will be the 4th narrow alleyway on the right, just before San Polo 740). **Amenities:** Restaurant; bar; babysitting; concierge; room service; free Wi-Fi. *In room:* A/C, TV, hair dryer, minibar.

Inexpensive
Pensione Guerrato ★★★ (Value)(Kids)   The Guerrato is as reliable and clean a budget hotel as you're likely to find at these rates. Brothers-in-law Roberto and Piero own this former *pensione* in a 13th-century convent and manage to keep it almost always booked (mostly with Americans). The firm mattresses, good modernish bathrooms, and flea-market finds (hand-carved antique or Deco headboards and armoires) show their determination to run a top-notch budget hotel in pricey Venice. They don't exaggerate when they call their breakfast, accompanied by classical music, *buonissimo.* The Guerrato is in the Rialto's heart, so think of 7am noise before requesting a room overlooking the marketplace (with a peek down the block to the Grand Canal and Ca' d'Oro). Piero and Roberto have also renovated the building's top floor (great views; no elevator, 70 steps) to create five new rooms—with air-conditioning (for which you will pay 10€).

San Polo 240A (on Calle Drio or Dietro la Scimia, near the Rialto Market), 30125 Venezia. ℭ **041-522-** **123**
7131. Fax 041-528-5927. www.pensioneguerrato.it. 14 units, 95€ double with shared bathroom; 140€ double with private bathroom; 120€ triple with shared bathroom; 155€ triple with private bathroom; 185€ quad with private bathroom. Pay in cash, get 10% off. Rates include buffet breakfast. AE, MC, V. Closed Dec 22–26 and Jan 10–31. *Vaporetto:* Rialto (from the north side of the Ponte Rialto, walk straight ahead through the stalls and market vendors; at the corner of Banca di Roma, go 1 more short block and turn right; the hotel is halfway down the narrow street). **Amenities:** Babysitting; concierge; smoke-free rooms. *In room:* A/C (top floor only), hair dryer.

IN SANTA CROCE
Moderate
Hotel San Cassiano Ca'Favretto ★★ Call this place a moderate splurge choice, which gets two stars for its location and views. About half the rooms look across the Grand Canal to the gorgeous Ca' d'Oro (accounting for the highest rates listed below) and tend to be larger than the others, most of which open onto a side canal. Built into a 16th-century palace, the hotel is steeped in dusty old-world elegance, with Murano chandeliers (but no elevator). The rooms are outfitted in modest, dark-wood 1970s-style faux antiques. The breakfast room is done in 18th-century-style pastels and stuccoes— get to breakfast early to snag one of the two tiny tables on the wide balcony overlooking the Grand Canal. There's also a wood-beam bar and TV lounge with a canal-view window and a few small tables on the private boat launch where you can sip an *aperitivo* in the evening and gaze at the Ca' d'Oro.

Santa Croce 2232 (Calle della Rosa), 30135 Venezia. ℭ **041-524-1768.** Fax 041-721-033. www.san cassiano.it. 35 units. 299€ double; 319€ superior double; 399 double with Grand Canal view. Rates include breakfast. AE, DC, MC, V. *Vaporetto:* San Stae (turn left to cross in front of the church, take the bridge over the side canal and turn right; then turn left, cross another canal, turn right, and then left again; cross yet another canal and turn right, then immediately left and then left again toward the Grand Canal and the hotel). **Amenities:** Bar; babysitting; concierge; room service; smoke-free rooms; Wi-Fi. *In room:* A/C, TV, hair dryer, minibar.

Inexpensive
Hotel Ai Due Fanali ★★ (Finds) Ai Due Fanali's 16th-century altar-turned-reception-desk is your first clue that this is the hotel of choice for lovers of aesthetics with impeccable taste but restricted budgets. The hotel is located on a quiet square in the residential Santa Croce area, a 10-minute walk across the Grand Canal from the train station but a good 20-minute stroll from the Rialto Bridge. Signora Marina Stea and her daughter Stefania have beautifully restored a part of the 14th-century *scuola* of the Church of San Simeon Grando with their innate *buon gusto,* which is evident wall-to-wall, from the lobby furnished with period pieces to the third-floor breakfast terrace with a glimpse of the Grand Canal. Guest rooms boast headboards painted by local artisans, high-quality bed linens, chrome and gold bathroom fixtures, and good, fluffy towels. Prices drop considerably from November 8 through March 30 with the exception of Christmas week and Carnevale. Ask about the four classy waterfront apartments with a view (and kitchenette), near Vivaldi's Church (La Pietà) east of Piazza San Marco, which sleep four to five people.

Santa Croce 946 (Campo San Simeone Profeta), 30125 Venezia. ℭ **041-718-490.** Fax 041-718-344. www. aiduefanali.com. 20 units. 95€–230€ double; 185€–380€ apt. (minimum 3-day stay). Rates include break-fast, though not at apartments. AE, MC, V. Closed most of Jan. *Vaporetto:* A 10-min. walk from the train station, or get off at the Riva di Biasio stop. **Amenities** (at hotel only): Bar; concierge; room service. *In room:* A/C, TV, hair dryer, minibar, Wi-Fi.

Expect most (but not all) of the least expensive suggestions to be in or near the train-station neighborhood, an area full of trinket shops and budget hotels. It's comparatively charmless (though safe), and in the high season it's wall-to-wall with tourists who window-shop their way to Piazza San Marco, an easy half-hour to 45-minute stroll away. *Vaporetto* connections from the train station are convenient.

Expensive

Hotel Bellini ★   By far the classiest hotel I'm listing near the train station, the Bellini is convenient if you have an early train. Though mere steps away from the station, it's well insulated from the neighborhood's tourist bustle. Rooms are midsize to large, with high ceilings (some stuccoed), done in a rich 19th-century decor with modern amenities. Several on the front have views of the Grand Canal, some from small balconies. Junior suites on the canal side are great for families—each comes with a loft with twin beds and its own bathroom and TV. Most "deluxe" rooms come with a view; those that do not are larger and nicer by way of compensation. Special offers can sometimes bring rates below even the lower prices listed below, depending on the time of year and availability.

Cannaregio 116A (Lista di Spagna), 30121 Venezia. ℂ **041-524-2488.** Fax 041-715-193. www.bellini. boscolohotels.com. 97 units. 295€–420€ superior double; 320€–440€ deluxe double; 310€–420€ junior suite. Rates include buffet breakfast. AE, DC, MC, V. *Vaporetto:* Ferrovia (turn left from the *vaporetto*—or right if you're exiting the train station—to walk down Lista di Spagna). **Amenities:** Bar; babysitting; concierge; Internet; room service; smoke-free rooms. *In room:* A/C, TV, hair dryer, minibar.

Moderate

Hotel Adua   It's not pretty, but it's cheap (for Venice), conveniently located near the station, clean, and very well run. Owned by the Adua family, who has been in the low-end hotel business for more than 30 years, this hotel has largish rooms with contemporary wood furnishings painted pale green. At an independent *palazzo* across the street, the six refurbished rooms (with a shared bathroom, TV, or air-conditioning) cost 20% less.

Cannaregio 233A (on Lista di Spagna), 30121 Venezia. ℂ **041-716-184.** Fax 041-244-0162. www.adua hotel.com. 13 units, 9 with private bathroom. 85€ double with shared bathroom; 130€ double with private bathroom. Off-season rates 10%–15% less. Breakfast not included. AE, DC, MC, V. *Vaporetto:* Ferrovia (exit train station and turn left onto Lista di Spagna). **Amenities:** Bar; concierge; room service. *In room:* A/C, TV, hair dryer.

Hotel Giorgione ★★ (Finds)   Original columns and huge wood beams decorate the salons off the reception area of this 16th-century *palazzo.* The best rooms overlook the private brick courtyard, a shaded breakfast nook with a small, decorative pool, a hushed oasis save for the splashing of the fountain. "Standard" rooms are carpeted, with an early-19th-century style. In "superior" rooms, some beds have a small canopy curtain at the head, others are slightly lofted above the sitting area and flanked by twisting columns; some furnishings are 18th-century Venetian reproductions refreshingly done in brighter modern hues (in fact, each room follows its own, overwhelmingly strict, color scheme). Suites, with midsize sitting rooms and bedrooms, are done in a vaguely romantic style— matching embroidered fabrics, half-testers, and the like. No. 105 has a great private flower-fringed terrace.

Cannaregio 4587 (Campo SS. Apostoli), 30131 Venezia. ℂ **041-522-5810.** Fax 041-523-9092. www. hotelgiorgione.com. 76 units. 170€–285€ standard double; 190€–340€ superior double; 245€–370€ junior suite; 250€–390€ suite. Rates include buffet breakfast. AE, DC, MC, V. *Vaporetto:* Ca' d'Oro (walk straight up Calle Ca' d'Oro and turn right onto broad Strada Nuova, which ends in Campo SS; Apostoli is

Inexpensive

Albergo Santa Lucia   Bordered by roses, oleander, and ivy, the flagstone patio/ter-
race of this contemporary building is a lovely place to enjoy breakfast, with coffee and
tea brought to the table in sterling silver pots. The kindly owner, Emilia Gonzato, her
son Gianangelo, and his wife, Alessandra, oversee everything with pride, and it shows:
The large rooms are simple but bright and clean, with modular furnishings and a print
or pastel to brighten things up.

Cannaregio 358 (on Calle della Misericordia), 30121 Venezia. ✆ **041-715-180.** Fax 041-710-610. www.
hotelslucia.com. 18 units, 12 with private bathroom. 50€–90€ double with shared bathroom, 70€–115€
double with private bathroom; 90€–145€ triple with private bathroom. Rates include continental breakfast. AE, DC, MC, V. Generally closed Dec 15–Feb 15. *Vaporetto:* Ferrovia (exit the train station, turn left
onto Lista di Spagna, and take the 2nd left onto Calle della Misericordia). **Amenities:** Concierge; Internet;
room service. *In room:* A/C, TV, hair dryer (on request).

Hotel Bernardi-Semenzato ★★★ (Value) (Kids)   Don't be misled by the weather-
worn exterior of this *palazzo;* inside, there are exposed hand-hewn ceiling beams, air-
conditioned rooms outfitted with antique-style headboard/spread sets, and bright
modern bathrooms. The enthusiastic, young English-speaking owners, Maria Teresa and
Leonardo Pepoli, offer three-star style at one-star rates (prices get even better in the off
season). The *dépendance* (annex), 3 blocks away, offers you the chance to feel as if you've
rented an aristocratic apartment, with parquet floors and Murano chandeliers—room no.
5 is on a corner with a beam ceiling and fireplace, and no. 6 (a family-perfect two-room suite)
looks out on the confluence of two canals, and no. 2 overlooks the lovely garden of a
palazzo next door. The Pepolis also opened yet another annex nearby consisting of just
four rooms, all done in a Venetian style, including one large family suite (two guest
rooms, one of which can sleep four, with a common bathroom).

Cannaregio 4366 (on Calle de l'Oca), 30121 Venezia. ✆ **041-522-7257.** Fax 041-522-2424. www.hotel
bernardi.com; for annex, www.locandaleo.it. Hotel: 18 units, 11 with private bathroom. Main annex 7
units. New annex 6 units. *Frommer's* readers take 8% off these official rates: 70€ double with shared
bathroom; 110€ double with private bathroom; 90€ triple with shared bathroom; 118€ triple with private
bathroom; 100€ quad with shared bathroom; 150€ quad with private bathroom. Rates include breakfast.
AE, DC, MC, V. *Vaporetto:* Ca' d'Oro (walk straight ahead to Strada Nova, turn right toward Campo SS.
Apostoli; in the campo, take 1st side street on your left, which is Calle de l'Oca). **Amenities:** Babysitting
(on request); concierge; room service; Wi-Fi. *In room:* A/C, TV, hair dryer.

Hotel Dolomiti ★   For those who prefer to stay near the train station, this is an old-
fashioned, reliable choice. Because it has large and clean but ordinary rooms spread over
four floors (no elevator), your chances of finding availability are better here, one of the
larger places I suggest. It's been in the Basardelli family for generations—the current head
manager, Graziella, was even born in a second-floor room—and they and their efficient
staff supply dining suggestions, umbrellas when necessary, and big smiles after a long day
of sightseeing. Rooms with shared bathrooms always come with sinks.

Cannaregio 72–74 (on Calle Priuli ai Cavalletti), 30121 Venezia. ✆ **041-715-113** or 041-719-983. Fax 041-
716-635. www.hoteldolomiti-ve.it. 32 units, 22 with private bathroom. 70€–110€ double with shared
bathroom; 100€–180€ double with private bathroom; 90€–120€ triple with shared bathroom; 135€–210€
triple with private bathroom. Extra bed, add 20%. Inquire about off-season discounts. Rates include continental breakfast. MC, V. Closed Nov 15–Jan 31. *Vaporetto:* Ferrovia (exit train station, turn left onto Lista di
Spagna, and take 1st left onto Calle Priuli). **Amenities:** Bar; concierge. *In room:* A/C (in some), hair dryer.

VENICE

5

WHERE TO STAY

Hotel San Geremia ★★ (Finds)   If this gem of a two-star hotel had an elevator and was in San Marco, it would cost twice as much and still be worth it. Consider yourself lucky to get one of the tastefully renovated rooms—ideally, one of the seven overlooking the *campo* (better yet, one of three top-floor rooms with small terraces). The rooms have blond-wood paneling with built-in headboards and closets, or whitewashed walls with deep-green or burnished rattan headboards and matching chairs. The small bathrooms offer hair dryers and heated towel racks, and rooms with shared bathrooms have been renovated. Everything is overseen by an English-speaking staff and the owner/manager Claudio, who'll give you helpful tips and free passes to the winter Casino.

Cannaregio 290A (on Campo San Geremia), 30121 Venezia. ℂ **041-716-245.** Fax 041-524-2342. 20 units, 14 with private bathroom. 55€–85€ double with shared bathroom; 85€–125€ double with private bathroom. Rates include breakfast. AE, DC, MC, V. *Vaporetto:* Ferrovia (exit the train station, turn left onto Lista di Spagna, and continue to Campo San Geremia). **Amenities:** Babysitting; concierge; room service. *In room:* TV, hair dryer.

ON GIUDECCA

You don't stay on Giudecca—the only one of Venice's main islands you must access by boat—for the atmosphere, the sights, or the hotel scene (though it does host the official IYH Hostel, an utterly average hostel that's terribly inconvenient, especially with its curfew). You come for only two reasons: the Cipriani and the new Palladio Hotel and Spa.

Very Expensive

Hotel Cipriani ★★★   Long regarded as Venice's top hotel, the Cipriani is a gorgeously elegant inn set into a string of Renaissance-era buildings on 1.2 hectares (3 acres) at the tip of Giudecca. Although by staying here you give up a central location and easy access to central Venice's sights, shops, and restaurants (it's a 10-min. boat ride to Piazza San Marco), that's the whole point: The Cipriani is a gilded retreat. The hotel was opened in 1959 by Giuseppe Cipriani, who founded Harry's Bar and Torcello's Locanda Cipriani, and was such a good buddy to Ernest Hemingway that he appeared in one of the master's novels *(Across the River and into the Trees).* Room decor varies greatly, from full-bore 18th-century Venetian to discreetly contemporary, but all are among Venice's most stylish accommodations. The amenities-filled rooms overlook some combination of the gardens and Olympic-size pool, the lagoon, San Giorgio Maggiore, and St. Mark's Square across the wide mouth of the Grand Canal. The 15th-century Palazzo Vendramin annex, connected via a garden, is for guests who desire more privacy (not unusual, given their celebrity guest list), a more homelike feel, and a private butler.

Giudecca 10, 30133 Venezia. ℂ **041-520-7744.** Fax 041-520-3930. www.hotelcipriani.com. 95 units. Hotel Cipriani: 690€–920€ standard double; 820€–1,350€ superior double; 910€–1,525€ deluxe double; 1,330€–1,950€) standard junior suite; 1,490€–2,300€ deluxe junior suite; 1,810€–2,700€ standard suite; 2,300€–3,150€ superior suite; 2,950€–4,750€ deluxe suite; 3rd person 200€; 5,300€–8,000€ Palladio suite with 1 bedroom; 7,000€–9,950€ Palladio suite with 2 bedrooms. Rates include full American breakfast. AE, DC, MC, V. Closed Nov 2–Apr 11. *Vaporetto:* Zitelle. **Amenities:** 3 restaurants (excellent Italian Cipriani w/lagoon views, bar eatery, poolside lunch); 3 bars; babysitting; courtesy boat (back and forth to Piazza San Marco 24 hr.); concierge; docking facilities; golf course; exercise room; Olympic-size outdoor pool; room service; sauna; spa; indoor tennis courts. *In room:* A/C, TV/VCR (free movies), fax (on request), hair dryer, kitchenette (only in junior suites and suites of the Palazzo Vendramin), minibar, Wi-Fi.

Palladio Hotel & Spa ★★   Francesca Bortolotto Possati, owner of the Hotel Bauer/Bauer il Palazzo (p. 111), opened the Palladio Hotel & Spa in 2006 almost adjacent to the Cipriani, giving the venerable hotel some competition. Venice can seem a long way off from here as you immerse yourself in what seems to be another world, but with a solar-powered shuttle boat (free for clients of any of the three Bauer hotels) continually running back and forth between the Hotel Bauer and the Palladio, you are just minutes away from San Marco. There are few other places in Venice—the only one that comes to mind is the Cipriani next door—where you can relax as completely as you can here and yet quickly be in the midst of it all. The hotel is located in what was a crumbling 16th-century convent designed by Palladio. All rooms are spacious; the rooms with the garden views are relaxing, but as long as you are splurging, you may want to opt for a lagoon-view room, where you will be afforded stunning views of the bell tower in Piazza San Marco.

Giudecca 33, 30133 Venezia. ✆ **041-520-7022.** Fax 041-520-7557. www.palladiohotelspa.com. 50 units (13 are suites). 750€ double; 930€ double with lagoon view; 1,050€ junior suite; 1,350€ junior suite with lagoon view; 1,200€ suite; 1,570€ suite with lagoon view. Continental breakfast 18€. AE, DC, MC, V. Closed Nov–Apr. *Vaporetto:* Zitelle. **Amenities:** Venetian/Mediterranean restaurant; bar; babysitting; courtesy boat (back and forth to the Hotel Bauer); concierge; Jacuzzi; room service; sauna; spa w/massage and facial; smoke-free rooms. *In room:* A/C, TV, hair dryer, minibar, Wi-Fi.

ON THE LIDO

The Lido offers an entirely different Venice experience. The city is relatively close at hand, but you're really here to stay at an Italian beach resort and day-trip into the city for sightseeing. Although there are a few lower-end, moderately priced hotels here, they are entirely beside the point of the Lido and its jet-set reputation.

If you are looking for a more reasonable option—and one that's open year-round—check out the modern **Hotel Belvedere,** Piazzale Santa Maria Elisabetta 4 (✆ **041-526-0115;** fax 041-526-1486; www.belvedere-venezia.com). It's right across from the *vaporetto* stop, has been in the same family for nearly 150 years, and sports a pretty good restaurant and a free beach cabana. It charges 80€ to 311€ for a double.

Very Expensive

Hotel Excelsior ★★★ The Excelsior is the first place most celebs phone for film festival or Biennale accommodations. The hotel was the first successful attempt to turn the grassy wilds between the Lido's fishing villages into a bathing resort. Its core was built a century ago in a faux-Moorish style, with horseshoe arches peeking out all over; lots of huge, ornate salons and banquet halls; and a fountain-studded Arabian-style garden. As a purpose-built hotel, the rooms were cut quite large, with nice big bathrooms. Standard rooms keep the Moorish look going, with latticework doors, richly patterned wall fabrics, flamboyant bentwood headboards, and tented ceilings. Even if you don't have a sea view from your balcony, you might overlook the gorgeous garden or the private boat launch. Even junior-level suites are huge, with sitting areas, an entrance hall, and double sinks. A modern bar spills onto a large terrace overlooking the beach.

Lungarno Marconi 41, 30126 Venezia Lido. ✆ **041-526-0201.** Fax 041-526-7276. www.hotelexcelsior venezia.com. 197 units. 920€ double; 1,020€ double with sea or lagoon view; 2,100€ junior suite; 3,500€ sea-view suite. Rates include buffet breakfast. AE, DC, MC, V. Closed mid-Oct to mid-Mar. *Vaporetto:* Lido, then bus A. **Amenities:** 3 restaurants (Venetian/international terrace restaurant for dinner, lunch restaurants poolside and at beach); 2 bars; babysitting; bikes; courtesy boat (from airport and from central Venice); children's program; concierge; executive-level rooms; exercise room (at sister Hotel des Bains, nearby); special rates at nearby golf course; outdoor pool; room service; smoke-free rooms; outdoor lighted tennis courts; watersports equipment/rentals; Wi-Fi. *In room:* A/C, TV w/pay movies, hair dryer, minibar.

Expensive

Hotel des Bains ★★★ Its sister, Hotel Excelsior (see above), may be the last word in luxury on Lido, but the Belle Epoque Hotel des Bains beats it for sheer style, with its creaky, polished-wood floors and high, airy salons scattered with Oriental rugs. Not for nothing did Des Bains *habitué* Thomas Mann set his dreamy, decadent *Death in Venice* (and Visconti filmed it) here. The large rooms are fitted with the original, discreetly elegant, if worn, furnishings. Definitely ask for a sea-view room, since that's what the Lido is all about, though there's nothing wrong with pool- or parkview rooms. When the wood-paneled, two-story banquet room is not being used for a conference, you can take tea there or out on the broad tiled Pompeian terrace opening off it. There's a private beach across the street, connected by a tunnel, but unfortunately, you have to pay for access.

Lungomare Marconi 17, 30126 Venezia Lido. (℃ **041-526-5921.** Fax 041-526-0113. www.grandhotel debainsvenezia.com. 191 units. 710€ double with garden view; 845€ double with sea view; 1,205€ junior suite; 1,390€ suite with sea view. Rates include buffet breakfast. AE, DC, MC, V. Closed Oct–Feb. *Vaporetto:* Lido, then bus A. **Amenities:** Elegant Venetian/Italian restaurant; bar; babysitting; bikes; courtesy boat (from airport, to Excelsior, and from central Venice); children's program; concierge; exercise room; special rates at nearby golf course; 2 outdoor pools (May–Sept); room service; smoke-free rooms; spa; outdoor tennis courts; watersports equipment/rentals; Wi-Fi. *In room:* A/C, TV w/pay movies, hair dryer, minibar.

4 WHERE TO DINE

Eating cheaply in Venice is not easy, though it's by no means impossible. So plan well and don't rely on the serendipity that may serve you in other cities. If you've qualified for a Rolling Venice card, ask for the discount guide listing dozens of restaurants offering 10% to 30% discounts for cardholders. Bear in mind that, compared with Rome and other points south, Venice is a city of early meals: You should be seated by 7:30 to 8:30pm. Most kitchens close at 10 or 10:30pm, even though the restaurant may stay open until 11:30pm or midnight.

BUDGET DINING   Pizza is the fuel of Naples, and bruschetta and *crostini* (small, open-face sandwiches) the rustic soul food of Florence. In Venice it's *tramezzini*—small, triangular white-bread half-sandwiches filled with everything from thinly sliced meats and tuna salad to cheeses and vegetables; and *cicchetti* (tapaslike finger foods such as calamari rings, speared fried olives, potato croquettes, or grilled polenta squares), traditionally washed down with a small glass of wine, or *ombra* ("some shade from the sun"). Venice offers countless neighborhood bars called *bacari* and cafes where you can stand or sit with a *tramezzino,* a selection of *cicchetti,* a *panino* (sandwich on a roll), or a *toast* (grilled ham and cheese sandwich). All of the above will cost approximately 1.50€ to 4€ if you stand at the bar, as much as double when seated. Bar food is displayed on the countertop or in glass counters and usually sells out by late afternoon, so don't rely on it for a light dinner, though light lunches are a delight. A concentration of popular, well-stocked bars can be found along the Mercerie shopping strip that connects Piazza San Marco with the Rialto Bridge, the always lively Campo San Luca (look for **Bar Torino, Bar Black Jack,** or the character-filled **Leon Bianco** wine bar), and Campo Santa Margherita. Avoid the tired-looking pizza (revitalized only marginally by microwaves) you'll find in most bars; informal sit-down neighborhood pizzerias everywhere offer savory and far fresher renditions for a minimum of 4€, plus your drink and cover charge—the perfect lunch or light dinner.

CULINARY DELIGHTS   Venice has a distinguished culinary history, much of it based on its geographical position on the sea and, to a lesser degree, its historical ties with the Orient. You'll see things on Venetian menus you won't see elsewhere, together with local versions of time-tested Italian favorites. For first courses, both pasta and risotto (more liquidy in the Veneto than usual) are commonly prepared with fish or seafood: Risotto

Fishy Business

Eating a meal based on the day's catch (restaurants are legally bound to print on the menu when the fish is frozen) will be a treat but never inexpensive. Keep in mind that the price indicated on the menu commonly refers to *l'etto* (per 100g), a fraction of the full cost (have the waiter estimate the full cost before ordering); larger fish are intended to feed two. Also, avoid splurging on fish or seafood on Mondays, when the Fish Market is closed (as are most self-respecting fish-serving restaurants). Those restaurants open on Mondays will be serving you fish bought on Saturday.

alla sepie or *alla seppioline* (tinted black by the ink of cuttlefish, also called *risotto nero* or black risotto) or *spaghetti alle vongole* or *alle vorace* (with clams; clams without their shells are not a good sign!) are two commonly found specialties. Both appear with *frutti di mare,* "fruit of the sea," which can be a little bit of whatever shellfish looked good at the market that morning. *Bigoli,* homemade pasta of whole wheat, is not commonly found elsewhere, while creamy polenta, often served with *gamberetti* (small shrimp) or tiny shrimp called *schie,* or as an accompaniment to *fegato alla veneziana* (calves' liver with onions Venetian style), is a staple of the Veneto. Some of the fish and seafood dishes they do particularly well include *branzino* (a kind of sea bass), *rombo* (turbot or brill), *moeche* (small soft-shelled crab) or *granseola* (crab), and *sarde in saor* (sardines in a sauce of onion, vinegar, pine nuts, and raisins).

From a host of good local wines, try the dry white Tocai and pinot from the Friuli region and the light, champagnelike *prosecco* that Venetians consume almost like a soft drink (it is the base of Venice's famous Bellini drink made with white peach purée). Popular red wines include merlot, cabernet, Raboso, and Refosco. The quintessentially Italian Bardolino, Valpolicella, and Soave are from the nearby Veneto area. *Grappa,* the local firewater, is an acquired taste and is often offered in a dozen variations. Neighborhood *bacari* wine bars provide the chance to taste the fruits of leading wine producers in the grape-rich regions of the Veneto and neighboring Friuli.

IN SAN MARCO
Very Expensive
Antico Martini ★★ VENETIAN/INTERNATIONAL   One of Venice's top restaurants started out in 1720 as a cafe, and the Baldi family has since 1921 retained its airy, clubby atmosphere, especially at the outdoor tables in summertime. Venetian specialties such as *risotto di frutti di mare* and *fegato alla Veneziana* are prepared perfectly here, but the food, reputation, and location across from the opera house all come at a stiff price. If you want to dine as if you were at a classic Italian wedding, then try the tasting menu, which comes with both a fish and meat secondo broken up by a lemon sorbet. The price of the tasting menu might not even seem that expensive when you consider you probably won't have to dine for the next 24 hours. They also run a piano bar nearby at San Marco 2007 Wednesday through Monday from 10pm.

Campo San Fantin (on the square occupied by La Fenice opera house). ℂ **041-522-4121.** www.antico martini.com. Reservations required. Primi 19€–28€; secondi 24€–40€; fixed-price tasting menu 110€. AE,

VENICE

5

WHERE TO DINE

VENICE

5 WHERE TO DINE

DC, MC, V. Daily noon–midnight. *Vaporetto:* Santa Maria del Gilgio (walk up into Campo Santa Maria Zobenigo, turn right to cross the footbridge; the road on the other side makes a sharp left, and then right to open into the Calle Larga/Via XXII Marzo; turn left up Calle delle Veste into Campo San Fantin).

Do Forni ★★ VENETIAN/INTERNATIONAL

The dining rooms in this place have a split personality: The main room is decorated country style—perhaps a throwback to its origins as a monastic bakery—and the front room does its best to imitate an *Orient Express* car. The food is purely Venetian, with a huge menu that promises all the bounty of the sea, along with select specialties from world cooking. It's not cheap, though. Do Forni keeps busy, and the bustling sometimes detracts from the posh atmosphere.

San Marco 468 (Calle dei Specchieri). © **041-523-2148.** www.doforni.it. Reservations required. Primi 19€–25€; secondi 27€–39€. AE, DC, MC, V. Daily noon–3pm and 7–11pm. *Vaporetto:* San Marco (walk through Piazza San Marco and around the left flank of the basilica into Piazzetta dei Leoncini; take the 3rd left and continue straight across Calle Larga San Marco).

La Cusina ★★ MODERN VENETIAN

Excepting maybe the Cipriani, newcomer La Cusina is the only hotel restaurant in Venice that deserves singling out on its own. The service is stellar, and the seating is in that most sought-after of spots: a terrace right on the Grand Canal overlooking floodlit Santa Maria della Salute across the water. They reserve a page in the menu for dishes made fresh from what the chef found that morning at the market. You may find ravioli stuffed with sea bass in a light cream sauce with wild fennel; *maltalgiati* noodles in a duck and truffle ragù; or rabbit saddle with sun-dried tomatoes and grilled leeks.

San Marco 2159 (in the Westin Hotel Europa & Regina off Via XXII Marzo). © **041-240-0001.** Reservations highly recommended. Primi 23€–28€; secondi 38€–46€. AE, DC, MC, V. Daily 7–10:30am, 12–2:30pm, and 7:30–10pm. *Vaporetto:* San Marco (head west out of the southwest corner of Piazza San Marco down Saliz San Mose; cross the bridge to continue straight on Calle Larga XXII Marzo; you'll see hotel signs directing you down the alleyways to the left).

Ristorante Quadri ★ VENETIAN

Dine by candlelight with a view across St. Mark's Square. That's the selling point of this restaurant, which is almost kitschily romantic—a single red rose, silver dish lids removed with a flourish, threadbare velvet benches, pop ballads by Andrea Bocelli, silk wall coverings, and painted wood ceilings, all in dusty rose shades. The cooking is good, if generally uninspired, and service can be a little sour and short. But the place has got history: In 1725, Giorgio Quadri, from Corfu, and his wife bought this spot and started serving "khava," a dark, caffeinated Turkish drink served hot. As such, "cafes" became popular—the restaurant sits above an elegant, still-functioning cafe—Austrian officers made the Quadri their hangout; Italians preferred the Florian across the way. Definitely call ahead—if possible, a few days in advance—to get one of the few tables next to a window so you can get that view; otherwise, it's really not worth the prices.

Piazza San Marco 120. © **041-522-2105** or 041-528-9299. www.quadrivenice.com. Reservations highly recommended. Primi 19€–26€; secondi 24€–49€. AE, DC, MC, V. Tues–Sun noon–2:30pm and 7–10:30pm. *Vaporetto:* San Marco (it's on the north side of the square).

Vini da Arturo ★★ (Finds) VENETIAN

This narrow dining room has long been one of my favorite hidden gems in Venice (and it is, indeed, very hard to find), even if prices have skyrocketed over the past several years. Aside from the friendly service (the owner usually sits and chats with the last few diners at the end of the evening) and excellent cooking, this place sells itself on being perhaps the only restaurant in Venice with no seafood. Primi are limited and often targeted toward vegetarians—spaghetti with tomatoes and artichokes, or *alla siciliana* with mozzarella, eggplant, and tomatoes—but they are perfectly **133** prepared. Mostly it is known for its meats, such as *stracetti di filetto alla rucola* (beef strips tossed with arugula), *filetto al pepe verde* (steak in a green-peppercorn sauce), and veal scaloppine. It has fewer than 10 tables, so book ahead, and remember to bring lots of cash, since credit cards aren't accepted here.

San Marco 3656A (Calle degli Assassini). ℂ **041-528-6974.** Reservations highly recommended. Primi 12€–18€; secondi 25€–36€. No credit cards. Mon–Sat noon–3pm and 7–10:30pm. Closed for a week in Aug. *Vaporetto:* Sant'Angelo, Rialto.

Expensive

Le Bistrot de Venise ★★★ VENETIAN/FRENCH   This relaxed spot offers indoor and outdoor seating, young English-speaking waiters, and a varied, eclectic menu. It's a popular meeting spot for Venetians and young artists, and you're made to feel welcome to sit and write postcards over a cappuccino, enjoy a simple lunch of risotto and salad, or dine when most of Venice is shutting down. Linger over an elaborate meal that may include local favorites like *figa' de vedelo a la venexiana* (Venetian calves' liver) or the odd *morete a la caorlotta* (tagliolini made with cocoa, topped with a festival of crustaceans), or unique dishes made from historic 15th-century Venetian recipes or a classic French cookbook. Peek in the back room to see what's going on in the evening—the place hosts art exhibits, wine tasting, and poetry readings.

San Marco 4687 (on Calle dei Fabbri), below the Albergo al Gambero. ℂ **041-523-6651.** www.bistrotde venise.com. Reservations not necessary. Primi 19€–24€; secondi 27€–34€; classic Venetian tasting menu 45€; historical Venetian menu 65€. AE, MC, V. Daily noon–1am. Usually closes Dec. 10–25. *Vaporetto:* Rialto (turn right along canal, cross small footbridge over Rio San Salvador, turn left onto Calle Bembo, which becomes Calle dei Fabbri; Bistrot is about 5 blocks ahead in the direction of St. Mark's Sq.).

Trattoria da Fiore ★★ VENETIAN/TRATTORIA   Don't confuse this laid-back trattoria with the expensive Osteria da Fiore. You might not eat better here, but it'll seem that way when your relatively modest bill arrives. Start with the house specialty, the *pennette alla Fiore* for two (with olive oil, garlic, and seven in-season vegetables), and you may be happy to call it a night. Or try the *frittura mista,* over a dozen varieties of fresh fish and seafood. This is a great place to snack or make a light lunch out of *cicchetti* at the Bar Fiore next door (10:30am–10:30pm).

San Marco 3461 (on Calle delle Botteghe). ℂ **041-523-5310.** Reservations recommended. Primi 12€–19€; secondi 14€–25€. AE, MC, V. Wed–Mon noon–3pm and 7–10pm. Closed 2 weeks in Jan and 2 weeks in Aug. *Vaporetto:* Accademia (cross bridge to San Marco side and walk straight ahead to Campo Santo Stefano; exit *campo* at northern end, take a left at Bar/Gelateria Paolin onto Calle delle Botteghe).

Moderate

Osteria alle Botteghe ITALIAN   Casual, easy on the palate, not too hard on the wallet (by Venetian standards), and even easy to find (again, for Venice), this is a decent choice for pizza, a light snack, or an elaborate meal. You can have stand-up *cicchetti* and sandwiches at the bar or window-side counter, while more serious diners head to the tables in back to enjoy the pizzas, pastas, or *tavola calda,* a glass counter–enclosed buffet of prepared dishes like eggplant *parmigiana,* lasagna, and fresh-cooked vegetables in season, reheated when you order.

San Marco 3454 (on Calle delle Botteghe, off Campo Santo Stefano). ℂ **041-522-8181.** www.ristorante lafeluca.com/allebotteghe/ristorante.htm. Reservations not necessary. Pizza and primi 6€–12€; secondi 8€–25€; menu turistico 15€. DC, MC, V. Mon–Sat 11am–11pm; open Sun in high season. *Vaporetto:* Accademia or Sant'Angelo (find your way to Campo Santo Stefano by following stream of people or asking; take narrow Calle delle Botteghe at Gelateria Paolin [in northwest corner] across from Santo Stefano).

Family-Friendly Restaurants

Ai Tre Spiedi (p. 135)   There's nothing in particular that flags this as kid-friendly, but its genial atmosphere, friendly service, and good cookin' make it welcoming for families. Admittedly, most tables are taken by couples.

Da Sandro (p. 139)   This place offers good pizza and pasta, seating outdoors, and low prices. What more can you ask for?

Pizzeria ae Oche (p. 140)   If the kids are hankering for home and you (rightly) refuse to set foot in a McDonald's, this place is a good compromise; it serves great pizza and pumps rock music through the speakers, and even looks vaguely American—or at least trattoria–meets–Cracker Barrel.

Pizzeria/Trattoria al Vecio Canton (p. 137)   This spot offers plenty of seating, a good location near San Marco, low prices, and an extensive menu of both pastas and some of the best pizzas in Venice.

Rosticceria San Bartolomeo (p. 134)   There's not much that isn't served at this big, efficient, and bustling fast-food *emporio* in the Rialto Bridge area. Much of it is displayed in glass cases to pique the fussy appetite, and you won't raise any eyebrows if you eat too little, too much, or at hours when the natives have either finished or haven't yet started.

Taverna San Trovaso (p. 138)   Here you'll find a bustling atmosphere, good-natured waiters, and a lengthy menu that covers all sorts of dishes and pizzas to please finicky youngsters and more adventurous palates alike. Good value-priced menus, too.

VENICE

5

WHERE TO DINE

Ristorante Teatro Goldoni ITALIAN/INTERNATIONAL/FAST FOOD   Bright and modern (though it has been here for over 50 years), this showcase of Venetian-style fast food tries to be everything: bar, cafe, *rosticceria,* and *tavola calda* (hot foods deli) on the ground floor and a pizzeria upstairs. A variety of sandwiches and pastries beckons from a downstairs display counter, and another offers prepared foods (eggplant *parmigiana,* roast chicken, *pasta e fagioli,* lasagna) that'll be reheated when ordered; there are also a dozen pasta choices. A number of combination salads are a welcome concession to the American set and are freshest and most varied for lunch. This won't be your most memorable meal in Venice, but you won't walk away hungry or broke.

San Marco 4747 (at the corner of Calle dei Fabbri). ⓒ **041-522-2446.** Reservations not accepted. Pizza and primi 7.50€–15€; secondi 9€–18€; menu turistico with meat 18€; menu turistico with fish [22]. AE, DC, V. Daily 9am–midnight. *Vaporetto:* Rialto (walk from San Marco side of bridge to Campo San Bartolomeo and exit it to your right in direction of Campo San Luca).

Rosticceria San Bartolomeo ★ Kids ITALIAN/DELI   With long hours and a central location, this refurbished old-timer is Venice's most popular *rosticceria,* so the continuous turnover guarantees fresh food. With a dozen pasta dishes and as many fish, seafood, and meat entrees, this place can satisfy most any culinary desire. Since the ready-made food is displayed under a glass counter, you don't have to worry about mistranslations—you'll know exactly what you're ordering. There's no *coperto* (cover charge) if you take your meal standing up or seated at the stools in the aroma-filled ground-floor eating area. If you prefer to linger, head to the dining hall upstairs, though it costs more and, frankly, for the money you can do much better elsewhere than this institutional setting.

San Marco 5424 (on Calle della Bissa). (© **041-522-3569.** Pizza and primi 5.80€–8€; secondi 10€–16€; *menù turistico* 8€–23€. Prices are about 20%–30% higher upstairs, and there is a discount if you order to take away. AE, MC, V. Daily 9:30am–10pm (until 3:30pm Mon). *Vaporetto:* Rialto (with bridge at your back on San Marco side of canal, walk straight ahead to Campo San Bartolomeo; take underpass slightly to your left marked SOTTOPORTEGO DELLA BISSA; you'll come across the *rosticceria* at 1st corner on your right; look for GISLON [its old name] above the entrance).

Inexpensive

Vino Vino ★★★ (Value WINE BAR/ITALIAN   Vino Vino is an informal wine-bar archetype serving simple, well-prepared food, but its biggest pull is the impressive selection of local and European wines sold by the bottle or glass. The Venetian specialties are written on a chalkboard but are also usually displayed at the glass counter. After placing your order, settle into one of about a dozen wooden tables squeezed into two storefront-style rooms. Credit the high-quality food to the fact that Vino Vino shares a kitchen (and an owner) with the eminent and expensive Antico Martini restaurant (p. 129) a few doors down. It's also a great spot for a leisurely self-styled wine tasting (around 3.50€ per glass), with great *cicchetti* bar food. At dinner the food often runs out around 10:30pm, so don't come too late.

San Marco 2007 (on Ponte delle Veste near La Fenice). (© **041-241-7688.** www.vinovino.co.it. Reservations not accepted. Primi 8€–12€; secondi 13€–16€. AE, DC, MC, V. Daily 11:30am–11:30pm. *Vaporetto:* San Marco (with your back to basilica, exit Piazza San Marco through arcade on far left side; keep walking straight, cross canal, and then take 2nd right, Calle delle Veste).

IN CANNAREGIO

Very Expensive

Fiaschetteria Toscana ★★ VENETIAN   One hundred years ago this was a Tuscan wine outlet and social center of the neighborhood, so the Busatto family couldn't very well change the name even if their cuisine is strictly traditional Venetian and fish based. Albino heads up the dining room, wife Mariuccia makes desserts, and son Stefano mans the kitchen. They care about quality here, draping choice San Daniele prosciutto over slices of ripe melon or figs, stuffing ravioli with seafood and coating it with a light parsley sauce, or tossing zucchini flowers with the scampi and homemade *tagliolini.* The *frittura della serenissima* mixes a fry of seafood, sole, zucchini, artichokes, shrimp, baby squid, and octopus.

Cannaregio 5719 (Salizzada San Giovanni). (© **041-528-5281.** www.fiaschetteriatoscana.it. Reservations recommended. Primi 13€–22€; secondi 15€–37€. AE, DC, MC, V. Closed the last week of July and the first 3 weeks of August. Thurs–Mon 12:30–2:30pm; Wed–Mon 7:30–10:30pm. *Vaporetto:* Rialto (from the *vaporetto* launch, walk left to the bridge, and then right down Salita Pio X to Campo San Bartolomeo; hang a left, past the post office and over a bridge, and the street becomes Salizzada San Giovanni).

Moderate

Ai Tre Spiedi ★★ (Kids VENETIAN   Once upon a time, Venetians brought their visiting friends here to make a *bella figura* (good impression) without breaking the bank, and then swore them to secrecy. Well, the secret is out, and the prices have surely crept up, roughly coinciding with a change in ownership in 2006. Still, it is a very pleasant setting and the meal is just as appetizing as ever in this small, casually elegant trattoria with great, fresh fish. (When a restaurant is filled exclusively with French tourists, you know the cuisine can't be bad.) Try the traditional *bisato in umido con polenta* (braised eel), or, for a less daring but excellent choice, you can't go wrong with the grilled *orata* (John Dory). This and Trattoria da Fiore (see above) are the most reasonable choices for an authentic Venetian dinner of fresh fish; careful ordering needn't mean much of a splurge, either.

Cannaregio 5906 (on Salizzada San Cazian). ✆ **041-520-8035.** Reservations not accepted. Primi 7€–10€; secondi 11€–20€; menu turistico 13€. AE, MC, V. Tues–Sat noon–3pm and 7–10pm; Sun 7–10pm. Closed July 20–Aug 10. *Vaporetto:* Rialto (on San Marco side of bridge, walk straight ahead to Campo San Bartolomeo and take a left, passing post office, Coin department store, and San Crisostomo; cross 1st bridge after church, turn right at shoe store onto Salizzada San Cazian).

Osteria da Robia ★★ VENETIAN   Located along a pleasant canal, this place oozes Venice. It offers various local favorites on the menu, such as numerous preparations of cod with polenta and fresh squid ink pasta. Weather permitting, insist on sitting outside, if at all possible, though the simple yet classic decor inside the restaurant will make for a pleasant dining experience as well. If you are outside, beware that 27m (90 ft.) away there is a bar that often features loud live music.

Cannaregio 2553 (Fondamenta della Misericordia). ✆ **041-524-4379.** Reservations highly recommended. Primi 8€–14€; secondi 16€–24€. MC, V. Tues–Sun 11am–3pm and 6–10pm. *Vaporetto:* San Marcuola (go around the church that's right at the stop, then go straight about 5 blocks until you get to the first bridge; cross and turn right on Fondamenta della Misericordia).

IN CASTELLO
Expensive

Al Covo ★★★ VENETIAN/SEAFOOD   For years this lovely restaurant has been deservingly popular with American food writers, putting it on the short list of every food-loving American tourist. There are nights when it seems you hear nothing but English spoken here. But this has never compromised the dining at this warm and welcoming spot, where the preparation of superfresh fish and an excellent selection of moderately priced wines is as commendable today—perhaps more so—as it was in its days of pretrendiness. Much of the tourist-friendly atmosphere can be credited to the naturally hospitable Diane Rankin, the co-owner and dessert whiz who hails from Texas. She will eagerly talk you through a wondrous fish-studded menu. Her husband, Cesare Benelli, is known for his infallible talent in the kitchen. Together they share an admirable dedication to their charming gem of a restaurant—the quality of an evening at Al Covo is tough to top in this town.

Castello 3968 (Campiello della Pescheria, east of Chiesa della Pietà in the Arsenale neighborhood). ✆ **041-522-3812.** www.ristorantealcovo.com. Reservations required. Primi 14€–22€; secondi 23€–35€; 47€ for menu with choice of 1 primo, 1 secondo, and dessert. MC, V. Fri–Tues 12:45–2pm and 7:30–10pm. Closed Dec 20–Jan 20 and 2 weeks in Aug. *Vaporetto:* Arsenale (walk a short way back in the direction of Piazza San Marco, turning right at the bar/cafe il Gabbiano; the restaurant is on your left; otherwise, it is an enjoyable 20-min. stroll along the waterfront Riva degli Schiavoni from Piazza San Marco, past the Chiesa della Pietà and the Metropole Hotel).

Da Aciugheta ★ VENETIAN/WINE BAR/PIZZERIA   A long block north of the chic Riva degli Schiavoni hotels lies one of Venice's best wine bars, expanded to include an elbow-to-elbow trattoria/pizzeria in back. Its name refers to the marinated anchovies that join other *cicchetti* lining the popular front bar of this friendly *bacaro,* where you can enjoy an excellent selection of Veneto and Italian wines by the glass. It's a good place for a light meal: A pasta and glass of wine (or pizza and beer) will do just fine. There's an unusually long list of half-bottles of wine, and an even more unusual nonsmoking room. Tables move out onto the small piazza when the warm weather moves in.

Castello 4357 (in Campo SS. Filippo e Giacomo east of Piazza San Marco). Ⓒ **041-522-4292.** Primi 7.50€–14€; secondi 13€–18€. MC, V. Daily 8am–midnight (closed sometimes Wed Nov–Mar). *Vaporetto:* San Zaccaria (walk north on Calle delle Rasse to Campo SS. Filippo e Giacomo).

Osteria alle Testiere ★★ VENETIAN/ITALIAN   The limited seating for just 24 savvy (and lucky) patrons at butcher paper–covered tables, the relaxed young staff, and the upbeat tavernlike atmosphere belie the seriousness of this informal *osteria*. This is a guaranteed choice if you are a foodie curious to experience the increasingly interesting Venetian culinary scene without going broke. Start with the carefully chosen wine list; any of the 90 labels can be ordered by the half-bottle. The delicious homemade *gnocchetti ai calamaretti* (with baby squid) makes a frequent appearance, as does the traditional "secondo" specialty *scampi alla busara,* in a "secret" recipe some of whose identifiable ingredients include tomato, cinnamon, and a dash of hot pepper. Cheese is a rarity in these parts, except for Alle Testiere's exceptional cheese platter.

Castello 5801 (on Calle del Mondo Novo off Salizzada San Lio). Ⓒ **041-522-7220.** www.osteri!alletestiere. it. Reservations required for each of 2 seatings. Primi 18€; secondi 25€ and many types of fish sold by weight. MC, V. Mon–Sat 2 seatings at 7 and 9:15pm. *Vaporetto:* Equidistant from either the Rialto or San Marco stops. Find the store-lined Salizzada San Lio (east of the Campo Santa Maria Formosa), and from there ask where to turn off on the Calle del Mondo Novo.

Ristorante Corte Sconta ★★ VENETIAN/SEAFOOD   The bare, simple decor doesn't hint at the trendiness of this out-of-the-way trattoria, nor at the high quality of its strictly seafood cuisine. The emphasis is on freshness here; they put the shrimp live on the grill. Seafood fans will want to make reservations here on their very first night to hang with the foodies, artists, and writers who patronize this hidden gem. There's seafood-studded spaghetti, risotti with scampi, and a great *frittura mista all'Adriatico* (mixed Adriatic seafood fry). In nice weather, you can dine under a canopy of grapevines in the courtyard.

Castello 3886 (Calle del Pestrin). Ⓒ **041-522-7024.** Reservations recommended. Primi 16€–18€; secondi 20€–25€. MC, V. Tues–Sat 11am–4pm and 7pm–midnight. Closed Jan 7–Feb 7 and July 15–Aug 15. *Vaporetto:* Arsenale (walk west along Riva degli Schiavoni and over the footbridge; turn right up Calle del Forno, and then as it crosses Calle va in Crosera, veer right up Calle del Pestrin where it branches to the left).

Moderate

Pizzeria/Trattoria al Vecio Canton (Kids) ITALIAN/PIZZA   Good pizza is hard to find in Venice, and I mean that in the literal sense. Tucked away in a northeast corner behind Piazza San Marco on a well-trafficked route connecting it with Campo Santa Maria Formosa, the Canton's wood-paneled tavernlike atmosphere and great pizzas are worth the time you'll spend looking for the place. There is a full trattoria menu as well, with a number of pasta and side dishes *(contorni)* of vegetables providing a palatable alternative.

Castello 4738a (at the corner of Ruga Giuffa). Ⓒ **041-528-5176.** Reservations not accepted. Primi and pizza 6€–11€; secondi 12€–20€. AE, DC, MC. Wed–Mon noon–2:30pm and 7–10:30pm. *Vaporetto:* San Zaccaria (from the Riva degli Schiavoni waterfront, walk straight ahead to Campo SS. Filippo e Giacomo, then right and continue east to Campo San Provolo; take a left on the Salizzada San Provolo, cross the 1st footbridge, and you'll find the pizzeria on the 1st corner on the left).

Trattoria alla Rivetta ★★ SEAFOOD/VENETIAN   Lively and frequented by gondoliers (always a clue of quality dining for the right price), merchants, and visitors

VENICE

5

WHERE TO DINE

drawn to its bonhomie and bustling popularity, this is one of the safer bets for genuine Venetian cuisine and company in the touristy San Marco area, a 10-minute walk east of the piazza. All sorts of fish—the specialty—decorate the window of this brightly lit place. Another good indicator: There's usually a short wait, even in the off season.

Castello 4625 (on Salizzada San Provolo). ✆ **041-528-7302.** Reservations recommended. Primi 8€–10€; secondi 10€–15€. AE, MC, V. Tues–Sun noon–2:30pm and 7–10pm. *Vaporetto:* San Zaccaria (with your back to water and facing Hotel Savoia e Jolanda, walk straight ahead to Campo SS. Filippo e Giacomo; trattoria is tucked away next to a bridge off the right side of *campo*).

Inexpensive

Trattoria da Remigio ★★ ⓥalue ITALIAN/VENETIAN   Famous for its straight-forward renditions of Adriatic classics, Remigio is the kind of place where you can order simple *gnocchi alla pescatora* (homemade gnocchi in tomato-based seafood sauce) or *frittura mista* (a cornucopia of seafood fried in clean oil for a flavorful but light secondo) and know that it will be memorable. It bucks current Venetian trends by continuing to offer exquisite food and excellent service at reasonable prices. The English-speaking co-owners, Pino, Fabio, and Gianluca, will talk you through the day's perfectly prepared fish dishes (John Dory, sole, monkfish, cuttlefish). You'll even find a dozen meat choices, such as Venetian liver. Dine in one of two pleasant but smallish rooms. Remigio—less abuzz and more sedate than Alla Madonna (see below)—is well known though not as easy to find; just ask a local for directions.

Castello 3416 (on Salizzada dei Greci near Scuola San Giorgio dei Greci). ✆ **041-523-0089.** Reservations recommended for dinner. Primi 8€–11€; secondi 8€–16€. AE, DC, MC, V. Wed–Mon 12–2:30pm; Wed–Sun 7:30–10pm. *Vaporetto:* San Zaccaria (follow Riva degli Schiavoni east until you come to white Chiesa della Pietà; turn left onto Calle della Pietà, which jogs left into Calle Bosello).

IN DORSODURO

Moderate

Taverna San Trovaso ★ ⓚids VENETIAN   Wine bottles line the wood-paneled walls, and low vaulted brick ceilings augment the sense of character in this canal-side tavern, always packed with locals and visitors. The *menù turistico* includes wine, an ample *frittura mista* (assortment of fried seafood), and dessert. The gnocchi is homemade; the local specialty of calves' liver and onions is great, and the simply grilled fish is the taverna's claim to fame. There are also a variety of pizzas. For a special occasion that'll test your budget but not bankrupt you, consider the four-course menu: It starts with a fresh antipasto of seafood followed by pasta and a fish entree (changing with the day's catch) and includes side dishes, dessert, and wine.

Dorsoduro 1016 (on Fondamenta Priuli). ✆ **041-520-3703.** www.tavernasantrovaso.it. Reservations recommended. Pizza and primi 7€–13€; secondi 9.50€–18€. AE, DC, MC, V. Tues–Sun noon–2:45pm and 7pm–midnight. *Vaporetto:* Accademia (walk to right around Accademia and take a right onto Calle Gambara; when this street ends at small Rio di San Trovaso, turn left onto Fondamenta Priuli).

Trattoria ai Cugnai ★★ ⓕinds VENETIAN   The unassuming storefront of this longtime favorite does little to announce that herein lies some of the neighborhood's best dining. The name refers to the brothers-in-law of the women chefs, sisters, who serve classic *cucina veneziana,* like the reliably good *spaghetti alle vongole verace* (with clams) or *fegato alla veneziana.* The homemade gnocchi and lasagna would meet any Italian grandmother's approval (you won't go wrong with any of the menu's *fatta in casa* choices of daily homemade specialties, either). Equidistant from the Accademia and the Guggenheim, Ai Cugnai is the perfect place to recharge after an art overload.

Dorsoduro 857 (on Calle Nuova Sant'Agnese). ℂ **041-528-9238.** Reservations not necessary. Primi 9€–14€; secondi 10€–18€. AE, MC, V. Tues–Sun 12:30–3pm and 7–10:30pm. *Vaporetto:* Accademia (head east of bridge and Accademia in direction of Guggenheim Collection; on straight street connecting 2 museums; restaurant is on your right).

IN SAN POLO
Moderate

Alla Madonna (Overrated) ITALIAN/VENETIAN   This bright and busy trattoria is a classic and has been packing them in for more than 50 years. A Venetian institution, it has a convenient location near the Rialto Bridge, five large dining rooms to accommodate the demand, an encouraging mix of loyal local regulars and foreign patrons, a characteristic decor of high-beam ceilings and walls frame-to-frame with local artists' work, and decent fresh fish and seafood. With all of this, and (by Venetian standards) moderate prices, to boot, it's no surprise that this place is always jumping. Don't expect the waiter to smile if you linger too long over dessert, though. Most of the first courses are prepared with seafood, such as the spaghetti or risotto with *frutti di mare* (seafood) or pasta with *sepie* (cuttlefish), blackened from its own natural ink. Most of the day's special fish selections are best simply and deliciously prepared *alla griglia* (grilled). Despite the good food and reasonable prices for Venice, I mark this restaurant as "overrated" since you'll be rushed through your meal and made to feel like you're part of an assembly line, with waiters caring more about the money you're going to leave on the table than about the quality of your dining experience.

San Polo 594 (Calle della Madonna) ℂ **041-522-3824.** www.ristorantellamadonna.com. Reservations accepted only for parties of 8 or more. Primi 10€–12€; secondi 10€–15€. AE, DC, MC, V. Thurs–Tues noon–3pm and 7–10pm. Closed 2 weeks in Aug and all of Jan. *Vaporetto:* Rialto (from the foot of the Rialto Bridge on the San Polo side of the Grand Canal, turn left and follow the Riva d. Vin along the Grand Canal; Sottoportego della Madonna [which will then become Calle della Madonna] will be the 2nd calle on your right [look for the big yellow sign]; the restaurant is on your left).

Da Sandro ★ (Kids) ITALIAN/PIZZERIA   Like most *pizzerie/trattorie,* Sandro offers dozens of varieties of pizza (his specialty), as well as a full trattoria menu of pastas and entrees. If you're looking for a 10€ pizza-and-beer meal where you can sit outside, this is a reliably good spot on the main drag linking the Rialto to Campo San Polo. Although Italians are very careful about counting carbs, you won't raise any eyebrows if you order a pasta and pizza and pass on the meat or fish: This city has seen it all. There's communal seating at a few wooden picnic tables placed outdoors, with just a handful of small tables stuffed into the two dining rooms—which, unusually, are on opposite sides of the street.

San Polo 1473 (Campiello dei Meloni). ℂ **041-523-4894.** Reservations not necessary. Primi and pizza 6€–9€; secondi 10€–20€. AE, MC, V. Sat–Thurs 11:30am–11:30pm. *Vaporetto:* San Silvestro (with your back to Grand Canal, walk straight to store-lined Ruga Vecchia San Giovanni and take a left; head toward Campo San Polo until you come on Campiello dei Meloni).

Do Spade ★ VENETIAN   From 1415 until just a few years ago, workers, fishmongers, and shoppers from the nearby Mercato della Pescheria flocked to this spot, once a characterful wine bar, with bonhomie galore. After a change of ownership in 2007 and a widely divergent approach to dining, it became an upscale restaurant, with lobster flown in twice weekly from Maine, specializing in risotto with foie gras and truffles. The rich and elaborate menu was out of place in this spot in Venice, and in 2008 there was another change in management and a return to the place's modest roots, with it being reborn as an excellent place to get moderately priced local favorites.

San Polo 860 (on Sottoportego do Spade). ☎ **041-521-0574.** Reservations not necessary. Primi 8€–14€; secondi 11€–16€. No credit cards. Tues–Sun 10am–3pm and 6–10pm. Closed 1 week in Jan and 1 week in Aug. *Vaporetto:* Rialto or San Silvestro (at San Polo side of Rialto Bridge, walk away from bridge and through open-air market until you come to an intersection with a pharmacy and Cassa di Risparmio di Venezia bank on 2 corners, here take a left and then take 2nd right onto Sottoportego do Spade).

Inexpensive

Cantina do Mori ★★★ (Value) WINE BAR/LIGHT FARE   Since 1462, this has been the local watering hole of choice in the market area; legend even pegs Casanova as a habitué. *Tramezzini* are the fuel of Venice—sample them here where you're guaranteed fresh combinations of thinly sliced meats, tuna, cheeses, and vegetables, along with tapaslike *cicchetti.* They're traditionally washed down with an *ombra.* Venetians stop to snack and socialize before and after meals, but if you don't mind standing (there are no tables), for a light lunch this is one of the best of the old-time *bacari* left. And now that it serves a limited number of first courses, like *melanzane alla parmigiana* (eggplant Parmesan) and *fondi di carciofi saltati* (lightly fried artichoke hearts), my obligatory stop here is more fulfilling than ever.

San Polo 429 (entrances on Calle Galiazza and Calle Do Mori). ☎ **041-522-5401.** Sandwiches and *cicchetti* bar food around 3€ per serving. No credit cards. Mon–Sat 8:30am–8pm. *Vaporetto:* Rialto (cross Rialto Bridge to San Polo side, walk to end of market stalls, turn left and then immediately right, and look for small wooden cantina sign on left).

IN SANTA CROCE

Inexpensive

Pizzeria ae Oche ★★ (Kids) PIZZERIA   It's nice to know that some things haven't changed in Venice: This is still the Baskin-Robbins of Venice's pizzerias, an American-style tavern restaurant of wood beams and booths decorated with classic 1950s Coca-Cola signs and the like, and still at honest pizza prices. Italians are zealously unapologetic about tucking into a good-size pizza and a pint of beer (with more than 20 here from which to choose); the walk to and from this slightly peripherally located hangout (with outside eating during warm weather) allays thoughts of calorie counts. What you count here are the 85 varieties of imaginative pizza that fill the menu, including a dozen of the tomato-sauce-free "white" variety *(pizza bianca).* The clientele is a mixed bag of young and old, students and not, Venetians and visitors. (At economy prices like these, you should note that a 12% service charge is automatically added to the bill.)

Santa Croce 1552 (on Calle del Tintor south of Campo San Giacomo dell'Orio). ☎ **041-52-41-161.** www.aeoche.com. Reservations recommended for weekends. Pizza 4.70€–9.50€; primi 5.50€–9.50€; secondi 9€–17€. MC, V. Tues–Sun noon–midnight (daily in summer). *Vaporetto:* Equidistant from Rio San Biasio and San Stae. (You can walk here in 10 min. from the nearby train station; otherwise, from the *vaporetto* station find your way to the Campo San Giacomo dell'Orio and exit the *campo* south on to the well-trammeled Calle del Tintor.)

PICNICKING

You don't have to eat in a fancy restaurant to have a good time in Venice. Prepare a picnic, and while you eat alfresco, you can observe the life of the city's few open piazzas or the aquatic parade on its main thoroughfare, the Grand Canal. And you can still indulge in a late dinner *alla Veneziana.* Plus, doing your own shopping for food can be an interesting experience—the city has very few supermarkets as we know them, and small *alimentari* (food shops) in the highly visited neighborhoods (where few Venetians live) are scarce.

MERCATO RIALTO   Venice's principal open-air market is a sight to see, even for non-shoppers. It has two parts, beginning with the produce section, whose many stalls, alternating with that of souvenir vendors, unfold north on the San Polo side of the Rialto Bridge (behind these stalls are a few permanent food stores that sell delicious cheese, cold cuts, and bread selections). The vendors are here Monday to Saturday 7am to 1pm, with a number who stay on in the afternoon.

At the market's farthest point, you'll find the covered **fresh-fish market,** with its carnival atmosphere, picturesquely located on the Grand Canal opposite the magnificent Ca' d'Oro and still redolent of the days when it was one of the Mediterranean's great fish markets. The area is filled with a number of small *bacari* bars frequented by market vendors and shoppers where you can join in and ask for your morning's first glass of *prosecco* with a *cicchetto* pick-me-up. The fish merchants take Monday off and work mornings only.

CAMPO SANTA MARGHERITA   On this spacious *campo,* Tuesday through Saturday from 8:30am to 1 or 2pm, a number of open-air stalls set up shop, selling fresh fruit and vegetables. You should have no trouble filling out your picnic spread with the fixings available at the various shops lining the sides of the *campo,* including an exceptional *panetteria* (bakery), **Rizzo Pane,** at no. 2772; a fine *salumeria* (deli) at no. 2844; and a good shop for wine, sweets, and other picnic accessories next door. There's even a conventional supermarket, **Merlini,** just off the *campo* in the direction of the quasi-adjacent *campo* San Barnabà at no. 3019. This is also the area where you'll find Venice's heavily photographed **floating market** operating from a boat moored just off San Barnabà at the Ponte dei Pugni. This market is open daily from 8am to 1pm and 3:30 to 7:30pm, except Wednesday afternoon and Sunday. You're almost better off just buying a few freshly prepared sandwiches (panini when made with rolls, *tramezzini* when made with white bread).

THE BEST PICNIC SPOTS   Alas, to stay behind and picnic in Venice means you won't have much in the way of green space (it's not worth the boat ride to the Giardini Publici past the Arsenale, Venice's only green park). An enjoyable alternative is to find some of the larger piazzas or *campi* that have park benches, and in some cases even a tree or two to shade them, such as Campo San Giacomo dell'Orio (in the quiet *sestiere* of Santa Croce). The two most central are **Campo Santa Margherita** (*sestiere* of Dorsoduro) and **Campo San Polo** (*sestiere* of San Polo). For a picnic with a view, scout out the **Punta della Dogana area (Customs House)** near La Salute Church for a prime viewing site at the mouth of the Grand Canal. It's located directly across from the Piazza San Marco and the Palazzo Ducale—pull up on a piece of the embankment here and watch the flutter of water activity against a canvaslike backdrop deserving of the Accademia Museum. In this same area, the small **Campo San Vio** near the Guggenheim is directly on the Grand Canal (not many *campi* are) and even boasts a bench or two.

If you want to create a real Venice picnic, you'll have to take the no. 12 boat out to the near-deserted island of **Torcello,** with a hamper full of bread, cheese, and wine, and reenact the romantic scene between Katharine Hepburn and Rossano Brazzi from the 1950s film *Summertime.*

But perhaps the best picnic site of all is in a **patch of sun on the marble steps** leading down to the water of the Grand Canal, at the foot of the Rialto Bridge on the San Polo side. There is no better ringside seat for the Canalazzo's passing parade.

5 EXPLORING VENICE

Venice is notorious for changing and extending the opening hours of its museums and, to a lesser degree, its churches. Before you begin your exploration of Venice's sights, ask at the tourist office for the season's list of museum and church hours. During the peak months, you can enjoy extended museum hours—some places stay open until 7 or even 10pm. Unfortunately, these hours are not released until approximately Easter of every year. Even then, little is done to publicize the information, so you'll have to do your own research.

IN PIAZZA SAN MARCO

Basilica di San Marco (St. Mark's Basilica) ★★★ Venice for centuries was Europe's principal gateway between the Orient and the West, so it should come as no surprise that the architectural style for the sumptuously Byzantine Basilica di San Marco, replete with five mosquelike bulbed domes, was borrowed from Constantinople. Legend has it that, in 828, two enterprising Venetian merchants smuggled the remains of St. Mark the Evangelist from Egypt by packing them in pickled pork to bypass the scrutiny of Muslim guards. Thus, St. Mark replaced the Greek St. Theodore as Venice's patron saint, and a small chapel was built on this spot in his honor. Through the centuries (much of what you see was constructed in the 11th c.), wealthy Venetian merchants and politicians alike vied with one another in donating gifts to expand and embellish this church, the saint's final resting place and, with the adjacent Palazzo Ducale, a symbol of Venetian wealth and power. Exotic and mysterious, it is unlike any other Roman Catholic church.

And so it is that the Basilica di San Marco earned its name as the Chiesa d'Oro (Golden Church), with a cavernous interior exquisitely gilded with Byzantine mosaics added over some 7 centuries and covering every inch of both ceiling and pavement. For a closer look at many of the most remarkable ceiling mosaics and a better view of the Oriental carpet–like patterns of the pavement mosaics, pay the admission to go upstairs to the **Galleria** (the entrance to this and the Museo Marciano is in the atrium at the principal entrance); this was originally the women's gallery, or *matroneum.* It is also the only way to access the outside Loggia dei Cavalli (see below). More important, here you can mingle with the celebrated *Triumphal Quadriga* of four gilded bronze horses (dating from the 2nd or 3rd c. A.D.), brought to Venice from Constantinople (although probably cast in Imperial Rome) in 1204, together with the Lion of St. Mark (the patron saint's and the former republic's mascot) and other booty from the Crusades; they were symbols of the unrivaled Serene Republic and are the only *quadriga* to have survived from the classical era. The restored originals have been moved inside to the small museum.

A visit to the outdoor **Loggia dei Cavalli** is an unexpected highlight, providing an excellent view of the piazza and what Napoleon called "the most beautiful salon in the

VENICE

5

EXPLORING VENICE

Tips **Church Tours**

Check with a tourist office for free tours being offered (erratically and usually during high season) in some of the churches, particularly the Basilica di San Marco and occasionally the Frari.

world" upon his arrival in Venice in 1797 (he would later cart the *quadriga* off to Paris, but they were returned after the fall of the French Empire). The 500-year-old **Torre dell'Orologio (Clock Tower)** stands to your right; to your left is the **Campanile (Bell Tower)** and, beyond, the glistening waters of the open lagoon and Palladio's **Chiesa di San Giorgio** on its own island. It is a photographer's dream.

The church's greatest treasure is the magnificent altarpiece known as the **Pala d'Oro (Golden Altarpiece),** a Gothic masterpiece encrusted with close to 2,000 precious gems and 255 enameled panels. It was created as early as the 10th century and embellished by master Venetian and Byzantine artisans between the 12th and 14th centuries. It is located behind the main altar, whose green marble canopy on alabaster columns covers the tomb of St. Mark. Also worth a visit is the **Tesoro (Treasury),** with a collection of the Crusaders' plunder from Constantinople and other icons and relics amassed by the church over the years. Much of the Venetian booty has been incorporated into the interior and exterior of the basilica in the form of marble, columns, capitals, and statuary. Second to the Pala d'Oro in importance is the 10th-century ***Madonna di Nicopeia,*** a bejeweled icon taken from Constantinople and exhibited in its own chapel to the left of the main altar. She is held as one of present-day Venice's most protective patrons.

FREE TOURS In July and August (with much less certainty the rest of the year), church-affiliated volunteers give free tours Monday to Saturday, leaving four or five times daily (not all tours are in English), beginning at 10:30am; groups gather in the atrium, where you'll find posters with schedules.

San Marco, Piazza San Marco. © **041-522-5697.** www.basilicasanmarco.it. Basilica, free admission; Museo Marciano (St. Mark's Museum, also called La Galleria, includes Loggia dei Cavalli) 4€, Pala d'Oro 2€, Tesoro (Treasury) 3€. Basilica, Tesoro, and Pala d'Oro: Summer Mon–Sat 9:45am–5pm, Sun 2–4pm; in winter, closes an hour earlier. Museo Marciano: Summer daily 9:45am–4:45pm. *Vaporetto:* San Marco.

Campanile di San Marco (Bell Tower) ★★ It's an easy elevator ride up to the top of this 97m (318-ft.) bell tower for a breathtaking view of the cupolas of St. Mark's. It is the highest structure in the city, offering a pigeon's-eye view that includes the lagoon, its neighboring islands, and the red rooftops and church domes and bell towers of Venice—and, oddly, not a single canal. On a clear day, you may even see the outline of the distant snowcapped Dolomite Mountains. Originally built in the 9th century, the bell tower was then rebuilt in the 12th, 14th, and 16th centuries, when the pretty marble loggia at its base was added by Jacopo Sansovino. It collapsed unexpectedly in 1902, miraculously hurting no one except a cat. It was rebuilt exactly as before, using most of the same materials, even rescuing one of the five historical bells that it still uses today (each bell was rung for a different purpose, such as war, the death of a doge, religious holidays, and so on).

VENICE

5

EXPLORING VENICE

VENICE

5

EXPLORING VENICE

San Marco, Piazza San Marco. ℂ **041-522-4064.** Admission 8€. Easter to June 9am–5pm; July–Sept 9am–9pm; Oct 9am–7pm; Nov to Easter 9:30am–3:45pm. *Vaporetto:* San Marco.

Museo Civico Correr (Correr Civic Museum) ★   This museum, which you enter through an arcade at the west end of Piazza San Marco opposite the basilica, is no match for the Accademia but does include some interesting paintings of Venetian life and a fine collection of artifacts, such as coins, costumes, the doges' ceremonial robes and hats, and an incredible pair of 38cm (15-in.) platform shoes that gives an interesting feel for aspects of the day-to-day life in La Serenissima in the heyday of its glory. Bequeathed to the city by the aristocratic Correr family in 1830, the museum is divided into three sections: the **Painting Section,** the **History Section,** and the **Museum of the Risorgimento** (1797–1866). The latter two aren't worth much mention. Of the painting collection from the 13th to 18th centuries, Vittorio Carpaccio's *Le Cortigiane (The Courtesans),* in room no. 15 on the upper floor, is one of the museum's most famous paintings (are they courtesans or the respected elite?), as are the star-attraction paintings by the Bellini family, father Jacopo and sons Gentile and Giovanni. For a lesson in just how little this city has changed in the last several hundred years, head to room no. 22 and its anonymous 17th-century bird's-eye view of Venice. Most of the rooms have a sign with a few paragraphs in English explaining the significance of the contents.

San Marco, west end of Piazza San Marco. ℂ **041-271-5911.** www.museiciviciveneziani.it. Admission only on San Marco cumulative ticket (see "Venice Discounts," p. 107). Daily 10am–7pm (until 5pm Nov–Mar). *Vaporetto:* San Marco.

Palazzo Ducale and Ponte dei Sospiri (Ducal Palace and Bridge of Sighs) ★★★   The pink-and-white marble Gothic-Renaissance Palazzo Ducale, residence and government center of the doges ("dukes," elected for life) who ruled Venice for more than 1,000 years, stands between the Basilica di San Marco and St. Mark's Basin. A symbol of prosperity and power, it was destroyed by a succession of fires and was built and rebuilt in 1340 and 1424 in its present form, escaping the Renaissance fever that was in the air at the time. Forever being expanded, it slowly grew to be one of Italy's greatest civic structures. A 15th-century **Porta della Carta (Paper Gate),** the entrance adjacent to the basilica where the doges' official proclamations and decrees were posted, opens onto a splendid inner courtyard with a double row of Renaissance arches.

Ahead you'll see Jacopo Sansovino's enormous **Scala dei Giganti (Stairway of the Giants),** scene of the doges' lavish inaugurations and never used by mere mortals, which leads to the wood-paneled courts and elaborate meeting rooms of the interior. The walls and ceilings of the principal rooms were richly decorated by the Venetian masters, including Veronese, Titian, Carpaccio, and Tintoretto, to illustrate the history of the puissant Venetian Republic while at the same time impressing visiting diplomats and emissaries from the far-flung corners of the maritime republic with the uncontested prosperity and power it had attained.

If you want to understand something of this magnificent palace, the fascinating history of the 1,000-year-old maritime republic, and the intrigue of the government that ruled it, take the **Secret Itineraries tour** ★★★ (see "An Insider's Look at the Palazzo Ducale," below). Failing that, at least shell out for the infrared audio-guide tour (at entrance: 6€) to help make sense of it all. Unless you can tag along with an English-speaking tour group, you may otherwise miss out on the importance of much of what you're seeing.

The first room you'll come to is the spacious **Sala delle Quattro Porte (Hall of the Four Doors),** whose ceiling is by Tintoretto. The **Sala del Anti-Collegio** (adjacent to the

(Map of Piazza San Marco)

Labels on map:
N

Mercerie

Torre dell'Orologio (Clock Tower)

Piazzetta dei Leoni

Patriarchal Palace

Basilica di San Marco (St. Mark's Basilica)

Procuratie Vecchie

Scala dei Giganti (Stairway of the Giants)

Ponte dei Sospiri (Bridge of Sighs)

Campanile di San Marco (Bell Tower)

Quadri

Piazza San Marco

Porta della Carta (Paper Gate/ main entrance)

Palazzo Ducale (Ducal Palace)

Rio di Palazzo

Caffè Florian

Ala Napoleonica

Entrance to museum

Procuratie Nuove

Museo Civico Correr (Correr Civic Museum)

Sansovino Library

Piazzetta San Marco

South facade of the palazzo

Ponte della Paglia

GIARDINETTI REALI

Zecco (Mint)

Tourist Information Office (Palazzina del Santi)

Canal Grande

Pontile di S. Marco

Vaporetto Stop

VENICE

5

EXPLORING VENICE

College Chamber, whose ceiling is also decorated by Tintoretto), the next main room, is where foreign ambassadors waited to be received by this committee of 25 members: It is decorated with works by Tintoretto, and Veronese's *Rape of Europe,* considered one of the *palazzo*'s finest. It steals some of the thunder of Tintoretto's *Three Graces* and *Bacchus and Ariadne*—the latter considered one of his best by some critics. A right turn from this room leads into one of the most impressive of the spectacular interior rooms, the richly adorned **Sala del Senato (Senate Chamber),** with Tintoretto's ceiling painting, *The Triumph of Venice.* Here laws were passed by the Senate, a select group of 200 chosen from the Great Council. The latter was originally an elected body, but from the 13th century onward, it was an aristocratic stronghold that could number as many as 1,700. After passing again through the Sala delle Quattro Porte, you'll come to the Veronese-decorated **Stanza del Consiglio dei Dieci (Room of the Council of Ten,** the republic's dreaded security police), of particular historical interest. It was in this room that justice was dispensed and decapitations ordered. Formed in the 14th century to deal with emergency situations, the Ten were considered more powerful than the Senate and feared by all. Just outside the adjacent chamber, in the **Sala della Bussola (The Compass Chamber),** notice the **Bocca dei Leoni ("lion's mouth"),** a slit in the wall into which secret denunciations and accusations of enemies of the state were placed for quick action by the much-feared Council.

The main sight on the next level down—indeed, in the entire palace—is the **Sala del Maggior Consiglio (Great Council Hall).** This enormous space is made special by Tintoretto's huge *Paradiso* at the far end of the hall above the doge's seat (the painter was in his 70s when he undertook the project with the help of his son; he died 6 years later). Measuring 7×23m (23×75 ft.), it is said to be the world's largest oil painting; together with Veronese's gorgeous *Il Trionfo di Venezia (The Triumph of Venice)* in the oval panel on the ceiling, it affirms the power emanating from the council sessions held here. Tintoretto also did the portraits of the 76 doges encircling the top of this chamber; note that the picture of the Doge Marin Falier, who was convicted of treason and beheaded in 1355, has been blacked out—Venice has never forgiven him. Although elected for life since sometime in the 7th century, over time *il doge* became nothing but a figurehead (they were never allowed to meet with foreign ambassadors alone); the power rested in the Great Council. Exit the Great Council Hall via the tiny doorway on the opposite side of Tintoretto's *Paradiso* to find the enclosed **Ponte dei Sospiri (Bridge of Sighs),** which connects the Ducal Palace with the grim **Palazzo delle Prigioni (Prisons).** The bridge took its current name only in the 19th century, when visiting northern European poets romantically envisioned the prisoners' final breath of resignation upon viewing the outside world one last time before being locked in their fetid cells awaiting the quick justice of the Terrible Ten. Some attribute the name to Casanova, who, following his arrest in 1755 (he was accused of being a Freemason and spreading antireligious propaganda), crossed this very bridge. He was one of the rare few to escape 15 months after his imprisonment, returning to Venice 20 years later. Some of the stone cells still have the original graffiti of past prisoners, many of them locked up interminably for petty crimes.

Note: At press time the Palazzo Ducale was partially covered for restoration, which is unbothersome until you realize that both sides of the building that frame the Bridge of Sighs are completely covered in an enormous advertisement. The bridge, one of the most

An Insider's Look at the Palazzo Ducale

I cannot recommend highly enough the **Itinerari Segreti (Secret Itineraries)** ★★★ guided tours. The tours offer an unparalleled look into the world of Venetian politics over the centuries and are the only way to access the otherwise restricted quarters and hidden passageways of this enormous palace, such as the doges' private chambers and the torture chambers where prisoners were interrogated. The story of Giacomo Casanova's imprisonment in, and famous escape from, the palace's prisons is the tour highlight (though a few of the less-inspired guides harp on this aspect a bit too much). I strongly recommend you reserve in advance, by phone if possible—tours are often sold out at least a few days ahead, especially from spring through fall—or in person at the ticket desk. Tours in English are daily at 9:55am and 10:45am and cost 16€ for adults, 10€ for children ages 6 to 14 and students ages 15 to 29. There are also tours in Italian and French interspersed between 9:30am and 12:25pm.

Basilica di San Marco

Chapel of the Madonna di Nicopeia **10**

Creation of Eve **5**

Mosaics depicting the relics of St. Mark being carried into the church **1**

Narthex/entrance to upstairs museum and Loggia dei Cavalli **6**

Nave **7**

Pala d'Oro **11**

Pietra del Banda **3**

Principal facade **2**

Sanctuary barrier and pulpits **9**

South facade **4**

Treasury **8**

photographed sights in the city, is still there and still visible, but the usual effect is completely lost. The restoration should be done by the end of 2010.

San Marco, Piazza San Marco. ℂ **041-271-5911.** Admission only on San Marco cumulative ticket (see "Venice Discounts," p. 107). For Itinerari Segreti guided tour in English, see "An Insider's Look at the Palazzo Ducale" box, below. Daily 9am–7pm (until 5pm Nov–Mar; ticket office closes 1 hr. earlier). *Vaporetto:* San Marco.

Torre dell'Orologio (Clock Tower)   As you enter the magnificent Piazza San Marco, it is one of the first things you see, standing on the north side, next to and towering above the Procuratie Vecchie (the ancient administration buildings for the republic). The Renaissance tower was built in 1496, and the clock mechanism of that same period still keeps perfect time—and a lengthy restoration that finished in 2005 has helped keep the rest of the structure in top shape. The two bronze figures, known as "Moors" because of the dark color of the bronze, pivot to strike the hour. The tower has always been a favorite *punto di incontro* ("meet me at the tower") for Venetians and is the entryway to the ancient Mercerie (from the word for "merchandise"), the principal souklike retail street of both high-end boutiques and trinket shops that zigzags its way to the Rialto Bridge. Guided tours are required and are included in the price of entrance.

San Marco, Piazza San Marco. Admission 12€, 7€ for children ages 6–14 and students ages 15–29; the ticket also gets you into the Museo Correr, the Museo Archeologico Nazionale, and the Biblioteca Nazionale Marciana (but not Palazzo Ducale, as you get with the San Marco Museum Pass, see "Venice Discounts," p. 107). Daily 10am–3:30pm; tours in English Mon–Wed at 10 and 11am and Thurs–Sun 2 and 3pm. There are also tours in Italian and French. *Vaporetto:* San Marco.

TOP ATTRACTIONS BEYOND SAN MARCO

Canal Grande (Grand Canal) ★★★   A leisurely cruise along the "Canalazzo" from Piazza San Marco to the Ferrovia (train station), or the reverse, is one of Venice's (and life's) must-do experiences. Hop on the no. 1 *vaporetto* in the late afternoon (try to get one of the coveted outdoor seats in the prow), when the weather-worn colors of the former homes of Venice's merchant elite are warmed by the soft light and reflected in the canal's rippling waters, and the busy traffic of delivery boats, *vaporetti,* and gondolas that fills the city's main thoroughfare has eased somewhat. The sheer number and opulence of the 200-odd *palazzi,* churches, and imposing republican buildings dating from the 14th to the 18th centuries is enough to make any boat-going visitor's head swim. Many of the largest canal-side buildings are now converted into imposing international banks, government or university buildings, art galleries, and dignified consulates.

2 most popular stations located at Piazzale Roma/Ferrovia (train station) and at Piazza San Marco. Tickets 6.50€. *Vaporetto:* 1.

Collezione Peggy Guggenheim (Peggy Guggenheim Collection) ★★★ Considered to be one of the most comprehensive and important collections of modern art in the world, and one of the most visited attractions in Venice, this collection of painting and sculpture was assembled by the eccentric and eclectic American expatriate Peggy Guggenheim. She did an excellent job of it, with particular strengths in cubism, European abstraction, surrealism, and abstract expressionism since about 1910. Max Ernst was one of her early favorites (she even married him), as was Jackson Pollock.

Among the major works here are Magritte's *Empire of Light,* Picasso's *La Baignade,* Kandinsky's *Landscape with Church (with Red Spot),* and Pollock's *Alchemy.* The museum is also home to several haunting canvases by Ernst, Giacometti's unique figures, Brancusi's fluid sculptures, and numerous works by Braque, Dalí, Léger, Mondrian, Chagall, and Miró.

Directly on the Grand Canal, the elegant 18th-century Palazzo Venier dei Leoni was purchased by Peggy Guggenheim in 1949 and was her home in Venice until her death in 1979. The graves of her canine companions share the lovely interior garden with several

---

Venice's Newest Bridge

After years of disputes about its utility and design, the **Ponte della Costituzione,** the fourth bridge spanning the Grand Canal, opened for business in 2008. Venice's newest bridge is an impressive sight. To visit it, come out of the Santa Lucia train station and turn right at the Grand Canal, where you'll encounter this futuristic creation of famed Spanish architect Santiago Calatrava. The bridge connects the train station with the Piazzale Roma parking lot, so it's probably not of much use to you if you have arrived by train, but that doesn't mean you can't cross it in awe anyway.

prominent works of the Nasher Sculpture Garden, while the canal-side patio watched over by Marino Marini's *Angel of the Citadel* is one of the best spots to simply linger and watch the canal life. An interesting book and gift shop and cafe/bistro is located in a separate wing across the inside courtyard where temporary exhibits are often housed.

Don't be shy about speaking English with the young staff working here on internship; most of them are American. Free presentations on the history of Peggy Guggenheim and the museum are held daily at noon and 4pm.

Dorsoduro 701 (on Calle San Cristoforo). ℂ **041-240-5411.** www.guggenheim-venice.it. Admission 12€ adults, 10€ over 65 and holders of an Ikea Family Card, 7€ students under 26 and children ages 10–18. Wed–Mon 10am–6pm. *Vaporetto:* Accademia (walk around left side of Accademia, take 1st left, and walk straight ahead following signs—you'll cross a canal and then walk alongside another, until turning left when necessary).

Galleria dell'Accademia (Academy Gallery) ★★★ The glory that was Venice lives on in the Accademia, the definitive treasure house of Venetian painting and one of Europe's great museums. Exhibited chronologically from the 13th through the 18th centuries, the collection features no one hallmark masterpiece in this collection; rather, this is an outstanding and comprehensive showcase of works by all the great master painters of Venice, the largest such collection in the world.

It includes Paolo and Lorenzo Veneziano from the 14th century; Gentile and Giovanni Bellini (and Giovanni's brother-in-law Andrea Mantegna from Padua) and Vittore Carpaccio from the 15th century; Giorgione (whose *Tempest* is one of the gallery's most famous highlights), Tintoretto, Veronese (see his *Feast in the House of Levi* here), and Titian from the 16th century; and, from the 17th and 18th centuries, Canaletto, Piazzetta, Longhi, and Tiepolo, among others.

Most of all, the works open a window to the Venice of 500 years ago. Indeed, the canvases reveal how little Venice has changed over the centuries. Housed in a deconsecrated church and its adjoining *scuola,* the church's confraternity hall, it is Venice's principal picture gallery, and one of the most important in Italy. Because of fire regulations, admission is limited, and lines can be daunting (check for extended evening hours in peak months), but put up with the wait and don't miss it.

Dorsoduro, at foot of Accademia Bridge. ℂ **041-520-0345.** www.gallerieaccademia.org. Admission 6.50€ adults, 3.25€ EU citizens 18–25 and free for EU citizens younger than 18, free for children under 12. Paying 1€ more a ticket, you can call ahead and reserve tickets, thereby saving yourself from potential lines. Mon 8:15am–2pm; Tues–Sun 8:15am–7:15pm; last admission 45 min. before closing. *Vaporetto:* Accademia.

Scuola Grande di San Rocco (Confraternity of St. Roch) ★★★ Jacopo Robusti (1518–94), called Tintoretto because his father was a dyer, was a devout, unworldly man who traveled only once beyond Venice. His epic canvases are filled with phantasmagoric light and intense, mystical spirituality. This museum is a dazzling monument to his work—it holds the largest collection of his images anywhere. The series of the more than 50 dark and dramatic works took the artist more than 20 years to complete, making this the richest of the many confraternity guilds or *scuole* that once flourished in Venice.

Begin upstairs in the Sala dell'Albergo, where the most notable of the enormous, powerful canvases is the moving *La Crocifissione (The Crucifixion).* In the center of the gilt ceiling of the great hall, also upstairs, is *Il Serpente di Bronzo (The Bronze Snake).* Among the eight huge, sweeping paintings downstairs—each depicting a scene from the

For Church Fans

The **Associazione Chiese di Venezia** (📞 **041-275-0462;** www.chorusvenezia. org) now curates most of Venice's top churches. A visit to one of the association's churches costs 3€; most are open Monday to Saturday 10am to 5pm and Sunday 1 to 5pm. The churches are closed Sundays in July and August. If you plan to visit more than three churches, buy the 9€ ticket (valid for 1 year), which allows you to visit all of the following churches: Santa Maria del Giglio, Santo Stefano, Santa Maria Formosa, Santa Maria dei Miracoli, Santa Maria Gloriosa dei Frari (reviewed here), San Polo, San Giacomo dell'Orio, San Stae, Sant'Alvise, Madonna dell'Orto, San Pietro di Castello, Il Redentore (reviewed here), San Sebastiano (reviewed here), Santa Maria del Rosario (Gesuati; reviewed here) and San Giobbe. The association also has audio guides available at some of the churches for 1€.

New Testament—*La Strage degli Innocenti (The Slaughter of the Innocents)* is the most noteworthy, so full of dramatic urgency and energy that the figures seem almost to tumble out of the frame. As you enter the room, it's on the opposite wall at the far end of the room.

There's a useful guide to the paintings posted inside on the wall just before the entrance to the museum. There are a few Tiepolos among the paintings, as well as a solitary work by Titian. The works on or near the staircase are not by Tintoretto.

San Polo 3058 (on Campo San Rocco adjacent to Campo dei Frari). 📞 **041-524-2820.** www.scuola grandesanrocco.it. Admission 7€ adults, 5€ ages 18–26, under 18 free. Daily 9:30am–5:30pm. *Vaporetto:* San Tomà (walk straight ahead on Calle del Traghetto and turn right and immediately left across Campo San Tomà; walk as straight ahead as you can, on Ramo Mandoler, Calle Larga Prima, and Salizzada San Rocco, which leads into *campo* of the same name—look for crimson sign behind Frari Church).

IN SAN MARCO

Chiesa di San Salvador ★   The interior is classic Renaissance, built by Giorgio Spavento, Tullio Lombardo, and Sansovino between 1508 and 1534; the facade is 1663 baroque. It includes a pair of sculptures *(Charity and Hope)* by an elderly Jacopo Sansovino, who may also have designed the third altar, which supports one of the church's treasures, Titian's *Annunciation* (1556). Titian also painted the *Transfiguration* (1560) on the high altar. Ask the sacristan to lower the painting so that you can see the ornate 14th-century silver reredos (ornamental partition) hidden behind. In the right transept rests Bernardino Contino's tomb for Caterina Cornaro (d. 1510), the one-time queen of Cyprus who abdicated her throne to Venice and ended up with Asolo (see chapter 6) as a consolation prize.

Campo San Salvador (just south from the Rialto Bridge on Via 2 Aprile). 📞 **041-523-6717** or 041-270-2464. Free admission. Daily 9am–noon and 3–6pm. *Vaporetto:* Rialto.

Rialto ★★.   This graceful arch over the Grand Canal is lined with overpriced boutiques and is teeming with tourists and overflow from the daily market along Riga degli Orefici on the San Polo side. Until the 19th century, it was the only bridge across the Grand Canal, originally built as a pontoon bridge at the canal's narrowest point. Wooden versions of the bridge followed; the 1444 one was the first to include shops, interrupted by a drawbridge in the center. In 1592, this graceful stone span was finished to the designs of Antonio da Ponte, who beat out Sansovino and Palladio, and Michelangelo with his plans that called for a single, vast, 28m-wide (92-ft.) arch in the center to allow trading ships to pass.

Ponte del Rialto.

IN CASTELLO

Chiesa di San Zaccaria (Church of St. Zachary) ★

Behind (east of) St. Mark's Basilica is a 9th-century Gothic church with its original 13th-century campanile and a splendid Renaissance facade designed by the Venetian architect Mario Codussi in the late 15th century. Of the interior's many artworks is the important *Madonna Enthroned with Four Saints,* painted by Giovanni Bellini in 1505. Art historians have long held this as one of Bellini's finer Madonnas. Ask the sacristan to see the Sisters' Choir, with works by Tintoretto, Titian, Il Vecchio, Anthony Van Dyck, and Bassano. The paintings aren't labeled, but the sacristan will point out the names of the artists. In the fan vaults of the Chapel of San Tarasio are the faded ceiling frescoes of the Florentine-born artist Andrea del Castagno, who was the first to bring the spirit of the Renaissance to Venice.

Castello, Campo San Zaccaria. ℂ **041-522-1257.** Free admission. Mon–Sat 10am–noon; daily 4–6pm. *Vaporetto:* San Zaccaria.

Museo Storico Navale and Arsenale (Naval History Museum and the Arsenal) ★★

The Naval History Museum's most fascinating exhibit is its collection of model ships. It was once common practice for vessels to be built not from blueprints, but from the precise scale models that you see here. The prize of the collection is a model of the legendary *Bucintoro,* the lavish ceremonial barge of the doges. Another section of the museum contains an array of historic vessels. Walk along the canal as it branches off from the museum to the Ships' Pavilion, where the historic vessels are displayed.

Occupying one-fifth of the city's total acreage, the arsenal was once the very source of the republic's maritime power. It is now used as a military zone and is as closed as Fort Knox to the curious. The marble-columned Renaissance gate, with the republic's winged lion above, is flanked by four ancient lions, booty brought at various times from Greece and points farther east. It was founded in 1104, and at the height of Venice's power in the 15th century, it employed 16,000 workers who turned out merchant and wartime galley after galley on an early version of massive assembly lines at speeds and in volume unknown until modern times.

Castello 2148 (Campo San Biasio). ℂ **041-520-0276.** Admission 3€. Mon–Fri 8:45am–1:30pm; Sat closes at 1pm. *Vaporetto:* Arsenale.

Scuola di San Giorgio degli Schiavoni ★

At the St. Antonino Bridge (Fondamenta dei Furlani) is the second-most-important guild house to visit in Venice. The Schiavoni were an important and wealthy trading colony of Dalmatian merchants who built their own *scuola,* or confraternity (the coast of Dalmatia—the former Yugoslavia—was once ruled by the Greeks, hence the *scuola's* alternative name of San Giorgio dei Greci).

Between 1502 and 1509, Vittore Carpaccio (himself of Dalmatian descent) painted a pictorial cycle of nine masterpieces illustrating episodes from the lives of St. George (patron saint of the *scuola*) and St. Jerome, the Dalmatian patron saints. These appealing pictures freeze in time moments in the lives of the saints: St. George charges his ferocious dragon on a field littered with half-eaten bodies and skulls (a horror story with a happy ending); St. Jerome leads his lion into a monastery, frightening the friars; St. Augustine

Back to Scuola

Founded in the Middle Ages, the Venetian *scuole* (schools) were guilds that brought together merchants and craftspeople from certain trades (for example, the dyers of Scuola dei Carmini), as well as those who shared similar religious devotions (Scuola Grande di San Rocco). The guilds were social clubs, credit unions, and sources of spiritual guidance. Many commissioned elaborate headquarters and hired the best artists of the day to decorate them. The *scuole* that remain in Venice today house some of the city's finest art treasures.

has just taken up his pen to reply to a letter from St. Jerome when he and his little dog are transfixed by a miraculous light and a voice telling them of St. Jerome's death.

Castello 3259, Calle Furlani. ✆ **041-522-8828.** Admission 5€. Tues–Sun 9am–noon; Tues–Sat 3–6pm. *Vaporetto:* San Zaccaria.

SS. Giovanni e Paolo ★ This massive Gothic church was built by the Dominican order from the 13th to the 15th century and, together with the Frari Church in San Polo, is second in size only to the Basilica di San Marco. An unofficial Pantheon where 25 doges are buried (a number of tombs are part of the unfinished facade), the church, commonly known as Zanipolo in Venetian dialect, is also home to a number of artistic treasures.

Visit the **Cappella del Rosario ★** through a glass door off the left transept to see the three recently restored ceiling canvases by Paolo Veronese, particularly *The Assumption of the Madonna.* Also recently restored is the brilliantly colored *Polyptych of St. Vincent Ferrer* (ca. 1465), attributed to a young Giovanni Bellini, in the right aisle. You'll also see the foot of St. Catherine of Siena encased in glass.

Anchoring the large and impressive *campo,* a popular crossroads for this area of Castello, is the **statue of Bartolomeo Colleoni ★★**, the Renaissance condottiere who defended Venice's interests at the height of its power and until his death in 1475. The 15th-century work is by the Florentine Andrea Verrocchio; it is considered one of the world's great equestrian monuments and Verrocchio's best.

Castello 6363 (on Campo Santi Giovanni e Paolo). ✆ **041-523-7510** or 041-235-5913. Admission 3€. Mon–Sat 8:30am–12:30pm and 3:30–7pm. *Vaporetto:* Rialto.

IN DORSODURO

The **Accademia** and the **Peggy Guggenheim museums** are the top two sights in this neighborhood and, as such, are both covered above.

Ca' Rezzonico (Museo del '700 Veneziano; Museum of 18th-Century Venice) ★★ This museum, in a handsome *palazzo* on the Grand Canal, reopened after a complete restoration in 2001. It offers an intriguing look into what living in a grand Venetian home was like in the final years of the Venetian Republic.

Begun by Baldassare Longhena, 17th-century architect of La Salute Church, the Rezzonico home is a sumptuous backdrop for this collection of period paintings (most important, works by Venetian artists Tiepolo and Guardi, and a special room dedicated to dozens of works by Longhi), furniture, tapestries, and artifacts. This museum is one of the best windows into the sometimes-frivolous life of Venice of 200 years ago, as seen

through the tastes and fashions of the wealthy Rezzonico family of merchants—the lavishly frescoed ballroom alone will evoke the lifestyle of the idle Venetian rich. The English poet Robert Browning, after the death of his wife, Elizabeth Barrett Browning, made
this his last home; he died here in 1889.

Dorsoduro (on the Grand Canal on Fondamenta Rezzonico). © **041-241-0100.** Admission 6.50€ adults,
4.50€ children 6–14 and students under 30, or free with Musuem Pass cumulative ticket (see "Venice
Discounts," p. 107). Wed–Mon 10am–5pm (ticket office closes at 4pm). *Vaporetto:* Ca' Rezzonico (walk
straight ahead to Campo San Barnabà, turn right at the piazza and go over 1 bridge; then take an immediate right for the museum entrance).

Dogana da Mar ★★ (**Moments**)   The eastern tip of Dorsoduro is covered by the triangular 15th-century (restructured with a new facade in 1676–82) customs house that once
controlled all boats entering the Grand Canal. It's topped by a statue of Fortune holding
aloft a golden ball. Now it makes for remarkable, sweeping views across the *bacino* San
Marco, from the last leg of the Grand Canal past Piazzetta San Marco and the Ducal
Palace, over the nearby isle of San Giorgio Maggiore, La Giudecca, and out into the
lagoon itself.

Fondamenta Dogana alla Salute. *Vaporetto:* Salute.

I Gesuati (Santa Maria del Rosario) ★   Built from 1724 to 1736 to mirror the
Redentore across the wide Canale della Giudecca, the Jesuits' church counters the Palladian sobriety of the Redentore with rococo flair. The interior is graced by airy 1737–39
ceiling frescoes (some of the first in Venice) by Giambattista Tiepolo, celebrating Donen-
ticna scenes. Tiepolo also did the *Virgin in Glory with Saints Rosa, Catherine of Siena,* and
Agnes of Montepulciano on the first altar on the right. The third altar has a Tintoretto
Crucifixion.

Fondamenta Zattere ai Gesuati. © **041-275-0462.** www.chorusvenezia.org. Admission 3€ adults, free for
children under 5, or 9€ on cumulative ticket (see "For Church Fans," above). Mon–Sat 10am–5pm; Sun
1–5pm. *Vaporetto:* Zattere.

San Sebastiano   Way out in the boondocks of Dorsoduro rises a 16th-century
church for Paolo Veronese fans. Veronese, who lived nearby, scattered it with paintings
from 1555 to 1570 and is buried in the majolica-floored chapel, left of the high altar.
The colorful Renaissance master provided the ceiling with paintings on the *Story of
Esther,* the choir with a bevy of St. Sebastian–themed works, the organ with painted
panels, the sacristy's ceiling with his earliest commissions, the nun's choir with St. Sebastian frescoes, and the third altar on the left with a *Madonna with Saints.* Titian makes a
guest appearance with a late *St. Nicholas* (1563) on the first altar on the right.

Fondamenta di San Sebastiano. © **041-275-0462.** 3€ or 9€ on cumulative ticket (see "For Church Fans,"
above). Mon–Sat 10am–5pm. *Vaporetto:* San Basilio.

Santa Maria della Salute (Church of the Virgin Mary of Good Health) ★
Generally referred to as "La Salute," this crown jewel of 17th-century baroque architecture proudly reigns at a commercially and aesthetically important point, almost directly
across from the Piazza San Marco, where the Grand Canal empties into the lagoon.

The first stone was laid in 1631 after the Senate decided to honor the Virgin Mary of
Good Health for delivering Venice from a plague. They accepted the revolutionary plans
of a young, relatively unknown architect, Baldassare Longhena (who would go on to
design, among other projects, the Ca' Rezzonico). He dedicated the next 50 years of his

VENICE

5

EXPLORING VENICE

The Art of the Gondola

Putting together one of the sleek black boats is a fascinatingly exact science that is still done in the revered traditional manner at boatyards such as the **Squero di San Trovaso** (see above). The boats have been painted black since a 16th-century sumptuary law—one of many passed by the local legislators as excess and extravagance spiraled out of control. Whether regarding boats or baubles, laws were passed to restrict the gaudy outlandishness that, at the time, was commonly used to "outdo the Joneses."

Propelled by the strength of a single *gondoliere,* these boats, unique to Venice, have no modern equipment. They move with no great speed but with unrivaled grace. The right side of the gondola is lower because the *gondoliere* always stands in the back of the boat on the left. Although the San Trovaso *squero,* or boatyard, is the city's oldest and one of only three remaining (the other two are immeasurably more difficult to find), its predominant focus is on maintenance and repair. They will occasionally build a new gondola (which takes some 40–45 working days), carefully crafting it from the seven types of wood—mahogany, cherry, fir, walnut, oak, elm, and lime—necessary to give the shallow and asymmetrical boat its various characteristics. After all the pieces are put together, the painting, the *ferro* (the iron symbol of the city affixed to the bow), and the wood-carving that secures the oar are commissioned out to various local artisans.

Although some 10,000 of these elegant boats floated on the canals of Venice in the 16th century, today there are only 350. But the job of *gondoliere* remains a coveted profession, passed down from father to son over the centuries.

life to overseeing its progress (he would die 1 year after its inauguration but 5 years before its completion).

The only great baroque monument built in Italy outside Rome, the octagonal Salute is recognized for its exuberant exterior of volutes, scrolls, and more than 125 statues and rather sober interior, though one is highlighted by a small gallery of important works in the sacristy. (You have to pay to enter the sacristy; the entrance is through a small door to the left of the main altar.) A number of ceiling paintings and portraits of the Evangelists and church doctors are all by Titian. On the right wall is Tintoretto's *Marriage at Cana,* often considered one of his best.

Dorsoduro (on Campo della Salute). ℂ **041-522-5558.** Free admission to church; sacristy 2€. Daily 9am–noon and 3–5:30pm. *Vaporetto:* Salute.

Squero di San Trovaso ★★ (Finds) One of the most interesting (and photographed) sights you'll see in Venice is this small *squero* (boatyard), which first opened in the 17th century. Just north of the Zattere (the wide, sunny walkway that runs alongside the Giudecca Canal in Dorsoduro), the boatyard lies next to the Church of San Trovaso on the narrow Rio San Trovaso (not far from the Accademia Bridge). It is surrounded by Tyrolean-looking wooden structures (a true rarity in this city of stone built on water) that are home to the multigenerational owners and original workshops for traditional Venetian boats (see "The Art of the Gondola," below). Aware that they have become a tourist site themselves, the gondoliers don't mind if you watch them at work from across the narrow Rio di San Trovaso, but don't try to invite yourself in. *Tip:* It's the perfect midway photo op after a visit to the Gallerie dell'Accademia and a trip to the well-known gelateria, Da Nico (Zattere 922), whose chocolate *gianduiotto* is not to be missed.

Dorsoduro 1097 (on the Rio San Trovaso, southwest of the Accademia Gallery). No phone. Free admission. *Vaporetto:* Zattere.

IN SAN POLO & SANTA CROCE

Ca' Pesaro   Tired of Venice's one-two punch of baroque and Byzantine? Check out the two museums housed in this late Renaissance *palazzo* on the Grand Canal. The first collection is the **Museo d'Arte Moderna (Museum of Modern Art),** which houses works—most of them bought during Venice's own Biennale over the years—by the likes of Chagall, Kandinsky, Klimt, Miró, Henry Moore, Umberto Boccioni, Morandi, and Filippo De Pisis.

Up on the top level, also partially closed, is the **Museo d'Arte Orientale,** a collection of mostly Japanese artifacts, but also Chinese, Javanese, Siamese (Thai), Cambodian, and Indonesian pieces. Rumors that this collection may eventually move, perhaps to the Palazzo Marcello, have persisted for several years, but for the moment nothing has happened.

Santa Croce 2076 (Fondamenta Ca' Pesaro). (℗ **041-524-1173.** Admission 5.50€, 3€ for ages 6–14 and students under 30. Tues–Sun 10am–5pm (ticket office closes at 4pm). *Vaporetto:* San Stae.

Santa Maria Gloriosa dei Frari (Church of the Frari) ★★   Known simply as "i Frari," this immense 13th- to 14th-century Gothic church is easily found around the corner from the Scuola Grande di San Rocco—make sure you visit both when you're in this area. Built by the Franciscans (*frari* is a dialectal distortion of *frati,* or "brothers"), it is the largest church in Venice after the Basilica of San Marco. The Frari has long been considered something of a memorial to the ancient glories of Venice. Since St. Francis and the order he founded emphasized prayer and poverty, it is not surprising that the church is austere both inside and out. Yet it houses a number of important works, including two Titian masterpieces. The more striking is his *Assumption of the Virgin* over the main altar, painted when the artist was only in his late 20s. His *Virgin of the Pesaro Family* is in the left nave; for this work commissioned by one of Venice's most powerful families, Titian's wife posed for the figure of Mary (and then died soon afterward in childbirth).

The church's other masterwork is Giovanni Bellini's important triptych on wood, the *Madonna and Child,* displayed in the sacristy; it is one of his finest portraits of the Madonna. There is also an almost primitive-looking woodcarving by Donatello of St. John the Baptist. The grandiose tombs of two famous Venetians are also here: Canova (d. 1822), the Italian sculptor who led the revival of classicism, and Titian, who died in 1576 during a deadly plague.

Another Cumulative Ticket

One ticket covers entrance to both the **Ca' d'Oro** and the **Ca Pesaro** for 5.50€; a cumulative ticket including the **Accademia** costs 11€.

Free tours in English are sometimes offered by church volunteers during the high-season months; check at the church.

San Polo 3072 (on Campo dei Frari). ☏ **041-522-2637.** Admission 3€ or 9€ on cumulative ticket (see "For Church Fans," earlier in this chapter). Mon–Sat 9am–6pm; Sun 1–6pm. *Vaporetto:* San Tomà (walk straight ahead on Calle del Traghetto; then turn right and left across Campo San Tomà; walk as straight ahead as you can, on Ramo Mandoler, then Calle Larga Prima, and turn right when you reach beginning of Salizzada San Rocco).

IN CANNAREGIO

Ca' d'Oro (Galleria Giorgio Franchetti) ★★   The 15th-century Ca' d'Oro is one of the best preserved and most impressive of the hundreds of *palazzi* lining the Grand Canal. After the Palazzo Ducale, it's the city's finest example of Venetian Gothic architecture. Its name, the Golden Palace, refers to the gilt-covered facade that faded long ago and is now pink and white. Inside, the beam ceilings and ornate trappings provide a backdrop for the collection of former owner Baron Franchetti, who bequeathed his home and artworks to the city during World War I.

The core collection, expanded over the years, now includes sculptures, furniture, 16th-century Flemish tapestries, an impressive collection of bronzes (12th–16th c.), and a gallery whose most important canvases are Andrea Mantegna's *San Sebastiano* and Titian's *Venus at the Mirror,* as well as lesser paintings by Tintoretto, Carpaccio, Van Dyck, Giorgione, and Jan Steen. For a delightful break, step out onto the *palazzo*'s loggia, overlooking the Grand Canal, for a view up and down the waterway and across to the Pescheria, a timeless vignette of an unchanged city. Off the loggia is a small but worthy ceramics collection, open 10am to noon.

Cannaregio btw. 3931 and 3932 (on Calle Ca' d'Oro north of Rialto Bridge). ☏ **041-520-0345.** www.cadoro.org. Admission 5.50€, 3€ for ages 6–14 and students under 30. Mon 8:15am–2pm; Tues–Sun 8:15am–7:15pm. *Vaporetto:* Ca' d'Oro.

Chiesa Santa Maria dei Miracoli   Hidden in a quiet corner of the residential section of Cannaregio northeast of the Rialto Bridge, the small 15th-century Miracoli is one of the most attractive religious buildings in Europe, with one side of the precious polychrome-marbled facade running alongside a canal, creating colorful and shimmering reflections. The architect, Pietro Lombardo, a local artisan whose background in monuments and tombs is obvious, would go on to become one of the founding fathers of the Venetian Renaissance.

The less romantic are inclined to compare it to a large tomb with a dome, but the untold couples who have made this perfectly proportioned jewel-like church their choice for weddings will dispel such insensitivity. The small square in front is the perfect place for gondolas to drop off and pick up the newly betrothed. The inside is intricately decorated with early Renaissance marble reliefs, its pastel palette of pink, gray, and white marble making an elegant venue for all those weddings. In the 1470s, an image of the Virgin Mary was responsible for a series of miracles (including bringing back to life someone who spent half an hour at the bottom of the Giudecca Canal) that led pilgrims to leave gifts and, eventually, enough donations to have this church built. Look for the icon now displayed over the main altar.

Cannaregio, Rio d. Miracoli. No phone. Admission 3€ or 9€ on cumulative ticket (see "For Church Fans," earlier). Mon–Sat 10am–5pm; Sun 3–5pm. *Vaporetto:* Rialto (located midway between the Rialto Bridge and the Campo SS. Giovanni e Paolo).

The Jews of Venice

Jews began settling in Venice in great numbers in the 16th century, and the republic soon came to value their services as moneylenders, physicians, and traders. For centuries, the Jewish population was forced to live on an island that now encompasses the Campo Ghetto Nuovo, and drawbridges were raised to enforce a nighttime curfew. By the end of the 17th century, as many as 5,000 Jews lived in the Ghetto's cramped confines. Today the city's Jewish population is comprised of only about 500 people, few of whom live in the Ghetto.

Il Ghetto (the Jewish Ghetto) ★★ Venice's relationship with its longtime Jewish community fluctuated over time from acceptance to borderline tolerance, attitudes often influenced by the fear that Jewish moneylenders and merchants would infiltrate other sectors of the republic's commerce under a government that thrived on secrecy and control. In 1516, 700 Jews were forced to move to this then-remote northwestern corner of Venice, to an abandoned site of a 14th-century foundry (*ghetto* is old Venetian dialect for "foundry," a word that would soon be used throughout Europe and the world to depict an area where isolated minority groups lived).

As was commonplace with most of the hundreds of islands that make up Venice, this *ghetto* neighborhood was totally surrounded by water. Its two access points were controlled at night and early morning by heavy gates manned by Christian guards (paid for by the Jews), both protecting and segregating its inhabitants. Within 1 century, the community grew to more than 5,000, representing many languages and cultures. Although the original Ghetto Nuovo (New Ghetto) was expanded to include the Ghetto Vecchio (Old Ghetto; the names are confusing, but remember that *ghetto* meant "foundry," so when the Jews moved into the area occupied by its ruins, they first occupied the newer part of the former foundry and then the older part) and later the Ghetto Nuovissimo (Newest Ghetto), land was limited and quarters always cramped. In 1797, when Napoleon rolled into town, the *ghetto* as an institution was disbanded and Jews were free to move elsewhere. Still, it remains the center of Venice's ever-diminishing community of Jewish families; although accounts vary widely, it's said that anywhere from 500 to 2,000 Jews live in all of Venice and Mestre.

Aside from its historic interest, this is also one of the less touristy neighborhoods in Venice (though it has become something of a nightspot) and makes for a pleasant and scenic place to stroll.

Venice's first kosher restaurant, **Gam Gam,** opened several years ago on Fondamenta di Cannaregio 1122 (© **041-523-1495**), near the entrance to the Jewish Ghetto and close to the Guglie *vaporetto* stop. Owned and run by Orthodox Jews from New York, it serves lunch and dinner Sunday through Friday, with an early Friday closing after lunch.

Cannaregio (Campo del Ghetto Nuovo). *Vaporetto:* Guglie or San Marcuola (from either of the 2 *vaporetto* stops, or if walking from the train station, locate the Ponte delle Guglie; walking away from the Grand Canal along the Fondamenta di Cannaregio, look for a doorway on your right with Hebrew etched across the threshold; this is the entrance to the Calle del Ghetto Vecchio that leads to the Campo del Ghetto Nuovo).

Museo Communità Ebraica ★ The only way to visit any of the area's five 16th-century synagogues is through one of the Museo Communità Ebraica's frequent

VENICE

5

EXPLORING VENICE

organized tours conducted in English. Your guide will elaborate on the commercial and political climate of those times, the unique "skyscraper" architecture (overcrowding resulted in many buildings having as many as seven low-ceiling stories with no elevators), and the daily lifestyle of the Jewish community until the arrival of Napoleon in 1797. You'll get to visit historic temples dedicated to the rites of all three major Jewish groups who called Venice home: Italian (Scola Italiana), Sephardic (Scola Levantina), and Ashkenazi (Scola Canton).

Cannaregio 2902B (on Campo del Ghetto Nuovo). ℂ **041-715-359.** www.museoebraico.it. Museum 3€ adults, 2€ children; museum and synagogue tour 8.50€ adults, 7€ children. Museum June–Sept Sun–Fri 10am–7pm, Oct–May Sun–Fri 10am–6pm; synagogue tours hourly 10:30am–4:30pm (until 5pm Apr–Sept). Closed on Jewish holidays. *Vaporetto:* Guglie.

ON GIUDECCA & SAN GIORGIO

Chiesa di San Giorgio Maggiore ★★ (Moments) This church sits on the little island of San Giorgio Maggiore. It is one of the masterpieces of Andrea Palladio, the great Renaissance architect from nearby Vicenza. Most known for his country villas built for Venice's wealthy merchant families, Palladio was commissioned to build two churches (the other is the Redentore on the neighboring Giudecca island), beginning with San Giorgio, designed in 1565 and completed in 1610. To impose a classical facade on the traditional church structure, Palladio designed two interlocking facades, with repeating triangles, rectangles, and columns that are carefully and harmoniously proportioned. Founded as early as the 10th century, the interior of the church was reinterpreted by Palladio with whitewashed surfaces, stark but majestic, and unadorned but harmonious space. The main altar is flanked by two epic paintings by an elderly Tintoretto, *The Fall of Manna,* to the left, and the more noteworthy *Last Supper,* to the right, famous for its chiaroscuro. Through the doorway to the right of the choir leading to the Cappella dei Morti (Chapel of the Dead), you will find Tintoretto's *Deposition.*

To the left of the choir is an elevator that you can take to the top of the campanile—for a charge of 3€—to experience an unforgettable view of the island, the lagoon, and the Palazzo Ducale and Piazza San Marco across the way.

A handful of remaining Benedictine monks gather for Sunday Mass at 11am, sung in Gregorian chant.

On the island of San Giorgio Maggiore, across St. Mark's Basin from Piazzetta San Marco. ℂ **041-522-7827.** Free admission. Mon–Sat 9:30am–12:30pm; daily 2–6pm. *Vaporetto:* Take the Giudecca-bound *vaporetto* (no. 82) on Riva degli Schiavoni and get off at the 1st stop, the island of San Giorgio Maggiore.

Il Redentore ★ Perhaps the masterpiece among Palladio's churches, Il Redentore was commissioned by Venice to give thanks for being delivered from the great plague (1575–77), which claimed over a quarter of the population (some 46,000 people). The doge established a tradition of visiting this church by crossing a long pontoon bridge made up of boats from the Dorsoduro's Zattere on the third Sunday of each July, a tradition that survived the demise of the doges and remains one of Venice's most popular festivals.

The interior is done in grand, austere, painstakingly classical Palladian style. The artworks tend to be workshop pieces (from the studios or schools, but not the actual brushes, of Tintoretto and Veronese), but there is a fine *Baptism of Christ* by Veronese himself in the sacristy, which also contains Alvise Vivarini's good *Adoration* and *Angels* alongside works by Jacopo da Bassano and Palma il Giovane, who also did the *Deposition* over the right aisle's third chapel. Recent renovations to the interior have now been completed, and the sacristy is to be next.

Campo del Redentore, La Giudecca. (© **041-523-1415.** Admission 3€ or 9€ on cumulative ticket (see "For Church Fans," earlier). Mon–Sat 10am–5pm; Sun 1–5pm. *Vaporetto:* Redentore.

ESPECIALLY FOR KIDS

It goes without saying that a **gondola ride** will be the thrill of a lifetime for any child or adult. If that's too expensive, consider the convenient and far less expensive alternative: a **ride on the no. 1 *vaporetto*.** They offer two entirely different experiences: The gondola gives you the chance to see Venice through the back door (and ride past Marco Polo's house); the *vaporetto* provides a utilitarian—but no less gorgeous—journey down Venice's aquatic Main Street, the Grand Canal. Look for the ambulance boat, the garbage boat, the firefighters' boat, the funeral boat, even the Coca-Cola delivery boat. Best sightings are the special gondolas filled with flowers and rowed by *gondolieri* in livery delivering a happy bride and groom from the church.

Judging from the squeals of delight, **feeding the pigeons in Piazza San Marco** (purchase a bag of corn and you'll be draped in pigeons in a nanosecond) could be the epitome of your child's visit to Venice, and it's the ultimate photo op. Be sure your child won't be startled by all the fluttering and flapping. When I was 11, my parents had me do it; all I remember is the scrabbly little feet of the pigeons.

A jaunt to the neighboring **island of Murano** can be as educational as it is recreational—follow the signs to any *fornace,* where a glass-blowing performance of the island's thousand-year-old art is free entertainment. But be ready for the guaranteed sales pitch that follows.

Before you leave town, take the elevator to the **top of the Campanile di San Marco** (the highest structure in the city) for a pigeon's-eye view of Venice's rooftops and church cupolas, or get up close and personal with the four bronze horses on the facade of the Basilica San Marco. The view from its **outdoor loggia** is something you and your children won't forget.

Some children enjoy the **Museo Navale & Arsenale,** with its ship models and old vessels, and the many historic artifacts in the **Museo Civico Correr (Correr Civic Museum),** tangible vestiges of a time when Venice was a world unto itself.

The **winged lion,** said to have been a kind of good luck mascot to St. Mark, patron saint of Venice, was the very symbol of the Serene Republic and to this day appears on everything from cafe napkins to T-shirts. Who can spot the most flying lions? They appear on facades, atop columns, over doorways, as pavement mosaics, on government stamps, and on the local flag.

6 ORGANIZED TOURS

Most of the central travel agencies and the tourist information offices will have posters in their windows advertising half- and full-day walking tours of the city's sights, and should cost about 35€ for a 2-hour tour and 50€ for a full day, per person.

Organized 3- to 4-hour visits to "The Islands of the Venetian Lagoon" include brief stops on Murano, Burano, and Torcello. See "Exploring Venice's Islands," later in this chapter.

7 FESTIVALS & SPECIAL EVENTS

Venice's most special event is the yearly pre-Lenten **Carnevale** ★★★ (✆ **041-241-0570;** www.carnivalofvenice.com), a 2-week theatrical resuscitation of the 18th-century bacchanalia that drew tourists during the final heyday of the Serene Republic. Most of today's Carnevale-related events, masked balls, and costumes evoke that time. Many of the concerts around town are free, when baroque to samba to gospel to Dixieland jazz music fills the *piazze* and byways; check with the tourist office for a list of events.

The masked balls are often private; those where (exorbitantly priced) tickets are available are sumptuous, with candlelit banquets calling for extravagant costumes you can rent by the day from special shops. If you can score tickets, splurge some 350€ per person on the **Ballo del Doge,** or **Doge's Ball** (✆ **041-523-3851**). They throw a real jet-set party (accessible to all) in the 16th-century Palazzo Pisani-Moretta on the Grand Canal (between the Rialto and the Foscari), sumptuously outfitted with Tiepolo frescoes and all the other accouterments of 18th-century Venetian style. Different ballrooms feature minuets, waltzes, baroque chamber orchestras—there's even a modern disco (acoustically self-contained)—all catered by posh Do Forni restaurant. Those not invited to any ball will be just as happy having their face painted and watching the ongoing street theater from a ringside cafe. There's a **daily market of Carnevale masks and costumes** on Campo Santo Stefano (10am–10pm).

Carnevale builds for 10 days until the big blowout, **Shrove Tuesday** (Fat Tuesday for Mardi Gras), when fireworks illuminate the Grand Canal, and Piazza San Marco is turned into a giant open-air ballroom for the masses. Book your hotel months ahead, especially for the 2 weekends prior to Shrove Tuesday. See "Carnevale a Venezia," below, for more info.

The **Voga Longa** ★ (literally "long row"), a 30km (19-mile) rowing "race" from San Marco to Burano and back again, has been enthusiastically embraced since its inception in 1975, following the city's effort to keep alive the centuries-old heritage of the regatta. It takes place on a Sunday in mid-May; for exact dates, consult the tourist office or www. vogalonga.com. It's a colorful event and a great excuse to party, plus every local seems to have a relative or next-door neighbor competing.

Stupendous fireworks light the night sky during the **Festa del Redentore** ★, on the third Saturday and Sunday in July. This celebration marking the July 1576 lifting of a plague that had gripped the city is centered on the Palladio-designed Chiesa del Redentore (Church of the Redeemer) on the island of Giudecca. A bridge of boats across the Giudecca Canal links the church with the banks of Le Zattere in Dorsoduro, and hundreds of boats of all shapes and sizes fill the Giudecca. It's one big, floating *festa* until night descends and an awesome half-hour *spettacolo* of fireworks fills the sky.

The **Venice International Film Festival** ★★★, in late August and early September, is the most respected celebration of celluloid in Europe after Cannes. Films from all over the world are shown in the Palazzo del Cinema on the Lido as well as at various venues—and occasionally in some of the *campi*. Ticket prices vary, but those for the less-sought-after films are usually modest.

Venice hosts the latest in modern and contemporary painting and sculpture from dozens of countries during the prestigious **Biennale d'Arte** ★★★ (✆ **041-521-8711;** www.labiennale.org), one of the world's top international modern art shows. It fills the pavilions of the public gardens at the east end of Castello and in the Arsenale from late

May to October every odd-numbered year. In the past, awards have gone to Jackson Pollock, Henri Matisse, Alexander Calder, and Federico Fellini, among others. Tickets (20€; 11€ students) can be reserved online or by calling ✆ **199-199-100** (Mon–Fri 9am–6pm, Sat 9am–2pm) in Italy.

The **Regata Storica** ★★ that takes place on the Grand Canal on the first Sunday in September is an extravagant seagoing parade in historic costume as well as a genuine regatta. Just about every seaworthy gondola, richly decorated for the occasion and piloted by *gondolieri* in colorful livery, participates in the opening cavalcade. The aquatic parade is followed by three regattas along the Grand Canal. You can buy grandstand tickets through the tourist office or come early and find a piece of embankment near the Rialto Bridge for the best seats in town.

Other notable events include **Festa della Salute** ★ on November 21, when a pontoon bridge is erected across the Grand Canal to connect the churches of La Salute and Santa Maria del Giglio, commemorating delivery from another plague in 1630. The Festa della Sensa, on the Sunday following Ascension Day in May, reenacts the ancient ceremony when the doge would wed Venice to the sea. April 25 is a local holiday, the **feast day of Saint Mark,** beloved patron saint of Venice and of the ancient republic. A special High Mass is celebrated in the Basilica of San Marco, and Venetians exchange roses with those they love.

Finally, the ultimate anomaly: Venice's annual **October Maratona (Marathon),** starting at Villa Pisani on the mainland and ending up along the Zattere for a finish at the Basilica di Santa Maria della Salute on the tip of Dorsoduro. It's usually held the last Sunday of October.

8 SHOPPING

A mix of low-end trinket stores and middle-market-to-upscale boutiques line the narrow zigzagging **Mercerie** running north between Piazza San Marco and the Rialto Bridge. More expensive clothing and gift boutiques make for great window-shopping on **Calle Larga XXII Marzo,** the wide street that begins west of Piazza San Marco and wends its way to the expansive Campo Santo Stefano near the Accademia. The narrow **Frezzeria,** also west of the piazza and not far from Piazza San Marco, offers a grab bag of bars, souvenir shops, and tony clothing stores.

In a city that for centuries has thrived almost exclusively on tourism, remember this: **Where you buy cheap, you get cheap.** There are few bargains to be had; the nonproduce

VENICE

5

SHOPPING

Ⓣ**ips** **Venice Shopping Strategies**

There are two rules of thumb for shopping in Venice: If you have the good fortune of continuing on to Florence or Rome, shop for clothing, leather goods, and accessories with prudence in Venice, because most items are more expensive here. If, however, you happen on something that strikes you, consider it twice on the spot (not back at your hotel), and then buy it. In this web of alleys, you may never find that shop again.

Carnevale a Venezia

Venetians once more are taking to the open piazzas and streets for the pre-Lenten holiday of Carnevale. The festival traditionally was the celebration preceding Lent, the period of penitence and abstinence prior to Easter; its name is derived from the Latin *carnem levare*, meaning "to take meat away."

Today Carnevale lasts no more than 5 to 10 days and culminates in the Friday to Tuesday before Ash Wednesday. In the 18th-century heyday of Carnevale in La Serenissima Republic, well-heeled revelers came from all over Europe to take part in festivities that began months prior to Lent and crescendoed until their raucous climax at midnight on Shrove Tuesday. As the Venetian economy declined and its colonies and trading posts fell to other powers, the Republic of Venice in its swan song turned to fantasy and escapism. The faster its decline, the longer, and more licentious, became its anything-goes merry-making. Masks became ubiquitous, affording anonymity and the pardoning of a thousand sins. Masks permitted the fishmonger to attend the ball and dance with the baroness, the properly married to carry on as if they were not. The doges condemned it and the popes denounced it, but nothing could dampen the Venetian Carnevale spirit until Napoleon arrived in 1797 and put an end to the festivities.

Resuscitated in 1980 by local tourism powers to fill the empty winter months when tourism comes to a screeching halt, Carnevale is calmer nowadays, though just barely. The born-again festival got off to a shaky start, met at first with indifference and skepticism, but in the years since has grown in popularity and been embraced by the locals. In the 1980s, Carnevale attracted an onslaught of what was seemingly the entire student population of Europe, backpacking young people who slept in the piazzas and train station. Politicians and city officials adopted a middle-of-the-road policy that helped establish Carnevale's image as neither a backpacker's free-for-all outdoor party nor a continuation of the exclusive private balls in the Grand Canal *palazzi* available to a very few.

part of the Rialto Market is as good as it gets, where you'll find cheap T-shirts, glow-in-the-dark plastic gondolas, and tawdry glass trinkets. Venetians, centuries-old merchants, aren't known for bargaining. You'll stand a better chance of getting a bargain if you pay in cash or buy more than one item.

Venice is uniquely famous for local crafts that have been produced here for centuries and are hard to get elsewhere: the **glassware** from Murano, the **delicate lace** from Burano, and the *cartapesta* (papier-mâché) **Carnevale masks** you'll find in endless *botteghe,* where you can watch artisans paint amid their wares.

Now here's the bad news: There's such an overwhelming sea of cheap glass gewgaws that buying Venetian glass can become something of a turnoff (shipping and insurance costs make most things unaffordable; the alternative is to hand-carry anything fragile).

Carnevale is now a harlequin patchwork of musical and cultural events, many of them free of charge, which appeals to all ages, tastes, nationalities, and budgets. At any given moment, musical events are staged in some of the city's dozens of piazzas—from reggae and zydeco to jazz and baroque. Special art exhibits are mounted at museums and galleries. The recent involvement of international corporate commercial sponsors has met with a mixed reception, although it seems to be the direction of the future.

Carnevale is not for those who dislike crowds. Indeed, the crowds are what it's all about. All of Venice becomes a stage. Whether you spend months creating an extravagant costume or grab one from the countless stands set up about the town, Carnevale is about giving in to the spontaneity of magic and surprise around every corner, the mystery behind every mask. Masks and costumes are everywhere, though you won't see anything along the lines of Teletubbies or Zorro. Emphasis is on the historical, for Venice's Carnevale is the chance to relive the glory days of the 1700s when Venetian life was at its most extravagant. Groups travel in coordinated getups that range from a contemporary passel of Felliniesque clowns to the court of the Sun King in all its wigged-out, over-the-top, drag-queen glory. There are the three musketeers riding the *vaporetto;* your waiter appears dressed as a nun; sitting alone on the church steps is a Romeo waiting for his Juliet; late at night, crossing a small, deserted *campo,* a young, laughing couple appears out of a gray mist in a cloud of crinoline and sparkles, and then disappears down a small alley. The places to be seen in costume (only appropriate costumes need apply) are the historical cafes lining the Piazza San Marco, the **Florian** being the unquestioned command post. Don't expect a window seat unless your costume is straight off the stage of the local opera house.

The city is the perfect venue; Hollywood could not create a more evocative location. This is a celebration of history, art, theater, and drama that one would expect to find in Italy, the land that gave us the Renaissance and Zeffirelli—and Venice, an ancient and wealthy republic that gave us Casanova and Vivaldi. Venice and Carnevale were made for each other.

There are so few women left on Burano willing to spend countless tedious hours keeping alive the art of lace-making that the few pieces you'll see not produced by machine in Hong Kong are sold at stratospheric prices; ditto the truly high-quality glass (though trinkets can be cheap and fun). Still, exceptions are to be found in all of the above, and when you find them you'll know. A discerning eye can cut through the dreck to find some lovely mementos.

ANTIQUES

The interesting **Mercatino dell'Antiquariato (Antiques Fair)** takes place three times annually in the charming Campo San Maurizio between Piazza San Marco and Campo Santo Stefano. Dates change yearly for the 3-day weekend market but generally fall the first weekend of April, mid-September, and the weekend before Christmas. More than

100 vendors sell everything from the sublime piece of Murano glass to quirky dust collectors. Early birds might find reasonably priced finds such as Murano candy dishes from the 1950s, Venetian-pearl glass beads older still, vintage Italian posters advertising Campari-sponsored regattas, or antique postcards of Venice that could be from the 1930s or the 1830s—things change so little here. Those for whom price is less an issue might pick up antique lace by the yard or a singular museum-quality piece of hand-blown glass from a local master.

BOOKS

Libreria Studium, San Marco 337 (✆ **041-522-2382**), carries lots of travel guides and maps as well as books in English. Two other centrally located bookstores are the **Libreria Sansovino,** in the Bacino Orseolo 84, just north of the Piazza San Marco (✆ **041-522-2623**), carrying a good selection of books about Venetian art, history, and literature; and the **Mondadori,** San Marco 1346 (✆ **041-522-2193**), on Salizzada San Moise, which stocks travel guides and English-language books.

For art books and other colorful hardbacks on history and Italian sights to hold down your coffee table at 40% to 50% off, head to **Libreria Bertoni Mario,** San Marco 3637B (Rio Terrà dei Assassini; ✆ **041-522-9583**), or **Libreria Beronti Alberto,** San Marco 4718 (Calle dei Fabbri; ✆ **041-522-4615**).

CRAFTS

The **Murano Art Shop,** at San Marco 1232 (on the store-lined Frezzeria, parallel to the western border of, and close to, the Piazza San Marco; ✆ **041-523-3851**), is a cultural experience. At this small shop, every inch of wall space is draped with the whimsical crafts of the city's most creative artisans. Fusing the timeless with the contemporary—with a nod to the magic and romance of Venice past—the store offers a dramatic and evolving collection of masks, puppets, music boxes, costume jewelry, and the like. It's all expensive, but this rivals a visit to the Doge's Palace.

When it seems as if every gift-store window is awash with collectible bisque-faced dolls in elaborate pinafores and headdresses, head to **Bambole di Trilly,** at Castello 4974 (Fondamenta dell'Osmarin, off the Campo San Provolo on your way east out of Piazza San Marco in the direction of the Church of San Zaccaria; ✆ **041-521-2579**), where the hand-sewn wardrobes of rich Venetian fabrics and painstakingly painted faces are particularly exquisite. The perfect souvenir starts at about 20€ in this well-stocked workspace north of Campo San Zaccaria.

FOODSTUFFS

Food lovers will find charmingly packaged food products for themselves or friends at the well-known pasta manufacturer **Giacomo Rizzo,** near the major Coin department store, northeast of the Rialto Bridge at Cannaregio 5778 at Calle San Giovanni Grisostomo (✆ **041-522-2824**). You'll find pasta made in the shape of gondolas, colorful carnival hats, and dozens of other imaginatively shaped possibilities (colored and flavored with squash, beet, and spinach).

Those with a sweet tooth should head in the opposite direction, to Giancarlo Vio's **Pasticceria Marchini,** just before Campo Santo Stefano (San Marco 2769 at Ponte San Maurizio; ✆ **041-522-9109**), where the selection of traditional cookies are beautifully prepackaged for traveling—delicate *baicoli,* cornmeal raisin *zaleti,* and the S-shaped *buranelli.*

GLASS

If you're going to go all out, look no further than **Venini,** Piazzetta dei Leoni 314 (*C* **041-522-4045**), since 1921 one of the most respected and innovative glassmakers in all of Venice. Their products are more works of art than merely blown glass. So renowned are they for their quality, Versace's own line of glass objets d'art are done by Venini. Their **workshop** on Murano is at Fondamenta Vetrai 50 (*C* **041-273-7211**). Cheap they are not, but no one else has such a lovely or original representation of hand-blown Murano glassware.

You should also visit the spacious emporium of quality glass items at **Marco Polo** (San Marco 1644; *C* **041-522-9295**), just west of the Piazza San Marco. The front half of the first floor offers a variety of small gift ideas (candy dishes, glass-topped medicine boxes, paperweights).

Glass beads are called "Venetian pearls," and an abundance of exquisite antique and reproduced baubles are the draw at **Anticlea,** at Castello 4719A (a bit off Campo San Provolo going north on Calle San Provolo; *C* **041-528-6946**). Once used for trading in Venice's far-flung colonies, they now fill the coffers of this small shop east of Piazza San Marco, sold singly or already strung. The open-air stall of **Susie and Andrea** (Riva degli Schiavoni, near Pensione Wildner; just ask) has handcrafted beads that are new, well made and strung, and moderately priced. The stall operates from February through November.

JEWELRY

Chimento, San Marco 1460 (Campo San Moisè; *C* **041-523-6010;** www.chimento.it), carries gold and silver jewelry of their own manufacture as well as items from top international designers, including Faberge.

Tiny **Antichità Zaggia,** Dorsoduro 1195 (Calle della Toletta; *C* **041-522-3159**), specializes in genuine antique jewelry (and glassware) of the highest quality and beautiful designs.

The jewelers at **Esperienze,** Cannaregio 326B (Ponte delle Guglie; *C* **041-721-866**), marry their own art with the local glass-blowing traditions to create unique pins, necklaces, and other jewelry.

LEATHER & SHOES

One usually thinks of Florence when thinking of Italian leather goods. But the plethora of mediocre-to-refined shoe stores in Venice is testimony to the tradition of small shoe factories along the nearby Brenta canal that supply most of Italy, and much of the world, with made-in-Italy footwear. Venice has plenty of fine shoe stores—including **Bruno Magli,** San Marco 1302 (Calle dell'Ascensione; *C* **041-522-7210**), and **Mori e Bozzi,** Cannaregio 2367 (Rio Terrà della Madonna; *C* **041-715-261**)—but one store deserves singling out for sheer oddness. Even if you're not in the market for shoes, stop by **Rolando Segalin,** San Marco 4365 (Calle dei Fuseri; *C* **041-522-2115**), for fantastical footwear in an acid trip of colors and shapes, including curly-toed creations; many are intended for Carnevale costumes.

LINENS & LACE

Frette, San Marco 2070A (Calle Larga/Via XXII Marzo; *C* **041-522-4914;** www.frette.com), is another long-respected place to head for classy linens, bedclothes, and silk jammies. They'll even do custom work for you.

For hand-tatted lace from the only school still teaching it in Venice, ride out to Burano to visit the **Scuola dei Merletti,** Piazza B. Galuppi (✆ **041-730-034**), founded in 1872, closed in 1972, and reopened in 1981. (*Note:* The Scuola dei Merletti and the museum are closed for restoration until mid-2010.)

MASKS

A shortage of mask *bottegas* in Venice is not a problem; the challenge is ferreting out the few exceptionally talented artists producing one-of-a-kind theatrical pieces. Only the quality-conscious should shop at **La Bottega dei Mascareri** (San Polo 80—at the northern end of the Rialto Bridge amid the tourist booths; ✆ **041-522-3857**), where the charming Boldrin brothers' least elaborate masks begin at about 20€. Anyone who thinks a mask is a mask is a mask should come here first for a look-see.

Not only does **Il Canovaccio,** Castello 5369–70 (Calle delle Bande; ✆ **041-521-0393**), produce high-quality artisan work, but it's undeniably cool. Rolling Stone guitarist Ron Wood has shopped here, and the shop provided the masks and costumes for the orgy scene in Stanley Kubrick's *Eyes Wide Shut.*

PAPER PRODUCTS

Biblos, with shops in San Marco at 739 (Mercerie San Zulian), 2087 (Via XXII Marzo), and 221 (Mercerie de l'Orologio; ✆ **041-521-0714;** www.biblos-venezia.com), carries leather-bound blank books and journals, marbleized paper, enamel pill boxes, watercolor etchings, and fountain pens.

WINE

For a broad selection of wines from the Veneto and across Italy at truly decent prices, head to **Bottiglieria Colonna,** Castello 5595 (Calle della Fava; ✆ **041-528-5137**), which will put together gift packets of wines in packs of six, and also handles liqueurs from around the world. There's a more down-to-earth cantina called **Nave de Oro,** Cannaregio 4657 (Rio Terrà dei SS. Apostoli; ✆ **041-522-7872**), where locals bring empty bottles to have them filled with a variety of Veneto table wines at low, low prices—1.80€ to 2.30€ per liter.

9 VENICE AFTER DARK

Visit one of the tourist information centers for current English-language schedules of the month's special events. The monthly *Ospite di Venezia* is distributed free or online at **www.unospitedivenezia.it** and is extremely helpful but usually available only in the more expensive hotels. If you're looking for serious nocturnal action, you're in the wrong town. Your best bet is to sit in the moonlit Piazza San Marco and listen to the cafes' outdoor orchestras, with the illuminated basilica before you—the perfect opera set.

THE PERFORMING ARTS

Venice has a long and rich tradition of classical music, and there's always a concert going on somewhere. Several churches regularly host classical music concerts (with an emphasis on the baroque) by local and international artists. This was, after all, the home of Vivaldi. One of the more popular spots to hear the music of Vivaldi and his contemporaries is **Chiesa San Vidal,** between Campo Santo Stefano and the Accademia bridge. Unfortunately, the Chiesa di Vivaldi (officially, the Chiesa Santa Maria della Pietà), once the most popular venue for hearing Vivaldi's works, no longer hosts concerts. Though this was the best venue to attend a Vivaldi concert, there are still many other places to catch a show. A number of other churches and confraternities (such as San Stae, the Scuola di San Giovanni Evangelista, and the Scuola di San Rocco) host concerts. People dressed in period costumes stand around in heavily trafficked spots near San Marco and Rialto passing out brochures advertising the classical music concerts, so you'll have no trouble finding up-to-date information.

The city still remembers well when the famous **Teatro La Fenice** ★★★ (San Marco 1965, on Campo San Fantin; ℂ **041-2424** or 041-786-511; www.teatrolafenice it) went up in flames in January 1996. For centuries it was Venice's principal stage for world-class opera, music, theater, and ballet. Carpenters and artisans were on standby to begin working around the clock to re-create the teatro (built in 1836) according to archival designs. Finally, on December 14, 2003, La Fenice (which means "the Phoenix") arose from the ashes as Ricardo Muti conducted the Orchestra and Chorus of La Fenice in an inaugural concert in a completely renovated hall. Its performances now follow a regular schedule.

CAFES

Venice is a quiet town in the evening and offers very little in the way of nightlife. For tourists and locals alike, Venetian nightlife mainly centers on the many cafe/bars in one of the world's most remarkable piazzas: Piazza San Marco. It is also the most expensive and touristed place to linger over a Campari or cappuccino, but it's a splurge that should not be dismissed too readily.

One of the most atmospheric and hidden places to have a *spritz* (soda water, white wine, and your choice of Campari or Aperol) is **Taverna del Campiello Remer** (Cannaregio 5701; ℂ **349-336-5168**), in the courtyard of the same name, right on the Grand Canal close to the Rialto bridge. The nightly live music—feel free to get up and sing, if you're any good—along with the expertly staffed bar, extensive wine list, and big portions of prosciutto and melon, are a recipe for a romantic night out, especially in this magically restored cantina, right by the canal. It generally stays open until at least 1am (closed Wed).

The nostalgic 18th-century **Caffè Florian** ★★ (San Marco 56A–59A; ℂ **041-241-7286**), on the south side of the piazza, is the most famous (closed Wed in winter) and most theatrical inside; have a Bellini (*prosecco* and fresh peach nectar) at the back bar for half what you'd pay at an indoor table; alfresco seating is even more expensive when the band plays on, but it's worth every cent. It's said that when Casanova escaped from the prisons in the Doge's Palace, he stopped here for a coffee before fleeing Venice.

On the opposite side of the square at San Marco 133–134 is the old-world **Caffè Lavena** (ℂ **041-522-4070;** closed Tues in winter), and at no. 120 is **Caffè Quadri** ★ (ℂ **041-522-2105;** www.quadrivenice.com; closed Mon in winter), the first to introduce coffee to Venice, with a restaurant upstairs that sports Piazza San Marco views. See p. 132 for more on Quadri's restaurant. At all spots, a cappuccino, tea, or Coca-Cola at a table will set you back about 7€. But no one will rush you, and if the sun is warm and the orchestras are playing, there's no more beautiful public open-air salon in the world. Around the corner (no. 11) and in front of the pink-and-white marble Palazzo Ducale is the best deal, **Caffè Chioggia** ★★★ (ℂ **041-528-5011;** closed Sun). Come here at midnight and watch the Moors strike the hour atop the Clock Tower from your outside table, while the quartet or pianist plays everything from quality jazz to pop until the wee hours.

If the weather is chilly or inclement, or for no other reason than to revel in the history and drama of Venice's grand-dame hotel, dress up and stroll into the landmark lobby of the Danieli hotel and **Bar Dandolo** (Castello 4196 on Riva degli Schiavoni, east of Piazza San Marc; © **041-522-6480**). Tea or coffee will set you back only 7.50€, and you can sit forever, taking in the former residential *palazzo* of a 15th-century doge. A pianist plays from 7 to 9pm and from 10pm to 12:30am. Drinks are far more expensive; ask for the price list before ordering.

CLUBS, BIRRERIE & GELATERIE

Although Venice boasts an old and prominent university, clubs and discos barely enjoy their 15 minutes of popularity before changing hands or closing down (some are open only in the summer months). Young Venetians tend to go to the Lido or mainland Mestre.

For just plain hanging out in the late afternoon and early evening, popular squares that serve as meeting points include **Campo San Bartolomeo,** at the foot of the Rialto Bridge, and nearby **Campo San Luca;** you'll see Venetians of all ages milling about engaged in animated conversation, particularly from 5pm until dinnertime. In late-night hours, for low prices and low pretension, I'm fond of the **Campo Santa Margherita,** a huge open *campo* about halfway between the train station and Ca' Rezzonico. Look for the popular **Green Pub** (no. 3053; closed Thurs), **Bareto Rosso** (no. 2963; closed Sun), and **Bar Salus** (no. 3112). **Campo Santo Stefano** is also worth a visit to sit and sample the goods at the **Bar/Gelateria Paolin** (no. 2962; closed Fri), one of the city's best ice cream sources. Its runner-up, **Gelateria Nico,** is on the Zattere in Dorsoduro 922, south of the Gallerie dell'Accademia. For occasional evenings of live music, cabaret, or just a relaxed late-night hangout, consider the ever-popular **Le Bistrot de Venise** (p. 133).

Note: Most bars are open Monday to Saturday from 8pm to midnight.

The **Devil's Forest Pub** ★, San Marco 5185, on Calle Stagneri (© **041-520-0623; www.devilsforest.com**; *vaporetto:* San Marco), offers the outsider an authentic chance to take in the convivial atmosphere and find out where Venetians hang out. It's popular for lunch with the neighborhood merchants and shop owners, and ideal for relaxed socializing over a beer and a host of games like backgammon, chess, and Trivial Pursuit. A variety of simple Irish dishes are served. It's open daily 10am to 1am.

Bácaro Jazz ★★ (© **041-285-249;** *vaporetto:* Rialto) is a happening cocktail bar (the Bellinis are great) with restaurant seating in the back (tasty Venetian cuisine from 8€), across from the Rialto post office at San Marco 5546, just north of Campo San Bartolomeo (the San Marco side of Rialto Bridge). It's a mix of jazzy music (a bit too loud), rough plank walls, industrial-steel tables, and a corrugated aluminum ceiling. It's open Thursday to Tuesday 11am to 2am (happy hour 2–7:30pm).

Being the only real pub in town, the **Inishark Irish Pub** ★, at Castello 5787 (Calle Mondo Novo just off Salizzada San Lio, near Santa Maria Formosa; © **041-523-5300;** *vaporetto:* Rialto) is a big draw for young locals as well as tourists. As in every self-respecting Irish pub this side of Dublin, here you'll find Guinness on tap and the walls full of Irish paraphernalia. There is an enormous flat screen television where they show soccer matches and other sporting events.

Good food at reasonable prices would be enough to regularly pack **Paradiso Perduto** ★★, Cannaregio 2540, on Fondamenta della Misericordia (© **041-720-581;** *vaporetto:* Ferrovie), but its biggest draw is the live jazz performed on a small stage several nights a week. Popular with Americans and other foreigners living in Venice, this bar was once largely devoid of tourists, primarily because of its hard-to-find location, but lately it looks as if the word is out. The good selection of well-prepared pizzas and pastas goes for under 10€; arrive early for a table. It's open Thursday to Tuesday 7pm to 1 or some-times 2am.

The party spills well out from the plate-glass windows of **Bar Torino,** San Marco 459 (Campo San Luca; ✆ **041-522-3914**), a bar that has brought this square to life after dark with live jazz many nights, unusual beer from Lapland, and good panini. It's open Tuesday to Sunday 7am to 2am.

In 1932, famed restaurateur and hotelier Giuseppe Cipriani opened **Harry's Bar** ★★ right at the San Marco–Vallaresso *vaporetto* stop, San Marco 1323 (Calle Vallaresso; ✆ **041-528-5777**). Named for his son Arrigo (Italian for Harry), it has been a preferred retreat for everyone from Hemingway—when he didn't want a bloody mary, he mixed his own drink: 15 parts gin, 1 martini—to Woody Allen. Regulars prefer the elegant front room to the upstairs dining room (the cooking is decent, and they invented carpac-cio, a dish of thinly sliced raw beef now served throughout Italy). Harry's is most famous for inventing the Bellini, a mix of champagne and peach juice. Prices—for both drinks and the fancy cuisine—are rather extravagant.

Dance Clubs

Venice is a quiet town at night and offers little in the line of dance clubs. Evenings are best spent lingering over a late dinner, having a pint in a *birrerie,* or nursing a glass of *prosecco* in one of Piazza San Marco's tony outdoor cafes.

If you really need that disco fix, you're best off at **Piccolo Mondo** ★, Dorsoduro 1056, near the Accademia (✆ **041-520-0371;** *vaporetto:* Accademia). Billed as a disco/pub, it serves sandwiches during lunch to the sounds of America's latest dance music, offers a happy hour in the late afternoon in winter, and often features live music. But the only reason you'd want to come is if you want a disco night (summer only); the club is frequented mostly by curious foreigners and the young to not-so-young Venetians who seek them out. It's open daily from 10pm to 4am in summer, and 10am to 4pm and 5 to 8pm in winter.

THE CASINO

From May to October, **Casino Municipale di Venezia,** located at Palazzo Vendramin Calergi, Cannaregio 2040 (Fondamenta Vendramin; ✆ **041-529-7111;** www.casino venezia.it; *vaporetto:* San Marcuola), moves to its nondescript summer location on the Lido, where a visit is not as strongly recommended as during the winter months, when it is housed in this handsome 15th-century *palazzo* on the Grand Canal. Venice's tradi-tion of gambling goes back to the glory days of the republic and lives on in this august Renaissance palace built by Mauro Codussi. Though not of the caliber of Monte Carlo and, on a midweek winter's night, occasionally slow, this is one of only four casinos on Italian territory—and what a remarkable stage setting it is! Richard Wagner lived and died in a wing of this *palazzo* in 1883.

Check with your hotel before setting forth; some offer free passes for their guests. Otherwise, if you're not a gambler or a curiosity seeker, it may not be worth the admis-sion cost of 5€ to get in. *Tip:* If you pay a higher 10€ admission fee, the casino will provide you with a 10€ credit for gambling, so your admission could actually be free—and perhaps, if you're lucky, better than free. *Note:* A passport and jacket are required for entrance (you can rent the jacket there, the passport you have to bring yourself), and the casino is open daily from 3:30pm (11am for the slots) to 2:45am (3:45am Fri and Sat).

10 EXPLORING VENICE'S ISLANDS

Venice shares its lagoon with three other principal islands: Murano, Burano, and Torcello. Guided tours of the three are operated by a dozen agencies with docks on Riva degli Schiavoni/Piazzetta San Marco (all interchangeable). The 3- and 4-hour tours run 15€ to 26€, usually include a visit to a Murano glass factory (you can easily do that on your own, with less of a hard sell), and leave daily around 9:30am and 2:30pm (times change; check in advance).

You can also visit the islands on your own conveniently and easily using the *vaporetti.* Line nos. 12, 13, 14, 41, and 42 make the journey to Murano from Fondamente Nove (on the north side of Castello), and line no. 12 continues on to Burano and Torcello. The islands are small and easy to navigate, but check the schedule for the next island-to-island departure (usually hourly) and your return so that you don't spend most of your day waiting for connections.

MURANO & ITS GLASS

The island of **Murano ★★** has long been famous throughout the world for the products of its glass factories, but there's little here in variety or prices that you won't find in Venice. A visit to the **Museo del Vetro (Museum of Glass),** Fondamenta Giustinian 8 (✆ **041-739-586**), will put the island's centuries-old legacy into perspective and is recommended for those considering major buys. Hours are Thursday to Tuesday 10am to 6pm (to 5pm Nov–Mar), and admission is 5.50€ for adults and 3€ children 6 to 14 and students under 30, or free with the cumulative Museum Pass (see "Venice Discounts," on p. 107).

Dozens of *fornaci* (furnaces) offer free shows of mouth-blown glassmaking almost invariably hitched to a hard-sell ("No obligation! Really!") tour of the factory outlet. These retail showrooms of delicate glassware can be enlightening or boring, depending on your frame of mind. Almost all the places ship, often doubling the price. On the other hand, these pieces are instant heirlooms.

Murano also has two worthy churches: **San Pietro Martire ★**, with its altarpieces by Tintoretto, Veronese, and Giovanni Bellini, and the ancient **Santa Maria e Donato ★**, with an intricate Byzantine exterior apse and a 6th-century pulpit and columns inside resting on a fantastic 12th-century inlaid floor.

BURANO & ITS LACE

Lace is the claim to fame of tiny, colorful **Burano ★★★**, a craft kept alive for centuries by the wives of fishermen waiting for their husbands to return from sea. It's still worth a trip if you have time to stroll the island's back streets, whose canals are lined with the brightly colored simple homes of the *buranesi* fisherman. The local government continues its attempt to keep its centuries-old lace legacy alive with subsidized classes.

Visit the **Museo del Merletto (Museum of Lace Making),** Piazza Galuppi (✆ **041-730-034**), to understand why something so exquisite should not be left to fade into extinction. It's open Wednesday to Monday 10am to 5pm (to 4pm Nov–Mar), and admission is 4€ adults and 2.50€ children 6 to 14 and students under 30, or free with the cumulative Museum Pass (see "Venice Discounts," on p. 107). (*Note:* The museum is closed until mid-2010 for restoration.)

TORCELLO

Nearby **Torcello** ★ is perhaps the most charming of the islands. It was the first of the lagoon islands to be called home by the mainland population fleeing Atilla and his Huns (from here they eventually moved to join the growing area around what is now Rialto Bridge), but today it consists of little more than one long canal leading from the *vaporetto* landing past sad-sack vineyards to a clump of buildings at its center.

Torcello boasts the oldest Venetian monument, the **Cattedrale di Torcello (Santa Maria Assunta)** ★★★, whose foundation dates from the 7th century (*©* **041-730-084**). It's famous for its outstanding 11th- to 12-century Byzantine mosaics—a *Madonna and Child* in the apse and *Last Judgment* on the west wall—rivaling those of Ravenna's and St. Mark's basilicas. The cathedral is open daily 10:30am to 6pm (shorter hours in winter), and admission is 3€. You can climb the bell tower for a panorama for 2€. Also of interest is the adjacent **11th-century church** dedicated to St. Fosca and a **small archaeological museum;** the church's hours are the same as the cathedral's, and the museum is open Tuesday to Sunday 10am to 12:30pm and 2 to 4pm. Museum admission is 2€. A combined ticket for all three sights is 6€.

Peaceful Torcello is uninhabited except for a handful of families and is a favorite picnic spot (you'll have to bring the food from Venice—there are no stores on the island and only one bar/trattoria and one rather expensive restaurant, the Cipriani, of Hemingway fame). Once the tour groups have left, it offers a very special moment of solitude and escape when St. Mark's bottleneck becomes oppressive.

THE LIDO & ITS BEACHES

Although a convenient 15-minute *vaporetto* ride away from San Marco, Venice's **Lido beaches** are not much to write home about. The Adriatic waters have had pollution problems in recent years, and for bathing and sun-worshipping there are much nicer beaches nearby—in Jesolo, to the north, for example. But the parade of wealthy Italian and foreign tourists (plus a good number of Venetian families with children) who frequent this *litorale* (coastal area) throughout summer is an interesting sight indeed, though you'll find many of them at the elitist beaches affiliated with such deluxe hotels as the legendary Excelsior and the Des Bains.

There are two beach areas at the Lido. **Bucintoro** is at the opposite end of Gran Viale Santa Maria Elisabetta (referred to as the Gran Viale) from the *vaporetto* station Santa Elisabetta. It's a 10-minute stroll; walk straight ahead along Gran Viale to reach the beach. **San Nicolò,** 1.6km (1 mile) away, can be reached by bus B. You'll have to pay 10€ per person (standard procedure at Italy's beaches) for use of the cabins and umbrella rental. Alternatively, you can patronize the more crowded and noisier **public beach,** Zona A at the end of Gran Viale. Keep in mind that if you stay at any of the hotels on the Lido, most of them have some kind of agreement with the different beach establishments *(bagni).*

The Lido's limited sports amenities, such as golf and tennis, are affiliated with its deluxe five-star hotels. Although there is car traffic, the Lido's wide, shaded boulevards are your best bet for jogging while you're visiting Venice. A number of bike-rental places along the Gran Viale rent bicycles for 4€ to 8€ an hour. *Vaporetto* line nos. 1, 6, 52, and 82 cross the lagoon to the Lido from the San Zaccaria–Danieli stop near San Marco.

VENICE

5

EXPLORING VENICE'S ISLANDS

The Veneto

For centuries the Venetian Republic ruled most of the northeastern region called the Veneto, but many of those inland cities had been around for centuries when the city of Venice was officially founded with the election of its first doge in A.D. 726. As ancient Roman strongholds, these cities had already lived through a glorious period. Verona has even been called "Little Rome" for its wealth of Roman sites and magnificent ancient amphitheater.

Until Napoleon arrived in 1797—whereupon he donated Venice to Austria (where it would remain until 1866) and broke up the regional power structure—the Veneto shared in the bounty of the Serene Republic, its countryside a mixture of vineyards, fields, and summer villas. Many of the Palladian villas that dot the hills of the Veneto were once the extravagant legacy of wealthy Venetian merchants whose urban *palazzi*-cum-warehouses lined Venice's Grand Canal. The Veneto also boasts buildings that show the Byzantine-Oriental influence so prominent in Venice's Gothic architecture, some adorned with frescoes by Giotto, and later by the Venetian masters Tiepolo, Veronese, Titian, and Tintoretto. Columns topped by the winged-lion mascot of St. Mark and representing the Serene Republic—a symbol of those distant, often glorious times—still stand in the main squares of the Veneto's three great city centers: Padua, Vicenza, and Verona.

Indeed, the first architectural movement to sweep through the entire Western world has its roots in the Veneto. The geometric and classical form of the High Renaissance that local architect Andrea Palladio practiced became the model for the rest of the world's Renaissance builders—from England's Inigo Jones to Thomas Jefferson's Monticello. Throughout the Veneto you'll find a wealth of Venetian Renaissance *palazzi,* frescoed churches, and basilicas, which makes a tour through the region a rewarding and fascinating trip.

The Veneto even had a hold on those who knew of its enchantments only from afar. Shakespeare may have never set foot in these parts, but "fair Verona" and the surrounding area so fascinated him that he chose to set some of his best works *(Romeo and Juliet, Two Gentlemen of Verona)* there.

Geographically, the Veneto is a region of great diversity. It abuts the Adriatic Sea to the east and shares Lake Garda with Lombardy to the west. Its northern boundaries reach up to the pale, pink-tinged mountain range of the regal Dolomites that separate Italy from the Austrian Tirol. The southern boundary is the mighty Po River, its relentlessly flat alluvial plains punctuated by the Berici Mountains south of Vicenza and the Euganean Hills near Padua. But the Veneto is really defined by the valleys flowing down from the Dolomites and Alps in the north: The Adige, Brenta, Piave, and other rivers make fertile the Veneto's middle hills, rich with the vineyards, fruit orchards, and small-scale farms that create the agricultural wealth that has been the Veneto's sustenance.

The Veneto's three major cities, **Padua, Vicenza,** and **Verona,** hold the most historical and artistic interest in the region, and they are all accessible by public transportation. Trains between these cities run on the Milan-Venice line and, hence, are inexpensive, frequent, and user-friendly. In fact, the distances between the cities are so small that you could very well stay put in Venice and tool into Verona—the most distant of the three—for an easy day trip. But this would be a great shame, since each of the cities warrants a slow exploration.

Enjoy the Veneto in the late afternoon and early evening hours when the day-trippers have gone; sip an *aperitivo* or take a leisurely *passeggiata* along streets lined with tiny boutiques. End your day with a moderately priced meal of home-cooked regional specialties in a characteristic wine tavern amid much bonhomie and brio, followed by a good night's rest in a small, friendly hotel located just off the postcard-perfect main square.

Spend time in the region's lesser-explored cities and small towns such as **Treviso, Bassano del Grappa,** and **Asolo.** All offer a host of excursions into the real countryside, where you need only a car or the slightest sense of adventure to jump on a local bus and enjoy the back roads and backwaters of the Veneto. Top it off with a leisurely cruise down the Brenta Canal to return to Venice.

REGIONAL CUISINE The Veneto's food products are as diverse as its geography. From the mountains and their foothills come a proliferation of **mushrooms** and **game.** The northerly reaches around Treviso produce wild **white asparagus** and

cherries in the spring and, in the late fall, **radicchio,** a red chicory that was renowned in ancient Roman times. Much of the cuisine is based on the rice and corn grown here; on most menus here you'll find **polenta,** which is served with a hearty game stew with hints of Austrian influence. **Risotto** is often served as a first course along with the season's vegetables or, more characteristically, offerings from the Adriatic on the east.

Unlike in Tuscany, olive oil is used sparingly here—it is not unusual to see **butter** instead, which is so commonly associated with Emilian food. But above all, it is the Adriatic that dictates even the landlocked cuisines of the Veneto.

The proliferation of desserts is a throwback to when the Veneto was ceded to Austria—sweet reminders are evident in many pastry shops. **Tiramisù** (lady fingers soaked in espresso and liqueur, layered with sweetened mascarpone cheese and dusted with cacao), is said to have originated in the Veneto and remains a favorite at Italian restaurants the world over.

The Veneto—and Verona especially—plays an all-important role in the production and exportation of wines: **Soave, Bardolino, Valpolicella,** and **Amarone** are world-recognized varieties that originate in these acclaimed vineyards. No other region in Italy produces as many DOC (Denominazione di Origine Controllata, zones of controlled name and origin) red wines as the Veneto. The rich volcanic earth of the Colli Euganei produces a good number of these, while a light and fizzy **prosecco** hails from the hills around Asolo. Wine is an integral element in any meal, and it's no compromise to limit yourself to the local regional wines that are some of Europe's finest.

For more information on the Veneto, check out this good regionwide website: **www.venetonet.com**.

1 PADUA (PADOVA)

42km (26 miles) W of Venice, 81km (50 miles) E of Verona, 32km (20 miles) E of Vicenza, 234km (145 miles) E of Milan

The University of Bologna had already grown to 10,000 students by the time Padua (Padova) founded its university in 1222. Padua was long the academic heartbeat of the powerful Venetian Republic—and far before that, an ancient Roman stronghold—and for this reason one of the most important medieval and Renaissance cities in Italy. Dante and Copernicus studied here, and Petrarch and Galileo taught here. When you wander the narrow, cobbled, arcaded side streets in the timeless neighborhoods surrounding the "Bo" (named after a 15th-c. inn that once stood on the present-day site of the university), you will be transported back to those earlier times.

Padua is a vital city, with a young university population that gets about by bicycle and keeps the city's piazzas and cafes alive. The historic hub of town still evokes the days when the city and its university flourished in the late Middle Ages and the Renaissance as a center of learning and art, although you'll have to visit during the scholastic year to witness it: Padua in summer is something of a ghost town.

Most visitors bypass Padua in their rush to Venice. During peak season, when Venice's hotels are full, some travelers stay here but see little except for the train station. You can spend a few hours or a few days in Padua, depending on your schedule. Its most important

A Pilgrimage for the Absent Minded

Giotto's frescoes attract art lovers and the city's university students, but pilgrims of another ilk have long secured Padua's place on the map. For more than 700 years, the enormous **Basilica di Sant'Antonio** has drawn millions from around the world. A mendicant Franciscan monk born in Lisbon, Antonio spent his last years in Padua. He died here in 1231 and was canonized almost immediately, and the basilica—a fantastic mingling of Romanesque, Byzantine, and Gothic styles—was begun within a year.

St. Anthony is one of the Roman Catholic Church's most beloved saints—and one of Italy's most popular namesakes—universally known for his powers to locate lost keys or sunglasses, lost causes, lost everything. Countless handwritten messages left in a kind of mailbox in the side of his tomb within the church call upon this power to help find everything from lost love to lost limbs. For example, I lost something rather important in Padua—my annotated copy of this book! A quick visit to St. Anthony did the trick: When I left the church and switched my cellphone back on, I received a call from the cafe where I had been that morning. The proprietor had found the missing book.

Both the church and the miracle worker are simply referred to as "il Santo," and the church warrants a visit for its artistic treasures and architectural importance, as well as for its religious significance.

sights for those with limited time are Giotto's magnificent **frescoes** in the Scrovegni Chapel (fully restored between 1999 and 2001) and the revered pilgrimage site of the eight-domed **Basilica of Sant'Antonio di Padova,** whose important **equestrian statue** by Donatello stands in the piazza before it.

FESTIVALS & MARKETS   The beloved Sant'Antonio (see "A Pilgrimage for the Absent Minded," above) is celebrated with a **feast day** on June 13, when his relics are carried about town in an elaborate procession joined in by the thousands of pilgrims who come from all over the world.

The **outdoor markets** (Mon–Sat) in the twin Piazza delle Erbe (for fresh produce) and Piazza della Frutta (dry goods) that flank the enormous Palazzo della Ragione are some of Italy's best. The third Sunday of every month sees the area of the Prato della Valle inundated by more than 200 antiques and collectibles dealers, one of the largest **antiques and collectibles fairs** in the region. Only early birds will beat the large number of local dealers to the worm.

Antiques lovers with a car might want to visit Italy's second-largest **Mercato dell'Antiquariato** at the 18th-century Villa Contarini (in Piazzola sul Brenta, a lovely 30-min. drive that can be combined with visiting some of the other Palladian and Palladian-inspired country villas along the Brenta Canal; see "Day Trips from Padua," later in this chapter), held the last Sunday of every month. There an estimated 350 vendors hawk their wares; the villa is open for visits during those hours.

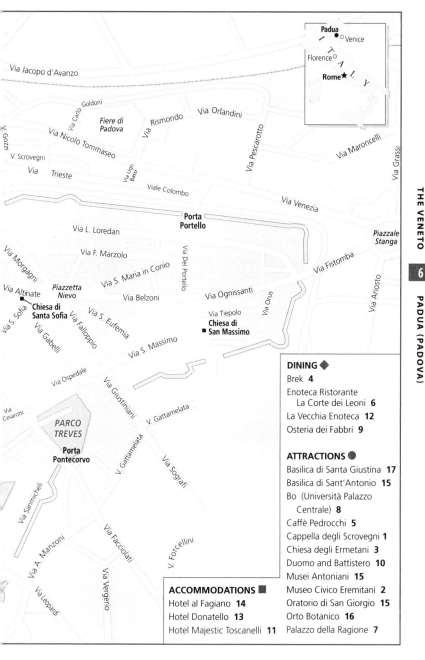

DINING ◆
Brek **4**
Enoteca Ristorante
  La Corte dei Leoni **6**
La Vecchia Enoteca **12**
Osteria dei Fabbri **9**

ATTRACTIONS ●
Basilica di Santa Giustina **17**
Basilica di Sant'Antonio **15**
Bo (Università Palazzo
  Centrale) **8**
Caffè Pedrocchi **5**
Cappella degli Scrovegni **1**
Chiesa degli Ermetani **3**
Duomo and Battistero **10**
Musei Antoniani **15**
Museo Civico Eremitani **2**
Oratorio di San Giorgio **15**
Orto Botanico **16**
Palazzo della Ragione **7**

ACCOMMODATIONS ■
Hotel al Fagiano **14**
Hotel Donatello **13**
Hotel Majestic Toscanelli **11**

> **(Finds) Shoes & Spoons**
>
> A less important street market is the weekly **Saturday outdoor market of non-antique goods** (selling clothes, pet food, household goods—nothing fascinating, but an interesting peek into local life and a good place to pick up kitchen items to re-create your own *cucina italiana* back home) in the Prato della Valle. It has a number of inexpensive shoe stands hawking goods from the many factories for which the nearby Brenta Canal area has long been renowned. Both the antiques fair (listed above) and this weekly market will give you a reason to visit the 18th-century **Prato della Valle,** said to be one of the largest piazzas in Europe. Located just southwest of the Basilica di Sant'Antonio, it is ringed by a canal and populated by more than 80 statues.

ESSENTIALS

GETTING THERE   By Train   The main train station is at Piazza Stazione (© 049-875-1800; www.ferroviedellostato.it), in the northern part of town, just outside the 16th-century walls. Padua is well connected by frequent train service to points directly west and east: Verona (1 hr.), Venice (30 min.), Vicenza (25 min.), and Milan (2½ hr.).

By Bus   The main **APS bus station** is located east of the Scrovegni Chapel and the Arena Gardens area on Via Rismondo 28 © 049-824-1111; www.apsholding.it/mobilita). Frequent bus service to Venice and Verona costs approximately the same as train tickets, though tourists and locals alike seem to use this station principally for the smaller outlying cities such as Bassano del Grappa.

By Car   Padua is located directly on the principal Autostrada A4 that links Venice with Milan. All the points of interest listed below are located in the city's historic center, which is closed to traffic. When booking at your hotel, ask about the closest parking lot. Hotels usually have an agreement with their neighborhood parking lot and pass those savings along to hotel guests.

VISITOR INFORMATION   The **tourist office** is in the train station (© 049-875-2077; fax 049-875-5008; www.padovanet.it or www.turismopadova.it). April to October, it's open Monday to Saturday 9am to 7pm and Sunday 9am to noon; November to March, hours are Monday to Saturday 9:30am to 6pm and Sunday 9am to noon. From the train station, bus nos. 3 and 8 head downtown (as do nos. 12 and 18 Mon–Sat and no. 32 Sun). There's another **office** on Piazza del Santo (© 049-875-3087). It's open April to October 9am to 1:30pm and 3 to 6pm. A third office can be found behind the Caffè Pedrocchi (© 049-876-7927). You can also visit the **APT office** at Riviera Mugnai 8 (© 049-876-7911) for information.

CITY LAYOUT   Pick up a map from the tourist office and plan your attack. The train station marks the city's northernmost point, and the Prato della Valle and Basilica di Sant'Antonio mark the southernmost. The following sites of interest can be organized into three clusters and are all within walking distance of one other: The Cappella degli Scrovegni (also called the Arena Chapel) and the adjacent Museo Civico are across a small piazza from the Eremitani Church; the Caffè Pedrocchi can be found near the Palazzo della Ragione in the Piazza Cavour area (the Piazza della Frutta sits to the north

and Piazza delle Erbe just to the south of the *palazzo,* with the Piazza dei Signori bringing
up the west); and the Basilica di Sant'Antonio caps the southern end of town, with the
enormous Piazza Prato della Valle just beyond.

GETTING AROUND   Hotels, restaurants, and major points of interest all fall inside the
historic center and can be reached on foot. Public buses service many of the center's
streets, which are otherwise limited to traffic (pick up a bus map from the tourist office).
Single tickets cost 1€ and are valid for 75 minutes; a family ticket is 2€. March through
October, a **sightseeing bus** runs about every hour, with a midday break (9:50 and 11am,
noon, 2:45, 4, 5, and 6pm); it departs from in front of the Basilica di Sant'Antonio, costs
15€, and includes a small discount at museums. Look for the red double-decker buses.

WHAT TO SEE & DO

Basilica di Sant'Antonio ★★   This enormous basilica's imposing interior is richly
decorated, filled with tombs, works of art, and inlaid checkerboard marble flooring. It's
all there to honor one man, Padua's patron Saint Anthony. Simply and commonly
referred to as "il Santo," Anthony was born in Lisbon in 1195 and died just outside of
Padua in 1231. Work began on the church almost immediately but was not completed
until 1307. Its eight domes bring to mind the Byzantine influence found in Venice's St.
Mark's Basilica. A pair of octagonal, minaret-like bell towers enhances its Eastern appearance. Donatello's seven **bronze statues** and towering central *Crucifixion* (1444–48) that
adorn the main altar are the basilica's artistic highlights.

   The faithful could care less about the architecture and art; they flock here year-round
to caress the **tomb ★** holding the saint's body (off the left aisle) and pray for his help in
finding what they've lost. The tomb is always covered with flowers, photographs, and
handwritten personal petitions left by devout pilgrims from every corner of the globe.
The series of nine bronze bas-reliefs of scenes from the saint's life are some of the finest
works by 16th-century northern Italian sculptors.

   In his lifetime, St. Anthony was known for his eloquent preaching, so interpret as you
will the saint's perfectly (some say miraculously) preserved **tongue, vocal chords,** and
jawbone on display in the Cappella del Tesoro in the back of the church, directly behind
the main altar. These treasured relics are carried through town in a traditional procession
every June 13 to celebrate the feast day of il Santo. You'll also see one of his original tat-
tered tunics dating from 1231.

(Value) Cumulative Tickets

If you plan on taking in all the sights of Padua during a short visit—or even if you
plan on visiting the Scrovegni Chapel and only one other sight—a **PadovaCard**
is a worthwhile investment. In addition to free use of the city's buses and free
parking in some areas, the 15€ card gets you admission to the Cappella degli
Scrovegni (you must call to make reservations), Musei Civici Eremitani, the Palazzo della Ragione, and other sites in Padua and the province as well as a seat
in Caffè Pedrocchi. The card is valid for 48 hours and can be shared by both an
adult and a child younger than 12. You'll find the card for sale at tourist offices
and at sites at which you can use the card. A 72-hour card costs 20€. See www.
padovacard.it.

In front of the basilica across the large piazza, standing out amid the smattering of stalls selling St. Anthony–emblazoned everything, is Donatello's famous **Gattamelata equestrian statue ★★**. The first of its size to be cast in Italy since Roman antiquity, it is important for its detail, proportion, and powerful contrast between rider (the inconsequential Venetian condottiere Erasmo da Narni, nicknamed the "Spotted Cat") and horse. It was a seminal work that influenced Renaissance sculpture and casting and restored the lost art of equestrian statuary.

Piazza del Santo (east of Prato della Valle). ℂ **049-878-9722.** www.santantonio.org. Free admission. Summer daily 6:20am–7:45pm; winter daily 6:20am–7pm. Bus: 3, 8, 12, 18, 32, or 43.

Bo (Università Palazzo Centrale)   Galileo's battered desk and podium, from which he taught from 1592 to 1610, are still on display in Italy's second-oldest university (after Bologna). His name joins a legendary honor roll of students and professors— Petrarch, Dante, the poet Tasso, and Copernicus—who came here from all over Europe. The University of Padua was founded in 1222 and grew to become one of the most famous and ambitious learning centers in Europe, reaching its zenith in the 16th and 17th centuries. Today a number of buildings are spread about town, but the Palazzo del Bo (named after the "Bo," or Ox, Inn—a favorite student hangout that stood on this spot in the 15th c.) is the university's main seat. The perfectly preserved **Teatro Anatomico ★**, where professors did autopsies on cadavers, gives a vivid picture of how students learned the intricacies of the human body centuries ago. Built in 1594, it was here that William Harvey most probably developed his theory of the circulation of blood while earning his degree in 1602.

Via VIII Febbraio (south of Piazza Cavour). ℂ **049-827-5111.** www.unipd.it/en. Admission 5€ by guided tour only, some in English. Ask at tourist office for status of an ongoing renovation and visitor hours. Bus: 3, 8, 12, 16, 18, or 22.

Caffè Pedrocchi ★★   The Pedrocchi is a historic landmark, as beloved by the Padovans as "their" own St. Anthony (who actually hailed from Lisbon). When it first opened in 1831, it was the largest cafe in Europe. Famous literary and political characters and local luminaries made this their command post—French-born Henri Beyle, better known as Stendhal, had it in mind when he wrote, "The best Italian cafe is almost as good as the Parisian ones." Countless others were less reserved, calling it arguably the most beautiful coffeehouse in the world. Heavily damaged during World War II, it has been completely rebuilt in its original neoclassical, 19th-century stage-set splendor, and, after a laborious renovation and heralded 1998 reopening that was, for Padua, the event of the year, it is again the social heartbeat of the city.

It has the nicest restrooms in town, for the use of cafe patrons. They're worth the cost of a coffee. In warm weather, Pedrocchi opens wide its doors (and, hence, its curious description as a "doorless cafe") onto the pedestrian piazza; sit here for a while to absorb the Padovan spirit. As is always the case, drinks cost less when you're standing at the bar, but then you will have missed the *dolce far niente* (sweetness of doing nothing) experience for which Pedrocchi has always been known. A cappuccino, tea, beer, or glass of *prosecco* will cost 3€ at your table (half that price at the bar), and hunger can be held at bay with a plate of dainty teatime pastries or a grilled ham-and-cheese toast, each 3.50€. Pedrocchi often hosts live music in the evenings.

Via VIII Febbraio 15 (at Piazza Cavour). ℂ **049-878-1231.** www.caffepedrocchi.it. AE, DC, MC, V. Historical salon upstairs: Daily 9:30am–12:30pm and 3:30–8pm. Bar: Sun–Wed 9am–9pm, Thurs–Sat 9am–midnight. Closed 2 weeks in mid-Aug. Bus: 3, 8, 12, 16, 18, or 22.

Cappella degli Scrovegni (Scrovegni Chapel or Arena Chapel) ★★★ This
is the one uncontested must-see during your stay in Padua, so be prepared for lengthy lines
in high season, a wait made even longer by the small numbers of controlled groups (25 people
maximum) allowed to enter the chapel at any one time. Scandalously brief 15-minute visits
are the limit imposed during peak periods; check when buying your ticket so you can plan
accordingly. Another 15 minutes are spent in a separate room beforehand, watching a mandatory but decent documentary on the frescoes, in order to give the air temperature in the
chapel a chance to stabilize in between visits. Art lovers armed with binoculars behold the
scene in awe—the recently renovated cycle of **vibrant frescoes** by Giotto that revolutionized
14th-century painting is considered among the most important art leading up to the Renaissance. While some experts have questioned whether the famed frescoes in Assisi are entirely
by Giotto, here there is no equivocation: These are the master's works. Cobalt blue is the
dominant color; the illustrations are in that typical easy-to-understand medieval comic-strip
format, but here they take on an unprecedented degree of realism and emotion.

This cycle is even larger, more complete, and better preserved than the famed St.
Francis frescoes in Assisi. Giotto worked from 1303 to 1306 to completely cover the
ceiling and walls with 38 scenes illustrating the lives of the Virgin and of Christ from
floor to ceiling. With your back to the front door, the three bands that cover the walls
are: top right, *Life of Joachim;* top left, *Life of the Virgin;* right center, *The Childhood of
Christ;* left center, *Christ's Public Life;* right bottom, *The Passion of Christ* (the third panel
of Judas kissing Christ is the best known of the entire cycle); left bottom, *Christ's Death
and Resurrection.* Above the entrance is the fresco of the *Last Judgment:* Christ, as judge,
sits in the center, surrounded by the angels and apostles. Below him, to the right, are the
blessed, while to the left, Giotto created a terrible hell in which devils and humans are
condemned to eternal punishment.

Note: Each online reservation—even for holders of the PadovaCard, which allows for
free admission—incurs a 1€ reservation fee. If you want to be assured that you will have
more time in the chapel, consider visiting between 7 and 9:30pm on the 11€ "Double
Turn" ticket, which allows you 30 minutes in the chapel.

Piazza Eremitani 8 (off Corso Garibaldi). ✆ **049-201-0020** for required reservations (call center lines open
Mon–Fri 9am–7pm, Sat 9am–6pm). www.cappelladegliscrovegni.it. For reservations: musei.comune@
padovanet.it. Admission (joint ticket with the Museo Eremitani; add 1€ per ticket to reservations made
online) 12€ adults (includes a 1€ reservation fee), 5€ ages 6–17, free for children younger than 6 (although
admission still requires a reservation); free with purchase of PadovaCard (see "Cumulative Tickets," above).
Daily 9am–7pm; until 10pm Mar–Nov. Entrance through the Museo Eremitani. Bus: 3, 8, 10, 12, 32, or 42.

Chiesa degli Eremitani (Church of the Hermits) ★ Padua's worst tragedy was
the complete destruction of this church by Allied bombs in 1944; some art historians
consider it the country's greatest artistic wartime loss. It has been remarkably restored to its
original early-13th-century Romanesque style, but the magnificent frescoes by the 23-year-
old Andrea Mantegna could not be salvaged, except for a corner of the Ovetari Chapel.
Here you'll find enough fragments left in the rubble of the frescoes he painted from 1454
to 1457 to understand the loss of what was considered one of the great artistic treasures of
Italy. Mantegna was born in Padua (1431–1506) and studied under the Florentine master
Donatello, who lived here while completing his commissions for the Basilica di
Sant'Antonio, as well as the famous equestrian statue that now stands in the piazza before
it. Classical music concerts occasionally are held in the church.

Piazza Eremitani (off Corso Garibaldi). ✆ **049-875-6410** or 049-876-1855. Free admission. Daily 8:30am–
12:30pm and 4:30–7pm. Bus: 3, 8, 10, 12, 32, or 42.

Museo Civico Eremitani ★ These centuries-old cloisters that were once home to the monks (*eremitani* means "hermits") who officiated in the adjacent Scrovegni Chapel have been renovated to provide an airy display space as the city's civic museum. Its collection begins on the ground floor with the Archaeological Museum's division of Egyptian, Roman, and Etruscan artifacts. The upstairs collection represents an impressive panorama of minor works from major Venetian artists from the early 15th century to the 19th century: You'll find works by Titian, Tiepolo, and Tintoretto, whose *Crucifixion* is the museum's finest work. Special mention is given to Giotto's unusual wooden crucifix and Bellini's *Portrait of a Young Senator.*

Piazza Eremitani 8 (off Corso Garibaldi and adjacent to the Cappella Scrovegni). © **049-820-4551** or 049-820-4551. www.padovanet.it/museicivici. Admission to Musei Civico Eremitani only: 10€ adults, 8€ ages 6–17, free for children younger than 6 and seniors older than 65. Joint ticket with the Cappella Scrovegni (add 2€ per ticket to reservations made online) 12€ adults, 10€ ages 6–17, free for children under 6 (although admission to the Scrovegni Chapel still requires a reservation); free with purchase of PadovaCard (see "Cumulative Tickets," above). Tues–Sun 9am–7pm. Bus: 3, 8, 10, 11, 12, 32, or 42.

Palazzo della Ragione (Law Courts) ★ Located just south of the historic Caffè Pedrocchi, and a necessary destination for those meandering about the historic center of town, the picturesque open-air markets of **Piazza delle Erbe (Square of the Herbs)** ★★ and **Piazza della Frutta (Square of Fruit)** frame this massive 13th-century *palazzo* and have stood as the town's political and commercial nucleus for centuries.

Before being distracted by the color, smells, and cacophony of the sprawling outdoor fruit and vegetable market stalls, turn your attention to the magnificent Palazzo della Ragione, whose interior is as impressive as its exterior. Food shops by the dozen fill its ground floor, and stand-up bars and outdoor cafes make this lunchtime central. The two-story loggia-lined "Palace of Reason" is topped with a distinctive sloped roof that resembles the inverted hull of a ship, the largest of its kind in the world. It was built in 1219 as the seat of Padua's parliament and was used as an assembly hall, courthouse, and administrative center to celebrate Padua's newly won independence as a republican city. Considered a masterpiece of civil medieval architecture, it was heavily damaged by a fire in 1420 that destroyed, among other things, an elaborate cycle of frescoes by Giotto and his students that adorned **il Salone (the Great Hall).** The hall, 81m (266 ft.) long, was almost immediately rebuilt and today is the prime draw, for both its floor-to-ceiling 15th-century frescoes—commissioned immediately after the fire—and a large wooden sculpture of a horse attributed to Donatello (although many art historians don't agree). The 15th-century frescoes are similar in style and astrological theme to those that had been painted by Giotto, and comprise one of the very few complete zodiac cycles to survive until modern times.

ⓘ Tips **When Venice Overflows**

Padua is convenient to both Venice and Verona. There isn't a wide choice of desirable hotels in the *centro storico* (historic center), but you'll pay close to half the rates of comparable accommodations in Venice and find the commute, just 34km (21 miles), an easy and inexpensive one (and often a necessary one when Venice is fully booked).

On the far (west) side of the adjoining piazzas' canvas-topped stalls, flanking the Palazzo della Ragione, is the **Piazza dei Signori,** most noteworthy for the 15th-century clock tower that dominates it, the first of its kind in Italy. (*Note:* At press time, portions of the building were under restoration and may or may not be completed by 2010.)

Piazza delle Erbe/Piazza della Frutta. (C) **049-820-5006.** www.turismopadova.it. Admission to *palazzo* 4€ adults, 2€ children (8€ adults and 5€ children when there are exhibitions in the *palazzo.* Tues–Sun 9am– 7pm (until 6pm in winter). Bus: 3, 5, 6, 8, 9, 10, 11, 12, 13, 15, 18, 22, or 42.

WHERE TO STAY

When making reservations, note that low season is considered December and January, and July and August. Inquire about discounts if you'll be in Padua at this time of year.

Hotel al Fagiano ★   Although small, this family-run hotel is a great value for your money. Located just a few steps off the expansive Piazza del Santo (its most appealing asset), it doesn't exactly ooze coziness and charm, but given the less-than-encouraging hotel situation in town, the Fagiano's clean, bright, modern rooms are still a standout choice. Bathrooms have been freshly redone and include such niceties as hair dryers and bright lighting. Also, you rarely find air-conditioning and TVs at these rates. Don't confuse this Fagiano with the Hotel Buenos Aires, formerly known as the Fagiano and just a block away.

Via Locatelli 45 (west of Piazza del Santo), 35123 Padova. (C) **049-875-0073.** Fax 049-875-3396. www. alfagiano.com. 29 units. 70€–100€ double; 90€–110€ triple. Continental breakfast 8€. AE, DC, MC, V. Private parking. From train station: Bus no. 8, 12, 18, or 22. **Amenities:** Bar; bikes; concierge; Internet. *In room:* A/C, TV, hair dryer.

Hotel Donatello ★   This is a modern hotel in an old building, flush with amenities and enjoying a great location right at the Basilica di Sant'Antonio. More than half the rooms overlook the basilica, though those on the inner courtyard are quieter. Guest quarters vary as the owners slowly refresh and update a few each year. Some feature plush modular furnishings, some retro-Empire style. Some of the older bathrooms have tubs with hand-held shower nozzles, but most are modernized. Apartments sleeping three to four come with two bedrooms and a common bathroom.

Via del Santo 102–104, 35123 Padova. (C) **049-875-0634.** Fax 049-875-0829. www.hoteldonatello.net. 44 units. 198€ double; 231€ triple; 312€ apt for 4. Breakfast 14€. AE, DC, MC, V. Parking in garage included. **Amenities:** International restaurant; bar; concierge; room service. *In room:* A/C, TV w/pay movies, hair dryer, minibar.

Hotel Majestic Toscanelli ★★   A four-star hotel this nice would cost a great deal more in nearby Venice, which is why the Toscanelli often finds itself with guests who make this their home base while they visit neighboring cities and the surrounding area. The hotel has old-world charm, with rooms tastefully done in classic decor with coordinated pastel themes, burnished cherrywood furniture, and large, bright bathrooms with white ceramic and marble tiles. Off the lobby, a bright and attractive breakfast room serves a good buffet breakfast. This quiet, historic neighborhood, with porticoed alleyways lined with antiques shops and wine bars, is entirely closed to traffic. From here it's an easy walk to the Via Roma and the Piazza delle Erbe.

Via dell'Arco 2 (2 blocks west of Via Roma and south of the Piazza delle Erbe), 35122 Padova. (C) **049-663-244.** Fax 049-876-0025. www.toscanelli.com. 34 units. 139€–192€ double; 169€–227€ junior suite; 189€–290€ suite. Rates include buffet breakfast. Rates discounted mid-July to Aug. AE, DC, MC, V. Valet garage parking 19€. **Amenities:** Bar; babysitting; concierge; room service; smoke-free rooms. *In room:* A/C, TV w/pay movies, hair dryer, kitchenette (in 2 units), minibar, Wi-Fi.

Brek (**Value**) ITALIAN/CAFETERIA   Brek is self-service *all'italiana,* a homegrown northern Italian chain of upscale cafeterias that make concessions to the time-pressed modern world without sacrificing old-world quality. Put your language problems and calorie-counting aside and help yourself to pastas, made fresh while you wait, that are topped with your choice of sauce. There's a counter just for omelets made express, another for entrees and pizza. The dessert cart groans under an array of cheeses, fresh fruits, fruit salads, tarts, and cobblers. Join the thoroughly local eat-on-the-run lunch crowd from the university and surrounding shops, and save your day's budget for dinner.

Piazza Cavour 20. (✆) **049-875-3788.** www.brek.it. Reservations not accepted. Primi and pizza 3.90€– 9.50€; secondi 3.50€–9.90€. AE, DC, MC, V. Daily11:30am–3pm and 6:30–10pm.

Enoteca Ristorante La Corte dei Leoni ★ (**Finds**) WINE BAR/PADOVAN   After a heady wander among the sights, sounds, and smells of Padua's open-air marketplace, one of Italy's most colorful and authentic, head for a respite at this *enoteca.* A stylishly minimal decor in the cream-and-rose-petal interior is attractive, but the outdoor court-yard where centuries-old horse stables have been converted for modern-day grazers is the warm-weather draw—especially when the restaurant hosts its monthly jazz concerts in summer. Only a handful of dishes are offered—and the menu changes seasonally—but each is excellently prepared, such as *cavatelli* in a white ragout. For a more lingering and a memorable meal in these relaxing settings, try the tasting menu (40€).

Via Pietro d'Abano 1 (on a side street just north of the Piazza della Frutta). (✆) **049-875-0083.** www.corte deileoni.com. Reservations suggested. Primi 8.50€–12€; secondi 17€–22€. AE, DC, MC, V. Tues–Sun 11:30am–2:30pm; Tues–Sat 6:30pm–midnight. Closed 1 week in Aug and most of Jan.

La Vecchia Enoteca ★★ PADOVAN   The sophistication of the Veneto's prodigious viticulture is shown off here in an appropriately refined venue. Cozy, in a rustic and elegant kind of way, La Vecchia Enoteca is for that special evening of white linen and smooth service when you'd like the full-blown experience of Padovan cuisine and award-deserving wines. Prices are contained enough to encourage diners to leave caution at the door and indulge in a delicious menu and commendable selection of regional and Italian wines. The menu showcases the bounty-rich Veneto: The traditional polenta and risotto change with the season, as does the light, homemade gnocchi. Meat possibilities are numerous and tempting, while the influence of the Adriatic appears in such entrees as the favored *branzino in crosta di patate,* sea bass roasted in a light potato crust.

Via San Martino e Solferino 32 (just south of Piazza delle Erbe). (✆) **049-875-28-56.** Reservations recom-mended. Primi 12€–18€; secondi 20€–22€. MC, V. Tues–Sat 12:30–2:30pm; Mon–Sat 7:30–10:30pm. Closed 3 weeks in Aug.

Osteria Dei Fabbri ★ PADOVAN   Simple, well-prepared food is the draw here. This rustic, old-fashioned tavern, or *osteria,* is a lively spot where intellectual types share tables with Zegna-suited bankers, and students stop by for a tipple or to find a quiet corner in which to pore over the newspaper (a pastime not encouraged during hours when meals are served). There's always at least one homemade pasta choice to start with, and *osso buco,* the specialty of the house, is especially memorable when accompanied by any of the local (and excellent) Venetian wines available by the bottle or glass. The *seppia al nero* (squid in its own ink) served on polenta is faithful to its Veneto roots but maybe just a little too rich for the uninitiated. If you don't come here for dinner, consider stop-ping by for the *dopo cena* (after-dinner drink) to top off your day in Padua.

Reservations recommended. Primi 8.50€–11€; secondi 12€–17€. AE, DC, MC, V. Mon–Sat 12:30–3pm and 7:30–10:30pm. Closed Dec 25–Jan 4.

PADUA AFTER DARK

The classical music season usually runs from October to April at different venues around town. The historic **Teatro Verdi,** at Via dei Livello 32 (☎ **049-877-7011** or 049-8777-0213; www.teatroverdipd.it), is the most impressive location. Programs are available at the tourist office. Look for posters advertising performances by the world-class Solisti Veneti, who are Padovans but spend most of the year traveling abroad.

As a university city, Padua has a large, very visible student population. You can network with the student crowd at any of the popular cafes along Via Cavour, or in the *osterie,* wine bars, and beer dives in the porticoed medieval side streets encircling the Palazzo della Ragione (the area around the Bo) and its bookend Piazza delle Erbe and Piazza della Frutta. In the summer, the toned-down nightlife is to be found mostly around Prato della Valle.

DAY TRIPS FROM PADUA

The **Euganean Hills (Colli Euganei)** are at the center of a small but renowned wine industry located southwest of Padua. You can pick up a *Strada dei Vini* wine route map from the tourist office. It also leads you to the small city of **Terme di Abano** (12km/7½ miles south of Padua), famous as a center for radioactive springs and mud treatments unique to this volcanic range.

The Forgotten Riviera: The Brenta Canal

The navigable **Brenta Canal** ★★ links Padua with Venice in the east. Ambitiously called "the Forgotten Riviera" because of the dozens of historic summertime villas built here by Venice's aristocracy and wealthy merchants, it can be visited by car or by boat—you can even stay in a few of the villas (see "Where to Stay on the Brenta," below). Only one was designed by 16th-century master architect Palladio (the Villa Foscari), but many are Palladian-inspired (see "Vicenza," later in this chapter, for background on Palladio and how to visit his villas). The best way to see the villas is on a cruise down the Brenta (see below). Call the **Brenta Canal tourist office** at ☎ **041-424-973** for more information.

More than 30 villas can be viewed from the boats (some just partially or at a great distance), but only three are visited. The important 18th-century **Villa Pisani** ★★ (☎ **0425-920-016;** www.villapisani.com) in Stra was commissioned by the family of a Venetian doge and is famous for its ballroom frescoes by Tiepolo and its extensive gardens. The hedge maze here—something to engage youngsters bored with having to tour all these frescoed mansions—sprouts a tower at the center so that you can get a bird's-eye view of the trip back out; during the crowded summer season, a young man stands up here calling out instructions to maze-goers to hurry them along so the next group can get in. The villa is open Easter to September, Tuesday to Sunday 9am to noon and 1:30 to 6pm (to 4pm in winter). Admission is 6€ for the villa, or 5€ for just the park and gardens. It's free for seniors older than 60 and children younger than18.

The other two biggies are in Mira, and fair warning: Both keep erratic hours (see notes after each). The 18th-century **Villa Valmarana** ★★ (☎ **044-321-803**) is dramatically set amid weeping willows; it's open Tuesday to Sunday from March to November (Dec–Feb open only on weekends) and costs 8€, free for children younger than 12. The **Villa Foscari** (also known as Villa Malcontenta, "The Unhappy Woman"; ☎ **041-547-0012**

> (Moments) **A Perfect Picnic Spot**
>
> The secondary road S11 runs alongside the canal in spots; it departs from the canal here and there but remains the best roadway for viewing the villas as it skirts the little canal-side villages. If you take a right-branching street through any of the towns, you'll come upon grassy verges leading down to the water—a perfect spot for a **picnic** ★ (though you might want to bring bug repellent).

or 041-520-3966; www.lamalcontenta.com) is one of Palladio's finest works. It's open May to October Tuesday to Saturday 9am to noon and costs 10€.

TOURING THE CANAL   There are a number of companies willing to take you up the river for anywhere between 50€ and 95€. The tourism office promotes two of them: **I Battelli del Brenta,** Via Porciglia 34 (*(C)* **049-876-0233;** fax 049-876-3410; www. battellidelbrenta.it), and **Delta Tour,** Via Toscana 2 (*(C)* **049-870-0232;** www.deltatour. it). Other companies come in and out of the market. For more info on plying the rivers, canals, and other watery byways of the region, check out the local river-craft consortium's website at www.padovanavigazione.it.

I Battelli del Brenta embarks in Padua from the Scalinata del Portello at 8:30am on Wednesday, Friday, Saturday and Sunday, arriving in Venice at 7pm; from Venice's Zattere ai Gesuati, they leave Tuesday, Thursday, and Saturday at 8:30am, finishing in Padua at 7pm. The trip costs 85€ for a full day, including lunch and entrance to all of the above-mentioned villas, while a half-day, at 48€, includes a visit to the Villa Pasani, but not the optional fish lunch that adds another 27€.

Delta Tour greets passengers at the Villa Pisani at 8:30am (Tues–Fri), visits each of the estates, along with a tour guide, and finishes up at Fusina on the coast south of Venice. For an extra 3€, the boat will take you for a panoramic view of Piazza San Marco. The 65€ fee includes a fish lunch, the tour guide's services, and entrance to the villas.

If you want to do the tour yourself, the largest concentration of country villas can be found between Stra and Mira. A car tour does require some planning, since visiting hours and days differ from villa to villa and season to season. See the tourist office about a map. *Note:* If you want to try this by bus, know that difficult, erratic visiting hours and public bus connections may make this close to impossible for those without their own wheels.

Where to Stay on the Brenta

An excellent budget alternative to the admittedly pricey villa hotels below is the **Ostello di Mira,** Via Giare 169 (*(C)* **041-567-9203;** fax 041-567-6457; www.casasoleluna.it), a bare-bones hotel just outside Mira; it charges 18€ for a bed in an eight-bed dorm or 25€ per person in a shared double, breakfast included. It's open March to September; the reception desk is open 7:30 to 9:30am and 4:30 to 10:30pm.

Villa Ducale ★★   This hotel occupies an 1884 villa built atop an older structure amid a lovely park of gravel paths, fountains, and flowering bushes under the shade of exotic palms, magnolias, and pines. Rooms feature marvelous inlaid wood floors, Persian rugs, and Murano chandeliers hanging from high, frescoed ceilings. Wrought-iron bedsteads are surrounded by (mostly) antiques, and the marble bathrooms feature antique brass fittings. "Standard" rooms are smaller (some almost cramped—but those cost less), with simpler parquet floors and smaller bathrooms. "King" rooms are larger and overlook the park from balconies or a small terrace. The breakfast room/restaurant is intimate—in fact, the Ducale has a generally classier setting in its public areas than the Margherita (see below), but the Margherita tends to have classier rooms.

Riviera Martiri della Libertà 75, 30031 Dolo (Venezia). ✆/fax **041-560-8020.** www.villaducale.it. 11 units. 90€–180€ standard double; 125€–210€ "king" double with park view. Rates include breakfast. AE, DC, MC, V. Free parking. **Amenities:** Seafood restaurant; bar; babysitting; bikes; concierge; Internet; room service; smoke-free rooms. *In room:* A/C, TV, hair dryer, minibar.

Villa Margherita ★★★ This 17th-century villa, expanded in the 19th century, once served as guest quarters for the noble Contarini family of Venice. Today it is run with refined gusto by the Dal Corso family, who provide fresh fruit and flowers in your room and a highly polished professional courtesy. All rooms overlook the large, pine-shaded lawn and are soundproofed against the noise of passing cars. "Standard" rooms, on the smaller side of medium size, have rugs scattered over wood floors. "Deluxe" rooms are larger (except for no. 218, which is a cozy lovers' nook with a spacious terrace), with more interesting antiques and richer fabrics, and are more frequently blessed with balconies. "Junior suites" are larger still and feature double sinks. The salons downstairs are appropriately furnished in the manner of a rich country villa, with chessboards fronting fireplaces and plush armchairs.

The Dal Corsos also run Brenta hotel in Mira, about 5 minutes away. **Villa Franceschi** (Via Don Minzoni 28, Mira Porte, Venezia; ✆ **041-426-6531;** fax 041-560-8996; www.villafranceschi.com), in the late-16th-century Villa Palladiana, features 27 guest rooms (mostly junior suites), lush gardens, a swimming pool, and an on-site restaurant. Grand doubles run 265€, grand deluxe doubles are 290€, junior suites cost 305€, and suites run 390€.

Via Nazionale 416–417 (on the Venice side of Mira), 30030 Mira Porte (Venezia). ✆ **041-426-5800.** Fax 041-426-5838. www.villa-margherita.com. 19 units. 220€ standard double; 240€ deluxe double; 258€ junior suite. Rates often discounted in slower periods and off season. Rates include breakfast. AE, DC, MC, V. Parking free. Public bus stop, with half-hourly service to Venice, 15km (9¹/₄ miles) away, is a 5-min. walk. **Amenities:** Frescoed Venetian/fish restaurant across the street; bar; bikes; concierge; room service; smoke-free rooms. *In room:* A/C, TV, hair dryer, minibar.

2 TREVISO

25km (16 miles) N of Mestre/Venice, 50km (31 miles) NE of Padua

Treviso is a bustling, prosperous small city and center in the northern Veneto. It seems to have changed little from its early days as a medieval market town and staunch ally to Venice. Much of the city had to be rebuilt after severe World War II damage, but it was done well. Treviso's medieval *palazzi* and houses with painted facades, churches frescoed by Giotto's follower Tomaso da Modena (1325–79), and pleasant streets cut across by pretty canals together make for a lovely, genuine-Italy break from the tourist beat of Padua-Vicenza-Verona.

FESTIVALS & MARKETS Treviso leads up to the **Feast of the Assumption** with a week of street theater, dance, music competitions, and other performances (Aug 6–14). The daily **fish market** ★★, on the islets in the Cagnan canal, is a picturesque slice of old Treviso (mornings are best). Treviso hosts an **antiques fair** the fourth Sunday of each month (except July) on Borgo Cavour (② **0422-419-195**).

ESSENTIALS

GETTING THERE **By Train** There are trains two to four times an hour from Venice (25–35 min.). Fifteen runs daily (10 on Sun) come from Vicenza (40–80 min.).

By Bus Ten buses (② **0422-577-311**) run daily from Asolo (55 min.).

By Car From Venice, the quick way is Autostrada A27 to the Treviso Sud exit, but the more direct route is the SS13 (though that can be slow going at rush hour and midday). From Padua, take Autostrada A4 past Venice to the A27. When booking at your hotel, ask about the closest parking lot.

VISITOR INFORMATION The **tourist office** is just behind the main Piazza dei Signori at Piazza Monte di Pietà 8 (② **0422-547-632;** fax 0422-419-092; http://tourism. provincia.treviso.it) and is open daily from 9am to 12:30pm, plus Tuesday to Friday 2:30 to 6:30pm and Saturday and Sunday 3:30 to 6pm. There's also a provincial **tourist office** at Via Turazza 7a (② **0422-541-052;** fax 0422-540-366; www.trevisotour.org), though it's mostly administrative.

WHAT TO SEE & DO

The center of town is **Piazza dei Signori,** lined with arcades that run under the retro-medieval **Palazzo del Podestà,** rebuilt in the 1870s with a tall clock tower, and spread into a loggia under the 13th-century brick council hall **Palazzo dei Trecento.**

Just beyond this square, on Piazza San Vito, sits a pair of medieval churches: **Santa Lucia,** with Tomaso da Modena frescoes in the first alcove on the right, and **San Vito,** with its rather faded Byzantine-style frescoes from the 12th or 13th century. Both are open daily 9am to noon and 4 to 6pm.

The overbearing facade of the **Duomo** ★ is from 1836, but it's flanked by Romanesque lions that, coupled with the seven green copper domes, speak to the cathedral's 12th-century origins in the Venetian-Byzantine style. The second pilaster features a late-1400s relief of the *Visitation,* by Lorenzo Bregno. The chapel altarpiece at the end of the right aisle is an unusually bright and open *Annunciation,* by Titian (chapel founder Broccardo Malchiostro was painted in later, crouching behind the classical building to peep at the scene). The crypt contains a forest of columns and fragments of 14th-century fresco and mosaic. It's open Monday to Saturday 7:30am to noon and 3:30 to 7pm, Sunday 7:30am to 1pm and 3:30 to 8pm.

Via Canoniche, next to the cathedral, runs past an ancient paleo-Christian mosaic of the 4th century to a Gothic priory housing the **Museo Diocesano d'Arte Sacra** (② **0422-416-707**). Inside are 13th-century frescoes, a Tomaso da Modena that used to decorate the bishop's palace, and plenty of medieval sculpture along with vestments and holy silverware—though frankly, if admission weren't free, it wouldn't be worth it. It's open Monday to Thursday 9am to noon, Saturday 9am to noon and 3 to 6pm.

More interesting is the **Museo Bailo,** Borgo Cavour 24 (② **0422-580-567**), previously the Museo Civico, which holds the civic museum's remarkable collection of ancient bronze relics—including swords and ritualistic disks from the 5th century B.C., alongside Roman remains—as well as the city's collection of lesser-known works by the likes of Titian, Tiepolo, and Tintoretto. On the other side of town, across the wide Cagnan canals, whose islands host a daily fish market (see above), stands a (deconsecrated) church that's now well worth seeking out. The highlight of **Santa Caterina** (② **0422-591-337**)

ATTRACTIONS ●
Duomo **2**
Museo Bailo **1**
Museo Diocesano
   d'Arte Sacra **3**
Palazzo del Podestà **10**
Piazza dei Signori **10**
Palazzo dei Trecento **10**
Sala del Capitolo **14**

Santa Caterina **7**
Santa Lucia **6**
San Nicolò **14**
San Vito **6**

ACCOMMODATIONS ■
Albergo il Focolare **8**
Hotel Continental **13**
Hotel Scala **5**

DINING ◆
Biffi **10**
Brek **12**
Caffè Beltrame **10**
Da Pino **9**
Toni del Spin **4**
Toulà-Da Alfredo **11**

is its frescoes by Tomaso da Modena, including a Madonna and (detached from a now-destroyed church and kept here) a series on the life of St. Ursula. Admission is 3€ for adults, 2€ for students, and 1€ for kids under 10; it's open every Tuesday to Sunday from 9am to 12:30pm and 2:30 to 6pm.

   Down in the southwest corner of town, the big brick 13th- to 14th-century Dominican church of **San Nicolò** ★ houses some good Gothic frescoes. Tomaso da Modena decorated the huge round columns with a series of saints; Antonio da Treviso did the absolutely gargantuan St. Christopher—his .9m-long (3-ft.) feet strolling over biting fish—in 1410. On the right side of the apse, the tomb of Agostino d'Onigo from 1500 has courtly *Pages* frescoed by Lorenzo Lotto, who also did the altarpiece of the *Incredulity of St. Thomas with Apostles* in the chapel right of the altar. The late-14th-century Sienese School frescoes lining the walls include an *Adoration of the Magi,* complete with camels. San Nicolò is open daily 8am to 12:30pm and 3:30 to 7pm. Next door to the (unused) front door of the church is the entrance to the adjoining seminary's **Sala del Capitolo,** Piazzetta Benedetto XI 2 (© **0422-3247**), frescoed in 1352 by Tomaso da Modena with 40 Dominicans busily studying and copying out manuscripts at their desks. It's open 8am to 6pm daily; admission is free (ring the bell if the door is shut).

WHERE TO STAY

Treviso doesn't have much of a hotel industry. If the places below are full, consider a lovely option about a 10-minute drive north of the town walls: the **Hotel Scala** ★, Viale Felissent (☏ **0422-307-600;** fax 0422-305-048; www.hotelscala.com), a suburban villa with 20 comfortable bedrooms—all with air-conditioning, TV, telephone, and mini-bar—and a good restaurant. Doubles go for 85€ to 95€, including breakfast.

Albergo il Focolare ★   This simple hotel sits smack in the center of town, on a little street off the main drag a half-block from the Palazzo Podestà. Three of the largest rooms come with three beds: No. 29 has a small sitting area, no. 30 sits in the narrow end of the buildings with windows on three sides overlooking a canal, and the similar no. 34 lies directly above no. 30 on the top floor, so its windows have views over two canals. This won't be the quietest place you'll ever sleep, but it's clean.

Piazza Ancilotto 4, 31100 Treviso. ☏/fax **0422-56-601.** www.albergoilfocolare.net. 14 units. 100€–120€ double. Breakfast included. AE, DC, MC, V. Free parking in public lot. **Amenities:** Room service; smoke-free rooms. *In room:* A/C, TV, hair dryer.

Hotel Continental   The Continental is a large, well-worn hotel 3 blocks from the train station at the city walls, a 10-minute walk from the central piazza. The modular furnishings are a bit faded, but there are parquet floors and some nice old touches such as ornate wood entablatures, chandeliers, or mirrored closet doors silk-screened with Oriental prints. A few rooms have small vestibule sitting areas, and corner units are larger and tend to be more nicely furnished. There is, however, a bit of street noise from the busy road below, and while some bathrooms are new, others are aging, and many have shower nozzles you have to hold and no shower curtains.

Via Roma 16, 31100 Treviso. ☏ **0422-411-216.** Fax 0422-55-054. www.hcontinental.it. 80 units. 120€–205€ double; 150€–256€ triple. Rates include breakfast. AE, DC, MC, V. Parking 8€–10€ in nearby lots; hotel offers 20% discount. **Amenities:** Nearby restaurant; bar; babysitting; concierge; room service. *In room:* A/C, TV, hair dryer.

WHERE TO DINE

In addition to the choices below, you can get classy, made-to-order cafeteria fare at the Treviso branch of the excellent **Brek** chain, Corso del Popolo 25 (☏ **0422-590-012**), open daily. For pizza and people-watching, **Da Pino,** Piazza dei Signori 23 (☏ **0422-56-426**), has tables set under the high, wood-coffered arcade of the main square; it's closed Tuesday.

Toni del Spin ★★ (Finds) VENETIAN   Blackboards with the daily list of dishes hang from the rough crossbeams beneath high, sloping wood ceilings of this legendary eatery. The kitchen prepares a carefully considered mix of simple but intriguing dishes such as *gazbacho andaluz* (cold tomato vegetable soup), *panzerotti di funghi al burro* (fried mushroom pastries), *fegato alla veneziana* (Venetian-style liver), and *faraona con polenta* (guinea fowl with polenta). The house wine is good, and they charge decent prices on a select list of regional bottles—they even run a wine shop across the street.

Via Inferiore 7. ☏ **0422-543-829.** www.ristorantetonidelspin.com. Reservations not necessary. Primi 6€–8€; secondi 8€–14€. AE, MC, V. Tues–Sat 12:30–2:30pm; Mon–Sat 7:30–10:30pm. Closed 3 weeks in July and 1 week in Aug.

Toulà-Da Alfredo ★ NORTHERN ITALIAN/INTERNATIONAL   This chain of upmarket northern-cuisine restaurants, founded at the ski resort of Cortina about 2 hours north of Treviso in the Dolomites, is set in a modern series of rooms with odd murals and a ceiling *trompe l'oeil* frescoed with vines. The cuisine is refined yet traditional, and extremely

pricey. The specialty is *linguine verdi tradizione toulá* (green noodles in a cream and prosciutto sauce baked under *parmigiano*), though they also feature risotto with clams and wild asparagus, spaghetti with caviar and cherry tomatoes, and chateaubriand in a béarnaise sauce.
Via Collalto 26. ✆ **0422-540-275.** www.toula.it. Reservations recommended. Primi 11€–26€; secondi 21€–34€. AE, DC, MC, V. Tues–Sun 12:30–2:30pm; Tues–Sat 7:30–11pm. Closed Aug 2–25. Bus: 1 or 7.

3 ASOLO

73km (45 miles) N of Padua, 52km (32 miles) NE of Treviso, 16km (10 miles) E of Bassano del Grappa

Known as the "Town of a Hundred Horizons" because of its panoramic views, this nub of a medieval hill town (though it was founded during the twilight of Imperial Rome) has become the secret hideaway for true Veneto aficionados. It's a required stop for folks interested in meandering the backcountry or driving the wine roads, and it's a great place for those on bike tours to take a midday break.

Asolo was the Renaissance-era home of Caterina Cornaro of Venice, who was awarded the realm of Asolo for her help in (unsuccessfully) keeping the Turks out of Cyprus. Much of the 15th-century charm you see today is a result of her 12-year presence and patronage in the town. Other VIP residents were the English poet Robert Browning and Italy's early-20th-century grande dame of the stage, Eleonora Duse.

FESTIVALS & MARKETS There's an **antiques market** the second Sunday of each month, with a special books and prints edition the third Sunday in October. The local **folk festival** is in honor of San Gottardo on May 5, with a market, procession, and the sale of traditional terra-cotta shepherd flutes. Asolo holds a **Palio race** the third Sunday of September, pitting the town's six *contrade* (neighborhoods) against each other to pull up the hill a Roman-style chariot bearing a local damsel dressed as Caterina Cornaro. There's also a **Festival of Chamber Music** in August and September.

ESSENTIALS

GETTING THERE **By Train** Since the nearest train station is in Cornuda, a 17-minute bus ride away, buses are a better bet. There are a dozen trains into Cornuda daily from Padua (40–60 min.). From Treviso there are only three direct trains (30 min.), at 8:23am, 12:33pm, and 5:28pm, but you can get 1 of 20 or so daily trains to Montebelluno (20–30 min.) and change to 1 of 14 trains on to Cornuda (a bit over 10 min.), though the wait may be anywhere from a few minutes to over an hour.

By Bus A dozen **buses** (✆ **0423-493-464**) run daily from Bassano del Grappa (25 min.), and about 10 daily from Treviso (✆ **0422-577-311;** 55 min.). Buses stop at Asolo's Ca' Vescovo station on the main highway down in the valley, from which frequent shuttles climb the long hill into the Old Town.

By Car   From Padua, take SS47 north to Bassano di Grappa, and then drive east to Asolo on SS248. From Treviso, take the SS348 to Montebelluno, and then the SS248 west.

VISITOR INFORMATION   The genuinely helpful **tourist office** is at Piazza Garibaldi 73 (✆ **0423-529-046;** fax 0423-524-137). Another can be found at Piazza Gabrielle d'Annunzio 3 (✆ **0423-55-045;** www.asolo.it or www.comune.asolo.tv.it; hours vary, so call ahead).

WHAT TO SEE & DO

Though the area's top sight is the **Villa Barbaro,** outside town (see below), Asolo has a few diversions beyond merely strolling its streets and enjoying its "hundred horizons." Asolo was the seat of a bishopric until 969 and remained a countryside escape for rich Venetians thereafter, so it's no surprise that its cathedral, rebuilt in the 18th century, contains several artistic treasures. They apparently had a thing for paintings of the Assumption. There's one by Lorenzo Lotto (1506; on the left aisle), another by Jacopo "da Ponte" Bassano (1549; next to the last on the left aisle), and a bad 19th-century copy of a Titian version on the high altar. Breaking the theme is Lazzaro Bastiani's stiffly formal *St. Jerome* (1488), which features a pretty countryside in the background.

On the main square, the frescoed **Loggia del Capitano** houses a small museum that contains memorials to Robert Browning (whose son is buried in the local cemetery) and to Caterina Cornaro. Caterina was the queen of Cyprus until her husband died and she abdicated. She sought refuge in the Republic of Venice, which gave her Asolo to rule from 1489 to her death in 1510. Her home was the medieval **Castello,** begun in the late 6th century (there's nothing special to see there now; it just has a cafe tucked against the inside of the old castle's towering wall), which became known as the "Queen's Palace."

WHERE TO STAY

Hotel Duse (Value)   The Hotel Duse, named for Italian actress Eleonora Duse, offers a perfect location at decent prices. This small, relatively inexpensive (for Asolo) hotel occupies a 16th-century house right on the corner of the main square. The rooms are tight but nicely furnished with a few art prints on the walls. Top-floor rooms have sloping plank ceilings and a cozy feel.

Via R. Browning 190, 31011 Asolo. ✆ **0423-55-241.** Fax 0423-950-404. www.hotelduse.com. 14 units. 100€–130€ double; 120€–140€ junior suite. Extra bed 26€. Breakfast 8€. MC, V. Parking 4€. **Amenities:** Golf (nearby); room service; smoke-free rooms. *In room:* A/C, TV, Wi-Fi.

Hotel Villa Cipriani ★★   One of the town's beautiful 16th-century villas, once owned by Robert and Elizabeth Barrett Browning, was turned into the area's most sought-after deluxe hotel in 1962 by Giuseppe Cipriani (owner of Venice's Harry's Bar). It retains that private villa feel; its main building wraps around a lovely garden centered on a rose-trimmed well, with an 11-room annex and views spilling down a terraced park

Impressions

I assure you that, even though I have knowledge of and have seen with my own eyes the most beautiful panoramas in Italy and elsewhere, I have found nothing quite like the view one can enjoy from the tower of the Queen's Palace.

—Robert Browning

(Moments) A Glass of Wine

The best place in town to duck in for a glass of wine with the locals is **Antica Osteria Al Bacaro,** Via R. Browning 165 (⚞ **0423-55-150**), where townsfolk have gathered since 1892. Enjoy the breathtaking views from the lovely terrace bar for the cost of an iced tea or cocktail.

---

and slopes of olive trees. "Superior" rooms—with worn Oriental carpets on parquet floors; stylish, subdued furnishings; and hand-painted Vietri tiles in the bathrooms—are slightly smaller than "Deluxe" accommodations, which often feature beam ceilings, brass chandeliers, painted antiques mixed with discreetly modern TV chests, and a small sitting area of overstuffed easy chairs. Room nos. 101 and 102 enjoy large private terraces with valley views.

Via Canova 298. ⚞ **0423-523-411.** Fax 0423-952-095. www.villacdiprianiasolo.com. 31 units. 319€ double; 379€ superior double; 438€ deluxe double. Extra bed 80€. Continental breakfast 20€; buffet breakfast 35€. AE, DC, MC, V. Parking 17€. **Amenities:** Restaurant; elegant bar; babysitting; bikes; concierge; exercise room; golf (nearby); room service; smoke-free rooms; Wi-Fi. *In room:* A/C, TV, hair dryer, minibar.

WHERE TO DINE

Hosteria Ca' Derton ★★ VENETIAN   This haven of fine dining sits in a 17th-century *palazzo* on a quiet *piazzetta* just off the busy main square. The menu changes with the season and whim of chef-owner Nino Baggio, whose wife, Antoinetta, and grown children Guido, Enrico, and Cristina wait tables in the antiques-filled dining room. Nino looks to local culinary traditions and the freshest of ingredients to create such dishes as *bigoli al torchio con ragù d'anatra* (fat strands of handmade spaghetti in a duck ragù), *lasagnetta con zucchine e gamberoni* (delicate pasta casserole with zucchini and jumbo shrimp), or simple *tagliata di manzo* (steak perfumed with rosemary). Secondi may look pricey, but, unlike in most Italian restaurants, they come with a *contorno* (side dish)—as Antoinetta explains it, "a vegetable Nino thinks appropriate . . . or sometimes just polenta!" The house merlot and Colli Asolani white are both excellent.

Piazza d'Annunzio 11. ⚞ **0423-529-648.** www.caderton.com. Reservations recommended. Primi 6€–9€; secondi 13€–18€. AE, DC, MC, V. Tues–Sun 12:30–2pm; Tues–Sat 7:30–9:45pm.

A VILLA OUTSIDE TOWN

The **Villa Barbaro** ★★ (⚞ **0423-923-004;** www.villadimaser.it), also called Villa di Maser, is one of Palladio's most celebrated. It lies down in the valley, east of Asolo outside the hamlet of Maser. Probably the most famous of the Palladian villas (after Vicenza's Villa Rotonda), not to mention one of the most beautiful, the 1560 Barbaro is a standout for its gorgeous frescoes by Veronese (which La Rotonda lacks). It's privately owned by some very, very lucky folks who make you wear giant slippers to shuffle around and admire the frescoes on the ground floor. The hours change almost monthly: March, July, and August, it's open Tuesday, Thursday, and Saturday 10am to 6pm and Sunday 11am–6pm; April, May, June, September, and October, add Wednesday and Friday 10am to 6pm; November to February, Saturday and Sunday 2:30 to 5pm; closed December 24 to January 6. Admission is 6€.

At least 10 to 15 daily **buses** (⚞ **0422-577-311**) between Bassano (30 min.) and Treviso (50 min.), with stops at Asolo (15–20 min.), also stop in Maser. If you're coming by car from Asolo, drive down to the main road and turn left; turn left again when you see a pretty church squatting in the middle of the road.

4 BASSANO DEL GRAPPA

35km (22 miles) NE of Vicenza, 43km (27 miles) N of Padua, 16km (10 miles) W of Asolo, 47km (29 miles) W of Treviso

This picturesque town on the Brenta River is renowned for its centuries-old production of handcrafted ceramics and of grappa, Italy's national firewater of choice (see box below). Its Palladian covered wooden bridge is a highlight of the small *centro storico*. The city's arcaded homes, whose facades are painted in the traditional manner, and small squares make this a lovely break from the larger towns described in this chapter.

FESTIVALS In June, Bassano invites international street musicians to perform in a festival. Bassano's annual **Opera Estate Festival** ★ takes place from early July through August, with alfresco performances of opera, concerts, a mini–jazz fest, and dance (ballet, modern, and folk). For information, contact the tourist office (Largo Corona d'Italia 35; ✆ **0424-524-214;** fax 0424-525-138; www.comune.bassano.vi.it).

ESSENTIALS

VISITOR INFORMATION For information, call the **tourist office,** Lgo. Corona d'Italia 35 (✆ **0424-524-351;** fax 0424-525-301; www.comune.bassano.vi.it). It's open daily from 9am to 1pm and Monday to Saturday from 2 to 6pm.

GETTING THERE   By Bus To get here from Vicenza, you can take one of two dozen daily **FTV buses** (✆ **0424-30-850;** www.ftv.vi.it) that make the 1-hour trip. Frequent buses from Padua take half the time, making fewer stops. There are also a dozen **buses** (✆ **0423-493-464** or 0423-529-966) daily from nearby Asolo (25 min.).

By Car From Asolo, head west on the SS248; from Vicenza, north on the SS248; from Padua, north on the SS47. From Treviso, the more scenic route follows the SS348 northwest to Montebelluno, where you pick up the smaller SS248 west; the faster route is west along the SS53 toward Vicenza, turning north onto the SS47 at Cittadella.

WHAT TO SEE & DO

Bassano's historic center is just a half-dozen or so blocks in either direction; its medieval buildings and baroque *palazzi* snuggle along the Brenta River. Andrea Palladio designed Bassano's lovely symbol, the wooden **Ponte degli Alpini** ★★ covered bridge, in 1569, and every time floods or disaster have struck, it has been rebuilt precisely along the original plan.

The stars of the **Museo Civico** ★, Piazza Garibaldi (✆ **0424-522-235** or 0424-523-336; www.museobassano.it), are the Bassano family. Patriarch Jacopo was clearly the most talented, evident in his early *Flight into Egypt* and faded frescoes from local house facades to later works such as *St. John the Baptist* (1558) and *Pentecost* (1559), which are looser and show the influence of Titian. His sons Leandro and Francesco il Giovane (responsible for the nice *Lamentation*) had less success, as did their less talented sibling, Gerolano, who stayed in Bassano to run the family workshop. Admission—which also covers the ceramics museum (see below)—is 5€ for adults and 3.80€ for children under 18 or seniors older than 60. It's open Tuesday to Saturday from 9:30am to 6:30pm and Sunday from 3:30 to 6:30pm.

Italian Firewater: Grappa

As best as we can figure, grappa was invented by 11th-century Italian monks fiddling with the leftovers of the winemaking process: grape pulp, seeds, stems, and juices. Distilled and purified, the resulting after-dinner liqueur can range from clear to amber (which is usually aged), *morbido* ("soft" and smooth) to *duro* ("hard" and quite harsh to the uninitiated).

This Italian firewater was long known as *aqua vitae,* the "water of life," for its purported medicinal and restorative properties. Over the ages, it was believed to do everything from reviving the vital spirits, warming the belly (undoubtedly), relaxing the brain, sharpening the intellect, and clearing the vision to removing bodily impurities, repairing memory, prolonging life, and even curing the plague. The only benefit now touted—aside from inflicting raging intoxication—is its role as the ultimate *digestivo,* capable of helping settle your stomach after a huge Italian meal. And, scientific evidence aside, I can confirm from personal experience that grappa does indeed cure the common cold.

Nowadays, grappa is distilled from Piedmont in the west to Friuli in the east and as far south as Tuscany. You'll find bottles in all shapes and sizes; some seem to be sold more as works of glass blowers' art than for the liqueur inside. There are labels hailing from renowned grappa distilleries, high-grade *aqua vitae* produced by vineyards (which have often raised the bar on grappa quality by forgoing the winemaking process entirely, distilling the stuff from whole grapes rather than just the scraps), and homemade hooch made in copper stills that are wheeled from farm to farm.

The most renowned producer in Bassano is **Nardini,** Ponte Vecchio 2 (② **0424-227-741;** www.nardini.it), run by the same family since 1779. It is the leader in grappa production, responsible for 25% of the Italian market, and its wood-beam *taverna* at the base of the Ponte degli Alpini is on the register of Italy's Historic Locales. Most people order a Rosso, the house version of Campari and soda, using Nardini's own "Rosso" hair-tonic liqueur. Walk out onto the bridge a bit to look back at the building's wall to see the bullet marks in the plaster from French rifles giving chase to the Archduke of Austria on May 3, 1889.

Just up the street sits **Poli** (② **0424-524-426;** www.poligrappa.com), founded in 1898 at nearby Schiavon, where its production is still centered. This Bassano sales outlet is a slick operation, with less atmosphere than Nardini, but it does incorporate a small but very informative grappa museum. It's all in Italian, but if you recall the basics of distillation from high-school science (or your college dorm), it all makes sense—and the elegant glass and copper machinery is beautiful in its own way. Plus, tastings here are free.

Palazzo Sturm (1765–66), overlooking the Brenta River on Via Schiavonetti, retains some original frescoes and stuccoes, and houses a ceramics museum heavy on 18th- and 19th-century porcelains, with a contemporary collection downstairs. Admission is cumulative with the Museo Civico, above, and its hours are also the same.

Bonotto Hotel Belvedere ★ It looks modern out front, but this has been Bassano's premier hotel since the 15th century. The Belvedere sits on the busy main road skirting the walls of the historic center, 4 blocks from the central Piazza Garibaldi, but the windows' double set of double panes cuts out most noise. Standard rooms in the 1985 wing have modular '80s-style units in baby blue or wood veneer and mirrors to make the midsize rooms feel larger. Superior accommodations are larger, with sturdy dark-wood furnishings and Jacuzzi tubs. Junior suites are spruced up with 17th- and 18th-century Venetian-style antiques and double sinks, though some are done in a modern but still classy style, with embroidered sofas.

Should the Belvedere be full, they may put you up in their modern, 66-room **Hotel Palladio,** around the corner at Via Gramsci 2 (© **0424-523-777;** fax 0424-524-050). There a double runs from 138€ to 160€.

Piazzale Giardino 14, 36061 Bassano del Grappa (VI). © **0424-529-845.** Fax 0424-529-849. www. bonotto.it. 87 units. 180€ standard ("Silver") double; 212€ superior ("Gold") double; 280€ junior suite. Rates include breakfast. AE, DC, MC, V. Parking 10€ in garage. **Amenities:** Excellent Veneta restaurant; bar; babysitting; free bikes; concierge; discount at golf course in nearby Asolo; exercise room and sauna at sister Hotel Palladio around the corner; room service; smoke-free rooms. *In room:* A/C, TV w/pay movies, hair dryer, Internet, minibar.

Hotel Al Castello ★ (Value) This is the best semibudget option in town, its rooms situated above a neighborhood bar in a goldenrod building against a tower of the half-ruined castle, just 3 blocks from the Ponte degli Alpini. Accommodations are medium to largish, with wood floors, box showers, thick beams, and a touch of class in the wood furnishings. Among the thoughtful touches are heated towel racks in the freshly tiled bathrooms. Room no. 10 is the best, with a small flower-bedecked balcony.

Piazza Terraglio 19, 36061 Bassano del Grappa (VI). ©/fax **0424-228-665.** www.hotelalcastello.it. 11 units. 70€–100€ double. Breakfast 6€. AE, DC, MC, V. Free parking. **Amenities:** Bar. *In room:* A/C, TV.

Villa Palma ★★ (Finds) Don't be put off by the industrial zone you drive through to get to this 1680 countryside villa 5km (3 miles) outside Bassano. Once inside the gates, it's a quiet walled retreat of birdsong, manicured garden lawns, and pine trees onto which the marble-floor bar opens. Regular rooms are midsize with rattan furnishings, chipped stone floors, thick carpets, and doubled sinks (in most). Junior suites are larger, with elegant period-style furnishings, silk wall coverings, and Murano chandeliers. The most requested suite, no. 39, has a Jacuzzi; no. 53 lacks the Jacuzzi but enjoys long garden vistas. Even singles come with extra-wide *francesina* beds.

Via Chemin Palma 30, 36065 Mussolente (VI; 5km/3 miles from Bassano off the road to Asolo/Montebelluno). © **0424-577-407.** Fax 0424-87-687. www.villapalma.it. 21 units. 110€ double; 180€ junior suite. Rates include breakfast. AE, DC, MC, V. Free parking. **Amenities:** Elegant Veneto restaurant; bar; concierge; heated indoor pool at nearby sports center; room service. *In room:* A/C, TV, hair dryer, minibar, Wi-Fi.

WHERE TO DINE

Bassano has long been known for its white asparagus, green peas, and blend of Venetian and mountain cuisines. Unfortunately, few of Bassano's current crop of restaurants live up to its traditions. Along with the excellent restaurant at Bonotto Hotel Belvedere (see above), here are the best of what you will find.

Al Sole VENETIAN This is one of the more refined restaurants in town, serving elegant dishes of seasonal fresh ingredients such as *bigoli al sugo d'anatra* (thick homemade pasta in a duck ragù), *risotto agli asparagi bianchi* (risotto with the tender local white asparagus), or *baccalà con polenta* (salt cod served with creamy polenta).

Beer in Boot-Shaped Glasses

Bassanese love to spend their time out of the house and in each other's company, and Bassano is flush with spots to enjoy an espresso, linger over a beer with buddies, or indulge in a grappa-tasting marathon. On the main piazza, **Caffè Danieli,** Piazza Garibaldi 39 (© **0424-529-322**), retains its stuccoed ceilings and chandeliers from 1927. The beer, according to "an old, old tradition," is served in boot-shaped glasses, and there are lots of tables out on the square.

There are plenty of places on Piazza Garibaldi to grab a gelato, but most of the action is down by the Ponte degli Alpini. At the base of Via Gamba sits **Birreria da Ponte,** no. 1 (© **0424-521-613**), with Spaten on tap, toasted sandwiches, beam ceilings, and tables spilling down the marble steps toward the bridge. Across the street at no. 4 is **Al Saiso** (© **0424-521-838**), bigger than its cozy neighbor, with more food (*bruschette* along with panini) and a better view down the bridge from outdoor tables.

For the best vistas, however, cross to the spare, crowded **Taverna al Ponte,** Via Angarano 2 (© **0424-503-662**), flush against the far end of the *ponte* with a tiny balcony of three tables overhanging the river in the shade of the bridge.

Via Vittorelli 41–43. © **0424-523-206.** Reservations recommended. Primi 6.50€–10€; secondi 10€–17€. AE, DC, MC, V. Tues–Sun noon–2:30pm and 7:30–10pm.

Birreria Ottone ★ AUSTRIAN/ITALIAN   This popular 1870 beer hall inhabits a 13th-century *palazzo*, which lent its stone walls to the elegant dining room. Bassano friends and families gather here sometimes just to drink in good company, sometimes for a full meal of grub that runs the gamut from traditional Italian dishes and local Veneto specialties to the best of Tyrolean and Austrian cuisines.

Via Matteotti 48–50. © **0424-522-206.** Reservations suggested on weekends. Primi 6€–7€; secondi 7.50€–15€. AE, DC, MC, V. Wed–Mon noon–3pm; Wed–Sun 7–11:30pm. Closed 2nd week of Aug.

A SIDE TRIP TO MAROSTICA

The delightful medieval-walled village of Marostica, 30km (19 miles) north of Vicenza (7km/4¼ miles west of Bassano), comes alive every other summer (in even years only): The entire town dresses up to commemorate a true centuries-old chess game between two knights vying for the hand of Lionora, daughter of a 15th-century local lord. The chivalric **Partita a Scacchi ★★★** is reenacted on the main piazza with real people as the pieces, dressed in elaborate Renaissance costume, preceded by a flag-throwing procession. The whole town takes part, and the torch-lit nighttime setting is gorgeous.

Performances are repeated over the course of the second weekend of September. A few of the worst seats are usually available each day of performance, but it's best to purchase tickets months in advance. **Tourist information** is at Piazza Castello 1 (© **0424-72-127;** fax 0424-72-800; www.marosticascacchi.it). Marostica's engaging **Sagra del Ciliege (Cherry Festival)** takes place in June. You can get here on one of two dozen daily buses from Vicenza in 40 minutes. Dozens of local buses do the short run daily from Bassano to Marostica. By car, head west on S248.

5 VICENZA

32km (20 miles) W of Padua, 74km (46 miles) W of Venice, 51km (32 miles) E of Verona, 204km (126 miles) E of Milan

Vicenza pays heartfelt homage to Andrea di Pietro della Gondola (born in Padua in 1508, died in Maser in 1580). He came to Vicenza at the age of 16 and lived out his life and dreams here under the name Palladio at a time when Vicenza was under the sway of the still-powerful Venice Republic. Palladio was the most important architect of the High Renaissance, one whose living monuments have inspired and influenced architecture in the Western world over the centuries to this very day.

Vicenza and its surroundings are a mecca for the architecture lover, a living museum of Palladian and Palladian-inspired monuments—and, consequently, Vicenza was designated a UNESCO World Heritage Site in 1994. But even if you've never heard of Palladio, you'll find an evening stroll through illuminated piazzas and boutique-lined streets plenty enjoyable. Plan on taking home a wealth of knowledge about architecture—a day in Vicenza is worth a semester back in school.

Today Vicenza is one of the wealthiest cities in Italy, thanks in part to the recent burgeoning of the local computer-component industry (Federico Faggin, inventor of the silicon chip, was born here). It is also the center of the country's gold-manufacturing industry (one-third of Italy's gold is made here, and each year three prestigious international gold fairs make finding a hotel in these parts impossible) and is one of Europe's largest producers of textiles. The average Vicentino is well off, and it shows.

FESTIVALS   The well-established summertime series of **Concerti in Villa** ★ (© 0444-399-104) takes place in June and July; a few concerts are held outdoors at Vicenza's famed Villa la Rotonda; for others, you will need a car. The tourist office will have the schedule and availability of seats; tickets usually cost around 15€ to 20€. The stage of the delightful **Teatro Olimpico** (© 347-492-5005; www.olimpico.vicenza.it) hosts shows in September and October, often classical plays or Shakespeare, though in 2009 it presented operas by Rossini and Piccinni and music by Bach.

ESSENTIALS

GETTING THERE   **By Train**   The **train station** is in Piazza Stazione, also called Campo Marzio (© 0444-326-707; www.ferroviedellostato.it), at the southern end of Viale Roma. There's frequent service (2–3 per hr.) connecting Vicenza with Venice (52–67 min.), Padua (20 min.), and Verona (30 min.).

By Bus   The **FTV bus station** (© 0444-223-111; www.ftv.vi.it) is located on Viale Milano, just to the west (left) of the train station. Buses leave frequently for all the major cities in the Veneto and to Milan; prices are comparable to train travel.

By Car   Vicenza is on Autostrada A4, linking Venice to Milan. Coming from Venice (about 1 hr.), you'll bypass Padua before arriving in Vicenza.

VISITOR INFORMATION   The main **tourist information office** is at Piazza Matteotti 12 (© 0444-320-854; fax 0444-327-072; www.vicenzae.org), next to the Teatro Olimpico. The office is open daily from 9am to 1pm and Monday to Saturday from 2 to 6pm. A second office can be found at Piazza dei Signori 8 (© 0444-544-122; fax 0444-325-001), and it is open daily 10am to 2pm and 2:30 to 6:30pm.

Value Seeing Vicenza by Cumulative Ticket

The Card Musei costs 8€ for adults, 6€ for students, and includes admission to the **Teatro Olimpico, Museo Civico, Museo Naturalistico Archeologico,** and the **Galleria di Palazzo Leoni.** Children younger than 14 get into every museum for free. For more information, see www.vicenzae.org.

CITY LAYOUT   The city's layout is quite straightforward and easy to navigate on foot. The train station lies at its southernmost point. From here, head straight ahead on Viale Roma; it ends at a turnabout with gated gardens beyond. Head right (east) into the *centro storico,* marked by the **Piazza Castello,** from which the main thoroughfare, the **Corso Palladio,** starts. Lined with shops, offices, and banks, the arrow-straight Corso cuts through town, running southwest (from Piazza Castello) to northeast (Piazza Matteotti), site of the Teatro Olimpico. Along the Corso you'll find urban *palazzi* by Palladio and his students; midway, the **Piazza dei Signori** (and its Basilica Palladiana) will be found on your right (south). Perpendicular to the Corso is the important **Contrà Porti,** a lovely *palazzo*-studded street, on your left (north).

GETTING AROUND   There is limited traffic (for taxis, buses, and residents) once you enter the Piazza del Castello and the *centro storico.* Everything of interest can be easily reached on foot; pick up a map at the tourist office. Even the two villas just outside town (see "Villas & a Basilica Nearby," below) can be reached by foot (not suggested in the heat of high season) or bike, as well as by bus or car.

PIAZZA DEI SIGNORI

South of Corso Palladio on the site of the ancient Roman Forum and still the town hub, this central square is your first introduction to the city and local boy wonder Palladio.

The magnificent bigger-than-life **Basilica Palladiana** ★★ is not a church at all and was only partially designed by Palladio. Beneath it stood the Gothic-style Palazzo della Ragione (Law Courts and Assembly Hall) that Palladio was commissioned to convert to a High Renaissance style befitting a flourishing late-16th-century city under Venice's benevolent patronage. It was Palladio's first public work and secured his favor and reputation with the local authorities. He created two superimposed galleries, the lower with Doric pillars, and the upper with Ionic. The roof was destroyed by World War II bombing but has since been rebuilt in its original style. It's open from Easter to September Tuesday to Saturday from 9:30am to noon and from 2 to 7pm; Sunday from 9:30am to 12:30pm and from 2 to 7pm. Off season, it's closed Sunday afternoon; admission is free. *Note:* The Basilica Palladiana is currently undergoing a lengthy restoration, which will likely last well into 2010.

The 12th-century **Torre Bissara** (or **Torre di Piazza**) bell tower belonged to the original church and stands near two columns in the piazza's east end (the Piazza Blade), one topped by the winged lion of Venice's Serene Republic, the other by the *Redentore* (Redeemer). Also of note in the piazza is the Loggia del Capitaniato (1570), begun but never finished according to plans by Palladio, except for the four massive red-brick columns. Behind the basilica (to the south) is the **Piazza delle Erbe** ★, site of the daily produce market.

THE VENETO

6

VICENZA

This is Vicenza's main street, and what a grand one it is, lined with the magnificent *palazzi* of Palladio and his students (and *their* students, who, centuries later, were still influenced by Palladio's work), today converted into cafes, swank shops, and imposing banks. The first one of note, starting from its southwest cap near the Piazza Castello, is the **Palazzo Valmarana,** at no. 16, begun by Palladio in 1566. On the right (behind which stands the Piazza dei Signori and the Basilica Palladiana) is the **Palazzo del Comunale,** the Town Hall built in 1592 by Scamozzi (1552–1616), a native of Vicenza and Palladio's protégé and star pupil. This is said to be Scamozzi's greatest work.

Heading northeast from the Corso Palladio, take a left onto the Contrà Porti, the second most important street for its Palladian and Gothic *palazzi.* The two designed by Palladio are the **Palazzo Barbarano Porto,** at no. 11, and (opposite) **Palazzo Thiene,** at no.12 (now the headquarters of a bank); **Gothic** *palazzi* of particular note can be found at nos. 6 to 10, 14, 16, 17, and 19. Parallel, on Corso Fogazzaro, look for no. 16, **Palazzo Valmarana,** perhaps the most eccentric of Palladio's works.

Returning to Corso Palladio, look for no. 145/147, the pre-Palladian **Ca d'Oro (Golden Palace),** named for the gold leaf used in the frescoes that once covered its facade. The simple **16th-century** *palazzo* at no. 163 was Palladio's home.

Before reaching the Piazza Matteotti and the end of the Corso Palladio, you'll see signs for the **Church of Santa Corona** ★, set back on the left on the Via Santa Corona 2 (daily 8:30am–noon and 2:30–6pm). An unremarkable 13th-century Gothic church, it shelters two masterpieces (and Vicenza's most important church paintings) that make this worth a visit: Giovanni Bellini's *Baptism of Christ* (fifth altar on left) and Veronese's *Adoration of the Magi* (third chapel on right). This is Vicenza's most interesting church, far more so than the cavernous Duomo southwest of the Piazza dei Signori, but worth seeking out only if you've got the extra time. At the end of the Corso Palladio at its northeastern end is Palladio's world-renowned **Teatro Olimpico** and, across the street, the **Museo Civico** in the Palazzo Chiericati.

Teatro Olimpico & Museo Civico ★★★ The splendid Teatro Olimpico was Palladio's greatest urban work, and one of his last. He began the project in 1580, the year of his death, at the age of 72; it would be completed 5 years later by his student Vicenzo Scamozzi. It was the first covered theater in Europe, inspired by the theaters of antiquity. The seating area, in the shape of a half-moon, as in the old arenas, seats 1,000. The stage seems much deeper than its actual 4.2m (14 ft.), thanks to the permanent stage "curtain" and Scamozzi's clever use of *trompe l'oeil.* The stage scene represents the ancient streets of Thebes, while the faux clouds and sky covering the dome further the impression of being in an outdoor Roman amphitheater. Drama, music, and dance performances are still held here year-round; check with the tourist office.

Across the Piazza Matteotti is another Palladian magnum opus, the **Palazzo Chiericati,** which houses the Museo Civico (Municipal Museum). Looking more like one of the country villas for which Palladio was equally famous, this major work is considered one of his finest and is visited as much for its two-tiered, statue-topped facade as for the collection of Venetian paintings it houses on the first floor. Venetian masters you'll recognize include Tiepolo, Tintoretto, and Veronese, while the lesser known include works from the Vicenzan (founded by Bartolomeo Montagna) and Bassano schools of painting.

cumulative ticket (see "Seeing Vicenza by Cumulative Ticket," above); it is not possible to buy a ticket just
for the Teatro Olimpico or Palazzo Chiericati. Apr–Sept Tues–Sun 9am–7pm; Oct–Mar Tues–Sun 9am–
5pm. Bus: 1, 2, 5, or 7.

VILLAS & A BASILICA NEARBY

To reach the two important villas in the immediate environs of Vicenza, southeast of the
train station, you can walk, bike, or take the no. 8 bus. First stop by the tourist office for
a map, and check on visiting hours, which tend to change from year to year. The following two villas are generally open from mid-March to early November.

The **Villa Rotonda** ★★★ (© **0444-321-793;** fax 0444-879-1380), alternatively
referred to as Villa Capra Valmarana after its owners, is considered one of the most perfect buildings ever constructed and has been added to the World Heritage List by
UNESCO; it is a particularly important must-do excursion for students and lovers of
architecture. Most authorities refer to it as Palladio's finest work. Inspired by ancient
Greek and Roman designs, Palladio began this perfectly proportioned square building,
topped by a dome, in 1567; Scamozzi completed it between 1580 and 1592, after Palladio's death. It is worth a visit if only to view it from the outside (in fact, you can really
see much of it from the gate). Admission to the grounds for viewing is 4€; admission to
visit the lavishly decorated interior is 8€. The grounds are generally open from about
March 15 to November 4, Tuesday to Sunday 10am to noon and 3 to 6pm, the interior
only Wednesday during the same hours. The villa is private, like many others around
Vicenza, and can be closed for a day or week on short notice, so it's always a good idea
to call before going, if possible.

From here, it is only a 10-minute walk to the **Villa Valmarana** ★★ (© **0444-543-
976**), also called *ai Nani* (dwarves) after the statues that line the garden wall. Built in the
17th century by Mattoni, an admirer and follower of Palladio, it is an almost commonplace structure whose reason to visit is an interior covered with remarkable 18th-century
frescoes by Giambattista Tiepolo and his son Giandomenico. Admission is 8€, and the
villa is open mornings as follows: March 15 to November 5 Wednesday, Thursday, Saturday, and Sunday 10am to noon. It's open afternoons Tuesday to Sunday as follows:
March 15 through April, 2:30 to 5:30pm; May through September, 3 to 6pm; and
October to November 5, 2 to 5pm. These hours are fungible so it's a good idea to check
with the tourist information office.

Also in this area is the **Santuario di Monte Berico** ★ (© **0444-559-411**), built in 1668
by a Bolognese architect. If you've already visited the Villa Rotonda, you will understand
where the architect got his inspiration. The interior's most important work is in a chapel to
the right of the main altar, *Lamentation,* by Bortolomeo Montagna (1500), one of the
Veneto's most famous artists. The terrace in front of the church affords beautiful views of

THE VENETO

6

VICENZA

(Fun Facts   A Model for Monticello

Villa Rotonda may seem vaguely familiar, for it is the model that inspired Thomas
Jefferson's home Monticello, the Chiswick House near London, myriad plantation
homes in America's Deep South, and countless other noble homes and government buildings in the United States and Europe.

Touring the Villas

In addition to visiting the two villas located in the immediate outskirts of Vicenza, a tour of the dozens of country *ville venete* farther afield is the most compelling outing from Vicenza. Check at the tourist office for availability of organized tours, something that has been on again and (more frequently) off again for the last few years. You most probably will have to do it yourself (this means having access to wheels). Many of the villas are still privately owned, and each has its own hours and restrictions (not all the villas can be visited; others permit visits only to the grounds but not the interiors, and so forth). The tourist office can help you plan your trip around these restrictions, and it also has maps and a host of varied itineraries outlining the most important villas (not all of them 16th-c. Palladian designs), many of which are UNESCO-protected sites. Public transportation for these visits is close to nonexistent. If you do have access to a car, ask about the summer concert series in June and July, Concerti in Villa (see "Festivals," above), which draws first-class talent in the classical music world.

Vicenza, the Monti Berici, and the distinct outline of the nearby Alps. The basilica is open in summer months Monday to Saturday from 6am to 12:30pm and 2:30 to 6:30pm, Sunday 6am to 8pm (it closes earlier in winter months); admission is free.

ORGANIZED TOURS

Each summer brings a different sort of guided tour of the city by the local tourism authorities, often free of charge—but only if you buy the Card Musei (see "Seeing Vicenza by Cumulative Ticket," above). Saturday walking tours start at 12€. Check with the tourist office upon your arrival, or in advance by visiting its website (see "Visitor Information," above). Architecture buffs may want to splurge for an accredited multilingual tour guide through **Guide Turistiche Autorizzate** (*©* **348-677-1271;** www.vicenza tourguide.it). Rates are 105€ for a half-day, for up to 30 people.

WHERE TO STAY

Unlike the tourism-magnet Verona, Vicenza can be very quiet in high season, August, or winter months when trade fairs are not in town; some hotels close without notice for a few weeks if there's little demand. Make sure you call in advance; the number of hotels in the city is limited.

Due Mori ★ Due Mori's history as the oldest family-run hotel in Vicenza and its convenient location on a quiet side street just west of the sprawling Piazza dei Signori make this the (deservedly) most popular spot in town for the budget-minded. Which is to say: Book early. In a modernized shell of a centuries-old *palazzo*, tasteful and authentic 19th-century pieces distinguish otherwise plain rooms whose amenities are kept at a minimum—but, then, so are the prices. This is as good as it gets in the very center of Palladio's hometown.

Via Do Rode 24 (1 block west of Piazza dei Signori), 36100 Vicenza. *©* **0444-321-886.** Fax 0444-326-127. www.hotelduemori.com. 30 units, 27 with private bathroom. 55€ double with shared bathroom, 80€

double with private bathroom. Breakfast 5€. AE, MC, V. Free parking. **Amenities:** Bar; Wi-Fi. *In room:* Hair dryer (on request).

Giardini   There is nothing particularly friendly or charming about the Hotel Giardini, but its location can't be beat: It is one of the few moderately priced choices in the city center. The exterior is symmetrical and innocuous, with flowerpots arranged with Swiss precision. Rooms are very clean, with modern furniture, and there's a businesslike atmosphere here such as you might find in an American motel. The staff is similarly efficient and to the point. As you can imagine, it caters to business travelers, so the place fills up quickly and the rates rise when there is a convention in town. Also, inexcusably, the hotel closes for the month of August.

Viale Giuriolo (next to Piazza Matteotti and the Teatro Olimpico), 36100 Vicenza ☎ **0444-326-458.** Fax 0444-326-458. www.hotelgiardini.com. 18 units. 114€ double (rates can be much higher if there is a convention in town). Rate includes breakfast. AE, DC, MC, V. Free parking. Closed Aug. Bus from station: 1, 2, 5, or 7. **Amenities:** Bar. *In room:* A/C, satellite TV, hair dryer, minibar.

Hotel Cristina   Located west of the Piazza Castello and the green Giardino Salvi, this recently refurbished hotel is within easy walking distance of the historic center's principal sites. It's a good choice for those with wheels and a few extra dollars. A contemporary approach with occasional exposed beams and marble and parquet flooring results in a handsome, well-maintained lodging and makes this one of Vicenza's preferred three-star properties. A courtyard provides welcome parking space, and guests have access to bicycles for touring the traffic-free center of town as well as the nearby villas. After all that cycling, coast back to the hotel and its Finnish sauna.

Corso San Felice e Fortunato 32 (west of Salvi Gardens), 36100 Vicenza. ☎ **0444-323-751** or 0444-324-297. Fax 0444-543-656. www.hotelcristinavicenza.it. 33 units. 90€–170€ double. Rates include buffet breakfast. Discounts possible in off season. AE, DC, MC, V. Parking 7€. **Amenities:** Bar; bikes; concierge; room service; sauna; smoke-free rooms. *In room:* A/C, TV, hair dryer, minibar, Wi-Fi.

WHERE TO DINE

Antica Casa della Malvasia ★ VICENTINO   This ever-lively, taverna-like *osteria* sits on a quiet, characteristic side street that links the principal Corso Palladio with the Piazza dei Signori. Service comes with a smile and is informal, the cooking homemade and regional. The food is reliably good, but it's just an excuse to accompany the selection of wines (80), whiskeys (100), grappas (150), and teas (over 150). No wonder this place always buzzes. Even if you don't eat here, at least stop in for a late-night toddy, Vicentino style—it's a favorite spot for locals and visitors alike, and there's often live music on Tuesday and Thursday evenings.

Contrà delle Morette 5 (off Corso Palladio). ☎ **0444-543-704.** Reservations suggested during high season. Primi 5€–8€; secondi 7€–13€. Weekday lunch special: primi 4€; secondi 6€. AE, MC, V. Tues–Sun noon–3pm and 7pm–midnight (sometimes later).

Gran Caffè Garibaldi CAFE   If it's a lovely day, set up camp here in the shade of a table with an umbrella overlooking Vicenza's grand piazza. The most historically significant cafe in town is as impressive inside as you would imagine. The upstairs restaurant is expensive for what it offers, but the outside terrace gives you the chance to sit and gaze upon the wonders of the basilica, yet another Palladian masterpiece, while sipping a drink or having an ice cream. The cuisine is nothing to write a postcard to Grandma about, but the front-row seats on the beautiful Piazza dei Signori are.

Piazza dei Signori 5. ☎ **0444-542-455.** Primi 8.50€; secondi 15€. MC, V. Wed–Mon noon–2:30pm and 7–10:30pm.

Righetti ⓥ̲a̲l̲u̲e̲ VICENTINO/ITALIAN   For a self-service operation, this place is a triple surprise: The diners are all local (and loyal); the food is reliably good, of the home-cooked, generous-portions kind; and the interior is rustic, welcoming, and pleasant, considering its inexpensive profile. But it's the opportunity to sit outdoors in the quiet, traffic-free Piazza Duomo that's the biggest draw. First stake out a table by setting your place, and then order your food at the counter (prepared fresh on the spot); when you're finished eating, just tell the cashier what you had and he'll add up the bill. There are three or four first courses to choose from (Tues and Fri are risotto days) and as many entrees. Evenings offer the option of grilled meats (which makes eating indoors in the cold winter months more enjoyable), though this is the perfect relaxed place to revel in a simple lunch of pasta and a vegetable side, opting for a more special dinner venue.

Piazza Duomo 3–4. Ⓒ **0444-543-135.** Primi 4.50€; secondi 5€–8€. No credit cards. Mon–Fri noon–2:30pm and 7–10pm.

Trattoria Tre Visi ★★ VICENTINO/ITALIAN   Operating, from the early 1600s until 1997, around the corner from the current address, this Vicentino institution is now located on an important *palazzo*-studded street in a setting somewhat less dramatic than the previous 15th-century *palazzo.* The menu has stayed unchanged, however, and this is good: Ignore items that concede to foreign requests and concentrate on the regional dishes they know how to prepare best. Almost all the pasta is made fresh daily, including the house specialty, *bigoli con anitra,* fat, spaghetti-like pasta served with duck ragout. The region's signature dish is *baccalà alla Vicentina,* a tender salt codfish simmered in a stew of onions, herbs, anchovies, garlic, and *parmigiano* for 8 hours before arriving at your table in perfection. Ask your waiter for help in selecting from Veneto's wide spectrum of very fine wines: It will enhance your bill but also the memories you'll bring home.

Corso Palladio 25 (near Piazza Castello). Ⓒ **0444-324-868.** Reservations suggested. Primi 10€–15€; secondi 16€–21€. AE, DC, MC, V. Tues–Sun 12:30–2:30pm; Tues–Sat 7:30–10pm. Closed July.

6 VERONA

114km (71 miles) W of Venice, 80km (50 miles) W of Padua, 61km (38 miles) W of Vicenza, 157km (97 miles) E of Milan

Suspend all disbelief regarding the real-life existence of Romeo and Juliet, and your stay in Verona can be magical. After Venice, this is the Veneto's most-visited city. Verona reached a cultural and artistic zenith during the 13th and 14th centuries under the puissant, often cruel, and sometimes quirky della Scala, or Scaligeri, dynasty that took up rule in the late 1200s. In 1405 it surrendered to Venice, which remained in charge until the invasion of Napoleon in 1797.

During the time of Venetian rule, Verona became a prestigious urban capital and controlled much of the Veneto and as far south as Tuscany. You'll see the emblem of the *scala* (ladder) around town, heraldic symbol of the Scaligeri dynasty. The city has a locked-in-time character that recalls its medieval and Renaissance heyday, and the magnificent medieval *palazzi,* towers, churches, and stagelike piazzas you see today are picture-perfect testimony to its centuries-old influence and wealth.

For some reason, visitors spend remarkably little time in this beautiful medieval city. While it has a short list of attractions, it is a handsome town to stay in and visit at a leisurely pace. Statistics indicate that most tourists stop here for a night (or less)—I'd say try for at least 2 nights.

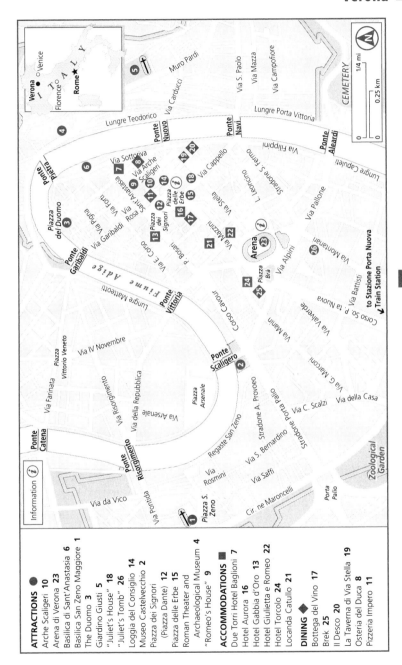

THE VENETO

6 VERONA

ATTRACTIONS ●
Arche Scaligeri **10**
Arena di Verona **23**
Basilica di Sant'Anastasia **6**
Basilica San Zeno Maggiore **1**
The Duomo **3**
Giardino Giusti **5**
"Juliet's House" **18**
"Juliet's Tomb" **26**
Loggia del Consiglio **14**
Museo Castelvecchio **2**
Piazza dei Signori
  (Piazza Dante) **12**
Piazza delle Erbe **15**
Roman Theater and
  Archaeological Museum **4**
"Romeo's House" **9**

ACCOMMODATIONS ■
Due Torri Hotel Baglioni **7**
Hotel Aurora **16**
Hotel Gabbia d'Oro **13**
Hotel Giulietta e Romeo **22**
Hotel Torcolo **24**
Locanda Catullo **21**

DINING ◆
Bottega del Vino **17**
Brek **25**
Il Desco **20**
La Taverna di Via Stella **19**
Osteria del Duca **8**
Pizzeria Impero **11**

(Fun Facts) Art Thou, Truly, Romeo?

Though the city has plenty else to recommend it as a sightseeing capital of the Veneto, the local tourism economy is underpinned by hordes of bus groups, Shakespearian pilgrims, and hopeless romantics. They come to wander the streets where Capulets and Montagues once fought, Romeo pined, and Juliet sighed from her (completely false) balcony.

Wealthy Veronese families called Capuleti and Montecchi did exist. Did they feud? Probably. That often was the way with local clans vying for city power in the Middle Ages. But did their two houses, so alike in dignity, ever harbor secret, star-crossed lovers? Did Romeo and Juliet really exist?

The story is based in an ancient legend; the core tragic elements go back at least to the Greeks. To trace the Shakespeare version: The basic story was put into novella form (based on a medieval Sienese version) in 1476 and then subsequently retold in 1524 by Veneto-born Luigi da Porto. He chose to set it in Verona in the years 1302 to 1304 during the reign of the Scaligeri, and renamed the young couple Romeo and Giulietta. The popular *storia d'amore* was translated into English, at which point Shakespeare obviously got hold of it and worked his own magic.

With the genius of Shakespeare's pen, the story turned into theatrical gold. Translated into dozens of languages and performed around the world (check out the number of Asian and eastern European tourists who flock to Juliet's House), this universal and timeless tale of pure love has forever since been set in the tempestuous days of this medieval city—notwithstanding that version with Leo DiCaprio.

That said, Zeffirelli chose to film his classic 1968 interpretation in the tiny Tuscan town of Pienza, south of Siena. And, of course, the story emigrated to the New World and took up in the mean streets of New York as *West Side Story.*

FESTIVALS & MARKETS   The Teatro Romano is known for its **Festival Shakespeariano (Shakespeare Festival)** ★ June through August, which celebrated its 61st anniversary in 2009. Festival performances usually begin in late May with jazz concerts, while performances of the Bard's plays generally kick off toward the end of June. In July and August, there are a number of ballets (occasionally, Prokofiev's *Romeo and Juliet*) and modern-dance performances. Check the schedule (ⓒ **045-807-7500** or 045-806-6485, www.estateteatraleveronese.it, or the tourist office). Last-minute tickets go on sale at the Teatro Romano box office at 8:15pm (most performances start at 9pm). Tickets are in the neighborhood of 25€.

During Verona's summer-long festival of the arts, see what's happening in the Piazza dei Signori, where frequent **free concerts** (jazz, tango, classical) keep everyone out until the wee hours. And for something truly unique, check out **Sognando Shakespeare (Dreaming Shakespeare):** Follow this *teatro itinerante* (traveling theater) of young, talented actors in costume as they wander about the medieval corners of Verona from site to site, reciting *Romeo e Giulietta* (in Italian only) *in situ,* as Shakespeare would have loved it to be. For information, contact the tourist office. For information about performances July through September, call ℂ **045-800-0065.**

Other important events are the famous 4-day **horse fair,** Fieracavalli, in early November, and the important 5-day **VinItaly wine fair** (that overlaps with the Olive Oil Fair) in mid-April. (Verona's schedule of fairs is long and varied; while few may be of interest to those outside the trades involved, their frequency can create problems for tourists in regard to hotel availability.) The Piazza San Zeno hosts a **traveling antiques market** the third Saturday of every month; come early.

ESSENTIALS

GETTING THERE   By Train   Verona is easily accessed on the west-east Milan-Venice line, as well as on the north-south Brennero-Rome line. At least 30 trains daily run east from Venice (1½–2 hr.). Even more arrive from Milan (1½–2 hr.). Trains also connect Verona with Vicenza (30–50 min.), Padua (35–50 min.), and Bologna (⅔–2 hr.).

The **Stazione Porta Nuova train station** (ℂ **045-534-221**) is located rather far south of the Piazza Brà (and Arena) area and is serviced by at least half a dozen local bus lines. The bus network within the historic center is limited, so if you have luggage, you'll probably want a taxi to get to your hotel.

To get downtown from the train station, walk straight out to the bus island marked MARCIAPIEDE F (parallel to the station) to catch minibus no. 72 or 73 (tickets on sale at the newsstand in the station or the AMT booth on MARCIAPIEDE A). Get off on Via Stella at Via Cappello for the center. Alternatively, over half the buses from the station stop at Piazza Brà, so just peruse the posted route signs.

By Bus   The bus station, **A.P.T.** (Azienda Provinciale Trasporti), is at Piazza XXV Aprile (ℂ **045-805-7911;** www.aptv.it), across from the train station. Buses leave from here for all regional destinations, including Largo di Garda. Although there is bus service to Vicenza, Padua, and Venice (only the summertime departures for Venice are direct; in other months, there's a change), it is generally easier to travel by train.

By Car   The Serenissima autostrada (A4) links Venice and Milan; the exit for downtown Verona is Verona Sud. Coming from the north or south, use the A22 autostrada, taking exit Verona Nord.

VISITOR INFORMATION   A **central tourist office** is at Via degli Alpini 9, adjacent to the Arena off Piazza Brà (ℂ **045-806-8680;** fax 045-801-0682), open Monday to Saturday 9am to 7pm and Sunday 10am to 4pm. A **small office** at the train station (ℂ **045-800-0861**) is open Monday to Saturday 9am to 7pm and Sunday 9am to 3pm. Visit their website at www.tourism.verona.it.

Guided Tours   An air-conditioned *bus turistico,* called "Romeo," departs thrice daily for a 1½-hour Giro Turistico tour of the city's historic center every day except Monday from June 1 until September 28. The cost is 15€ for adults and 7€ for children under 18 for a recorded spiel in four languages; you can buy your ticket on the bus. It leaves from the Gran Guardia in the Piazza Brà at 10am, 11:30am, 1pm, and 3:30pm (an evening tour leaves at 9pm on Sat and Sun). The 3:30pm Saturday afternoon tour has a real, live tour guide that ups the cost to 20€. I think you'll do just as well (if not better) with this guidebook, however.

CITY LAYOUT   The city lies alongside the banks of an S-shaped curve in the Adige River. As far as the average visitor is concerned, everything of interest—with the exception of the Teatro Romano—is found in the *centro storico* on the south side of the river's loop; there's no site that cannot be easily and enjoyably reached by foot.

Will the Fat Lady Sing?

Verona's renowned **opera season** ★★★ begins in late June and extends through August in Verona's Arena, the ancient amphitheater. It began in 1913 with a staging of *Aïda* to commemorate the 100th anniversary of Verdi's birth, and *Aïda* in all of its extravagant glory has been performed yearly ever since. Expect to see other Verdi works such as *Nabucco, La Traviata,* and *Rigoletto,* as well as other big-name crowd pleasers (the 2010 season, which begins on June 18, will have *Aïda, Turandot, Madama Butterfly, Il Trovatore,* and *Carmen*).

Those seated on the least expensive, unreserved stone steps costing 23€ to 28€ Friday and Saturday and 21€ to 26€ otherwise, enjoy fresh air, excellent acoustics, and a view over the Arena's top to the city and surrounding hills beyond. The rub is that Jose Carreras will only appear to be 1 inch high, and if it was a sunny day, the stones will have stored up enough heat to keep a small town humming for days and that heat will pass to you during your 3 hours at the Arena. Numbered seats below cost from 73€ to 183€ during the week and 84€ to 198€ on Friday and Saturday (there are slightly reduced prices for those under 27 and over 65). All tickets are subject to an advance booking fee that varies depending on how much you spend and is 7.50€ for a purchase of up to 150€ and 12€ for a purchase of up to 250€—worth it, unless you're willing to tough it out by lining up at 4 or 5pm for the 6pm opening of the gates for unreserved seating (and the show doesn't even start until 9:15pm).

The **box office** is located on Via Dietro Anfiteatro 6b; credit card purchase accepted by phone or online (📞 **045-800-5151;** www.arena.it). You pick up tickets the night of the performance. If you hope to find tickets upon arrival, remember that *Aïda* is everyone's most requested performance; weekend performances are usually sold out. As a last resort, be nice to your hotel manager—everyone has a connection. And even on the most coveted nights (weekend performances by top names), scalpers abound. If you want to plan early, tickets generally go on sale at the beginning of October for the season that begins the following June.

The massive ancient Roman amphitheater, the **Arena,** sits at the southern end of the city's hub in the airy cafe-ringed **Piazza Brà.** The piazza is linked by the popular **Via Mazzini** pedestrian thoroughfare to the **Piazza delle Erbe** and its adjacent **Piazza dei Signori.** The grid of pedestrian-only streets between is lined with shops and cafes that make up the principal strolling and window-shopping destinations in town.

Slightly out of this loop (though still an easy walk) is the **Basilica San Zeno Maggiore,** west of the Arena, and **Juliet's Tomb,** southeast of the Arena (only die-hard Juliet fans will appreciate the trek here). Both the **train station** and the **Fiera di Verona conference center** are located in the southern part of town beyond the Porta Nuova.

GETTING AROUND   Verona lends itself to walking and strolling, and most sites are concentrated within a few history-steeped blocks of each other. Venture off the store-lined treadmill and seek out the narrow, cobblestoned side streets that are evocative of

eras past. Little to no traffic is permitted in town, so upon arrival, stash your car in a
parking area suggested by your hotel (where they'll most likely have a special arrangement), and let your feet do the transporting.

WHAT TO SEE & DO
Top Attractions

If you're in town the **first Sunday** of any month, note that entrance is free for the following sites: Castelvecchio Museum, the Roman Theater, and Juliet's Tomb.

Because there are so many churches in Verona, an admission charge has been imposed in an attempt to cover custodian charges and offer longer hours.

Arena di Verona ★★★　The best-preserved Roman amphitheater in the world and the best known in Italy after Rome's Colosseum, the elliptical Arena was built in a slightly pinkish marble in the 1st century A.D. and stands in the very middle of town, with the Piazza Brà on its southern flank. Built to accommodate more than 20,000 people (outdone by Rome's contender that could seat more than twice that), it is in remarkable shape today (despite a 12th-c. earthquake that left only four arches of the outer ring standing), beloved testimony to the pride and wealth of Verona and its populace.

Its acoustics (astoundingly good for an open-air venue) have survived the millennia and make it one of the most fascinating venues for live performances today, conducted without microphones. If you're in town during the summer opera performances in July and August, do everything possible to procure a ticket (see "Will the Fat Lady Sing?" above) for any of the outdoor evening performances. Even opera-challenged audience members will take home the memory of a lifetime. Other events, such as orchestral concerts, are staged here whenever the weather permits. Check with the tourist office for more information.

The cluster of outdoor cafes and *trattorie*/pizzerias on the western side of the Piazza Brà line a wide marble esplanade called Il Liston; they stay open long after the opera performances end. Enjoy some serious post-opera people-watching here.

Piazza Brà. (*C*) **045-800-3204.** www.arena.it. Admission 6€, 4€ for students and 1€ for children 8-14. Mon 1:30–7:30pm; Tues–Sun 8:30am–7:30pm (last admission 45 min. before close); July–Aug summer opera season 9am–3:30pm (and sometimes a little later).

Casa di Giulietta (Juliet's House) ★★　There is no proof that a Capuleti (Capulet) family ever lived here (or, if they did, that a young girl named Juliet ever existed), and it wasn't until 1905 that the city bought what was an abandoned, overgrown garden and decided its future. Rumor is that this was once actually a whorehouse.

(Value)　**Verona by Cumulative Ticket**

The **VeronaCard,** a *biglietto cumulativo* (cumulative ticket), will help you visit several of the city's sites for just one fee. Two versions of the card are available. The 10€ card, valid for just 1 day, allows you to ride the city's buses and enter its museums, monuments, and churches. The 15€ card offers the same places but allows you 3 consecutive days rather than 1. You'll find the VeronaCard for sale at the sites below, or call (*C*) **045-807-7774.**

So powerful is the legend of Juliet that over half a million tourists flock here every year to visit the simple courtyard and home that are considerably less affluent-looking than the sumptuous Franco Zeffirelli version as you may remember it (the movie was filmed in Tuscany). Many are those who leave behind layer upon layer of graffiti along the lines of *"Valentina, ti amo!"* or who engage in the peculiar tradition (whose origin no one can seem to explain) of rubbing the right breast (now buffed to a bright gold) of the 20th-century bronze statue of a forever nubile Juliet.

The curious might want to fork over the entrance fee to see the spartan interior of the 13th-century home, restored in 1996. Ceramics and furniture on display are authentic to the era but did not belong to Juliet's family—if there ever was a Juliet at all. No one is willing to confirm (or deny) that the balcony was added to the *palazzo* as recently as 1928 (though that doesn't stop many a young lass from posing on it, staring dreamily at the sky).

La Tomba di Giulietta (Juliet's Tomb; ✆ 045-800-0361) is about a 15-minute walk south of here (near the Adige River on Via delle Pontiere 5; admission 4.50€ adults, 3€ students and those over 65, 1€ children 8–14, and free first Sun of each month; hours are Mon 1:30–7:30pm and Tues–Sun 9am–7pm; last admission is 45 min. before closing). The would-be site of the star-crossed lovers' suicide is found within the graceful medieval cloisters of the Capuchin monastery of San Francesco al Corso. Die-hard romantics may find this tomb, with its surely posed "sarcophagus," rather more evocative than the crowded scene at Juliet's House and worth the trip. Others will find it overrated and shouldn't bother. The adjacent church is where their secret marriage was said to have taken place. A small museum of frescoes is also adjacent.

Via Cappello 23 (southeast of Piazza delle Erbe). ✆ 045-803-4303. Admission (to building only; courtyard is free) 6€ adults, 4.50€ children. Mon 1:30–7:30pm; Tues–Sun 8:30am–7:30pm. (Last admission 45 min. before closing.)

Museo Castelvecchio ★★   A 5-minute walk west of the Arena on the Via Roma and nestled on the banks of the swift-flowing Adige River, the "Old Castle" is a crenelated fairy tale of brick towers and turrets, protecting the bridge behind it. It was commissioned in 1354 by the Scaligeri warlord Cangrande II to serve the dual role of residential palace and military stronghold. It survived centuries of occupation by the Visconti family, the Serene Republic of Venice, and then Napoleon, only to be destroyed by the Germans during World War II. Its restoration was initiated in 1958 by the acclaimed Venetian architect Carlos Scarpa, and it reopened in 1964.

The ground-floor rooms, displaying statues and carvings of the Middle Ages, lead to alleyways, vaulted halls, multileveled floors, and stairs, all as architecturally arresting as the Venetian masterworks from the 14th to 18th centuries—notably those by Tintoretto, Tiepolo, Veronese, Bellini, and the Verona-born Pisanello—found throughout. Don't miss the large courtyard with the equestrian statue of the warlord Cangrande I, with a peculiar dragon's head affixed to his back (actually his armor's helmet, removed from his head and resting behind him).

A stroll across the pedestrian bridge behind the castle affords you a fine view of the castle, the **Ponte Scaligeri** (built in 1355 and also destroyed during World War II; it was reconstructed using the original materials), and the river's banks.

Corso Castelvecchio 2 (at Via Roma, on the Adige River). ✆ 045-806-2611. www.comune.verona.it/Castelvecchio/cvsito. Admission 6€, 2€ children 8–14. Free 1st Sun of each month. Mon 1:45–7:30pm; Tues–Sun 8:30am–7:30pm (last admission 45 min. before closing).

Piazza delle Erbe ★★ This bustling marketplace—the *palazzi*-flanked Square of
the Herbs—sits on the site of the Roman Forum where chariot races once took place.
The herbs, spices, coffee beans, and bolts of silks and damasks that came through Verona
after landing in Venice from faraway Cathay have given way to the fresh and aromatic
produce of one of Italy's wealthiest agricultural regions—offset by the presence of T-shirt
and french-fry vendors, as the piazza has become something of a tourist trap. But the
perfume of fennel and vegetables fresh from the earth still assaults your senses in the early
morning, mixing with the cacophony of vendors touting plump tomatoes, dozens of
different variations of salad greens, and fruits that can't possibly taste as good as they
look, but do. Add to this the canary lady, the farmer's son who has brought in a half a
dozen puppies to unload, and the furtive pickpocket who can spot a tourist at 50 paces—
and you have one of Italy's loveliest little outdoor markets. Take a rest on one of the steps
leading up to the small 14th-century fountain in the piazza's center and a Roman statue
dubbed *The Virgin of Verona.*

Btw. Via Mazzini and Corso Porta Borsari. Open-air produce and flower market Mon–Sat 8am–7pm.

Piazza dei Signori (Piazza Dante) ★ To reach the Piazza dei Signori from the
Piazza delle Erbe, exit under the Arco della Costa (see "Liar, Liar," below). The perfect
antidote to the color and bustle of the Piazza delle Erbe, the serene and elegant Piazza dei
Signori is a slightly somber square, one of Verona's innermost chambers of calm. Its
center is anchored by a large 19th-century statue of the "divine poet" Dante, who found
political exile from Florence in Verona as a guest of Cangrande I and his Scaligeri family
(in appreciation, Dante wrote of his patron in his poem *Paradiso*).

If entering from the archway, you'll be facing the Scaligeri's 13th-century crenelated
residence. Left of that, behind Dante's back, is the Loggia del Consiglio (Portico of the
Counsel), a 15th-century masterpiece of Venetian Renaissance style. Opposite that and
facing Dante is the 12th-century Romanesque Palazzo della Ragione, whose courtyard
and fine Gothic staircase should be visited. This piazza is Verona's finest microcosm, a
balanced and refined assemblage of historical architecture. Secure an outdoor table at the
square's legendary command post, the Antico Caffè Dante, and take it all in over a late-
afternoon Campari and soda.

Piazza dei Signori, adjacent to Piazza delle Erbe.

More Attractions
Arche Scaligeri (Scaligeri Tombs)/Torre dei Lamberti ★ Exit the Piazza dei
Signori opposite the Arch of the Rib, and immediately on your right, at the corner of Via
delle Arche Scaligeri, are some of the most elaborate Gothic funerary monuments in

---

(Fun Facts) Liar, Liar

You'll be able to spot the Arco della Costa (Arch of the Rib) by the enormous
whalebone hanging overhead. It was placed here 1,000 years ago when it was
said to have been unearthed during excavations on this spot, indicating this area
was once underwater. Local legend goes that the rib will fall on the first person
to pass beneath it who has never told a lie—thus explaining the nonchalance
with which every Veronese passes under it.

City of Love

If no romantic comedy is too saccharine for your tastes and no love letter too sappy, you might just want to make your visit to Verona coincide with Valentine's Day so that you can participate in the city's weeklong **Verona in Love** festival. Yes, that's really the name. The festival is 7 days devoted to devotion, and sponsored by local florists. Events include a competition to see who can write the best love letter to Juliet, and merchants' stands in Piazzale Bra are set up in the shape of a heart for the occasion. The city center is decked out with twinkling lights, and a sort of holiday spirit pervades the medieval alleys. If you and your significant other happened to meet at the track or in the gym, you might want to celebrate *Verona in Love* by running the city's annual marathon or the Giulietta and Romeo Half Marathon. An added bonus for cash-strapped lovers: Entrance to Juliet's house and tomb is free for most of the week during the festival. For information: www.veronainlove.com.

Italy—the raised outdoor tombs of the canine-obsessed Scaligeri family (seen behind the original decorative grillwork), powerful and often ruthless rulers of Verona.

The most important are those by the peculiar names of Mastino I (Mastiff the First, founder of the dynasty, date of death unknown), Mastino II (Mastiff the Second, d. 1351), and Cansignorio (Head Dog, d. 1375). The most interesting is found over the side door of the family's private chapel, Santa Maria Antica—the tomb of Cangrande I (Big Dog, d. 1329), with *cani* (dogs) holding up a *scala* (ladder), both elements that figure in the Scaligeri coat of arms. That's Cangrande I—patron of the arts and protector of Dante—and his steed you see above (the original can be seen in the Museo Castelvecchio). Recently restored, these tombs are considered one of the country's greatest medieval monuments. Entry is only to the neighboring **Torre dei Lamberti;** the tomb area itself is closed to visitors. The view from atop the 83m (272-ft.) tower is the best in the city and takes in all the vibrant colors of the surrounding landscape.

Around the corner, on Via delle Arche Scaligeri 2, is the alleged 13th-century home of Juliet's significant other, **Romeo Montecchi** (Montague, in Shakespearian), which incorporates the popular Osteria del Duca (see "Where to Dine," below).

Via della Costa 1. ℂ **045-927-3027.** Admission 6€, 4.50 students and those over 65, 1€ children 8-14. Mon 1:45–7:30pm; Tues–Sun 9:30am–7:30pm (last admission 30 min. before closing).

Basilica di Sant'Anastasia Built between 1290 and 1481, this is Verona's largest church, considered the city's finest example of Gothic architecture, even though the facade remains unfinished. A lovely 14th-century campanile bell tower is adorned with frescoes and sculptures. The church's interior is typically Gothic in design, highlighted by two famous *gobbi* (hunchbacks) that support the holy-water fonts, an impressive patterned pavement, and 16 side chapels containing a number of noteworthy paintings and frescoes from the 15th and 16th centuries.

Most important is Verona-born Pisanello's *St. George Freeing the Princess of Trebisonda* (1433). This is considered one of his best paintings and is of the armed-knight-and-damsel-in-distress genre—with the large white rump of St. George's steed as one of

its focal points. Also worth scouting out are the earlier 14th-century frescoes by the
Giotto-inspired Altichiero in the Cavalli Chapel next door.

Piazza Sant'Anastasia at Corso Sant'Anastasia. ℂ **045-592-813.** www.chieseverona.it. Admission 2.50€.
Mar–Oct Mon–Sat 9am–6pm, Sun 1–6pm; Nov–Feb Tues–Sat 10am–4pm, Sun 1–4pm.

Basilica San Zeno Maggiore ★★   This is one of the finest examples of Romanesque architecture in northern Italy, built between the 9th and 12th centuries. Slightly
out of the old city's hub but still easily reached by foot, San Zeno (as it's often referred
to), dedicated to the city's patron saint, is Verona's most visited church. Spend a moment
outside to appreciate the fine, sober facade, highlighted by the immense 12th-century
rose window, the *Ruota della Fortuna* (Wheel of Fortune).

This pales in importance compared to the **facade** ★★ below—two pillars supported by
marble lions and massive doors whose 48 bronze panels were sculpted from the 9th to the
11th centuries and are believed to have been some of the first castings in bronze since Roman
antiquity. They are among the city's most cherished artistic treasures and are worth the trip
here even if the church is closed. Not as sophisticated as those that would adorn the Baptistery
doors of Florence's Duomo in the centuries to come, these are like a naive illustration from a
children's book and were meant to educate the illiterate masses with scenes from the Old and
New Testaments and the life of San Zeno. They are complemented by the stone bas-reliefs
found on either side of the doors, the 12th-century work of Niccolo, who was also responsible
for the Duomo's portal. The 14th-century **tower** on the left belonged to the former abbey,
while the free-standing slender **campanile** on the right was begun in 1045.

The massive **interior** ★ is filled with 12th- to 14th-century frescoes and crowned by
the nave's ceiling, designed as a wooden ship's keel. But the interior's singular highlight
is the famous triptych of the *Madonna and Child Enthroned with Saints,* by Andrea
Mantegna (1459), behind the main altar. Napoleon absconded with the beautiful centerpiece—a showcase for the Padua-born Mantegna's sophisticated sense of perspective and
architectural detail—which was eventually returned to Verona, although two side panels
stayed behind in the Louvre and in Tours. Look in the small apse to the left of the altar
for the colored marble statue of a smiling San Zeno, much loved by the local Veronesi,
in an act of blessing.

Piazza San Zeno. ℂ **045-592-813.** www.chieseverona.it. Admission 2.50€. Mar–Oct Mon–Sat 8am–6pm,
Sun 1–6pm; Nov–Feb Tues–Sat 10am–1pm and 1:20–4pm, Sun 1–5pm.

**Teatro Romano (Roman Theater) and the Museo Archeologico (Archaeo-
logical Museum)** ★   The oldest extant Roman monument in Verona dates from the
time of Augustus, when the Arena was built and Verona was a strong Roman outpost at

---

ⓘ **Tips**   **A Church Tip**

Verona's churches have banded together as the **Associazione Chiese Vive**
(ℂ **045-592-813;** www.chieseverona.it). Admission to any one church is 2.50€,
or you can buy a cumulative ticket for 5€ for adults, granting admission to
Sant'Anastasia, San Zeno, San Fermo, and the Duomo complex. *Note:* If you're
only going to visit Verona's churches, this is the deal for you. Otherwise, if you
want to see all or most of the city's attractions, stick with the **VeronaCard** (see
the "Verona by Cumulative Ticket" box, p. 211.)

(Moments) Beautiful Views

The panorama from the Torre dei Lamberti is not the only perspective of Verona from on high. The view from the Roman Theater is beautiful any time of day, but particularly during the evening performances—the ancient Romans knew a thing or two about dramatic settings. For other views, you can take a rickety elevator to the 10th-century Church of Santa Libera above the theater, or to the former monastery and cloisters of San Girolamo, which now houses a small archaeological museum. Above this is the Castel San Pietro, whose foundations date from the times of the Romans and whose terraces offer one of the best views in town.

THE VENETO

6

VERONA

the crossroads of the Empire's ancient north-south, east-west highways. There is something almost surreal about attending an open-air performance of Shakespeare's *Two Gentlemen of Verona* or *Romeo and Juliet* here—even if you can't understand a word (see "Festivals & Markets," earlier in this section). Classical music, ballet, and jazz performances are also given here, with evocative views of the city beyond. A small archaeological museum (same hours as the site itself) housed in a lovely old monastery is included in the ticket price. On Sunday (only), the promenade is open to the public.

Via Rigaste Redentore (over the Ponte Pietra bridge behind the Duomo, on the north banks of the river Adige). ℭ **045-800-0360**. www.estateteatraleveronese.it. Admission 4€; free 1st Sun of each month. Mon 1:30–6:45pm; Tues–Sun 8:30am–6:45pm; during theater season 9am–3pm. Bus: 31, 32, 33, or 73.

The Duomo ★ Begun in the 12th century and not finished until the 17th century, the city's main church still boasts its original main doors and portal, magnificently covered with low reliefs in the Lombard Romanesque style that are attributed to Niccolo, whose work can be seen at the Basilica of San Zeno Maggiore. The church was built upon the ruins of an even more ancient paleo-Christian church dating from the late Roman Empire. Visit the **Cappella Nichesola,** the first chapel on the left, where Titian's serene but boldly colorful *Assumption of the Virgin* is the cathedral's principal treasure, with an architectural frame by Sansovino (who also designed the choir). Also of interest is the semicircular screen that separates the altar from the rest of the church, attributed to Sanmicheli. To its right rises the 14th-century tomb of Saint Agatha.

The excavations of Sant'Elena church, also in the Duomo complex, reveal a bit of 6th-century mosaic floor; the Baptistery contains a Romanesque font carved with scenes from the Nativity cycle.

Don't leave the area without walking behind the Duomo to the river: Here you'll find the 13th-century Torre di Alberto della Scala tower and nearby Ponte della Pietra bridge, the oldest Roman monument in Verona (1st c. B.C.; rebuilt in the 14th c.). There has been a crossing at this point of the river since Verona's days as a 1st-century Roman stronghold when the Teatro Romano was built on the river's northern banks and the Arena at its hub.

Piazza Duomo (at Via del Duomo). ℭ **045-592-813**. www.chieseverona.it. Single admission 2.50€. Mar–Oct Mon–Sat 10am–5:30pm, Sun 1:30–5:30pm; Nov–Feb Tue–Sat 10am–1pm and 1:30–4pm, Sun 1–5pm.

Close to the Castel San Pietro is the well-known, multitiered **Giardino Giusti** gardens (✆ **045-803-4029**), whose formal 16th-century layout and geometrical designs of terraces, fountains, statuary, and staircases inspired, among many, Mozart and Goethe. The gardens are open daily from 9am to dusk; admission is 6€.

SHOPPING

Unlike in Venice, most of the people walking Verona's boutique-lined pedestrian streets are locals, not tourists. Come to Verona to spend some time doing what the locals do, shopping and stopping in any of the myriad cafes and *pasticcerie.* Shopping is mostly for the Veronesi, and upscale clothing and accessories boutiques line the two most fashionable shopping streets, **Via Mazzini** (connecting the Arena and the Piazza delle Erbe) and **Via Cappello,** heading southeast from the piazza and past Juliet's House. There's also **Corso Borsari** to check out, and **Corso Sant'Anastasia** (heading west and east, respectively, out of the Piazza delle Erbe), the latter having a concentration of interesting antiques stores.

WHERE TO STAY

Although the following prices reflect peak-season rates, expect inflated prices during the July/August opera season or when one of the major trade fairs is in town. With this exception, low season is November through mid-March. The **C.A.V.** (Cooperativa Albergatori Veronesi), at Via Patuzzi 5, is an organization of dozens of hotels that will help you with bookings for a fee determined by your choice of hotel category (✆ **045-800-9844;** fax 045-800-9372; www.cav.vr.it).

Due Torri Hotel Baglioni ★★   Verona's top hotel occupies a 14th-century *palazzo* that was reopened in the 1950s. It's where rock stars and opera singers stay when they play in town, picking up where Mozart, Goethe, and Garibaldi left off—perhaps because they're among the few who can afford it. The airy lobby looks like a stage set, with original 1370s columns and carvings and contemporary frescoes of medieval scenes, the ceilings set with oil paintings. The room furnishings range from Louis XIV to Biedermeier, and even standard rooms are luxurious, with patterned wall coverings, Murano chandeliers, and large, marble-sheathed bathrooms with double sinks. Windows are double-paned, so even on the piazza things are quiet. The hotel is in the narrow end of Verona formed by the tight river bend, so many rooms, especially on the third floor, and the rooftop terrace have great views to the hills beyond.

Piazza Sant'Anastasia 4, 37121 Verona. (✆ **045-595-044.** Fax 045-800-4130. www.baglionihotels.com. 90 units. 280€–595€ double; 535€–900€ junior suite. Discounts with online booking. Rates include breakfast. AE, DC, MC, V. Valet parking 26€. **Amenities:** Veronese/international restaurant; bar; babysitting; concierge; smoke-free rooms; Wi-Fi. *In room:* A/C, TV/VCR, hair dryer, Internet, minibar.

Hotel Aurora ★   It used to be location, location, location that had loyal guests returning to the Aurora. But after a refurbishing of all guest rooms and en suite bathrooms, it is the decor that brings them in as well. Six doubles are blessed with views of one of the world's great squares, the Piazza delle Erbe and the white-umbrella stalls that make up the daily marketplace. Consider yourself lucky if you snag the top-floor double (there is an elevator!) with a small balcony. There's another terrace, overlooking the *mercato* (market), for the guests' use on the second floor, just above the breakfast room where the hotel's free daily ample buffet is served.

Piazza delle Erbe 2 (southwest side of the piazza), 37121 Verona. ℂ **045-594-717** or 045-597-834. Fax 045-801-0860. www.hotelaurora.biz. 19 units, 16 (including all doubles) with private bathroom. 100€–150€ double (prices higher when a convention is in town). Rates include buffet breakfast. AE, DC, MC, V. Parking 10€. Bus: 72 or 73. **Amenities:** Bar; concierge; room service. *In room:* A/C, TV, hair dryer.

Hotel Gabbia d'Oro ★★

One wall dates to 1320 at this cozy hotel of stone-trimmed doorways, rustic beams, and smart liveried service around the corner from the main piazza, but most of the *palazzo* is 18th century. The atmosphere hovers between medieval and eclectic, vaguely 19th-century Victorian romantic. It's all a bit put on—falsified fresco fragments, half-testers, and collectibles in little glass cases on wall brackets—but the result is more or less effective. Most rooms are terribly snug, but artfully placed mirrors help open up the space. Careful touches abound, from comfy couches in the sitting areas to extra-large shower heads and stone reliefs set in the tubs. A few rooms have small "Romeo-o-Romeo" balconies. The lovely winter garden is half-enclosed and half-open for nice weather.

Corso Porta Borsari 4A, 37121 Verona. ℂ **045-800-3060.** Fax 045-590-293. www.hotelgabbiadoro.it. 27 units. 220€–380€ double; 285€–530€ junior suite. Breakfast included, except during opera season (June 29–Sept 2), when it's 23€. AE, DC, MC, V. Valet parking 28€. Bus: 72 or 73. **Amenities:** Bar; babysitting; bikes; concierge; room service. *In room:* A/C, TV/VCR, hair dryer, Internet, minibar.

Hotel Giulietta e Romeo ★★

A block from the Arena is this handsomely refurbished *palazzo*-hotel recommended for its upscale ambience, cordial can-do staff, and location in the heart of the *centro storico*. Brightly lit rooms are warmed by burnished cherrywood furnishings, and the large marble-tiled bathrooms are those you imagine finding in tony first-class hotels. The hotel takes its name seriously; there are two small marble balconies à la Juliet on the facade, but their view is unremarkable. The hotel is located on a narrow side street that is quiet and convenient to everything.

Vicolo Tre Marchetti 3 (south of Via Mazzini, 1 block east of the Arena), 37121 Verona ℂ **045-800-3554.** Fax 045-801-0862. www.giuliettaeromeo.com. 30 units. 105€–230€ double; 125€–230€ triple. Rates include buffet breakfast. Mention Frommer's when booking and show book upon arrival for a 10% discount. Add approximately 30% to all above rates during the opera season and major trade fairs. AE, DC, MC, V. Parking nearby 10€–15€. From train station: Buses going to Piazza Brà. **Amenities:** Bar; babysitting; bikes; concierge; room service; smoke-free rooms. *In room:* A/C, TV, hair dryer, minibar, Wi-Fi.

Hotel Torcolo ★

Lifelong friends Signoras Silvia and Diana are much of the reason behind the deserving success of this small, comfortable hotel just 1 block off the lively Piazza Brà. Each guest room is individually done. Room no. 31 is a country-style sunny top-floor room (the hotel has an elevator) with exposed ceiling beams; nos. 16 (a triple), 18, 21, and 34 are done with original Liberty-style furnishings. They truly care about your comfort here: Rooms are equipped with orthopedic mattresses on stiff springs, double-paned windows (though it's quiet already), extra air-conditioners on the top floor, and extra-wide single beds. They even keep different typical national travel tastes in consideration: They accept pets in a nod to Swiss travel habits, have a few rooms with tubs for Japanese, and offer some softer beds for the French. You can take the rather expensive breakfast outdoors on the small patio if the weather is pleasant, in a breakfast nook, or in your room.

Vicolo Listone 3 (just 1 block off the Piazza Brà), 37121 Verona. ℂ **045-800-7512.** Fax 045-800-4058. www.hoteltorcolo.it. 19 units. 70€–127€ double; 155€ double during the opera season. Buffet breakfast 8€ (included during the opera season). MC, V. Parking in nearby garage 12€; 20€ during the opera season. Closed Dec 16–26 and Jan 26–Feb 8. From train station: Buses to Piazza Brà. **Amenities:** Babysitting; concierge; room service; smoke-free rooms. *In room:* A/C, TV, hair dryer, minibar.

Locanda Catullo (Value) It's a three-floor hike to this homey *pensione*-like place that has been run by the affable Pollini family for more than 30 years, and it seems that nothing ever changes—from the prices to the decor. However, it's centrally located and the rooms are spacious and clean, the bathrooms nice and bright. The prices attract the 20- and 30-something euro-counters who make up the majority of the hotel's clientele. With impressive details such as decorative plaster molding, French doors, and marble or parquet floors, the superfluous tapestries and dried flower arrangements become almost too much. Single rooms are large and come equipped with a sink; solo travelers feel comfortable in the prevailing family atmosphere. There's no breakfast service available, but the bar downstairs couldn't be more convenient.

Via Catullo 1 (just north of the Via Mazzini; entrance from the alleyway Vicolo Catullo), 37121 Verona. © 045-800-2786. locandacatullo@tiscali.it. 21 units, 5 with private bathroom. 60€ double with shared bathroom; 70€ double with private bathroom; 85€ triple with shared bathroom; 100€ triple with private bathroom; 135€ mini-apt (2 doubles, shared bathroom). No credit cards. Parking free on the street. From train station: Buses going to Piazza Brà. **Amenities:** Bar. *In room:* No phone.

WHERE TO DINE

Bottega del Vino ★ VERONESE/WINE BAR Oenophiles can push an evening's meal here into the stratosphere if they succumb to the wine cellar's unmatched 80,000-bottle selection, the largest in Verona. This atmospheric *bottega* first opened in 1890, and the old-timers who spend hours in animated conversation seem to have been here since then. The ambience and conviviality are reason enough to come by for a tipple at the well-known bar, where five dozen good-to-excellent wines are for sale by the glass for 3.50€ to 12€. There's no mistaking Verona's prominence in the wine industry here. At mealtimes the regulars head home and the next shift arrives: Journalists and local merchants fill the few wooden tables ordering simple but excellent dishes where the Veneto's wines have infiltrated the kitchen, such as the *risotto al Amarone,* sauced with Verona's most dignified red.

Via Scudo di Francia 3 (off Via Mazzini), Verona. © 045-800-4535. www.bottegavini.it. Reservations necessary for dinner. Primi 11€–15€; secondi 16€–28€. AE, DC, MC, V. Wed–Mon noon–3pm (bar 10:30am–3pm) and 7pm–midnight (bar 6pm–midnight).

Brek (Value) PIZZERIA/CAFETERIA The Veronesi (and Italians in general; Brek is part of a northern Italian restaurant chain) are forever dismissing this place as a mediocre tourist spot. But then who are all these Italian-speaking, local-looking patrons with their trays piled high, cutting in line at the pizza station and clamoring for all the best tables outside with a brilliant view of the sun-kissed Arena? This strip of the Piazza Brà is lined with pleasant alfresco alternatives such as the more serious Olivo and Tre Corone, but Brek is an informal, inexpensive preference for a casual lunch where you can splurge (a lot) and walk away satisfied and solvent. Yes, this is fast-food *alla Veronese*—but do the Italians ever really go wrong in the culinary department? Inside it's a food fest, with various pastas and fresh vegetables made up as you wait and some self-service where fruit salads and mixed green salads are displayed.

Piazza Brà 20. © 045-800-4561. www.brek.it. Reservations not accepted. Primi and pizzas 3.50€–6€; secondi 4.20€–11€. AE, MC, V. Daily 11:30am–3pm and 6:30–10pm.

Il Desco ★ VERONESE Il Desco offers highly creative cuisine made with a variety of the best ingredients the Veneto has to offer, with warm fresh-baked rolls and odd *amuse-bouches* such as olive-oil gelato with a tomato coulis. They tend to serve all meat dishes—from venison with pearl onions to salmon on a bed of lentils—extremely rare, so order it *ben cotto* (well done) if you want it cooked beyond merely flame-kissed. Some examples of the kitchen's rich creations include papardelle with sea snails, pork ravioli soup with shrimp, and stuffed pigeon and salt cod. Desserts are stupendous. Though the service is refined and the food of the highest quality, the inflated prices keep me from recommending it beyond a single star.

Via Dietro San Sebastiano 7. ℂ **045-595-358.** www.ildesco.com. Reservations highly recommended. Primi 26€–32€; secondi 40€–45€; tasting menu 130€. AE, DC, MC, V. Tues–Sat 12:40–2pm and 7:40–10:30pm; open Mon in July, Aug, and Dec. Closed 15 days in June and 15 days btw. Dec and Jan.

La Taverna di Via Stella (Finds) VERONESE   Opened in 1999 by the Vantini brothers and their two friends, this taverna already has the feel of a popular neighborhood *osteria* that has been around for much longer, likely because all of the antique furniture was recouped from older taverns in the area. The small wooden tables are packed in tightly to seat the locals (the whole fire squad stopped in one time I visited), who come for huge portions of Veronese cuisine. To go with their 180 labels in the wine cellar, try *bigoli al torchio* with shredded duck, *coniglio alla veronese con pesto* (rabbit served in a crushed-basil-and-garlic pesto), or *pastise de' caval con polenta* (horse goulash with polenta).

Via Stella 5C. ℂ **045-800-8008.** Reservations recommended. Primi 7.50€–9€; secondi 9€–15€; fixed-price menu 22€. AE, DC, MC, V. Tues–Sun noon–3pm and 7–11pm.

Osteria del Duca ★★ VERONESE   There are no written records to confirm that this 13th-century *palazzo* was once owned by the Montecchi (Montague) family, and, thankfully, the discreet management never considered calling this place the Ristorante Romeo. But here you are, nonetheless, dining in what is believed to be Romeo's house, a characteristic medieval *palazzo,* and enjoying one of the nicest meals in town amid a spirited and friendly neighborhood ambience. You might find *penne con pomodoro e melanzane* (fresh tomato sauce with eggplant) or a perfectly grilled chop or filet with rosemary-roasted potatoes. It will be simple, it will be delicious, you'll probably make friends with the people sitting next to you, and you will always remember your meal at Romeo's Restaurant. If you don't have an adventurous palate, avoid anything on the menu that has *cavallo* or *asino* in it, unless you want to sample horsemeat, a local specialty, or donkey.

Via Arche Scaligeri 2 (east of Piazza dei Signori). ℂ **045-594-474.** Reservations not accepted. Primi 5€–7€; secondi 9€–12€; *menù turistico* 15€. MC, V. Mon–Sat 12:30–2:30pm and 7–10:30pm.

Pizzeria Impero (Kids) PIZZERIA/TRATTORIA   Location is not everything, but to sit with a pleasant lunch or moonlit dinner in this most elegant piazza will be one of those Verona memories that stays with you. Impero makes an okay pizza—especially for undiscerning tourist tastes—but any of the two dozen or so varieties will taste pretty heavenly if you're sharing an outdoor table with your Romeo or Juliet.

If Impero is full and the Arena area is more convenient to your day's itinerary, try the well-known and always busy **Pizzeria Liston,** a block off Piazza Brà at Via Dietro Listone 19 (ℂ **045-803-4003**), which also serves a full trattoria menu (all major credit cards accepted; closed Wed). Its pizzas are said to be better, but its side-street setting—even with outdoor tables—doesn't quite match that of the Impero.

Piazza dei Signori 8. ℂ **045-803-0160.** Reservations not accepted. Primi and pizzas 6€–9€; secondi 7€–16€. DC, MC, V. Summer daily noon–1am; winter Thurs–Tues noon–3:30pm and 7pm–midnight.

CAFES, PASTRIES & WINE BARS

When all is said and done in Verona, one of the most important things to consider is where you'll stop to sip, recharge, socialize, nibble, and revel in this handsome town.

CAFES & PASTRIES   Verona's grande dame of the local cafe society is the **Antico Caffè Dante** ★, in the beautiful Piazza dei Signori (no phone). Verona's oldest cafe, it is rather formal indoors (read: expensive) where meals are served. But it's most recommended for those who want to soak up the million-dollar view of one of Verona's loveliest ancient squares from the outdoor tables smack in the middle of it all. During the Arena summer season, this is the traditional après-opera spot to complete—and contemplate—the evening's experience. It's open from 9am to 4am.

The oldest of the cafe/bars lining Verona's market square is **Caffè Filippini,** at Piazza delle Erbe 26 (✆ **045-800-4549**). Renovations have left little of yesteryear's character or charm, but centuries-old habits die hard: It's still the command post of choice whether indoors or (preferably) out, a lovely spot to take in the cacophony and colorful chaos of the market. It's open daily from 8am to 1am (closed Wed in winter).

An old-world temple of caffeine, **Caffè Tubino** (Corso Porta Borsari 15/D, 1 block west of the Piazza delle Erbe; ✆ **045-803-2296**) is stocked with packaged blends of Tubino-brand teas and coffees displayed on racks lining parallel walls in a small space made even smaller by the imposing crystal chandelier. The brand is well known, is nicely packaged, and makes a great gift. It's open daily from 7am to 11pm. On the same street is **Pasticceria Bar Flego** (Corso Porta Borsari 9; ✆ **045-803-2471**), a beloved institution with eight tiny tables. Accompany a frothy cappuccino with an unbridled sampling of their deservedly famous bite-size pastries by the piece at 1€ each. *Zaletti* are a regional specialty, traditional cookies made with corn flour, raisins, and pine nuts—much better tried than described! It's closed on Monday.

One of Verona's oldest and most patronized *pasticcerie* is **Cordioli,** a stroll from Juliet's House on Via Cappello 39 (✆ **045-800-3055**). There are no tables and it's often crowded at the bar, but with coffee this good and pastries this fresh, it's obvious why the crowds come. Verona's perfect souvenir? How about homemade *baci di Giulietta* (Juliet's kisses, vanilla meringues) and *sospiri di Romeo* (Romeo's sighs, chocolate hazelnut cookies)? It's closed Sunday afternoon and Wednesday.

WINE BARS   Verona is the epicenter of the region's important viticulture, but the old-time wine bars are decreasing in number and atmosphere. Recapture the spirit of yesteryear at **Carro Armato,** in a 14th-century *palazzo* at Vicolo Gatto 2A/Vicolo San Piero Martire (1 block south of Piazza Sant'Anastasia; ✆ **045-803-0175**), a great choice when you want to sit and sample some of 30 or so regional wines by the glass (2€–5€) and make an informal meal out of fresh, inexpensive bar food. Oldsters linger during the day playing cards or reading the paper at long wooden tables, while a younger crowd fills the place in the evening. A small but good selection of cheeses and cold cuts or sausages might be enough to take the edge off, but there is always an entree or two and a fresh vegetable side dish. It's open Monday to Friday from 10am to 2pm and 5pm to 2am, Saturday and Sunday 10am to 2am without a lunch break.

The wonderful old wine bar **Enoteca dal Zovo,** on Vicolo San Marco in Foro 7/5 (off Corso Porta Borsari near Caffè Tubino; ✆ **045-803-4369**), is run by Oreste, who knows everyone in town, and they all stop by for his excellent selection of Veneto wines averaging 2€ a glass, or you can go for broke and start with the very best at 4€. Oreste's *simpatica* American-born wife, Beverly, can give you a crash course. Salami, olives, and finger foods will help keep you vertical, since the few stools are always occupied by senior gentlemen who are as much a part of the fixtures as the hundreds of dusty bottles of wines and grappa that line the walls. It's open Tuesday to Sunday from 9am to 8pm.

WINE SIDE TRIPS FROM VERONA

The ancient Greeks called Italy *Enotria*—the land of wines. It produces more wine than anywhere else, so the annual **VinItaly** ★★ wine fair held every April in Verona is an understandably prestigious event, drawing vintners from around the world. The Veneto produces more DOC (Denominazione di Origine Controllata, zones of controlled name and origin) wines than anywhere else in Italy, particularly the Veronese trio of Bardolino and Valpolicella (reds) and soave (white).

The costly, dry Valpolicello wine known as Amarone comes from the vineyards outside Verona. **Masi** ★ is one of the most respected producers, one of many in the Verona hills, whose *cantine* are open to the public for wine-tasting stops. Visit Verona's tourist information office for a listing of wine estates open to the public. No organized tours are available, and you'll need your own wheels, but oenologically minded visitors will want to taste some of Italy's finest wines at the point of their origin.

Trentino–Alto Adige: The Dolomites & South Tirol

Mountains dominate much of this region, which stretches north along the Adige River valley from the intersection of Lombardy and the Veneto. The soaring landscape of the Alps and the Dolomites (Dolomiti) presides over a different Italy, one that often doesn't seem very Italian at all.

Most of the Dolomites and Südtirol (the South Tirol, which encompasses the Trentino and Alto Adige regions) belonged to Austria until it was handed over to Italy at the end of World War I. In fact, many residents, especially in and around Bolzano, Merano, and Brixen, still prefer the ways of the north to those of the south. They eat Austrian food, go about life with Teutonic crispness, and, most noticeably, tend to avoid speaking Italian in favor of their native German-based dialect. Some villages even speak Ladin, a vestigial Latin dialect related to Switzerland's Romansch. And they live amid mountain landscapes that are more suggestive of Austria than of Italy.

The eastern Alps that cut into the region are gentle and beautiful. A little farther to the east rise the Dolomites—dramatically craggy peaks that are really coral formations that only recently (in geological terms) reared up from ancient seabeds. Throughout Trentino–Alto Adige, towering peaks, highland meadows, and lush valleys provide a paradise for hikers, skiers, and rock climbers. Set amid these natural spectacles are pretty, interesting towns and castles to explore and a hybrid Teutonic-Latin culture to enjoy.

REGIONAL CUISINE The cuisine of the Alto Adige is more or less Austrian, with a few Italian touches. *Canederli* (bread dumplings) often replace pasta or polenta and are found floating in rich broths infused with liver; *speck* (smoked ham) replaces prosciutto; and Wiener schnitzel *Grostl* (a combination of potatoes, onions, and veal—the local version of corned beef hash) and pork roasts are among preferred secondi (second courses).

1 TRENT (TRENTO)

230km (143 miles) NW of Milan, 101km (63 miles) N of Verona, 57km (35 miles) S of Bolzano

Surrounded by mountains, this beautiful little city, founded by the Romans on the banks of the Adige River, definitely has an Alpine flair. It spent most of its history, from the 10th century though 1813, as a German-Austrian bishopric ruled by powerful princely bishops from their seat in the Castello del Buonconsiglio. In fact, the town's status as an Italian city at the crossroads of the Teutonic and Latin worlds, along with the bishop's dual role as subject both to the pope and to the German Emperor, made Trent the ideal compromise site for the Council of Trent called in the 16th century to address the Protestant Reformation (see "Europe Divided: Protestant Reformation & the Council of Trent," below).

Napoleon's imperial sweep through Italy sent the last prince-bishop packing in 1796, and by 1813, Trent came under a century of direct Austrian rule. Austria's hegemony was constantly challenged by the local pro-Italian *Irredentist* movement, which was delighted when the treaties ending World War I landed Trent on the Italian side of the border in 1918.

And indeed, unlike other towns up here in the far north, which tend to lean heavily on their Austrian heritage, Trent is essentially Italian. The *piazze* are broad and sunny, the palaces are ocher-colored and tile-roofed, Italian is the lingua franca, and pasta is still a staple on menus. With its pleasant streets and the remnants of its most famous event, the 16th-century Council of Trent, Trent is a nice place to stay for a night or to visit en route to Bolzano (discussed later) and other places in the Trentino–Alto Adige.

FESTIVALS & MARKETS   In May and June, churches around the city are the evocative settings of performances of the ***Festivale di Musica Sacra*** **(Festival of Sacred Music).** Its final performances coincide with **Festive Vigiliane,** a medieval pageant for which townspeople turn up in the Piazza del Duomo appropriately decked out. Call the tourist office (☎ **0461-839-000**) for performance dates.

An ambitious program aptly named **Superfestival** stages musical performances, historic dramas, and reenactments of medieval and Renaissance legends in castles surrounding Trent; it runs late June through September.

A small daily **food market** covers the paving stones of Piazza Alessandro Vittorio every day from 8am to 1pm. A **larger market,** this one with clothing, crafts, and bric-a-brac as well, is held Thursday 8am to 1pm in Piazza Arogno near the Duomo; this same piazza hosts a **flea market** the third Sunday of every month.

ESSENTIALS

GETTING THERE   **By Train**   Strategically located on a main north-south rail line between Italy and Austria, Trent is served by some 21 trains a day to and from Verona (55–69 min.), a major transfer point for trains to Milan, Florence, Rome, Venice, Trieste, and all points south. There are about two dozen trains a day from Bolzano (32–49 min.). To reach the center of town from the train station, follow the Via Pozzo through several name changes until it reaches the Piazza del Duomo as Via Cavour.

By Bus   Trentino Trasporti (☎ **0461-821-000;** www.ttesercizio.it), which leaves from a terminal next to the train station, is the major link to outlying mountain towns. There's also hourly service to and from Riva del Garda on Lago di Garda (1 hr., 40 min.; see chapter 10, "The Lakes").

By Car   Autostrada A22 connects Trent with Verona in about an hour; from Verona, you can connect with the A4 for Milan (total trip time btw. Milan and Trent is about 2½

 Trentino–Alto Adige on the Web

In addition to the city websites listed under each town throughout this chapter, the Trentino province around Trent maintains its own site at **www.provincia. tn.it**. The South Tirol is also represented by private sites such as **www.sudtirol. com** and **www.suedtirol.info**, while the Dolomites can be researched at various sites claiming to be "the official" one (all are loaded with good information, at any rate); the most reputable site is **www.dolomiti.it**.

hr.), and with the A22 to Modena and, from there, the A1 for Florence and Rome. (Trent is a drive of about 3½ hr. from Florence and about 6½ hr. from Rome.) A22 also runs north to Bolzano, a little over half an hour away; the slower S12 also connects Trent and Bolzano, and from it you can get on the scenic Strada di Vino.

VISITOR INFORMATION   The local **tourist office,** near the Duomo at Via Manci 2 (✆ **0461-216-000;** fax 0461-232-426; www.apt.trento.it), is open daily 9am to 7pm.

WHAT TO SEE & DO

Castello di Buonconsiglio ★   Many Council of Trent sessions were held in this bishop's palace/fortress on the north edge of town, which you can reach by walking north from the Duomo along Via Belenzani, and then east on Via Roma (though it's a bit of a trek from the rest of the center and the train station)—both streets, especially the former, are lined with the palaces, many with faded frescoes on their facades, built to house the church officials who came to Trent to attend the council sessions. The mazelike *castello* incorporates the 13th-century Castelvecchio, surrounded by medieval fortifications, and the elegant Magno Palazzo, a palace built for a prince-bishop in the 15th century.

Europe Divided: Protestant Reformation & the Council of Trent

As you amble around this lovely town, you'll quickly learn that much of what is notable about it is in some way connected with the historic 16th-century Council of Trent, in which the Catholic church closed ranks against the waves of Protestant reform coming from the north.

In late medieval Europe, power was carefully balanced between the pope and the various kings and emperors. Power was consolidated through an intricate network wherein the secular alliances and post-feudal loyalties of princes, answerable to the Holy Roman Emperor, intersected with an overlying ecclesiastical structure of churches and monasteries, run by powerful bishoprics and answerable to the pope.

In short, by the 16th century, the system had developed to the point where not only the Vatican's strength, but also that of the emperor and other kings, relied heavily on the power structure of the Catholic Church. Therefore, the Protestant revolutions being fired in the north by Martin Luther and other reformers—who were distressed by the corruption on the part of the official church and its pope in regard to worldly interests—were seen as much more than a mere argument over style of worship: They threatened Europe's entire power base.

Germanic Holy Roman Emperor Charles V—who had brought that office to the heights of its power, ruling or controlling much of Europe—recognized this threat, both to Catholicism and to his domain. But he spent so much of his time and effort fighting wars with France and others that, despite holding his own

Among the many small collections contained within the vast complex is the Museo Provincale d'Arte, where the pride of the collection is the *Ciclo dei Mesi* (Cycle of the Months) ★★, an enchanting fresco cycle painted around 1400. It presents a detailed look at life at court and in the countryside, showing amusements among the lords and ladies and much hard work among the peasants. It's housed in the Torre dell'Aquila, or Eagle's Tower; for admission, ask the guards at the Loggia del Romanino, an atrium named for the Renaissance artist who frescoed it.

You can also visit the cell where native son Cesare Battiste was held in 1916 for his part in the *Irredentist* movement, which sought to return Trent and other parts of the region to Italy—which, indeed, came to pass with the Treaty of Versailles in 1919, but not before Battiste was hanged in the moat that surrounds the Castelvecchio.

Via Bernardo Clesio 3. ℂ **0461-233-770** or 0461-492-840. www.buonconsiglio.it. Admission 7€ adults, 4€ children. Apr–Sept Tues–Sun 9am–5:30pm; Oct–Mar Tues–Sun 9am–5pm. Bus: 5, 7, 10, or B.

Duomo   The outcomes of many Council of Trent sessions were announced in this 13th- to 16th-century cathedral, delightfully situated on the wide expanse of the cafe-filled Piazza Duomo. This square, with a statue of Neptune at its center, is referred to as the city's *salotto* (sitting room), so popular is it as a place to pass the time. The decrees that came out of the council were read in the Duomo's Chapel of the Crucifix, beneath diets to stamp out Luther's ideas, Protestantism kept growing in Germany. Charles eventually pressured the pope into instituting a great council to refute the reformers, and the Vatican called the council in 1536. But it took another 9 years to settle on Trent as the ideal compromise location in which to hold it, during which time Swiss reformer John Calvin introduced and perfected his own version of Protestantism. On and off for 18 years, from 1545 to 1563, the council held its debates and meetings, to which the Protestants were not really welcome and from which, probably wisely, they stayed away. The Great Council outlasted five popes, Martin Luther (who died in its second year), and Charles V himself (he died in 1556). Calvin passed on in 1564.

Far from taking Protestant complaints to heart, the council took a hard line, becoming more of a defensive strategy session. The Vatican dug in its heels and its doctrine, reorganizing church structure and policies to *tighten* control rather than loosen it. This became the Counter-Reformation, which, while not quite reaching the terrifying extremes of the Spanish Inquisition, brought the yardstick of conservatism down hard on the knuckles of Catholic Europe.

Still, it was all too late to stem the tide of Protestantism—and a general progressive slide away from the remnants of feudal power structures. The Germanic countries, soon to be followed by England, increasingly turned their backs on the Vatican. Charles V was the last German emperor to be crowned by the pope. The Papal States and the continent's secular kingdoms drifted apart, and the old power system gradually unraveled as Europe groped its way toward the system of nation-states we know today.

an enormous 15th-century cross. Beneath the altar of the main church is the crypt-cum-basilica Paleocristiana, a 6th-century church later used as a crypt for the city's powerful prince-bishops. A few scraps of mosaic and carvings remain.

Piazza Duomo. ℂ **0461-234-419.** Admission to the crypt 1€, or free with the Museo Diocesano ticket (see below). Mon–Sat 9:30am–12:30pm and 2:30–6pm; crypt 10am–noon and 2:30–6pm. Bus: A.

Museo Diocesano Tridentino   The cathedral's museum is housed in the adjoining, heavily fortified palace of these bishops. The museum displays some fascinating paintings of council sessions that serve almost as news photos of the proceedings (one provides a seating plan for delegates), as well as 16th-century tapestries and statuary, objects from the Duomo's treasury, and a collection of medieval and Renaissance paintings. The latter often showcase local Saint Vigilio, Trent's 4th-century bishop and a literal iconoclast whose destruction of a Saturn idol earned him his martyrdom as enraged pagans beat him to death with their wooden shoes. By the Renaissance, these nail-studded sandals had inexplicably become the *zoccolo,* a silken slipper, which the hapless saint is always holding up in paintings as the symbol of his martyrdom.

Piazza Duomo 18. ℂ **0461-234-419.** www.museodiocesanotridentino.it. Admission (includes Duomo's crypt; see above) 4€ adults, 1€ ages 12–18. Wed–Mon 9:30am–12:30pm and 2:30–5:30pm (6pm June–Sept). Bus: A.

Trent on Two Wheels

The city offers bikes to those who sign up for the **TrentoCard,** which also offers discounts for municipal museums and transportation. A 1-day card costs 10€, and a 2-day card costs 15€. Pick one up at the tourist office, which also offers guided cycling tours on weekend mornings in warmer months. For example, on a recent September morning they were offering a mountain bike tour of the local trails: 12€ for the day. Tours are usually limited to 20 people and depart from the tourist office at 9:30am (although they ask that you arrive 15 min. earlier). Call ℂ **0461-216-000** to reserve a space.

Santa Maria Maggiore   The pretty little church is a set piece of Lombard Renaissance architecture, designed and decorated almost entirely in the second quarter of the 16th century. Inside is an organ gallery ornately carved by Vincenzo Grandi in 1534. The church hosted several Council of Trent sessions, including the last ones.

Piazza Santa Maria Maggiore (btw. Via Rosimini and Via Cavour). ℂ **0461-239-888.** Free admission. Mon–Sat 9:30am–12:15pm and 3:30–7:30pm. Bus: NP.

WHERE TO STAY

Trent, despite its history, has a pretty sorry hotel crop, with most of the nicer joints outside the center and focused mainly on conference centers and corporate rates. If you want a bit more class and a full complement of amenities in your hotel, you might check out the **Grand Hotel Trento,** Via Alfieri 1–3 (ℂ **0461-271-000;** fax 0461-271-001; www.grandhoteltrento.com), a large and elegant but somewhat bland business-oriented hotel near the bus and train station, a few blocks from the Duomo. Doubles go for between 110€ and 165€; prices depend on availability. All major credit cards are accepted. The hotels listed below are located in the *centro storico,* much of which is closed to traffic. Inquire about the closest parking when making your reservation.

Accademia Hotel ★   This simple but nice hotel is the best choice in the center, though prices are a bit steep. It's set in a restored medieval house on an alley about a block from the Duomo and Piazza Santa Maria Maggiore (whose bell tower some rooms overlook). The reception area's whitewashed vaulted ceilings and stone doorjambs don't really carry over into the rooms, which are a bit spartan, if well equipped with modular or rattan furnishings, sometimes under nice sloping ceilings. The one drawback to its central location is its proximity to the church bells.

Vicolo Colico 4–6, 38100 Trento (off Via Cavour). ℂ **0461-233-600.** Fax 0461-230-174. www.accademia hotel.it. 50 units. 160€–180€ double; 190€–208€ triple; 175€–280€ suite. Rates include buffet breakfast. AE, DC, MC, V. **Amenities:** Restaurant; woodsy *enoteca* (wine bar); bikes; concierge; room service; Wi-Fi. *In room:* A/C, TV, hair dryer, Internet, minibar.

Hotel Aquila D'Oro ★   A 2007 renovation of a hotel that once occupied a centuries-old *palazzo* has created some of the nicest rooms in Trent, with a new spalike focus on health and fitness in the same ancient location right around the corner from Piazza Duomo. Each of the doubles has either a Roman sauna or a therapeutic shower known as a "water paradise," as well as either stationary bikes or treadmills. Decor throughout is stylishly contemporary, with a nice smattering of Oriental carpets, vaulted ceilings, and other interesting and cozy architectural touches in public rooms.

Via Belenzani 76, 38100 Trento. ℂ/fax **0461-986-282.** www.aquiladoro.it. 19 units. 90€–250€ double. (Prices vary greatly depending on the individual room you choose.) Rates include buffet breakfast. AE, DC, MC, V. **Amenities:** Bar; concierge; room service; smoke-free rooms. *In room:* A/C, TV, hair dryer, mini-bar, Wi-Fi.

Hotel Garni (aka Hotel Venezia)   This old hotel is very basic. It is rather less charming than its next-door neighbor, Aquila D'Oro (see above), and its "amenities" consist entirely of toilet paper and one towel, but it's cheap. Marked by 1950s-style furnishings, the simple, high-ceiling rooms are a bit dowdy but offer solid, old-fashioned comfort (unfortunately, some beds still bear the sags left by generations of travelers). Its selling point: Those rooms in the front come with stunning views over the Piazza Duomo. For the reception, walk around the corner to the "unofficial" entrance, on Piazza Duomo, to find someone to check you in. *Note:* Though the hotel's official name is now Hotel Garni, the name painted on the side of the building still says HOTEL VENEZIA (since it's a historic landmark, they can't change the outside!).

Via Belenzani 70/Piazza Duomo 45, 38100 Trento. ℂ/fax **0461-234-559.** www.hotelveneziatn.it. 50 units, 28 with private bathroom. 57€ double without private bathroom; 72€ double with private bathroom; 88€ triple with private bathroom. Rates include continental breakfast. MC, V. Free parking 200m (656 ft.) from hotel. **Amenities:** Wi-Fi. *In room:* Hair dryer, no phone.

WHERE TO DINE

It's almost a requirement to stroll down Trent's Renaissance streets with a gelato from **Torre Verde-Gelateria Zanella,** on Via Suffragio 6 (ℂ **0461-232-039**). Many flavors are made from fresh, local fruits in season, while others make no such attempt at wholesomeness and incorporate the richest chocolate and cream.

Birreria Pedavena BEER HALL/PIZZA   This hip beer hall and cafe draws a big crowd for coffee and pastries in the morning and keeps serving a huge mix of pastas, *Würstel,* and its own beer all day. You will probably be happiest if you order simply, maybe a plate of *Würstel* (sausages) or goulash. Additionally, it keeps some of the latest hours in town, making Pedavena something of a late-evening spot in a town where the nightlife is scarce, especially as there is a separate room for smokers.

Piazza Fiera 13 at Via Santa Croce. ℂ **0461-986-255.** www.birreriapedavena.com. Primi 4€–6€; secondi 4.50€–10€; pizza 4€–6€. MC, V. Mon and Wed–Thurs 9am–12:30am; Fri–Sat 9am–1am; Sun 9am–midnight. Sometimes closed in July.

La Cantinota ITALIAN   With its white tablecloths, excellent service, and reasonably priced menu, La Cantinota may be the most popular restaurant in Trent. The fare includes Italian and Tyrolean dishes and is truly inspired, making use of fresh local ingredients: wonderful homemade gnocchi, *strangola preti* (spinach dumplings coated in

Getting a Lift out of Town

For a breezy view of Trent and a heart-thumping aerial ride as well, take the **cable car** from Ponte di San Lorenzo near the train station up to Sardagna, a village on one of the mountainsides that encloses the city. You may want to provision yourself at the market and enjoy a picnic on one of the grassy meadows nearby. The cable car (ℂ **0461-822-075**) runs daily every 30 minutes from 7am to 10:30pm (7:30pm on weekends), and the fare is 1€ each way.

melted butter), rich risottos with porcini mushrooms, and venison with polenta. The adjoining piano bar is popular with local talent who tend to intersperse Frank Sinatra renditions with yodeling.

Via San Marco 24. ℂ **0461-238-527.** Reservations recommended. Primi 6.50€–8€; secondi 11€–13€. Tasting menus 25€–30€. AE, MC, V. Fri–Wed noon–3pm and 7–11pm (piano bar 10:30pm–2am).

Scrigno del Duomo ★★ ⟨Value⟩ WINE BAR/ITALIAN   This stylish wine bar and restaurant is a surprisingly good value, considering the quality of the creative cooking, immaculate service, and stellar location. From the front courtyard, with tables set under the frescoed facade, you can peek through the gate at the fountain splashing away on Trent's main piazza. The interiors mix the antique with postmodern: Renaissance-painted beams or baroque stuccoed ceilings, aluminum chairs, and sconces. There are more than 35 wines available by the glass (2.50€–6.50€). Dishes change constantly with the seasons and chef's whims but usually include pasta or gnocchi with some combination of lake fish and zucchini, and its signature cheek of beef, stewed in merlot with cream of celery sauce and candied baby carrots.

Piazza Duomo 29. ℂ **0461-220-030.** www.scrignodelduomo.com. Reservations recommended. Primi 6.50€–8€; secondi 10€–13€; tasting menu 47€ without wine. MC, V. Daily 11am–2:30pm and 6pm–midnight.

THE SOUTHERN TRENTINO: ROVERETO & CASTELLO SABBIONARA

CASTELLO DI AVIO   The first historical mention of the spectacular Castello Sabbionara (ℂ **0464-684-453**), at the town of Avio 21km (13 miles) south of Rovereto, is from the 13th century, though the castle dates back at least to the 11th century. It was built on the ever-shifting battle line between the dominions of Austrian emperors and the Venetian Republic—so it's no surprise that, during a 13th-century period of Venetian control when the castle was enlarged, the Casa delle Guardie (Guard's House) was frescoed with marvelous medieval battle scenes featuring the castle in the background. Local folklore whispers that public executions were once carried out inside the imposing Picadòra tower, which defends the north side. A more pleasant part of the house is the beautifully frescoed Room of Love on the top floor. The castle is open February to December 17, Tuesday to Sunday 10am to 1pm and 2 to 6pm (to 5pm Oct–Dec 17); admission 4€ adults, 2.50€ children ages 6 to 10.

ROVERETO   There are two main reasons to visit this noble, medieval town 24km (15 miles) south of Trent. One is simply to stroll through its winding streets and elegant, quiet piazza, both of which lie in the shadow of the 15th-century **Castello di Rovereto** (ℂ **0464-438-100**). This Venetian-built castle reminds its visitors that this is as far north as Venice got (by 1418) in its long battle with Austrian powers over control of the Tirol. By 1487, the Austrian factions had control again, but Italian hopes, and the native pro-Italy *Irrendentisti,* never truly disappeared. This brings us to the other reason to visit: to pay homage to the thousands of mostly Italian and Austrian soldiers who died in the surrounding hills during some of the fiercest fighting of World War I.

These soldiers are commemorated mainly by two sites: the daily sunset ringing of the **Campana della Pace,** or Bell of Peace (ℂ **0464-434-412;** daily 9am–6:30pm; 3€ adults, 2€ ages 6–18), which perches atop the hillside near a neoclassical rotunda temple to the fallen, and the **Museo Storico Italiano della Guerra** (ℂ **0464-438-100**). The latter occupies part of the castle, at Via Castelbarco 7, and displays photographs, weaponry,

Tuesday to Sunday 10am to 8pm. Admission is 6.50€ adults, 2€ ages 6 to 18.

Another reason to come to Rovereto is to attend one of its much-heralded cultural events: The **Rovereto Festival,** in early September, features dance performances and a major exhibition of contemporary art; and the late-September **Festival Internazionale Mozart** (✆ **0464-439-988**) features world-renowned performances of the composer's work.

Rovereto is less than half an hour south of Trent via A22. About two buses an hour make the 45-minute trip; contact **Trentino Trasporti** (✆ **0461-821-000;** www.ttspa.it) for more information. The **APT tourist office,** at a park on the Leno River at Corso Rosmini 6A (✆ **0464-430-363;** fax 0464-435-528; www.apt.rovereto.tn.it), is open Monday to Friday 8:30am to 12:15pm and 2:30 to 6pm, and Saturday (summer only) 8:30am to 12:15pm.

EN ROUTE TO BOLZANO: THE STRADA DI VINO

Some of Italy's finest wines are produced on the vines that cloak the hillsides between Trent and Bolzano. (These local wines include many pinot grigios and pinot noirs, and Vernatsch, the most common red of the region.) If you are traveling by car between the two cities, you can make the trip on the well-marked *Strada di Vino (Weinstrasse),* or Wine Road. Leave Trent on S12; 15km (9¼ miles) north, you will come to the main turnoff for the village of Lavis; take this turnoff, and from here, easy-to-follow yellow signs will lead you along a series of twisting roads past vineyards and around Lago di Caldaro to Bolzano. Many of the vineyards have tasting rooms open to the public and sometimes offer cheese, sandwiches, and other refreshment as well.

The **Vini Josef Hofstätter** cantina, on Piazza Municipio 5 in Termeno (✆ **0471-860-161**), welcomes drop-ins for free tastings, but for most vineyards you must book ahead; keep in mind that most are closed from around noon to 2pm. Check out **Georg Baron Widmann,** Via im Feld 1 in Cortaccia (✆ **0471-880-092**); **Alois Lageder** in Magrè (✆ **0471-809-500;** www.lageder.com); and **Castel Schwanburg** in Nalles (✆ **0471-678-622**). There's the small **Südtiroler Weinmuseum** (✆ **0471-963-168**) in the Caldaro village outside Termeno at Goldgasse 1, open Monday to Saturday 9:30am to noon and 2 to 6pm, Sunday 10am to noon. If you don't have your own wheels, the tourist offices in Trent and Bolzano can provide lists of local tour companies that lead wine tours.

2 BOLZANO/BOZEN

154km (95 miles) N of Verona, 118km (73 miles) S of Innsbruck, 57km (35 miles) NE of Trent

Without even crossing a border, by heading north from Trent into the Alto Adige region, you'll find yourself in a place that doesn't resemble Italy at all. During its long history, this pretty town at the confluence of the Talvera and Isarco rivers has been ruled by the bishops of Trent, the counts of Tirol, and the Habsburgs, to name but a few of its lords. Bolzano (Bozen in German) has been part of Italy only since the end of World War I. As you explore the narrow streets and broad *platzen (piazze)* and stroll through the parks that line the town's two rivers, you get the sense that, with its gabled, Tirolean-style houses and preference for Germanic dialect, the city is still more Teutonic than Italian.

Bolzano's foundation dates back to the Iron Age—and now there's even a full-fledged (and famous) Ice Man cooling his 5,000-year-old heels in the excellent local archaeology museum. But Bolzano didn't really pick up steam until the Middle Ages, when its situation at a river confluence just south of an Alpine pass made it an important small market town.

FESTIVALS & MARKETS Bolzano celebrates spring with **weekend concerts** throughout April and May in Piazza Walther, and adds a **flower show,** with more music, around the first of May. The city's most serious musical event is the **Concorso Internazionale Piantistico F. Busoni,** an international piano competition held the last 2 weeks of August. The **Festival del Teatro di Strada** draws wandering musicians, mimes, puppeteers, and other performers to the streets of the Old City in October. One of the more colorful events in the region is the **Bartolomeo Horse Fair,** which brings together the region's most beautiful equines on the Renon plateau, which can be reached by funicular (see "Cable Cars" on p. 235).

One of the most enjoyable walks in the Old City takes you through the stalls of the **fruit-and-vegetable market** in Piazza delle Erbe, which operates Monday through Saturday from 8am to 7pm. From November 28 to December 23, the city hosts a much-attended **Mercatino di Natale (Christkindlmarkt),** in which handmade ornaments, wooden toys, and other seasonal crafts, along with Christmas pastries and mulled wine, are sold from booths in a festively decorated Piazza Walther.

A **flea market** fills the Passeggiata del Talvera along the River Talvera (follow Via Museo from the center of town) the first Saturday of the month (except July–Aug), opening at 8am and closing at 5pm.

ESSENTIALS

GETTING THERE   By Train Bolzano is on the north-south rail line that links Verona with Innsbruck, Austria, via the Brenner Pass. There are some 17 trains daily from Verona (1½–1¾ hr.) and 25 trains a day from Trent (32–45 min.). Hourly train service links Bolzano with Merano (38 min.).

By Bus Bolzano is the hub of the excellent **SAD bus** network, serving even the most remote mountain villages (© **0471-450-111;** www.sad.it). There are hourly buses to and from Merano (1 hr.) and Bressanone (1 hr.). Two daily morning buses (currently departing at 9:15 and 11:10am) make the trip to Cortina, with a change in Dobbiaco (about 4 hr.). The extremely helpful staff at the bus station, the round building 1 block up from the train station and on the left, will help you make sense of the routing.

By Car Autostrada A22 connects Bolzano with Trent in a little over half an hour and with Verona (where you can connect with the A4 for Milan and Rome) in a little over an hour; and, farther south, Modena (where you can connect with the A1 for Florence and Rome); A22 runs north to Innsbruck. Avoid parking in the criminally expensive public garages; most hotels have arrangements for considerably less.

By Plane Bolzano's dinky **airport** (© **0471-254-070;** www.abd-airport.it), on the south side of the Isarco River, a few minutes' taxi ride from the center, is the Dolomite's official airport and has daily flights from Rome and Frankfurt, as well as service from Vienna.

VISITOR INFORMATION The **city tourist office,** near the Duomo at Piazza Walther 8 (© **0471-307-000;** fax 0471-980-128; www.bolzano-bozen.it), dispenses a wealth of information on Bolzano and the South Tirol. It's open Monday to Friday from 9am to 6:30pm and on Saturday from 9am to 12:30pm. The local events calendar *BoBo* can also be found online at **www.bobo.it.**

Bolzano by Bike . . . for a Buck!

The best way to get about town—certainly out to the castles and to Gries—is on one of the bikes offered by the municipality. There's a stand on the left side of Viale Stazione just before Piazza Walther, and another on Piazza Gries. Just leave 1€ for 6 hours, 2€ for the day, and have a passport or driver's license handy. Unfortunately, this initiative is guaranteed only from Easter through October. Those who would prefer a little mechanical advantage can rent an electric bike from **Sport Ler,** Via Portici 1 ((℃ **0471-977-719**).

A STROLL AROUND BOLZANO

With its two rivers, surrounding hills, expansive greens, and medieval center, Bolzano is an extremely appealing city that seems to effortlessly meld urban sophistication with an appreciation for nature. The compact medieval Old City is still the heart of town, and at its center is **Piazza Walther,** honoring a 12th-century wandering minstrel. The piazza captures the mood of its lighthearted historical associations with a fringe of cafe tables to one side and the brightly tiled roof and lacy spire of the **Duomo** on the other. The interior of this 12th- to 14th-century edifice is far more plain, enlivened somewhat by some much-faded frescoes and an intricately carved pulpit ((℃ **0471-978-676;** Mon–Fri 9:45am–noon and 2–5pm, Sat 9:45am–noon; Sun for services only).

A far more enticing church is the **Chiesa dei Domenicani** ((℃ **0471-973-133**), just a few steps west of the Duomo. Inside the 13th-century church are two sets of frescoes, the city's greatest artistic treasures. One from the 15th century, on the walls of the cloisters, depicts court life. The other, in the Capella di San Giovanni (under the arch behind the altar and to the right), is a 14th-century religious cycle attributed to the school of Giotto, including the *Triumph of Death.* In these rich frescoes, you can see the beginnings of the use of such elements as perspective and foreshortening, suggesting the influence of the early Renaissance. It's open Monday to Saturday 9:30am to 6pm, Sunday for services only.

There is one more church to see in Bolzano, but before you reach it, you will be distracted by the considerable worldly pleasures this city offers. If you walk north from Piazza Walther, you will soon come to the lively clamor of **Piazza dell'Erbe,** actually one long, wide street that winds past a statue of Neptune through the Old Town and is so called because it has hosted the city's **fruit-and-produce market** for centuries. The piazza is lined with shops selling bread, cheese, strudel, wine, and other comestibles, which spill into stalls along the pavement to create a cheerful, open-air supermarket. At the north end is Bolzano's atmospheric main shopping street, **Via dei Portici,** also closed to traffic and lined with 15th-century houses whose porticoes overhang the sidewalk to create a cozy effect that is definitely more northern European than Italian.

The **Chiesa dei Francescani** ((℃ **0471-977-293**) is across Via dei Portici on Via Francescani. Inside there's a sumptuously carved **altar** ★ from 1500, one of the Gothic masterpieces of the Trentino–Alto Adige. The 14th-century cloisters are charming—intimate, frescoed on one side, gracefully vaulted, and beautifully planted—and are open Monday to Saturday 10am to noon and 2:30 to 6pm, Sunday for services only.

Bolzano's most popular attraction by far is the thoroughly modernized **South Tyrol Museum of Archaeology** ★★★, Via Museo at Via Cassa di Risparmio (℅ **0471-320-100;** www.iceman.it), better known as Ötzi's House, since it was remodeled in 1998 to house the famed 5,300-year-old "Ice Man." This mummy made headlines in 1991 when a pair of German hikers discovered him sticking out of a melting glacier high in the Tirol mountains—though whether he was of Alpine origin or merely trying to cross the Alps is still being debated. His equipment and one of his last meals seem to have come from lower-altitude valleys, nearer Verona.

Forensic analysis brought the surprise revelation that, apparently, he was shot in the shoulder with an arrow shortly before he died. Further research, published in 2003 (and based on blood samples, microscopic fibers, and re-creations of wound placements—real *CSI* kinda stuff) revealed that the Ice Man was killed in a battle or skirmish of some sort—shot in the back and then carried off by a companion who must have removed the arrow for him.

Along with the mummy were preserved remnants of clothing (including shoes and a bearskin hat), a flint dagger, a copper ax, and a quiver with flint-tipped arrows he was in the process of making. The museum is open Tuesday to Sunday 10am to 6pm, daily in December, July, and August. Admission is 9€ adults, 7€ students under 28 and seniors over 65. The audio guides, which I highly recommend, are an extra 2.50€.

A walk across the **River Talvera** (follow Via Museo west across the Ponte Talvera) brings you into the newer "Italian" section of Bolzano, constructed in the 1920s when the Mussolini government encouraged workers from other parts of Italy to settle here in the newly won territory. Those who bid the call were either inspired or intimidated by the imposing Fascist-era structures put up along Corso Libert (including the Monumento della Vittoria, a triumphal arch that is frequently the target of attacks by German-speaking groups that want the region to revert to Austrian rule).

In a few blocks, though, the Corso brings you into the pleasant confines of **Gries** ★, once an outlying village and now a quaint, leafy neighborhood built around the Abbazia dei Benedettini di Gries, a Benedictine abbey (not usually open to the public) prettily surrounded by vineyards and gardens. Just beyond is the **Vecchia Parrochiale di Gries,** the village's parish church, whose treasures include a 12th-century crucifix and an elaborately carved 15th-century altar (℅ **0471-283-089;** Mon–Fri 10:30am–noon and 2:30–4pm; closed Nov–Mar).

If you wish to continue walking or biking, Gries contains one end of the **Passeggiata del Guncina,** a beautifully maintained 8km-long (5-mile) trail that leads through parklike forests planted with many botanical specimens to a belvedere and a waterfall before dumping you back into town. You wind up at the northerly end of the park stretched along the north bank of the Talvera River.

CASTLES Of the many castles that surround Bolzano, the closest to the center is the **Castel Mareccio,** just a short walk along the River Talvera (from the Piazza delle Erbe, follow the Via Museo west to the Ponte Talvera and, from there, the Lungo Talvera Bozen north for less than .5km/¼ mile). Though it is now used as a convention center and its five towers rise from a residential neighborhood of recent vintage, this 13th-century fortress is a stunning sight, all the more so because it is surrounded by a generous swath of vineyards that have been saved from urban encroachment and backed by forested hills. You can step inside for a glimpse at the stone-walled medieval interior and enjoy a beverage at the bar; the castle is open to the public Wednesday through Monday 9am to 6pm (hours vary when conferences are in session; ℅ **0471-976-615**).

A longer walk of about 2km (1¼ mile, or take the free bus from Piazza Walther, which goes back and forth only between the piazza and the castle) leads out of town north to the **Castel Roncolo** ★★ (𝄜 800-210-003 or 0471-329-808; www.roncolo.info), beautifully ensconced high above the town and beneath a massive, foreboding cliff face. The interior of this 13th-century castle is decorated with faded but fascinating frescoes from the 14th and 15th centuries that depict secular scenes from the story of *Tristan and Isolde* and other tales of romantic love and chivalry. These painted scenes are remarkably moving in their almost primitive craftsmanship that nonetheless reveals a certain worldliness. Admission is 8€ adults, 5.50€ students and seniors over 60; hour-long guided tours in English cost an extra 3€ per person (minimum six people). The castle is open Tuesday to Sunday 10am to 6pm (July–Sept to 8pm). To get here, follow the Via Castel Roncolo north from the Chiesa dei Francescani; you will pass one side of the Castel Mareccio, at which point signposts will lead you along Via Beatro Arrigo and Via San Antonio for a gradual uphill climb to Castel Roncolo.

CABLE CARS   Several **cable cars** will whisk you right from the center of Bolzano into the surrounding mountains. The most dramatic ride takes you from a terminal near the train station 900m (2,952 ft.) up to the **Altopiano del Renon** (www.renon.com), a pasture-covered plateau that provides dizzying views down to Bolzano and up to higher Dolomite peaks. The ride deposits you in SopraBolzano (aka Oberbozen), where you can sip a beer, enjoy the view, and then venture farther by footpath or an electric tram into a bizarre landscape of spindly rock spires—worn needle-thin by erosion, each seeming to balance a boulder on the top—that surrounds the village of Collabo. The cable car (𝄜 0471-978-479) makes the ascent in 15 minutes and operates daily from a terminus about 450m (1,476 ft.) east of the train station on Via Renon; it operates hourly from 7am to 8pm. Costs are 2.50€ from Bolzano to Soprabolzano and 2.50€ for the tram between SopraBozen and Collabo.

The **Funivia di San Genesio** takes you up a forested hillside to the pretty village of San Genesio Atesino, surrounded by woods and mountain peaks. Cable cars (𝄜 0471-978-436) leave hourly from 7am to 7pm (from 8am on Sun) from a terminus on Via Sarentino on the northern outskirts of Bolzano (take bus no. 12 or 14). The trip takes 15 minutes, and the round-trip fare is 3.20€. San Genesio's little **tourist office** (𝄜 0471-354-196; fax 0471-354-085; www.jenesien.net), at Schrann 7, is open Monday to Friday 9am to 1pm (July–Oct also 4–6pm). It can set you up with one of the horseback rising schools that offer rides across the high Alpine meadows for about 20€; call ahead.

WHERE TO STAY

Hotel Feichter   This charming little inn is one of the few hotels in the Old City itself and, for the location and atmosphere it provides, is one of the city's better lodging values. On the main floor there's a restaurant that resembles a *Weinstube* (tavern). The rooms may not be full of mountain ambience (and the bathrooms are cramped), but they contain serviceable, modern, comfortable furnishings. The extremely firm beds are equipped with that wonderful local luxury: thick down comforters. There's also a narrow courtyard set with picnic tables and shaded by a grape arbor.

Via Grappoli 15, 39100 Bolzano. (𝄜 **0471-978-768.** Fax 0471-974-803. www.hotelfeichter.it. 49 units. 85€ double; 105€ triple. Rates include breakfast. MC, V. Parking 5€ in garage (10 spots). Closed 3 weeks in Feb. **Amenities:** Tirolese restaurant; bar; concierge. *In room:* TV, hair dryer (on request).

Hotel Greif ★★★   The boutique hotel has a motto, "very personal," and it shines through—from the laptop PC with free Internet access in every room to an extraordinary attention to detail (the silver umbrellas ranked by the doors match the burnished steel and glass of the entryway). Each überstylish, modern room is unique, featuring an original work by a Tirolese artist (each key chain is a tiny catalog for that room's artist). Most accommodations are spacious, some with lofted bedrooms, others with Jacuzzi tubs and views over the main square. The furnishings are a mix of modern and late-19th-century antiques, including gorgeous inlaid wood dressers and desks. Room no. 211 is like a musician's studio apartment, with deep sloping ceilings, dormer windows onto Piazza Walther, and even a baby grand.

Piazza Walther, 39100 Bolzano. ☏ **0471-318-000.** Fax 0471-318-148. www.greif.it. 33 units. 180€ comfort double; 220€ superior double; 255€ deluxe double; 310€ junior suite; 360€ junior suite with sauna and grand piano. Buffet breakfast 20€ extra. AE, DC, MC, V. Parking 17€. **Amenities:** Restaurant; bar (at Parkhotel Laurin, see below); babysitting; children's center at Laurin; concierge; golf (nearby); pool at Laurin; room service; smoke-free rooms. *In room:* A/C, TV, free movies, hair dryer, laptop w/Internet connection, minibar.

Hotel Regina A. (Kids)

For pleasant and affordable lodgings in Bolzano, you need look no further than this modern hotel across the street from the train station—a decent location, as you're still only 3 blocks from the main square, but the rate disparity below reflects the noisiness of the busy main street out front. *Families take note:* The bright rooms are unusually large, and there are several quads and one mansard quintuplet on hand. Although accommodations are quite plain, they're nicely decorated with streamlined Scandinavian furnishings, and all offer a level of comfort and have amenities you would expect in a much more expensive hotel—including large bathrooms nicely equipped with stall showers.

Via Renon 1, 39100 Bolzano. ☏ **0471-972-195** or 0471-974-099. Fax 0471-978-944. www.hotelreginabz it. 40 units. 85€–130€ double; 110€–155€ triple; 130€–175€ quad. Rates include breakfast. MC, V. Free on-street parking. **Amenities:** Bar; concierge; smoke-free rooms. *In room:* A/C, TV, hair dryer, Internet.

Parkhotel Laurin ★

This early-20th-century Liberty-style edifice takes up an entire city block just a few hundred meters from both the train station and Piazza Walther. Though it's full of modern comforts, the quirky old structure gives it character and style (and plenty of windows). The modern furnishings reinterpret antique styles, such as angular postmodern settees or exaggeratedly swooping Empire-style chairs lacquered black and red. Rooms are spacious. "Comfort" rooms are roughly the same as "superior," but they're smaller and all face the street. About half the "superior" rooms overlook the garden, while the others face downtown. Suites are like mini-apartments with a hall off of which open the bedroom, a tiny sitting room (often with a balcony), and the bathroom (in brown marble with double sinks and separate tub and shower stalls); one even has its own sauna. The hotel's real selling point is its large, landscaped garden of flower-lined and tree-shaded gravel paths.

Via Laurin 4, 39100 Bolzano. ☏ **0471-311-000.** Fax 0471-311-148. www.laurin.it. 96 units. 138€–170€ comfort double; 160€–210€ superior double; 280€ junior suite. Children under 13 stay free in parent's room. Breakfast 15€. AE, DC, MC, V. Parking 13€. **Amenities:** Italian restaurant; period bar; babysitting; children's center and small playground; outdoor heated pool; room service for a 5€ service fee; smoke-free rooms. *In room:* A/C, TV, hair dryer, Internet, minibar.

Stadt Hotel Citta ★★

This modernized old hotel, with an attractive arcaded facade typical of this city's distinctive architecture, commands a sunny corner of Bolzano's main piazza. Its location and the sleek new feel of the hotel are good reason to gravitate here, especially if you are partial to waterbeds, which some superior doubles have. The large and bright guest rooms have been done in a contemporary style; top-floor rooms are cozier. The best rooms overlook the square and the Duomo; Mussolini stayed in one of them (no. 303), a suite with a corner balcony. The ground-floor bar and cafe, which opens to the square, is a popular gathering spot.

Piazza Walther 21, 39100 Bolzano. (€) **0471-975-221.** Fax 0471-976-688. www.hotelcitta.info. 102 units. 136€–180€ double; 160€–220€ waterbed double; 220€–350€ family apt for up to 5. Rates include breakfast. AE, DC, MC, V. Parking 13€ in garage. **Amenities:** Mediterranean/Tirolese restaurant; bar under the arcades of Piazza Walther; babysitting; concierge; room service; large sauna/baths complex in basement w/Turkish baths and huge whirlpool tub; smoke-free rooms. In room: A/C, TV, hair dryer, Wi-Fi.

MOUNTAIN HOTELS EN ROUTE TO BRESSANONE

High on the eastern wall of the Adige valley, halfway up the Siusi Alps above the road from Bolzano to Bressanone, lies the **Schlern plateau** (Sciliar in Italian). Its summertime meadows and forest trails for hiking and mountain biking, modestly decent winter skiing, half-ruined castles, colorful folk festivals, and cute Tirolean villages draw a small clutch of devoted vacationers. It's also got some great hotel deals in a perfect Tirol setting that gets you away from it all, but is still just a half-hour from the large towns down in the valley.

Cavallino d'Oro/Goldenes Rössl ★★ This 15th-century inn right on the main square of its little village does an excellent job of marrying traditional and cozy Tirolean style with modern comforts—the parquet-floored lounge has a picture window overlooking the Alps in the backyard right next to a widescreen TV with 300 channels. The nicest rooms have four-poster beds with carved wood canopies, and all have new widescreen TVs. Room no. 24 is simply huge, featuring a four-poster bed and a small terrace. All rooms on the back have balconies with mountain vistas, while rooms on the front overlook the cobblestone main square and fountain. Off the excellent restaurant, with its mountain views, is a wood-paneled *Stuben* (beer nook) that's 18th century right down to the filament bulbs. Guests receive a warm, friendly reception from the owners, the Urthalers, who love Frommer's (they made a 32-state U.S. odyssey using Frommer's guides).

Piazza Kraus, 39040 Castelrotto/Kastelruth (BZ). (€) **0471-706-337.** Fax 0471-707-172. www.cavallino.it. 20 units. 96€–110€ double. Add about 10€ per person for half-board, 20€ over the Christmas/New Year's period. AE, DC, MC, V. Parking free. Closed Nov. **Amenities:** Fine restaurant; old-fashioned tavern w/food; babysitting; bikes; children's center nearby; concierge; room service; sauna and tanning bed; smoke-free rooms. In room: TV, hair dryer.

Romantik Hotel Turm ★★ At the very top of this medieval hamlet and modest mountain resort lies the Turm, a series of buildings dating in part to the 13th century that have served time as a tribunal, a prison, and an *osteria.* During blizzards, the whole village would come to the *osteria* and shut themselves in together to feast, play cards, and wait out the storm. This tradition gave rise to its role as an inn, which stands today as a collection of three towers and a *"wagenhaus,"* sort of like an upscale garage, the most prized property today. Stefan Pramstrahler has gradually morphed this communal tradition into the modern concept of a "wellness" retreat to accompany the luxurious suites. Choose from hay baths (apparently a long-standing tradition), a massage on a heated stone bed, or a candlelight bath for two in the "emperor's" tub.

39050 Fié allo Sciliar/Völs am Schlern (BZ). (€) **0471-725-014.** Fax 0471-725-474. www.hotelturm.it. 35 units. 170€–280€ double without balcony; 226€–310€ double with balcony; 250€–335€ suite in the main tower; 270€-360€ deluxe suite. Half-board add 30€ per person. MC, V. Free parking. **Amenities:** Tirolean restaurant; Stube bar; babysitting (book ahead); 3 free bikes; concierge; Jacuzzi; 2 pools (indoor and outdoor heated); room service; sauna; tennis courts (in town); extensive "wellness" center. In room: TV, hair dryer, minibar.

Some of the least expensive (and tasty) meals in town are supplied by the vendors who dispense a wide assortment of *Würstel* from carts in the Kornplatz and Piazza dell'Erbe.

Batzenhaüsl TYROLEAN   The two floors of dining rooms here are charming and cozy, with dark carved Tirolean benches, hardwood floors, and heavily beamed ceilings; downstairs is primarily a *Weinstube,* a tavernlike room where you are welcome to linger over a beer and a plate of cheese. On both floors you can also order from a menu that, like those in many other restaurants in town, is typically Tirolean, which means mostly Austrian with some Italian touches. While an excellent minestrone is sometimes available, this is also the place to sample *Leberknödelsuppe,* a thick broth with a liver dumpling floating in it. Pork loin, roast beef with potatoes, and other heavy northern fare dominate the entree choices.

Via Andreas Hofer/Andreas Hoferstrasse 30. ⓒ **0471-050-950.** Reservations not accepted. Primi 4.50€–6.50€; secondi 10€–13€. No credit cards. Wed–Mon 6:30pm–2am (Sun to 1am).

Cavallino Bianco TYROLEAN   This atmospheric *Stube* (beer hall) is darkly paneled and decorated with carved wooden furniture to create a cozy, typically Tirolean atmosphere. The restaurant opens early to operate as a cafe, dispensing coffee and pastry for breakfast, and remains open well into the night, sending out hearty lunches and dinners of local fare with only a slight Italian influence. Fried Camembert, herrings, and assorted salami are among the dozens of appetizers, while a pasta dish (and there are many to choose from) is likely to be followed by a main course of Wiener schnitzel or *Würstel.*

Via dei Bottai/Bindergasse 6. ⓒ **0471-973-267.** Reservations not accepted. Primi 3.50€–8€; secondi 4€–15€. No credit cards. Mon–Fri 8am–1am; Sat 8am–3pm.

Ristorante Hostaria Argentieri SEAFOOD   You'll feel like you've come back to Italy when you step into this attractive cream-colored, tile-floored room. There are several risottos and a grilled steak on the menu, but most of the offerings are fishy—unusual and much in demand up here in the Dolomiti. You can start with tasty *tagliolini al salmone* or *bigoli alla veneta* (homemade pasta with anchovies and capers), followed by grilled *branzino, rombo,* or *trancio di spada* (swordfish steak). In good weather, you can dine on a tiny terrace in front of the restaurant, facing an attractive cobblestone street that is indeed Tirolean in character.

Via Argentieri 14. ⓒ **0471-981-718.** Reservations highly recommended. Primi and secondi 12€–20€. DC, MC, V. Mon–Sat noon–2:30pm and 7–10:30pm.

Scheune TYROLEAN/PIZZA   This welcoming and cozy *Bierhalle* (beer hall) has remarkable rough-hewn beams; the log-cabin looks of the place are genuine—its name is Tirolese dialect for "hayloft," and the interior was lifted, intact, from an abandoned hayloft high up in the mountains. A cherry tree is planted in the middle of the bar, where Warsteiner beer flows from the taps. The tables in back wrap around a big, square, rustic room-heating stove. Along with the 20-odd pasta dishes and typical Tirolean fare, such as goulash and Wiener schnitzel, they have added decent pizzas.

Weintraubengasse 9. ⓒ **0471-978-838.** Reservations not accepted. Primi 5.50€–7€; secondi 6.50€–15€; DC, MC, V. Daily 11am–11pm. Closed last 2 weeks of June.

Vogele TYROLEAN   If you ask someone in Bolzano where to eat, there's a very good chance you will be sent to this attractive, always busy *Weinstube* and restaurant in the center of the Old City just off Piazza Erbe. (Its original name translated to "The Eagle," but the locals always referred to it as the *"vogele,"* or the "little bird.") Like many such places in Bolzano, it is open continuously all day and night, and some of the patrons seem to stop by for every meal and for coffee and a beer in between. One of the two long cross-vaulted rooms is set up as a cafe, and the other as a dining room (or you can eat under the arcade out front). Both have traditional, woody Tirolean furnishings, and wherever you sit you can order from the long appetizer menu: maybe a platter of *speck* (ham) or *affumicato della casa* (smoked meats). First and second courses include many traditional favorites; a wonderful *zuppa di vino* (a soup with a white wine and cream base) or different kinds of *canederli* (dumplings that here are laced with liver, bacon, or ham) are the ways to begin, followed by a *stinco di maiale* (roast pork shank) or other roast meat dish.

Via Goethe 3. (C) **0471-973-938.** Primi 4€–8€; secondi 8.50€–17€. MC, V. Mon–Fri 9am–midnight; Sat 9am–3pm.

BARS & CAFES

Nightlife in Bolzano is certainly not its greatest draw, but what life there is mostly centers around the long curve of Piazza delle Erbe. There you'll find a few other wine bars, pubs, *Stube,* and tiny live-music venues in addition to the following establishments.

The chic **Café Exil,** at Piazza del Grano/Kornplatz 2 ((C) **0471-971-814**), is filled with a young crowd night and day for whom it probably provides a welcome alternative to the many *Weinstubes* around town. Exil has the ambience of a coffeehouse (excellent coffee, pastries, and sandwiches are served) and a bar as well, with many kinds of beers from Italy and north of the Alps on tap. On weekend evenings, the elegant **Laurin Bar,** in the Parkhotel Laurin ((C) **0471-311-000;** see above), turns its Art Nouveau lobby—a sumptuous room overlooking the hotel's private park—into a jazz club. An enthusiastic crowd shows up, making this one of the most popular places in town.

In Bolzano, you won't find a more distinctive locale in which to bend your elbow than **Fishbanke,** at Via Dr. Streiter 26A ((C) **0471-971-714**); in fact, a stop at this outdoor wine bar run by a gregarious artist is mandatory, and a unique experience in an otherwise homogenous field of beer halls and taverns. Wine, beer, and a few snacks (cheese and bruschetta) are served on the well-worn stone slabs of Bolzano's centuries-old former fish market, an unusual experience that attracts a friendly crowd of regulars who are always pleased to welcome strangers into their midst.

3 MERANO/MERAN

86km (53 miles) N of Trent, 28km (17 miles) NW of Bolzano

This well-heeled resort, tucked into a valley half an hour west of Bolzano, sports Europe's northernmost palm trees—the product of a mild microclimate ensuring that summers are never too hot or humid and that winter temperatures remain above freezing even when the surrounding slopes fill with snow.

Austrian nobility and, in their wake, bourgeois vacationers from all over the Continent have been descending on Merano since the 19th century for their famous grape cure (see "Taking the Cure," below). But the town flourished long before that. In fact, the counts of Venosta were lords of what would become Austria through much of the 13th and 14th centuries; the name "Tirol" came from the Castel Tirolo, just above Merano, from which they ruled. The capital of the territories that passed from the house of Venosta to the Habsburgs was moved from Merano to Innsbruck until 1420.

With its handsome shop-lined streets, riverside promenades, and easy access to mountainous wilderness, Merano is a nice place to visit for a day or two of relaxation or hiking.

FESTIVALS & MARKETS   The Piazza del Duomo is the scene of Merano's civic life. A morning **fruit-and-produce market** is held here from 8am to 1pm Monday to Saturday. From late November through Christmas, the piazza fills with stalls selling carved ornaments and other seasonal paraphernalia during the town's **Christkindlmarkt.** From late August through September, the town hosts **Settimane Musicali Meranesi** in several concert halls and churches around town (© **0473-221-447;** www.meranofestival.com). On the second Sunday of October, enthusiasts of the grape take over the square for a **wine festival,** honoring the wines and grape juice yielded by local vineyards.

ESSENTIALS

GETTING THERE   **By Train**   Hourly train service links Merano with Bolzano (40 min.).

By Bus   SAD buses (© **0471-450-111** in Italy; www.sad.it) arrive and depart from the train station and stop in the center of town, connecting Merano with Bolzano hourly (1 hr.) and with villages throughout the region.

By Car   Route S38, a pretty road that cuts through vineyards and mountain meadows, links Merano and Bolzano in less than half an hour.

VISITOR INFORMATION   The **tourist office,** Corso Libertà/Freiheistrasse 45 (© **0473-272-000;** fax 0473-235-524; www.meran.eu), is open March through September, Monday to Friday 9am to 6:30pm, Saturday 9:30am to 6pm, and Sunday 10am to 12:30pm; October through February, Monday to Friday 9am to 12:30pm and 2:30 to 6:30pm, Saturday 9:30am to 12:30pm.

A good source of information on hiking the region is the local office of the **Club Alpino Italiano,** at Via K. Wolf 15 (© **0473-448-944;** www.cai.it). It's open Monday to Friday from 9am to 1pm, plus Thursday from 7 to 8:30pm.

WHAT TO SEE & DO

The charming Old Town, a vestige of Merano's noble past, clusters around the **Piazza del Duomo,** where the namesake 14th-century cathedral has a crenelated facade and heavy buttresses that make it look almost like a castle. Nearby, just to the west on Via Galilei, is a dollhouse-size castle—**Castello Principesco** or **Landesfürstliche Burg,** built by the counts of Tirol in 1470 and still filled with the austere furnishings they installed, along with a collection of armor and musical instruments. The castle (© **0473-250-329**) is open Tuesday to Saturday 10am to 5pm, Sunday 10am to 1pm (closed Jan–Feb). Admission is 2€ adults, 1.50€ students and those over 60.

Merano's picturesque main shopping street, **Via Portici** (leading west from Piazza del Duomo), is lined with Tirolean-style houses whose porticoes extend over the sidewalk. The preferred places to stroll in Merano, though, are along any number of scenic

Free Wheels

Late May through September, the town provides free bikes at the main parking lot (near the Terme, across the river from the center) and at the train station. Just leave a 5€ deposit and a driver's license, and return the bike by 7pm.

Taking the Cure

With its mild climate and mineral-rich springs bubbling up from beneath the town, Merano has long enjoyed a reputation as a spa town. To this day, one of Merano's most popular pastimes is taking the cure. You can take a complete treatment (mud bath, mineral wrap, hydrotherapy) at the **Terme di Merano** (© **0473-237-724;** www.termemerano.com), in the center of town, across the river at Via Piave 9, or just take a dip in the pool of mineral-rich water. There is a wide range of prices for individual treatments such as apple aroma therapy and hay baths, but a 2-hour pass for the pool alone costs 11€, 12€ for 3 hours, and 16€ for the day. Add about 5€ for the sauna (so you're not shocked: no bathing suits allowed in the sauna). A poor man's version of an elaborate spa regimen—but one you can follow only when grapes from the vineyards surrounding the town ripen in late September and early October—is Merano's famous *cura delle uva* **(grape cure).** One drastic form of the grape cure, which is allegedly beneficial for digestive disorders, requires eating 2 pounds of grapes a day. A more palatable approach calls for drinking several glasses a day of the delicious fresh *spremuta di uva fresca/traubensaft* **(grape juice)** that's available in cafes in the early fall.

promenades. Two follow the banks of the River Passer: the **Passeggiata d'Inverno** (Winter Walk, which faces south) and **Passeggiata d'Estate** (Summer Walk, which faces north).

The top of the Passeggiata is just below **Castel Tirolo** ★ (© **0473-220-221**), which you can also reach by car or by walking along Via Monte San Zeno for 5km (3 miles) from Merano. Here, amid stony splendor, you can see the throne room from which the counts of Tirol ruled much of present-day Austria and northern Italy, and a beautifully frescoed Romanesque chapel with a 1330 carved wood crucifix (and enjoy a magnificent view that hasn't changed much since then). The castle is open Easter through November, Tuesday to Sunday 10am to 5pm. Admission is 6€ adults, 3€ students under 28, and 12€ for a family ticket (two adults with kids under 14); there's no admission fee for children under 6. Occasional guided tours are available for a 2€ supplement. To get here without too much hoofing, you can take a half-hourly bus from Merano's train station or center to the village of Tirol, and then finish the beautiful 15-minute walk along a trail amid grapevines and apple groves.

THE NATIONAL PARKS

Merano is the gateway to two national parks. The tourist office in town provides information on them, as does the Club Alpino Italiano (see "Visitor Information," above); both parks also have visitor centers within their boundaries.

PARCO NAZIONALE DELLA STELVIO In this vast 520,000-hectare (1.3-million-acre) wilderness east of Merano, elk and chamois roam the mountainsides, and craggy, snowcapped peaks pierce the sky. A network of trails crisscross almost virgin wilderness, and some of Europe's largest glaciers provide year-round skiing. The official **park office** (© **0342-903-030**), in the center of the park, is open March to November daily 9am to 1pm and 4 to 6pm; in winter, call © **0342-903-300.** The office dispenses maps and lists of hiking trails and *rifugi* (huts where hikers can overnight) within the park; several buses a day travel from Merano to Silandro, at the park entrance, about 30km (19 miles) east via route S38.

PARCO NAZIONALE DI TESSA This Alpine wonderland surrounds Merano with a pleasant terrain of meadows and gentle, forest-clad slopes. A relatively easy path, the southern route of the Meraner Hohenweg allows even the most inexperienced hikers to cross the park effortlessly (in 2 days if you wish to follow the entire route) and is conveniently interspersed with restaurants and farmhouses offering rooms. The northern route is much more isolated, difficult, and scenic, with snack bar–equipped *rifugi* conveniently placed every few hours or so along the route. The **park office** in Naturno, about 15km (9¼ miles) west on Route S44 (Via dei Campi 3; ℂ **0473-668-201**), provides a wealth of information on hiking trails, meals, and accommodations. Hourly buses run between Merano and Naturno in about half an hour.

WHERE TO STAY

April, August through October, and the Christmas holidays constitute high season in Merano, when rates are most expensive and rooms are scarce. The two hotels in the center of town are easy enough to find; for the Castel Rundegg and Hotel Castello Schloss Labers, follow the yellow arrows on *alberghi* road signs (Merano has a complicated color-coded, geographical breakdown for all its hotels; just trust me and follow the yellow arrows) until a small brown-on-white sign for the hotels tells you otherwise.

Castel Rundegg ★ Unlike most Merano castle hotels, the Rundegg is barely outside town, offering the convenience of downtown with the atmosphere of a restored 1152 castle. It bills itself as a "Hotel & Beauty Farm," and many guests come to avail themselves of the spa and its programs, which make good use of the large exercise room, sauna, Turkish steam baths, various body treatments, Jacuzzi, tanning beds, and beauty center. The cross-vaulted reception halls and restaurant stuffed with painted wood statues set the tone of the hotel. Even the standard rooms are large and perfectly nice, with rich tapestries upholstering the 18th-century-style chairs and bed frames, small lofted sitting areas or nooks, and tiled bathrooms with double sinks. Some "deluxe" rooms, such as no. 20, have balconies over the courtyard with views of the mountains; a few even have small private gardens. A *molto particolari* (very unique) room is no. 15, with tented windows on three sides and views over the valley and the hotel's own large park, where goldfish ponds and small lawns set with sunning chairs highlight the garden paths lined with trees, plants, and flowers. This place would get a second star if the rates weren't so darn high.

Via Scena 2 (at the end of Via Cavour), 39012 Merano. ℂ **0473-234-100.** Fax 0473-237-200. www.rundegg. com. 30 units. 330€–380€ double; 390€–440€ suite. Rates include buffet breakfast. Half-board add about 30€. Discounts, but with half-pension included, for stays of 3 days or more. Aug 4–25 and Dec 22–Jan 6 minimum stay 7 nights; Easter minimum stay 5 nights. AE, DC, MC, V. Parking free in lot or 6€ in garage. Bus: 1, 3, or 5. **Amenities:** Mediterranean restaurant; bar; bikes; 9-hole golf course 4km (2½ miles) away; large health club and spa; indoor pool; room service; nearby tennis courts. *In room:* TV/VCR (in some), hair dryer, minibar.

Garni Domus Mea Simple little bed-and-breakfasts are just about the only alternative to Merano's high-priced lodging, and this pleasant *pensione* in a modern multiuse building is one of the nicer of them. It is well located, on a major street about a 10-minute walk on the other side of Ponte Teatro from the center of town, and the prices never seem to go up. The friendly proprietor keeps the premises immaculate (cleanliness is her watchword) and welcoming, with cut flowers and freshly waxed floors. The rooms are basically but nicely furnished with wood dressers and armoires, and some have balconies overlooking the peaks. A small living room sports a TV. Places like this tend to fill up quickly, so be sure to reserve in advance.

Via Piave 8, 39012 Merano. ⓒ **0473-236-777.** www.domusmea.com. 13 units, all with bathroom. 75€–86€ double. Rates include breakfast. MC, V. Parking free in courtyard or 2.50€ in garage. **Amenities:** Room service. *In room:* TV, hair dryer, high-speed Internet connection.

Hotel Castello Schloss Labers ★★

The Stapf-Neubert family turned its pitch-roofed castle (begun in the 11th c.) into a remarkable hotel in 1885. The dark, airy, hunting lodge–style salons, library, and billiards and dining rooms of the former residence have been seamlessly converted to guest use. Upper floors house distinctive and gracious accommodations, many with small terraces, no two of which are alike—in some, cozy conversation nooks are tucked into towers; others are luxurious garretlike arrangements under the eaves, and some are simply commodious, high-ceilinged, and elegantly appointed. The grounds wander down toward the surrounding grapevine-covered hillside, with a pleasant rose garden terrace overlooking the valley below and the peaks that hem it in. It's a good 10-minute drive high above downtown, so you'll need a car.

Via Labers 25 (in Maia Alta, 3km/1³⁄₄ miles east of town), 39012 Merano. ⓒ **0473-234-484.** Fax 0473-234-146. www.castellolabers.it or www.schlosslabers.it. 36 units, 25 with private bathroom. 200€ small double; 230€ regular double; 270€ double with terrace; 340€ suite. Rates include breakfast. Stays of 3 nights or more include half-pension (meals available a la carte if your stay is fewer than 3 nights). MC, V. Free parking. Closed Nov 9–Apr 1. Bus: 1a. **Amenities:** Tirolean/Italian restaurant; bar; babysitting; billiards room; outdoor heated pool; room service; sauna; smoke-free rooms; tennis court. *In room:* TV, hair dryer, Internet.

Hotel Europa Splendid ★

Conveniently located in the center of town a block off the Passer River, the Europa is an old-fashioned hotel that caters to guests who return year after year. The decor is charmingly faded, with an elegant, Regency-style salon and Tirolean-style bar downstairs. The large, bright guest rooms upstairs haven't been redecorated since the 1960s, but they're very comfortable, with handsome, sturdy furnishings and old but well-maintained bathrooms. A few accommodations are even Art Deco. Many of the rooms have small balconies, and a large, sunny hotel terrace is on the first floor. The rates reflect both season and room type (cheaper category "B" rooms suffer from less space, a poorer view, or more noise). Corner rooms (nos. 208, 308, and 408) are choice, with windows on two sides and small balconies.

Corso Liberta 178, 39012 Merano. ⓒ **0473-232-376.** Fax 0473-230-221. www.europa-splendid.com. 52 units. 98€–130€ standard double; 112€–143€ comfort double; 124€–155€ deluxe double. Rates include buffet breakfast. AE, DC, MC, V. Parking 9.50€. **Amenities:** Tirolese/Italian restaurant; bar; concierge; room service; smoke-free rooms. *In room:* TV, hair dryer, minibar.

WHERE TO DINE

Yes, with all the grapes around, this region produces excellent, crisp wines. But be sure to set aside at least one *"Prost!"* (German for "cheers!") for a frosty glass of **Forst,** a rich and slightly bitter golden beer brewed here in Merano.

Caffè Darling CAFE The so-called "Winter Walk" along the banks of the Passer River is lined with cafes, and this one is especially pleasant. There's an awning out front, but the tables stretch much farther along the cobblestones to where they're practically hanging over the river. The interior room has a casual ambience that's not too common

Sampling the Local Grape in Wine Bars

Merano doesn't leave all its famous grapes unfermented for the cure, and you can sample local wine at *Weinstuben* (*enoteche* in Italian), or wine bars. **Rothaler Weinstube,** Via Portici 41 (no phone), is a cozy Tirolean tavern, on Merano's arcaded main street, with a simple bar upfront and a teensy, dimly lit back room half-paneled and heavily frescoed with images of grapes and vineyards. Cheese and meat platters run about 3.50€ to 6€; it's closed Sunday and Saturday afternoon.

For less historical atmosphere but a larger choice, head to **Enoteca Claudia,** Piazza del Duomo 13 (② **0473-230-693**), where over three dozen wines are available by the glass for 1.75€ to 5€. There's a smattering of round tables outside in the shadow of the Duomo's bell tower and apse, plus more seating lined against the shelves upon shelves of wine inside. The various mixed platters of meats, cheeses with olives and artichokes, homemade sausages with vinegar-pickled veggies, and a sandwich or two (such as *speck,* cheese, tomatoes, and peppers), cost from 4€ to 9€.

in this staid, refined resort area. You'll probably feel comfortable passing some time reading a book here while sipping a beer or a glass of the house grape juice. Pastries and light sandwiches are also available.

Passeggiata d'Inverno 5–9. ② **0473-237-221.** Pastries from 1€; sandwiches from 2€. MC, V. Thurs–Tues 7:30am–1am.

Kavalier ITALIAN/TIROLEAN   Just a few steps off the river (you can hear it from the terrace) near Piazza Teatro, this informal restaurant, with a pleasant arbor-shaded terrace to one side, is a handy stop and can accommodate any level of hunger. A full menu of mostly Tirolean fare is served, featuring heaping platters of *speck;* a hearty beef goulash; the odd *Kavalierplatte* (Wiener schnitzel with pineapple, banana, rice, and mushrooms); and an amazingly filling pasta dish, *gnocchetti alla spinachi con prosciutto e panna* (little spinach gnocchi filled with ham in a cream sauce). You can also dine lightly on salads and omelets, or just stop by for a pizza.

Via Carducci 29. ② **0473-236-561.** Primi 7€–8€; secondi 10€–20€; pizza 5€–10€. MC, V. Thurs–Tues 11am–2:30pm and 5:30–9:30pm.

4 BRESSANONE/BRIXEN

40km (25 miles) N of Bolzano, 68km (42 miles) E of Merano

Tucked neatly in the Val d'Isarco between the Eisack and Rienz rivers, and surrounded by orchards and vineyards that climb the lower flanks of the surrounding peaks, Bressanone is a gem of a Tirolean town with a hefty past that today's quaint, small-town atmosphere belies. From 1027 to 1803, it was the center of a large ecclesiastical principality, and its bishop-princes ruled over much of the South Tirol. Their impressive monuments preside over the town's heavily gabled, pastel-colored houses and narrow cobblestone streets.

FESTIVALS & MARKETS   With its cozy, twisting medieval lanes and snug Tirolean-style houses, Bressanone is especially well suited to Christmas celebrations. The main holiday event is a **Christkindlmarkt (Christmas market)** from late November to Christmas Eve; stalls on and around Piazza Duomo sell hand-carved ornaments, crafts, holiday pastries, and other seasonal merchandise. A **fruit-and-vegetable market** enlivens Piazza Parrocchia near the Duomo Monday through Saturday from 8am to noon and 3 to about 6pm.

ESSENTIALS

GETTING THERE   By Train   Bressanone lies on the same north-south rail line as Bolzano and Verona, making connections between those cities extremely easy, with more than 18 trains a day from Bolzano (25–35 min.). From Trent, trains run almost hourly (1–1¼ hr.).

By Bus   STI buses (© **0472-801-075** or 800-846-047; www.sii.bz.it) leave from the front of the train station and connect Bressanone and Bolzano (1 hr.) and outlying villages, including several daily (half-hourly in ski season) to Sant'Andrea, a good base for hiking and skiing (see below; 20 min.). Service is augmented by a ski bus that is free for pass holders. There are also two daily buses to Cortina, with a change at Dobbiaco (about 2¾ hr.).

By Car   Bressanone is about a half-hour drive north of Bolzano on A22. It's easy to get around Bressanone by foot—the town is compact, and many of its streets are closed to cars. If you arrive by car, you will probably use the large parking lot south of the city on Via Dante (you will pass it as you drive into the city from the autostrada); the center is 5 minutes away up the Via Roma. From the train station, follow Viale Stazione for about 10 minutes to the center.

VISITOR INFORMATION   The **tourist office,** at the *centro storico* end of Via Stazione leading from the train station at no. 9 (© **0472-836-401;** fax 0472-836-067; www. brixen.org), is open Monday to Friday 8:30am to 12:30pm and 2:30 to 6pm, Saturday 9am to 12:30pm. The provincial website, **www.provinz.bz.it**, has a section with tourism links.

WHAT TO SEE & DO

The center of town is the **Piazza Duomo,** a long, rectangular tree-shaded square with cafes on one side and the white facade of the Duomo on the other. A baroque renovation to the tall exterior, flanked by two bell towers, has masked much of the cathedral's original 13th-century architecture, which you'll see more of in the interior and in the crypt. The heavily frescoed cloisters (entered through a door to the right of the main one) are especially charming, even though the view of Judgment Day they portray is gloomy. The cathedral is open daily 6am to noon and 3 to 6pm; there are guided tours (in Italian and German) Monday through Saturday at 10:30am and 3pm.

Just south of the Piazza del Duomo, on the adjoining Piazza Vescovile, stands the **palace of the prince-bishops,** whose power over the region—and the fragility of that power—is made clear by the surrounding moat and fortifying walls. The massive 14th-century palace now houses the **Museo Diocesano,** where more than 70 rooms display wooden statuary, somewhat unremarkable Renaissance paintings by local artists, and what is considered to be the museum's treasure and the objects most likely to capture your attention—an extensive and enchanting collection of antique Nativity scenes, filling

Hitting the Slopes

Bressanone's major playground is Monte Plose, and the gateway to ski slopes and hiking trails alike is the outlying village of **Sant'Andrea** (see "By Bus," above). Skiing here is not as glamorous as it is in better-known resorts like Cortina, but it is excellent and much less expensive. A ski pass is 30€ to 40€ a day and can be purchased at one of the outlets near the **Sant'Andrea funicular** (*©* **0472-200-433**), which costs 10€ round-trip for adults and 8€ for children ages 8 to 14. The funicular runs from July through September weekdays 9am to noon and 1 to 6pm, Saturday and Sunday 9am to 6pm; and December through May daily 9am to 4:30pm. (Winter schedules vary considerably with snow conditions; a summer ascent will take you to a network of Alpine trails near the stop at Valcroce.) The tourist board in Brixen provides maps and information on skiing, mountain refuges, and other details you need to know to enjoy this mountain wilderness.

eight rooms and one of the largest such assemblages anywhere. The museum (*©* **0472-830-505;** www.dioezesanmuseum.bz.it) is open March 15 to October 31, Tuesday through Sunday 10am to 5pm; the Nativity-scene galleries are open only from December 1 to January 31, Tuesday through Sunday from 2 to 5pm (closed Dec 24–25); admission, including the Nativity scenes, is 7€. Note that frequent exhibits often double the admission price.

WHERE TO STAY

Goldene Krone Vital Stadthotel   Everything about this amiable hotel at the edge of the old city suggests solid comfort, from the homey, wood-paneled lounge to the *Weinstube*-style bar to the breakfast room and restaurant, where booth tables are lit by pretty shaded lamps. There are two categories of guest rooms, hence the range of prices. Those in the lower range are pleasant enough, with streamlined modern furnishings, and many have terraces. The more expensive rooms are really quite special, though, and well worth the extra money. They're actually suites, with separate sitting and sleeping areas, equipped, respectively, with roomy couches and armchairs and king-size beds. The bathrooms are grand, with double sinks and large tubs equipped with Jacuzzi jets. A comprehensive remodeling in 2003 preserved the hotel's style and added a sauna.

Via Fienili 4, 39042 Bressanone. *©* **0472-835-154.** Fax 0472-835-014. www.goldenekrone.com. 35 units. 144€–198€ double. Rates include breakfast. Half-board 25€ more per person. MC, V. Free parking. Closed Jan 6–Feb 6. **Amenities:** Italian/Tyrolese restaurant; bar; babysitting; free bikes; children's program; concierge; gym; room service. *In room:* TV, hair dryer, Internet, minibar.

Hotel Angerer   Like many of the other well-heeled resorts in this part of the world, downtown Brixen offers few inexpensive beds. So it's well worth a taxi ride across the river, in the direction of the skiing, to find better value. That's where the Angerer resides, a typical chalet with all the right amenities for a reasonable price, and a great location for those who are looking for a mixture of city and slopes. The rooms offer an Alpine feel—pinewood surroundings, firm beds, and cool mountain air—and spacious bathrooms.

The sauna and heated pool are good therapy for ski-worn muscles, and the selection of
beers at the hotel's tavern doesn't hurt, either.

Via Plose, 48, 39042 Bressanone. (C) **0472-833-279.** Fax 0472-834-004. www.hotel-angerer.com. 28 units. 80€–96€ double. Rates include breakfast. Half-board 12€ more per person. MC, V. Closed early Jan to mid-Feb. **Amenities:** Tavern; concierge; indoor/outdoor pool; room service; sauna. *In room:* TV, hair dryer.

Hotel Elephant   One of the Tirol's oldest and most famous inns (also sometimes spelled Hotel Elefant) is named for a 16th-century guest—an elephant accompanying Archduke Maximilian of Austria on the long trek from Genoa to Vienna, where the beast was to become part of the royal menagerie. During its 2-week stay, the pachyderm attracted onlookers from miles around, and the innkeeper renamed his establishment and commissioned a delightful elephant-themed fresco that still graces the front of the building. Today's hotel matches its provenance with excellent service and extraordinary environs that include dark-paneled hallways and grand staircases. The distinctive old rooms are furnished with heavy old Tirolean antiques and tasteful modern pieces. The buffet breakfast emphasizes delicious Austrian pastries.

Via Rio Bianco 4, 39042 Bressanone. (C) **0472-832-750.** Fax 0472-836-579. www.hotelelephant.com. 44 units. 160€–212€ comfort double; 212€–234€ deluxe double; 244€–268€ junior suite. Half- and full-pension available. Ask about discounted rates for stays of more than 3 nights. Breakfast 13€. AE, DC, MC, V. Parking 6€. Closed Jan 7–Feb 28 and Nov 5–30. **Amenities:** Tirolese restaurant; bar; babysitting; bikes; concierge; small exercise room; outdoor heated pool; room service; 2 saunas; tennis courts. *In room:* TV, hair dryer, Internet, minibar.

WHERE TO DINE

Caffè Duomo   CAFE   These minimalist walls hold a contemporary version of the woody taverns that prevail in this part of the world (there are still little nooks off to one side for intimate conversation). No attempt is made at serious cuisine here, but there is a nice selection of panini made with local hams and mountain cheeses, and sumptuous cakes and pastries. The coffee is excellent, and the wine-and-beer list extensive.

Piazza Parocchia 3. (C) **0472-838-277.** Sandwiches and snacks from 3€. No credit cards. Mon–Fri 8am–8pm; Sat 12:30–8pm.

Fink   TYROLEAN   It only seems right that Brixen's charmingly arcaded main street should have a restaurant that looks like this, with paneling hung with antlers and oil paintings, while dishing out excellent local cuisine. Fink offers many mountain-style dishes that you are likely to encounter only within a close radius of Brixen, including a *piatto alla Val d'Isarco,* a platter of locally cured hams and salamis, and a *zuppa di vino,* a traditional Tirolean soup made with white wine and, here, crusty pieces of cinnamon toast. The *miale gratinato,* a pork roast topped with a cheese sauce, is surprisingly light and absolutely delicious, as are the local cheeses served for dessert. If in doubt about what to order, just ask—the English-speaking staff is extremely gracious.

Via Portici Minori 4. (C) **0472-834-883.** Primi 5€–10€; secondi 7€–16€. AE, DC, MC, V. Thurs–Tues noon–2:30pm; Thurs–Mon 7–10pm. Closed July 1–14.

Finsterwirt   WINE BAR   Occupying the same quarters as Oste Scuro (see below) and run by the same family, this ground-floor tavern near the cathedral has the same dark paneling and leaded-window ambience as the aforementioned restaurant. The fare and service, however, are much more casual, though excellent, and you are welcome to settle into one of the nooklike tables for as long as you'd like to enjoy a beer or a glass of local wine and a plate of fresh goat cheese or a platter of *speck* and salami. A lovely rear garden, candlelit at night, is open throughout the summer and well into chillier days when people from more southerly climes wouldn't think of sitting outdoors.

Vicolo Duomo 3. © **0472-835-343**. www.finsterwirt.com. Salads and light meals from 7€. AE, DC, MC, V. Tues–Sat 10am–midnight; Sun 10am–3pm. Closed Jan 10–Feb 2 and June 15–30.

Oste Scuro TYROLEAN   What may be Brixen's temple of gastronomy (Fink, above, is a close contender) occupies a welcoming series of intimate candlelit rooms above the Finsterwirt *Weinstube* (see above). This is a favorite of the Germany-born reigning pope, who last stopped by here in 2008. A *terrina di formaggio di capra fresco* is a concoction of creamy cheese atop a bed of lightly sautéed spinach and greens; even if you have found the region's steady diet of *canederli* (dumplings) heavy, try them here, where they are light and infused with fresh wild mushrooms. The kitchen excels at meat dishes, including an herb-infused veal roast. For dessert, fresh, seasonal berries top off a meal, and the strudels are done to perfection.

Vicolo Duomo 3. © **0472-835-343**. www.finsterwirt.com. Reservations recommended. Primi 9€–11€; secondi 15€–18€. AE, DC, MC, V. Tues–Sun noon–2pm; Tues–Sat 7–9pm. Closed Jan 11–Feb 2 and June 21–July 5.

EN ROUTE TO CORTINA: THE GREAT DOLOMITE ROAD

The **Grande Strada delle Dolomiti,** the scenic route between Bolzano (follow signs to Eggental/Val d'Ega) and Cortina going east, S241 and S48, is 110km (68 miles) of stunning views. The road curves around some of the highest peaks in the Dolomites, including 3,000m-tall (9,840-ft.) **Marmolda,** and goes through a scattering of mountain villages and ski resorts before dropping out of a high pass into Cortina. Some tour buses follow this route (the tourist offices in Bolzano and Cortina can provide a list of tour operators; check with the bus station in Bolzano), as do two daily buses of the **STI network** July through September (check with the bus station in Bolzano or call © **0471-450-111;** www.sii.bz.it). You may want to rent a car, if only for a day, to make the spectacular round-trip, one of Europe's most scenic drives (allow at least 2½ hr. each way over the twists and turns of the passes). Keep in mind that the Grande Strada delle Dolomiti is often closed to vehicles because of heavy snow in the winter months, and you will often need chains on your tires between November and April.

5 CORTINA D'AMPEZZO

133km (82 miles) E of Bolzano, 166km (103 miles) N of Venice

Technically, Cortina d'Ampezzo is part of the Veneto, not Alto-Adige, but it is grouped here alongside other Dolomite landmarks with the same Teutonic flavor.

Italy's best-known mountain resort, put on the international map when it hosted the 1956 Winter Olympics, is often associated with wealth and sophistication. Long before the Olympics, though, Cortina was attracting European Alpine enthusiasts, who began coming here for stays in the town's first hotels as early as the 1860s. In 1902, Cortina hosted its first ski competitions, and in 1909, the completion of the first road in and out of the town, the magnificent Strada di Dolomiti (built by the Austro-Hungarian military), opened the slopes to more skiers.

Even without its 145km (90 miles) of ski runs and 50 cable cars and chairlifts that make the slopes easily accessible, Cortina would be one of Europe's most appealing Alpine towns. The surrounding Dolomite peaks are simply stunning. Eighteen of them rise more than 3,000m (9,840 ft.), ringing Cortina in an amphitheater of craggy stone. In full light the peaks are a soft bluish gray, and when they catch the rising and setting sun, they take on a welcoming rosy glow.

True to its reputation for glamour, Cortina can be expensive (especially in Aug and the high-ski-season months of Jan–Mar). Many well-to-do Italians have houses here, and a sense of privilege prevails. What's often forgotten, though, is that for all of the town's fame, strict zoning has put a damper on development; as a result, Cortina is still a mountain town of white timbered houses, built aside a rushing stream and surrounded by forests, meadows, and, of course, stunning Dolomite peaks.

FESTIVALS & MARKETS The **Piazza Italia** near the bus station doubles as Cortina's marketplace. Stalls sell produce, mountain cheeses, clothing, housewares, and other items on Tuesday and Friday mornings from 8:30am to 1pm. While chic Cortina concerns itself mostly with secular pursuits, the town turns out for a solemn religious procession down the main street, Corso Italia, on **Good Friday.**

ESSENTIALS

GETTING THERE **By Train** The closest train station to Cortina is the one at **Calalzo di Cadore,** 30km (19 miles) south. From Calalzo, 30 daily buses connect with Cortina. There are 10 trains a day to Calalzo from Venice, but only two are direct (2½ hr; with connections, allow 3–4 hr.). There are also six daily direct runs from Padua (3 hr.).

By Bus Frequent **STI bus service** provides the only public transportation in and out of Cortina (✆ 800-846-047 in Italy; www.sii.bz.it). There are two daily buses each from Bolzano (about 4 hr.), stopping in Bressanone (about 2¾ hr.), that head to Cortina, but with a change in Dobbiaco. There is also one daily bus to and from Venice (✆ 035-237-641; 4½ hr.) and a daily bus to and from Milan (✆ 02-801-161; 6½ hr.). The bus station in Cortina is located in the former train station on Via Marconi.

By Car The spectacularly scenic Grande Strada delle Dolomiti (see above) links Bolzano and Cortina, while S51 heads south toward Venice, connecting south of Belluno to Autostrada A27, for a total trip time of about 3 hours between Cortina and Venice.

VISITOR INFORMATION The **APT tourist office,** Piazetta San Francesco 8 (✆ 0436-3231; fax 0436-3235; www.cortina.dolomiti.com or www.dolomiti.com), is open daily 9am to 12:30pm and 4 to 7pm. In addition to a list of accommodations, the English-speaking staff will provide a wealth of information on ski slopes, hiking trails, and bus schedules.

WHAT TO SEE & DO

The primary activity in Cortina appears to be walking up and down the main street, the pedestrian-only **Corso Italia,** in the most fashionable skiwear money can buy. Most of the buildings are pleasingly low-scale and Alpine in design, and at the town center is the pretty 18th-century church of **Santi Filippo e Giacomo,** with a charming bell tower eclipsed in height only by the majestic peaks. It is on these peaks that most visitors set their sights, enjoying an array of outdoor activities on the slopes.

EXPLORING PEAKS Skiers and nonskiers alike will enjoy the eye-popping scenery on a trip up the surrounding mountainsides on the funicular systems that leave right from town. The most spectacular trip is the ascent on the **Freccia nel Cielo (Arrow in the Sky),** which departs from a terminus near the Stadio Olimpico del Ghiaccio (Olympic Ice-Skating Stadium), about a 10-minute walk north and west of the town center. It has three segments. The top station is at **Cima Tofana,** at 3,163m (10,375 ft.); the round-trip is 26€. It is a little less expensive (21€)—and just as satisfying, if mountain scenery and not high-Alpine skiing is your quest—to make the trip only as far as **Ra Valles,** the second stop, at 2,550m (8,364 ft.). The views over glaciers and the stony peaks are magnificent, and a bar serves sandwiches and other refreshments on an outdoor terrace. Or, for 12€, you could take the tramway as far as **Col Druscie,** whose views are still nothing to sneeze at, and there is a decent restaurant there as well. The funicular runs from mid-July to late September and mid-December to May 1, with departures every 20 minutes from 9am to 4 or 5pm, depending on the time of sunset; call ✆ **0436-5052** for information.

The **Funivia Faloria** (✆ **0436-2517**) arrives and departs from a terminus on the other side of town, about a 10-minute walk southeast of the town center. The ride is a little less dramatic than the one on the longer Freccia nel Cielo. Even so, the ascent over forests and meadows and then up a sheer cliff to the 2,100m-high (6,888-ft.) ski station at Faloria is not without thrills, and the view from the terrace bar at Faloria, down to Cortina and to the curtain of high peaks to the north, is one you won't soon forget. Like the Freccia nel Cielo, the Funivia Faloria runs from mid-July to late September and mid-December to May 1, with departures every 20 minutes from 9am to 4 or 5pm, depending on the time of sunset; round-trip fare is 16€.

Another trip for cable car enthusiasts is the one from the top of **Passo Falzarego,** 25km (16 miles) west of Cortina, to Lagazoul, a little skiing and hiking station at the 2,550m (8,364-ft.) level. In summer, you can follow a network of trails at the top and scamper for miles across the dramatic, rocky terrain. The ride is a nearly vertical ascent up the rocky face of the mountain, and as an eerie alternative to the funicular, you can make the climb up or down through a series of tunnels dug into the cliff during World War I battles. Falzarego is the last pass through which you descend if you follow the Strada di Dolomiti into Cortina, so you may want to stop and board the funicular for a scenery-filled introduction to the region. If you are not driving, five buses a day make the 35-minute trip between Cortina and the funicular stop at the top of the Passo Falzarego; the fare is 1.50€ each way. The funivia runs from mid-July to late September and mid-December to May 1, with departures every 30 minutes; round-trip fare is 12€; call ✆ **0436-867-301** for information.

DOWNHILL SKIING Cortina is Italy's leading ski resort, and it lives up to its reputation with eight exceptional ski areas that are easily accessible from town. Two of the best, **Tofana-Promedes** and **Faloria-Tondi,** are accessible by funiculars that lift off from the edges of town (see "Exploring Peaks," above), as are the novice slopes at **Mietres.** You can enjoy these facilities fairly economically with one of the comprehensive Dolomiti Superski passes that provide unlimited skiing (including all chairlift and funicular fees, as well as free shuttle bus service to and from Cortina and the ski areas) at all eight of Cortina's ski areas and those at 10 outlying resorts. You can get passes for any number of days, up to 21. A few sample prices: During high season, December 21 to January 6 and February 1 to March 13, the cost is 45€ for 1 day, 113€ for 3 days, and 210€ for 7 days; shave off about 5€ per day for low season, January 7 to January 31 and March 13 to March 27. For more information, contact the **tourist office** or **Dolomiti Superski,** Via Marconi 15b, 32043 Cortina (✆ **0436-866-525** or 0471-867-448; www.dolomitisuperski.com).

For **lessons,** contact the **Scuola di Sci Cortina,** Corso Italia (✆ **0436-2911;** www.scuola scicortina.it). Prices start at 40€ per hour in low season, 53€ per hour in the holiday season, though cheaper weeklong rates are available.

You can **rent skis** at many outlets throughout town, including stands at the lower and upper stations of the Freccia nel Cielo cable car and other funiculars; rentals average 15€ to 25€.

HIKING & ROCK CLIMBING   In this mountainous terrain, these two activities are often synonymous. The tourist office can provide maps of hiking trails throughout the surrounding region. For high-altitude hiking, canyoning, and rock climbing, you may want to join one of the excursions led by **Gruppo Guide Alpine Cortina,** Corso Italia 69A (ⓒ **0463-868-505;** www.guidecortina.com), open daily 8am to noon and 4 to 8pm. A 3-day climbing course, for example, is 270€.

ICE-SKATING   At the **Stadio Olimpico del Ghiaccio,** just to the northwest of the town center on Via del Stadio (ⓒ **0436-866-342**), you can practice turns on the two recently refurbished rinks where Olympians tried for the gold in the 1956 games. Admission plus skate rental is 7€.

MOUNTAIN BIKING   The roads and tracks leading up to the peaks provide arduous biking terrain; cyclists from all over the world come to Cortina to practice for events. If you want to test your mettle, rent a bike from the **Mountain Bike Center,** Corso Italia 294. Contact them on their mobile phone (ⓒ **347-128-1607**). Rentals are 30€ for a day and half-price in the off season, for which there are no set dates but roughly correspond to spring and fall. (No one rides here in the winter.) The staff will try to point you in the direction of routes that match your abilities.

WHERE TO STAY

Cortina is booked solid during the high season: August, Christmas, and late January through March. You should reserve well in advance. Rates are lowest in late spring and early fall. It's closed down tight in June. Keep in mind that many innkeepers prefer to give rooms to guests who will stay several days or longer and will take meals at the hotel. Given the scarcity of reasonably priced restaurants in town, you will probably be happy settling for a half- or full-board plan. The tourist board provides a list of private homes that take in guests, a way to keep costs down while enjoying the local hospitality, which is considerable.

Hotel Bellaria   The Majoni family owns this pleasant hotel a short walk from the center on the northern edge of town, and they choose to keep prices down for the benefit of the patrons who come here year after year. (In ski season, the hotel generally rents out doubles by the week.) They provide some of Cortina's most reasonably priced accommodations, and they house their guests in handsome, sunny rooms that overlook the mountains and have fresh Alpine-style pine furnishings, firm new beds, and crisp fabrics. All of the bathrooms are fitted with heated towel racks. Downstairs there's a lovely paneled lounge, a dining room, a pleasant terrace in front of the house, and a lawn out back.

Corso Italia 266, 32043 Cortina d'Ampezzo. ⓒ **0436-2505.** Fax 0436-5755. www.hbellaria.it. 22 units. 90€–160€ double; in winter, half-board and long stays may be required: weekly rates 500€–610€. DC, MC, V. Free parking. Closed 1 month in fall or spring. **Amenities:** Tirolese/Italian restaurant; bar; babysitting; concierge; room service; smoke-free rooms. *In room:* TV, hair dryer.

Hotel Menardi   One of the oldest and most charming hostelries in Cortina successfully combines the luxury and service of a fine hotel with the homelike comfort of a mountain inn. The Menardi family, which converted its farmhouse into a guesthouse in the 1920s, has beautifully appointed the public rooms with antiques and comfortable furnishings, and done up the high-ceilinged, wood-floored guest rooms simply but tastefully with painted or pine armoires and bedsteads, down quilts, and floral fabrics. Rooms in the rear of the house are especially quiet and pleasant, looking across the hotel's spacious lawns to the forests and peaks; some newer (but still panel-and-pine Alpine) rooms are located in an annex next door; many have large balconies with picnic tables. Most guests take half-board to avail themselves of the excellent meals in a dining room converted from former stalls, but it is also possible to make bed-and-breakfast arrangements when the hotel is not fully booked. A pretty foot trail leads from the back lawn into town in 15 minutes.

Via Majon 110, 32043 Cortina d'Ampezzo. ☎ **0436-2400.** Fax 0436-862-183. www.hotelmenardi.it. 49 units. 100€–220€ double; 190€-260€ in winter, including requisite half-board. Rates include breakfast. Add 20€–23€ per person for half-board; add 30€–32€ per person for full board. DC, MC, V. Parking free or 8€ in garage. Closed Apr 10–June 15 and Sept 21–Dec 20. **Amenities:** International/Tirolese restaurant; bar; bikes; children's playground; concierge; golf course (9 holes, 3km/1³/₄ miles away); room service; smoke-free rooms. In room: TV, hair dryer, minibar, Wi-Fi.

Hotel Montana ★   Right in the center of town, this hotel occupies a tall, pretty Alpine-style house and is run by the amiable Adriano and Roberta Lorenzi, who provide some of the resort's nicest lodgings for the price. Guest rooms are pleasant and cozy, with old-style armoires, hardwood floors, and down quilts on the beds, and many open onto balconies overlooking the peaks. Most of the doubles are quite large, and many are beautifully paneled and have separate sitting areas. Half the rooms here are singles, making this an ideal spot for solo travelers. Breakfast is served in a pleasant room where guests tend to linger through much of the morning.

Corso Italia 94, 32043 Cortina d'Ampezzo. ☎ **0436-862-126.** Fax 0436-868-211. www.cortina-hotel.com. 30 units. In winter 590€–1,000€ double per week; in summer 80€–148€ double per night. Rates include breakfast. AE, DC, MC, V. Free parking. Closed Nov and June. **Amenities:** Babysitting; bikes; concierge; room service. In room: Satellite TV, high-speed Internet connection, hair dryer.

Miramonti Majestic Grand Hotel   The top deluxe spot in town since 1893, this enormous golden-age beauty of a hotel is set just outside and above the village, backed up against the pine forests with sweeping views of the cut-glass peaks. The decor, if uninspired, is perfectly pleasant, where 19th century meets modern, classy lines, and rooms contain a full complement of amenities. Public spaces devoted to après-ski fun include a piano bar, a billiards room, and even a small cinema, and it calls a (separately managed) golf course its next-door neighbor.

Loc. Peziè 103, 32043 Cortina d'Ampezzo. ☎ **0436-4201.** Fax 0436-867-019. www.miramontimajestic.it. 105 units. 350€–620€ superior double with half-board. (Over Christmas/New Year's holidays, prices are almost doubled. Even in off-season, a 3-day minimum is often required.) AE, DC, MC, V. Parking 40€ in garage. Closed Apr–June and Sept–Nov. **Amenities:** Regional/international restaurant; piano bar; babysitting; free bikes; children's center; exercise room; golf course; indoor heated pool; sauna; smoke-free rooms; tennis courts (lighted at night). In room: TV w/pay movies, VCR, hair dryer, Internet.

Villa Nevada   On a grassy hillside overlooking the town, valley, and mountains, the Villa Nevada is a low-slung Alpine building that has the appearance of a private home. The same ambience prevails inside, where an attractive paneled lounge is grouped around a hearth and opens to a sunny terrace, inviting guests to linger as they might in a living room. The guest rooms are large and bright, and afford wonderful views over the Alpine landscape; they are nicely furnished with dark-stained pine pieces and thick rugs or carpeting, and all have large balconies. Located on the road to the outlying settlement of Ronco, this is probably a better option for those with a car than for those without—the center of Cortina is a pleasant 20-minute walk downhill, but it could be a long uphill trek home in bad weather or late at night.

nevada. 11 units. In winter 700€–980€ double per week; in summer 530€–700€ double per week. Rates include buffet breakfast. No credit cards. Free parking. Closed first Sun Oct–Dec 1 and after Easter to mid-June. **Amenities:** Bar; room service. *In room:* TV, hair dryer.

WHERE TO DINE

Inexpensive meals are hard to come by in Cortina—even pizzerias are few and far between. For a low-cost meal, you might want to equip yourself for a picnic at **La Piazzetta,** Corso Italia 53, with a mouthwatering assortment of salamis, cheeses, breads, and other fare. Another source of supplies is the department store **La Cooperativa,** Corso Italia 40 (ⓒ **0436-861-245**), the largest, best-stocked supermarket for miles around.

Al Camin ALPINE   If you follow the Via Alverà along the Ru Bigontina, a rushing mountain stream, about 10 minutes east from the center of town, you'll come to this charming restaurant, rustic in appearance, but the cuisine is anything but unrefined. Tables in the wood-paneled dining room are grouped around a large stone fireplace, and the menu includes local favorites like *kenederli* (these dumplings flavored with liver are known as *canederli* outside Cortina) *in brodo* or *al formaggio,* as well as dishes that you may not encounter elsewhere, like *radicchio di prato,* a mountain green that appears in early spring and is served dressed with hot lard; and, in winter *formaggio fuso con funghi e polenta,* a lush combination of creamy melted mountain cheese and wild mushrooms served over polenta. The wine list is extensive.

Via Alverà 99. ⓒ **0436-862-01.** www.alcamincortina.dolomiti.org. Reservations recommended. Primi 6€–9.50€; secondi 7€–18€. MC, V. Tues–Sun noon–3pm and 7–11:30pm.

Caffè Royal CAFE   The Corso Italia, Cortina's pedestrians-only main street, is the center of the town's social life. This cafe is one of several that occupy the ground floor of large hotels along the street, and it is one of the more pleasant. As soon as it's even remotely possible to sit outdoors, tables are set out front on a sunny terrace. At other times, patrons are welcome to sit for hours over coffee, pastries, or light fare such as sandwiches in a pleasant room off the lobby of this hotel of the same name.

Corso Italia. ⓒ **0436-867-045.** Sandwiches and snacks from about 2€. MC, V. Wed–Mon 8am–9pm.

La Tavernetta ALPINE   A former barn, just steps from the Olympic ice-skating stadium, has been delightfully converted to a very stylish yet reasonably priced restaurant, with handsome paneled walls, timber ceilings, and tile floors. The menu relies on local ingredients and typical dishes of the Alto Adige, and the rustic environs may inspire you to eat heartily. You might want to begin with a dish of polenta delicately infused with *asparagi selvatici* (the tips of fresh wild asparagus) or *gnocchi di spinachi* (filled with spinach and topped with a rich wild-game sauce), and then move on to a robust *stinco di vitello con patate* (veal shank served with creamy potato) or *cervo in salsa di mirtilli* (venison with a sauce of myrtle berries with polenta).

Via del Stadio 27 a/b. ⓒ **0436-867-494.** Reservations recommended. Primi 6.50€–12€; secondi 11€–20€. AE, MC, V. Thurs–Tues noon–2:30pm and 7:30–11pm.

Ospitale ALPINE   A trip out to this roomy restaurant in a high-gabled house (about 8km/5 miles north of Cortina on the road to the village and lake of Dobbiaco) is a favorite outing for residents of Cortina. Many members of the Alvera family are on hand in the comfortable, wood-floor dining rooms and in the kitchen, preparing and serving

TRENTINO–ALTO ADIGE

7

CORTINA D'AMPEZZO

local specialties. In season, fresh vegetables appear in such pasta dishes as *pappardelle ai porcini* (flat noodles with porcini mushrooms) and *casunziei rossi,* a short, local pasta mixed with beets, or *gnocchi di zucca con ricotta* (gnocchi made from squash and stuffed with ricotta). The *goulash con polenta* is one of any number of substantial main courses. If you don't have a car, you can take one of the hourly buses out here from the bus station in Cortina, but that is an option only at lunch.

Locale Ospitale. ☎ **0436-4585.** Reservations recommended. Primi 5€–7€; secondi 8€–15€. AE, MC. Tues–Sun noon–2:30pm and 7–10pm.

Friuli-Venezia Giulia

Trieste's Friuli-Venezia Giulia region is a sliver of coastline across the Adriatic Sea from Venice. Any glance at a map will show you that it would probably be part of Slovenia today were it not for the border juggling that followed World War I. Though primarily known for the shipping industry and naval yards around the Habsburgs' old port city of **Trieste,** this region was actually a major center of both ancient Rome and the Dark Ages' Lombards.

The Friuli-Venezia Giulia region comprises Venezia Giulia, of which Trieste is the capital, and the much larger Friuli, with Udine as its capital. There's an interesting inverse proportion between the size of the Friuli-Venezia Giulia's most interesting centers and each one's era of domination over local affairs. Rule by the sprawling free port and current capital of Trieste dates back only through Austro-Hungarian control and the 16th century. The midsize city of **Udine** held the patriarchy and regional power from the 13th century, until it came under Venetian control in the 15th century. Udine had wrested that patriarchal seat, and control of it, from what is today the oversize town of **Cividale,** where in the early Middle Ages the Lombards inaugurated their ruling system of duchies. Even the sleepy backwater town of **Aquileia,** with its ruins and early Christian mosaics, once held a position of power as the fourth-most-important city of the Roman Empire.

Almost every town in the region has a museum or two devoted to the Risorgimento and/or World War I. Well worth a visit to help understand the history of this region (a history, unfortunately, rarely explained in English), these museums trace the Italian national movement from its mid-19th-century beginnings through the intense fighting that took place in Friuli's mountains to the border disputes involving the line separating Italy from Yugoslavia. Even then, these disputes were not always happily resolved. The Treaty of Paris plopped the national boundary right through the town of **Gorizia.** It wasn't until later compromises in the 1970s that the line was finally moved over so that only Gorizia's eastern suburbs, just beyond the medieval Castello's hill, remained Slovenian (called Nova Gorica).

REGIONAL CUISINE The cuisine of Friuli-Venezia Giulia ranges from the firmly Alpine mountain fare of the borderland **Tirol** (see chapter 7) to some exotic and hard-to-pronounce variations reflecting the region's mixed cultural heritage, coastal region, and Slovenian slant. Among these are *cevapcici,* Trieste's signature meatball dish; *jota,* minestrone with sauerkraut; and *brovada,* a secondo that combines turnips, grape skins, and pork sausage—a farmer's supper if ever there was one. The town of **San Daniele** produces what is widely acknowledged as the best prosciutto in all of Italy—no small claim.

Friuli wines (celebrated on the website www.mtvfriulivg.it) range from local varieties such as the common **tocai,** sweeter **verduzzo, malvasia,** and beefier **collio** to more international grapes such as merlot, cabernet sauvignon and cabernet franc, all the pinots, and chardonnay.

1 TRIESTE

158km (98 miles) E of Venice, 68km (42 miles) SE of Udine, 408km (253 miles) E of Milan

Trieste faces west, toward the rest of Italy, to which it is connected only by a strip just a few miles wide of what might otherwise be Slovenian beachfront if either of last centuries' world wars had ended differently. For many of its traditions—from the Slavic dialects you are likely to hear in the streets to the appearance of goulash and Viennese pastries on its menus—this handsome city of medieval, neoclassical, and modern buildings turns to other parts of Europe and is rightly considered a Habsburgian Adriatic port, tied more to Vienna than to Venice.

Already a thriving port by the time it was absorbed into the Roman Empire in the 2nd century A.D., Trieste competed with Venice for control of the seas from the 9th through the 15th centuries. For several centuries it thrived under the Habsburgs; in the late 18th century, Maria Theresa, and later her heirs and successors, gave the city its grandiose neoclassical look. Trieste was the chief seaport of the Austro-Hungarian Empire until the conclusion of World War I, when Trieste became part of Italy. At the end of World War II, Allied forces and Yugoslavia jointly occupied Trieste, which became a free city issuing its own stamps and currency until 1954, when it was given back to Italy.

Politics continue to shape this city—today you're likely to notice the recent influx of refugees from the former Yugoslavia. You're also likely to notice that Trieste is a seagoing city. The traditional *passeggiata* here means a stroll along the waterfront to enjoy a sea breeze and watch the sun set over the Adriatic.

In the cafes that remain (fewer now than before World War I), you can experience the city's history as one of Europe's intellectual centers. James Joyce arrived in 1904 and stayed for more than a decade, teaching English and writing *A Portrait of the Artist as a Young Man, Dubliners,* and at least part of *Ulysses;* the poet Rainer Maria Rilke lived nearby; Sigmund Freud spent time here; and the city was home to Italo Svevo, one of Italy's greatest 20th-century novelists, and to Umberto Saba, one of its greatest 20th-century poets.

FESTIVALS & MARKETS   The city celebrates summer with a **series of concerts and films,** many free and held in the outdoor theater in the Castello di San Giusto. If you are going to be in Trieste at this time, ask the tourist office for a copy of *Eventi Luglio-Agosto.* The **International Operetta Festival** presents three or four noted masterworks (and a new piece or two) in June and July in the Teatro Lirico Giuseppe Verdi (© **040-672-2500;** www.teatroverdi-trieste.com). The **Barcolana Autumn Cup,** held in the Golfo di Trieste on the second Sunday in October, is the largest sailing regatta in Southern Europe. The regatta celebrated its 41st anniversary in 2009. For more information, call © **040-411-664** or visit www.barcolana.it.

An **antiques market** fills the streets of the Old City the third Sunday of every month, while early November brings an important **antiques fair,** especially noted for Liberty (plus its Austrian cousin Jungendstil) and Biedermeier pieces, to the conference center of the Stazione Marittima (© **040-304-888**). Trieste's two **food markets** provide colorful surroundings and a chance to eye the local cuisine. The covered market, at the corner of Via Carducci and Via della Majolica, is open Monday from 8am to 2pm and Tuesday through Saturday from 8am to 7pm. The open-air market is on Ponte Ponterosso, alongside the canal that cuts into the center of the city from the harbor, and it operates Tuesday through Saturday from 8am to 5:30pm.

ESSENTIALS

GETTING THERE   By Train   Trains arrive at and depart from **Stazione Centrale** on Piazza della Libertà (✆ **040-412-695**), northwest of the historic center. There are, on average, two trains an hour to and from Venice (2½–3 hr.), where you can make connections to Milan and other Italian cities. There are also twice-hourly connections to and from Udine (1–1½ hr.). Two trains a day connect Trieste to Budapest, Hungary (11 hr.), three daily to Ljubljana, Slovenia (3 hr.).

By Bus   The **bus station** is on Corso Cavour, to the left of the train station (✆ **800-915-303;** www.saf.ud.it). Frequent buses (28 a day) link Trieste and Udine (1½ hr.), and many other towns throughout the region. There's also one bus Monday to Saturday (check for the schedule, as it often changes) to Ljubljana, Slovenia (2¾ hr.).

By Car   Trieste is a 2-hour trip from Venice along Autostrada A4.

VISITOR INFORMATION   The **tourist office** is at Piazza dell'Unità d'Italia 4B near the waterfront (✆ **040-347-8312;** fax 040-437-8320; www.triestetourism.it; daily 9am–7pm, Sun 9am–1pm).

CITY LAYOUT   The **center** of Trieste, which is snuggled between the hills and the sea, is compact and easy to get around on foot. The bus and train stations are at the northern end of the center, on the **Piazza della Libertà.** From there, follow the harbor south for about 10 minutes along Corso Cavour (you'll soon cross Trieste's Canal Grande) and its continuation, Riva III Novembre, to the **Piazza dell'Unità d'Italia.** This dramatic space—with Habsburg-commissioned, neoclassical buildings on three sides, the sea on one side, and a fountain in its center—is the heart of old Trieste and the present-day city as well. **Via Carducci,** Trieste's main shopping street, cuts through the center of the orderly 19th-century city. It begins in Piazza Oberdan (a few blocks east of the train station on Via Ghega) and cuts a straight swath south to Piazza Goldoni; from there the Corso Italia leads west to Piazza dell'Unità d'Italia and the sea.

GETTING AROUND   Central Trieste is easily navigable on foot, but the footsore can use the extensive network of **TT buses and trams** (© **040-425-001** or 800-016-675 in Italy; www.triestetrasporti.it) that runs throughout the city. You can purchase tickets at any *tabacchi* (tobacconist) for 1.05€ for 60 minutes (valid for 4 hr. on Sun) or 3.50€ for a day pass. One foot-saving route is the no. 24 line from the train station to the hilltop Castello di San Giusto and its adjoining cluster of remarkable buildings (see below), or call a **taxi** at © **040-307-730.**

WHAT TO SEE & DO

The oldest part of Trieste climbs the **Colle Capitolino (Capitoline Hill),** just behind the grandiose **Piazza dell'Unità d'Italia ★.** This is where many of the city's most interesting museums and monuments (including Roman remains) are located. A good way to approach the hill is to leave the southeastern end of Piazza dell'Unità d'Italia and step into Piazza Cavana.

In contrast to the assemblage of 18th- and 19th-century buildings on the main piazza, this part of Trieste, a warren of tiny streets climbing the hillside away from the sea, is medieval. From Piazza Cavana, follow Via Felice Veneziano to Piazza Barbacan, where you take a left to duck under the 1st-century A.D. **Arco di Riccardo,** then turn right up Via Cattedrale, and follow that for about 10 minutes up the flanks of the Colle Capitolino to the **Cattedrale di San Giusto** (see below). Just above that is the **Castello di San Giusto** (see below), from which Trieste and the Adriatic unfold in an unforgettable view at your feet.

For a quicker descent, you can take the 265-step **Scala dei Giganti (Steps of the Giants)** back down the hill to Piazza Goldoni and Via Carducci, Trieste's main shopping street.

Castello di San Giusto ★   The tall walls of this bastion, built between 1470 and 1630, rise just behind the cathedral. Within the walls are an open-air theater, the **Cortile delle Milizie,** where a summer film-and-concert festival is held (see "Festivals & Markets," above), and a museum. But the walls themselves steal the show. A walk along them affords views over Trieste and the Adriatic, making this a popular spot just before its sunset closing time. The **Civic Museum** provides an interesting, if not profound, experience—among a series of period rooms is a "Venetian chamber" filled with antique chests, 17th-century Flemish tapestries, and other furnishings—as does the **Appartamento del Capitano,** the residence of the castle's 18th-century commander. A collection of antique weaponry is housed in the rooms of the castle watch.

Piazza Cattedrale, Colle Capitolino. © **040-309-362.** www.triestecultura.it. Castle ramparts 1€; Civico Museo del Castello 5€. Castle daily 9am–7pm (until 5pm Oct–Mar). Museum Tues–Sun 9am–1pm. Bus: 24.

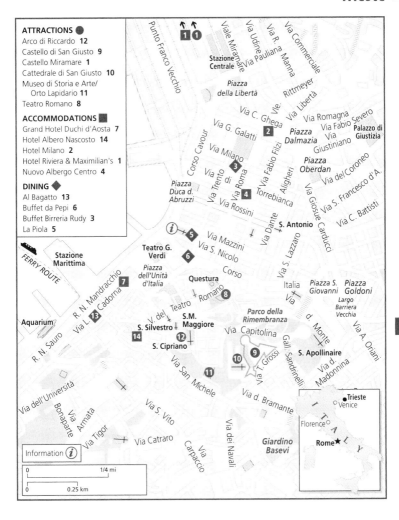

ATTRACTIONS ●
Arco di Riccardo **12**
Castello di San Giusto **9**
Castello Miramare **1**
Cattedrale di San Giusto **10**
Museo di Storia e Arte/
   Orto Lapidario **11**
Teatro Romano **8**

ACCOMMODATIONS ■
Grand Hotel Duchi d'Aosta **7**
Hotel Albero Nascosto **14**
Hotel Milano **2**
Hotel Riviera & Maximilian's **1**
Nuovo Albergo Centro **4**

DINING ◆
Al Bagatto **13**
Buffet da Pepi **6**
Buffet Birreria Rudy **3**
La Piola **5**

FRIULI-VENEZIA GIULIA

8

TRIESTE

Cattedrale di San Giusto ★   This hilltop basilica is one of several remarkable buildings atop the Capitoline Hill, which is littered with Roman ruins, evidence of the city's
long history as an important port. In fact, the cathedral's squat, 14th-century **campanile**
rises from the ruins of a 1st-century-A.D. Roman temple. Pleasingly asymmetrical, the
cathedral is dedicated to Saint Just, Trieste's patron. It incorporates two 5th-century
Romanesque basilicas, one already dedicated to San Giusto, the other to Santa Maria
Assunta. You'll see what remains of both as you step inside: The two right aisles belong
to the original San Giusto, the two left aisles to Santa Maria Assunta, and in the center
is the 14th-century nave that was added to bring them together. The apse mosaics at the
ends of the aisles are from the 13th century; those in the main apse date from 1932.

Trieste Walking Tours

If you don't have a friend to show you the sights of Trieste, make a new one at the tourist office: a local tour guide. The tourism office offers three walking tours, including a comprehensive 2-hour tour of the historic center. For those who can't get enough of James Joyce, there is a 2-hour walking tour that shows you where the Dublin native lived, walked, ate, drank coffee, taught English, and took his son for dips in the sea. For foodies, there is a 3-hour guided bus tour that focuses on the wine, cheese, olive oil, and prosciutto producers in the nearby hills.

All three tours start at 10am at the tourist office in Piazza dell'Unità d'Italia. Admission is 5€ for the first two tours and 10€ for the tasting tour. (Historic center tour: daily from Apr to mid-Oct and Sat, Sun, and holidays for the rest of the year. James Joyce tour: usually two Sat a month Apr–Sept. Food tour: usually two Sat a month Apr–Oct.) See the tourist office or check www.turismofvg. it for details.

Piazza Cattedrale 3, Colle Capitolino. ℂ **040-302-874** or 040-309-666. Free admission. Daily 8:30am–noon and 4–7pm. Bus: 24.

Museo di Storia e Arte/Orto Lapidario   This is Trieste's archaeological collection, and it includes prehistoric finds, exquisite Greek pieces (including some fine vases and a 4th-century-B.C. silver Rhyton, a chalice shaped as a deer's head, from Taranto), and remnants of the city's Roman past. Most of the Roman architectural fragments, though, are scattered about the **Orto Lapidario (Lapidary Garden).** A few rooms of the museum house a growing Egyptian collection, including a female mummy.

Another outdoor remnant of Roman Trieste lies near the bottom of the Colle Capitolino. On Via Teatro Romano, you'll find the **Teatro Romano (Roman Theater),** built in the 2nd century A.D. Only partially unearthed, the ruins can be glimpsed for free through a fence; let your imagination take you to the days when 6,000 spectators packed in for gladiatorial contests.

Piazza Cattedrale 1. ℂ **040-310-500.** www.triestecultura.it. Admission 3.50€ adults, 2.50€ students under 25 and seniors older than 65. Tues–Sun 9am–1pm (until 7pm on Wed). Bus: 24.

NEARBY SIGHTS

Castello di Miramare ★★   This vision of gleaming white turrets looms over the coast north of the city, 7km (4¼ miles) from the center. Archduke Maximilian, brother of Austrian Emperor Franz Joseph, built this castle in the late 1850s when he was sent to Trieste to command the Austrian Navy. The interior reflects the somewhat insipid royal taste of the day, with room after room of gilt and velvet. Far more romantic are the adjoining gardens, where oaks, firs, and cypresses sway in sea breezes. Alluring, too, is the legend that those who sleep in the castle will meet a violent end, a belief to which history has given some credence—the same Maximilian went to Mexico in 1864 to assume the brief role of emperor and was shot there in 1867; Archduke Ferdinand spent the night here before journeying to Sarajevo, where he was assassinated on the eve of World War I; and a later owner, Duke Amadeo of Austria, was also assassinated in 1938.

Cumulative Tickets

The region of Friuli-Venezia Giulia offers a cumulative ticket called the FVG Card, which includes admission to all regional museums and guided tours; discounts on natural parks, boat rides, and ski lifts; and free transport on Udine city buses and trams. It costs 15€ for 48 hours, 20€ for 72 hours, and 29€ for a week. See **www.turismofvg.it** for more information.

For sheer theatrics in such a theatrical setting, you can attend one of the campy sound-and-light shows in July and August. They depict Maximilian's final days in Mexico and are staged Tuesday, Thursday, and Sunday at 9:30 and 10:45pm; tickets begin at 10€.

Via Miramare, Grignano. (℃ **040-224-143.** www.castello-miramare.it. Castle 4€ adults, 2€ E.U. citizens ages 18–24, free for E.U. children under 18 and seniors older than 65; grounds free. English-language tours available for 21€ for 1–10 people. Castle: Daily 9am–6pm (last admission 30 min. before closing). Grounds: Apr–Sept daily 8am–7pm; Mar and Oct daily 8am–6pm; Nov–Feb daily 8am–5pm. Oct–Mar admission to the Castello after 5pm is from Viale dei Lecci only. Bus: 36 (catch at train station). Parking .50€ per hour, or free along road and walk 5 min.

Grotta Gigante The "Gigantic Cave" lives up to its name: 114m high, 924m long, and 65m wide (374 ft.×3,031 ft.×213 ft.), this single-chamber cave is the world's largest underground cavern open to the public. *Warning:* The requisite guided tours descend and ascend about 500 stairs total. Tours are in Italian, though if your group is mixed, they may play English and German recordings. The cave is about 15km (9¼ miles) north of the city near Opicina. An exciting way to get here is via the rickety tram that climbs into the hills from Piazza Oberdan (just west of the train station) and ends at Opicina, where you can catch the no. 42 bus to the cave. The tram runs every 20 minutes from 7:30am to 8pm, and the fare is 1.05€.

Opicina. (℃ **040-327-312.** Admission 8.50€ adults, 6.50€ ages 6–12. Tues–Sun tours every hour Nov–Feb 10am–noon and 2–4pm, Mar and Oct 10am–4pm; tours every half-hour Apr–Sept 10am–6pm. Bus: 42.

WHERE TO STAY

The **C.A.T.** (℃ **040-630-286;** www.cat-trieste.com) office inside the train station will help you find a room if the choices below are full. Also, if you stay at one of their associate hotels (all of the ones listed below except the Hotel Riviera & Maximilian's and the Grand Hotel Duchi d'Aosta), you get a special shopping card good for the reduced price at most museums in town (and a reduction on the audio guide at Castello Miramare), plus 10% off at more than three dozen shops and restaurants.

Grand Hotel Duchi d'Aosta ★ This is Trieste's best hotel, installed in one of the neoclassical buildings right on Piazza dell'Unità d'Italia. It is business oriented and modernized—with snappy service, a thermal pool, and Jacuzzi box showers in the marble bathrooms—but retains plenty of class in the stylish wood furnishings and old-world charm of its reception and Harry's Grill, which has tables on the square.

Piazza dell'Unità d'Italia 2, 34121 Trieste. (℃ **040-760-0011.** Fax 040-366-092. www.grandhotelduchi daosta.com. 53 units. 330€ double. Breakfast 20€. AE, DC, MC, V. Parking 21€ in nearby garage. **Amenities:** International restaurant; bar; babysitting; concierge; indoor pool; room service; smoke-free rooms. *In room:* A/C, TV w/pay movies, VCR (on request), hair dryer, minibar, free Wi-Fi.

Hotel Albero Nascosto ★ (Finds)   The "hidden tree" hotel is a secluded gem in the historic center by the seafront. For the price, the rooms are very well equipped (compact apartments, really), with ample bathrooms and a kitchenette in most units. The recently restored rooms have a sleek but charming feel, with hardwood floors, exposed beams, and modern art gracing the walls, with sophisticated touches such as stocked bookshelves. Beyond its convenient but quiet location and excellent wine bar/tavern downstairs, the most compelling reason to stay at the Albero Nascosto may be the friendly and genteel staff.

Via Felice Venezian 18, 34124 Trieste. ✆ **040-300-188.** Fax 040-303-733. www.alberonascosto.it. 10 units. 95€–135€ double; 135€–165€ triple. Rates include breakfast. AE, DC, MC, V. No parking. **Amenities:** Wine bar; concierge. *In room:* A/C (in some rooms), TV, hair dryer, kitchenette, minibar, Wi-Fi.

Hotel Milano   Quiet and geared to business travelers as well as foreigners, this modern hotel is near the train station but within an easy walk to most of the sights in the city center. There's a spacious lounge and bar on the ground floor, as well as a breakfast room where a generous buffet, the only meal served, is laid out in the morning. The bright, cheerful guest rooms are decorated in contemporary style with wood-veneer furnishings to provide a comfortable ambience. The small bathrooms are completely up-to-date.

Via Ghega 17, 34132 Trieste. ✆ **040-369-680.** Fax 040-369-727. www.hotel-milano.com. 44 units. 140€ double; 170€ triple. Rates include breakfast. AE, DC, MC, V. Parking 12€ in garage. **Amenities:** Bar; concierge; room service. *In room:* A/C (in some rooms), TV, hair dryer, minibar, Wi-Fi (3€ for 1 hr. and 5€ for 2 hr.).

Hotel Riviera & Maximilian's ★★   This seaside retreat has been steadily expanded since it opened in 1910. Rooms in the older half have parquet floors, blue-tiled bathrooms, and carved wood furnishings with modern prints, and many neighboring doubles can be connected to make suites. Number 101 is a family suite, though it is one of only three rooms without a sea view. In the new half, rooms have balconies that are shaded by umbrella pines, cypress, and palms, and are cooled by Adriatic breezes. Rooms on the first floor have terraces opening directly onto the garden; those on the side have less of a sea view but more greenery.

The Maximilian's separate residence is made up of 12 apartments, rented by the week. They have stylish, modern furnishings in burnished steel and light wood tones, minimalist and low to the ground for a vaguely Japanese-industrial look. In the single-bedroom apartments and in one of the bedrooms in the two- or three-room units, the bed folds away and an end table unfolds into a large desk. The kitchenettes are slipped behind pocket doors, so the rooms can be sold as doubles as well. The hotel's catwalk leads from the panoramic terrace with umbrella-shaded tables to an elevator tower down to two private beaches (the second, which includes the pools, is a 5-min. walk along the coast).

Strada Costiera 22 (just north of Castello Miramare, 8km/5 miles from Trieste's center), 34010 Trieste. ✆ **040-224-551.** Fax 040-224-300. www.hotelrivieraemaximilian.com. 70 units. 195€–240€ double; 420€–1,250€ 1-room apt for 2 guests per week; 665€–2,100€ 2-room apt for 2 guests per week. Rates include breakfast. AE, DC, MC, V. Free parking. **Amenities:** International/Italian terrace restaurant; beach buffet in summer; bar; babysitting; children's center at beach; concierge; golf course; 2 outdoor pools (1 for adults, 1 for kids); room service; smoke-free rooms; nearby tennis courts; watersports equipment/rentals. *In room:* A/C, TV w/pay movies, hair dryer, kitchenette (in apts), minibar, Wi-Fi.

Nuovo Albergo Centro   New ownership has made this formerly down-at-the-heels *pensione* very livable while maintaining the low prices and simple comforts, including Internet access in each room and private bathrooms. Rooms have firm orthopedic beds, modular furnishings, high ceilings, and linoleum-that-looks-like-wood floors. The shared bathrooms (four showers, six toilets) are of recent vintage, and a wide spot in the hall contains a small sitting area with TV. The Centro occupies a floor of a large building about midway between the train station and the Piazza dell'Unità d'Italia, and it is less than a 10-minute walk from either.

Via Roma 13, 34132 Trieste. ⓒ **040-347-8790.** Fax 040-347-5258. www.hotelcentrotrieste.it. 15 units, 10 with private bathroom. 55€ double with shared bathroom; 75€ double with private bathroom. Rates include buffet breakfast. AE, DC, MC, V. Parking 15€ in garage. **Amenities:** Bikes; concierge; smoke-free rooms. *In room:* TV, hair dryer, Internet.

WHERE TO DINE

Al Bagatto ★★ SEAFOOD   The best fish restaurant in Trieste occupies simply decorated quarters, overseen by a staff that seems to have been working the perpetually crowded dining room for decades. The emphasis is clearly on the freshest fish in simple but tasty preparations. *Risotto ai frutti di mare* is laden with tiny shrimp and squid from the Gulf of Trieste, and they also find their way into the *zuppa di pesce.* It would be a shame, though, to come this far and not join most of the other diners in ordering the house's *frittura mista,* a delicately fried sampling of the sea creatures that were fresh at the market that morning.

Via Felice Venezian 2/Via Cadorna. ⓒ **040-301-771.** Reservations required. Primi 12€–20€; secondi 20€–30€. AE, DC, MC, V. Mon–Sat noon–2:30pm and 7pm–midnight. Closed Aug 15–30 and Dec 15–31.

Buffet Birreria Rudy TRIESTINO/AUSTRIAN   Just because Trieste is currently part of Italy doesn't mean you can't indulge in the cuisines of its former identities. This small Austrian/Bavarian *Bierhalle* serves Spaten beer on tap and sausages, wurst, and goulash alongside pastas, soups, and boiled meats. If you can't choose between a primo or a secondo, get both at once; the gnocchi with goulash is memorable. Otherwise, stand at the bar and choose nibblers from behind the glass—roasted peppers, fried zucchini, rice croquettes, frankfurters in pastry—or grab a straw-bottomed chair at the little tables under Bavarian banners and pick from the chalkboard menu.

Via Valdirivo 32. ⓒ **040-639-428.** www.buffetrudyspaten.it. Primi 4€–5€; secondi 9€–10€. AE, DC, MC, V. Mon–Sat 11am–midnight.

Buffet da Pepi ★ TRIESTINO   Trieste has many such *tavola caldi* (hot-foods delis) like this one, though none compare to century-old Pepi, a much-beloved institution. You can get a panino of cold cuts or splurge on a 10€ platter of the house specialty, many varieties of pork: spicy *cotechini* (pork sausages), *porchetta* (roast pork), *bollito di maiale* (a Trieste dish of boiled pork), and prosciutto, all served with *crauti* (sauerkraut) and other vegetables.

Via della Cassa di Risparmio 3 (near Piazza della Borsa, 1 block from the water and 2 blocks north of Piazza dell'Unità d'Italia). ⓒ **040-366-858.** Sandwiches and dishes 4€–11€. AE, DC, MC, V. Mon–Sat 9am–9pm. Closed July 15–Aug 7.

La Piola ★ TRIESTINO   This animated trattoria in the center of town near Trieste's Greek Orthodox church of San Nicolò dei Greci is popular with workers from the surrounding offices. The *jota,* a soup of beans and cabbage; *cevapcici* (Trieste's special meatballs, a Croatian tradition); and *gnocchi di patate* (potato gnocchi filled with cheese), as well as many pastas, are excellent, especially those topped with fresh porcini mushrooms. Main courses concentrate on meat, including *bistecche di cavallo* (horsemeat steak) or *costine di miale* (roast pork ribs), though fresh grilled Adriatic fish is often available. While in the evenings the trattoria provides table service, for lunch it functions as a buffet.

FRIULI-VENEZIA GIULIA

8

TRIESTE

Via San Nicolò 1B. (✆ **040-366-354.** Primi 8€–9€; secondi 8€–14€. DC, MC, V. Mon–Sat noon–3pm and 6–11pm. Closed July 15–Aug 7.

COFFEE & GELATO

Coffee is one of Trieste's most important products—Illy and many other major Italian brands are located here (in fact, an Illy family member has even served as the city's mayor). More to the point for travelers, drinking coffee is a local pastime, and Trieste's exquisite blends can be enjoyed in any number of august cafes.

Caffè degli Specchi, at Piazza dell'Unità d'Italia 7 (✆ **040-365-777;** www.caffespecchi. it), enjoys a marvelous position on the city's main, seafront piazza, making its terrace a prime spot to linger. In bad weather, a series of elegant rooms fill with shoppers and businesspeople. The pastries are excellent, as is the coffee. James Joyce spent much of his 12 years in Trieste at **Caffè-Pasticceria Pirona** ★, at the east end of Via Carducci at Largo Barriera Vecchia 12 (✆ **040-636-046**). It was here that he allegedly wrote part of *Ulysses*. With its photographs of old Trieste and gilded mirrors, the premises bear the mark of one of Europe's great remaining literary cafes. **Caffè San Marco** ★★, at Via Battisti 18 (✆ **040-371-373**), is one of Trieste's most elegant cafes; it dates from 1914, with a Liberty-style (as Art Nouveau is called in Italy) interior. A pianist puts the final touches on the ultimate cafe experience.

Gelateria Zampolli, at Via Ghega 10 (✆ **040-364-868**), is reputed to be the best gelateria in Trieste. It's located near Stazione Centrale and the city center, serving more than 50 flavors made on the premises daily. Another Zampolli, owned by a different member of the same family, is located on Piazza Cavana 6 (✆ **040-306-003**), just south of Piazza dell'Unità d'Italia.

AN ANCIENT DIVERSION EN ROUTE TO GORIZIA

Aquileia ★★ is one of those perfect Italian sites. This tiny village of just over 3,000 souls was once a major Roman city and early Christian stronghold, with a rich heritage that has left it littered with ruins and some of the best paleo-Christian mosaics in Europe. The Roman colony was founded in 181 B.C. and witnessed such momentous ancient events as Emperor Augustus's meeting with King Herod of Judea in A.D. 10, the murders of would-be Emperor Maximinus (by his own army) and Emperor Constantine II (by his brother), and the sacks of Attila the Hun in 452.

Remains of the **Roman colony** ★ are open sites (open 8:30am to an hour before sunset; free admission), some still being excavated, that lie scattered north of the current town. Just to the north of the main Piazza Capitolo, behind the tourist office, are a set of Roman houses and Christian oratories with excellent floor mosaics. From here, walk right (east) a bit to turn north up Via Sacra alongside the river, which leads to the remains of the Roman harbor. Turn left on Via Gemina then left again on Via Giulia Augusta to pass, on the right, a stretch of ancient road and, on the left, a row of standing columns marking one edge of the **Forum** ★ (among the items displayed here, look for the Gorgon's head). The road forks at the **Grande Mausoleo,** a 1st-century-A.D. tomb hauled here from the edge of town. The right fork (Via XXIV Maggio) will lead you past the remaining scraps of the amphitheater and baths (still being excavated).

The left fork (really straight on down Via Giulio Augusto) takes you in a few blocks to Via Roma and the **Museo Archeologico** ★ (✆ **0431-91-016** or 0431-91-035), which houses some nice statuary, mosaics, bronzes, and glassware, plus the excellently preserved hull of a Roman ship. Admission to the museum is 4€ for adults, 2€ for E.U. citizens ages 18 to 25, and free for those younger than 18 and older than 65; it's open Monday

Sept). The last admission is half an hour before closing.

Christianity is also ancient in Aquileia. A major church council called here in 381 was attended by such towering early theologians as saints Jerome and Ambrose. The fabulously mosaic-filled **Basilica** ★★ on Piazza Capitolo (© **0431-919-719**) is precisely as old as the official church in Italy, founded in A.D. 313, the same year Emperor Constantine declared Christianity to be the state religion. In the early 20th century, the church's original 4th-century **mosaic floor** ★★★ was uncovered to reveal a colorful cornucopia of early Christian iconography mixed with pagan symbols and portraits of 4th-century congregants spreading over 700 sq. m (7,535 sq. ft.). The basilica was substantially rebuilt in the early 11th century, when the now-faded apse frescoes were painted. In the chapel, to the left of the altar, is a **bas-relief** ★, from 1170, of Christ with St. Peter and the freshly martyred St. Thomas of Canterbury. Later frescoes also litter the church, including some lovely Byzantine 12th-century ones in the **main crypt** ★★.

The **Cripta Affreschi** ★★ is entered next to the medieval reconstruction of the Holy Sepulcher at the entrance end of the basilica's left aisle. The mosaics here hail from three eras: Augustan ones from a Roman house (just to the left), an early-4th-century floor laid at the same time as the Basilica's (this was once a neighboring church), and later-4th-century ones as well. Admission to the Basilica is free, though the Cripta charges a fee (some years it is tied into the Museo Archeologico ticket); both are open daily from 9am to 5pm (until 6pm on Sat and Sun). April to October, they are open from 9am to 7pm. Admission is 3€ for adults and free for children younger than 10.

Aquileia lies on local road 352 (take the Palmanova exit from the A4) some 11km (6¾ miles) inland from Grado, a low-key Venice Lido–like semi-island resort where Aquileia's population, and fortunes, moved to escape Dark Ages barbarian raids by the likes of Huns and Lombards. The easiest way here without your own wheels is the bus from Udine to Grado, though you can also catch a bus here from the Cervignano del Friuli train station 8km (5 miles) to the north on the Trieste-Venice line.

Aquileia's **tourist office** is on the main Piazza Capitolo (© **0431-91-087** or 0431-919-491; www.aquileia.net).

2 UDINE

71km (44 miles) NW of Trieste, 127km (79 miles) NE of Venice

Surrounded by the green, rolling plains of the Friuli, Udine is a delightful small city with a vibrant air, captivating medieval squares and Gothic and Renaissance monuments, and some stunning artworks by the rococo painter Tiepolo. A possession of the Venetian Republic from the 14th century, Udine has enjoyed great prosperity as a major trading center and a crossroads for trade across the Alps, just to the north. The late 18th century saw an Austrian takeover, the 19th century witnessed unification with Italy, and the 20th century brought intense World War II bombings. Through it all, the city's landmarks and distinct character (reflecting Italian, Nordic, and central European influences) have remained intact.

FESTIVALS & MARKETS **Udine d'Estate** is the city's major festival, running from July to mid-September, with concerts and theatrical performances in churches and on Udine's beautiful *piazze*. An **outdoor food market** fills the atmospheric Piazza Matteotti daily from 8am to 1pm.

GETTING THERE **By Train** About two trains an hour leave from Udine's station on Viale Europa Unità to both Venice (1¾–2 hr.) and Trieste (1–1½ hr.). Two trains an hour also arrive from each of the nearby cities.

By Bus The bus station is 1 block east of the train station on Viale Europa Unità. There is extensive service to other cities and towns in Friuli-Venezia Giulia, but little outside it, provided by **SAF** (✆ **800-915-303;** www.saf.ud.it). Hourly buses (more frequent between 7–9am and 4–7pm) make the hour-long trip to and from Trieste.

By Car Udine is an easy 2-hour drive northeast of Venice first east on the A4, then north on the A23. From Trieste, it's a trip of a little under an hour west on the A4 and then north on A23. If you are driving from Cortina d'Ampezzo or another Dolomite resort, you will drop down from the mountains toward Belluno on SS51 as if you were going to Venice, but at Vittorio Veneto head east on the state roads toward Pordenone and then Udine. Allow about 3 hours for the drive.

VISITOR INFORMATION The **tourist office** is at Piazza I Maggio 7 (the other side of the Castello from Piazza della Libertà; ✆ **0432-295-972;** fax 0432-504-743; www.turismo.fvg.it) and is open Monday to Saturday 9am to 1pm and 3 to 6pm.

CITY LAYOUT Much of the center of Udine is closed to traffic and surrounded by ring roads. The train and bus stations are at the southern end of this ring network, on Viale Europa Unità. From there it is about a 15-minute walk into the center, following Via Aquileia and its continuation, Via Veneto, to Piazza della Libertà. Bus no. 1 makes the trip from the train station to the center (1€).

WHAT TO SEE & DO

In Udine's center, handsome streets open every few blocks or so onto another stunning piazza and sometimes even cross little streams. The effect is like walking from one stage set to another. The heart of the city is the elegant **Piazza della Libertà** ★★, which bears the telltale marks of the Venetian presence in Udine: On one side is the **Loggia del Lionello,** the town hall, built in the mid–15th century in Venetian style with a pink-and-white-striped facade. Across the piazza is the Renaissance **Porticcato di San Giovanni** ★★, with a long portico supported by slender columns and, rising above it, a Venice-inspired clock tower emblazoned with the Venetian lion and topped with two Moors who strike the hours.

The great Renaissance architect Palladio designed the **Arco Bollani,** located to one side of the clock tower. Pass through it and make the short climb through verdant gardens to the somber 16th-century **Castello** ★★, which rises above the Piazza della Libertà on a hillock. Many Udinese come up here just to admire the view over the town and countryside, but you can also venture into the castle and visit the **Musei Civici.** While many of the galleries house an eclectic collection that includes coins, ancient pottery, and old photographs of Udine, the real treasures can be found in the **Galleria d'Arte Antica** ★. Here you'll get a taste of the work of Giambattista Tiepolo, who came to Udine from Venice in 1726, when he was 30 and already regarded as a master of a rococo style that was the last great burst of Italian painting. His *Consilium in Arena* is pure Tiepolo, a swirl of lush skies and plump putti. The museum (✆ **0432-271-591**) is open Tuesday to Sunday 10:30am to 5pm and until 7pm from May to September; admission is 5€ and 3€ for under 18 and over 65, respectively.

Many visitors come to Udine just to enjoy the Tiepolos that grace many of its buildings. To follow in their footsteps, descend again to Piazza della Libertà and follow Via Veneto south for a block or so to Piazza Duomo. The **Cathedral** ★ (daily 7am–noon and 4–8pm) dominates the square with its 14th-century Gothic facade, but the interior is theatrically baroque. The first, second, and fourth altars in the right nave are adorned with Tiepolo paintings; in the fourth chapel, his airy version of *Christ's Ascension* imparts lightness and a sense of exhilaration at leaving Earth (Tiepolo also did the frescoes here).

Tiepolo also frescoed the **Oratorio della Purità** ★ across the piazza (☎ **0432-506-830**). In *Fall of the Angels,* the plummeting cherubs look like children who have just been scolded. An *Assumption,* appropriately adorning the ceiling, is so light that it seems to draw the viewer right off the floor. To enter the oratory, rustle up a sacristan in the Duomo (but not on Sun), or try ringing the bell (mornings only).

Udine's largest collection of the artist's works adorns the **Palazzo Patriarcale** or **Palazzo Arcivescovile** ★★ (☎ **0432-25-003**), just north of the Duomo on Piazza Patriarcato. This palace was once home to Udine's patriarchal bishops. One of the last (before the position was dissolved) was Dionisio Delfino (1699–1734), from a wealthy and influential Veneto family (they produced several Udine patriarchs; look for their "three dolphins on a blue field" coat of arms all over the *palazzo*). Delfino was the guy who brought Tiepolo to Udine to paint the second floor's airy frescoes, which depict Old Testament scenes full of familiar biblical characters wearing fashionable 18th-century clothing. The most impressive room is the narrow **Galleria degli Ospiti,** though the balustraded **Biblioteca (library)** and double-decker **Sala del Trono (Throne Room)** are also notable. The Sala del Trono is plastered with portraits of the patriarchs, many redone by Tiepolo. Dionisio is the one on the bottom at the far left of the window wall. The *palazzo,* which also houses the Duomo's Museo Diocesano on the first floor containing Friuliana-School wood statues spanning the 13th to 18th centuries, is open Wednesday to Sunday 10am to noon and 3:30 to 6:30pm. Admission is 5€ for adults and 3€ for children under 10.

One more museum here deserves a visit, the **Galleria d'Arte Moderna** ★ (☎ **0432-295-891**), on the other side of the city on Piazza Diacono (from Piazza della Libertà, follow Via Mazzini and Via Anton Morro north to the edge of the old center). Here you will be shaken out of the reverie induced by Tiepolo's airy views of miracles and the afterlife—the galleries are filled with the works of 20th-century powerhouses such as Picasso and Giorgio de Chirico, as well as 1970s works by the likes of Lichtenstein and De Kooning. It's open Wednesday to Monday 10:30am to 5pm and until 7pm from May to September. Admission is 5€ for adults, 2.50€ for those younger than 18 and older than 65.

WHERE TO STAY

Astoria Hotel Italia   This is a classy business hotel, smack in the center of town, that, unfortunately, charges expense-account rates. The rooms are smallish but not cramped, with firm enough beds and a mix of furnishings from cherry-veneer mod and 1980s vintage floral-print-on-black to restructured 18th- and 19th-century antiques. Oddly, the bathrooms are old-fashioned (some outright old and in need of renovation), with nowhere to hang the shower nozzle.

Piazza XX Settembre 24, 33100 Udine. ☎ **0432-505-091.** Fax 0432-509-070. www.hotelastoria.udine.it. 75 units. 120€–207€ standard double; 130€–224€ superior double; 168€–290€ suite. Rates include breakfast. AE, DC, MC, V. Parking 16€ in garage. **Amenities:** Highly refined restaurant; bar; babysitting; concierge; room service. *In room:* A/C, TV, hair dryer, minibar, free Wi-Fi.

Hotel Clocchiatti ★★ The Clocchiatti family has provided this hotel, installed in a Liberty-style 19th-century villa, with a wonderfully warm family reception since 1965. It's 10 minutes from the town center, close to the ring road, and offers a bit of quiet from Udine. The historic villa setting means guest quarters vary widely in size, shape, and decor, though all enjoy rich fabrics and carpets. One of the nicest is suite no. 102, large and on a corner, with floor-to-ceiling windows and a sofa that can be replaced by a double or twin beds for families. Upper-floor rooms have low, vaguely rustic sloping plank ceilings. The only drawbacks are that there's no elevator (they're quite proud of the hotel's grand stairway), and most bathrooms, while fully adequate, are cramped.

Via Cividale 29, 33100 Udine. ©/fax **0432-505-047.** www.hotelclocchiatti.it. 14 units. 140€–180€ double; 180€–200€ junior suite. Rates include breakfast. AE, DC, MC, V. Parking free in small lot. Closed 2 weeks around Christmas. **Amenities:** Bar; bikes; concierge; room service. *In room:* A/C, TV, hair dryer, minibar, Wi-Fi (3 hr. for 2€ or 12 hr. for 3€).

Hotel Europa The blocks in front of Udine's train station make up a pleasant residential neighborhood where many of the city's hotels are clustered. The Europa is one of the nicest, with the exception of sometimes-rude staff. The guest rooms are handsomely outfitted with sleek wood cabinetry and headboards, thick carpeting, and some nice touches that include brass wall lamps and framed reproductions. All the bathrooms are new and equipped with generous basins and stall showers. The quietest rooms are those in the back, facing a sunny courtyard, but double-glazing on the front-room windows keeps noise there to a minimum as well.

Viale Europa Unità 47, 33100 Udine. © **0432-508-731** or 0432-294-446. Fax 0432-512-654. www.hotel europa.ud.it. 48 units. 68€–92€ double; 89€–110€ triple. Breakfast included. AE, DC, MC, V. Parking 10€ and sometimes included for stays of more than 1 day. **Amenities:** Regional restaurant next door; bar; concierge; room service. *In room:* A/C, TV, hair dryer, minibar, Wi-Fi.

WHERE TO DINE

Al Vecchio Stallo ★★ TRATTORIA In the 1920s, this served as a post station, offering refreshments and fresh horses to mounted mail carriers. Today it has been transformed into a full-fledged *osteria,* serving simple, filling, cheap traditional dishes, along with lots of local wine. Things haven't changed much, though a token national Italian dish such as *penne amatriciana* is often added to the daily menu. Those in the know, however, recommend that you stick to local specialties like *orzo e fagioli* (barley and bean soup), *frico con polenta* (cheese melted over potatoes), *nervetti con cipolla* (cow leg tendons and veins tossed with onions—I think you have to be from Udine to appreciate them), or the ever-popular *polpettone con pure* (slices of giant meatball with mashed potatoes). Service is brisk but jocular.

Via Viola 7 (off Viale Marco Volpe, near Piazza XXVI Luglio). © **0432-21-296.** Reservations recommended. Primi 6€–11€; secondi 8€–12€. No credit cards. Mon–Sat 11am–3pm and 6pm–midnight. Closed Wed.

Caffè Bistrot CAFE This welcoming cafe faces Udine's oldest square, which is surrounded by tall old houses with porticos and which is the site of a colorful morning produce market. You can take in these atmospheric surroundings from a table on the terrace, though the interior rooms, which spread across two floors, are inviting. Students, businesspeople, and neighborhood residents alike sit for hours chatting and reading while they sip cups of coffee or one of the excellent local wines served by the glass. The delicious homemade pastries make this a popular breakfast spot. Sandwiches and a few other dishes, including an *insalata caprese* (with mozzarella, basil, and tomato) and crepes filled with ham and cheese, are also served throughout the day and night (after dark, in fact, this cafe often becomes a focal point of Old City nightlife; on some nights, a DJ spins records while students dance on the flagstones of the raised square).

Piazza Matteotti. No phone. Reservations not accepted. Sandwiches and snacks from 2.50€. MC, V. Tues–Fri 7:45am–2am; Sat 9am–2am.

Ristorante-Pizzeria Al Portici ★ PIZZERIA   Udine has a large and energetic population of students, and they seem to spend much of their time in this large trattoria with red-checked tablecloths. The pizza oven turns out the most popular fare, but you can also dip into some of the city's simple, casual cuisine here, such as *cialzons*—as gnocchi are called here—which are often stuffed with smoked ricotta cheese, and *brovada* (a poor man's dish of turnips and pork sausage). Given the establishment's long open hours, you can stop by any time during the day for a coffee or beer, or a glass of some of the excellent Friuli wines.

Via Veneto 8. (© **0432-508-975.** Reservations not accepted. Primi 5€–9€; secondi 7€–18€; pizza 5€–10€. MC, V. Wed–Mon 9am–1am.

A DAY TRIP TO CIVIDALE DEL FRIULI

When the Lombards founded their first Italian duchy in the Dark Ages, it was centered on this pretty little city, so the entire region became known as Friuli after a corrupt elision of this Roman colony's original name, Forum Iulii (Caesar had modestly founded it as "Julius' Forum"). It later produced a few Lombard "Kings of Italy" from the 8th to 10th centuries, and until the Middle Ages, it was the seat of the local patriarch, after which its fortunes fell off. These days it's a largely medieval town perched on the lip of an impressive river gorge, where some of the best Lombard-era stone carving in Italy is preserved.

VISITOR INFORMATION   The **tourist office,** Corso Paolino d'Aquileia 10 (© **0432-731-398** or 0432-731-461; fax 0432-731-398; www.comune.cividale-del-friuli.ud.it), is open Monday to Friday 9am to 1pm and 3 to 7pm.

A Stroll Through Town

From the train station, turn left on Viale Libertà to Via C. Alberto, where you can take a right and follow it (it becomes Corso Mazzini) into the heart of town. After Piazza Duomo, the road becomes Corso Paolino d'Aquileia, and then you cross the Ponte del Diavolo over the deep and seriously impressive limestone gorge carved by the Natisone River.

The current **Duomo** (backtrack from the bridge to the central Piazza Duomo) is largely of the 16th and 17th centuries, though its bare interior does house a fantastic silver altarpiece set with gold-backed enameled scenes from the 12th century. A small series of rooms opens on the right aisle, with detached frescoes and several gorgeously carved stone relief panels, including a cobbled-together 8th-century baptistery, an 11th-century throne for the patriarch, and the **altar of the Duke of Ratchis** (A.D. 744–49) ★★, duke of the Friuli and king of Italy, featuring gibbon-armed angels surrounding a beardless Christ, with side panels of the *Visitation* and *Adoration of the Magi*. The cathedral is open daily 9am to noon and 3 to 6pm (to 7pm Apr–Oct) and is closed Sunday morning.

Around the corner on Piazza Duomo sits the **Palazzo dei Provveditori Veneti,** designed by Andrea Palladio (but construction began only after his death, in 1581; the building was finished in 1596). It now houses the **Museo Archeologico Nazionale** ★ (© **0432-700-700**), whose treasures include ancient bronzes (look for the fragment of a toga-wearing man from the early 1st c. A.D.), a Roman mosaic of Oceanus, and numerous early medieval pieces. Among the latter, standouts include the 6th-century Treasure of Duke Gisulfo (gold accouterments and a gem-studded cross, all found in his sarcophagus), and the Pace of Duke Ursus, an A.D. 800 ivory crucifixion scene surrounded by a silver frame. Admission is 2€, free for children under 18 and seniors over 65. It's open Tuesday to Sunday 8:30am to 7:30pm, Monday 9am to 1:30pm.

Medieval streets behind the Palazzo dei Provveditori Veneti lead under the Romanesque Porta Patriarchale to Piazzetta San Biagio and the entrance to Cividale's top sight, the **Tempietto Longobardo** ★★★ (© **0432-700-867**). The Lombards carved this cliff-side church directly into the limestone in the 8th century, decorating it with saintly high-relief statues and stuccoes. The stalls date to the 14th century. Admission is 4€ for adults, 3€ for seniors over 65 and 1.50€ for students. It's open daily April to September 9:30am to 12:30pm and 3 to 6:30pm; October to March, the closing is pushed up to 5pm.

For kicks, ask the guy at **Bar all'Ippogeo,** on Corso Paolino d'Aquileia at the corner with Via Monastero (on Mon, when the bar is closed, ask at the tourist office), for the *chiave all'Ippogeo Celtico* ("key to the Celtic Tomb"), an artificial grotto of uncertain date with a few highly worn carvings at Via Monastero 6 (© **0432-701-211**). It's free, but relaxing with an espresso or Campari at the bar when you return the key never hurts!

Where to Dine

For a quick bite or a sampler platter of meats and cheese near the Tempietto Longobardo, pop into the **Osteria Bar Al Tempietto,** Via Michele della Torre 2 (© **0432-731-071;** www.altempietto.it).

Osteria d'Italia/Enoteca de Feo ★★ MODERN ITALIAN   This wood-paneled modern joint has old-fashioned values. There's a wine-tasting bar down below and just five tables in the lofted dining nook (three more are squirreled away in the basement). Because this place is *vino* driven, you can order a dozen red and white wines by the glass for 1.50€ to 6€ each. The music is jazz, the service professional, and the food impeccable. Start off with a "salad" of prosciutto from San Daniele, *caprino* (soft goat cheese), and figs before moving on to a primo such as a *zuppa di orzo* (pasta soup with potatoes, asparagus, and summer vegetables) or *cannoli di crespelle alla ricotta di bufala* (pasta crepes stuffed with buffalo-milk ricotta). Secondi are hearty and come with side dishes: steak alongside oven-roasted potatoes, or sea bass filets with steamed veggies.

Via Adelaide Ristori 29. © **0432-701-425.** Reservations recommended. Primi 8€–10€; secondi 9€–16€. AE, DC, MC, V. Tues–Sun 11am–3pm and 5pm–midnight.

Milan & Lombardy

There's a lot more to Italy's most prosperous region than the factories that fuel its economy. Many of the attractions here are urban—in addition to Milan, a string of Renaissance cities dots the Lombardian plains, from Pavia to Mantua. To the north the region bumps up against craggy mountains and romantic lakes (see chapter 10, "The Lakes"), and to the south Lombardy spreads out in fertile farmlands fed by the Po and other rivers. The Lombardians, originally one of the Germanic barbarian hordes who crossed the Alps during Rome's decline and ended up staying to settle down, have been ruled over the centuries by feudal dynasties, the Spanish, the Austrians, and the French. They tend to be a little more Continental than their neighbors to the south, faster talking, and more fast-paced as well. They even dine a little differently, eschewing olive oil for butter and often forgoing pasta for polenta and risotto.

REGIONAL CUISINE A meal in Lombardy will probably include polenta or risotto, and both are served in variations that can sometimes stand in for an entire meal. *Polenta alla Bergamasca,* for one, is cooked with tomatoes, sausage, and cheese. Creamy risottos are often embellished with fish (in Mantua, perhaps with pikelike *luccio*) or any other ingredients an innovative chef might find at hand; one of the simplest and ever-so-common preparations here is *risotto alla Milanese,* infused with saffron. In Mantua you have a third choice of pasta—*tortelli,* little envelopes that are folded over and stuffed most commonly with *zucca* (pumpkin). Meat dishes tend to be plain and hearty. Best known and most typical of the region are *osso buco,* slowly braised veal shank served with *gremolada,* a sauce of lemon and parsley, and *cotoletta alla milanese,* a veal cutlet that is breaded, dipped in egg, and sautéed in butter—not what would be considered a healthy dish, but so delicious it warrants a departure from a diet at least once during a stay in the region.

1 MILAN (MILANO)

552km (342 miles) NW of Rome, 288km (179 miles) NW of Florence, 257km (159 miles) W of Venice, 140km (87 miles) NE of Turin, 142km (88 miles) N of Genoa

True, Italy's financial center, business hub, fashion capital, and one of the world's most industrialized major cities is not a traditional vacation spot. It's hot and empty in the summer and damp and foggy in the winter, it's surrounded by bland apartment buildings (it was heavily bombed in World War II), and it's generally less beautiful than its counterparts to the east and south. Milan, though, reveals its long and event-filled history downtown, in monuments, museums, and churches. It sets one of the finest tables in Italy, features art by such towering geniuses as Michelangelo (his final sculpture) and Leonardo da Vinci *(The Last Supper),* and supports a cultural scene that embraces La Scala, fashion shows, and nightlife, not to mention two top soccer teams, Inter and AC Milan. With its dazzling shop windows, ethnic diversity, proud cocktail hour, and other sophisticated ways, Milan is more cosmopolitan than anywhere else in Italy, an urban treasure that remains hidden from the casual tourist.

Milan was chosen to host the **Expo 2015** (www.milanoexpo-2015.com), a large international exhibition held every few years in a different country. The theme of the Milan Expo, which will run from May to October in 2015 and is expected to attract millions of visitors to the city, is "Feeding the Planet, Energy for Life." As a result, the city has an enormous opportunity to give itself a major makeover that will, among other things, make the city more tourist friendly. A new Metro line is being built, and several very big construction sites are open around town, though they are mostly outside of the city center, so visitors likely won't notice. What you will notice, though, are some recent positive changes that are making the notoriously industrial city more eco-friendly in the run up to the Expo; Milan has implemented a new bike-sharing program (see "Milan on Two Wheels," later in this chapter) and new traffic regulations that discourage drivers from entering the city with their cars during weekdays.

FESTIVALS & MARKETS   Though it's overshadowed by the goings-on in Venice, Milan's pre-Lenten **Carnevale** is becoming increasingly popular, with costumed parades and an easygoing good time, much of it focusing around Piazza del Duomo beginning a week or so before Ash Wednesday. Milan's biggest holiday, however, is December 7, the **feast of its patron saint,** Sant'Ambrogio (St. Ambrose). Those who don't leave the city for their sacrosanct day off generally spend the afternoon wrapping their mittens around a hot *vin brule* at an **outdoor fair** in, you guessed it, Piazza Sant'Ambrogio. Just before the city shuts down in August, the city council stages a series of June and July **dance, theater, and music events** in theaters and open-air venues around the city; call ☏ **02-7740-4343** for more information.

In a city as well dressed as Milan, it only stands to reason that some great-looking cast-offs are bound to turn up at **street markets.** Milan's largest street market is the one held on Via Papiniano in the Ticinese/Navigli district (Metro: Sant'Agostino) on Tuesday mornings from 8am to 1pm and on Saturday from 9am to 7:30pm; some stalls sell designer seconds as well as barely used high-fashion ware, though most offer basic staples like underwear and belts, usually cheaper than in department stores.

There's an **antiques market** on Via Fiori Chiari in the Brera district (Metro: Moscova) the third Saturday of each month, from 9am to about 7:30pm, but not in August, and another the last Sunday of each month on the quays along the Canale Grande in the Navigli district, from 9am to about 7:30pm (☏ **02-8940-9971;** Metro: Porta Genova).

Each Sunday morning, there's a large **flea market,** with everything from books to clothing to appliances, at the San Donato Metro stop.

The city's largest **food market** is at Piazza Wagner, just outside the city center due west of the church of Santa Maria delle Grazie (follow Corso Magenta and its extension, Corso Vercelli, to Piazza Piemonte; the market is 1 block north; Metro: Piazza Wagner). It's held Monday through Saturday from 8am to 1pm and Tuesday through Saturday from 4 to 7:30pm; the displays of mouthwatering foodstuffs fill an indoor market space and stalls that surround it.

ESSENTIALS

GETTING THERE   By Train   Milan is one of Europe's busiest rail hubs, with connections to all major cities on the Continent. Trains arrive and depart about every half-hour to and from Venice (2½ hr.), hourly to and from Rome (4 hr.), and hourly to and from Florence (2 hr.). **Stazione Centrale,** a vast structure of Fascist-era design,

ATTRACTIONS ●

Castello Sforzesco **15**
Chiesa di San Lorenzo Maggiore **22**
Chiesa di Sant'Ambrogio **19**
Chiesa Santa Maria Presso
di San Satiro **31**
Civic Gallery of Modern Art **6**
Civic Museum of Contemporary Art **20**
Civic Museo Archeologico **18**
Duomo & Baptistery **34**
Duomo Museum **33**
Galleria Vittorio Emanuele II **35**
Leonardo da Vinci National Museum
of Science & Technology **20**
Museo Diocesano **22**
Museo Poldi-Pezzoli **9**
Museo Teatrale alla Scala **10**
Pinacoteca Ambrosiana **29**
Pinacoteca di Brera **4**
Santa Maria delle Grazie
(The Last Supper) **17**
Teatro alla Scala **10**

ACCOMMODATIONS ■

Antica Locanda Solferino **1**
Ariosto Hotel **16**
Doria Grand Hotel **45**
Four Seasons Hotel Milano **8**
Grand Hotel et De Milan **5**
Hotel Aliseo **30**
Hotel America **39**
Hotel Due Giardini **42**
Hotel Giulio Cesare **13**
Hotel Gran Duca di York **28**
Hotel Kennedy **41**
Hotel Manzoni **7**
Hotel Paganini **47**
Hotel Pavone **37**
Hotel Rovello **12**
Hotel Santa Marta **26**
Le Meridien Gallia **44**
London Hotel **14**

DINING ◆

Al Pont de Ferr **23**
Brek **43**
Da Abele **46**
Da Claudio **11**
Dongiò **38**
Il Verdi **3**
Joia **40**
La Crêperie **21**
Latteria **2**
Luini Panzerotti **36**
Peck **32**
Ponte Rosso **24**
Premiata Pizzeria **25**
Trattoria Milanese **27**

MILAN & LOMBARDY

9

MILAN (MILANO)

is about a half-hour walk northeast of the center, with easy connections to Piazza del Duomo by Metro, tram, and bus. The station stop on the Metro is Centrale F.S.; it is only 10 minutes (and 1€) away from the Duomo stop, in the heart of the city. If you want to see something of the city en route, take the no. 60 bus from the station to Piazza del Duomo. If you walk (a good half-hour), follow Via Pisani through the district of high-rise office buildings that have sprung up around the station in the past several decades to the equally cheerless Piazza della Repubblica, and from there continue south on busy Via Turati and Via Manzoni to Piazza del Duomo.

Chances are, you will arrive at Stazione Centrale, but some trains serve Milan's other train stations: **Cadorna** (with service to and from Como and Malpensa airport, for example), **Stazione Lambrate** (with service to and from Bergamo and other points east), and **Porta Garibaldi** (with service to and from Lecco and other points north). Conveniently, all three of these stations, along with Stazione Centrale, are on the same subway line: Linea 2, the green one.

By Bus   Given Milan's excellent rail links with other cities in Lombardy and throughout Italy, it's usually unnecessary to travel by long-distance buses, which tend to take longer and cost more than the trains do. If you choose to travel by intercity bus, expect to arrive at and depart from Autostradale, in front of the Castello Sforzesco on Piazza Castello (Metro: Cairoli). The ticket office is open daily 6:30am to 9:30pm (✆ **166-845-010** is a special toll number for which you are charged .30€ a minute). A few common runs are the 12 daily buses to and from Turin (2½ hr.) and, for Milanese ski and outdoor enthusiasts, the two daily buses (more in the winter) to and from the hard-to-reach-by-train Aosta (allow 3½ hr.).

By Car   Milan is well served by Italy's superhighway (autostrada) system. The A1 links Milan with Florence and Rome (Florence is a little over 3 hr. away by car, Rome is a little under 6 hr.), and the A4 connects Milan with Verona and Venice to the east and Turin to the west (Venice is about 2½ hr. from Milan by car; Turin is a little over 1 hr.). Driving and parking in Milan are not experiences to be relished, and much of the central city is closed to traffic. Many hotels make parking arrangements for guests; ask when you reserve a room.

By Plane   Both of Milan's major airports are operated by **SEA** (✆ **02-7485-2200;** www.sea-aeroportimilano.it).

Milan Malpensa, 45km (28 miles) northwest of the center, is Milan's major international airport and an important hub for southern Europe. When it was unveiled in 2000, it was crowned worst major airport in Europe by the continent's official oversight committee in terms of flight delays and convenience, and while many of the kinks have been worked out since then, it's home to Alitalia and its strike-prone staff. (For general information about Malpensa, call ✆ **02-7485-2200.**) Conveniently, a 40-minute express train heads half-hourly to Cadorna train station, which is, frankly, just as central as the so-named Stazione Centrale. Then there are the Malpensa shuttle buses, which will take you directly to Centrale in 50 minutes without traffic. The train, known as **Malpensa Express** (✆ **02-8511-4382** or 199-151-152), costs 11€, while two bus companies run a combined five times per hour (**Malpensa Shuttle** ✆ **02-5858-3185** or **Malpensa Bus Express** ✆ **02-3391-0794**), and cost 7.50€. The buses may be cheaper, but you run the risk of hitting the legendary traffic of the Northern 'burbs. By taxi, the trip into town costs a wallet-stripping 75€, but it's the best choice when you are running late and it's not rush hour, or else after midnight, when it is indeed the only choice.

Bus Tours

CitySightseeing Milano (✆ **02-867-131;** www.milano.city-sightseeing.it) has a choice of two 90-minute bus tours of Milan's major sights, with buses leaving every 30 minutes from in front of the Castello, daily 9:30am to 6:30pm. Each tour costs 20€, and commentary is available in English.

Milan Linate, only 7km (4¼ miles) east of the center, handles some European flights and many domestic flights. Call ✆ **02-7485-2200** for information. *Starfly* (✆ **02-5858-7237**) runs from Linate to Stazione Centrale every 30 minutes from 6am to 10pm; allow 30 minutes for the trip. Purchase tickets (4.50€) on the bus. You can also take a city bus, no. 73, to and from Linate, from the southeast corner of Piazza San Babila, a few blocks east of the Duomo (1€). The trip into town by taxi costs about 18€ to 20€.

Malpensa Shuttle buses (✆ **02-5858-3185**) also connect Malpensa and Linate about every 2 hours from 9:30am to 4:30pm. The trip takes 1¼ hours and costs 10€.

Budget-minded flyers should consider a third option, **Orio Al Serio** (www.orioaeroporto.it) airport. Located just outside Bergamo and about an hour from Milan, Orio al Serio is a hub for discount airline Ryanair and a number of other budget airlines. Direct buses run to and from Stazione Centrale several times an hour.

VISITOR INFORMATION   The main **Azienda di Promozione Turistica (APT) tourist office** is on the north side of Piazza del Duomo at the corner of Via Silvio Pellico (✆ **02-7740-4343;** www.visitamilano.it). Hours are Monday to Saturday from 8:45am to 1pm and 2 to 6pm, Sunday from 9am to 1pm and 2 to 5pm. There is also an **office in Stazione Centrale** (✆ **02-7740-4318**), open Monday to Saturday 9am to 6pm, and Sunday 9am to 1pm and 2 to 5pm.

These offices issue free maps, museum guides, hotel and restaurant listings, and a wealth of other useful information, including the free *Milano Mese.* The Piazza del Duomo APT office recently installed a computer that lets you download audio guides—in English and Italian—via Bluetooth to your cellphone, which you can listen to while you are walking around town. The free monthly events brochure *Hello Milano* (www.hellomilano.it) and expatriate monthly *EasyMilano* all have listings of museum exhibitions, performances, and other events.

CITY LAYOUT   Think of Milan as a series of concentric circles radiating from the Piazza del Duomo at the center. Within the inner circle, once enclosed by the city walls, are many of the churches, museums, and shops that will consume your visiting hours. For a general overview of the lay of the land, obtain one of the serviceable maps, with indices, that the tourist offices provide for free.

The city's major neighborhoods encircle the hub, **Piazza del Duomo.** Looking west from the Duomo, you can see the imposing **Castello Sforzesco** at one end of the well-heeled Magenta neighborhood. You can walk to the Castello in about 15 minutes by following first Piazza dei Mercanti or Via Orefici to Piazza Cordusio and, from there, Via Dante. The other major tourist draw in Magenta is the church of **Santa Maria delle Grazie;** to reach it, you'll leave Via Dante at Via Meravigli, which becomes Corso Magenta and leads to the church (total walking time from Piazza del Duomo to the church is about 20 min.).

Cruising the Canals

Milan's *navigli,* or canals, are a focal point of the preparation for **Expo 2015,** but you can already start exploring these canals. **Navigli Lombardi** (© 02-3322-7336;** www.naviglilombardi.it) offers **canal tours** which bring visitors around Milan's historic canals and offer a new perspective on the historic Navigli neighborhood. Tour boats leave seven times a day from the top of the Naviglio Grande where it meets the Darsena, Milan's old port that connects the Naviglio Grande with the Naviglio Pavese. Cruises are 55 minutes long and cost 12€ for adults, 10€ for seniors, and 8€ for children 11 and under; children 5 and under ride free.

Heading north from the Piazza del Duomo, walk through the glass-enclosed shopping center (the world's first), the **Galleria Vittorio Emanuele II.** Emerging from the northern end of the Galleria, you'll be just steps away from **Piazza della Scala** and Milan's famous **opera house.** A 5-minute walk northeast along Via Manzoni takes you to Via Montenapoleone and the city's **high-fashion shopping district,** the epicenter of Italian design. A walk of about 10 minutes north of Piazza della Scala along Via Brera brings you into the atmospheric **Brera neighborhood**—once home to the city's brothels, which has gentrified over the last 3 or 4 decades—where cobblestone streets and old *palazzi* surround the city's major art collection, the **Pinacoteca di Brera.**

Another neighborhood to set your sights on is **Ticinese/Navigli,** usually referred to by the last word in that combination, which translates as "canals." Beyond the central city and due south of Piazza del Duomo, the Navigli's old quays follow what remains of an elaborate canal system, designed in part by Leonardo da Vinci, that once laced through the city. The moody charm of these waterways is not lost on young Milanese who are converting old lofts and moving into former quarters of the working classes. The attendant bars, shops, and restaurants on the ground floors have appeared to serve their needs, making this a great neighborhood to head to for dinner and then stay for the nightlife (it's also the only bit of town open through Aug, when cars are banned and all the eateries and bars move tables outside to fill the boisterous quays). You can walk to the Navigli in about 30 minutes from Piazza del Duomo by following Via Torino southwest to Corso di Porta Ticinese, but a Metro ride to Porta Genova will get you there more quickly.

GETTING AROUND   An extensive **subway system (Metropolitana Milanese), trams,** and **buses** make it very easy to move around Milan. The Metro closes at midnight (1am on Sat nights); buses and trams run all night. Tickets good for one Metro ride (or 1¼ hr. of surface transportation) cost 1€. You can also purchase a ticket good for unlimited travel for 1 day (3€) or 2 days (5.50€). Tickets are available at Metro stations and at newsstands. Stamp your ticket when you board a bus or tram—you can be slapped with a hefty fine if you don't. For information about Milan public transportation, visit the ATM information office in the Duomo Metro stop, open Monday through Saturday 7:45am to 7:15pm (© **800-808-181;** www.atm-mi.it).

(Fast Facts Milan

American Express The office is a few blocks from the Duomo, at Via Larga 4, on the corner with Via dell'Orso (℃ **02-721-041**), and is open Monday to Friday from 9am to 5:30pm (Metro: Duomo). Card members can arrange cash advances, receive mail (the postal code is 20121), and wire money.

Bookstores Milan has two English-language bookshops. The **American Bookstore,** between the Duomo and Castello Sforzesco at Via Camperio 16, at the corner with Via Dante (℃ **02-878-920**), is open Monday 1 to 7pm, Tuesday to Saturday 10am to 7pm (Metro: Cardusio). The **English Bookshop,** Via Ariosto at Via Mascheroni 12 (℃ **02-469-4468**), is open Monday to Saturday 9am to 8pm. **Rizzoli,** the glamorous outlet of one of Italy's leading publishers, in the Galleria Vittorio Emanuele (℃ **02-8646-1071**), also has some English-language titles, as well as a sumptuous collection of art and photo books; it's open daily 9am to 9pm (opens at 10am Sun and closes at 8pm Sun and Mon). For English-language newspapers and magazines, check out the **newsstands** in Stazione Centrale and around Piazza del Duomo.

Consulates The **U.S. Consulate** is at Via Principe Amedeo 2/10 (℃ **02-290-351**); it's open Monday through Friday from 8:30am to 12:30pm and 1:30 to 5:30pm (Metro: Turati). The **Canadian Consulate** closed its office in Milan in 2007; emergencies can be directed to the embassy in Rome at ℃ **06-854-441.** The **British Consulate,** Via San Paolo 7 (℃ **02-723-001**), is open Monday to Friday from 9:15am to 12:15pm and 2:15 to 3:45pm (Metro: Duomo). The **Australian Consulate,** at Via Borgogna 2 (℃ **02-777-041**), is open Monday to Friday 9am to 5pm (Fri closes at 4:15pm; Metro: San Babila). And the **New Zealand Consulate,** at Via Terraggio 17 (℃ **02-721-70001**), is open Monday to Friday from 9 to 11am (Metro: Cadorna or Sant'Ambrogio).

Crime For police emergencies, dial ℃ **113** (a free call); you can reach the English-speaking staff of the tourist police at ℃ **02-863-701.** There is a police station in Stazione Centrale; and the main station, the **Questura,** is just west of the Giardini Pubblici, at Via Fatebenefratelli 11 (℃ **02-622-61;** Metro: Turati). Milan is generally safe, with some exceptions, especially at night, including the public gardens, Parco Sempione, and the area to the west of Stazione Centrale.

Drugstores Pharmacies rotate 24-hour shifts; dial ℃ **192** to find pharmacies that are open around the clock on a given day, or look for signs posted in most pharmacies announcing which shop is keeping a 24-hour schedule. The **Farmacia Stazione Centrale** (℃ **02-669-0735**), in the train station, is open 24 hours daily and some of the staff speak English.

Emergencies The general number for emergencies is ℃ **113.** For the police, call ℃ **112;** for first aid or an ambulance, dial ℃ **118.** All are free calls.

Hospitals The **Ospedale Maggiore Policlinico** (℃ **02-5503-1**) is centrally located a 5-minute walk southeast of the Duomo at Via Francesco Sforza 35 (Metro: Duomo or Missori). Some of the medical personnel here speak English.

Internet As you exit the front of the Centrale train station, on your left is **Grazia Internet Café** (Piazza Duca D'Aosta 14; ℃ **02-670-0543**), with some 30 PCs and the possibility to pay for Wi-Fi access, open Monday to Friday 8am to midnight and Saturday and Sunday 9am to midnight. Also **FNAC** (☎ **02-869-541**), on Via Torino about a 10-minute walk south of the Duomo, is open Monday to Saturday 9:30am to 8pm and Sunday 11am to 8pm.

Laundry Self-service laundromats are sprinkled all over the city; one chain is **Ondablu** (www.ondablu.net), which has several locations in Milan.

Lost Property The lost-baggage number for **Malpensa** and **Linate** airports is ☎ **02-7485-2200.** The English-speaking staff at these offices handles luggage that has gone astray on most airlines serving the airports, though a few airlines maintain their own lost-baggage services. The **lost and found at Stazione Centrale** is open daily from 8am to 4pm.

Luggage Storage The luggage storage office in Stazione Centrale is open daily from 6am to 11:50pm; the fee is 4€ per piece of baggage for the first 5 hours. It is an additional .60€ per hour for the next 6 hours and then an additional .20€ per hour after that.

Post Office The main post office, **Poste e Telecommunicazioni,** is just west of Piazza del Duomo at Via Cordusio 4 (☎ **02-7248-2126;** Metro: Cardusio). Windows are open Monday to Friday 8am to 7pm and Saturday 8:30am to 1:50pm. Most branch offices are open Monday to Saturday 8:30am to 1:30pm and some until 7pm. There is a post office in Stazione Centrale, open Monday through Friday 8am to 5:30pm and Saturday 8:15am to 3:30pm.

Taxis To find a taxi in Milan, walk to the nearest taxi stand, usually located near major *piazze* and major Metro stops. In the center, there are taxi stands at Piazza Duomo and Piazza della Scala. Or call a **radio taxi** at ☎ **02-4040,** 02-6767, 02-8585, 02-5353, or 02-8383 (the desk staff at many hotels will be happy to do this for you, even if you are not a guest). Cab meters start at 3.10€ and add a nighttime surcharge of 3.10€ and a Sunday surcharge of 1.55€.

Telephones Throughout Milan, you'll find public telephones that accept phone cards *(carta telefonica),* which you can purchase at tobacco shops in denominations of 5€. You can also make calls from the Telecom Italia offices in Stazione Centrale and in the Galleria Vittorio Emanuele, both open daily from 8am to 9:30pm. Some phones in these offices also accept major credit cards, and you can buy Italian phone cards on the premises. The area code for Milan is ☎ **02.**

Travel Services For budget travel options, including low-cost flights, contact **Zani Viaggi,** Foro Bonaparte 76 near the castle (☎ **02-867-131**), open Monday through Saturday from 9am to 7pm. Students and those under 25 should try **CTS (Centro Turistico Studentesco),** Piazza Santo Stefano 12 (☎ **02-7621-2311**), open Monday through Friday from 9:30am to 6:30pm and Saturday 10am to 1pm. This is the most centrally located CTS, but there are five others sprinkled around town.

WHAT TO SEE & DO
The Top Sights
Castello Sforzesco ★★ ⓥ Though it's been clumsily restored many times, most recently at the end of the 19th century, this fortresslike castle continues to evoke Milan's

Shopping Binges & Soccer Pilgrimages

Bus trips organized by **Zani Viaggi** are tailored to all sorts of appetites, especially those that Milan cultivates so well, namely fashion and soccer. Excursions to the Serravalle outlet village (about 90 min. outside town); FoxTown (just across the border in Switzerland, about 1 hr. drive); and the Meazza stadium, also know as San Siro (home to Inter and AC Milan, in the outskirts), leave from Foro Bonaparte 76, in front of the Castello. The shopping trip to Serravalle departs at 1:30pm daily and costs 20€ round-trip, with return buses leaving Serravalle at 7pm. There is a daily bus to FoxTown (20€) at 2pm, with a return at 7pm. The 3-hour trip to Meazza stadium (28€) leaves Thursday at 10:30am, though it is sometimes can-celled if there are not enough people signed up. For more info, call ☎ **02-867-131** or visit www.zaniviaggi.it.

two most powerful medieval and Renaissance families, the Visconti and the Sforza. The Visconti built the castle in the 14th century, and the Sforza, who married into the Vis-conti clan and eclipsed them in power, reconstructed it in 1450. The most influential residents were Ludovico il Moro and Beatrice d'Este (he of the Sforza and she of the famous Este family of Ferrara). After ill-advisedly calling the French into Italy at the end of the 15th century, Ludovico died in the dungeons of a château in the Loire valley—but not before the couple made the Castello and Milan one of Italy's great centers of the Renaissance. It was they who commissioned the works by Bramante and Leonardo da Vinci, and these splendors can be viewed on a stroll through the miles of salons that surround the Castello's enormous courtyard.

The salons house a series of small city-administered museums known collectively as the Civici Musei Castello Sforzesco. They include a *pinacoteca* with works by Bellini, Correggio, and Magenta, and the extensive holdings of the Museo d'Arte Antica, filled with Egyptian funerary objects, prehistoric finds from Lombardy, and the last work of 89-year-old Michelangelo, his unfinished ***Rondanini Pietà*** ★★.

Piazza Castello. ☎ **02-8846-3700.** Free admission to the castle courtyard daily 7am–6pm (7pm in sum-mer). Civici Musei Castell Sforzesco Tues–Sun 9:00am–5:30pm. Metro: Cairoli, Cadorna, or Lanza.

Duomo ★★★   When Milanese think something is taking too long, they refer to it as *la fabbrica del duomo*—the making of the Duomo, a reference to the 5 centuries it took to complete the magnificent Gothic cathedral that rises from the center of the city. (This turn of phrase could also describe the church's recent 6-year renovation, which kept the building behind scaffolding until 2009.) The last of Italy's great Gothic structures— begun by the ruling Visconti family in 1386—is the fourth-largest church in the world (after St. Peter's in Rome, Seville's cathedral, and a new one on the Ivory Coast), with 135 marble spires, a stunning triangular facade, and 3,400-some statues flanking the massive but airy, almost fanciful exterior.

The cavernous **interior,** lit by brilliant stained-glass windows, seats 40,000 but is unusually spartan and serene, divided into five aisles by a sea of 52 columns. The poet Shelley used to sit and read Dante here amid monuments that include a gruesomely graphic statue of ***St. Bartholomew Flayed*** ★ and the tombs of Giacomo de Medici, two Visconti, and many cardinals and archbishops. Another British visitor, Alfred, Lord Ten-nyson, rhapsodized about the **view** of the Alps from the **roof** ★★★ (elevators on the church's exterior northeast corner; stairs on the exterior north side), where you get to wander amid the Gothic pinnacles, saintly statues, and flying buttresses. You are joined high above Milan by the spire-top gold statue of *Madonnina* (the little Madonna), the city's beloved protectress.

Back on terra firma, the **crypt** contains the remains of San Carlo Borromeo, one of the early cardinals of Milan. A far more interesting descent is the one down the staircase to the right of the main entrance to the **Battistero Paleocristiano,** the ruins of a 4th-century baptistery believed to be where Saint Ambrose baptized Saint Augustine.

The Duomo houses many of its treasures across the piazza from the right transept in the *Museo del Duomo* section of Milan's Palazzo Reale—closed for restoration in 2009 without a definite reopening date. Among the legions of statuary saints is a gem of a painting by Jacopo Tintoretto, *Christ at the Temple,* and some riveting displays chronicling the construction of the cathedral. Adjoining this is the **Museo Civico d'Arte Contemporanea (Civic Museum of Contemporary Art),** with works by living artists and such masters as De Chirico and Modigliani.

Though the scaffolding from its most recent restoration is down, visitors may still encounter some restoration work. The most recent restoration, completed in 2009, brought luster back to the church's white marble. Other restoration projects will continue on the sides and interior of the Duomo in a never-ending bid to keep the building looking its best.

Piazza del Duomo. ✆ **02-7202-3375.** Duomo: Free admission; daily 8:30am–6:45pm. Roof: Admission 5€ by stairs, 8€ with elevator; daily 7am–5:45pm (until 9pm Apr–Sept). Crypt: Admission 2€; daily 9am–noon and 2:30–6pm. Baptistery: Admission 2€; Tues–Sun 10am–noon and 3–5pm. Museum: Before its closing, admission was 6€ adults, 3€ children younger than 18 and seniors over 65; Tues–Sun 9:30am–12:30pm and 3–6pm. Metro: Duomo.

Galleria Vittorio Emanuele II ★★ Milan's late-19th-century version of a mall is this wonderful steel-and-glass-covered, cross-shaped arcade. The elegant Galleria is the prototype of the enclosed shopping malls that were to become the hallmark of 20th-century consumerism. It's safe to say that none of the imitators have come close to matching the Galleria for style and flair. The designer of this urban marvel, Giuseppe Mengoni, didn't live to see the Milanese embrace his creation: He tripped and fell from a girder a few days before the Galleria opened in 1878. His shopping mall par excellence provides a lovely route between the Duomo and La Scala and is a fine locale for watching the flocks of well-dressed Milanese—you'll understand why the Galleria is called *Il Salotto di Milano* (Milan's drawing room).

Just off Piazza del Duomo and Piazza della Scala. Metro: Duomo.

Pinacoteca di Brera ★★★ This 17th-century *palazzo* houses one of Italy's finest collections of medieval and Renaissance art; it's inarguably the world's finest collection of northern Italian painting. The concentration of so many masterpieces here is the work of Napoleon, who used the *palazzo* as the repository for the art he confiscated from public and private holdings throughout northern Italy; fittingly, a bronze likeness of the emperor greets you upon entering the courtyard. Just as a sampling of what you'll encounter in these 40 or so rooms, three of Italy's greatest masterpieces hang here: Andrea Mantegna's amazingly foreshortened *Dead Christ* ★★★, Raphael's **Betrothal of the Virgin** ★★★, and Piero della Francesca's *Madonna with Saints* ★★ (the *Montefeltro Altarpiece*). It is an indication of this museum's ability to overwhelm visitors that the last

Tuscan and Umbrian painters.

Paintings are continually being rearranged; in the first rooms, you will encounter the museum's sizeable collection of 20th-century paintings. From there you enter several galleries of sumptuous Venetian works, including Jacopo Tintoretto's *Finding of the Body of St. Mark* ★, in which the dead saint eerily confronts appropriately startled grave robbers who come upon his corpse. Caravaggio (*Supper at Emmaus* ★★ is his masterpiece here) is surrounded by works of his followers, and just beyond is a room devoted to works by foreigners; among them is Rembrandt's *Portrait of a Young Woman.* Given Napoleon's fondness for the Venetian schools, the final rooms are again filled with works from that city, including Canaletto's *View of the Grand Canal.*

You can rent an audio guide for 3.50€, or 5.50€ for two. Cheap guided tours are available weekdays if you book at least 2 to 3 days ahead, Saturday at 3pm and 5pm, and Sunday at 10am, noon, 3pm, and 5pm.

Via Brera 28. (✆ **02-722-631** or 02-8942-1146 (for reservations). www.brera.beniculturali.it. Admission 10€. Tues–Sun 8:30am–7:15pm. Bus: 61 or 97. Metro: Lanza or Montenapoleone. Tram: 1, 4, 8, 12, 14, or 27.

Santa Maria delle Grazie/The Last Supper ★★

What draws so many visitors to Milan is the *Cenacolo Vinciano,* Leonardo da Vinci's *The Last Supper.* From 1495 to 1497, Leonardo painted this poignant portrayal of confusion and betrayal for the far wall of the refectory when this was a Dominican convent. Aldous Huxley called this fresco the "saddest work of art in the world," a comment in part on the deterioration that set in even before the paint had dried on the moisture-ridden walls. (It probably didn't help that the monks cooked their meals here.) The fresco got a lot of well-intentioned but poorly executed "touching up" in the 18th and 19th centuries, though a recent lengthy restoration has done away with these centuries of overpainting, as well as tried to undo the damage wrought by the clumsy patching and damage inflicted when Napoleon's troops used the wall for target practice, and from when Allied bombing during World War II tore off the room's roof, leaving the fresco exposed to the elements for 3 years.

In short, *The Last Supper* is a mere shadow of the work the artist intended it to be, but the work, which captures the moment when Christ told his Apostles that one of them would betray him, remains amazingly powerful and evocative nonetheless. Only 25 people are allowed to view the fresco at one time, and they must pass through a series of devices that remove pollutants from clothing. Accordingly, lines are long and tickets usually sold out days in advance. I'm serious: If you don't book ahead, you'll likely be turned away at the door, even in the dead of winter when you'd expect the place to be empty (tour bus groups swallow up inordinately large batches of tickets, leaving precious few for poor do-it-yourself travelers).

Often overlooked are the other treasures of the late-15th-century church itself, foremost among them the fine dome and other architectural innovations by one of the great architects of the High Renaissance, Donato Bramante (one of the first architects of St. Peter's in Rome). To one side of the apse, decorated in marble and terra cotta, is a lovely cloister.

Piazza Santa Maria delle Grazie. *The Last Supper:* (✆ **02-9280-0362.** www.cenacolovinciano.org. Admission 6.50€ plus a booking fee of 1.50€; 3.25€ plus 1.50€ booking fee for EU citizens 18 to 25; EU citizens under 18 and over 65 pay only the booking fee. Tues–Sun 8:15am–7pm. Church: (✆ **02-467-6111.** Free admission. Mon–Sat 7:30am–noon and 3–7pm; Sun 7:20am–12:15pm and 3:30–9pm (may close earlier in winter). Metro: Cadona or Conciliazione.

A Last-Minute Invitation to The Last Supper

The Cenacolo Viniciano, the building that holds *The Last Supper,* is one of the most popular museums on a tourist's itinerary of Milan—if not the only museum some tourists see. Space is limited, and thus so are reservations, so lots of folks leave the ticket booth disappointed. If you can't get a reservation, in a pinch you can take a guided 3-hour bus and walking tour of Milan's top attractions and take advantage of the guaranteed admission to *The Last Supper* as part of the package. **Autostradale** (*C* **02-3391-0794**) tours leave every day except Monday at 9:30am from near the taxi stand in Piazza Duomo; tours cost 55€. **Zani Viaggi** has a similar tour with guaranteed admission to *The Last Supper* that also costs 55€ and leaves from Foro Buonaparte in front of the castle Tuesday to Sunday at 9:30am and 2:30pm.

More Sights

Chiesa di San Lorenzo Maggiore ★
The oldest church in Milan attests to the days when the city was the capital of the Western Roman Empire. This 4th-century, early-Christian structure has been rebuilt and altered many times over the centuries (its dome, the highest in Milan, is a 16th-c. embellishment), but it still retains the flavor of its roots in its octagonal floor plan and a few surviving remnants. These include 5th-century mosaics in the Cappella di Sant'Aquilino, which you enter from the atrium. A sarcophagus in the chapel is said to enshrine the remains of Galla Placidia, sister of Honorius, last emperor of Rome and wife of Ataulf, king of the Visigoths. Ironically, her mausoleum is one of the mosaic masterworks of Ravenna, and she is most likely buried in Rome, where she died. You'll be rewarded with a glimpse at even earlier history if you follow the stairs from behind the altar to a cryptlike room that contains what remains of a Roman amphitheater.

Corso di Porta Ticinese *C* **02-8940-4129.** www.sanlorenzomaggiore.com. Church: Free admission. Cappella di Sant'Aquilino: 2€ adults, 1€ children. Mon–Sat 7:30am–12:30pm and 2:30–6:45pm; Sun 7:30am–6:45pm. Bus: 94. Metro: Missori. Tram: 3.

Chiesa di Sant'Ambrogio ★
From the basilica that he constructed on this site in the 4th century A.D.—when he was bishop of Milan and the city, in turn, was briefly capital of the Western Roman Empire—Saint Ambrose had a profound effect on the development of the early church. Little remains of Ambrose's church, but the 11th-century structure built in its place, and renovated many times since, is remarkable. It has a striking atrium, lined with columned porticos and opening on the side to the brick facade, with two ranks of loggias and, on either side, a bell tower. Look carefully at the door on the left, where you'll see a relief of Saint Ambrose. The church of Sant'Ambrogio set a standard for Lombard Romanesque architecture that you'll see imitated many times on your travels through Lombardy.

On your wanderings through the three-aisle nave you'll come upon a gold altar from Charlemagne's days in Milan, and, in the right aisle, the all-too-scant remains of a Tiepolo fresco cycle, most of it blown into oblivion by World War II bombs. The little that remains of the original church is the Sacello di San Vittore in Ciel d'Oro, a little

Milan on Two Wheels

The city began a bike-sharing program at the end of 2008 that, though directed at locals and commuters, can actually provide an excellent way for tourists to see more of the city. For 2.50€ a day and 6€ a week, you can buy a pass that gives you unlimited use of the bikes for 30-minute increments. You pick up a bike in one of the many racks around town and leave it at another. Buy your pass at the **ATM offices** at the Duomo Metro stop or at the Centrale and Cadorna train stations (✆ **800-80-8181**). Milan has also managed to cut down on traffic by instituting a fee for cars to enter the city center during the day from Monday to Friday.

chapel in which the cupola glows with 5th-century mosaics of saints (enter from the right aisle). The skeletal remains of Ambrose himself are on view in the crypt. As you leave the main church from the left aisle, you'll see one of the "later" additions: another work of the great architect Bramante—his Portico dell Canonica, lined with elegant columns, some of which are sculpted to resemble tree trunks.

Piazza Sant'Ambrogio 15. ✆ **02-8645-0895.** www.santambrogio-basilica.it. Church: Free admission. Sacello di San Vittore: 2€. Mon–Sat 9:00am–noon and 2:30–6:30pm. Bus: 50, 58, or 94. Metro: Sant'Ambrogio.

Chiesa Santa Maria Presso San Satiro   What makes this beautiful church, just south of Piazza del Duomo, so exquisite is what it doesn't have—space. Stymied by not being able to expand the T-shaped apse to classical Renaissance, cross-shaped proportions, the architect Bramante created a marvelous relief behind the high altar. The effect of the *trompe l'oeil* columns and arches is not entirely convincing, but it is nonetheless magical. Another gem lies to the rear of the left transept: the Cappella della Pietà, so called for the 15th-century terra-cotta *Pietà* it now houses; the Cappella was built in the 9th century to honor Saint Satiro, the brother of Saint Ambrose. The namesake statue is not the most alluring adornment in this charming little structure; it's the lovely Byzantine frescoes and Romanesque columns that will catch your eye. While this little-visited complex is now eclipsed by other, more famous Milan churches, it was an important pilgrimage site in the 13th and 14th centuries, after news spread through Christendom that an image of the Madonna here shed real blood when stabbed.

Via Torino (at Via Speronari). Free admission. Daily 9am–noon and 2:30–6pm. Metro: Duomo or Missori.

Civica Galleria d'Arte Moderna (Civic Gallery of Modern Art)   This sumptuous *palazzo,* where Napoleon and his stepson, Eugene de Beauharnais, lived, houses a collection that is "modern" in the true 19th-century sense. The salons are filled with works by Lombardians and other Italian painters who embraced trends from France. More familiar are works by Cézanne, Gauguin, and other non-Italian modernists also included in the galleries (in a section housing the noted Grassi Collection), but it's fascinating to see the same dreamy landscapes and the flight from creeping industrialism reflected in the works of lesser-known Italian artists. The upper floors of the museum house the equestrian works of 20th-century sculptor Marino Marini.

MILAN & LOMBARDY

9

MILAN (MILANO)

In the Villa Reale. Via Palestro 16. ℂ **02-7634-0809.** www.gam-milano.com. Free admission. Daily 9am–1pm and 2–5:30pm. Metro: Porta Venezia.

Civico Museo Archeologico ★ (Value)

The most fascinating finds in this sizable repository of civilizations past are the everyday items from Milan's Roman era—tools, eating utensils, jewelry, and some exquisite and remarkably well-preserved glassware. The exhibits, which seem to fill every corner of the 16th-century monastery in which the museum is housed, also include Greek, Etruscan, and Roman pieces from throughout Italy; there's even a section devoted to ancient remains from Ghandara, India. You can get a glimpse of Roman architecture in the garden, where two Roman towers, a section of a road, and part of the walls enclosing the settlement of Mediolanum (once capital of the Western Roman Empire) remain on their original setting. Rarely in Italy do museums this good (even if the collections are relatively modest in size) come so cheap, so take full advantage.

Corso Magenta 15. ℂ **02-8645-0011.** Admission: 2€ adults, 1€ over 65, free 17 and under. Tues–Sun 9:00am–1pm and 2–5:30pm. Metro: Cadorna.

Museo Diocesano ★ (Finds)

This museum is set just inside the Parco delle Basiliche—a collection of grass-fringed paths, playgrounds, and volleyball courts created just after World War II on the site of Milan's ancient execution grounds. It brings together the best works from small church museums and treasuries across Milan and Lombardy, from the Church of Sant'Ambrogio on down, alongside works of religious significance donated from various private collections. Among the works from the now-defunct Museo di Sant'Ambrogio is an important 10th-century carved wooden tondo of *S. Ambrogio.*

The Crespi collections include many 14th- and early-15th-century Gothic works by such Tuscan-school masters as Bernardo Daddi, Sano di Pietro, Agnolo Gaddi, Taddeo di Bartolo, Bicci di Lorenzo, and Nardo di Cione. The giant, excellently preserved 1510 altarpiece of saints by Marco d'Oggiono came from the church of S. Stefano.

Other paintings include works by the prolific 16th-century Campi clan of Cremona; a Tintoretto *Christ and the Adulterer;* a luminous *Crucifixion with Mary Magdalene* by Francesco Hayez; many late-15th-century paintings by local boy Il Begognone; 17th- and 18th-century landscapes by Panini, Zuccarelli, and others; and Previati's important Via Crucis cycles from the 1880s. And what would a church museum be without a passel of 17th-century Flemish tapestries?

Corso di Porta Ticinese 95. ℂ **02-8942-0019.** www.museodiocesano.it. Admission 8€ adults, 5€ ages 6–18 and seniors over 65 (all visitors pay 4€ on Tues). Tues–Sun 10am–6pm (to 10pm Thurs). Metro: Missori or Sant'Ambrogio.

Museo Nazionale della Scienza e della Tecnologia Leonardo da Vinci (Leonardo da Vinci National Museum of Science and Technology) ★

The heart and soul of this engaging museum are the **working scale models** ★★ of Leonardo's submarines, airplanes, and other engineering feats that, for the most part, the master only ever invented on paper (each exhibit includes a reproduction of his drawings and a model of his creations). This former Benedictine monastery and its beautiful cloisters are also filled with planes, trains, carriages, sewing machines, typewriters, optical devices, and other exhibits, including some enchanting re-creations of workshops, all of which makes up one of the world's leading mechanical and scientific collections.

Via San Vittore 21. ℂ **02-485-551.** www.museoscienza.org. Admission 8€ adults, 6€ younger than 18 and older than 60. Tues–Fri 9:30am–5pm; Sat–Sun 9:30am–6:30pm. Metro: Sant'Ambrogio.

Museo Poldi-Pezzoli ★★ The pleasant effect of seeing the Bellinis, Botticellis, and Tiepolos amid these salons is reminiscent of a visit to other private collections, such as the Frick Collection in New York City and the Isabella Stewart Gardner Museum in Boston. This stunning treasure trove leans a bit toward Venetian painters (such as Francesco Guardi's elegantly moody *Grey Lagoon*), but also ventures widely throughout Italian painting and into the northern and Flemish schools. It was amassed by 19th-century collector Giacomo Poldi-Pezzoli, who donated his villa and its treasures to the city in 1881. Antonio Pollaiuolo's *Portrait of a Young Woman* is often likened to the *Mona Lisa,* in that it is a haunting image you will recognize immediately upon seeing it. The collections also include porcelain, watches, jewels, and many of the *palazzo*'s original furnishings.

Computer terminals let you explore bits of the collections not currently on display, especially arms and armor, the best of which are housed in an elaborate *pietra serena* room designed by Pomodoro. The museum offers free audio guides.

Via Manzoni 12. (𝄐 **02-794-889.** www.museopoldipezzoli.it. Admission 8€ adults, 5.50€ for ages 11–18 and seniors under 60. Tues–Sun 10am–6pm. Metro: Duomo or Montenapoleone. Tram: 2.

Pinacoteca Ambrosiana ★★ Much to the appreciation of art lovers who waited through the late 1990s for the museum to reopen, this exquisite collection is housed in newly restored galleries. The collection focuses on treasures from the 15th through 17th centuries: An *Adoration* by Titian, Raphael's cartoon for his *School of Athens* in the Vatican, Botticelli's *Madonna and Angels,* Caravaggio's *Basket of Fruit* (his only still life), and other stunning works hang in a series of intimate rooms. Notable (or infamous) among the paintings is *Portrait of a Musician,* attributed to Leonardo but, according to many scholars, of dubious provenance; if it is indeed a Leonardo, the haunting painting is the only portrait of his to hang in an Italian museum. The adjoining Biblioteca Ambrosiana—open (except for special exhibitions) only to scholars—houses a wealth of Renaissance literaria, including the letters of Lucrezia Borgia and a strand of her hair. The most notable holdings, though, are Leonardo's *Codice Atlantico,* 1,750 drawings and jottings the master did between 1478 and 1519. These and the library's other volumes, including a rich collection of medieval manuscripts, are frequently put on view to the public; at these times, an entrance fee of 10€ allows entrance to both the library and the art gallery.

Piazza Pio XI 2. (𝄐 **02-806-921.** www.ambrosiana.it. Admission 8€ adults, 5€ children. Tues–Sun 10am–5:30pm. Metro: Cordusio or Duomo.

SHOPPING

The best fashion gazing is to be done along four adjoining streets north of the Duomo known collectively as the **Quadrilatero d'Oro (Golden Quadrilateral): Via Montenapoleone, Della Spiga, Via Borgospesso,** and **Via Sant'Andrea,** lined with Milan's most expensive high-fashion emporia. From Piazza della Scala, follow Via Manzoni a few blocks north or take the Metro to Via Montenapoleone. The main artery of this shopping heartland is Via Montenapoleone, lined with the most chichi boutiques and most elegant fashion outlets, with parallel Via della Spiga running a close second.

For more Milanese shopping, cruise wide Corso Buenos Aires (northeast of the center and just east of Stazione Centrale—follow Via Vitruvio from Piazza Duca d'Aosta in front of the station; Metro stops Lima and Loreto are the gateways to this bargain stretch), home to a little bit of everything, from shops that hand-sew men's dress shirts to CD megastores. As it crosses Piazza Oberdan/Piazza Venezia heading south, it becomes Corso Venezia and the stores move up the scale very quickly.

Milan is home to the flagship stores of a litany of designers: Armani, Krizia, Versace, Ermenegildo Zegna, Missoni, Moschino, Mila Schön, and Trussardi.

With high fashion, chillingly expensive boutiques, and designer labels, it all comes down to personal taste, so I'll just let you know where to find the top names in town (but largely only Italian names—who comes to Milan to shop for Calvin Klein?), and you can steer your shopping cravings whither you will.

One store, though, deserves a visit whether you're into his übertrendy designs or not: The Grand Central of Italian fashion is the flagship **Armani Megastore,** Via Manzoni 31, near La Scala (✆ **02-7231-8600;** Metro: Montenapoleone). This flagship store (and offices) covers 743 sq. m (8,000 sq. ft.) with outlets for Giorgio Armani's high-fashion creations: the Emporio Armani and Armani Jeans lines, plus the new Armani Casa selection of home furnishings, as well as flower, book, and art shops; a high-tech Sony electronics boutique/play center in the basement; and an Emporio Café and branch of New York's Nobu sushi bar. An Armani hotel being built on the top floors is scheduled to open in 2010.

Of course, other major labels also have Milan addresses. Here are some of the most popular: **Dolce e Gabbana** carries women's wear at Via della Spiga no. 2 (✆ **02-7600-1155;** www.dolcegabbana.it; Metro: San Babila); menswear is nearby at Via della Spiga no. 26 (✆ **02-799-950;** Metro: Montenapoleone), and its youth-oriented fashions are at Corso Venezia 7 (✆ **02-7600-4091;** Metro: Palestro). **Etro** has its lines of clothing for men and women, along with accessories, at Via Montenapoleone 5 (✆ **02-7600-5450;** www.etro.it; Metro: Montenapoleone), with a discount outlet at Via Spartaco 3.

Ermenegildo Zegna began as a textile house in 1910 (they still weave their own fabrics) and, since the late 1960s, has turned to making elegant, ready-to-wear men's suits that look custom tailored, sold in Milan at Via P. Verri 3 (✆ **02-7600-6437;** www.zegna.com; Metro: Montenapoleone or San Babila).

Though in the past few years it has finally started to go out of fashion, a fur coat has long, long been de rigueur for all Italian women heading out for an evening. Without a doubt, one of Italy's top purveyors of furs is **Fendi,** Via Sant'Andrea 16 (✆ **02-7602-1617;** www.fendi.com; Metro: Montenapoleone or San Babila).

The firm that shod Hollywood's stars during its later golden era, **Ferragamo** has an outlet for men's shoes at Via Montenapoleone 20 (✆ **02-7600-3117** or 02-7600-6660; www.ferragamo.it; Metro: Montenapoleone), and for women's shoes at Via Montenapoleone 3 (✆ **02-7600-0054;** Metro: Montenapoleone or San Babila).

Gianfranco Ferré sells women's wear and accessories at Via Sant'Andrea 15 (✆ **02-794-864;** www.gianfrancoferre.com; Metro: Montenapoleone or San Babila); the men's lines are at Corso Venezia 6. Florentine leather specialist **Gucci** has a Milan outlet for bags, accessories, and clothing for men and women at Via Montenapoleone 27 (✆ **02-771-271;** Metro: San Babila or Montenapoleone).

Several designer boutiques in Milan are devoted to women's wear, and women's wear only. They include **Krizia,** Via della Spiga 23 (✆ **02-7600-8429;** www.krizia.it; Metro: Montenapoleone or San Babila); **Laura Biagiotti,** Via Borgospesso 19 (✆ **02-799-659;** Metro: Montenapoleone or San Babila); and **Max Mara,** on Corso Vittorio Emanuele where it crosses Galleria de Cristoforis (✆ **02-7600-8849;** Metro: San Babila).

Mila Schön's elegant clothing for women and men is displayed in a neoclassical *palazzo,* along with accessories, perfumes, and linens, at Via Manzoni 45 (✆ **02-781-190;** www.milaschon.com; Metro: Montenapoleone or San Babila). **Miu Miu** carries women's

Last Shoe Shine in Milan

Charging about 2€ per customer and spending a lifetime bent over wingtips, the average shoe shiner has few illusions about a career of fame and fortune. But while fortune never did find Carlo Santacroce, fame finally landed on his footrests. For his last decade of his career, Santacroce was known far and wide as the last surviving **shoe shiner** in Milan. He retired in 2009.

Throughout his 30-year career in the city, he had seen southerners like himself carrying stools from one street corner to the next, only to be told by police that shoe shining is not allowed on the sidewalks. The peddlers were told to work out of a storefront, an expense that few could afford. When the market dried up—even Santacroce's celebrity customers no longer stopped by—competition disappeared, and he served the city's well-heeled on his own.

His chair and footrests sat by the restrooms in the **Palestro** subway station, in a space he rented from the city's transportation agency. A handwritten sign announced his price for shoes and boots.

"In Naples, when I was growing up, there'd be a long line for a shine," he said in an interview in his final years as a shoe shiner. "Now people do it on their own. Those hotel machines," he sniffed, "they only brush off the dust."

As a child, Carlo made a living in postwar Naples by polishing U.S. soldiers' boots. He knew his leather. From the condition of the material, Santacroce said he could tell what the wearer did for a living. Still, the dapper-dressed 76-year-old professed, with the proper maintenance, even the lowest underling can look like the boss. "My father once told me, and I'll never forget this, if someone has a clean-shaven face, wears a tie, and his shoes are well polished, he's a *signore,* even if he doesn't have a lira in his pocket."

Sadly, since he has retired, tourists now have to settle for the hotel shoe-shine machines.

wear and shoes at Corso Venezia 3 (© **02-7601-4448;** www.miumiu.com; Metro: Palestro). **Missoni**'s colorful sweaters for men and women can be found at Via Sant'Andrea at Via Bagutta (© **02-7600-3555;** www.missoni.com; Metro: Montenapoleone or San Babila). **Moschino** has men's and children's wear at Via Durini 14 (© **02-7600-4320;** Metro: San Babila) and women's wear at Via Sant'Andrea 12 (© **02-7600-0832;** www.moschino.com; Metro: Montenapoleone or San Babila).

Prada maintains several outlets across town for its minimalist red-stripe fashions, none of them cheap! There's a bit of everything (men's and women's wear, accessories, and jewelry) in their high-profile boutique at the crossing of the Galleria Vittorio Emanuele 63 (© **02-876-979;** www.prada.com; Metro: San Babila); menswear, shoes, and accessories at Via Montenapoleone 8 (© **02-7602-0273;** Metro: Montenapoleone or San Babila); women's wear and accessories at Via Sant'Andrea 21 (© **02-7600-1426;** Metro: Montenapoleone or San Babila); bags, shoes, and accessories at Via della Spiga 1 (© **02-7600-8636;** Metro: Montenapoleone or San Babila); and, nearby, even an underwear branch at Via della Spiga 5 (© **02-7601-4448;** Metro: Montenapoleone or San Babila).

Milan in Style

Everyone knows Milan to be a fashion hub, with visitors flocking to Armani superstores and Dolce & Gabbana boutiques while ticking off the **fashion shows** (www.cameramoda.it) on their calendars: late September and late February for women's apparel, January and June for men's apparel.

What many foreigners forget, though, is that Milan does not just draw the line for clothing. It also dreams up some of the sexiest cars, couches, and kitchenware that Italy has to offer.

You know that **Alfa Romeo,** while built in Turin, is designed in Milan by just taking a look at the logo: It sports the city's red cross on the left, taken from its Crusaders' tunics, and the serpent favored by the ruling Visconti family on the right. The names of Alfa's models should also give some indication of which city rules the roost: the Milano, the Visconti, the Monza, and so forth. (Chevrolet and GM would later borrow some of these model names, though unfortunately not the designs themselves.)

For just about any other type of household mechanical device, if it looks good, chances are it was also designed in Lombardy or Piedmont. For example, **Pininfarina, Alessi,** and the **Memphis Group** are all from Turin or Milan or somewhere in between.

Alessi, founded on the shores of Lake Orta, counted within its stable of architects such leading lights as Philippe Starck and Ettore Sottsass. But in 1980, the latter went on to form the Memphis Group, poaching some of the other top talent from his former employer as well. The event that launched the start-up group to fame was the 1981 edition of the Salone del Mobile, an annual furniture design show that draws industry leaders and tourists from around the globe.

Trussardi sells men's and women's wear as well as accessories at Via Sant'Andrea 5 (© 02-781-878; www.trussardi.com; Metro: Montenapoleone or San Babila). **Ungaro**'s full line of men's and women's wear, accessories, bags, and shoes is at Via Montenapoleone 27 (© 02-784-256; www.ungaro.com; Metro: Montenapoleone or San Babila). **Valentino** menswear is kept at Via Montenapoleone 20 (© 02-7602-0285; www.valentino.it; Metro: Montenapoleone or San Babila); the women's wear is sold at Via Santo Spirito 3 (© 02-7600-6478; Metro: Montenapoleone). **Versace** carries its men's and women's wear and accessories in its shop at Via Montenapoleone 11 (© 02-7600-1982; www.versace.com; Metro: Montenapoleone or San Babila).

Designer Discounts

If your fashion sense is greater than your credit line, don't despair: Even the most expensive clothing of the Armani ilk is usually less expensive in Italy than it is abroad, and citywide *saldi* (sales) run from early January into early February and again in late June and July.

Inspired by the window displays in the **Quadrilatero,** you can scour the racks of shops elsewhere for designer seconds, last year's fashions, imitations, and other bargains. The

The **Salone del Mobile** (www.cosmit.it) is nothing like what a casual customer would expect out of a furniture show. Held in mid-April, it brings a lot more than just the latest designs in kitchens, living rooms, bathrooms, and lighting fixtures. It is essentially a contemporary art museum, complete with installation art and spectacles that fascinate even the least design-conscious observer. Most of all, it is the top excuse for Milan to throw parties that regular people actually have a chance of attending.

If you're not here in April, not to worry—the latest models tend to make their way into galleries and design stores around the city right away, making for a nice, city-wide tour of the latest living-room curves. Start off at **Galleria Post Design,** Via della Moscova 27 (© **02-655-4731;** www.memphis-milano.it), which is the flagship store of the Memphis movement. Admire a multicolored bookshelf that could double as contemporary sculpture, and an assortment of rugs, lamps, and more. Even more avant-garde is **Dilmos,** Piazza San Marco 1 (© **02-2900-2437;** www.dilmos.com), which almost crosses the line as a museum space rather than a retail store.

If, on the other hand, you're just looking to pick up a sleek, spider-shaped juicer by Starck or a stainless-steel toothpick holder, check out **Alessi,** Corso Matteotti 9 (© **02-796-726;** www.alessi.com). If you just happen to be driving in the lakes region (or have a few hours to kill between flights at Malpensa), it might be worth stopping in for a few bargains at Alessi's **factory outlet** in Crusinallo, Via Privata Alessi (© **0323-868-611**). Your kitchen counter will thank you.

best place to begin is **Il Salvagente,** several blocks east of the Quadrilatero off Corso XXII Marzo at Via Fratelli Bronzetti 16 (© **02-7611-0328;** Metro: San Babila), where you can browse through an enormous collection of designer clothing for men, women, and children (mostly smaller sizes) at wholesale prices. **DMagazine,** Via Montenapoleone 26 (© **02-7600-6027;** Metro: Montenapoleone), may sit on the boutique-lined main shopping drag, but its merchandise is pure discount overstock from big labels such as Armani, Prada, and Fendi.

Another haven for fashionistas looking for slightly eccentric designer clothes on a budget is the **Ticinese/Navigli.** Women can shop at **Anna Fabiano** on Corso di Porta Ticinese 40 (© **02-5811-2348** or 5830-6111; Metro: Sant'Ambrogio). Fabiano, who learned her tricks while designing for Fiorucci, favors linear cuts and mixing different types of fabrics to create an original style with a 1960s feel. Another Navigli stop is *Mauro Leone,* on Corso di Porta Ticinese 60 and 103 (© **02-8942-9167;** www.mauroleone.com), where you will find all types of well-priced, Italian-made women's shoes. **Biffi,** on Corso Genova 5/6 (© **02-831-1601;** www.biffi.com; Metro: San Agostino), attracts fashion-conscious hordes of both sexes in search of designer labels and the store's own designs.

Some of the best Milanese fashion deals can be found in stores that are tucked into some of the less trodden and more atmospheric medieval alleys of the city center. On one of those streets, you will find **Donatella Pellini** (✆ **02-7201-0199**), at Via Morigi 9, selling her own line of beautiful costume jewelry that looks like the real deal. In the Morigi shop, she sells her romantic and minimalist creations made with glass and synthetic resin; for more flamboyant costume jewelry, visit Pellini's shops on Via Manzoni 20 (✆ **02-7600-8084**) and on Corso Magenta 11 (✆ **02-7201-0569**).

If you are fond of colors and not afraid to wear them, visit the two tiny **Gallo** shops on Via Manzoni 16/b (✆ **02-783-602**) and Via Durini 26 (✆ **02-7600-2023**), where you'll find their signature multicolored striped socks, along with multicolored scarves, gloves, and T-shirts. The socks won't seem cheap compared with what you buy at Target, but a pair will give you an affordable piece of Milan fashion to bring home—even if you couldn't afford that Armani suit or Prada bag you had your eye on. If you missed out while in town, don't despair, because Gallo also has a brightly colored distributor at Milan's Linate airport.

For designer shoes at a discount to go with the new socks, look no further than ***Rufus,*** Via Vitruvio 35 (✆ **02-204-9648;** Metro: Centrale or Lima), which carries men's and women's styles from lots of labels for under 80€.

Housewares

The top name in Italian houseware design since 1921 has been **Alessi,** which has hired the likes of Michael Graves, Philippe Starck, Frank Ghery, and Ettore Sottsass to design the latest in teakettles, bottle openers, and other housewares since the late 1980s. They maintain a main showroom at Corso Matteotti 9 (✆ **02-795-726;** Metro: San Babila) and a sales outlet at Via Montenapoleone 19 (✆ **02-7602-1199;** www.alessi.com; Metro: Montenapoleone).

The 1980s were really part of a renaissance of Italian industrial design. This is the era when design team **Memphis,** led by Ettore Sottsass, virtually reinvented the art form, recruiting the best and brightest architects and designers to turn their talents to lighting fixtures, kitchen appliances, office supplies, even furnishings. Italian style has stayed at the very top of the designer housewares market (sharing popularity space with Scandinavian furniture) ever since. Part of the Memphis credo was to create the new modern and then bow out before they became establishment (they self-destructed in 1988). You can still find their influential designs in many houseware shops and in the showroom **Post Design** at Via della Moscova 27 (✆ **02-655-4731;** Metro: Turati or Moscova).

Linens

For Milanese design to dress the bed, visit **Frette,** Via Visconti di Modrone (✆ **02-498-9756;** www.frette.it; Metro: San Babila). This outlet of the high-fashion linen house offers discounts on the tablecloths, towels, robes, and bedding that it supplies to the world's top hotels. They have other stores at Via Montenapoleone 21 (✆ **02-7600-8094;** Metro: Montenapoleone), Via Manzoni 11 (✆ **02-801-327;** Metro: Montenapoleone), Corso Buenos Aires 82 (✆ **02-2940-5016;** Metro: Lima), Corso Vercelli 23/25 (✆ **02-498-9756;** Metro: Conciliazione), and Via Torino 42 (✆ **02-8645-2281;** Metro: Duomo).

The elegant swirling paisleys of **Etro,** Via Montenapoleone 5 (✆ **02-7600-5049;** www.etro.it; Metro: Montenapoleone), have been decorating the walls, furniture covers, and accessories in some of Italy's richest and aristocratic homes since 1969. They've since expanded into full lines of clothing and leather goods, as well as perfumes and accessories

(the latter are available at the branch on the corner of Via P. Verri and Via Bigli;
© **02-7600-5450;** Metro: Montenapoleone).

Spacci Bassetti, Via Procaccini 32 (© **02-3450-125;** Metro: Garibaldi F.S., but closer on tram no. 33 or 94), is a discount outlet of the august Bassetti line of high-quality linen, and the huge space offers the luxurious towels and sheets at excellent prices. They have regular (nondiscount) stores at Corso Buenos Aires 52 (© **02-2940-0048;** Metro: Lima) and Via Botta 7A (© **02-5518-3191;** Metro: Porta Romana).

WHERE TO STAY

While you can pay more for a hotel room in Milan than you would almost anywhere else in Europe, there are also some decent accommodations at reasonable prices in good locations. It's difficult to find rooms in any price category when fashion shows and trade fairs are in full swing (often in Oct and Mar). Many hotels raise their prices at these times, too. August is low season, and hotels are often willing to bring prices down considerably, as they will sometimes on slow weekends. Rule of thumb: Always ask for the lowest possible rate when booking and be prepared to bargain.

Inveterate shoppers will want to stay in the Brera and Magenta neighborhoods, avid sightseers near the Duomo; budgeters will find the most options near the central train station and along Corso Buenos Aires.

Near the Duomo
Moderate
Hotel Gran Duca di York   This 19th-century *palazzo* was once used by the Duomo for housing visiting church officials. The midsize rooms are simple, with hideous 1970s built-in units, tile floors, and plush easy chairs—a few even get small terraces. The thin windows do not keep out all the traffic noise (which isn't constant, but is noticeable). What it lacks in style, it makes up for in location—just off the main pedestrian drag leading from the cathedral to Castello Sforzesco.

Via Moneta 1A (a block off Piazza Edison), 20123 Milano. © **02-874-863.** Fax 02-869-0344. www.ducadi york.com. 33 units. 175€–225€ double. Rates include continental breakfast. AE, MC, V. Parking in nearby garage 25€. Metro: Cordusio. **Amenities:** Bar; babysitting; concierge; room service. *In room:* A/C, TV, hair dryer, minibar.

Hotel Santa Marta   It's a shame this hotel is not as charming as the quiet cobblestone alley it inhabits, nor as spotless as the beautiful courtyards of its neighbors. It is in desperate need of a restoration and some better cleaners. Really the only reason it is included in this guide is the lack of decently priced alternatives downtown during the peak visitor weeks. If they're full, they'll send you to their sister hotel, the Hotel Rovello (see below).

Via Santa Marta 4, 20123 Milano. © **02-805-2090.** 15 units. 140€–190€ double; 170€–260€ triple. Rates include continental breakfast. AE, DC, MC, V. Parking in nearby garage 21€. Closed 15 days in Aug. Metro: Cordusio or Duomo. Tram: 1, 2, 3, 4, 12, 14, 15, 19, 20, 24, or 27. **Amenities:** Bar; smoke-free rooms. *In room:* A/C, TV, hair dryer.

Inexpensive
Hotel Aliseo   A 10-minute walk south of the Duomo, this attractive *pensione* (once known as the Hotel Ullrich) offers a lot of comfort in addition to its good location. The management is friendly, and rooms are furnished with pleasant modern pieces and decent beds. A renovation in 2005 added bathrooms to most of the doubles and all of the triples, though there are still doubles with shared bathrooms—large, spanking-clean bathrooms in the hallway. Rooms on the street side open to small balconies but are noisier than those

overlooking the *cortile* (courtyard). One of the bathrooms is equipped with a washing machine, and guests can do a load for 10€. As it is one of the few good-priced alternatives remaining in the city center, the Aliseo books up quickly, so be sure to call ahead.

Corso Italia 6, 21023 Milano. ℂ **02-8645-0156.** www.hotelaliseo.it. 12 units. 50€–75€ double with shared bathroom; 75€–110€ double with bathroom; 80€–110€ triple with shared bathroom; 100€–130€ triple with bathroom. Continental breakfast included. MC, V. Metro: Duomo. Tram: 15, 24, 65, or 94. **Amenities:** Concierge; Internet. *In room:* TV, hair dryer.

In Magenta & Brera
Very Expensive

Four Seasons Hotel Milano ★★★   Milan's top five-star deluxe hotel lies just off Via Montenapoleone, the city's swankiest shopping boulevard. Though lacking the antiques-drawn style of its competitor, the Grand Hotel et de Milan (see below), it offers more luxuries. Its central core retains many touches, including the lovely garden-planted cloisters, rediscovered during the 7-year restructuring that by 1993 had turned this 1476 convent into a hotel (the frescoes in the lobby hint that this room was once the convent's church). Rooms are spacious, with thick rugs on modern parquet; designer chairs in comfy sitting areas, large marble-sheathed bathrooms with heated floors, and walk-in closets. "Superior" rooms are on the street (protected from noise by effective double-paned windows), with queen-size beds. "Executive" suites have a midsize sitting area and can be connected to deluxe doubles to form a family suite. Five bi-level suites on the ground floor of the cloisters have vaulted ceilings, mostly re-frescoed (though one bit of the original painting remains), with a split-level sitting area and bedroom and the bathroom underneath, all overlooking a neighbor's quiet grassy garden. A wing in a *vecchia Milano* house features a central courtyard; a balcony runs along every level, each of which contains five rooms and suites.

Via Gesù 8, 20121 Milano. ℂ **800-332-3442** in the U.S., or 02-77-088 in Italy. Fax 02-7708-5000. www.fourseasons.com/milan. 118 units. 726€ superior double; 869€ deluxe double; 924€ junior suite; 1,595€ executive suite. (Prices do not include taxes and service charges.) AE, DC, MC, V. Valet parking 51€. Bus: 54, 64, 65, or 73. Metro: Montenapoleone. **Amenities:** 2 restaurants (elegant restaurant under celebrity chef, casual restaurant open lunch and dinner); bar; babysitting; bikes; children's program and kids' menu; concierge; executive-level rooms; small exercise room; room service; smoke-free rooms; Wi-Fi. *In room:* A/C, TV/VCR, hair dryer, Internet, kitchenette (in Royal and Presidential suites), minibar.

Grand Hotel et de Milan ★★★   Perhaps Milan's most intimate luxury hotel, the Grand Hotel et De Milan balances family management with refined service in an 1863 building. It's perfectly positioned near La Scala (3 blocks away) and the shopping of Via Montenapoleone just across the street. The bathrooms are done in marble; rooms feature king-size beds and heavy curtains, chipped stone floors, elegant upholstered furnishings, and muted skylight domes. "Deluxe" rooms are larger than "classic" rooms and have genuine antiques. The suites genuinely feel like small apartments rather than hotel rooms, with their homelike arrangement of antiques and piped-in opera (perhaps something by Maria Callas, once a regular guest). The presidential Giuseppe Verdi Suite is preserved with the same furnishings as when the composer spent his last 30 years here (he even died in this room), including the desk upon which he composed many operas.

Via Manzoni 29, 20121 Milano. ℂ **02-723-141.** Fax 02-8646-0861. www.grandhoteletdemilan.it. 95 units. 455€ classic double; 535€ deluxe double; 645€ junior suite; 900€–1,175€ suite. Breakfast 35€. AE, DC, MC, V. Garage parking 43€. Metro: Montenapoleone. **Amenities:** 2 Italian/Milanese restaurants; bar; babysitting; bikes; concierge; large exercise room; room service. *In room:* A/C, TV w/pay movies, hair dryer, minibar, Wi-Fi (12€ per hour or 27€ for 24 hr.).

Hotel Manzoni ★★ This was a simple, midscale, laid-back hotel relatively cheap for this high-rent neighborhood, but after a renovation that lasted more than 4 years, the Manzoni reopened in 2008 with a new sparkle and prices to match. Upon entering, you are greeted by an opulent lobby that includes slick marble floors, inviting couches, original paintings, and a grand piano. The rooms have also been renewed, with wood paneling, mirrors, and flatscreen televisions.

Via Santo Spirito 20, 20121 Milano. ☎ **02-7600-5700.** Fax 02-784-212. www.hotelmanzoni.com. 52 units. 300€–500€ double; 480€–650€ suite. AE, DC, MC, V. Parking 30€ in garage. Metro: Montenapoleone. **Amenities:** Home-cooking restaurant; bar; babysitting; concierge; exercise room; room service; smoke-free rooms. *In room:* A/C, TV, hair dryer, minibar, Wi-Fi.

Expensive

Antica Locanda Solferino ★★★ If this charming old hotel in the arty Brera neighborhood hadn't been discovered long ago by members of the fashion world and film stars (this was Marcello Mastroianni's preferred Milan hostelry), you would consider it a find. The rooms have more character than they do modern comforts, but, to the loyal guests, the eclectic smattering of country antiques and Art Nouveau pieces more than compensates for the absence of minibars. Nor do the repeat customers seem to mind that some of the bathrooms are minuscule (though modern). The rooms on the tiny courtyard are quieter, but those on the street have plant-filled balconies (the best is no. 10 on the corner, if you don't mind a tub rather than a shower). The management also rents two apartments in the neighborhood, each with a living room, a bedroom, and a Jacuzzi, with the decorations straight out of the 1960s.

Via Castelfidardo 2, 20121 Milano. ☎ **02-657-0129** or 02-659-2706. Fax 02-657-1361. www.anticalocanda solferino.it. 11 units. 180€–400€ double; 50€ extra bed. Rates include in-room breakfast. AE, DC, MC, V. Parking 25€ in nearby garage. Closed 2–3 weeks in mid-Aug. Metro: Moscova or Repubblica. Tram/Bus: 11, 29, 30, 33, 41, 43, or 94. **Amenities:** Concierge. *In room:* A/C (2 rooms), TV, hair dryer, free Wi-Fi.

Moderate

Ariosto Hotel ★★ Tucked away in a residential neighborhood of apartment houses and old villas near the Santa Maria delle Grazie church, the Ariosto is a refreshingly quiet retreat—all the more so because many of the newly refurbished rooms face a private garden, and some open onto balconies overlooking it. All the rooms are decorated with wood-and-wicker furnishings, shiny parquet floors, and hand-painted wallpaper. Most of the rooms are decently sized, but singles tend to be skinny. Many of the doubles have separate dressing areas off the tile or stone bathrooms, which are equipped with hair dryers and a few with Jacuzzis. There's free Internet access in the lobby and satellite movie channels on the televisions.

Via Ariosto 22, 20145 Milano. ☎ **02-481-7844.** Fax 02-498-0516. www.hotelariosto.com. 48 units. 99€–290€ double; 109€–310€ triple. Rates include breakfast. AE, DC, MC, V. Parking 25€ in garage. Closed 3 weeks in Aug. Metro: Conciliazione. Tram/Bus: 29, 30, 61, 67, or 68. **Amenities:** Restaurant (Italian); bar; bikes; concierge; room service; smoke-free rooms. *In room:* A/C, TV w/pay movies, hair dryer, minibar, Wi-Fi (15€ per 24 hr.).

Hotel Giulio Cesare Because of its somewhat worn-down appearance, this old establishment is not the sort of place that will provide a very memorable stay, but it is convenient. Some rooms are quirkily shaped, and a few singles are cramped, but the white tile floors and minimalist furnishings are starkly modern. The bathrooms are equipped with stall showers and flat towels. Management can be as brusque and unsmiling as the decor. This is one of several similarly priced hotels on the block, a generally quiet street tucked away off Via Dante between the Duomo and La Scala in one direction and the Castello in the other. (See the London Hotel and Hotel Rovello listings, below.)

Via Rovello 10, 20121 Milano. ☏ **02-7200-3915.** Fax 02-7200-2179. www.giuliocesarehotel.it. 25 units. 100€–150€ double. Rates include breakfast. AE, DC, MC, V. Metro: Cordusio. Tram/Bus: 1, 2, 3, 4, 12, 14, 18, 19, 20, 24, or 27. **Amenities:** Bar; room service. *In room:* A/C, TV, hair dryer, Wi-Fi.

Hotel Rovello   The Rovello is one of those hotels you recommend simply because when Milan is full, there aren't a whole lot of good options, but frankly, the place is a bit frayed at the edges these days. That said, it sits on a quiet street between the Duomo and the Castello. The unusually large guest rooms occupy the first and second floors of a centuries-old building and incorporate many of the original architectural details, including exposed timbers and beam ceilings. Many of the rooms have dressing areas and large bathrooms. A breakfast of rolls and coffee is served in a sunny room off the lobby.

Via Rovello 18, 20121 Milano. ☏ **02-8646-4654.** Fax 02-7202-3656. www.hotel-rovello.it. 10 units. 120€–220€ double; 150€–260€ triple. AE, DC, MC, V. Parking 15€ in nearby garage. Metro: Cordusio. Tram/Bus: 1, 2, 3, 4, 12, 14, 18, 19, 20, 24, or 27. **Amenities:** Bar; concierge; Internet. *In room:* A/C, TV, hair dryer.

London Hotel ★   Unlike its neighbor the Hotel Giulio Cesare (see above), the London sticks to its old-fashioned ways, and even the prices are hesitant to budge. The big fireplace and cozy green velvet furniture in the lobby say a lot about the friendly comfort level that brings guests back time after time. Just beyond the lobby, there's a bar where beverages are available almost 'round-the-clock; guests can purchase cappuccino or a continental breakfast in the morning. Upstairs the rooms look like they haven't been redecorated in a number of decades, but they're roomy and bright, and the heavy old furnishings lend a charm very much in keeping with the ambience of the hotel. Rooms on the first floor tend to be the largest, and they get smaller as you go up. Guests receive a 10% discount at the trattoria next door, the Opera Prima.

Via Rovello 3, 20121 Milano. ☏ **02-7202-0166.** Fax 02-8057-037. www.hotellondonmilano.com. 29 units. 110€–180€ double; 160€–200€ triple. Continental breakfast 8€. MC, V. Parking 25€ in nearby garage. Closed Aug and Christmas. Metro: Cordusio. Tram/Bus: 1, 2, 3, 4, 12, 14, 18, 19, 20, 24, or 27. **Amenities:** Bar; concierge; room service. *In room:* A/C, TV, hair dryer, Wi-Fi.

East of the Duomo
Moderate
Hotel Pavone   The family-run Pavone is good in a pinch, when everything else is full. It sits just off the Corso di Porta Vittoria, around the corner from the Palace of Justice, and about a 15-minute walk from the Duomo. The surrounding neighborhood is more geared to business than to the tourist trade, but the friendly staff is eager to point out nearby restaurants and other conveniences, which are plentiful. Rooms are spartan, with gray tile floors and no-nonsense Scandinavian-style furniture, but most are unusually large and cloaked in a silence unusual for big-city Milan. For the quietest rest, though, check in to no. 12, 14, 16, or 18, all of which overlook a garden. The beds in most singles are extra-wide. Many rooms are outfitted as triples and are large enough to accommodate an extra bed, making this a fine choice for families.

Via Dandolo 2 (off Corso di Porta Vittoria), 20122 Milano. ☏ **02-5519-2133.** Fax 02-5519-2421. www.hotelpavone.com. 24 units. 76€–260€ double; 112€–350€ triple. AE, MC, V. Parking 10€. Tram: 12, 20, 23, 27, 60, or 73. **Amenities:** Bar; concierge; room service. *In room:* A/C, TV, hair dryer, Internet.

Inexpensive
Hotel America   Though this establishment is a bit off the beaten track in a middle-class neighborhood due east of Piazza del Duomo, it remains one of the better lower-priced

lodgings in Milan. Rooms occupy the fourth floor of an apartment house. Several have private bathrooms, and all are bright and nicely decorated with streamlined, wood-veneer modern furnishings—many sporting a thematic stars-and-stripes color scheme. The Rolling Stone music club, a fixture on the Milan nightlife scene, is on the ground floor of the building, a good reason to ask for a room facing the quieter *giardino* (garden) courtyard (no. 10 even has a balcony). The Duomo is about 20 minutes away by foot or 10 minutes by tram.

Corso XXII Marzo 32 (the block east of Piazza Emilia), 20135 Milano. ℂ **02-738-1865.** Fax 02-738-1490. www.milanohotelamerica.com. 10 units. 90€ double; 105€ triple. Rates include breakfast. AE, MC, V. Tram/Bus: 12, 27, 45, 60, 66, 73, or 92. **Amenities:** Bar; Internet. *In room:* A/C, TV.

Near Stazione Centrale & Corso Buenos Aires
Very Expensive
Le Meridien Gallia ★   This 1937 bastion of Liberty-style luxury rises near the main train station—a thoroughly uninteresting area a 15-minute taxi ride from the center. It is convenient for late arrivals or early departures, and while the neighborhood is trafficky, the hotel is well soundproofed. It's oriented toward business clients and conferences, so it's flush with amenities, but also charges expense-account rates. The granite columns and murals in the salon lend the hotel an antique air balanced by the modern art in the hallways. Each floor is done in a different pastel color scheme. The spacious, comfortable rooms are done in modern parquet (some are carpeted), with classy antiques and the occasional quirky touch such as a TV atop a column stump or a ceiling frescoed with puffy clouds. Bathrooms are clad in a variety of marbles, with heated towel racks, large tubs, and double sinks in all but "superior" type rooms. Superior rooms are recently renovated, a bit smaller than the deluxe version, but only slightly less fashionable (they retain the old, fairly fussy, repro Deco look).

Piazzale Duca d'Aosta 9, 20124 Milano. ℂ **02-678-5716.** Fax 02-6698-6942. www.lemeridiengallia.com. 235 units. 510€ standard double; 535€ superior double; 585€ deluxe double; from 750€ suite; extra bed 100€. Continental breakfast 25€; buffet breakfast 35€. AE, DC, MC, V. Parking 15€ at hotel or 31€ valet in garage. Metro: Centrale F.S. **Amenities:** Refined Italian restaurant; piano bar; babysitting; bikes; concierge; small exercise room; Jacuzzi; room service; sauna; smoke-free rooms. *In room:* A/C, TV w/pay movies, hair dryer, minibar, Wi-Fi.

Expensive
Doria Grand Hotel ★   This luxury hotel offers enormously discounted weekend prices (the lower rates below, applied Fri–Sun nights) that make it reasonable on weekends, most of August, and the Christmas/New Year's holiday (check for exact dates before booking; never applied during trade fairs). The Doria Grand is a large hotel near the station and is far more comfortable and stylish than most hotels in its luxury class. The good-size guest rooms are exquisitely appointed with handsome wood and marble-topped furniture; rich fabric wall coverings and draperies; and amenities such as linen sheets, satellite channels and pay-per-view, and bedroom slippers and bathrobes. The beautiful marble bathrooms are equipped with generous-size tubs, vanities, and a good selection of toiletries. A sumptuous buffet breakfast is served in a stylish room (where they also serve 28€ fixed-price menus at mealtimes), and Thursday and Friday evenings the piano bar becomes a jazz club.

Viale Andrea Doria 22, 20124 Milano. ℂ **02-6741-1411.** Fax 02-669-6669. www.doriagrandhotel.it. 124 units. 150€–400€ double; 300€–500€ suite. Rates include buffet breakfast. AE, DC, MC, V. Parking 30€ in garage. Metro: Loreto or Caiazzo. Tram: 1, 90, 91, or 92. **Amenities:** Restaurant; cafe; babysitting; concierge; room service; smoke-free rooms. *In room:* A/C, TV w/pay movies, hair dryer, minibar, Wi-Fi.

Hotel Due Giardini   This is a clean and bright budget choice in a neighborhood near the train station, where such offerings are scarce. As the name suggests, it abuts a pleasant garden with chirping birds and colorful flowers, where breakfast is served in warmer weather, and, as its two-star rating suggests, that's about the extent of the perks. The buzzword here is functionality: 24-hour reception, a small bar, and a sitting room flesh out the rest of the services. The location, while not the most characteristic area of the city, is conveniently nestled between Stazione Centrale and the shops of Corso Buenos Aires.

Via Benedetto Marcello 47, 20129 Milano. ✆ **02-2952-1093.** Fax 02-2951-6933. www.hotelduegiardini. it. 70€–160€ double; 90€–225€ triple. Rates include breakfast. MC, V. Parking free on street. Metro: Lima or Centrale. Tram: 5 or 33. **Amenities:** Bar. *In room:* A/C, TV, hair dryer.

Hotel Kennedy ⟨Value⟩   The name reflects the English-speaking management's fondness for the late president, and the family is genuinely welcoming to the many Americans who find their way to their *pensione* a block off the southern end of Corso Buenos Aires. Their homey establishment on the sixth floor of an office-and-apartment building (there's an elevator) is sparkling clean and offers basic accommodations in large, tile-floored rooms. No. 13 has a terrace, while no. 15 has a small balcony that even glimpses the spires of the Duomo in the distance. Amenities include a bar in the reception area, where coffee and soft drinks are available, as is a light breakfast of brioche and coffee that doesn't cost much more than it would in a cafe.

Viale Tunisia 6 (6th floor), 20124 Milano. ✆ **02-2940-0934.** Fax 02-2940-1253. www.kennedyhotel.it. 13 units, 3 with shower only, 5 with private bathroom. 55€–100€ double with shared bathroom; 65€–150€ double with private bathroom; 80€–180€ triple with private bathroom; 100€–200€ quad with private bathroom. Breakfast 4€. AE, DC, MC, V. Parking 20€ in nearby garage. Metro: Porta Venezia. Tram: 5 or 11. **Amenities:** Bar. *In room:* TV, hair dryer (on request), Internet.

Hotel Paganini ★ ⟨Value⟩   Occupying an old house off the north end of Corso Buenos Aires, ground zero for some rather lonely looking women on the street corners after 9pm, the Paganini appears to be a dismal option as you are buzzed in and walk up to the front desk. Still, the management goes to great lengths to keep this a clean, no-nonsense budget hotel: The guest rooms are large and bright, with high ceilings and solid beds. The one room with a private bathroom has wood floors and a ceiling decorated with molded stuccoes. The shared facilities are modern enough and kept spanking clean by the owners. The best rooms are in the rear, overlooking a huge private garden. There is much to be said for this location: The station is only a 10-minute walk way down Via Pergolsi, and if shopping is on your agenda, the nearby Corso Buenos Aires is one of the city's bargain fashion meccas.

Via Paganini 6, 20131 Milano. ✆ **02-204-7443.** 8 units, 1 with private bathroom. 60€ double. No breakfast. AE, DC, MC, V. Parking in garage across street 15€, free on street. Metro: Loreto. Tram/Bus: 33, 55, 55, 56, 56, 90, 91, or 93. **Amenities:** Concierge. *In room:* Hair dryer.

WHERE TO DINE

Geared to business, as the city is, Milanese are more willing than Italians elsewhere to break the sit-down-meal tradition and grab a sandwich or other light fare on the run. And with so many students and young professionals underfoot, Milan has no shortage of pizzerias and other low-cost eateries alongside its world-class dining options.

Near the Duomo

La Crêperie CREPERIE   About a 10-minute walk southeast of Piazza Duomo, this busy creperie is an ideal stop for a light lunch or a snack while visiting the nearby church of Sant'Ambrogio or Museo Nazionale di Scienza e di Tecnica. The far-ranging offerings include meal-like crepes such as *prosciutto e formaggio* (ham and cheese) or more dessert-like options (the Nutella creamy chocolate nut spread is highly recommended). There are a few value menus: Before 3pm, you can get one nondessert crepe, one sweet one, and a drink for 7€; until 9pm, you can get two "salty" ones, one dessert crepe, and a drink for 8.50€. The Italians split food like this into two categories: "sweet," *dolci,* and "salty," *salati.* A "sweet" crepe might have Nutella in it, a "salty" one, ham and cheese. The menu at La Crêperie is divided accordingly.

Via C. Corenti 21. ℂ **02-839-5913.** Crepes 3.50€–5€. No credit cards. Mon–Sat 11am–1am; Sun 4pm–midnight. Metro: Sant'Ambrogio.

Luini Panzerotti ★★ LIGHT FARE   A Milan institution since 1948, it's so good they've even opened a branch in London. At this stand-up counter near the Galleria, you'll have to elbow your way through a throng of well-dressed patrons to purchase the house specialty: *panzerotto,* a pocket of pizza crust stuffed with all sorts of ingredients, including the basic cheese-and-tomato. You'll also find many different kinds of panini here.

Via Santa Radegonda 16. ℂ **02-8646-1917.** www.luini.it. Panzerotto 3.50€. No credit cards. Mon 10am–5pm; Tues–Sat 10am–8pm. Closed Aug. Metro: Duomo.

Magenta & Brera

Da Claudio ★★ RAW BAR   One of Milan's oft-repeated idiosyncrasies is that it is a landlocked city and yet has the freshest fish in the country: The best catch is trucked up here from the shore every night to chase those bankers' euros. The best place to enjoy Milan's maritime bounty without dispensing a fortune is at this Brera fish market, which becomes a popular raw bar at night. Almost everyone goes for the mixed plate, which includes raw tuna, sea bass, salmon, red snapper, sturgeon, shrimp, prawns, and cod, or whatever else didn't sell that day. Order a plate for 13€ and enjoy it standing up at the counter (there are no seats) with a glass of *prosecco,* which is on the house. After more than 100 years in the same spot, in late 2009, Da Claudio moved around the corner to its current, more spacious location.

Via Cusani, 1. ℂ **02-80-56-857.** www.pescheriadaclaudio.it. Reservations not accepted. Mixed raw plate 13€–14€; half-dozen oysters 18€. AE, MC, V. Mon–Sat 11am–9:30pm. Metro: Lanza or Cordusio.

Il Verdi ★ VEGETARIAN   This trendy but cozy restaurant has earned the distinction of spawning the city's first yuppie scene in the '90s. Some things have changed since then: The menu is still healthy and the clientele relatively young, but now there is something for all tastes. The most popular dish seems to have remained the risotto with pears drizzled with balsamic vinegar, though the salads are perhaps the best in the city, especially those with crabmeat and avocados. The wine selection is also very good.

Piazza Mirabello 5. ℂ **02-659-0979.** Reservations not necessary. Primi 10€–16€; salads from 10€. AE, MC, V. Mon–Sat 12:30–2:15pm and 7:30pm–midnight. Metro: Turati.

Latteria ★★ MILANESE   The main business here at one time was dispensing milk and eggs to a press of neighborhood shoppers, but now the emphasis is on serving the La Brera neighborhood delicious, homemade fare in a room decorated with paintings and photographs of roses. The minestrone and other vegetable soups are delicious, as are the many variations of risotto, including some otherwise hard-to-find variations such as *riso al salto,* a delicious dish of leftover *risotto alla Milanese* that is fried with butter. The menu changes daily, and the friendly staff, including owners Arturo and Maria, won't mind

A Taste of Bitter Love

For some people, the allure is the signature salt shaker–shaped, neon red bottle, often neatly lined up on windowsills in restaurants and bars. Others know it for its placement in vintage Art Deco posters. For many people, it's simply a bitter alcoholic concoction that tastes like cough medicine. But for any self-respecting Milanese, it's the reward at the end of a hard day at work and the beginning of a good night on the town.

Love it or hate it, **Campari** is the soul of Milan and is at the heart of all its signature cocktails. Campari is a bitter alcoholic drink that was invented in 1860 in Novara, a city in the Piedmont region. Today, Campari is manufactured in Piedmont at the home of its sweeter friend, Cinzano. (The vermouth company was purchased by Campari Group in the 1990s. The group is now headquartered just outside Milan in Sesto San Giovanni, though all the drinks are manufactured just outside Turin.)

Together, Campari, vermouth, and a splash of seltzer make up the *americano,* a drink that is usually served in streetside cafes with an orange slice on its rim. Its cousin, the *negroni,* skips the seltzer in favor of gin and is also often served with orange garnishes; however, the *negroni* is often served without fruit at swankier night spots as the night goes on.

What is it that gives Campari its unique bitter and tangy essence? Only two people know. Local lore says that the secret blend of herbs is guarded by the manufacturing director and one other undisclosed custodian. One thing that is known, and frankly should have remained a secret, is the ingredient behind its almost fluorescent red hue: the squashed skeletons of South American insects. *Negroni,* anyone?

explaining the different dishes. The place is tiny and doesn't take bookings, so if you want to get one of the popular tables, arrive when it opens or wait until 8:30pm or later, when a few tables will free up as the early-dining tourist clientele clears out and the locals take over.

Via San Marco 24. ℂ **02-659-7653.** Reservations not accepted (and it fills up fast). Primi 10€–12€; secondi 8€–15€. No credit cards. Mon–Fri 12:30–2:30pm and 7:30–10pm. Metro: Moscova.

Peck ★★ (Value) DELI   Milan's most famous food emporium offers a wonderful selection of roast veal, risottos, *porchetta,* salads, aspics, cheeses, pastries, and other fare from its exquisite larder in this natty snack bar around the corner from its shop. If you choose to eat here, you will do so at a stand-up bar where, especially around lunchtime, it can be hard to find elbowroom. This shouldn't discourage you, though, because the pleasure of having access to such a cornucopia of delicacies at a reasonable price will be a gourmand's vision of paradise. By the way, their full-fledged restaurant around the corner at Via Victor Hugò 4 (ℂ **02-876-774**), **Cracco-Peck,** serves high-test traditional and creative cuisine, but with fixed-price tasting menus cresting at more than 100€, we thought maybe we'd skip it.

Via Spadari 9. ℂ **02-802-3161.** www.peck.it. Primi around 7€; secondi 9€–15€. AE, DC, MC, V. Mon–Sat 9:15am–7:30pm. Closed Jan 1–10 and July 1–20. Metro: Duomo.

Trattoria Milanese ★★★ MILANESE   Giuseppe and Antonella Villa preside with a watchful eye over the centuries-old premises (a restaurant since 1933), tucked into a narrow lane in one of the oldest sections of Milan, just west of the Duomo. In the three-beamed dining room, Milanese families and other patrons share the long, crowded tables. Giuseppe, in the kitchen, prepares what many patrons consider to be some of the city's best traditional fare. The *risotto alla Milanese,* with saffron and beef marrow, not surprisingly, is excellent, as is the minestrone that's served hot in the winter and at room temperature in the summer. The *costolette alla Milanese,* breaded and fried in butter, is even better here because only the choicest veal chops are used and it's served with the bone in, and the *osso buco* is cooked to perfection. If you want to try their twin specialties without pigging out, the dish listed as *risotto e osso buco* buys you a half-portion each of their *risotto alla Milanese* and the *osso buco* for 20€. Polenta with rich Gorgonzola cheese is one of the few nonmeat second courses. The attentive staff will help you choose an appropriate wine.

Via Santa Marta 11. ✆ **02-8645-1991.** Reservations required. Primi 9€–11€; secondi 14€–24€; *menù turistico* 39€ without wine. AE, DC, MC, V. Wed–Mon noon–3pm and 7–11:30pm. Metro: Cordusio.

Near Stazione Centrale & Corso Buenos Aires

Brek CAFETERIA   This outlet of Italy's popular cafeteria chain is centrally located just off Piazza San Babila and should not to be dismissed too quickly. Brek takes food, and its presentation, seriously. Pastas and risotto are made fresh; pork, veal, and chicken are roasted to order; and the large selection of cheeses would put many a formal restaurant to shame. Excellent wines and many kinds of beer are also available. Behind-the-counter service is friendly and helpful, and the country-style decor is quite attractive.

Piazzetta Umberto Giordano 1. ✆ **02-7602-3379.** www.brek.it. Reservations not accepted. Primi and pizza 3.50€–4.60€; secondi 3.20€–6.80€. AE, MC, V. Daily noon–3pm and 6:30–10:30pm. Metro: Stazione San Babila.

Da Abele ★ MILANESE   Once you get away from the sights and shops of the city center, you'll find yourself in some middle-class neighborhoods. Da Abele is tucked away in one, in a pleasant enclave of shops and apartment houses east of Stazione Centrale and north of the Corso Buenos Aires shopping strip (a few blocks north of Piazzale Loreto). This plain trattoria caters to local residents (hence its evening-only hours—they schedule reservations only before 8:30pm; afterward it's first-come, first-served) and serves a nice selection of soups (including a hearty seafood *zuppa di pesce*) and many kinds of risotto, including one with *frutti di mare* (a selection of fresh seafood) and others with fresh porcini in season. The amiable staff doesn't mind if you venture no farther into the menu, but if you do, there is a nice selection of roast meats as well. Sadly, they've joined that large percentage of shameful Italian businesses that used the arrival of the euro as an excuse to drastically inflate their prices.

Via Temperanza 5. ✆ **02-261-3855.** Reservations recommended. Primi 9€; secondi 12€–15€. MC, V. Tues–Sun 8–11:30pm. Closed July 20–Sept 1. Metro: Pasteur.

Joia ★★ VEGETARIAN   Milanese, who tend to be carnivorous, have embraced this refined vegetarian restaurant, just north of the public gardens, with great enthusiasm. Travelers may welcome the respite from northern Italy's orientation to heavy foods and will appreciate the light atmosphere offered by the blond-wood, neutral-toned dining rooms. Here the innovative vegetarian creations of Swiss chef Pietro Leemann incorporate the freshest vegetables and herbs, which appear in many traditional pasta dishes, such as *lasagne con zucchine pomodoro* (layered with zucchini and fresh tomatoes and served at room temperature), *ravioli di melanzana* (stuffed with eggplant), or tagliolini with a simple tomato sauce. Any of these first courses can be ordered as a main course, and many of the main courses can be ordered as starters. These secondi (second courses) include some excellent fish choices, as well as elaborate vegetables-only creations such as *melanzani viola al vapore con finferli* (steamed eggplant with chanterelle mushrooms). There's also a wonderful assortment of cheeses and, likewise, a long wine list. Joia has a Michelin star, so you will pay accordingly.

Via P. Castaldi 18. ℂ **02-2952-2124.** www.joia.it. Reservations highly recommended. Primi 18€–22€; secondi 27€–30€; tasting menu 45€–60€. AE, DC, MC, V. Mon–Fri noon–2:30pm and 7:30–11:30pm. Closed Aug. Metro: Repubblica.

In the Navigli

Al Pont de Ferr ★★ (Finds) ITALIAN   This is one of the more culinarily respectable of the dozens of restaurants around the Navigli, with tables set out on the flagstones overlooking the canal (regulars know to bring tiny cans of bug spray to battle the mosquitoes in summer). The *paste e fagioli* is livened up with bits of sausage, and the ricotta-stuffed ravioli inventively sauced with a pesto of *rucola* (arugula) and veggies. For a second course, you can try the *tocchetti di coniglio* (oven-roasted rabbit with potatoes), *porchetta* (pork stuffed with spices), or vegetable *cous-cous alla Trapanesi*—or just sack the whole idea of a secondo and order up a *tavolozza* selection of excellent cheeses. There's a surprisingly good selection of half-bottles of wine, with most full bottles starting at 15€ and going senselessly higher. On the whole, portions could be a whole lot larger, but you gotta love a place whose menu opens with the quip, "Good cooking is the friend of living well and the enemy of a hurried life."

Ripa di Porta Ticinese 55 (on the Naviglio Grande). ℂ **02-8940-6277.** Reservations recommended. Primi 11€–16€; secondi 20€–25€ (prices cheaper at lunchtime). Daily 12:30–2:30pm and 8–11pm. AE, MC, V. Tram: 3, 15, 29, 30, or 59.

Dongiò ★★ SOUTHERN ITALIAN   The red hot chili pepper is native to the Americas, but few places in the world have learned to work with the plant better than the Calabrians in the toe of the Italian boot. For a taste of Calabrian cuisine far from its native land, Dongiò is the best in Milan, and it's hard to imagine there is any place better in all of northern Italy. All the pasta is made in-house and is coupled with Calabrian specialties, including sausage, sweet Tropea onions, *pancetta,* aged ricotta, and *n'duja,* a spicy, spreadable salami. For a mouthwatering taste of how these ingredients can be meshed into a *primo piatto* approaching perfection, try the *Spaghettoni alla Tamarro,* thick spaghetti topped with a red sauce that includes *n'duja* and a dash of the aged ricotta that has been worked into a cream. *N'duja* makes it onto the antipasto menu, and if you still haven't had enough of this most signature of Calabrian specialties, for your *secondo* you can get a large slice of grilled *Caciocavallo Silano* cheese filled with *n'duja.* There are also excellent fillet steaks.

Via Bernardino Corio 3 ℂ **02-551-1372.** Reservations highly recommended. Primi 7.20€; secondi 9.50€–16€. MC, V. Mon–Fri 12:30–3pm and 7:30–11pm; Sat 7:30–11pm. Metro: Porta Romana.

Ponte Rosso ★ MILANESE/TRIESTINO   This is an old-fashioned trattoria on the canal, a long railroad room crowded with tiny tables and a short, simple menu of unfussy, hearty home cooking. The owner hails from Trieste originally (which explains the old Triestino photos on the walls), so kick a meal off with *salumi friuliani,* a mixed platter of cured meats from the region famous for producing the most delicate prosciutto in Italy. The *insalata di pasta* is a cold pasta salad with olives, capers, and mozzarella. They do a

mean minestrone vegetable soup, Triestino *sarde in saor* (vinegar-kissed fried sardines),
manzo in salsa verde (beef in an herb sauce), and *torta di verdure* (vegetable quiche).

Ripa di Porta Ticinese 23 (on the Naviglio Grande). ☎ **02-837-3132.** Reservations recommended. Primi
10€–14€; secondi 16€–18€. AE, DC, MC, V. Daily 12:30–3pm and 7–10:30pm (closed Sun evening). Tram:
3, 15, 29, 30, or 59.

Premiata Pizzeria ★ PIZZA/ITALIAN   The most popular pizzeria in the Navigli, if
not in the entire city, stays packed from early dinnertime until the barhopping crowd
stops by for late-night munchies. The restaurant rambles back forever, exposed copper
pipes tracing across the ceilings of rooms wrapped around shaded outdoor terraces set
with long, raucous tables. Seating is communal and service hurried, but the wood-oven
pizzas are excellent. If you're hungrier, there's a long menu of pastas and meat courses,
while lighter appetites can enjoy a selection of salads or platters of cheese or *salumi* built
for two.

Via Alzaia Naviglio Grande 2. ☎ **02-8940-0648.** Reservations recommended. Primi 8€–18€; secondi
12€–24€; pizza 5€–10€. MC, V. Wed–Mon noon–3pm; daily 6pm–2am. Tram: 3, 15, 29, 30, or 59.

Cafes & Gelato

Bar Zucca/Caffè Miani, at the Duomo end of the Galleria Vittorio Emanuele II (☎ **02-
8646-4435;** www.caffemiani.it; Metro: Duomo), is best known by its original name, the
Camparino. It's the most attractive and popular of the Galleria's many bars and holds the
dubious distinction of having introduced Italy to what has become the country's ubiquitous red cordial, Campari, a viciously red liquid that tastes like hair tonic even when cut
with soda water, as is traditional. You can sample one—along with a selection of light
dishes to wipe the taste off your tongue (as you might gather, I'm not a fan of the popular Campari soda)—while lingering at the tables set up in the Galleria with a bit of
Duomo facade view, or in one of the Art Nouveau rooms inside.

   For gelato, some of the best in the city can be found at **Grom,** Via Santa Margherita
16 (☎ **02-80581041;** www.grom.it), right by La Scala; Corso di Porta Ticinese 51, near
the San Lorenzo church; and Corso Buenos Aires 13, perfectly placed for a break from
your shopping spree. I'm not a big fan of chain stores in any form (there is even one of
these in New York), but if there is better old-fashioned gelato anywhere in northern Italy,
I've yet to taste it.

   Strollers in the atmospheric Brera neighborhood sooner or later stumble upon the
Gelateria Toldo, Via Ponte Vetero 9 (☎ **02-8646-0863;** Metro: Cordusio or Lanza),
where the gelato is wonderfully creamy and many of the *sorbetto* selections are so fruity
and fresh, they seem healthy.

   The **Pasticceria Confetteria Cova,** Via Montenapoleone 8 (☎ **02-600-0578;** Metro:
Montenapoleone), is nearing its 200th year in refined surroundings near the similarly
atmospheric Museo Poldi-Pezzoli. It's usually filled with shoppers making the rounds in
this high-fashion district. You can enjoy a quick coffee and a brioche standing at the long
bar, or take a seat in one of the elegant adjoining rooms.

   The **Pasticceria Marchesi,** Via Santa Maria alla Porta 13 (☎ **02-862-770;** Metro:
Cardusio), is a distinguished pastry shop with an adjoining tearoom. Since it's only steps
from Santa Maria delle Grazie, you can enjoy the old-world ambience and a cup of excellent coffee (or one of the many teas and herbal infusions) as you dash off postcards of
The Last Supper. You'll want to accompany your beverage with elegant pastries, perhaps
a slice of the *panettone* (cake with raisins and candied citron) that's a hallmark of Milan.
No one prepares it better than Marchesi. It's open Tuesday to Sunday 8am to 8pm.

Strolling Through Milan

The prime spot for a *passeggiata* (stroll) is the Piazza Duomo and the adjoining Galleria, but many of the neighborhoods that fan out from the center are ideal for wandering and looking into the life of the Milanese. The **Golden Quadrilateral** (the city's center for high fashion), just north of the Piazza Duomo on and around Via Montenapoleone, is known for window shopping and trendy cafes and bars; **Magenta** is an old residential quarter, filled with some of the city's most venerable churches, west of Piazza Duomo (follow Via Orifici and its extension, Via Dante, toward the Castello Sforzesco); the **Brera,** a parcel of once-seedy, now-gentrified Milan, filled with bars and inexpensive restaurants along the streets clustered around the Pinacoteca Brera (follow Via Brera from the Teatro alla Scala); and the popular **Navigli** neighborhood, at the southern edge of the center city, a series of narrow towpaths running alongside the remaining *navigli* (canals) that once laced the city, the former warehouse entrances along them now housing hopping and unpretentious bars, *birrerie* (pubs), restaurants, and small clubs in the city (take the Metro to Porta Genova). A stroll in Milan almost always includes a stop at a cafe or gelateria (see above).

MILAN AFTER DARK

On Wednesday and Thursday, Milan's newspapers tend to devote a lot of ink to club schedules and cultural events. If you don't trust your command of Italian to plan your nightlife, check out the tourist office in Piazza Duomo—there are usually piles of fliers lying about that announce upcoming events. The tourist office also keeps visitors up-to-date with *Milano Mese,* a periodical it distributes for free with schedules of events, as well as listings of bars, clubs, and restaurants.

THE PERFORMING ARTS   On the other side of the Galleria from the Duomo is Italy's premier opera house, **Teatro Alla Scala ★★**, Piazza Scala (✆ **02-887-91**), known to everyone as "La Scala." The calendar of events and online ticket office can be found at www.teatroallascala.org. Tickets go on sale about 3 months before a performance and sell out quickly for popular performances. Tickets can also be had the day of a performance; check the ticket office at the Duomo metro stop for details on availability. Purchase tickets online (all major credit cards accepted) or at about a dozen travel agencies around the city, and at various travel agencies throughout the country. For a complete list, visit the website.

The adjacent museum, **Il Museo Teatrale Alla Scala** (✆ **02-8879-7473**), pays tribute to the leading Italian lights in opera and ballet, often hosting exhibits of costumes worn at La Scala performances long ago. Also of note for scholars is a library of more than 40,000 musical works. The museum and library are open daily from 9am to 12:30pm and from 1:30 to 5:30pm. Entrance is 5€.

MOVIES   In Italy, English-language films are almost always dubbed into Italian, providing English speakers with an opportunity to bone up on their Italian but taking some of the fun out of a night at the movies. Fortunately, there are always a few theaters that screen English-language films in the original version 1 night a week. These three theaters

While Brera is always happening and the Navigli certainly packs a (mostly suburban) crowd, for a more authentic Milanese experience, check out the other (northern) end of Corso di Porta Ticinese: the San Lorenzo district. There are great bars and cafes between there and Metro stop Sant'Ambrogio.

take turns showing the same film on different nights of the week (the film changes every week): **Anteo,** Via Milazzo 9 (☎ **02-659-7732;** Metro: Moscova), on Monday; **Arcobaleno,** Vle. Tunisia 11 (☎ **02-2940-6054;** Metro: Porta Venezia), on Tuesday; and **Mexico,** Via Savona 57 (☎ **02-4895-1802;** Metro: Porta Genova), on Thursday.

PUBS & BARS   One of the most storied Brera hangouts is **Bar Jamaica,** Via Brera 32 (☎ **02-876723;** Metro: Lanza), an old-school bar where Mussolini once sat to work on his newspaper articles, and now arty locals and literati tolerate the company of better-heeled partygoers at the outdoor tables. The owner, Carlina, stirs a stiff drink, making this a worthwhile stop on the way to the clubs at Porta Garibaldi.

A publike atmosphere, induced in part by Guinness on tap and a very crowded *aperitivo* hour (about 6–8pm), where you can load up on free pasta and other munchies, prevails at Liberty-style **Bar Magenta,** Via Carducci 13 at Corso Magenta (☎ **02-805-3808;** Metro: Cadorna), in the neighborhood from which it takes its name; it's open Tuesday to Sunday and has the best panini in the city, usually made by old men with an old-fashioned meat-slicing machine. The cafe also offers wireless Internet access to its patrons.

En route to the Navigli, you can't help noticing the huge crowd of 20-somethings milling around outside the basilica di San Lorenzo, maybe kicking around a soccer ball through the crowd, usually with cocktails and beers in hand: Chances are, those drinks came from **Luca's Bar,** Corso Porta Ticinese 51 (☎ **02-5810-0405;** Metro: Sant'Ambrogio, just under the arch by the basilica, which has a sort of takeout service). Note that if you want to pull up a chair outside, you pay 6€ for a drink rather than the 5€ takeout price.

At the Navigli, **Birreria La Fontanella,** Alzaia Naviglio Pavese 6 (☎ **02-837-2391;** Metro: Porta Genova), has canal-side tables outside and the oddest-shaped beer glasses around—that half-a-barbell kind everyone seems to order is called the "Cavalliere." It's open Tuesday to Sunday 7pm to 3am.

JAZZ CLUBS   Since Capolinea got ousted (*Note:* The club's name is still there at Via Lodovico il Moro 119, but it's *not* the old jazz club where the greats came to play; rather, it's some pathetic mimic of it slapped together by the next-door neighbors who forced the original owners out of this space), the best venue on the jazz-club scene is **Le Scimmie,** which has its own bar-boat moored in the canal. It's in the Navigli at Via Ascanio Sforza 49 (☎ **02-8940-2874;** www.scimmie.it; Metro: Porta Genova) and operates Monday to Saturday, with shows starting between 10 and 10:30pm.

MUSIC & DANCE CLUBS   The dance scene changes all the time in Milan, but at whatever club is popular (or in business) at the moment, expect to pay a cover of 10€ to 15€—sometimes more for big-name live acts. Models, actors, sports stars, and the attendant fashion set favor **Hollywood;** it's small, chic, and somewhat centrally located in Brera at Corso Como 15 (☎ **02-655-5574** or 02-659-8996, or 02-679-8896 after

10:30pm; Metro: Garibaldi). It closes Mondays and July 23 to September 7. Across the street, at Corso Como 14, is **Casablanca** (☏ **39-38-46-1607**), which has a nice Moroccan-flavor lounge in the back and caters to a slightly more mature clientele. For something a little funkier, try **Plastic,** Viale Umbria 120 (☏ **02-733-996;** no Metro), where the people are a bit more colorful and the music more alternative. It's open only Friday to Sunday.

Milan's most venerable live music club is **Rolling Stone,** Corso XXII Marzo 32 (☏ **02-733-172;** tram: 12, 27, 45, 60, 66, 73, or 92), in business since the 1950s. Most of the performers these days are of a rock bent, and the club is as immensely popular as ever. Cover charges, which vary widely depending on who's performing, are less expensive for women than for men, and more expensive on weekends than on weekdays; it's closed Sunday and Monday.

Note: There are no specific club hours in Milan. Opening and closing times vary with the seasons and with the crowds, with openings anywhere from 7 to 11pm and closings anywhere from 1am to dawn, later on weekend nights.

GAY CLUBS Milan's largest gay club is **Nuovo Idea,** Via de Castillia 30 (☏ **02-6900-7859;** www.dinet.it/nuovaidea; Metro: Gioia); it attracts a mostly male crowd of all ages and offers everything from disco to polkas in a huge techno room. It's open Thursday to Sunday. **Recycle,** Via Calabria 5 (☏ **02-376-1531**), is a women-only club Friday to Sunday 9pm to 2am, sometimes later (mixed crowd welcome Wed–Thurs nights). There is no Metro line nearby; use the intermittent Passante train, or blue line, to the Lancetti stop.

Via Sammartini, along the train station's left flank (Metro: Centrale), is a good street to hit. **Next Groove,** at no. 23 (☏ **02-6698-0450**), is a mixed gay and lesbian disco bar of the phone-on-the-table sort and thematic evenings; it's open daily. Next door at no. 25, **After Line Disco Pub** (☏ **02-669-2130**) is a bar/restaurant where a giant-screen TV and strobe light are switched on after dinner to turn it into a lesbian discothèque; it's open Tuesday to Sunday.

DAY TRIPS FROM MILAN
Pavia & the Certosa

At one time, the quiet and remarkably well-preserved little city of **Pavia,** 35km (22 miles) south of Milan, was more powerful than Milan. It was the capital of Lombardy in the 7th and 8th centuries, and by the early Renaissance, the Viscontis and later the Sforzas, the two families who so influenced the history of Milan and all of Lombardy, were wielding their power here. It was the Viscontis who built the city's imposing **Castello,** made Pavia one of Europe's great centers of learning (when they founded the university) in 1361, began construction on the **Duomo** (with the third-largest dome in Italy) in 1488, and founded the city's most important monument and the one that brings most visitors to Pavia, the Certosa.

The **Certosa** ★★★ is 8km (5 miles) north of Pavia. One of the most unusual buildings in Lombardy, if not in all of Italy, this religious compound was commissioned by Gian Galeazzo Visconti in 1396 as a Carthusian monastery and a burial chapel for his family—officially as thanks for curing his second sickly wife (the first died) and granting him children and heirs. It was completed by the Sforzas. The facade of colored marbles, the frescoed interior, and the riot of funerary sculpture is evidence that this brood of often-tyrannical despots were also dedicated builders with grand schemes and large coffers. The finest and most acclaimed statuary monument here, that of Ludivico il Moro (buried in France, where he died a prisoner of war) and Beatrice d'Este (buried in Milan's Santa Maria delle Grazie), sits in the left transept of the massive church, beneath lapis lazuli–rich frescoes by Bergognone. Its presence here is a twist of fate—the monks at Milan's Chiesa di Santa Maria delle Grazie (which houses *The Last Supper*) sold the tomb to the Certosa to raise funds. In the right transept is the 15th-century tomb of Gian Galeazzo Visconti.

Across from the tomb is the entrance to the enormous cloister, lined with the monks' cells, each of which is actually a two-story cottage with its own garden plot. Most are now inhabited by a small community of Cistercian monks. It is possible to visit their refectory and an adjoining shop, where they sell their Chartreuse liqueur and herbal soaps and scents.

Admission to the Certosa (© **0382-925-613**) is free; it's open Tuesday to Sunday 9 to 11:30am and 2:30 to 5:30pm (until 4:30pm Nov–Feb, 5pm Mar and Oct, and 6pm May–Aug).

GETTING THERE & TOURIST INFO   Half-hourly trains from **Milan** usually stop at the station near the Certosa, just before the main Pavia station (30 min.). To reach the Certosa from Pavia, take one of the half-hourly buses from the Autocorriere station (next to the train station); the trip takes about 15 minutes. By car, the Certosa is about half an hour south of Milan via Autostrada A7 (follow exit signs).

The **tourist office** is near the train station at Via Fabio Filzi 2 (© **0382-22-156**); it's open Monday to Saturday from 8:30am to 12:30pm and 2 to 6pm.

Cremona

Violins have been drawing visitors to this little city on the river Po, 92km (57 miles) southeast of Milan, since the 17th century, when fine string instruments began emerging from the workshops of Nicolo Amati and his more famous protégé, Antonio Stradivari. The tradition continues: Cremona's Scuola di Luteria (Violin School) is world renowned.

Cremona's charms extend far beyond the musical. Its central Piazza del Commune is one of the largest and most beautiful town squares in Italy, fronted by remarkable structures. Among these is the 12th-century **Duomo** (© **0372-26-707**), clad in pink marble and overshadowed by Italy's tallest campanile; inside, it is covered with 16th-century frescoes (admission is free and hours are daily 7:30am–noon and 3:30–7pm).

The **Palazzo del Comune** rises gracefully above a Gothic arcade and is embellished with terra-cotta panels. Its **Raccolta dei Violini** ★★ displays a small collection of 17th- and 18th-century violins by Amati, the Guarneri, and one Stradvari (© **0372-22-138**). The **Museo Stradivariano** ★, in the Museo Civico alongside an unimportant *pinacoteca* collection of paintings at Via Palestro 17 (© **0372-461-886**), displays the finest violins ever made, including those by Amatis, Stradivari, and Guarneri.

Admission to the Museo Civico is 7€, including the Stradivarius museum, and it's open Tuesday to Saturday 8:30am to 6:30pm, Sunday 10am to 6pm. Admission to the Raccolta dei Violini is 6€; it's open Monday to Saturday 8:30am to 5:15pm. The instruments are regularly bowed most mornings by local musicians to keep their coveted tones intact. These "concerts" are open to the public, though for this honor, you must call the Comune at © **0372-22-138** a few weeks ahead of time to book a seat for an extra 1.50€.

GETTING THERE & TOURIST INFO   Trains arrive almost hourly from **Milan** (65 min.). Hourly trains to **Brescia** (50 min.) also make it possible to combine an excursion from Milan to Cremona and Brescia (see below). If you are traveling by car, you can make the trip to Cremona by following A1 from Milan to Piacenza and A21 from Piacenza to Cremona.

The **tourist office** is near the Duomo at Piazza del Commune 5 (✆ **0372-23-233;** www.cremonaturismo.it); hours are Monday to Saturday 9:30am to 12:30pm and 3 to 6pm, Sunday 10am to 1pm.

Brescia

Ringed by industrialized suburbs, Brescia (97km/60 miles from Milan) doesn't readily beckon travelers to stop. Those who do, however, have the pleasure of wandering through a centuries-old town center where Roman ruins, not one but two duomos, and medieval *palazzi* line winding streets and gracious piazzas.

The center of Brescia is Piazza Paolo VI, better known as Piazza del Duomo after its two duomos—the 17th- to 19th-century Duomo Nuovo (New Duomo), which is pretty bland, and the much more charming (on the outside, though it's nearly bare inside) 11th- to 12th-century **Duomo Vecchio (Old Duomo)** ★, also called Rotonda, for its shape. Year round, the New Duomo is open Monday to Saturday 7:30am to noon and 4 to 7:30pm, and Sunday 8am to 1pm and 4 to 7:30pm. April to September, the Old Duomo is open Wednesday to Monday 9am to noon and 3 to 7pm; October to March, hours are Saturday and Sunday 9am to noon and 3 to 6pm. Next to the New Duomo rises the Broletto, Brescia's medieval town hall.

Brescia's Roman past emerges if you leave the piazza on Via dei Musei and follow it to the **Capitolino** ★, a temple erected in A.D. 73. Jog up Vicolo del Fontanone to its right to see the remains of the Teatro Romano (Roman Theater). A few blocks farther down the street is the **Monasterio di Santa Giulia** ★★, at Via dei Musei 1B (✆ **030-297-7834;** www.bresciamusei.com), where Charlemagne's ex-wife, Ermengarde, spent her last days. Admission is 8€ for adults, 4€ for those 14 to 18 or over 65. The monastery incorporates several churches and museums, together housing a rich collection of prehistoric, Roman, and medieval objects (lots of them high-quality pieces). It is divided into two itineraries, a history of the monastery and a history of the city, called the **Museo della Citta'.** Everything is well documented and explained in Italian and English. It's open Tuesday to Sunday June to September 10am to 6pm and October to May 9:30am to 5:30pm. Special exhibits raise the prices a tad and lengthen the hours.

If you leave Piazza del Duomo from the other direction, through the archways into Piazza Loggia, you come upon Brescia's most enchanting building, the Renaissance **Loggia** ★★, a two-story colonnade festooned with reliefs and statues, and dating to the turn of the 16th century (the bottom half) and the mid-1550s through 1570s (the top half). As beautiful and renowned as the Loggia is, oddly enough, we don't know who designed it, though great names such as Jacopo Sansovino and Andrea Palladio have been suggested. The Torre dell'Orologio, on the opposite side of the square, resembles the campanile on Piazza San Marco in Venice, bespeaking the days when Brescia was a Venetian stronghold.

Brescia's excellent painting collection, the **Pinacoteca Tosio-Matinengo** ★★, is at Piazza Moretto 4 (✆ **030-377-4999;** www.bresciamusei.com). From Piazza Loggia, walk south into the Fascist-era Piazza Vittorio and follow that south into Piazza dei Mercati; from there, Corso Zanardelli and Corso Magenta lead west to Via Crispi, which leads south to the museum. Works by Moretto, Foppa, and other painters of the school of Brescia hang alongside Raphaels and Tintorettos in an old *palazzo*. Admission is 5€ for adults, 4€ for students, and free for children under 17 and seniors over 65. It's open Tuesday to Sunday June to September 10:30am to 6pm and October to May 9:30am to

5pm. *Note:* The museum was closed for remodeling in 2009 and wasn't scheduled to reopen until at least mid-2010. If you visit while the museum is closed, you can still see at least some of the museum's works; many of the most important paintings have been temporarily moved to the museum at the Monasterio di Santa **Giulia** (see above), which is itself worth a visit.

GETTING THERE & TOURIST INFO   Trains arrive from Milan about every half-hour (45–65 min.). Brescia is linked to Milan by the A4, which continues east to Verona and Venice; the trip from Milan to Brescia takes a little under an hour. There's a **tourist info office** at Piazza Loggia 6 (✆ **030-240-0357**), open in summer Monday to Saturday 9am to 6:30pm, and in winter Monday to Saturday 9:30am to 12:30pm and Monday to Friday 2 to 5pm.

There is another tourist office on Via dei Musei in front of the entrance to the Santa Giulia Monastery (✆ **030-374-9916**), open Monday to Saturday 9am to 12:30pm and Monday to Friday 3 to 6pm. You can get more details on the Web at www.bresciaholiday. com and www.comune.brescia.it.

2 BERGAMO

47km (29 miles) NE of Milan, 52km (32 miles) NW of Brescia

Bergamo is two cities. Bergamo Bassa, the lower, a mostly 19th- and 20th-century city, concerns itself with everyday business. Bergamo Alta, a beautiful medieval/Renaissance town perched on a green hill, concerns itself these days with entertaining the visitors who come to admire its *piazze, palazzi,* and churches; enjoy the lovely vistas from its belvederes; and soak in the hushed beauty that inspired Italian poet Gabriel d'Annunzio to call old Bergamo "a city of muteness." The distinct characters of the two parts of this city go back to its founding as a Roman settlement, when the *civitas* (Latin for city) was on the hill and farms and suburban villas dotted the plains below.

ESSENTIALS
GETTING THERE   By Train   Trains arrive from and depart for Milan hourly (50 min.); service to and from Brescia is even more frequent, with half-hourly service during peak early-morning and early-evening travel times (50 min.). Given the frequency of train service, you can easily make a daylong sightseeing loop from Milan, arriving in Bergamo in the morning, moving on to Brescia in the afternoon, and returning to Milan from there. If you're coming from or going to nearby Lake Como, there's hourly service between Bergamo and Lecco, on the southeast end of the lake (40 min.).

By Bus   An extensive bus network links Bergamo with many other towns in Lombardy. There are five to six buses a day to and from Como (2 hr.) run by **SPT** (✆ **031-247-247**). Service to and from Milan by **Autostradale** (✆ **02-3391-0843**) runs every half-hour (1 hr. trip time). The bus station is next to the train station on Piazza Marconi.

By Car   Bergamo is linked directly to Milan via the A4, which continues east to Brescia, Verona, and Venice. The trip between Milan and Bergamo takes a little over half an hour. Parking in or near the Città Alta, most of which is closed to traffic, can be difficult. There is a parking lot on the northern end of the Città Alta near Porta Garibaldi (1€ per hour) and street parking along Viale delle Mura, which loops around the flanks of the walls of the Città Alta.

VISITOR INFORMATION The **Città Bassa tourist office,** Viale Vittorio Emanuele 20 (© **035-210-204;** fax 035-230-184; www.apt.bergamo.it), is 9 long blocks straight out from the train station; it's open Monday to Sunday 9am to 12:30pm and 2 to 5:30pm. The **Città Alta office,** Vicola Aquila Nera 2 (© **035-232-730;** fax 035-242-994), is just off Piazza Vecchia, open daily the same hours. If you are planning to travel farther afield and into the hills, ask either tourist office for the trail map of the Bergamo province.

FESTIVALS & MARKETS Bergamo is a cultured city, and its celebrations include the May-to-June **Festivale Piantistico,** one of the world's major piano competitions. In September, the city celebrates its native composer, Gaetano Donizetti, with **performances of his works,** most of them at the Teatro Donizetti in the Città Bassa (see below).

CITY LAYOUT Piazza Vecchia, the Colleoni Chapel, and most of the other sights that bring visitors to Bergamo are in the **Città Alta**—the exception is the Accademia Carrara, which is in the Città Bassa but on the flanks of the hillside, so within easy walking distance of the upper-town sights. **Via Colleoni** cuts a swath through the medieval heart of the Città Alta, beginning at **Piazza Vecchia.** To reach this lovely square from the funicular station at **Piazza Mercato delle Scarpi,** walk along **Via Gombito** for about 5 minutes. Most of the Città Alta is closed to traffic, but it's compact and easy to navigate on foot. Down below, the main square known as the **Sentierone** is the center of the **Città Bassa.** It's about a 5-minute walk from the train station north along **Viale Papa Giovanni XXIII.**

GETTING AROUND Bergamo has an extensive **bus system** that runs through the Città Bassa and to points outside the walls of the Città Alta; tickets are 1€ and are available from newsstands and tobacco shops. With the exception of the trip from the train or bus stations up to the Città Alta, you probably won't have much need of public transit, since most of the sights are within an easy walk of one another.

To reach the Città Alta from the train station, take bus no. 1 or 1A and make the free transfer to the **Funicolare Bergamo Alta,** connecting the upper and lower cities and running every 7 minutes from 6:30am to 12:30am. You can make the walk to the funicular in about 20 minutes (and see something of the pleasant new city en route) by following Viale Papa Giovanni XXIII and its continuations Viale Roma and Viale Vittorio Emanuele II straight through town to the funicular station.

If you're feeling hearty, a footpath next to the funicular winds up to Città Alta; the steep climb up (made easier by intermittent staircases) takes about 30 minutes. Bus no. 1A also continues up and around the Città Alta walls to end just outside Porta San Vigilio, and hence more convenient to hotels San Lorenzo and Gourmet.

EXPLORING THE CITTÀ BASSA

Most visitors scurry through Bergamo's lower, newer town on their way to the Città Alta, but you may want to pause long enough to enjoy a coffee along the **Sentierone,** the elongated piazza/street at the center of town. This spacious square graciously combines a mishmash of architectural styles (including 16th-c. porticos on one side, the Mussolini-era Palazzo di Giustizia and two imitation Doric temples on another). Locals sit in its gardens, lounge in its cafes, and attend classical concerts at the **Teatro Donizetti.** This 19th-century theater is the center of Bergamo's lively culture scene, with a fall opera season and a winter-to-spring season of dramatic performances; for details, check with the tourist office or call the theater at © **035-416-0611** (http://teatro.gaetano-donizetti.com).

The main draw for most visitors down here, though, is the **Galleria dell'Accademia** **Carrara** ★★, Piazza Carrara 82a (℗ **035-399-677;** www.accademiacarrara.bergamo.it). The city's exquisite art gallery is one of the finest in northern Italy, founded in 1795 when Napoleon's troops were busy rounding up the art treasures of their newly occupied northern Italian states. Many of these works ended up in Bergamo under the stewardship of Count Giacomo Carrara. The collection came into its own after World War I, when a young Bernard Berenson, the 20th century's most noted art connoisseur, took stock of what was here and classified the immense holdings, making sure "every Lotto [was] a Lotto." Lorenzo Lotto (1480–1556) was a Venetian who fled the stupefying society of his native city and spent 1513 to 1525 in Bergamo perfecting his highly emotive portraits. His works take their place in the salons of this neoclassical palace alongside a staggering inventory with paintings by Bellini, Canaletto, Carpaccio, Guardi, Mantegna, and Tiepolo. Most of these masterworks are in the 17 third-floor galleries.

It's easy to become overwhelmed here, but among the paintings you may want to view first is Lotto's *Portrait of Lucina Brembrati,* in which you'll see the immense sensitivity with which the artist was able to imbue his subjects. Look carefully at the moon in the upper-left corner—it has the letters *ci* painted into it, a playful anagram of the sitter's first name; in Italian, *moon* is *luna,* and this one has a *ci* in the middle. Botticelli's much-reproduced *Portrait of Giuliano de Medici* hangs nearby, as does Raphael's sensual *St. Sebastian.* You can visit the Accademia on foot from the Città Alta by following Via Porta Dipinta halfway down the hill to the Porto Sant'Agostino and then a terraced, ramplike staircase to the doors of the museum. From the Città Bassa, the museum is about a 10-minute walk from the Sentierone—from the east end of the square, take a left on Largo Belotti, then a right on Via Giuseppe Verdi, follow that for several blocks to Via Pignolo, and turn left to Via Tomaso, which takes you to Piazza Carrara (the route is well signposted). Admission is 5€, 3€ for those under 12 or over 60. It's open June to September Tuesday to Friday, Saturday until 10pm, and Sunday 10am to 9pm. From October to May the museum is open Tuesday to Friday 9:30am to 5:30pm and Saturday and Sunday 10am to 6pm. *Note:* The museum is closed for restoration until mid-2010, though many of the works are visible at the Palazzo della Ragione (see below) in the Citta Altà in the meantime.

Across the street is the **Galleria d'Arte Moderna e Contemporanea** (℗ **035-270-272;** www.gamec.it), containing works by such 20th-century masters as Boccioni, De Chirico, Morandi, and Kandinsky. Admission is free, and it's open Tuesday to Sunday 10am to 1pm and 3 to 7pm.

EXPLORING THE CITTÀ ALTA

The higher, older part of Bergamo owes its stone *palazzos,* proud monuments, and what remains of its extensive fortified walls to more than 3 centuries of Venetian rule, beginning in 1428, when soldiers of the Republic wrestled control of the city out of the hands of the Milan-based Visconti. The Venetians left their mark elegantly in the town's theatrically adjoining squares, **Piazza Vecchia** and **Piazza del Duomo,** which together create one of the most beautiful outdoor assemblages in Italy—actually, French writer Stendhal went so far as to call this heart of old Bergamo the "most beautiful place on earth."

On Piazza Vecchia, you'll see traces of the Venetian presence in the 12th-century **Palazzo della Ragione (Courts of Justice),** which has been embellished with a graceful ground-floor arcade and the Lion of San Mark's, symbol of the Venetian Republic, above a 16th-century balcony reached by a covered staircase (the bells atop its adjoining tower, the **Torre Civico,** sound the hours sonorously). The recently restored halls often host traveling art exhibits. Across the piazza, the **Biblioteca Civica** was modeled after the Sansovino Library in Venice. Piazza del Duomo, reached through one of the archways of the Palazzo della Ragione, is filled with an overpowering collection of religious structures that include the **Duomo** and the much more enticing **Cappella Colleoni** (see below), the **Baptistery,** and the **Basilica di Santa Maria Maggiore** (see below).

Bergamese strongman Colleoni (see the Cappella Colleoni entry, below) lent his name to the upper town's delightful main street, cobblestoned and so narrow you can just about touch the buildings on either side when standing in the center. If you follow it to its far western end, you'll emerge into **Largo Colle Aperto,** refreshingly green and open to the Città Bassa and valleys below. For better views and a short excursion into the countryside, board the **Funicolare San Vigilio** for the ascent up the San Vigilio hill; the funicular runs daily every 12 minutes or so between 7am and midnight and costs 1€. The strategic importance of these heights was not lost on Bergamo's medieval residents, who erected a summit-top **Castello** (© **035-236-284**), now mostly in ruin. Its keep, still surrounded by the old walls, is a park in which every bench affords a far-reaching view. It's open daily April to September 9am to 8pm, October and March 10am to 6pm, and November to February 10am to 4pm.

The Castello is a good place to begin a trek around the flanks of the Città Alta—go down the San Vigilio hill (or take the funicular) back into the Città Alta through the Porta San Alessandro. For a look at the old walls and some more good views, instead of following Via Colleoni back into the center of the town, turn left on Via della Mura and follow the 16th-century bastions for about .8km (½ mile) to the Porta Sant'Agostino on the other side of the town.

Basilica di Santa Maria Maggiore ★

Behind the plain marble facade and a portico whose columns rise out of the backs of lions lies an overly baroque gilt-covered interior hung with Renaissance tapestries. **Gaetano Donizetti,** the wildly popular composer of frothy operas, who was born in Bergamo in 1797 (see Museo Donizettiano, below) and returned here to die in 1848, is entombed in a **marble sarcophagus** that's as excessive as the rest of the church's decor. The finest works are the **choir stalls,** with rich wood inlays depicting landscapes and biblical scenes; they're the creation of Lorenzo Lotto. The stalls are usually kept under cloth to protect the sensitive hardwoods from light and pollutants, but they're unveiled for Lent. The octagonal **Baptistery** in the piazza outside the church was originally inside but removed, reconstructed, and much embellished in the 19th century.

Piazza del Duomo. © **035-223-327.** Free admission. May–Sept Mon–Sat 9am–12:30pm and 2:30–6pm, Sun 9am–1pm and 3–6pm; Oct–Apr the basilica closes at 5pm.

Cappella Colleoni ★★★

Bartolomeo Colleoni was a Bergamese *condottiere* (captain) who fought for Venice to maintain the Venetian stronghold on the city. In return for his labors, the much-honored soldier was given Bergamo to rule for the republic. If you've already visited Venice, you may have seen Signore Colleoni astride the Verrocchio equestrian bronze in Campo Santi Giovanni e Paolo. He rests for eternity in this elaborate funerary chapel designed by Amadeo, the great sculptor from nearby Pavia (where he completed his most famous work, the Certosa; see p. 306). The pink-and-white marble exterior, laced with finely sculpted columns and loggias, is airy and almost whimsical; inside, the soldier and his favorite daughter, Medea, lie beneath a ceiling frescoed by Tiepolo and surrounded by reliefs and statuary; here Colleoni appears on horseback again atop his marble tomb.

Museo Donizettiano   This charming little museum commemorates Gaetano Donizetti, who was born in Bergamo in 1797 and—little wonder, given the romance of his boyhood surroundings—became one of Italy's most acclaimed composers of opera. Fans can swoon over his sheet music, piano, and other memorabilia and see the deathbed where he succumbed to syphilis in 1848. Thus inspired, you can make the pilgrimage to the humble house where he claimed to have been born in a cellar, the **Casa Nateledi Gaetano Donizetti,** Via B. Canale 14 (ℂ **035-399-432**), a rural street that descends the hillside from the Porta Sant'Alessandro on the western edge of the city. It's open Saturday and Sunday only 11am to 6:30pm (donations requested).

Via Arena 9. ℂ **035-247-116.** www.museostoricobg.org. Admission 3€. June–Sept daily 9:30am–1pm and 2–5:30pm; Oct–May Tues–Sun 9:30am–1pm, Sat–Sun 2–5:30pm. Bus: 1 or 1A.

WHERE TO STAY

The charms of staying in the Città Alta are no secret. Rooms tend to fill up quickly, especially in summer and on weekends. Reserve well in advance.

Agnello d'Oro ★★ (Value)   In keeping with its location a few steps from Piazza Vecchia, the Agnello d'Oro looks like it's right out of an old tourist brochure extolling the quaint charms of Italy. The tall, narrow, ocher-colored building, with flower boxes at its tall windows, overlooks a small piazzetta where a fountain splashes next to potted greenery. The wood-paneled lounge and intimate dining room add to the charm quotient, which declines somewhat as you ascend in a tiny elevator to the rooms. These lean more toward serviceable comfort than to luxury, but warm color schemes and old prints compensate for the lack of space and amenities; the bathrooms are roomy and have been modernized. Front rooms (the ones to request) have balconies overlooking the piazza. This is the most popular hostelry in the Città Alta (even though the friendliness level of the staff can vary wildly), so reservations are mandatory.

Via Gombito 22, 24129 Bergamo Alta. ℂ **035-249-883.** Fax 035-235-612. www.agnellodoro.it. 20 units. 93€ double. Continental breakfast 6€. AE, DC, MC, V. **Amenities:** Concierge. *In room:* TV, hair dryer.

Gourmet ★   This pleasant hotel offers the best of both worlds—it's only steps away from the Città Alta (a few hundred feet outside the Porta Sant'Agostino on the road leading up to the Castello) but on a rural hillside, giving it the air of a country retreat. The villa-style building is set behind walls in a lush garden and enjoys wonderful views. A wide terrace on two sides makes the most of these views. Many of the very large, bright rooms look across the hillside to the heavily developed valley, too. They have plain, wood-paneled furniture, a fashion geared more to solid comfort than to style, and king-size beds. They also rent a large two-floor suite with a sitting area and kitchen downstairs. There's a highly reputed restaurant on the premises—hence the name—with indoor and outdoor tables and midrange prices on Bergamasco and Lombard cuisine.

Via San Vigilio 1, 24129 Bergamo. ℂ/fax **035-437-3004.** www.gourmet-bg.it. 11 units. 90€–110€ double; 130€–135€ triple; 170€–210€ apartment with two double rooms. Continental breakfast 10€. AE, DC, MC, V. Closed Dec 27–Jan 7. **Amenities:** International/Bergamasco restaurant; bar; room service. *In room:* A/C, TV, hair dryer, minibar.

Hotel San Lorenzo ★★   This stylish place in Bergamo Alta is located in a former convent building of Santa Agata. The centuries-old setting is tailor-made for this unusually pleasant inn—most of the rooms face a courtyard and open through French doors to a balcony that wraps around it. Though the hotel is right in town, just a few steps off Via Colleoni, its hillside location provides views over the green slopes flowing down to the valley below. The rooms are small but comfortable, with striped silk draperies and bed coverings and cane-backed lounge chairs; the marble bathrooms come with hand-held shower massagers and hair dryers. A sumptuous buffet breakfast is served in the breakfast room. The discovery of Roman ruins put the brakes on construction of an underground parking facility, though the hotel provides a permit allowing you to park for free in the adjoining square.

Piazza Mascheroni 9A, 24129 Bergamo. ✆ **035-237-383.** Fax 035-237-958. www.hotelsanlorenzobg.it. 25 units. 100€–170€ double. Rates include continental breakfast. AE, DC, MC, V. Free parking. **Amenities:** Bar; room service; smoke-free rooms. *In room:* A/C, TV, hair dryer, minibar.

WHERE TO DINE

Your gambols through the Città Alta can be nicely interspersed with fortifying stops at the city's many pastry shops and stand-up eateries. **Forno Tresoldi,** Via Colleoni 13, sells excellent pizzas and focaccia breads by the slice topped with cheese, salami, and vegetables (from 2€). It's open Tuesday to Sunday from 8am to 1:30pm and 4 to 10pm.

Al Donizetti ★ WINE BAR   This charming restaurant faces the upper city's old covered market, whose sole purpose these days is to look medieval and romantic. In good weather, tables are set out under the market's arcaded loggia, and meals are also served in the two small vaulted-ceiling dining rooms. The bulk of the menu is devoted to various kinds of salami, ham, and cheeses, though many dishes also rely on fresh vegetables— perhaps a light zucchini flan or *raddichio con gorgonzola* (the bitter red greens are lightly grilled and the creamy cheese is added at the last minute). There are also the tried-and-true battle horses of northern Italian cuisine, such as polenta with braised pork. More than 360 wines are available, including dozens by the glass, to accompany a meal, and the staff will help you choose the right one.

Via Gombito 17A. ✆ **035-242-661.** www.donizetti.it. Reservations not necessary. Panini from 3€; salads and platters of cheese and/or meats 10€–17€. MC, V. Daily 11am–1am.

Antica Hosteria del Vino Buono ★★★ NORTHERN ITALIAN   The new ownership of this wine bar–turned-restaurant near the top of the funicular takes its food and wine seriously. It's a pleasure to dine in the handsome surroundings of brick, refinished in 2006 to give an older feel. For an introduction to food from the region, try one of the several tasting menus. Polenta figures prominently and is served *alla bergamasca* (with wild mushrooms). The *taragna* version uses buckwheat and cornmeal as its base and is filled with Taleggio cheese. The main courses lean toward meat. A dish like roast quail or rabbit should be accompanied by a Valcalepio Rosso, a medium-strength red from local vineyards. The house wine, a local cabernet, is more economical, perhaps a little young but perfectly drinkable.

✆ **035-247-993.** Reservations recommended. Primi 8€; secondi 11€; *menù turistico* 23€, wine included. AE, DC, MC, V. Tues–Sun noon–2:30pm and 7–10:30pm (Tues closed for lunch).

Taverna del Colleoni & Dell'Angelo ★ NORTHERN ITALIAN   Pierangelo Cornaro and chef Odorico Pinato run one of Bergamo's top restaurants and possibly its priciest. It's right on the main square in a Renaissance *palazzo*—in summer the best tables are outside on the piazza; otherwise, you're in a refined medieval-looking space of high vaulted ceilings. The ingredients used here are fresh and the recipes inspired by local tradition, but the menu is a more creative *cucina nuova* (nouvelle portions, nouvelle prices). The best part of the menu is the back page, where they list some of their more typical dishes, such as *fiorade bergamesche ai porcini e mirtilli* (wide noodles with porcini and blueberries), *cannoli di farro al ragù di cinghiale, salsa di zucca e patate* (pasta tubes made of emmer flour stuffed with wild boar and served under a pumpkin-potato sauce), *stoccafisso gratinato alla moda dell'Angelo* (cod casserole with cheese and polenta), and *cous cous siciliano di gamberi allo zafferano* (couscous tinged with saffron and studded with shrimp). Desserts are good, too.

Piazza Vecchia 7. (© 035-232-596. Reservations recommended. Primi 16€–20€; secondi 25€–30€; "gourmand" menu 60€, excluding wine. AE, DC, MC, V. Tues–Sun noon–2:30pm and 7:30–10:30pm.

Vineria Cozzi ★★ (Value) NORTHERN ITALIAN/WINE BAR   Cozzi isn't just a wine bar but a Bergamo institution. Its cane chairs are well worn with use by Bergamese and visitors who can't resist stopping in for a glass of wine while walking down Via Colleoni. Hundreds of bottles from throughout Italy line the walls and are served by the glass (from 2€). Sandwiches are always available, as are several kinds of cheese, but the changing daily offerings usually include several pasta dishes and polenta with rich cheese folded into it, perhaps a torta stuffed with fresh vegetables and a main course or two—if the duck breast stuffed with cabbage is available, order it.

Via Colleoni 22. (© **035-238-836.** www.vineriacozzi.it. Primi 10€–12€; secondi 10€–15€; 20% discount on weekday lunches. AE, MC, V. Daily 11am–2am. Closed Wed in winter, Fri in summer, 10 days in Jan, and 12 days in Aug.

CAFES

Caffè del Tasso ★, Piazza Vecchia 3, is a prime piece of real estate on the main square of the Città Alta. It began life as a tailor's shop 500 years ago, but it's been a cafe and bar since 1581. Legend has it that Garibaldi's Red Shirts used to gather here (Bergamo was a stronghold of Italian independence, which explains why an edict from the 1850s on the wall of this cafe prohibits rebellion).

While the location of **Caffè della Funicolare** in the Piazza Mercato delle Scarpe, in the upper terminal of the funicular that climbs the hill from the Città Bassa to the Città Alta, doesn't suggest a memorable dining experience, the station dates from 1887 and has enough Belle Epoque flourishes and curlicues to make the surroundings interesting. Plus, the dining room and terrace look straight down the hill to the town and valley, providing some of the best tables with a view (accompanied by low-cost fare) in the upper town. Stop in for a coffee, 1 of the 50 kinds of beer on tap, a sandwich, or a salad.

3 MANTUA (MANTOVA): A GEM OF LOMBARDY

158km (98 miles) E of Milan, 62km (38 miles) N of Parma, 150km (93 miles) SW of Venice

One of Lombardy's finest cities is in the farthest reaches of the region, making it a logical addition to a trip to Venice or Parma as well as to Milan. Like its neighboring cities in Emilia-Romagna, Mantua (Mantova) owes its past greatness and its beautiful Renaissance monuments to one family, in this case the Gonzagas, who rose from peasant origins to conquer the city in 1328 and ruled benevolently until 1707. You'll encounter the Gonzagas—and, since they were avid collectors of art and ruled through the greatest centuries of Italian art, the treasures they collected—in the massive Palazzo Ducale that dominates much of the town center; in their refreshing suburban retreat, the Palazzo Te; and in the churches and *piazze* that grew up around their court.

One of Mantua's greatest charms is its location—on a meandering river, the Mincio, which widens here to envelop the city in a necklace of moodily romantic lakes. Often shrouded in mist and surrounded by flat, lonely plains, Mantua can seem almost melancholy. Aldous Huxley wrote of the city, "I have seen great cities dead or in decay—but over none, it seemed to me, did there brood so profound a melancholy as over Mantua." Since his visit in the 1930s, though, the Palazzo Ducale, the Galleria Museo Palazzo Valentia Gonzaga, and other monuments have been restored, and what will probably strike you more is what a remarkable gem of a city Mantua is.

ESSENTIALS

GETTING THERE   By Train   Ten trains daily arrive from Milan (2 hr.). There are hourly runs from Verona, with connections to Venice (30–40 min.).

By Car   The speediest connections from Milan are via the *autostrade*, the A4 to Verona, and the A22 from Verona to Mantua (the trip takes less than 2 hr.). From Mantua, it's also an easy drive south to Parma and other cities in Emilia-Romagna, on S420.

VISITOR INFORMATION   The **tourist office** is at Piazza Mantegna 6 (© **0376-432-432;** fax 0376-432-433; www.turismo.mantova.it), open Monday to Saturday from 8:30am to 12:30pm and 3 to 6pm, and Sunday 9:30am to 12:30pm (closed almost every Sun Jan–Feb).

FESTIVALS & MARKETS   Sadly, Mantua's music festival was canceled after 2008 due to a lack of interest and funding from sponsors, but the city continues to dedicate itself to festivals. Mantua fights the post-summer blues with a **literature festival** the second weekend of September. The ***Festival delle Passioni,*** or Festival of Passions (www.festival dellepassioni.it), brings together food, music, and theater in July; themes for the 2009 festival included meat, fried food, bubbly wine, spicy food, and ice.

Year-round, Piazza delle Erbe is the scene of a bustling **food market** Monday through Saturday from 8am to 1pm. On Thursday mornings, a **bigger market,** filled with clothing, housewares, and more food, spills through Piazza Magenta and adjoining streets.

CITY LAYOUT   Mantua is tucked onto a point of land surrounded on three sides by the **Mincio River,** which widens here into a series of lakes, named prosaically **Lago Superiore, Lago di Mezzo,** and **Lago Inferiore.** Most of the sights are within an easy walk of one another within the compact center, which is only a 10-minute walk from the lakeside train station. Follow **Via Solferino** to **Via Marangoni,** turn right, and follow that to **Piazza Cavallotti,** where a left turn on **Corso Umberto I** will bring you to **Piazza delle Erbe,** the first of the gracious *piazze* that flow through the city center to the palace of the Gonzagas. You can also make the trip on the no. 2 bus, which leaves from the front of the station.

EXPLORING THE CITY

As you wander around, you'll notice that Mantua's squares are handsomely proportioned spaces surrounded by medieval and Renaissance churches and *palazzi*. The *piazze* open one into another, creating the wonderful illusion that walkers in the city are strolling through a series of opera sets.

The southernmost of these squares, and the place to begin your explorations, is **Piazza delle Erbe (Square of the Herbs)** ★, so named for the produce-and-food market that transpires in stalls to one side (see "Festivals & Markets," above). Mantua's civic might is clustered here in a series of late-medieval and early Renaissance structures that include the **Palazzo della Ragione (Courts of Justice)** and **Palazzo del Podestà (Mayor's Palace),** from the 12th and 13th centuries, and the **Torre dell'Orologio,** topped with a 14th-century astrological clock. Also on this square is Mantua's earliest religious structure, the **Rotunda di San Lorenzo** ★, a miniature round church from the 11th century (summer daily 10am–noon and 2:30–4:30pm, winter daily 11am–noon, though hours may vary; free admission). The city's Renaissance masterpiece, **Sant'Andrea Basilica** (see below), is off to one side on Piazza Mantegna.

In the adjoining **Piazza Broletto** (just north as you work your way through the Old City), the statue of Virgil commemorates the poet who was born near here in 70 B.C. and celebrated Mantua's river Mincio in his *Bucolics.* The next square, **Piazza Sordello,** is huge, rectangular, and somberly medieval, lined with crenelated *palazzi.* Most notably, though, the massive hulk of the **Palazzo Ducale** (see below) forms one wall of the piazza. To enjoy Mantua's soulful lakeside vistas, follow Via Accademia through Piazza Arche and the Lungolago Gonzaga.

Galleria Museo Palazzo Valenti Gonzaga

After a restoration that lasted 2 decades, this 16th-century palace, which is still inhabited today, reopened its doors to visitors in 2008. The palace retains much of its former splendor, and visitors can wander through the public spaces, which are the *piano nobile* and the rooftop garden (the other floors are inhabited). This palace offers insight into how Mantuan noble families lived throughout the centuries; it is also home to a wonderfully restored cycle of 17th-century frescoes by Frans Geffels, which will appeal to fans of Flemish painting and subjects.

Via Pietro Frattini 7. Ⓒ **0376-364-524** or 348-441-9954. www.valentigonzaga.com. Admission 8€ adults; 6€ seniors over 65; free for children under 12. Tues–Fri 10am–1pm and 4–7pm. Sat–Sun, guided tours available at 10am, 11am, noon, 3pm, 4pm, 5pm, and 6pm. Reservations are necessary. Ticket booth is at Piazza Mantegna 9/a.

Palazzo d'Arco

Mantua's aristocratic D'Arco family lived in this elegant Renaissance *palazzo* until 1973, when the last member of the family donated it to the city. Though most of the extant *palazzo* is neoclassical (1780s), the gardens shelter a wing from the 15th century; the highlight of the rooms is the Sala dello Zodiaco, brilliantly frescoed with astrological signs by Giovanni Falconetto in 1520.

Piazza d'Arco 4. Ⓒ **0376-322-242.** www.museodarco.it. Admission 3€. Mar–Oct Tues–Sun 10am–12:30pm and 2:30–6pm; Nov–Feb Sat–Sun 10am–12:30pm and 2–5pm.

Palazzo Ducale ★★

Behind the walls of this massive fortress/palace lies the history of the Gonzagas, Mantua's most powerful family, and what remains of the treasure trove they amassed in a rule that began in 1328 and lasted into the early 18th century. Between their skills as warriors and their penchant for marrying into wealthier and more cultured houses, they managed to acquire power, money, and an artistic following that included Pisanello, Titian, and, most notably, Andrea Mantegna, their court painter, who spent most of his career working for his Mantua patrons.

The most fortunate of these unions was that of Francesco Gonzaga to Isabelle d'Este in 1490. This well-bred daughter of Ferrara's Este clan commissioned many of the art-filled frescoed apartments you see today, including the Camera degli Sposi in Isabella's apartments—the masterpiece, and only remaining fresco cycle, of Mantegna. It took the artist 9 years to complete the cycle, and in it, he included many of the visitors to the court; it's a fascinating account of late-15th-century court life.

Most of Mantegna's works for the palace, though, have been carted off to other collections; his famous *Parnassus,* which he painted for an intimate room known as the *studiolo,* is now in the Louvre, as are works that Perugino and Correggio painted for the same room (in one of the more compelling current stories from the art world, Mantua is demanding their return).

The Gonzagas expanded their palace by incorporating any structure that lay within reach, including the Duomo and the Castello di San Giorgio (1396–1406). As a result, it's now a small city of 500 rooms connected by a labyrinth of corridors, ramps, courtyards, and staircases, filled with Renaissance frescoes and ancient Roman sculpture. The Sala del Pisanello frescoes feature Arthurian legends (mostly Tristan and Isolde) painted by Pisanello between 1436 and 1444, which were discovered beneath layers of plaster only in 1969. The Sale degli Arazzi (Tapestry Rooms) are hung with copies—woven at the same time but by a different Flemish workshop—of the Vatican's tapestries designed by Raphael and his students (among them Giulio Romano). The Camera degli Sposi was frescoed by Mantegna (the *trompe l'oeil* oculus in the center of the ceiling is an icon of Renaissance art and a masterpiece of foreshortening).

Other highlights include the Galleria degli Specchi (Hall of Mirrors); the low-ceiling Appartamento dei Nani (Apartments of the Dwarfs), where a replica of the Holy Staircase in the Vatican is built to miniature scale (in keeping with noble custom of the time, dwarfs were part of Isabella's court); and the Galleria dei Mesi (Hall of the Months). Some of the mostly delightful chambers in the vast complex make up the Appartamento Estivale (Summer Apartment), which looks over a courtyard where hanging gardens provide the greenery.

Piazza Sordello. ✆ **0376-382-150.** www.mantovaducale.it. Admission 6.50€. Tues–Sun 8:30am–7:00pm.

Palazzo Te ★ Federico Gonzaga, the pleasure-loving refined son of Isabella d'Este, built this splendid Mannerist palace as a retreat from court life. As you enter the courtyard, you'll see that the purpose of this palace was to amuse—the keystone of the monumental archway is designed to look like it's falling out of place. Throughout the whimsical interior, sexually frank frescoes by Giulio Romano (who left a scandal behind him in Rome over his licentious engravings) depict *Psyche* and other erotically charged subject matter and make unsubtle reference to one of Frederico's favorite pastimes (horses and astrology, Federico's other passions, also figure prominently). The greatest and most playful achievement here, though, has to do with power: In the **Sala dei Giganti (Room of the Giants) ★★,** Titan is overthrown by the gods in a dizzying play of architectural proportion that gives the illusion that the ceiling is falling. The Palazzo Te is the home of the Museo Civico, whose permanent collections on the upper floor include the Gonzaga family's coins, medallion, and other displays of its wealth and power, alongside more recently donated works of art by such names as Spadini and Zandomeneghini.

The *palazzo* is a 20-minute walk from the center of town along Via Mazzini. En route, at Via Acerbi 47, sits **Casa di Mantegna,** the house and studio of Andrea Mantegna. Admission is free, so devotees of Mantua's most famous painter may choose to stop by for a look. It's open Tuesday to Sunday 10am to 12:30pm and 3 to 6pm (✆ **0376-360-506;** hours may vary).

Viale Te. ✆ **0376-323-266.** Admission 8€ adults, 3€ ages 12–18 and seniors over 65, free for children under 12. Mon 1–6pm; Tues–Sun 9am–6pm.

Sant'Andrea Basilica ★ A graceful Renaissance facade fronts this 15th-century church by Leon Battista Alberti, with an 18th-century dome by Juvarra. The simple arches seem to float beneath the classic pediment, and the unadorned elegance forms a sharp contrast to other Lombardy monuments, such as the Duomo in Milan, the Cappella Colleoni in Bergamo, and the Certosa in Pavia. Inside, the classically proportioned vast space is centered on a single aisle. The Gonzaga court painter Mantegna is buried in the first chapel on the left. The crypt houses a reliquary containing the blood of Christ (allegedly brought here by Longinus, the Roman soldier who thrust his spear into Jesus' side), which is carried through town on March 18, the feast of Mantua's patron, Sant'Anselmo.

Piazza Mantegna. Free admission. Daily 7:30am–noon and 3–7pm.

WHERE TO STAY

If you're interested in the lowest-priced accommodations, the tourist office can provide details and reserve rooms at five hostel-like farmhouses in the surrounding countryside. Rates are about 30€ to 35€ per person. Since several of the properties are within a few kilometers of town, you can reach them without too much trouble by bike or combination bus ride and trek.

ABC Moderno ★   The prices at this hotel across from the train station are remarkably low, considering the pleasant surroundings and the amenities. A nice lounge area and breakfast room open onto a sunny terrace. Upstairs, the renovated rooms have bright tile floors, fresh plaster and paint, new modular furnishings, and modern bathrooms. Architectural details, such as stone walls and patches of old frescoes, have been uncovered to provide decorative touches. The management is extremely helpful, and their hospitality extends to lending out the three bikes they have on hand for free (first-come, first-served). If the Moderno is full, bypass the other nearby hotels, which tend to be dreary and overpriced.

Piazza Don Leoni 25, 46100 Mantova. ⓒ **0376-323-347.** Fax 0376-322-349. 31 units. 66€–165€ double. Rates include buffet breakfast. MC, V. Parking 10€. **Amenities:** Restaurant (cafe); bar; free bikes; concierge. In room: TV, hair dryer, Wi-Fi.

Broletto ★★   This atmospheric old hotel is in the center of the Old City, only a few steps from the lake and the *castello*, making it a fine base for a late-night stroll through the moonlit *piazze*. The rooms have contemporary furnishings that are vaguely rustic in design, with orthopedic bed frames. Bright corner room no. 16 has balconies and windows on two sides. The most alluring features of the decor, though, are the massive beams on the ceilings and other architectural details from the *palazzo*'s 16th-century origins.

Via Accademia 1, 46100 Mantova. ⓒ **0376-326-784.** Fax 0376-221-297. www.hotelbroletto.com. 16 units. 90€–120€ double. Rates include continental breakfast. AE, DC, MC, V. Closed Dec 23–28. **Amenities:** Babysitting; concierge. In room: A/C, TV, hair dryer, minibar, Wi-Fi.

Mantegna   On a quiet side street, just a few steps south of the *centro storico*, the Mantegna offers solid comfort in surroundings that are thoroughly modern. The cozy narrow singles resemble ships' cabins, but the doubles are unusually roomy. Many of them face a sunny and quiet courtyard.

Via Fabio Filzi 10, 46100 Mantova. ⓒ **0376-328-019.** Fax 0376-368-564. www.hotelmantegna.it. 42 units. 140€ double. AE, MC, V. Parking free in courtyard. Closed Dec 24–Jan 7 and 2 weeks in Aug. **Amenities:** Bar; concierge. In room: A/C, TV, hair dryer, minibar.

Rechigi Hotel   This is a modern hotel 1 block down and 3 blocks over from the main piazza and Duomo. It's decorated with modern sculptures and paintings, with regular exhibits by contemporary artists filling the common spaces sheathed in tan marble panels for a minimalist look that permeates the hotel. It's got loads of amenities and a great location, but the rooms aren't all that outstanding. They're midsize to large, fitted with thin carpets, and have hand-held nozzles in some tubs of the generous-size bathrooms. Some do come with king-size beds, though. There's a small patio for alfresco summer breakfasts.

Via Pier Fortunato Calvi 30, 46100 Mantova. © **0376-320-781.** Fax 0376-220-291. www.rechigi.com. 59 units. 110€–190€ standard double; 180€–215€ deluxe double; 200€–235€ suite. Breakfast 15€. AE, DC, MC, V. Garage parking 20€. **Amenities:** Bar; concierge; room service; sauna; smoke-free rooms. *In room:* A/C, TV, hair dryer, minibar.

WHERE TO DINE

Mantovian cuisine is quite refined—an array of pastas stuffed with pumpkin and squash, a fine selection of fish from the surrounding lakes and rivers, and exquisite risotto dishes (rice has been cultivated here since the early 1500s; the tourist office even promotes a *strada del riso,* or "rice road," through the region modeling the "wine roads" of other regions, and showing how important rice is to the area).

Leoncino Rosso ★★ MANTOVANA This fine old restaurant with an attractive rustic dining room, just off Piazza Broletto (on a parallel street) in the center of the Old City, has been serving food since 1750. This is a good place to sample Mantua's distinctive cuisine. Topping the list is *tortelli di zucca,* a large ravioli pillow stuffed with pumpkin. If you want to continue to eat as the Mantovese do, move on to *stracotto Mantovano* (stewed donkey; that store next door is a horsemeat butcher). For more familiar fare from the barnyard, try the delicious *cotechino e fagioli* (pork sausage and beans). You can tell it's a local place by the TV in the corner (a bit loud, actually) that always manages to have a soccer game playing.

Via Giustiziati 33. © **0376-323-277.** Reservations recommended. Primi 9€; secondi 11€. AE, DC, MC, V. Mon–Sat noon–3pm and 7–10pm. Closed 15 days in Aug and 1 week in Jan.

Ochina Bianca ★★ MANTOVANA Gilberto and Marcella Venturini serve distinctive variations on the local cuisine in these simple yet elegant dining rooms a few blocks north of the center. Many of the dishes rely on fresh fish from the Mincio, which finds it way into such creations as *peperoni ripieni di pesce di fiume* (peppers filled with smoked fish and topped with a fresh tomato sauce) and many of the risotti. Grilled or sautéed freshwater fish is also often on the menu, as are traditional meat specialties like *coniglio alla porchetta* (roasted rabbit with pork stuffing). The zucchini flowers stuffed with ricotta and *parmigiano* and kissed with anchovy paste are almost as good an antipasto as the tiny salmon rolls (wrapped around fat so it melts and flavors as the fish cooks) and served on a potato purée as a main course. *Torta sabbiosa* is a local dessert, a raisined plum cake soaked in Guinness, and the homemade gelato is delicious. The carefully chosen wine list is extensive.

Via Finzi 2. © **0376-323-700.** Reservations required. Primi 10€–11€; secondi 13€–15€. MC, V. Tues–Sun 12:45–2pm and 7:45–10pm. Closed Sun evening and last 3 weeks in Aug.

Trattoria due Cavallini ★ (Value) MANTOVANA Your reward for the 10-minute walk south of the center (follow Via Trieste and its continuation, Corso Garibaldi, until you hit Via Salnitro) is a meal at one of Mantua's favorite informal *trattorie,* where, in good weather, you can eat in a shady courtyard. The menu is typically Mantovian, with excellent *tortelli di zucca* and an aromatic *stinco di maiale* (roasted pork joint, infused with fresh herbs). The *torta sbrisolona,* a traditional Mantovese cake of cornmeal, almonds, and butter, is served fresh from the oven.

Via Salnitro 5. © **0376-322-084.** Reservations not necessary. Primi 6€–10€; secondi 8€–11€. AE, MC, V. Wed–Mon noon–3pm and 7:15pm–midnight.

The Lakes

Poets, writers, composers, and mere mortals have been rhapsodizing about the Italian lakes for centuries—most vocally since the 18th century, when it became de rigueur for travelers taking the Grand Tour to descend through the Alps and enjoy their first days on Italian soil on the shores of the lakes. Everyone from Catullus to Ernest Hemingway has sung their praises.

The lakes are among northern Italy's greatest treasures. Stretching from the Piedmont border across northern Lombardy to the Veneto border, backed by the Alps and ringed by lush gardens and verdant forests, each has its own charms and, accordingly, its own enthusiasts. Not least among these charms are the lakes' easy accessibility to many Italian cities, making them ideal for short retreats: Lake Maggiore and Lake Como are both less than an hour's distance from Milan, and Lake Garda is tantalizingly close to Venice, Verona, and Mantua.

Note: For a map of The Lakes area, please see the "Lombardy & the Lakes" map on p. 273.

1 LAKE GARDA (LAGO DI GARDA)

Sirmione: 127km (79 miles) E of Milan, 149km (92 miles) W of Venice; Riva del Garda: 170km (105 miles) E of Milan, 199km (123 miles) NW of Venice, 43km (27 miles) S of Trent

Lake Garda ★★, the largest and easternmost of the lakes, laps against the flat plains of Lombardy and the Veneto at its southern extremes, and in the north becomes fjordlike and moody, its deep waters backed by Alpine peaks. Garda's shores are green and fragrant with flowery gardens, groves of olives and lemons, and forests of pines and cypress.

This pleasing, vaguely exotic landscape has attracted the likes of poet Gabriele d'Annunzio, whose villa near Gardone is one of the area's major attractions, and Benito Mussolini, whose Republic of Salo was headquartered here. Long before them, the Romans discovered the hot springs that still gush forth at Sirmione, the famed resort on a spit of land at the lake's southern reaches. Today's visitors come to swim (Garda is the cleanest of the major lakes), windsurf (Riva del Garda, at the northern end of the lake, is Europe's windsurfing capital), and enjoy the easygoing ambience of Garda's many pleasant lakeside resorts.

SIRMIONE

Garda's most popular resort juts several miles into the southern waters of the lake on a narrow peninsula of cypress and olive groves. Despite an onslaught of visitors, Sirmione manages to retain its charm. Vehicular traffic is kept to a minimum (the few motorists allowed onto the marble streets of the Old Town are required to switch off their cars' engines at traffic lights). The emphasis is on strolling, swimming in waters warmed in spots by underwater hot springs, and relaxing on sunny hotel terraces. *One caveat:* You may find Sirmione to be less than charming in July and August, when the crowds descend in full force.

GETTING THERE **By Train** There are no direct trains, but you can ride the rails to nearby Desenzano del Garda (a 20-min. bus ride from Sirmione; buses half-hourly), which is on the trunk line from Milan to Venice. Trains run almost every half-hour in either direction, stopping in Venice (1½–2 hr.), Verona (25–35 min.), Brescia (25 min.), and Milan (1½ hr.).

By Bus Hourly bus service links Sirmione with Verona (1 hr.) and Brescia (1 hr.). For more information, contact **SAIA buses** in Brescia (✆ **800-620-001**) or **APT** in Verona (✆ **045-800-4129**). In summer, a special bus makes a 35-minute 7pm run from Verona Monday, Wednesday, Friday, and Saturday.

By Boat Hydrofoils and ferries operated by **Navigazione Laghi** (✆ **030-914-9511** or 045-755-0036; www.navigazionelaghi.it) ply the waters of the lake. One to two hourly ferries and four daily hydrofoils connect Sirmione with Desenzano del Garda (20 min. by ferry; 10 min. by hydrofoil). Two daily ferries and three daily hydrofoils connect Sirmione with Gardone (1¼–2 hr. by ferry, 55 min. by hydrofoil), Limone sul Garda (two daily; 3 hr. by ferry, 1¾ hr. by hydrofoil), and Riva del Garda (almost 4 hr. by ferry, 2¼ hr. by hydrofoil). Service is curtailed October to April.

By Car Sirmione is just off the A4 between Milan and Venice. From Bologna, Florence, Rome, and other points south, take the A22 north from Modena to Verona, and from there the A4 west to Sirmione. The trip from Venice takes about 1½ hours, and the trip from Milan a little over an hour. There's ample parking in the lakeside lots lining Viale Marconi, the broad avenue that runs down the peninsula to the entrance of the Old Town.

VISITOR INFORMATION The **tourist office** is outside the Old Town near the castle, at Viale Marconi 2 (✆ **030-916-245**). Easter to October, hours are daily 9am to 12:30pm and 3 to 6pm (though the hotel reservations people actually keep it open all day long until 9pm); November to March, hours are Monday to Friday 9am to 12:30pm and 3 to 6pm, and Saturday 9am to 12:30pm. The helpful English-speaking staff dispenses a wealth of information about Sirmione and other sights on the lake and will reserve a room for you.

Exploring the Town

In addition to its attractive, albeit tourist-shop-ridden Old Town, Sirmione has many lakeside promenades, pleasant beaches, and even some open countryside where olive trees sway in the breeze. Anything you'll want to see can be reached easily on foot, though an open-air tram makes the short run out to the Roman ruins from the northern edge of the Old Town (but not btw. 12:30 and 2:30pm).

The moated and turreted **Castello Scaligero** (✆ **030-916-468**) marks the only landside entrance to the Old Town. Built in the 13th century by the della Scala family, who ruled Verona and many of the lands surrounding the lake, the castle warrants a visit mainly for the views from its towers. It's open Tuesday to Sunday April to October 9am to 8pm and November to March 9am to 1pm. Admission is 5€.

From the castle, Via Vittorio Emanuele leads through the center of the town and emerges after a few blocks into the greener, garden-lined lanes that wind through the tip of the peninsula to the **Grotte di Catullo** (✆ **030-916-157**). Whether or not these extensive ruins at the northern tip of the peninsula were really, as they're alleged to have been, the villa and baths of the pleasure-loving Roman poet Catullus is open to debate.

Even so, their presence here, on a hilltop fragrant with wild rosemary and pines, demonstrates that Sirmione has been a deservedly popular retreat for millennia, and you can wander through the evocative remains while enjoying wonderful lake views. March to October 14, the ruins are open Tuesday to Saturday 8:30am to 7pm and Sunday 9am to 5:30pm; admission is 4€.

If you want to enjoy the clean waters of the lake, the place to head is the small **Lido delle Bionde beach,** near the castle off Via Dante. In summer the beach concession rents lounge chairs with umbrellas for 10€ per day, as well as kayaks and pedal boats (8€ per hour).

Where to Stay

Sirmione has many pleasant, moderately priced hotels, all of which book up quickly in July and August, when they also charge higher rates (reflected in the higher end of the rates below). You aren't allowed to drive into the Old Town until a guard at the entrance near the castle confirms that you have a hotel reservation. The tourist office will help you find a room in your price range on the day you arrive, but they won't book ahead of time.

Corte Regina ★   This attractive older hotel is housed in a stone building on a narrow side street leading to the lake and a beach. While it doesn't have the same lakeside views the Grifone enjoys (see below), the Corte Regina, with its pleasant accommodations and friendly ambience, is an excellent alternative if that hotel is full, and it's a bit nicer as well. Outside there's a sunny terrace. Upstairs the large tile-floored rooms have contemporary furnishings and bathrooms with box showers, hair dryers, and even telephones.

Via Antiche Mura 11, 25019 Sirmione (BS). ✆ **030-916-147.** Fax 030-919-6470. www.corteregina.it. 14 units. 80€–110€ double; 100€–130€ triple; 130€–150€ family suite for 4. Rates include breakfast. AE, DC, MC, V. Free parking nearby or 10€ in garage. Closed Jan–Mar. **Amenities:** Home-cooking seafood restaurant; bar; babysitting; room service. In room: A/C, TV, hair dryer, minibar.

Eden ★   The American poet Ezra Pound once lived in this pink-stucco lakeside hotel, located on a quiet side street leading to the lake in the center of town. Despite its long history as a lakeside retreat, the Eden has been modernized with taste and an eye to comfort. You can see the lake from most of the attractive rooms, which are decorated with contemporary furnishings. The mirrored walls enhance the light and lake views. The large bathrooms are new, and many have big tubs. The marble lobby opens to a delightful shaded terrace and a swimming pier that juts into the lake.

Piazza Carducci 17/18, 25019 Sirmione (BS). ✆ **030-916-481.** Fax 030-916-483. www.hoteledenonline.it. 33 units. 110€–160€ double; 120€–190€ double with lake view. Rates include breakfast. AE, DC, MC, V. Free parking nearby or 10€ in garage. Closed Nov to Easter. **Amenities:** Bar; babysitting; concierge; room service; tennis courts nearby. In room: A/C, TV, hair dryer, minibar.

Grifone ★★ (Value)   One of Sirmione's best-value lodgings is also one of its most romantic—the vine-clad stone building next to the castle enjoys a prime piece of lake property. You can enjoy this setting from a shady patio off the lobby, from a small beach, or from any of the guest rooms with a view. Brother and sister Nicola and Christina Marcolini oversee the hotel and adjoining restaurant with a great deal of graciousness, carrying on several generations of a family business. The rooms are simple but pleasant, with tile floors and plain furnishings; top-floor rooms (nos. 36–42) have small balconies from which to survey the views. The tidy bathrooms have stall showers or curtainless tubs. The Grifone books up quickly, often with return guests, so reserve well in advance.

Via Bocchio 4, 25019 Sirmione (BS). ✆ **030-916-014.** Fax 030-916-548. 16 units. 67€ double; extra bed 23€. No credit cards. Free parking. Closed late Oct to Easter. **Amenities:** International-cuisine restaurant; bar. In room: Hair dryer (on request).

Hotel Speranza This modest hotel occupies the upper floors of an old building that arches across Sirmione's main street, providing a prime location near the castle and only a few steps in either direction from the lake. The emphasis here is on clean efficiency rather than luxury: Public rooms consist of a tiny lobby and breakfast room, and the bare-bones rooms are perfectly serviceable. In fact, the modern furnishings set against parquet floors and stark white walls make for a fairly chic look. Bathrooms are modernized (save for the flat waffle towels on heated racks), with box showers.

Via Castello 6, 25019 Sirmione (BS). ✆ **030-916-116.** Fax 030-916-403. http://hotelsperanza.sitonline.it. 13 units. 90€–105€ double. Rates include breakfast. AE, DC, MC, V. Free parking in square with permit, available from hotel. Closed mid-Nov to late Feb. **Amenities:** Concierge. *In room:* A/C, TV.

Olivi ★★ This pleasant modern hotel offers the chance to live the high life at reasonable rates. It's not directly on the lake, which you can see from most rooms and the sunny terrace, but instead commands a hilltop position near the Roman ruins amid pines and olive groves. The rooms are stunningly decorated in varying schemes of bold, handsome pastels and earth tones. There are separate dressing areas off the bathrooms, and most have balconies. There's a pool in the garden and, to bring a lakeside feeling to the grounds, an artificial river that streams past the terrace and glass windows of the lobby and breakfast room.

Via San Pietro 5, 25019 Sirmione (BS). ✆ **030-990-5365.** Fax 030-916-472. www.hotelolivi.it. 58 units. 178€–200€ standard double; 212€–228€ "quality" double. Rates include breakfast. AE, MC, V. Free parking on grounds. Closed Jan. **Amenities:** 3 restaurants; 2 bars; babysitting; concierge; Internet; pool; room service. *In room:* A/C, TV, hair dryer, minibar.

Palace Hotel Villa Cortine ★★★ This is clearly something special: You enter the gates and drive around a statue-lined lily pond lorded over by Neptune to a snaking, cypress-lined road that ends at a Palladian villa. Actually, it was built only in the early 20th century (the main hotel core behind it was added in 1957) by a German count who was forcibly repatriated back north of the Alps during World War I, but its neoclassical grandeur is nonetheless impressive for it. The small gravel parking lot is packed with luxury automobiles and limited-edition sports cars. There are views across the trees to the lake below, where there is a private beach with a motorboat launch. The staff prides itself on personalized service. The decor is a quirky mix of styles ranging from Renaissance and baroque to Empire and neoclassical, all of it terribly elegant and refined. Guests enjoy breezy meals on the colonnaded flagstone terrace and access to a landscaped 4.8-hectare (12-acre) park.

Via Grotte 6, 25019 Sirmione (BS). ✆ **030-990-5890.** Fax 030-916-390. www.palacehotelvillacortine.it. 54 units. 280€–430€ double; 400€–620€ deluxe double; 380€–580€ junior suite; 500€–650€ suite. Half-board adds 120€ per person. Rates include continental breakfast. AE, DC, MC, V. Free parking on grounds. Closed mid-Oct to Apr 1. **Amenities:** 2 restaurants; bars; babysitting; bikes; concierge; heated outdoor pool; room service; smoke-free rooms; outdoor clay tennis courts (lighted); watersports equipment rentals. *In room:* A/C, TV, VCR (on request), hair dryer, Internet, minibar.

Where to Dine

In addition to the choices below, you can get a quick pizza with a lake view from the terrace at **L'Arcimboldo,** Via Vittorio Emanuele 71 (✆ **030-916-409;** closed Tues).

La Roccia ITALIAN/PIZZA This trattoria/pizza parlor caters to the flocks of tourists who stream through Sirmione, but it does so with excellent food and unusually pleasant surroundings. In good weather, the best seating is in the garden to one side of the restaurant. The menu includes more than 20 excellent pizzas made in a wood-burning oven,

plus plenty of pastas, including lasagna and excellent cheese tortellini in a cream-and-
prosciutto sauce. The fish (try the trout roasted or fried in butter and sage) and meat are
excellent, and the best dishes are grilled over an open fire.

Via Piana 2. (✆ **030-916-392.** Reservations not necessary. Primi 8€–11€; secondi 11€–17€; pizza 6€–10€.
DC, MC, V. Fri–Wed 12:30–3pm and 7–10:30pm. Closed Nov–Mar.

Ristorante Al Progresso SEAFOOD/ITALIAN   This fan-cooled room on the main
street of the Old Town is appealingly plain but has a touch of style. The pastas include
excellent tortellini variations, and some come with shellfish from the not-too-distant
Adriatic. Fresh lake trout is often on the menu—grilled or *al Sirmionese* (boiled with a
house sauce of garlic, oil, capers, and anchovies)—as are some simple veal preparations,
including a *vitello al limone,* made with fresh lemons that grow on the shores of the lake.

Via Vittorio Emanuele 18–20. (✆ **030-916-108.** Reservations not necessary. Primi 7.50€–11€; secondi
10€–17€. AE, DC, MC, V. Fri–Wed (daily in summer) noon–2:30pm and 6:30–10:30pm. Closed either Nov–
Dec or Dec–Jan (depending on flow of tourism).

GARDONE RIVIERA

The little resort of Gardone Riviera, 47km (29 miles) south of Riva del Garda on the
western shore of the lake, has two interesting attractions. Once Italy's most famous sol-
dier/poet, Gabriele d'Annunzio is today remembered not for his lackluster verse, but
more for his adventures and grand lifestyle at **Il Vittoriale** (✆ **0365-296-511;** www.
vittoriale.it), a hillside estate that is one of Lake Garda's major sites. He bought the estate
(it's also alleged that Mussolini presented it to the poet as a way to coerce his sympathies)
in 1921 and died here in 1936. The claustrophobic rooms of this ornately and bizarrely
decorated villa are filled with bric-a-brac and artifacts from the poet's colorful life, including many mementos of his long affair with actress Eleanora Duse. Elsewhere on the
grounds, which cascade down the hillside in a series of luxuriant gardens, are the patrol
boat D'Annunzio commanded in World War I, a museum containing his biplane and
photos, and his pompous hilltop tomb.

Admission is 7€ for adults and 5€ for children ages 7 to 12 and seniors older than 65
to the grounds only; you pay 5€ adults, 3€ kids and seniors additional to tour the villa,
which you can visit only via a 25-minute guided tour (in Italian; even if you don't understand a word of the tour, it's worth taking to look inside the villa). April to September
the grounds are open daily 8:30am to 8pm, and the villa is open Tuesday to Sunday
9:30am to 7pm; October to March the grounds are open daily 9am to 5pm, the villa
Tuesday to Sunday 9am to 1pm and 2 to 5pm. The villa also hosts a July-to-August
season of concerts and plays; call (✆ **0365-296-519** (www.teatrodelvittoriale.it) for more
information.

Just down the hill on Via Roma is the **Giardino Botanica Hruska** (✆ **0336-410-
877**), a small but delightful bower planted a hundred years ago by the Swiss naturalist
Arturo Hruska (a dentist whose clientele included European royalty). More than 2,000
species of exotic flora from around the world continue to thrive in the balmy microclimate around the lake here. Admission is 6€. March 15 to October 15, the garden is open
daily from 9am to 7pm.

GETTING THERE   For ferry connections with Riva del Garda and Sirmione, see those
sections elsewhere in this chapter (from Limone sul Garda, prices are the same as from
Riva del Garda, but the trip is 30 min. quicker by hydrofoil and 45 min. faster by ferry).
You can also bus here from Riva del Garda in 65 minutes. From Sirmione, you have to
transfer at Desenzano del Garda for one of six daily runs (1 hr. total). Hourly buses also

make the 1-hour trip to and from Brescia, and two buses a day make the 3-hour trip to and from Milan.

VISITOR INFORMATION   Gardone's **tourist office** is at Corso Repubblica 8 (℃/fax **0365-20-347**). Hours in April to October: Tuesday to Saturday 9am to 12:30pm and 4 to 7pm, and Sunday 9am to 12:30pm. November to March: Monday to Wednesday and Friday 9am to 12:30pm and 3 to 6pm, and Thursday 9am to 12:30pm.

Where to Stay & Dine

Grand Hotel Fasano ★★   Signor Mayer, the owner of this lakeside retreat, exclaims, "We sell water and sun; everything else is just a frame around it." He and his brother must be doing something right to ensure a 90% return rate on their guests—all the more remarkable, since their clientele is made up entirely of private tourists (lots of them German), as they refuse to take tour groups or agency bookings. Terraces and balconies overlook the palm- and willow-shaded garden right on the lake, where guests can take breakfast or dinner and swim off the small pier. The terraces above the gardens host the awning-shaded, fan-cooled restaurant and bar, which feature live piano music several times a week. Rooms at either end of the villa are larger, those in the long connecting wing smaller but with larger terraces. "Classic" rooms are fitted with simple, homey furnishings but are very comfy, featuring modern bathrooms and paintings of putti. "Superior" rooms are larger, with small, curtained-off terrace/sitting areas. Accommodations in the separate Villa Principe, set amid the trees at one end of the property, are slightly more exclusive, with larger rooms but similar furnishings.

25083 Gardone Riviera (BS). ℃ **0365-290-220.** Fax 0365-290-221. www.ghf.it. 75 units in main hotel, 12 in Villa Principe. 100€–115€ standard double without lake view; 110€–135€ superior double without lake view; 115€–155€ standard double with lake view; 135€–175€ superior double with lake view; 165€–205€ deluxe double with lake view; 300€–380€ suite. Rates include breakfast. Half-board available for stays of at least 3 nights. MC, V. Free parking. **Amenities:** 4 restaurants; bar; babysitting; bikes; concierge; fitness center; nearby golf course; outdoor heated pool; room service; outdoor tennis courts; watersports equipment/rentals. *In room:* A/C, TV, hair dryer, Internet (in suites and deluxe rooms), minibar.

Villa Fiordaliso ★★★   This gorgeous villa is a mix of neoclassical and Liberty style, built in 1903 and later host to several very famous guests, including poet Gabriele d'Annunzio, from 1921 to 1923, and Mussolini's mistress, Claretta Petacci, from 1943 to 1945. The dictator visited his lover frequently here, and they spent the final weeks of their lives at the villa. It's been a hotel since 1990. To choose your room, head to the villa's website, which features 360-degree panoramic photos of each one. The most requested is the "Claretta" suite, where the doomed woman spent her final years surrounded by elaborate ceilings and marble-clad bath fixtures. All rooms have lake views except the "Mimosa," which overlooks the garden from a small terrace. The "Gardenia" and the "Magnolia" below it have windows on three sides (lake view, garden view, and a view overlooking the road). Children under 12 are not allowed. The exquisite restaurant (closed Tues at lunch and Mon all day) has earned itself a Michelin star for its refined cuisine. In warm weather, meals are served on a broad terrace where the lake laps almost to the tables; in winter you dine in a series of rooms with inlaid wood floors, coffered and decorated ceilings, and bottle-bottom windows. There's also a piano bar, Torre San Marco, in a fanciful minicastle on the property that's built half out over the water. It opens at 10:30 every evening.

Via Zanardelli 150, 25083 Gardone Riviera (BS). ℃ **0365-20-158.** Fax 0365-290-011. www.villafiordaliso. it. 7 units. 350€–500€ double; 700€ Claretta suite. Rates include continental breakfast. AE, DC, MC, V. Free

RIVA DEL GARDA

The northernmost town on the lake is not just a resort, but a real, prosperous Italian town, with medieval towers, a nice smattering of Renaissance churches and *palazzi,* and narrow cobblestone streets where everyday business proceeds in its alluring way.

Essentials

GETTING THERE **By Train** See "Getting There," under Sirmione, earlier in this chapter, for connections to Desenzano del Garda, from which you must take a bus (see below).

By Bus Six buses a day link Riva del Garda and Desenzano del Garda on the southern end of the lake, about a 2-hour trip. You can also travel between Sirmione and Riva del Garda by bus, though except for a 4:30pm direct run, you must transfer at Peschiera (2 hr.). From Limone sul Garda, there are 11 trips daily (18 min.). Twenty-five daily buses connect Riva del Garda and Trent (1⅔ hr.). From Verona there are 16 a day (2 hr.), and from Brescia five daily (2 hr.).

By Boat Navigazione Lago di Garda (see "Sirmione," earlier in this chapter, for more information) runs the boats. Fifteen ferries and four hydrofoils per day connect Riva del Garda with Limone sul Garda (35–45 min. by ferry, 30 min. by hydrofoil). Two ferries and four hydrofoils per day connect Riva del Garda with Gardone (2¼ hr. by ferry; 1 hr., 20 min. by hydrofoil), Sirmione (almost 4 hr. by ferry, 2¼ hr. by hydrofoil), and Desenzano del Garda (4¼ hr. by ferry, 2½ hr. by hydrofoil). Schedules vary with the season, with very limited service in the winter.

By Car The fastest link between Riva del Garda and points north and south is via the A22, which shoots up the east side of the lake (exit at Mori, 13km/8 miles east of Riva del Garda). A far more scenic drive is along the western shore, on the beautiful corniche between Riva del Garda and Salo that hugs cliffs and passes through mile after mile of tunnel. Depending on the route, by car Riva del Garda is about an hour from Verona and about 45 minutes from Sirmione.

VISITOR INFORMATION The **tourist office,** which supplies information on hotels, restaurants, and activities in the area, is near the lakefront Giardini di Porta Orientale 8 (✆ **0464-554-444;** fax 0464-520-308; www.trentino.to). June 16 to September 15, it's open Monday to Saturday 9am to noon and 3 to 6:30pm, and Sunday 10am to noon and 4 to 6:30pm; April to June 15 and September 16 to October, hours are Monday to Saturday 9am to noon and 3 to 6:15pm; November to March, hours are Monday to Friday 9am to noon and 2:30 to 5:15pm.

FESTIVALS & MARKETS Riva del Garda becomes a cultural oasis in July, when the town hosts an **international festival of classical music.**

Exploring the Town

Riva del Garda's Old Town is pleasant enough, though the only historic attractions of note are the 13th-century **Torre d'Apponale** (a picturesque medieval tower on the main square, which is sometimes open for climbing and sometimes not) and, nearby, the moated lakeside castle, **La Rocca.** Part of the castle interior now houses an unassuming collection of local arts and crafts (✆ **0464-573-869**). It's open Tuesday to Saturday 9:30am to 5:30pm and Sunday 9:30am to noon and 2 to 5:30pm; admission is 2.50€, though the prices have been erratic in recent years. The castle also occasionally hosts minor traveling exhibits.

The tourist office runs a few free guided tours (in many languages, including English). On weekends they do walking tours of the town; on Tuesdays and Fridays they offer walking tours of a few sights in the area. You must book in advance, by 5pm the previous day, at ℂ **0464-554-444.** The sights aren't of staggering interest or importance (and that's being kind), but they're a good activity if you happen to be in town and your lazy vacationing by the lakeside is getting boring or you want something cultural to do between windsurfing lessons.

The main attraction here is the **lake itself,** which Riva del Garda takes advantage of with a waterside promenade stretching for several miles past parks and pebbly beaches. The water is warm enough for swimming May to October, and air currents fanned by the mountains make Garda popular for windsurfing year-round.

WATER & LAND SPORTS   A convenient point of embarkation for a lake outing is the beach next to the castle, where you can rent rowboats or pedal boats for about 8.50€ per hour (buy 2 hr., get a 3rd free); from March to October, the concession is open daily 8am to 8pm.

For a more adventurous outing, check out the **sailing** and **windsurfing** at the **Sailing Du Lac** (formerly the Nautic Club Riva), Via Rovereto 44 (ℂ **0464-552-453;** www. sailingdulac.com), where you can rent windsurf equipment for 42€ per day, 37€ for a half-day, or 18€ for an hour. Multiday and weekly packages, as well as lessons, are also available.

You can rent **bikes** from Superbike Girelli, Viale Damiano Chiesa 15 (ℂ **0464-556-602**), for 12€ per day for a mountain bike; or from **Cicli Pederzolli,** Viale dei Tigli 24 (ℂ **0464-551-830**), which charges 8€ per day for a city bike and 12€ for a mountain bike.

Where to Stay

Montanara   It ain't fancy, but it's real cheap. The Montanara is squirreled away above its cheap trattoria in a quiet part of the *centro storico*. The wood-floor, midsize rooms occupy three stories of an old *palazzo* and are exceedingly basic—not to say a bit down at the heels—but are kept immaculate, with a picture or two framed on the whitewashed walls for relief from the spartan environs. Rooms with shared bathrooms at least have a sink. The two top-floor accommodations are the best for their general brightness and high ceilings.

Via Montanara 18–20, 38066 Riva del Garda (BS). ℂ/fax **0464-554-857.** 9 units, 6 with private bathroom. 46€ double with shared bathroom; 50€ double with private bathroom; 70€ triple with private bathroom. Rates include breakfast. MC, V. Parking on street 3€, in garage 8€. Closed Nov to Easter. **Amenities:** Restaurant; bar. *In room:* No phone.

Portici   The management pays much more attention to their ground-floor restaurant/ bar under a portico of the main square than they do to the hotel, but perhaps that's because it's mainly booked by tour groups—keeping this central and surprisingly reasonable choice off the radar of more independent travelers. Sadly, its location in the upper leg of the piazza's L-shape deprives almost all rooms of a lake view—and the functional units are boringly modern, to boot, done up in a monotonous blue tone. Still, for these prices, you can easily walk to a cafe to enjoy the view.

Piazza III Novembre 19, 38066 Riva del Garda (BS). ℂ **0464-555-400.** Fax 0464-555-453. www.hotel portici.it. 45 units. 78€–120€ double. Half-board available. MC, V. Parking on street 3€, in garage 8€. Closed Nov–Mar. **Amenities:** International-cuisine restaurant; bar. *In room:* TV, hair dryer.

Sole ★★   One of the finest hotels in town enjoys a wonderful location right on the lake at the main square. The management lavishes a great deal of attention on the public rooms and guest rooms and charges very fairly. The lobby is filled with rare Persian carpets and abstract art. The rooms reached via a sweeping circular staircase are warm and luxurious, with tasteful furnishings and marble-trimmed bathrooms; the best rooms have balconies hanging over the lake. Lakeview rooms are outfitted in antique style; those overlooking the square and town are done in modern functional. Amenities include a formal restaurant, a casual cafe/bar extending onto a lakeside terrace, a rooftop solarium with sauna, and a nearby gated parking lot.

Piazza III Novembre 35, 38066 Riva del Garda (TN). (℃) **0464-552-686.** Fax 0464-552-811. www.hotelsole. net. 81 units. 96€–160€ double without lake view; 116€–180€ double with lake view. Add 15€ per person for half-pension and 30€ for full pension. AE, DC, MC, V. Parking on street 3€, in garage 8€. Closed Nov to mid-Mar (except at Christmastime and during frequent trade fairs). **Amenities:** International-cuisine restaurant; bar; free bikes; concierge; small exercise room; room service; sauna. *In room:* A/C (in some rooms), TV, hair dryer, minibar, Wi-Fi.

Where to Dine

Birreria Spaten ITALIAN   This noisy indoor beer garden occupies the ground floor of an old *palazzo* and features a wide-ranging mix of food from the surrounding regions, so you can dine on the cuisine of Trent (Trento) or Lombardy or from the other side of the Alps. Many of the German and Austrian visitors who favor Riva del Garda opt for the schnitzel-sauerkraut-sauerbraten fare, but you can also enjoy a pasta like *strangolapreti* (spinach-and-ricotta dumplings in a butter sauce), 1 of 30 pizzas, or a simply grilled lake trout. If you can't decide, the *Piatto Spaten* is an ample 14€ sampler of their Tirolean specialties, including wurstel, *canederli* (a giant bread dumpling), a ham steak, and sauerkraut.

Via Maffei 7. (℃) **0464-553-670.** Primi 6€–8€; secondi 7.50€–15€; pizza 4.50€–9€. MC, V. Thurs–Tues 11am–3pm and 7pm–midnight. Closed Nov–Mar.

LIMONE SUL GARDA

Limone sul Garda is a pretty resort wedged between the lake and mountains just 10km (6¼ miles) south of Riva del Garda on the lakeside corniche. For ferry connections with Riva del Garda and Sirmione, see those earlier sections. Despite the onslaught of tourists who come down through the mountains from Austria and Germany, it's a pleasant place to spend some time and offers more moderately priced lakeside hotels than those found in Riva del Garda. Romans planted lemon groves here (hence the name); the ruins of the protective structures that once covered the groves are still visible on the hills around the town, and lemons continue to thrive on every available parcel of land.

There's a small **IAT tourist info office** at Via Comboni 15 ((℃) **0365-954 070;** fax 0365-954-689). From March to October, it's open daily 9am to 12:30pm and Monday to Saturday 3:30 to 7pm; November to February, hours are Monday to Saturday 9am to 12:30pm and 4:30 to 6pm. Also try the private website **www.limone.com**. *Note:* You'll find that most of the resorts in Limone, such as the two listed below, require a 3-night minimum stay, especially in high season.

Where to Stay

Capo Reamol ★ (Kids)   This is a modern, family-run hotel set just below the road, with a terrace swimming pool above the lake; they even host their own windsurfing school on a private pier. Type "A" rooms—the best—come with large terraces set with beach chairs so that you can gaze over the lake; modern, comfortable built-in furnishings;

Two-Wheeling Limone

Rent a mountain bike in Limone sul Garda at **Tombola Rent,** Via L. Einaudi 1B
(© **0365-954-051**). Rates are 11€ for 5 hours, 17€ for a full day (6am–10pm).
They also rent scooters (for two people) starting at 27€ for 3 hours, 37€ for 5
hours, and 50€ for a full day.

and nice bathrooms graced with heated towel racks. "B" category rooms are somewhat
smaller, with balconies rather than terraces, though some have connecting doors to turn
into family suites. Only four rooms, "C" type, overlook the garden rather than the lake.
Rooms in the *dipendence* at the end of an olive-shaded terrace come with slightly older
(but spick-and-span) bathrooms and lake views, but lack air-conditioning; some are large
enough for four. The restaurant occupies a panoramic room with picture windows overlooking the water, with an antipasto buffet and choice of dishes.

Via IV Novembre 92, 25010 Limone sul Garda (BS). © **0365-954-040.** Fax 0365-954-262. www.hotel
caporeamol.it. 58 units. 80€–144€ "C" double without lake view or balcony; 90€–154€ "B" double with
lake view and balcony; 102€–166€ "A" large double with lake view and terrace. Half-board available. AE,
DC, MC, V. Free private parking. Closed mid-Oct to Easter. **Amenities:** Italian restaurant; large modern
bar; babysitting; free mountain bikes; children's playground; concierge; small exercise room; Internet;
outdoor pool; room service; sauna; outdoor tennis courts nearby; watersports equipment/rentals. *In
room:* A/C (in main building), TV, hair dryer, minibar.

Le Palme ★★   This gracious hotel is one of the most pleasant places to stay on Garda.
It's on the lake at one end of Limone sul Garda's narrow main street and surrounded by
palm trees. Downstairs, a bar and reasonably priced restaurant flow onto a flowery terrace
right on the lake. Upstairs, the large, pleasant rooms are furnished in Venetian-style
antiques (some genuine, others reproduction), and all but a few face the lake; the three
best have small balconies over the water (if your room doesn't have a balcony, you can
enjoy the lake from the downstairs terrace or rooftop solarium). A small beach is just a
few steps down the road, and the hotel has a small pool amid lemon-shaded terraces
nearby. There's also a larger pool available at its sibling hotel, the hillside Splendid Palace,
where they'll be happy to reserve a room for you if Le Palme is full.

Via Porto 36, 25010 Limone sul Garda (BS). © **0365-954-681** or 0365-954-612. Fax 0365-954-120. www.
sunhotels.it. 28 units. 80€–152€ double. Rates include breakfast. Add 16€ per person for half-pension.
MC, V. Free private parking. Closed Nov to Easter. **Amenities:** International/Italian restaurant; bar; children's games; concierge; pool; room service; tennis courts nearby. *In room:* A/C, TV, hair dryer.

Where to Dine

Ristorante Gemma ITALIAN   In a town where many restaurants cater to tourists
with bland fish and chips and bratwurst, Gemma remains an authentic, family-style trattoria. It also enjoys a pretty lakeside location, and the waves lap right up against the
dining terrace. Gemma is the best place in town for grilled lake trout, which, like all
entrees, can be accompanied by a fine *spaghetti alla mare* (with seafood) and other delicious pastas.

Piazza Garibaldi 12. © **0365-954-814** or 0365-940-145. www.ristorantegemma.it. Primi 7€–10€; secondi
9€–20€. MC, V. Thurs–Tues 11:30am–2:30pm and 6:30–10:30pm. Closed mid-Oct to Mar.

2 LAKE COMO (LAGO DI COMO)

Como (town): 65km (40 miles) NE of Milan; Menaggio: 35km (22 miles) NE of Como and 85km (53 miles) N of Milan; Varenna: 50km (31 miles) NE of Como and 80km (50 miles) NE of Milan

The first sight of the dramatic expanse of azure-hued **Lake Como** ★★★, ringed by gardens and forests and backed by the snowcapped Alps, is likely to evoke strong emotions. Romance, soulfulness, even gentle melancholy—these are the stirrings that over the centuries the lake has inspired in poets (Lord Byron), novelists (Stendhal), composers (Verdi and Rossini), and plenty of other visitors, too—be they deposed queens, such as Caroline of Brunswick, whom George IV of England exiled here for her adulterous ways, well-heeled modern travelers who glide up and down these waters in the ubiquitous lake steamers, or, these days, the rich and überfamous (George Clooney owns a villa here).

Aside from its emotional pull, Como is also just an enjoyable place to spend time. Less than an hour from Milan by train or car, its deep waters and verdant shores provide a wonderful respite from modern life. Tellingly, Lake Como served as a backdrop for the romantic scenes in *Star Wars II: Attack of the Clones*—one of the very few settings in the film that was *not* created entirely by CGI computer programs. I guess even George Lucas realized that Como was a place of such unearthly beauty as to need little digital touching up.

COMO

The largest and southernmost town on the lake isn't likely to charm you off the bat for its slight sprawl, but the historic center is lovely if you take the time to stroll it and pop into its little churches. Long a center of silk making, this city traces its roots to the Gauls and, after them, the Romans, and bustles with commerce and industry. You'll probably want to stay in one of the more peaceful settings farther up the lake, but Como amply rewards a day's visit with some fine Renaissance churches and palaces and a nice lakefront promenade.

Essentials

GETTING THERE   By Train   One to three trains hourly connect Milan and Como's Stazione San Giovanni on Piazzale San Gottardo (regional: from Milan's Piazza Garibaldi station, 55–60 min.; high-speed: from Milan's Stazione Centrale station, 40 min.). There are also twice-hourly trains from Milan's Cadorna station to the more convenient Como Lago station right on the shorefront at Piazza Giacomo Matteotti. These trains take about an hour.

VISITOR INFORMATION   The **regional tourist office** dispenses a wealth of information on hotels, restaurants, and campgrounds around the lake from its offices at Piazza Cavour 17 (© **031-269-712** or 031-264-215; www.lakecomo.org). It's open Monday to Saturday 9am to 1pm and 2:30 to 6pm. There is also a **city tourist office** in a little trailer that has moved around a bit since it opened in 2000, but it stays near Piazza del Duomo and seems to have settled on a spot along Via Maestri Comacini around the right side of the cathedral (© **031-264-215**). It's open Monday to Friday 10am to 12:30pm and 2:30 to 6pm, Saturday and Sunday 10am to 6pm.

Exploring Como

Part Gothic and part Renaissance, the **Duomo,** Piazza del Duomo, in the center of town just off the lake (© **031-265-244**), is festooned with exuberant masonry and sculpture.

Fun Facts   Lake Como on the Big Screen

Picturesque Lake Como has been featured in several films. Parts of *Star Wars Episode II: Attack of the Clones* (2002) were filmed at a villa in Lake Como, including the scene in which Anakin Skywalker and Padmé secretly marry each other. *Ocean's Twelve* (2004) also featured Lake Como as home to infamous thief and rival to Daniel Ocean, The Night Fox. In *Casino Royale* (2006), James Bond spends some time recuperating at a hospital in Lake Como after being tortured; this is also where he starts to fall in love with Vesper Lynd, a Bond girl.

Statues of two of the town's famous native sons, Pliny the Elder and Pliny the Younger, flank the main entrance. Inside, beneath an 18th-century dome by Juvarra—the architect who designed much of Turin—is a lavish interior hung with mostly 16th-century paintings and tapestries, with lots of helpful leaflets in English to explain the major works of art. It's open daily 7:30am to noon and 3 to 7pm. The black-and-white-striped 13th-century **Broletto (Town Hall)** abuts the Duomo's left flank, and adjoining it is the **Torre del Comune.** As a study in contrasts, the starkly modernist and aptly named **Casa del Fascio,** built in 1936 as the seat of the region's Fascist government, rises just behind the Duomo.

Como's main street, **Corso Vittorio Emanuele II,** cuts through the medieval quarter, where wood-beamed houses line narrow streets. Just 2 blocks south of the Duomo, the five-sided, 12th-century **San Fedele** stands above a charming square of the same name; parts of the church, including the altar, date from the 6th century. It's open daily 8am to noon and 3:30 to 7pm. To see Como's most alluring church, though, it's necessary to venture into the dull outlying neighborhood southwest of the center, where, just off Viale Roosevelt, you'll come to the five-aisle heavily frescoed **Basilica of Sant'Abbondio** (© 631-338-8111), a Romanesque masterpiece from the 11th century with great 14th-century frescoes (bring coins so you can illuminate them). It's open daily 8am to 6pm (unless a wedding, which is popular here, is on).

Lakeside life revolves around Piazza Cavour and the adjoining Giardini Publici, where the circular **Tempio Voltiano** (© 031-574-705) houses memorabilia on the life and experiments of native son and electricity pioneer Alessandro Volta. Admission is 3€. It is open Tuesday to Sunday 10am to noon and 3 to 6pm (2–4pm Oct–Mar).

For a quick retreat and some stunning views, take the **funicular** (© 031-303-608) for a 7-minute ride up to the top of Brunate, the forested hill above the town (it leaves from the Lungo Lario Trieste every 15 min. or so, in summer every half-hour).

Where to Stay

The Hotel Metropole Suisse (see below) is actually a pretty good value—especially when you consider Como's sad, moderately priced hotel scene. But if you're really pinching pennies, you could do worse (not much worse, mind you) than the seven bare-bones rooms above the **Ristorante Sociale** (see below). Their big selling points are a prime location next door to the Duomo and price: The double rooms go for just 40€ with a shared bathroom, 52€ with a private bathroom.

Hotel Metropole Suisse ★   This massive 1892 hotel closes one side of Como's main square overlooking the lake. Accommodations vary; some rooms are carpeted and have

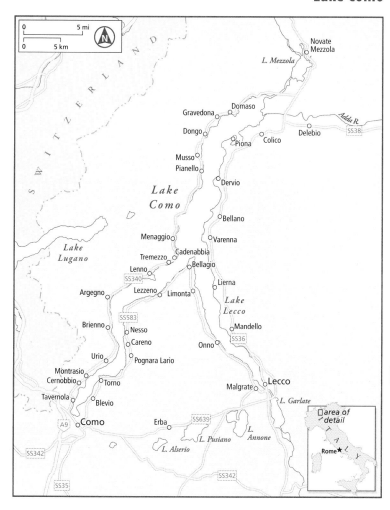

nice contemporary furnishings; others are older, with wood floors, brass beds, and embroidered upholstery. Almost all rooms overlook the lake at least partially—some full-on (the best with small balconies), some askance over the cafes ringing the piazza, and others beyond the tree-lined promenade leading to the city park. The corner bar/lounge has picture windows for lake views, and the restaurant (under separate management) has tables out on the piazza.

Piazza Cavour 19, 22100 Como. ✆ **031-269-444.** Fax 031-300-808. www.hotelmetropolesuisse.com. 71 units. 128€–226€ double; 160€–246€ junior suite. Rates include buffet breakfast. AE, DC, MC, V. Parking 12€. **Amenities:** International-cuisine restaurant; bar; babysitting; concierge; nearby golf course; room service; sauna; smoke-free rooms. *In room:* A/C, TV w/pay movies, Internet, hair dryer, minibar.

Pasticceria Monti CAFE   Above all, the busy Monti on the main lakefront piazza is one of Como's favorite places to gather and watch passersby. You can enjoy some of the excellent gelato or a coffee or cocktail, plus tasty sandwiches and some other light fare, including daily pasta dishes.

Piazza Cavour 21. ℂ **031-301-165.** Gelato from 2€ for a single scoop; pastries from 1.50€; sandwiches from 3.50€. MC, V. Wed–Mon 7am–2am (to 1am in winter).

Ristorante Sociale (Value) ITALIAN/TRATTORIA   Here you'll find simple dishes at low prices. This trattoria, tucked under an arcade next to the Duomo's right flank, is where Comashci go after a play or a concert at Como's Teatro Sociale (the walls are plastered with unsung heroes of the northern Italian stage and the yellowing posters of plays in which they appeared). It's where the local team celebrates victories, where the equivalent of the ladies' auxiliary meets to have long, voluble conversations while enjoying one of the best-priced fixed menus on the lake. The fixed menus give you your choice of four primi (first courses), four secondi (second courses), side dish, and water or wine (though they usually give you both at no extra charge). Just steer clear of the fish—it's frozen . . . rather scandalous for a place located just 2 blocks from the fishing boats bobbing in the lake harbor. They also rent rooms (see "Where to Stay," above).

Via Rodari 6. ℂ **031-264-042.** www.ristorantesociale.it. Primi 6€–12€; secondi 8€–16€. AE, DC, MC, V. Tues–Sun noon–2pm and 7:30–10:30pm.

A Top Hotel in Nearby Cernobbio

Villa d'Este ★★★   One of the most exclusive hotels in the world, this Renaissance villa is set amid 4 hectares (10 acres) of meticulously landscaped lakeside gardens. It has hosted everyone from Mark Twain to Joseph Heller, Clark Gable to Mel Gibson, Carreras to Madonna. Many guests arrive by helicopter or private boat (something which, incidentally, you can rent for yourself when you arrive). It's the sort of place that spares no expense, from the precious marbles in the spacious bathrooms and the genuine antique prints and oil paintings lining the halls and rooms, to the Como silk brocades covering the antiques and the Empire furnishings that actually date back to Napoleon's stay here when it was still a private villa. The villa is steeped in history: Russian Tsarina Maria Fedorowna was the last owner before it became a hotel in 1873. No two rooms here are alike, but rest assured, all are fit for royalty. The main pool floats out on the lake itself; the indoor pool is banked by the indoor tennis and squash courts. Villa d'Este is a member of the Leading Hotels of the World.

Via Regina 40, 22012 Cernobbio, Lago di Como. ℂ **031-3481** or 031-348-834. Fax 031-348-873. www.villadeste.it. 152 units. 490€–790€ double; 835€–1,650€ junior suite; call for rates on suites. Rates include buffet breakfast (or continental breakfast served in your room). AE, DC, MC, V. Free parking. Closed mid-Nov to Feb. **Amenities:** 3 restaurants (a formal, jacket-and-tie international-cuisine restaurant; casual dinner-only grill in Queen's Pavilion; Japanese dinner restaurant); 2 bars (1 elegant w/music, the other poolside); babysitting; free bikes; concierge; exercise room; 7 18-hole golf courses (14km/8¾ miles away); Jacuzzi; 2 heated pools (indoor and outdoor); room service; sauna; spa; 2 tennis courts (indoor and lighted outdoor); watersports equipment/rentals; Wi-Fi in public areas. *In room:* A/C, TV w/pay movies, VCR (on request), hair dryer, Internet, minibar.

BELLAGIO & THE CENTRAL LAKE REGION

By far the loveliest spot on the lake (and where travelers should definitely set their sights) is the section known as the Centro Lago. Three towns—**Bellagio, Varenna,** and **Menaggio**—sit across the water from one another on three different shorelines.

Essentials

GETTING THERE & GETTING AROUND **By Train** The closest train stations to Bellagio and the other Central Lake towns are in Como (see above)—from which you can continue by bus or boat—or, more conveniently, in Varenna, with trains hourly to Milan (about 70 min.). If you're planning to leave the central part of the lake after dinner, the 10:30pm train from Varenna to Milan (with an hour stopover in Lecco) will be your last chance to do so. *Tip:* The ticket window at Varenna's station is rarely, if ever, open, and the automatic ticket machine has been broken for about a decade. Get on without a ticket and find the ticket collector, who will have you pay a regular price ticket without tacking on the large onboard acquisition fee.

By Boat From Como, boats stop first at Bellagio: by ferry 2 hours, by hydrofoil 35 to 45 minutes. They continue on to Menaggio (by ferry another 15 min., by hydrofoil another 5 min.). About half the boats then stop in Varenna as well (plus there are about two dozen short-haul ferries each from Bellagio and Menaggio to Varenna; by ferry another 10 min.; by hydrofoil another 5 min.). You can also get day passes good for just the central lake or for the whole lake.

Many of the ferries carry cars for an additional fee. Schedules vary with the season, but from Easter through September a ferry or hydrofoil makes the trip from Como to Bellagio and other towns along the lake at least hourly. For more information, contact **Navigazione Lago di Como** (✆ **800-551-801** or 031-579-211); the office is on the lakefront in Como on Lungo Lario Trieste.

By Bus One to three **SPT buses** (✆ **031-304-744**) per hour travel from Como to Bellagio (a little more than 1 hr.). Hourly buses to Menaggio take a little more than an hour. Buses leave Como from the bus station in Piazza Matteotti next to the Como Lago train station. Buses to Menaggio and other towns on the western edge of the lake also stop at the San Giovanni train station; get bus tickets at the bar inside the train station.

By Car Bellagio is connected to Como by a picturesque lakeshore road, S583, which can be very crowded in summer. The A9 links Como with Milan in about an hour. To reach Menaggio from Como, follow route S340 along the western shore of the lake. For Varenna, follow S342 to Nibionno, a speck of a town where it intersects with S36, which runs north through industrialized Lecco and then along the lake's eastern shore. All these roads tend to be crowded, especially on weekends and in summer, so allow at least an hour of traveling time.

Bellagio

Bellagio ★★★ is at the tip of the peninsula at a point where the lake forks into three distinct basins: One long leg sweeps north into the Alps, Como is at the southern end of the western leg, and Lecco is at the southern end of the eastern leg. Boats from Bellagio make it easy to visit the nearby shores of the Centro Lago—not that you'll be in a great hurry to leave this pretty old town, with its steep narrow streets, lakeside piazza, and beautiful gardens.

FESTIVALS & MARKETS A pleasant way to spend a summer evening in Bellagio is at one of the concerts held in the Chiesa di Cappuccini, on the grounds of the Rockefeller Foundation between June and July. Bellagio's outdoor market fills the waterfront every third Wednesday of the month.

VISITOR INFORMATION The **Bellagio tourist office** is at Piazza della Chiesa 14 (✆/fax **031-950-204;** www.bellagiolakecomo.com). Its hours are Monday and Wednesday

Outdoor Adventures in Bellagio

The Bellagio region has a great outfitter that can treat you to some light adventurous exploration for decent prices. It runs mountain-bike treks, horseback rides through panoramic mountain passes, kayak excursions around the lake, canyoning (a combination of hiking, swimming, rappelling, and, well, jumping up and down a river gorge), and tandem paragliding lasting anywhere from an hour to 2 days. The price starts around 45€. Contact the **Cavalcalario Club,** Loc. Gallasco 1, Bellagio (✆ **031-964-814,** cellphone 339-530-8138; www.bellagio-mountains.it), for more information.

to Saturday from 9am to noon and 3 to 6pm, Tuesday and Sunday from 10:30am to 12:30pm and 3:30 to 5:30pm.

Exploring the Town

Bellagio is often called one of the most beautiful towns in Italy. Nestled amid cypress groves and verdant gardens, its earth-toned old buildings climb from the lakefront promenade along stepped cobbled lanes. While Bellagio is a popular retreat for everyone from Milanese out for a day of relaxation to British and Americans who come to relax for a week or two, the town has, for the most part, managed to keep its dignity despite the crush of tourists that arrive in the summer months.

One of Bellagio's famed gardens surrounds the **Villa Melzi** built by Francesco Melzi, a friend of Napoleon and an official of his Republic. The villa was the retreat of Franz Liszt and is now the home of a distinguished Lombardian family; they allow the public to stroll through their acres of manicured lawns and fountains and to visit a pavilion where a collection of Egyptian sculpture is on display. It's open from late March through October daily 9:30am to 6:30pm; admission is 6€ (for guided tours: ✆ **339-457-3838;** daniela@giardinidivillamelzi.it).

Bellagio's other famous gardens are those of the **Villa Serbelloni,** occupying land once owned by Pliny the Younger and now in the hands of the Rockefeller Foundation. You can visit the gardens on twice-daily guided tours (reserve ahead), about 1½ hours long, in Italian and English (tours require 6 people minimum, 20 people maximum). From April to October, tours are Tuesday to Sunday at 11am and 4pm and cost 6.50€; for more information and to book a spot on the tour, call ✆ **031-951-555.** You meet at the little tower on the back side of Piazza della Chiesa, a steep block and a half up from the port.

Where to Stay

For a wider selection of moderately priced hotels, you'd do best to head across the lake from Bellagio to Menaggio or Varenna (see below).

Du Lac ★★ The Leoni family ensures that an air of graciousness and old-fashioned comfort pervades its gracious 150-year-old hotel overlooking the lake from the main piazza. Downstairs, a bar spills onto the arcaded sidewalk in front and there are a series of pleasant sitting rooms. Meals are served in a nicely appointed dining room with panoramic views of the lake, and in the guest rooms, each of which is unique; cushy armchairs and a nice smattering of antiques and reproductions lend a great amount of charm. Many of the smallish rooms have balconies or terraces, and there's a rooftop sun terrace with sweeping lake views. They have a sports center nearby with a pool, tennis courts, and a children's center, free for guests.

Piazza Mazzini 32, 22021 Bellagio. ℂ **031-950-320.** Fax 031-951-624. www.bellagiohoteldulac.com. 39 units. 160€–190€ double; 200€–230€ superior double with lake view. Rates include buffet breakfast. Half-board available. MC, V. Parking 10€ in nearby garage. Closed early Nov to Easter. **Amenities:** Restaurant (Italian/international cuisine); bar; babysitting; concierge. In room: A/C, TV, hair dryer, minibar.

Giardinetto   The best lodging deal is at this little hotel at the top of town, reached from the lakefront by Bellagio's narrow stepped streets. A snug lobby, with a big fireplace, opens to a gravelly grapevine-covered terrace, where you're welcome to bring your own food for an alfresco meal. Most of the rooms also overlook the terrace (a flight and a half with no elevator). The majority of rooms are quite large and bright, with big windows (those on the upper floors provide nice views from balconies over the town and lake beyond, especially nos. 18–20) and furnishings like solid old armoires and, in the better rooms, box-spring-and-mattress beds rather than Italy's usual cots. Some are on the air-shaft, however, or come with no window whatsoever. All in all, this hotel is basic but comfortable enough.

Piazza della Chiesa, 22021 Bellagio. ℂ **031-950-168.** 13 units, 11 with private bathroom. 65€ double. Breakfast 6€. No credit cards. Parking 10€ in nearby garage. Closed Nov–Apr. In room: Hair dryer.

Grand Hotel Villa Serbelloni ★★   A grandiose 1850s villa lies at the core of this luxury hotel whose vast grounds expand from Bellagio's central square along the lake and up into the wooded hills. The tone is set by the high-ceilinged salons, frescoed with *grot-teschi* (fanciful stucco ornamentation) and blessed with lake views and live music on some evenings. Rooms vary widely in decor, with stucco ceilings in some, walnut furnishings in others, and oil paintings on the walls. Room categories boil down mostly to size, though almost all lakeview rooms are deluxe (not all deluxe rooms have the view, though), executive, or suite. They also run a health and beauty center with a large exercise room and full-body treatments. In the back of the property, over the spa, is the **Residence Ulivo,** a series of apartments recommended separately below.

Via Roma/Piazza Mazzini, 22021 Bellagio. ℂ **031-950-216.** Fax 031-951-529. www.villaserbelloni.com. 83 units. 375€–445€ classic double; 510€–590€ deluxe double; 750€–800€ executive double; 970€–1,030€ senior suite. Half-pension available. Rates include breakfast. AE, DC, MC, V. Free parking. Closed mid-Nov to Mar. **Amenities:** 2 Italian/international restaurants (1 jacket-and-tie terrace restaurant, 1 informal nautical-looking dinner-only restaurant); bar; babysitting; children's playground; concierge; exercise room; nearby golf course (in Menaggio); Internet; 2 heated pools (indoor and outdoor); room service; sauna; spa; outdoor tennis courts; watersports equipment/rentals. In room: A/C, TV, hair dryer, minibar.

Suisse ★   The simple rooms above this restaurant, in a 15th-century lakeside villa, have parquet floors and stylish solid wood furnishings with lovely details of inlay or carving. The bathrooms are plain and there's no elevator, but you're right on the harbor, and the midpriced restaurant is quite good. It offers Italian fare year-round, with an inventive fusion flair in summer; the downstairs room looks very plain (though you can also sit out front under the arcades), but the upstairs dining room is understatedly elegant, with a stucco ceiling and a lakeview terrace. (Mar–Oct the restaurant is open daily; Nov–Feb, it's open Thurs–Tues).

Piazza Mazzini 23, 22021 Bellagio. ℂ **031-951-755.** Fax 031-951-755. www.bellagio.co.nz/suisse. 10 units. 80€–130€ double; 130€ junior suite. Rates include breakfast. Half- and full-pension plans available. AE, DC, MC, V. Parking 10€ in nearby garage. Closed Dec–Feb. **Amenities:** Restaurant (international cuisine); bar; concierge; room service; smoke-free rooms; Wi-Fi. In room: TV, hair dryer, no phone.

Drinking with Dante

Bellagio has a great bar called **Divina Commedia** ★★, Salita Mella 43–45
(🕿 **031-951-680;** www.divinacommedia.com), modeled after Dante's epic poem:
Upstairs are frescoes with puffy clouds and cherubs as Paradise, the ground floor
is Purgatory, and the tiny basement room is a fantastical black-lit Inferno cave of
papier-mâché demons.

An Apartment Stay

Residence Ulivo ★★ (**Value**)   The Villa Serbelloni (see above) is one of Italy's grandest hotels, surrounded by beautiful gardens and manicured lawns on the lakeshore. For
those looking for less grandiose and expensive accommodations than those the main
hotel provides (while still enjoying all the hotel's amenities, including its lovely lakeside
pool, private beach, fitness club with sauna, game room, and frescoed salons), the Serbelloni rents these stylish apartments in an outbuilding on a hill above the lake. All have
sitting areas and either separate bedrooms or alcove sleeping areas, and are nicely decorated with terra-cotta floors and attractive rattan furniture. All have large kitchenettes;
the best have partial views of the lake (no. 10 gets the best vistas, while no. 8 is larger and
has some partial views, including from the bedroom). Although rentals are officially by
the week, shorter stays can be arranged when space is available. Even when the main hotel
is closed (mid-Nov to Mar) and the Residence stays open, there's also a section containing a covered grottolike pool, spa with massage and beauty treatments, and a lakeview
restaurant open to residence guests.

Via Roma/Piazza Mazzini, 22021 Bellagio. 🕿 **031-956-434.** Fax 031-951-529. www.residencelulivo.com.
13 apts. Weekly rates: 945€–1,295€ small apt; 1,120€–1,435€ medium apt; 1,505€–1,890€ large apt. Rates
are for 2 people, 105€–140€ for an additional bed. Buffet breakfast in main hotel (walk down a path to
get there) 22€. AE, DC, MC, V. Free parking. **Amenities:** Italian/international restaurant; bar; babysitting;
children's playground; concierge; exercise room; nearby golf course (in Menaggio); 2 heated pools
(indoor and outdoor); room service; sauna; spa; outdoor tennis courts; watersports equipment/rentals. *In
room:* A/C, TV, kitchenette.

Where to Dine

Bar Café Rossi ★★ LIGHT FARE   One of the nicest of Bellagio's pleasant lakefront
cafes is tucked under the arcades of the town's main square. You can dine at one of the
few outside tables or in the delightful Art Nouveau dining room, with intricate tile work,
carved wood cabinets, and stucco ceilings. Wine and the excellent house coffee are available all day, but a nice selection of pastries and sandwiches makes this a good stop for
breakfast or lunch.

Piazza Mazzini 22/24. 🕿 **031-950-196.** Sandwiches 6€. AE, DC, MC, V. Apr–Sept daily 7:30am–midnight;
Oct–Mar Fri–Wed 7:30am–10:30pm.

La Grotta ★ (**Value**) ITALIAN/PIZZERIA   Tucked away on a stepped street just off
lakefront Piazza Manzini, this cozy restaurant consists of a series of vaulted-ceiling dining
rooms. The service is extremely friendly, and the wide-ranging menu includes the Alps'
famous *pizzoccheri,* the sinfully rich buckwheat pasta with melted cheese from just north
of here. Most of the regulars, though, come for the fish specials, including lake trout, or
the delectable pizzas that are the best for miles around.

Salita Cernaia 14. (📞 **031-951-152.** Primi 7€–9€; secondi 7€–13€; pizza 5€–10€. AE, DC, MC, V (credit cards accepted only for bills totaling more than 20€). Daily noon–2:30pm and 7pm–1am (closed Mon Oct–June).

Ristorante Barchetta ★★ SEAFOOD   One of Bellagio's best restaurants specializes in fresh lake fish and other seafood. In all but the coldest weather, food is served on a bamboo-enclosed heated terrace. There is also a bar on the terrace. Most of the pastas don't use seafood but are innovative variations on traditional recipes, such as *ravioli caprino* (with goat cheese, topped with pear sauce) and savory risotto with hazelnuts and pistachios. For a main course, however, you should try one of the delicious preparations of local perch or angler fish; the meat entrees, including baby lamb chops with rosemary, are also excellent. You can enjoy a pasta dish, as well as a meat and a fish dish, on one of the set menus.

Salita Mella 13. (📞 **031-951-389.** Reservations highly recommended. Primi 10€–20€; secondi 16€–25€; tasting menu (for 2 only) 45€ per person, not including wine. AE, DC, MC, V. Thurs–Mon noon–2:30pm and 7–10:30pm. Closed Nov–Mar.

Varenna

You can happily spend some time clambering up and down the steep steps that substitute for streets in this charming village (on the eastern shore of the lake, about 10 min. by ferry from Bellagio) that, until not too long ago, made its living by fishing. The main attractions, though, are outside town.

The hilltop ruins of the **Castello di Vezio** (📞 **0341-831-000**) are about a 20-minute walk above the town on a gradually ascending path. The main reason for a visit is to enjoy the stunning views of the lake, its shoreline villages, and the backdrop of mountains at the northern end. May to June the castle is open daily 10am to 6pm, July to September 11am to 8pm; admission is 1€.

The **gardens of the Villa Monastero** (📞 **0341-830-129**) are more easily accessible, at the southern edge of town along Via 4 Novembre, and you can reach them by following the series of lakeside promenades through the Old Town from the ferry landing. This villa and the terraced gardens that rise up from the lakeshore were once a not-so-spartan monastery—until it was dissolved in the late 17th century when the nuns in residence began bearing living proof that they were on too-friendly terms with the priests across the way. If you find it hard to tear yourself from the bowers of citrus trees and rhododendrons clinging to terraces, you'll find equally enchanting surroundings in the adjoining gardens of the **Villa Cipressi** (📞 **0341-830-113**).

Both gardens are open daily March to October: Villa Monastero 10am to 7pm and Villa Cipressi 9am to 7pm. Admission is 3€ for adults (1.50€ for children under 10 and seniors over 60) to just one garden, 5.50€ adults (2.50€ kids and seniors) to visit both. Call 📞 **0341-830-113** for more details.

In season, **ferries** make the 10-minute run between Bellagio and Varenna about every half-hour (see "By Boat," earlier). There's a tiny **tourist office** at Piazza Venini, 1 (📞 **0341-830-367;** www.varennaitaly.com), open Tuesday to Sunday 10am to 12:30pm and Tuesday to Saturday 3 to 6pm.

Where to Stay

Milano ★★ (Value)   You'd have to look hard to find a more pleasant retreat by the lake. This old house hanging over Varenna's lakefront was taken over in 2002 by Bettina and Egidio Mallone, a friendly Italian-Swiss couple, and completely overhauled over the following 3 years, with new beds and antique-style furnishings, each room with its own

Chords & Canvas

In 2008, Bellagio held an exhibition of watercolor paintings that met with such success that the town has decided to make this festival an annual tradition. This week-long exhibition showcases the works of watercolor painters from around the world. It is held at the end of April or early May (contact the tourist office for the exact dates) and closes out with a competition to see who has created the most beautiful painting.

Across the lake, Menaggio held a guitar festival in 2007 that was repeated the following 2 years, and the town is now looking to make this a yearly event. Held the last weekend of August, the festival is 3 days of free concerts held in churches and a temporary tent pavilion. The festival has already begun to attract well-known international musicians, but lesser-known guitarists also perform in the local bars during the festival. There are also workshops where different playing styles are discussed and demonstrated. Menaggio recently instituted a shuttle service that makes the run on the state road to and from nearby Tremezzo and Cadenabbia late into the evening, giving those lodged farther down the lake a chance to enjoy an evening in Menaggio when public busses are no longer operating, without having to spring for a taxi to get back (4€ one-way, 6€ round-trip).

color scheme. All have balconies and views—nos. 1 and 2 open onto a wide terrace, and nos. 5 and 6 both have full-on lake vistas; the other half overlook the neighbor's pretty garden with askance lake views. The furnishings are a pleasant mix of old and unobtrusive modern pieces, brightened up with small Persian rugs. In summer, breakfast is served on the outdoor terrace.

A few years ago, the couple added two annexes, the Casa Rossa and the Casa Gialla, which enjoy all the services of the main hotel: breakfast, computer with Internet access, bar, and the like. The **Casa Gialla** is a two-bedroom apartment (two doubles and a sofa) accommodating up to five guests. Rates range from 120€ for two people to 260€ for five people. Views are of a quiet alley. The **Casa Rossa** rooms are on the third floor (walk-up) of an adjacent building: two doubles with a balcony and lake view (130€), and a more spacious double with the same view, terrace, and kitchenette (150€; add 35€ for a third person).

Via XX Septembre 29, 23829 Varenna. ℂ/fax **0341-830-298.** www.varenna.net. 8 units. 130€–140€ double with lateral lake view and balcony; 140€–150€ double with full lake view and balcony; 150€–160€ double with full lake view and terrace. Rates include buffet breakfast. 3-course dinner 27€ upon request (restaurant closed Tues and Sun). AE, DC, MC, V. Free parking on the street or 12€ in nearby garage. Closed mid-Nov through Mar. **Amenities:** Restaurant; bar; concierge; Internet; room service. *In room:* Hair dryer (on request).

Villa Cipressi ★★ (Finds) If you enjoyed your tour of Varenna's lush gardens, there's no need to leave. This 16th-century villa and several outbuildings were converted to a hotel in the early 1800s; it's now geared to conferences but takes other guests as well, space permitting. Though the rooms have been renovated without any attempt to retain historical character, they're extremely large and attractive. Suites take advantage of the high ceilings and contain loft bedrooms, with sitting areas below that can easily fit a couple of single beds for families. Although not every room gets a lake view, all save a few small ones on the roadside have marvelous views over the gardens, which you can also enjoy on the delightful terraces. Ten rooms on the top floor have lake views and high ceilings decorated with molded stuccoes—the best is the corner suite, with a coffered ceiling, alcove bed, four windows, and a nonworking fireplace. (Like most revered objects on the lake, the suite is named after Alessandro Manzoni, author of *The Betrothed,* which was set on these shores.) There are five more accommodations in a 15th-century building on the property.

Via IV Novembre 18, 22050 Varenna. © **0341-830-113.** Fax 0341-830-401. www.hotelvillacipressi.it. 32 units. 130€–145€ double without lake view; 150€–170€ double with lake view; 160€–180€ deluxe double with lake view; 250€–290€ suite. Rates include buffet breakfast. AE, DC, MC, V. Free parking. Usually closes late Oct to Mar, but some years open year-round. **Amenities:** Restaurant; bar; babysitting; concierge. *In room:* A/C, TV, hair dryer, Internet.

Where to Dine

Vecchia Varenna ★★ SEAFOOD   One of your most memorable experiences in this region could be a meal at this romantic restaurant, which combines refined local cuisine with the lakefront charm of Varenna's oldest section, all at reasonable prices. Dining is in a beautiful stone-floored room with white stone walls or on a covered terrace overhanging the water. The kitchen makes the most of local herbs and vegetables and, of course, the bounty of the lake—for starters, tagliolini laced with caviar, and one of the best of the many risottos combines wild mushrooms and *lavarello* (a white fish from the lake). Grilled lake trout stuffed with radicchio risotto is an excellent choice for a main course, though a half-dozen other local fish are available.

Contrada Scoscesa 10. © **0341-830-793.** www.vecchiavarenna.it. Reservations required. Primi 11€–12€; secondi 15€–16€. MC, V. Tues–Sun 12:30–2pm and 7:30–10pm. Closed Jan.

Menaggio

This lively resort town hugs the western shore of the lake, across from Bellagio on its peninsula and Varenna on the distant shore. Hikers should stop in at the **tourist office** on Piazza Garibaldi 8 (©/fax **0344-32-924;** www.menaggio.com), open Monday to Saturday 9am to noon and 3 to 6pm (July–Aug also Sun 7:30am–6:30pm). The very helpful staff distributes a booklet, *Hiking in the Area around Menaggio,* with descriptions of more than a dozen walks, with maps and instructions on what buses to take to trail heads. The town's bus stop is at Piazza Garibaldi (Sun on Via Mazzini); tickets are sold at Bar Centrale or the newsstand on Via Calvi at the piazza.

The major nearby attraction is about 2.5km (1½ miles) south of town: The **Villa Carlotta** (© **0344-40-405;** www.villacarlotta.it) is the most famous villa on the lake and was begun in 1643 for the Marquis Giorgio Clerici, who made his fortune supplying Napoleon's troops with uniforms; he spent much of it on this neoclassical villa and gardens. After a succession of owners, including Prussian royalty who lavished their funds and attention on the gardens, the villa is now in the hands of the Italian government. It's filled with romantic paintings, statues by Canova and his imitators, and Empire furnishings, but the gardens are the main attraction, with azaleas, orchids, banana trees, cacti, palms, and forests of ferns spreading in all directions. You can take the no. C10 bus from Menaggio or walk along the lake (about 30–45 min.). The nearest ferry landing is at Cadenabbia, just north of the gardens, though ferries to Menaggio are more frequent. The villa and gardens are open daily in March and October through mid-November from 9am to 4:30pm (the villa is closed from noon to 2pm), and April through September from 9am to 6pm. Admission is 8€ for adults and 4€ for seniors over 65 and students.

WATERSPORTS   The lido, at the north end of town, has an excellent **beach,** as well as a **pool,** and is open late June to mid-September daily 9am to 7pm. For information on water-skiing and other activities, contact **Centro Lago Service,** in the Grand Hotel Victoria along the lakeside Via Castelli (✆ **0344-320-03**). Also ask at the hostel (see below) about boat and bike rentals, which are available to nonguests during slow periods.

Where to Stay & Dine
Albergo-Ristorante Il Vapore ★   This very pleasant small restaurant/hotel faces a quiet square just off the lakefront. The rooms are comfortable, with rather nice modern furnishings (plus antiques in a few) and fuzzy towels in the cramped bathrooms. Six rooms open onto partial lake views: nos. 21 and 22 from tall windows, nos. 25 and 26 from small terraces, and nos. 28 and 29 (the biggest room, with windows on two sides for a breeze) from tiny balconies. They usually won't accept reservations for just 1 or 2 nights (but you can stop by and ask). Meals of local specialties from the nearby mountain valleys are normally served beneath the wisteria-shaded arbor of the entryway or in an attractive pale-blue dining room with paintings by local artists. It's best to call ahead in winter, as the owners' vacation can change from year to year.

Piazza Grossi 3, 22017 Menaggio. ✆ **0344-32-229.** Fax 0304-34-850. www.italiaabc.com/a/ilvapore. 10 units. 55€ double without lake view; 60€ double with lake view. Breakfast 7€. No credit cards. Free parking on street (though free spaces are hard to find). **Amenities:** Restaurant; bar. *In room:* No phone.

Grand Hotel Menaggio ★★   This 19th-century *palazzo* retains original stucco work and chandeliers in the main hall and salons. The spacious rooms are nicely furnished in a modern style. Superior ones are larger, have lake views, and come with Jacuzzi tubs in the bathrooms (some standard rooms have lake views, some have mountain views). Three superior rooms even have small terraces rather than balconies; the three junior suites also come with nice terraces whose stone balustrades overlook the pool. The restaurant's picture windows open to the lawn and the lake, which shares its view with the pool and pier, overlooking Lake Como to the less-developed eastern shore.

Via IV Novembre 77, 22017 Menaggio (CO). ✆ **0344-30-640.** Fax 0344-30-619. www.grandhotelmenaggio. com. 90 units. 200€ standard double without lake view; 240€ standard double with lake view; 280€ superior double with lake view; 320€ superior double with lake view and balcony. Half-pension available. Rates include breakfast. AE, MC, V. Free parking on street (though free spaces are hard to find). Closed Nov–Jan. **Amenities:** Italian/international restaurant; bar; babysitting; concierge; tiny exercise room; golf course 3km (1³/₄ miles) away; outdoor heated pool; room service; smoke-free rooms; outdoor tennis courts; watersports equipment/rentals; Wi-Fi. *In room:* A/C, TV, VCR (on request), hair dryer, kitchenette (in 2 apts), minibar.

Ostello La Primula (Value   As far as youth hostels go, this is one I would hang out in without hesitation: It is easily accessible from Bellagio and other towns on the Centro Lago by boat, and is frequented about evenly by frugal adults and backpacking students. The dorms are relatively cozy, with no more than six beds per room. Most of the rooms, admittedly a little run-down, have a view of the lake—nos. 3, 4, and 5 on the first floor even share a balcony. Everyone enjoys the view from the large, sunny communal terrace. *One drawback:* no luggage lockers. It's run by ex–social workers, and they serve a 12€ dinner that's so good it even attracts locals. (You're expected to set your own table on the porch, retrieve each course, as it's called, and wash your own dishes.)

Via IV Novembre 86 (on the south edge of town), 22017 Menaggio (CO). ✆/fax **0344-32-356.** www. menaggiohostel.com. 35 beds. 16€ per person in dorm; 18€ per person in family suites (sleep 4–6 people), with private bathroom; 60€ triple without a bathroom in the room; 65€ triple with a bathroom. Rates include breakfast. No credit cards. (Free parking on the street, though free spaces are hard to find.) Open Mar 15 to 1st weekend in Nov. Office open 8–10am and 5–11:30pm. **Amenities:** Restaurant; bar; bike, kayak, and rowboat rental. *In room:* No phone.

3 LAKE MAGGIORE (LAGO MAGGIORE) & THE BORROMEAN ISLANDS

Stresa: 90km (56 miles) NW of Milan

Anyone who reads Hemingway will know this lake and its forested shores from *A Farewell to Arms*. That's just the sort of place Lake Maggiore is—a pleasure ground that's steeped in associations with famous figures (Flaubert, Wagner, Goethe, and many of Europe's other great minds seem to have been inspired by the deep, moody waters, backed by the Alps) and not-so-famous wealthy visitors. Fortunately, you need not be famous or wealthy to enjoy Maggiore, the top bit of which is in Switzerland.

STRESA

The major town on the lake is a pretty, festive little place, with a long lakefront promenade, a lively and attractive commercial center, and a bevy of restaurants and hotels that range from the expensively splendid to the affordably comfortable.

Essentials

GETTING THERE   By Train   Stresa is linked with Milan by 20 trains a day (regional: 1¼ hr.; high-speed: 58 min.).

By Boat   Boats arrive and depart from Piazza Marconi, connecting Stresa with the Borromean Islands (Isole Borromee) and with many other lakeside spots; most boats on the lake are operated by **Navigazione Sul Lago Maggiore** (© 800-551-801 or 0322-233-200; www.navlaghi.it).

By Car   A8 runs between Milan and Sesto Calende, near the southern end of the lake; from there, Route S33 follows the western shore to Stresa. The trip takes a little over an hour.

VISITOR INFORMATION   The **tourist office** is at the ferry dock (©/fax **0323-31-308**) and is open Monday to Saturday (daily Mar–Oct) 10am to 12:30pm and 3 to 6:30pm. You can also get info from private websites (try www.lagomaggiore.it and www.stresa.it). For hiking information, ask for the booklet *Percorsi Verdi.*

FESTIVALS & MARKETS   July to September, Stresa draws visitors from around the world for its *Settimane Musicali,* or Festival of Musical Weeks, a major gathering of classical musicians. The festival has an info office at Via Canonica 6 (© **0323-31-095;** www.stresafestival.eu).

EXPLORING STRESA & THE ISLANDS

Stresa

Strolling and relaxing seem to be the main activities in Stresa. The action is at the lakeside promenade, running from the center of town north past the grand lakeside hotels, including the Iles des Borromees, where Hemingway set *A Farewell to Arms.* Sooner or later, though, most visitors climb into a boat for the short ride to the famed islands themselves, the Borromean Islands.

(i) **Tips** **Budgeting Your Time**

To squeeze as much of Stresa's sights as you can into a day, note that the ferry back from the Isole Borromee stops first at the Mottarone cable-car area before chugging down the coast to the center of Stresa and the main docks. You can hop off at this first stop to either ride the cable car up the mountain or simply walk back into Stresa itself along a pretty lakeside promenade, past crumbling villas and impromptu sculpture gardens, in about 20 minutes.

Borromean Islands (Isole Borromee)

These three islands, named for the Borromeo family, which has owned them since the 12th century, float in the misty waters off Stresa and entice visitors with their stunning beauty. Note that Isola Bella and Isola Superiore have villages you can hang out in for free, but Isola Madre consists solely of the admission-charging gardens.

Public **ferries** leave for the islands every half-hour from Stresa's Piazza Marconi; a 12€ **three-island pass** is the most economical way to visit them—and if you buy your admission tickets for the *isole* sights at the Stresa ferry office along with your ferry tickets, you'll save 1€ off each—though the generally grumpy ticket agents will not advise you of this; you have to ask. Buy tickets only from the public Navigazione Lago Maggiore (© **800-551-801** or 0322-233-200; www.navlaghi.it), in the big building with triple arches. Private boats also make the trip out to the island—at obscene rates; you'll see other ticket booths as well as hucksters dressed as sailors trying to lure you aboard (for large groups, the prices can be reasonable, but do your negotiating on the dock before you get on the boat). For more information, visit www.borromeoturismo.it.

Isola Bella Isola Bella (5 min. from Stresa) remains true to its name, with splendid 17th-century gardens that ascend from the shore in 10 luxuriantly planted terraces. The Borromeo *palazzo* provides a chance to explore opulently decorated rooms, including the one where Napoleon and Josephine once slept. It's open daily late March to mid-October, 9am to 5:30pm. Admission is 12€ for adults and 5€ for children ages 6 to 15. Audio tours help make sense of it all for 3.50€ each or 5€ to rent two sets of headphones. For more details, call © **0323-30-556.**

Isola Superiore Most of Isola Superiore, also known as Isola Pescatori (10 min. from Stresa), is occupied by a not-so-quaint old fishing village—every one of the tall houses on this tiny strip of land seems to harbor a souvenir shop or pizza stand, and there are hordes of visitors to keep them busy.

Isola Madre The largest and most peaceful of the islands is Isola Madre (30 min. from Stresa), every inch of which is covered with the exquisite flora and exotic colorful birds of the 3.2-hectare (8-acre) **Orto Botanico** (© **0323-31-261**). The map they hand out at the entrance/ticket booth details all the flora; you're on your own to ID the various peacocks, game fowl, exotic birds, funky chickens, and other avians that strut, flit, and roost amid the lawns around the central villa (1518–85), filled with Borromeo family memorabilia and some interesting old puppet-show stages. The botanical garden is open daily late March through mid-October 9am to 5:30pm; admission is 10€ for adults and 5€ for children ages 6 to 15. A joint 1-day ticket for the Isola Bella palazzo and the Isola Madre gardens costs 17€ for adults and 7.50€ for children.

THE LAKES

10

LAKE MAGGIORE & THE BORROMEAN ISLANDS

The forested slopes above Stresa are prime hiking and mountain biking terrain. To reach a network of trails, take the funivia from near the lakefront at the north end of town up **Monte Mottarone;** the funivia (📞 **0323-30-295;** www.stresa-mottarone.it) runs every 20 minutes from roughly 9am to 6pm (hours vary with the season). It costs 10€ one-way to take the funivia along with a bike, which you can rent at the station for 23€ for a half-day or 28€ for a full day. A round-trip ticket without a bike costs 18€ for adults and 11€ for children ages 4 to 12. The **Alpinia garden** halfway up is open daily April to October from 9:30am to 6pm. A round-trip ticket to Monte Mottarone gives you the right to stop off at the intermediate stop and gives free entry into the garden. If you don't want to venture too far from the lake, there's a nice **beach** near the station.

Where to Stay

Very Expensive

Grand Hôtel et des Iles Borromées ★★★   This is one of the grande dame hotels of the Italian lakes and a favorite of Ernest Hemingway, who set part of *A Farewell to Arms* here. Renovations over the past decade have restored the elegance to the decor—gilded stuccoes, mosaics lining the hall runners, giant Murano chandeliers—in the spirit and style of the 1860s era in which the hotel was built. Its Liberty-style facade is surrounded by well-manicured gardens of palms, flowers, ponds, fountains, and pools. Rooms come in various types. "Alla Stresa" means 19th-century-style furnishings in intricately inlaid wood; large, comfy beds; and marble bathrooms. "Al Impero" rooms are done in Empire style, with gilded Napoleon-type headboards and dressers, richly patterned carpets, *pietra dura* inlaid stone tabletops, and stucco decorations in the bathrooms. "Alla Baveno" rooms are mostly junior suites, some on the garden and some with lake views. Suites are sumptuous and vary widely; the Hemingway suite, in particular, is out of this world (and, at a cool 3,200€ per night, a wee bit out of most people's price range), with two bedrooms of half-tester king-size beds, three bathrooms (two with Jacuzzi tubs built for two), frescoed ceilings, and a large terrace.

Corso Umberto I 67, 28838 Stresa. 📞 **0323-938-938.** Fax 0323-32-405. www.borromees.it. 174 units. 250€ double with garden view; 390€ double with lake view; 500€ junior suite; 705€ junior suite deluxe; 795€ royal suite; 1,290€ imperial suite. Rates include breakfast. AE, DC, MC, V. **Amenities:** 2 restaurants (elegant Italian; poolside lunch bar); bar; babysitting; concierge; large exercise room; nearby golf course; Jacuzzi; 2 outdoor heated pools (1 for diving); indoor pool; room service; sauna; spa; outdoor tennis courts. *In room:* A/C, TV, hair dryer, Internet, kitchenette (in residence), minibar.

Expensive

La Palma ★★   The Palma is one of the nicest of Stresa's luxury hotels and, given the high-level comfort and the amenities, one of the most reasonably priced. Most of the large rooms, done in rich floral fabrics and wood tones, open to balconies overlooking the lake, and 98% of the spacious marble bathrooms have Jacuzzis. There's a rooftop sun terrace and fitness center, with a hot tub and sauna, but the most pleasant places to relax are in the flowery garden in front of the hotel and the terrace surrounding the lakeside pool.

Lungolago Umberto I, 33, 28838 Stresa. 📞 **0323-32-401.** Fax 0323-933-930. www.hlapalma.it. 128 units. 220€ standard double; 255€ superior double with lake view; 350€ junior suite with lake view. Rates include buffet breakfast. AE, DC, MC, V. Free parking. Closed mid-Nov to mid-Mar. **Amenities:** Restaurant; bar; babysitting; bikes; concierge; exercise room; Jacuzzi; pool; room service; sauna; smoke-free rooms; tennis courts. *In room:* A/C, TV, hair dryer, Internet, minibar.

Verbano ★★ (Finds) This dusty-rose villa has one of the most envied positions on all of Lago Maggiore, sitting at the tip of the Isola dei Pescatori, overlooking the back side of Isola Bella. The flower-fringed terrace, with its excellent restaurant (reviewed separately below), enjoys great lake views in three directions. Each room is named after the flower that drives the villa's color scheme; all feature parquet floors, big old-wood furnishings, real beds with wrought-iron bedsteads, and large tiled bathrooms. Nos. 1 and 2, on the front of the villa with Isola Bella views, have working fireplaces; highly requested no. 2 on the corner has a balcony on the front and a shared terrace on the side. Rooms on the first floor share a large terrace overlooking Isola Madre and the Lombard, eastern shore of the lake.

Isola Superiore dei Pescatori, 28838 Stresa. (🕻 **0323-32-534.** Fax 0323-33-129. www.hotelverbano.it. 12 units. 150€–185€ double; 190€–210€ triple. Half-pension 140€ per person. Rates include breakfast. AE, DC, MC, V. Closed Jan. **Amenities:** Excellent regional restaurant (see review below); bar; babysitting; courtesy boat from the mainland in the evenings after public ferry service ends; concierge; room service. *In room:* Hair dryer.

Inexpensive

Meeting ★ (Value) The name comes from the proximity of Stresa's small conference center, where a much-attended music festival is held from July to early September (see "Festivals & Markets," above). Although the lakefront is a 5-minute walk away, the setting here is quiet and leafy, though light sleepers on the back may notice the trains passing in the distance. The rooms, in a modern Scandinavian style, are big and bright, and many have terraces. There's a cozy bar and lounge downstairs, as well as a casual (but slightly impersonal) dining room.

Via Bonghi 9, 28838 Stresa. (🕻 **0323-32-741.** Fax 0323-33-458. www.stresahotels.net/meeting.asp. 29 units. 70€–115€ double. Half-pension add 13€ per day per person. Rates include breakfast. AE, DC, MC, V. Parking 7.50€. Closed Jan–Feb. **Amenities:** Restaurant (Italian cuisine); bar; bikes; concierge; room service. *In room:* TV, hair dryer.

Mon Toc ★ Just uphill from the train station, this family-run hotel, surrounded by a big private garden and lawn, is well short on charm but convenient to the lake and town (a 10- to 15-min. walk); indeed, it's enough removed to provide an almost countrylike atmosphere. With functional furniture, the rooms are unusually pleasant for a hotel in this price range and have tidy bathrooms (though a few are of the minuscule, molded, airplane variety). The friendly owner refuses, out of honesty, to call the sliver of lake visible over the rooftops from the second-floor rooms (no elevator) a "lake view."

Via Duchessa di Genova 69, 28838 Stresa. (🕻 **0323-30-282.** Fax 0323-933-860. www.hotelmontoc.com. 15 units, 12 with private bathroom. 85€ double; 100€ triple. Half-pension 60€ per person in a double room and 50€ in a triple. Rates include buffet breakfast. AE, DC, MC, V. **Amenities:** Home-cooking restaurant; bar; concierge; room service. *In room:* TV.

Primavera ★★ For much of the spring and summer, the street in front of this hotel is closed to traffic and filled with flowering plants and cafe tables. The relaxed air prevails throughout this bright little hotel, a block off the lake in the town center. A tiny lounge and bar are downstairs. Upstairs, the tile-floored rooms are furnished in functional walnut veneer; you can have a minifridge on request. Many rooms have balconies, just wide enough to accommodate a pair of chairs, with flower boxes overlooking the town. A few fourth-floor rooms get in a sliver of lake view around the apse and stone bell tower of the Duomo.

Via Cavour 30, 28838 Stresa. (🕻 **0323-31-286.** Fax 0323-33-458. www.stresahotels.net/primavera.asp. 34 units. 70€–115€ double. Rates include breakfast. AE, DC, MC, V. Parking 7.50€ at Hotel Meeting. Closed

Where to Dine

Hotel Ristorante Fiorentino (**Value**) ITALIAN/TRATTORIA   It's hard to find friendlier service or homier trattoria-type food in Stresa, especially at these prices. Everything that comes out of this family-run kitchen is made fresh daily, including cannelloni and other pastas. You can dine in a big cozy room or on a patio out back in good weather.

Via Bolongaro 9–11. ℂ **0323-30-254.** www.hotelfiorentino.com. Primi 6€–7€; secondi 9€–18€. AE, DC, MC, V. Mar–Oct daily 11am–3pm and 6–10pm. Closed Dec-Feb.

Osteria degli Amici ★★ (**Finds**) ITALIAN/PIZZERIA   This popular spot, beloved by locals and Italian vacationers alike, is tucked into a nook of a piazza with a tiny outdoor eating area shaded by vines. The rambling interior consists of tiny rooms with three to five tables each, so the overall effect is cozy. Pizzas come bubbling hot from a wood-fired oven, or you can try risotto enriched with porcini, *persico* (lake perch), or *rucola e gamberetti* (arugula and tiny shrimp). The *spaghetti montecarlo* puts on airs with its caviar and salmon cream sauce, while the *crespelle valdostane* comes back down to earth with a rib-sticking combo of ham and cheese wrapped in sheets of homemade pasta. Second courses are straightforward: *tagliata al rosmarino* (sirloin steak scented with rosemary), *filetto di persico alle mandorle* (broiled lake perch filet under almonds), and fresh grilled *i sogliola* (sole) or *orata* (bream).

Via A. M. Bolongaro 33. ℂ **0323-30-453.** Reservations highly recommended. Primi 6€–9€; secondi 10€–16€; pizza 5.50€–12€. MC, V. Thurs–Tues noon–2:30pm and 7pm–midnight. Closed Jan and Nov.

Taverna del Pappagallo ★ ITALIAN/PIZZERIA   Most of Stresa seems to congregate in this pleasant restaurant for the most popular pizza in town. But just about all the fare that comes out of this family-run kitchen is delicious, including delectable home-made gnocchi and dishes such as grilled sausage. Weather permitting, try to dine at one of the tables in the pleasant garden.

Via Principessa Margherita 46. ℂ **0323-30-411.** www.tavernapappagallo.com. Primi and pizza 5€–13€; secondi 8€–14€. No credit cards. Thurs–Tues 11:30am–2:30pm and 6:30–10:30pm (daily in summer).

Verbano ★★ ITALIAN   Verbano offers a fairy-tale location on the point of the "Fisherman's Isle," taking up the jasmine-fringed gravelly terrace next to the hotel (recommended above). The waters lap right up to the wall, and the views are over the back side of Isola Bella and the lake around you on three sides. The cooking needn't be anything special, given its location in a prime tourist spot, but, surprisingly, it is almost as lovely as the setting. The *zuppa di verdure* (vegetable soup) is hearty, with barley and grains; *paglia e fieno* ("hay and straw") is a mix of regular (yellow) and spinach (green) tagliatelle noodles in a ragù made of scorpion fish, carrots, and zucchini. The *crespelle con passato di melanzane e toma* are pasta sheets wrapped around a purée of eggplant and local cheese. For the secondo, definitely try grilled lake trout, or the *luccio percia* (lake perch) filet in a smoked-salmon-and-poppy crust sided with rice stained black from squid ink. Landlubbers can dig into *faraona dissosata farcita con spinaci e ricotta* (guinea fowl done up like ravioli, and stuffed with ricotta cheese and spinach).

Isola Superiore dei Pescatori. ℂ **0323-32-534.** www.hotelverbano.it/ristorante.html. Reservations recommended. Primi 7€–11€; secondi 10€–23€. AE, DC, MC, V. Daily noon–2:30pm and 7–10pm (closed Wed in winter). Closed Jan.

Piedmont & the Valle d'Aosta

Loosely translated, Piedmont (Piemonte) means "at the foot of the mountains." Those mountains, of course, are the Alps, which define the region and are part of Italy's northern and western borders. These dramatic peaks are visible in much of the province, most of which rises and rolls over fertile foothills that produce a bounty that is as rich as the region is green. Piedmont is a land of cheeses, truffles, plump fruit, and, of course, wine—among which are some of Italy's most powerful, complex, and delicious reds, including **Barolo** and **Barbaresco,** lighter reds **Barbera** and **Dolcetto,** and Italy's top sparkling white, **Asti Spumanti.**

Not that all of Piedmont is rural, of course. **Turin,** Italy's car town, is the region's capital. But within its ring of industrialized suburbs, rather than an Italian Detroit lies an elegant city of mannerly squares, baroque palaces, and stunning art collections. Torinese and their neighbors from other parts of Italy often retreat to the **Valle d'Aosta,** the smallest and most mountainous of Italian provinces.

REGIONAL CUISINE Given such vast geographic diversity, it's not surprising that the region's cuisine varies according to the topography. In the southern stretches of Piedmont, the palate turns primarily to those magnificent red wines from the wine villages around Asti and Alba. Barbaresco, Barbera, Barolo, Dolcetto, Nebbiolo—the names are legendary, and they often appear on the table to accompany meat dishes stewed in red wine; one of the most favored of these is *brasato al barolo* (beef or veal braised in Barolo).

The way to begin a meal here, but usually available in winter only, is with *bagna cauda,* literally, "hot sauce," a plate of raw vegetables that are dipped into a steaming sauce of olive oil, garlic, and anchovies. The Piemontese pasta is *tajarin,* and it is often topped with sauces made with walnuts or, for a special occasion, what is perhaps the region's greatest contribution to Italian cuisine, white truffles. As the land climbs higher toward the Valle d'Aosta, local mountain fare (a rib-sticking variant on Piemontese), called Valdostana, takes over—polenta is a popular primo (first course), stews are thick with beef and red wine (*carbonada* is the most common stew like this), and buttery fontina is the preferred cheese.

1 TURIN

669km (415 miles) NW of Rome, 140km (87 miles) E of Milan

It's often said that Turin is the most French city in Italy or the most Italian city in France. The reason is partly historical and partly architectural. From the late 13th century to Italy's unification in 1861 (when the city served very briefly as capital), Turin was the capital of the **House of Savoy.** The Savoys were as French as they were Italian, and their holdings extended well into the present-day French regions of Savoy and the Côte d'Azur, as well as Sardegna. The city's Francophile 17th- and 18th-century architects,

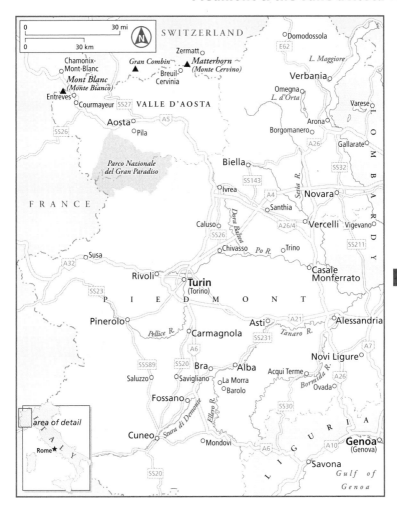

inspired by the tastes of the French court, laid out broad avenues and airy piazzas and lined them with low-slung neoclassical buildings.

After Napoleon's occupation, the city's intellectuals began percolating the ideas that would eventually blossom into the Risorgimento unification movement, with hometown king Vittorio Emanuele II of Savoy as its royal ruler. Italy's first prime minister was Torinese gentleman artist Massimo d'Azeglio, followed by the Risorgimento's political leader and another local hero, Camillo Cavour. Later the Italian Communist Party was born here on the Fiat factory floor under the leadership of poet Antonio Gramsci, though that same factory floor also gave rise to the ultraradical Red Brigades terrorist group in the 1970s.

Most visitors come to Turin with business in mind (often at Fiat, in the sprawling industrial outskirts). Those who take the time to look around the historic center, though, will find an elegant and sophisticated city that has changed little since more gracious centuries, with some fine museum collections and the charm of a place that, for all its Francophile leanings, is quintessentially Italian and perhaps the most pleasant big city in northern Italy.

FESTIVALS & MARKETS   Dance, opera, theater, and musical performances (mostly classical) are on the agenda all year long, but September is the month to really enjoy classical music—more than 60 classical concerts are held on stages around the city during the month-long **Settembre Musica** festival (✆ **011-442-4703;** www.mitosettembre musica.it).

Bric-a-brac of all kinds, be it household utensils, books, or used clothing, fills the stalls of the **Mercato del Balon,** held every Saturday at Piazza della Repubblica. **Gran Balon** fills the piazza the second Sunday of every month and is a larger affair, with some genuine antiques and artworks included in the mix. **Mercato della Crocetta,** at Largo Cassini, sells clothing at very low prices. For a look at the bounty of the surrounding farmlands, wander through the extensive outdoor food market at Porta Palazzo, open Monday through Saturday from 8:30am to 1:30pm and Saturday all day until 6:30pm.

In 2011, Italy will celebrate its 150th anniversary as a unified country. Turin and Piedmont were at the epicenter of the national movement that led to the foundation of modern-day Italy, so there will be many celebratory events in Turin and Piedmont. If you visit in 2011, be sure to check with the tourist office to find out about upcoming events—and don't forget to bring a green, white, and red flag to wave.

ESSENTIALS

GETTING THERE   By Plane   Domestic and international flights land at the **Caselle International Airport** (✆ **011-567-6361;** www.aeroportoditorino.it), 16km (10 miles) north of Turin. Buses run between the airport and the city's main train stations, Porta Nuova and Porta Susa. The trip takes about 40 minutes. A **taxi** from the airport takes about 30 minutes and costs around 35€.

By Train   Turin's main train station is **Stazione di Porta Nuova** (www.trenitalia.it), just south of the center on Piazza Carlo Felice, which marks the intersection of Turin's two major thoroughfares, Corso Vittorio Emanuele and Via Roma. From this station, there are two dozen trains a day to and from Milan—the trip takes 1¼ hours each way on the new fast trains; otherwise, it is closer to 2 hours (some trains to and from Milan also stop at Turin's other station, Stazione di Porta Susa). There are 16 trains a day to and from Venice (4½–5 hr.), 20 trains a day to and from Genoa (2 hr.), and 20 trains a day to and from Rome (6–7 hr.). **Stazione di Porta Susa,** west of the center on Piazza XVIII Dicembre, connects Turin with many outlying Piedmont towns; it is also the terminus for TGV service to and from Paris, with three trains a day making the trip in about 6 hours.

By Bus   Turin's main bus terminal is **Autostazione Terminal Bus,** Corso Vittorio Emanuele II 131 (near Stazione di Porta Susa; www.autostazionetorino.it). The ticket office is open daily from 6:30am to 1pm and 2 to 7pm. Buses connect Turin and Courmayeur (4 hr.), Aosta (3 hr.), Milan (3 hr.), Chamonix (3½ hr.), and many smaller towns in Piedmont.

By Car   Turin is at the hub of an extensive network of autostradas. A4 connects Turin with Milan, a little over an hour away; A6 connects Turin with the Ligurian coast (and,

Corso Francia

Piazza d. Statuto

Via Corte

Piazza Savoia

Via Garibaldi

d'Apello

Piazza d. Republica **1**

Stazione Autolinee (Bus Station)

Lungo Dora Firenze

Corso Dora Savoia

Corso Regina Margherita

Via Reggio

Corso Verona

Dora Riparia

Stazione di Porta Susa

Piazza XVIII Dicembre Autostazione Terminal Bus

Via Cernaia

Giardino Cittadella

Piazza San Giovanni

2

3 **4**

Via Maggio

Corso San Maurizio

Corso Inghilterra

Corso Bolzano

Corso Vinzaglio

Via G. Ferraris

Via Pietro Micca **(i)** **5**

Piazza Castello

Via Rossini

Via S. Teresa **6** **7**

Via Giuseppe Verdi

9

Corso Giacomo Matteotti

Corso Re Umberto

Via Roma

Piazza San Carlo

Via Maria

Via Princ. Amedeo

Via Po

8

Via Giulia di Barolo

Via Vanchiglia

Stamp Museum

Largo Vitt. **14** Eman. II

Piazza Carlo Alberto

Piazza Carlo Emanuele II

Via Giovanni Giolitti

Piazza Vittorio Veneto

Ponte Vitt. Eman. I

12 Piazza

10

11

ATTRACTIONS ●
Basilica di Superga **11**
Cattedrale di San Giovanni Battista/the Shroud of Turin (Museo della Sindone) **3**
GAM (Galleria Civica d'Arte Moderna) **14**
Mole Antonelliana & Museo Nazionale del Cinema (National Film Museum) **9**
Museo dell'Automobile **21**
Museo di Arte Orientale (MAO; Oriental Art Museum) **2**
Museo Egizio (Egyptian Museum) & Galleria Sabauda **6**
Museo Nazionale del Risorgimento Italiano **7**
Palazzina di Caccia di Stupinigi **21**
Palazzo Madama/Museo Civico di Arte Antica **5**
Palazzo Reale (Royal Palace) & Armeria Reale (Royal Armory) **4**

Piazza Carlo Felice **15**

Corso Vittorio Emanuele II

Stazione di Porta Nuova **(i)**

Via Sacchi

Via Nizza

Via Berthollet

Piazza Anthropology **13** Museum

Piazza Bodoni

Via dell'Accademia Albertina

Aiuola Balbo

Piazza Cavour

16

17

18

19

Corso Guglielmo Marconi

Via Cristina

Via Madama Cristina

Corso Cairoli

Via Frat Calandra

Po River

Gran Madre di Dio

Montagna Museum

Ponte Umberto I

C. Fiume

Corso Giov. Lanza

ACCOMMODATIONS ■
Hotel Bellavista **18**
Hotel Bologna **15**
Hotel Due Mondi **17**
Hotel Mobledor **8**
Victoria Hotel **13**
Villa Sassi **10**

Via Nizza

Via Valperga Caluso

Corso Raffaello

Pza. Nizza

Via Donizetti

Corso Massimo D'Azeglio

Parco del Valentino

Castello del Valentino

Parco del Valentino

Via Virgilio

Viale Virgilio

Corso Moncalieri

Corso Giov. Lanza

Viale E. Thovez

Via Sellimio Severo

Viale Cattone

Collegio S. Vito

0   1/4 mi
0   0.25 km

Torino Esposizioni

Corso Dante Alighieri

Corso Gal. Galilei **21**

Borgo Medioevale

Information **(i)**

DINING ◆
C'era Una Volta **16**
Dai Saletta **19**
L'Idrovolante **20**
Porto di Savano **12**
Ristorante Tre Galline **1**

PIEDMONT & THE VALLE D'AOSTA

11

TURIN

from there, with Genoa via A10, with a total travel time between the two cities of about 1½ hr.); A5 connects Turin with Aosta, about an hour away; and A21 connects Turin with Asti and Piacenza, where you can connect with the A1 for Florence (about 3½ hr. from Turin) and Rome (about 6½ hr. from Turin).

VISITOR INFORMATION   **Tourist offices** are at **Piazza Castello** (© **011-535-181;** fax 011-530-070; www.turismotorino.org) and are open daily from 9am to 7pm. There's also an office in the airport, open daily from 8am to 11pm. If you're coming to Turin on the weekend, check in with the tourist office's website, as you may be able to take advantage of a **"Torino Weekend"** deal, which offers 2 nights in a nice hotel room plus two Torino+Piemonte Cards (see below), often for as low as 64€ per person.

It's easy to get around central Turin **by foot.** There's also a vast network of GTT trams and buses (🕾 **800-019-152** in Italy, or 011-57-641; www.gtt.to.it). Tickets on public transportation are available at newsstands for 1€ and are valid for 70 minutes. With the **Torino+Piemonte Card** (see "What to See & Do," below), you can ride the city's public transportation for free for 48 hours. Longer periods are available as well.

CITY LAYOUT You will get a sense of Turin's refined air as soon as you step off the train into the mannerly 19th-century Stazione di Porta Nuova. The stately arcaded Via Roma, lined with shops and cafes, proceeds from the front of the station through a series of piazzas toward the Piazza Castello and the center of the city, about a 15-minute walk.

Directly in front of the station, the circular **Piazza Carlo Felice** is built around a garden surrounded by outdoor cafes that invite even business-minded Torinese to linger. Walking farther along the street will lead you into the **Piazza San Carlo,** which is flanked by the twin churches of San Carlo and Santa Christina. At the end of Via Roma, the **Piazza Castello** is dominated by the **Palazzo Madama,** so named for its 17th-century inhabitant Marie Christine. Just off the piazza is the **Palazzo Reale,** residence of the Savoys from 1646 to 1865, whose gardens now provide a pleasant respite from traffic and paving stones.

From here, a walk east toward the river along Via Po takes you through Turin's university district to one of Italy's largest squares, the much-elongated Piazza Vittorio Veneto and, at the end of this elegant expanse, the Po River.

ⒻFast Facts Turin

Bookstores **Libreria Internazionale Luxemburg,** Via C. Battisti 7 (🕾 **011-561-3896**), has a large selection of British books and a helpful English-speaking staff; it is open Monday through Saturday from 8am to 7:30pm, and Sunday from 10am to 1pm and 3 to 7pm. Another good bet for books in English is the chain **Libreria Feltrinelli,** Piazza Castello 19 (🕾 **011-541-627;** www.feltrinelli.it). Turin has many stores specializing in rare books and old prints, and many of these shops sell their wares from the secondhand-book stalls along the Via Po, which runs between Piazza Castello and the river.

Crime Turin is a relatively safe city, but use the same precautions you would exercise in any large city. Specifically, avoid the riverside streets along the Po at night, when they tend to be deserted. In an **emergency,** call 🕾 **113;** this is a free call. The **central police station** is near Stazione di Porta Susa at Corso Vinzaglio 10 (🕾 **011-558-81**).

Drugstores A convenient late-night pharmacy is **Farmacia Boniscontro,** Corso Vittorio Emanuele 66 (🕾 **011-541-271**); it is open most of the day and night, closing only between 12:30 and 3pm.

Emergencies The general emergency number is 🕾 **113;** for an ambulance, dial 🕾 **118.** Both are free calls.

Internet For Internet access, **1PC4YOU,** at Via Verdi 20/G (🕾 **011-835-908**), is open Monday through Friday 9am to 9pm, Saturday 10am to 8pm, and Sunday

2 to 8pm. Or try the **FNAC superstore,** on Via Roma 56 (📞 **011-551-6711**), which is open daily 9:30am to 8pm.

Laundry **Lavasciuga,** a laundromat/Internet point with seven locations across the city (📞 **011-2341-5015**; www.lavasciuga.torino.it), charges 7€ for a wash-and-dry of a small load. They're open daily from 8am to 10pm. The nearest location to the train station is Via San Anselmo 9.

Luggage Storage Luggage storage is available at the Porta Nuova train station: 4€ per bag for up to 5 hours, .60€ per hour for up to 12 hours, and .20€ per hour after that. The office is open daily from 6:30am to midnight.

Newspapers Your best bet for English-language newspapers is at the newsstands in Porta Nuova station. The major British and Irish papers are almost always available, as are the *International Herald Tribune,* the *Wall Street Journal Europe,* and sometimes *USA Today.* You may also find English-language magazines, commonly the *Economist* and *Wired,* as well as a Rome-based, American-run glossy called, appropriately enough, the *American.*

Post Office Turin's main post office is just west of Piazza San Carlo at Via Alfieri 10 (📞 **011-506-011**); it is open Monday through Friday from 8:30am to 7pm and Saturday from 8:30am to 1pm. The postal code for Turin is 10100.

Taxis You can find taxis at cabstands; especially convenient in the central city are the stands in front of the train stations and around Piazza San Carlo and Piazza Castello. Dial 📞 **011-5737,** 011-5730, or 011-3399 for a radio taxi.

WHAT TO SEE & DO

The tourist office sells an extremely worthwhile **Torino+Piemonte Card** for 19€, valid for one adult plus one child younger than 12. The card grants you 48 hours of free public transport within Turin; access to more than 160 museums, monuments, castles, royal residences, and the like; and discounts on car rentals, ski lifts, theme parks, concerts, and sporting events. The card is also available in 3-, 5 -, and 7-day versions. You can purchase the card at the tourist office at Piazza Castello; visit www.turismotorino.org for more information.

In December 2008, Turin welcomed a new museum: the **Museo di Arte Orientale** (Oriental Art Museum; see below). Italian newspapers have already dubbed it one of Italy's best museums for Asian art.

Since 2006, when Turin hosted the Winter Olympics, the city has been doing an excellent job of converting its Olympic venues into long-lasting structures that continue to be used. The **Palasport Olimpico (Olympic Arena),** designed by Japanese architect Arata Isozaki, was used for ice hockey competitions during the 2006 Olympics, but since then it has hosted performances by Bruce Springsteen, R.E.M., the Harlem Globetrotters, Depeche Mode, and many of the events in the Settembre Musica festival (see "Festivals & Markets," earlier in this chapter). Check the **Olympic Park** website (www.torinolympicpark.org) for a list of upcoming events.

Cattedrale di San Giovanni Battista ★★   The controversial **Shroud of Turin (Sacra Sindone)** and the chapel in which it is enshrined every jubilee year, **Cappella della Santa Sindone,** hold pride of place in this otherwise uninteresting, pompous 15th-century church. Even without the presence of one of Christianity's most precious relics

Tips   A Rare Glimpse: The Shroud of Turin

The Shroud of Turin—the garment that Christ was allegedly wrapped in when he was taken from the cross—is scheduled to be on display in the Museo della Sindone in spring 2010 for the first time in a decade.

(and it's only rarely on view in the silver casket elevated on an altar in the center of the room), the chapel is well worth a visit. Still under construction after a 1997 fire (one of many the shroud has miraculously survived, with an occasional singeing, over the centuries), the chapel is somberly clad in black marble. But, as if to suggest that better things await us in the heavens, it ascends to an airy, light-flooded, six-tiered dome, one of the masterpieces of Italian baroque architecture.

The shroud, of course, is allegedly the one in which the body of Christ was wrapped when taken from the cross—and to which his image was miraculously affixed. The image is of a man 1.7m tall (5 ft., 7 in.), with bloodstains consistent with a crown of thorns, a cut in the ribcage, cuts in the wrists and ankles, and scourge marks on the back from flagellation. Recent carbon dating suggests that the shroud was manufactured sometime around the 13th or 14th century, but the mystery remains, at least in part, because no one can explain how the haunting image appeared on the cloth. Also, additional radio carbon dating has suggested that, since the shroud has been exposed to fire (thus affecting carbon readings), it could indeed date from around the time of the death of Christ. Regardless of scientific skepticism, the shroud continues to entice hordes of the faithful.

The shroud is kept at the **Museo della Sindone (Holy Shroud Museum),** around the corner at Via San Domenico 28 (© **011-436-5832;** www.sindone.org), open daily from 8am to noon and 3 to 7pm; admission is 6€ for adults and 5€ for those under 12 or over 65 and students younger than 25. The shroud was last on view during Italy's Jubilee celebrations in 2000, and the Pope announced that it would be put on display in spring 2010. Technically, it is put on display only in Jubilee years, though it tends to pop up every 5 to 15 years for special occasions. Otherwise, you'll have to content yourself with a series of dramatically backlit photos of the relic near the entrance to the cathedral, and another in the church of San Lorenzo. The museum houses a plethora of information (including photos, X-rays, and history) relating to the shroud.

In front of the cathedral stand two landmarks of Roman Turin—the remains of a theater and the **Porta Palatina,** a Roman-era city gate, flanked by twin 16-sided towers. Piazza San Giovanni Battista. © **011-436-1540.** Free admission. Mon–Sat 7am–12:30pm and 3–7pm (opens at 8am on Sun). Bus: 12, 27, 50, or 51. Tram: 11, 13, 15, or 18.

GAM (Galleria Civica d'Arte Moderna e Contemporanea) ★   Turin's modern-art museum is one of the most important in Italy. It was founded in 1863, so its collections actually start with late-18th- and 19th-century neoclassical and Romantic works by Piemontese and other artists (Canova, Massimo d'Azeglio, Francesco Hayez)—in fact, the modern building itself makes a sharp point about our notions about art and its relevance with a glowing sign on the roof: ALL ART HAS BEEN CONTEMPORARY. The collections are largely arranged chronologically, with rooms focusing on specific movements or periods. Of the more than 600 works on display, you'll see art by Modigliani, Giorgio de Chirico, Gino Severini, Otto Dix, Max Ernst, Paul Klee, and Andy Warhol. On the first Friday of each month, you can take a free guided tour of the museum. Call for times.

Mole Antonelliana & Museo Nazionale del Cinema (National Film Museum) ★★

Turin's most peculiar building—in fact, one of the strangest structures anywhere—comprises a squat brick base and a steep conelike roof, which supports several layers of Greek temples piled one atop the other, topped in turn by a needlelike spire, all of it rising 167m (548 ft.) above the rooftops of the city center (a height that at one time made the Mole the world's tallest building). Begun in 1863 and designed as a synagogue, the Mole, now a monument to Italian unification and architectural hubris, is home to Italy's **National Film Museum.**

The museum's first section tracks the development of moving pictures, from shadow puppets to kinescopes. The rest is more of a tribute to film than a true museum, offering clips and stills to illustrate some of the major aspects of movie production, from *The Empire Strikes Back* storyboards to the creepy steady-cam work in *The Shining.* Of memorabilia, masks from the original *Planet of the Apes, Satyricon,* and *Star Wars* hang together near *Lawrence of Arabia*'s robe, *Chaplin*'s bowler, and *What Ever Happened to Baby Jane*'s dress. Curiously, most of the clips (all in Italian-dubbed versions), as well as posters and other memorabilia, are heavily weighted toward American movies, with exceptions mainly for the major players of European/international cinema like Fellini, Bertolucci, Truffaut, and Wim Wenders.

Even if you skip the museum, you can still ascend to an observation platform at the top, an experience that affords two advantages—the view of Turin and the surrounding countryside, backed by the Alps, is stunning—and, echoing Guy de Maupassant's famous comment on the Eiffel Tower, it's the only place in Turin where you won't have to look at the damned thingVia Montebello 20. ℭ **011-813-8560.** www. museocinema.it. Museum admission 7€; 5€ students 25 and under, and seniors 65 and over; 2€ children 6–18; free for children 5 and under. Observation platform 5€; 3.50€ students 25 and under, seniors 65 and over, and children 6–18; free for children 5 and under. Admission to both 9€, 6.50€ students 25 and under and seniors 65 and over, 4.50€ children 6–18, free for children 5 and under. Tues–Sun 9am–8pm (Sat until 11pm). Bus: 55, 56, 61, or 68. Tram: 13, 15, or 18.

Museo dell'Automobile (Automobile Museum)

As befits a city that is responsible for 80% of Italian car manufacturing, this shiny collection of mostly Italian automobiles, housed in a purpose-built, light-filled exhibition hall of classic 1960s design, draws car buffs from all over the world. Not too surprisingly, a century's worth of output from Fiat, which is headquartered in Turin, is well represented. The collection includes most of the cars that have done Italy proud over the years, including Lancias, Isotta Frashinis, and the Itala that came in first place in the 1907 Peking-to-Paris rally. Oddities include a roadster emblazoned with the initials ND that Gloria Swanson drove for her role as faded movie queen Norma Desmond in *Sunset Boulevard. **Note:*** The museum is closed for restorations until the end of 2010.

Corso Unita d'Italia 40. ℭ **011-677-666.** www.museoauto.it. Admission 7€ adults, 5€ children under 15 and seniors over 65. Tues–Sat 10am–6:30pm; Sun 10am–8:30pm. Bus: 1, 17, 18, 34, or 35.

Museo di Arte Orientale (MAO; Oriental Art Museum) ★

While you probably came to Italy dead set on seeing your favorite Botticelli, Raphael, or Caravaggio, you might want to set aside time for some non-Italian art and stop in at the MAO, Turin's newest museum, which opened in December 2008. With the opening of the MAO, Turin has quietly positioned itself as the premier place in the country to see Iranian porcelain, Chinese bronze art from 4,000 years ago, and Indian terracotta. The MAO has works from across Asia, including separate collections dedicated to southeast Asia, China,

India, Japan, the Himalayas, and Gandahara (an ancient kingdom located in what is now northwestern Pakistan and eastern Afghanistan). There is also an Islamic art gallery. The 1,500 pieces spread across the various galleries of the museum's 18th century Palazzo Mazzonis can be a bit much to take in on one visit, so you'd do well to choose a few areas to concentrate on.

Via San Domenico 11. (© **011-443-6927.** www.maotorino.it. Admission 7.50€ adults, 6€ ages 10–25 and seniors over 65; free 1st Tues of the month if it's not a national holiday. Tues–Sun 10am–6pm. Bus: 52.

Museo Egizio (Egyptian Museum) & Galleria Sabauda ★★★

Turin's magnificent **Egyptian collection** is one of the world's largest. This was, in fact, the world's first Egyptian museum, thanks to the fact that the Savoys ardently amassed artifacts through most of their reign, and the museum continued to mount collecting expeditions throughout the early 20th century. Of the 30,000 pieces on display, some of the more captivating exhibits are in the first rooms you enter on the ground floor. These include the **Rock Temple of Ellessiya,** from the 15th century B.C., which the Egyptian government presented to the museum in gratitude for Italian efforts to save monuments threatened by the Aswan Dam. The two statuary rooms nearby are staggering in the size and drama of the objects they house, most notably two sphinxes and a massive, richly painted statue of Ramses II. Smaller objects—mummies, funerary objects, and a papyrus *Book of the Dead*—fill the galleries on the next floor; the most enchanting exhibit here is the everyday paraphernalia, including eating utensils and shriveled foodstuffs, from the tomb of the 14th-century-B.C. architect Khaie and his wife.

The Savoys' other treasure trove, a magnificent collection of European paintings, fills the salons of the **Galleria Sabauda** above the Egyptian collection. The Savoys' royal taste ran heavily to painters of the Flemish and Dutch schools, and the works by Van Dyck, van Eyck, Rembrandt, and Van der Weyden, among others, make up one of Italy's largest collections of northern European paintings. In fact, two of Europe's most prized Flemish masterpieces are here, Jan van Eyck's *Stigmata of St. Francis* and Hans Memling's *Passion of Christ.* Italian artists, including those from Piedmont, are also well represented; one of the first canvases you see upon entering the galleries is the work of a Tuscan, Fra'Angelico's sublime *Virgin and Child.*

Via Accademia delle Scienze 6. Museo Egizio: (© **011-561-7776.** www.museoegizio.it. Admission 7.50€ adults, 3.50€ ages 18–25, free for children under 18 and seniors over 65. DC, MC, V. Tues–Sun 8:30am–7:30pm. Galleria Sabauda: (© **011-547-440.** Admission 4€ adults, 2€ for E.U. citizens ages 18–25, free for all those younger than 18 and older than 65. Tues and Fri–Sun 8:30am–2pm; Wed–Thurs 2–7:30pm. Bus: 4, 13, 18, 55, or 66.

Museo Nazionale del Risorgimento Italiano (National Museum of the Risorgimento)

Much of modern Italian history has been played out in Turin, and much of it, fittingly, in this *palazzo* that was home to the first king of a unified Italy, Vittorio Emanuele II, and the seat of its first parliament, in 1861. While any self-respecting town in Italy has a museum of the Risorgimento, the movement that launched Italian unification, this one is the best. Documents, paintings, and other paraphernalia recount the heady days when Vittorio Emanuele banded with Garibaldi and his Red Shirts to oust the Bourbons from Sicily and the Austrians from the north to create a unified Italy. The plaques that sum up each room are in English, and they will finally reveal to you the people behind the names of half the major streets and piazzas in Italy—including Mazzini, Vittorio Emanuele II, Massimo d'Azeglio, Cavour, and Garibaldi. The last rooms house a fascinating collection that chronicles Italian Fascism and the resistance against it. *Note:* The museum has been closed since 2006 for restorations, and **357** no reopening date has been announced.

Via Accademia delle Scienze 5. © **011-562-1147.** www.regione.piemonte.it. Admission 5€ adults; 3.50€ ages 10–18, students under 25, and seniors over 65. Tues–Sun 9am–7pm. Bus: 13, 15, 18, 55, 61, or 72.

Palazzo Madama—Museo Civico di Arte Antica (Civic Museum of Ancient Art) ★

Don't be misled by the baroque facade, added by architect Filippo Juvarra in the 18th century. If you walk around the exterior of the *palazzo* (named for its most popular resident, Madama Reale, aka Marie Christine of France), you'll discover that the massive structure incorporates a medieval castle, a Roman gate, and several Renaissance additions. Juvarra also added a monumental marble staircase to the interior, most of which is given over to the far-reaching collections of the Museo Civico di Arte Antica. The holdings focus on the medieval and Renaissance periods, shown off against the castle's unaltered, stony medieval interior. One of Italy's largest collections of ceramics is here, as well as some stunning canvases, including Antonello da Messina's *Portrait of a Man.*

In the Palazzo Madama, Piazza Castello. © **011-443-3501.** www.palazzomadamatorino.it. Admission 7.50€ adults, 6€ youths 10–25 and seniors 65 and over. Tues–Sat 10am–6pm; Sun 10am–8pm. Bus: 11, 12, 51, 55, 56, 61, or 68; or trams 4, 13, 15, or 18.

Palazzo Reale (Royal Palace) & Armeria Reale (Royal Armory) ★

The residence of the House of Savoy, begun in 1645 and designed by the Francophile count of Castellamonte, reflects the ornately baroque tastes of European ruling families of the time—a fact that will not be lost on you as you pass from one opulently decorated, heavily gilded room to the next. (The Savoys had a keener eye for paintings than for decor, and most of the canvases they collected are in the nearby Galleria Sabauda.) Most notable here are some of the tapestries, including the Gobelins depicting the life of Don Quixote, in the Sala delle Virtu (Hall of Virtues), and the collection of Chinese and Japanese vases in the Sala dell'Alcova. One of the quirkier architectural innovations, though not open to the public, is an antidote to several monumental staircases, a manually driven elevator from the 18th century.

One wing houses the **Armeria Reale,** one of the most important arms and armor collections in Europe, especially of weapons from the 16th and 17th centuries. Behind the palace, and offering a refreshing change from its frippery, are the **Giardini Reali (Royal Gardens),** laid out by Le Nôtre, more famous for Paris's Tuileries park and the gardens at Versailles.

Piazzetta Reale Palazzo: © **011-436-1455.** Admission 6.50€ adults, 3.25€ ages 18–25, free for children under 18. Tues–Sun 8:30am–7:30pm (sometimes to 11pm Sat in summer). Armeria: © **011-543-889.** Admission 4€. Tues–Fri 9am–2pm; Sat–Sun 1–7pm. Bus: 6, 11, 12, 27, 56, or 57.

PARKS & PIAZZAS

Piazza San Carlo, Turin's most beautiful square, is the city's outdoor living room, surrounded by arcaded sidewalks that house the terraces of the cafes for which Turin is famous (see "Cafes & Delicacy Shops," later). In the center is an equestrian statue of Duke Emanuele Filiberto of Savoy, and facing each other at the northern end of the piazza is a pair of 17th-century churches, San Carlo and Santa Cristina. The overall effect is one of elegant harmony.

The **Borgo e Rocca Medioevale** (© **011-443-1701**), built for Turin's 1884 world exposition, is a faithful reconstruction of a medieval village based on those in rural Piedmont and the Valle d'Aosta, with shops, taverns, houses, churches, and even a castle. The walk through the village is free, and pleasant enough, but since Piedmont and the rest of northern Italy are home to hundreds of bona fide fortresses, in the case of the Rocca, it's hard to find a good reason to pony up 5€ for a look around a make-believe castle.

The nearby **Castello del Valentino** is the real thing—a royal residence, begun in the 16th century but completed in the 17th century for Turin's beloved Marie Christine ("Madama Reale," wife of Savoy king Vittorio Amedeo) as a summer residence. It's a sign of Madama's Francophile leanings that, with its sloping roofs and forecourt, the castle resembles a French château. Used as a school of veterinary medicine, a military barracks, and currently as a university facility, the *castello* is continually undergoing renovations, and much of it, including many frescoed salons, is open to the public only on special occasions.

NEARBY ATTRACTIONS

Basilica di Superga ★★   As thanksgiving to the Virgin Mary for Turin's deliverance from the French siege of 1706, Vittorio Amedeo II commissioned Juvarra, the Sicilian architect who did his greatest work in Turin, to build this baroque basilica on a hill high above the city. The exterior, with a beautiful neoclassical porch and lofty drum dome, is more interesting than the gloomy interior, a circular chamber beneath the dome with six chapels. The church serves as a pantheon for the House of Savoy, whose tombs are scattered about, many in the Crypt of Kings beneath the main chapel. The building also includes some royal apartments. The name "Superga," however, in the Italian memory will forever be associated with a plane crash there in 1949 that killed the members of the Torino soccer club, the reigning champions, who were flying home from Portugal. A small museum there about the "Grande Torino" squad is a fitting tribute to players who have become almost patron saints of the city. The trip up to the hilltop on a narrow railway through a verdant park is a favorite Torinese outing.

Strada della Basilica di Superga 73, about 6.5km (4 miles) northeast of the town center in Parco Naturale della Collina di Superga. ℂ **011-899-7456.** www.basilicadisuperga.com. Free admission. Daily 9am–noon and 3–6pm (until 5pm Nov–Mar). Grande Torino Museum admission is 2€. Reached by rack railway (4€ round-trip) with a terminus at Stazione Sassi on Piazza Gustavo Modena (follow Corso Casale on east side of the River Po). Tram: 15 from Via XX Settembre to Stazione Sassi.

Palazzina di Caccia di Stupinigi ★   The other great work of the architect Juvarra (see Basilica di Superga, above) is this sumptuous, lavishly decorated hunting lodge that the Savoys commissioned in 1729. The main part of the lodge, to which the members of the House of Savoy retired for hunts in the royal forests that still surround it, is shaped like a Saint Andrew's cross (the lower arms extended and curved back inward like giant pincers), fanning out from a circular, domed pavilion topped with a large bronze stag. The lavish interior is filled with furniture, paintings, and bric-a-brac assembled from the many Savoy residences, technically comprising a **Museo d'Arte e Ammobiliamento (Museum of Art and Furniture).** Stroll through the acres of excessively decorated apartments to understand why Napoleon chose this for his brief residency in the region. Outstanding among the many, many frescoes are the scenes of a deer hunt in the King's Apartment and the triumph of Diana in the grand salon. The elegant gardens and surrounding forests provide lovely terrain for a jaunt. *Note:* The palace will remain closed for restoration until the end of 2010.

Piazza Principe Amedeo 7, Stupingi-Nichelino, 8.5km (5¼ miles) southwest of the city center. ℂ **011-358-1220.** www.mauriziano.it/arte/frsetpatr.htm. Admission 6.20€ adults, 5.15€ children 6–14. Tues–Sun 10am–6pm (to 5pm late Oct to late Mar). Bus: 63 from Porta Nuova train station to Piazza Caio Mario; change to bus 41.

Very Expensive

Victoria Hotel ★★ Step through the doors of this somewhat plain-looking building between the Via Roma and the river, and you'll think you're in an English country house. That's the whole idea, and the Anglophile decor works splendidly. The lobby is decorated as a country-house drawing room, with floral sofas, deep armchairs, and a view onto a garden; the room doubles as a bar and is an extremely pleasant place to enjoy a drink before setting out for one of the nearby restaurants. The glass-enclosed breakfast room, where a sumptuous buffet is served, resembles a conservatory. Accommodations are classified as deluxe or standard, depending on size and decor. "Standard" guest rooms are handsomely furnished in a chic style that soothingly combines contemporary and traditional styles, with mahogany bedsteads and writing desks, and rich fabric wall-coverings and draperies. "Deluxe" accommodations, each with its own distinctive look, are oversized and furnished with carefully chosen antiques and such flourishes as canopied beds and richly covered divans. A 2006 restoration added a Turkish steam room, a pool, and a selection of spa treatments available upon request.

Via Nino Costa 4, 10123 Turin. © **011-561-1909.** Fax 011-561-1806. www.hotelvictoria-torino.com. 106 units. 210€ standard double; 240€ deluxe double (150€ on weekends); 250€–270€ suite. Rates include breakfast. AE, DC, MC, V. Parking 20€ at hotel (you must reserve a space) or 18€ in nearby garage. **Amenities:** Bar; bikes; concierge; pool; room service; smoke-free rooms; spa w/hot tub, sauna, and massage and facial services; free Wi-Fi in common areas. *In room:* A/C, TV, hair dryer, minibar.

Expensive

Villa Sassi ★★ This early-17th-century villa is set in its own 20-hectare (49-acre) park east of town near the **Basilica di Superga.** Rooms on the first floor are larger, with Oriental rugs and semi-designer 1980s furnishings or antique dressers scattered across the parquet floors; a few open onto spacious terraces. Second-floor rooms have terra cotta–tiled floors and sloping ceilings, and better views over the surrounding forested hills. The bar opens onto a pleasant cobblestone terrace. Their restaurant (on the first floor, with large windows opening to tree views, and with the terrace to be enjoyed during the warmer weather) is highly regarded in the area, popular with Torinese for a breezy summer escape from the city.

Strada al Traforo di Pino 47 (about 4km/2¹⁄₂ miles from the center, near Superga), 10132 Torino. © **011-898-0556** or 011-898-0557. Fax 010-898-0095. www.villasassi.com/sassi_it. 15 units. 140€ double. Rates include continental breakfast. AE, DC, MC, V. Free parking. Bus: 61 or tram 15, then a 3km (1³⁄₄-mile) walk (better to take a taxi). **Amenities:** Highly regarded Piemontese restaurant; bar; babysitting; concierge; room service; smoke-free rooms. *In room:* A/C, TV, hair dryer, Internet, minibar.

Moderate

Hotel Bologna ★ (Value) This family-run hotel just across the street from the Porta Nuova train station offers location, affordable comfort, and a very attentive English-speaking staff. Each of the 45 rooms, spread over several floors of a gracious 18th-century apartment house, is different from the next. Some are quite grand, incorporating frescoes, fireplaces, and other original details (of these, nos. 52 and 64 are the largest and most elegant). Other rooms have been renovated in sleek modern style, with laminated, built-in cabinetry and neutral carpeting. Still others fall in between, with well-maintained 1970s-style furnishings and linoleum flooring. Whatever the vintage, all the rooms are spotlessly clean and nicely maintained. Two small suites with separate sitting rooms go for the same rates as regular rooms.

Corso Vittorio Emanuele II 60, 10121 Turin. ℭ **011-562-0193.** Fax 011-562-0193. www.hotelbolognasrl. it. 45 units. 95€ double; 120€ triple. Rates include breakfast. MC, V. Free parking (call ahead for a space). **Amenities:** Bar; concierge; room service. *In room:* A/C in some rooms, TV, hair dryer, minibar.

Hotel Due Mondi   This is a modern hotel 2 blocks east of the train station, with comfortable beds and modern units. Rooms are a wee bit cramped but retain some nice touches, such as faded remnants of frescoes on some ceilings. The wildly varying room rates below change with the season, and those high prices really apply only during trade fairs.

Via Saluzzo 3, 10125 Torino. ℭ **011-650-5084** or 011-669-8981. Fax 011-669-9383. www.hoteldue mondi.it. 42 units. 65€–180€ double. AE, DC, MC, V. Parking 15€ in hotel garage. **Amenities:** Italian restaurant; bar; concierge; room service; smoke-free rooms. *In room:* A/C, TV w/pay movies, hair dryer, Internet, minibar.

Inexpensive

Hotel Bellavista   The neighborhood between the Porta Nuova railway station and Parco del Valentino is pleasant and residential, and this *pensione* occupies the sixth floor of an apartment house on a quiet street. What is likely to strike you immediately is just how pleasant the surroundings are—step off the elevator and you will find yourself in a sun-filled corridor that's a garden of houseplants and opens onto a wide terrace. There's also a pleasant bar area. Rooms are airy and comfortable but a little less inspiring in decor, with banal, functional modern furnishings. Most, though, afford pleasant views over the surrounding rooftops—the best outlooks in the house are across the river toward the hills. What most rooms don't have is a private bathroom, though the several communal ones are well placed so most rooms are only a few steps away from a facility.

Via Galliari 15, 10125 Turin. ℭ **011-669-8139.** Fax 011-668-7989. www.bellavista-torino.it. 18 units. 40€–50€ double; 60€–70€ triple. Rates include breakfast. AE, MC, V. Free parking. **Amenities:** Bar; smoke-free rooms. *In room:* TV.

Hotel Mobledor   Located just steps from the Mole and close to both major train stations, the Mobledor is one of those quiet, unassuming places that puts the "star" in one-star hotels. It's ideal for those interested in only a nice, clean place to spend the night. The rooms are simply but tastefully decorated like the guest room of your grandmother's cottage, with plants and framed prints. Best of all, they have views of the Po River that normally can't be had for this price.

Via Accademia Albertina 1, 10123 Turin. ℭ **011-888-445.** Fax 011-812-5805. www.hotelmobledor.it. 10 units. 58€ double. No credit cards. Parking 20€ in nearby garage. *In room:* A/C, TV.

WHERE TO DINE

One of the great pleasures of being in Piedmont is sampling the cuisine that is unique to this region. Two new pastas you will encounter on menus are *agnolotti* (a type of ravioli often stuffed with an infusion of cheese and meat) and *tajarin,* a flat egg noodle that is often topped with porcini mushrooms. While chilly, foggy evenings call for grilled meat and game, truffles abound in the moist soil, and the farm gardens produce enough vegetables to make meatless meals a special occasion; one of the favorite preparations is *bagna cauda* (hot dip), in which raw vegetables are dipped into a heated preparation of oil, anchovies, and garlic. If you have a sweet tooth, you will soon discover that Turin and outlying towns can amply satisfy cravings for sweets, largely with pastries. Additionally, with wines as good as the Piedmont produces (see "Visiting the Wine Villages," later in this chapter), even a carafe of the house red is likely to be excellent.

C'era Una Volta ★★★ PIEMONTESE   To enter "Once Upon a Time," you must ring a bell at street level and then climb the stairs or take the elevator to a large, old-fashioned dining room filled with heavy old tables and chairs and dark credenzas. Until recently, they offered only the set-price tasting menu—and, for most of us, that was plenty (in fact, that was often more than plenty; we didn't have to make plans to eat anything for the next 24 hr.). However, due to popular demand by eager diners who just couldn't handle those massive meals, the restaurant has now introduced prices a la carte—though they've rigorously refused to change anything else about this classic Torinese establishment. The food, delivered by a highly professional waitstaff that has been here for years, is authentically Torinese and never seems to stop coming. A typical menu, which changes daily, might include crepes with ham and cheese, risotto with artichokes, a carrot flan, rabbit stew, a slice of beef with polenta, and any number of other wonderfully prepared dishes. You will want to accompany your meal with a fine Barolo or any other of the cellar's 300 local labels.

Corso Vittorio Emanuele II 41. ℂ **011-655-498.** www.ristorantecerraunavolta.it. Reservations recommended. Primi 8.50€–12€; secondi 14€–17€; tasting menu 26€–28€. AE, MC, V. Mon–Sat 8–10:30pm. Closed Aug.

Dai Saletta ★ PIEMONTESE   One of the few kitchens in Turin that remains open into the wee hours turns out a nice selection of homey trattoria fare, served in a tiny, cramped dining room near the train station. Homemade pasta dishes are delicious, and you may want to order some of them, such as *tortelloni alla salsiccia* (a large pasta shell stuffed with sausage) or *peposelle* (a thick pasta tossed with Gorgonzola and walnuts), as a main course. If you want to venture on, it may well be with a traditional favorite, like tripe.

Via Belfiore 37. ℂ **011-668-7867.** Reservations not accepted. Primi 9€; secondi 11€. AE, DC, MC, V. Mon–Sat 12:30–2:30pm and 8–10:30pm. Closed Aug. Bus: 1 or 16.

L'Idrovolante ★★ PIEMONTESE/ITALIAN   Situated in the city's medieval village, on the banks of the old embarcadero, the restaurant takes its name from the planes that landed on the water here from Trieste and Venice in the 1920s and 1930s, marking the beginning of Italian aviation. The owners are airplane enthusiasts and also masters of local cuisine. Start with a vegetable tart appetizer drizzled with fondue, followed by *cavatelli* pasta with white bean sauce and shellfish, or grilled veal stuffed with Taleggio cheese. Linger over one of the homemade desserts as you watch the city lights twinkle off the Po.

Viale Virgilio 105. ℂ **011-668-7602.** www.ristoranteidrovolante.com. Reservations recommended. Primi 7€–10€; secondi 14€–20€; sampling menus available for 30€. AE, DC, MC, V. Tues–Sat noon–2:30pm and 8–11pm.

Porto di Savona ★★ ⓥalue PIEMONTESE/TRATTORIA   What is probably the most popular trattoria in Turin is tucked under the arcades along the city's largest piazza. Seating is family style, at long tables that crowd a series of rooms beneath old photos and mementos, and the typically Piemontese fare never fails to please (all the more so on Sun, when many other restaurants in central Turin are closed). Several variations of gnocchi are usually made fresh daily, as is the Piemontese flat noodle, *tajarin,* and *pasticcio,* a pasta casserole with meat and cream. Another way to start a meal is with some variation of porcini mushrooms, which are perhaps best when simply sautéed. These starters can be nicely followed with a grilled meat dish—a house specialty.

Piazza Vittorio Veneto 2. ℂ **011-817-3500.** www.portodisavona.com. Reservations recommended. Primi 8€–8.50€; secondi 8€–19€. MC, V. Daily 12:30–2:30pm and 7:30–10:30pm. Bus: 53, 55, 56, or 61. Tram: 13 or 15.

Ristorante Tre Galline ★ PIEMONTESE   As one of Turin's most popular eateries for over 3 centuries, this bright wood-paneled room has friendly, professional service and a good-value tasting menu. The *salumi* are hand-carved at your table for an appetizer, and the daily, changing menu mixes Torinese and Piemontese specialties with slightly creative dishes using local ingredients. Some of their better creations include *agnolotti* (meat-filled pasta ringlets) in a pink ragù, risotto with basil and truffles, *carré d'agnello in crosta di erbette* (lamb cooked with herbs), and rabbit cooked in apple vinegar. One local dish that definitely takes some getting used to is the mix of zucchini, meatballs, a veal scallop, eggs, and a frog (an entire frog, not just the legs), all of it breaded and deep-fried, soaked in vinegar, and served cold.

Via Gian Francesco Bellezia 37. ☎ **011-436-6553.** www.3galline.it. Reservations highly recommended. Primi 10€–14€; secondi 16€–23€; tasting menu 58€, not including wine. AE, DC, MC, V. Tues–Sat 12:30–2:30pm and 7:30–10:30pm; Mon 7:30–10:30pm. Bus: 3, 4, 16, or 57.

CAFES & DELICACY SHOPS

Cafe sitting is a centuries-old tradition in sophisticated Turin. Via Roma and the piazzas it widens into are lined with gracious salons that have been serving coffee to Torinese for decades, even centuries. Below are some of the city's classic cafes. While espresso and pastries are the mainstays of the menu at all of them, most also serve chocolates—including the mix of chocolate and hazelnuts known as *gianduiotti*—that are among the city's major contributions to culinary culture.

Turin has a sizable sweet tooth, satisfied by any number of pastry and candy shops. Perhaps the best chocolatier north of Perugia is **Pfatisch/Peyrano** ★, Corso Vittorio Emanuele II 76 (☎ **011-538-765;** www.peyrano.com), open Tuesday through Saturday from 9am to 7:30pm and Sunday from 9am to 1pm. A wide variety of chocolates and other sweets, including sumptuous meringues, have been dispensed since 1836 at **Fratelli Stratta,** Piazza San Carlo 191 (☎ **011-547-920;** www.stratta1836.it), open Tuesday through Saturday from 9:30am to 1pm and Monday from 3 to 7:30pm.

The surrounding region is known not only for its wines but also for vermouth—the famed **Cinzano,** for instance, is produced south of the city in the town of Santa Vittoria d'Alba. Come evening, a glass of vermouth is the preferred drink at many of the city's cafes. **Paissa,** at Piazza San Carlo 196 (☎ **011-562-8462**), open Monday through Saturday from 9am to 1pm and 3:30 to 7:30pm, is an excellent place to purchase local vermouths by the bottle.

Caffè Confetteria al Bicerin ★ CAFE   What claims to be Turin's oldest cafe, in continuous operation (since 1763), is famous for its illustrious clientele, which has included Nietzsche, Dumas, and Puccini, as well as its signature drink—the Bicerin (local dialect for "something delicious"). It's a heady combination of coffee, hot chocolate, and cream—to be accompanied by one the house's exquisite pastries.

Piazza della Consolata 5. ☎ **011-436-9325.** www.bicerin.it. Sandwiches and pastries 3€. MC, V. Mon–Tues and Thurs–Fri 8:30am–7:30pm; Sat–Sun 8:30am–12:30pm and 3:30–7:30pm.

Caffè Fiorio ★ CAFE   Opened in 1780, the Fiorio was also a mainstay on the social circuit for aristocrats and other habitués with too much time on their hands and too many thoughts on their minds, giving it the nickname "the ponytail cafe." It serves a lunch buffet and some of the best ice cream in town.

Via Po 8. ☎ **011-817-3225.** www.fioriocaffegelateria.com. Sandwiches, pastries, ice cream, and dishes 3€–12€. AE, DC, MC, V. Daily 8:30am–1am.

Caffè-Pasticceria Baratti e Milano CAFE   No small part of the pleasure of sitting for a time in this stylish cafe, opened in 1875, is watching a clientele that includes auto executives, students from the nearby university, elegantly clad shoppers, and visitors to the nearby museums, all sipping espressos and munching on the delicious house pastries.

Piazza Castello 27. (✆ **011-561-3060** or 011-752-903. www.barattiemilano.it. Sandwiches and pastries 3€–6€. AE, MC, V. Tues–Sun 8am–8pm.

Caffè San Carlo ★ CAFE   One of the essential stops on any tour of Turin is this classic cafe. The San Carlo opened its doors in 1837 and ever since has been accommodating patrons beneath a huge chandelier of Murano glass in a salon that is a remarkable assemblage of gilt, mirrors, and marble. An adjoining, frescoed tearoom is quieter and only a little less grand.

Piazza San Carlo 156. (✆ **011-532-586** or 011-812-2090. Sandwiches, pastries, and dishes 2.50€–12€. AE, DC, MC, V. Tues–Sun 7am–1am; Mon 7am–8pm.

Caffè Torino ★★ CAFE   Although some of the mirrored and frescoed salons here serve full meals, we suggest you dine at another restaurant and enjoy only a light refreshment (one of the pastries or chocolates handsomely displayed in the main room) while soaking in the ambience of the classic, century-old Caffè Torino. Many mirrors, smoky oil paintings, and acres of carved wood create just the ambience you would expect to find in one of the city's most beloved institutions. This place is great for a cheap, fast, light meal: At lunch and dinner, bar plates are loaded with bite-size sandwiches, pizzas, stuffed olives, fried cheese and veggies, and other goodies—all yours for the gobbling with the purchase of a drink.

Piazza San Carlo 204. (✆ **011-547-356** or 011-546-690. www.caffe-torino.it. Sandwiches, pastries, and dishes 2.50€–10€. AE, DC, MC, V. Daily 7:30am–1am.

TURIN AFTER DARK

Turin has a lively classical music and opera scene, and you can get info on these and other cultural events at the **Vetrina Infocultura** office at Piazza San Carlo 159 (✆ **800-015-475** or 011-443-9040), open Monday to Saturday 11am to 7pm. Aside from the city's much-attended summer festivals (see "Festivals & Markets," earlier in this chapter), there are regular classical concerts by the National Symphonic Orchestra at **Auditorium della RAI,** Via Rossini 15 (✆ **011-810-4653;** www.orchestrasinfonica.rai.it). Other concerts, dance performances, and operas are staged at the city's venerable **Teatro Regio** (✆ **011-881-5241;** www.teatroregio.torino.it), in the center of the city on Piazza Castello.

DAY TRIPS FROM TURIN
Sacra di San Michele ★★★

Perched high atop Monte Pirchiriano—part of it projecting over the precipice on an elaborate support system that was one of the engineering feats of the Middle Ages—this dramatically situated abbey dedicated to Saint Michael provides views and an astonishing look at medieval religious life. It may well remind you of Mont Saint-Michel in France (both are laced with endless flights of stairs; the famous Mont Saint-Michel monastery and tourist site off the Normandy coast of France was one of the 176 religious institutions that once fell under the jurisdiction of Italy's San Michele, which today is all but forgotten). But with its dizzying views and scary drops, it just as easily may remind you of the abbey in the novel and film *The Name of the Rose* (probably because author Umberto Eco based his fictional abbey on this one). It was started in 983, but the extant church dates to the abbey's 12th-century heyday. A vast staircase hewn out of rock and clinging to the abbey's buttresses (known as *Scalone dei Morti* [Stairs of Death] because monks' corpses were once laid out here) leads to the massive carved doorway depicting the signs of the zodiac and the drafty Gothic and Romanesque church, decorated only with scraps of 16th-century frescoes by Secondo del Bosco. Another stairway leads down to three tiny chapels, carved into the rock, that contain tombs of some of the earliest members of the House of Savoy.

On Saturday evenings (and some Fri) from March to December, the atmospheric church hosts **concerts** of everything from chant and liturgical music to Renaissance chamber pieces, gospel, and traditional Celtic airs; check the website for schedules.

Outside Avigliana, 15km (9¼ miles) west of Turin's ring road. ✆ **011-939-130.** www.sacradisanmichele. com. Admission 4€ adults, 3€ children 6–14 and seniors over 65. Mon–Sat 9:30am–12:30pm and 2:30–5pm; Sun 9:30am–noon and 2:40–5pm.

GETTING THERE Take one of 15 trains a day from Turin to Sant'Ambrogio Torinese (30 min.); from there, it's a stiff 1½-hour trek up to the abbey. In summer only, call ahead to see about the once-daily bus that in past years has met trains from Torino at the Avigliana station (usually around 9am) to carry pilgrims up here. By car, follow the A32 from Turin's western ring highway toward Bardonecchia/Frejus. Get off at the Avigliana exit and follow the brown signs to the Sacra; the trip takes about an hour.

Savigliano & Saluzzo

Savigliano ★★ is one of those towns everyone dreams of stumbling upon in Italy—it's filled with Renaissance riches, but it's still undiscovered. The town center is the broad expanse of the Piazza Santa Rosa, surrounded by arcades, overlooked by a medieval tower, and lined with many of the town's grand palaces, which once housed summering members of the Savoy clan. Unfortunately, these and another fine collection of *palazzi* along the Via Jerusalem are closed to the public, so you'll have to settle for a gander at their gorgeous facades.

The pride of **Saluzzo** ★ is its sleepy upper town, huddled beneath its Castello di Manta. Along the warren of narrow lanes, you'll find the 13th-century Chiesa di San Giovanni and the Casa Cavassa, which is worth a look not for the musty civic museum it houses, but for its porticoed courtyard.

GETTING THERE Savigliano is 54km (33 miles) south of Turin, from which there are two to four trains per hour (35–50 min.). From there, hourly trains make the 13-minute run to Saluzzo. Saluzzo is also connected with Turin by 15 buses a day. The most direct driving route to Savigliano from Turin follows Autostrada A6 for 34km (21 miles) south to the exit near Brà. From the exit, follow S231 west for 9.5km (6 miles). Saluzzo is another 13km (8 miles) west on S231. If you are making the sweep through the wine country via Asti and Alba (see below), you can continue west from Alba for 34km (21 miles) on S231 to Savigliano.

---

2 THE PIEDMONT WINE COUNTRY

Asti is 60km (37 miles) SE of Turin, 127km (79 miles) SW of Milan; Alba is 60km (37 miles) S of Turin, 155km (96 miles) SW of Milan

South of Turin, the Po valley rises into the rolling Langhe and Roero hills, flanked by orchards and vineyards. You'll recognize the region's place names from the labels of its

Horses & Donkeys

Asti and Alba, bitter rivals through much of the Middle Ages, each celebrate the autumn harvest with equine celebrations that are horses of a very different color.

The **Palio** (✆ **0141-399-482**), Asti's annual horse race, is run the third Sunday of September. Like the similar but more famous horse race that the Tuscan city of Siena mounts, Asti's Palio begins with a medieval pageant through the town and ends with a wild bareback ride around the Campo del Palio. The race coincides with Asti's other great revel, the **Douja d'Or** (www.doujador.it), a weeklong fair-cum-bacchanal celebrating the grape.

On the first Sunday of October, Alba pulls a spoof on Asti with the **Palio degli Asini (Race of the Asses;** ✆ **0173-362-806**). The event, which coincides with Alba's annual truffle fair, is not as speedy as Asti's slicker horseback Palio, but it's a lot more fun. Good-natured as the event is, though, it is rooted in some of the darkest days of Alba's history. In the 13th century, Asti, then one of the most powerful republics of northern Italy, besieged Alba and burned the surrounding vineyards. Then, to add insult to injury, the victors held their *palio* in Alba, just to put the humbled citizenry further in its place. Alba then staged a *palio* with asses, a not-so-subtle hint of what they thought of their victors and their pompous pageantry.

excellent wines, among them **Asti Spumanti, Barbaresco,** and **Barolo.** Tasting these vintages at the source is one reason to visit the wine country, of course; another is to stroll through the medieval and Renaissance towns that rise from the vineyards and the picturesque villages that crown many a hilltop. And vines are not all that flourish in the fertile soil—truffles top the list of the region's gastronomic delights, which also include down-home country fare like rabbit and game dishes, excellent cheeses, and plump fruit.

ASTI

The Asti of sparkling-wine fame is a bustling city more concerned with everyday business than with entertaining visitors, but there are many treasures to be found in the history-drenched Old Town—medieval towers (120 of them still stand), Renaissance palaces, and broad *piazze* provide the perfect setting in which to sample the town's famous product.

Essentials

GETTING THERE   By Train   One to four trains an hour link Asti with **Turin** (30–60 min.). There are 14 trains daily between Asti and Alba, some of which require that you change trains at Nizza Monferrato or occasionally at Castagnole delle Lanze (35 min.–1 hr.).

By Bus   From Turin, **Arfea** (✆ **0144-322-023** or 0131-445-433; www.arfea.com) runs two buses per day, one morning and one midafternoon, on the hour-long ride to Asti. **Giachino** (✆ **0141-937-510;** www.giachino.it) makes the hour-long trip to and from Alba, about once per hour.

By Car   Asti, 60km (37 miles) east of Turin, can be reached from Turin in less than an hour via Autostrada 21.

VISITOR INFORMATION   The **APT tourist office** is near the train station at Piazza Alfieri 29 (✆ **0141-530-357;** fax 0141-538-300; www.terredasti.it). May to September, hours are Monday to Saturday 9am to 6:30pm and Sunday 9am to 1pm; October to April, hours are Monday to Saturday 9am to 1pm and 2:30 to 6:30pm, and Sunday 10am to 1pm. Among the office's offerings is a *Carta del Vini,* an annotated map that will point you to surrounding vineyards that provide wine tastings.

FESTIVALS & MARKETS   In late June and early July, Asti stages **Astiteatro** (✆ **0141-399-111** or 0141-399-032), a theater festival with performances that incorporate dance as well as music. September, though, is the town's busy cultural month, with townsfolk and horses alike donning medieval garb for its famous **Palio** on the third Sunday (see the "Horses & Donkeys" box, above). Local wine producers converge on the town the 2 weeks before the Palio for the **Douja d'Or** (www.doujador.it), an exhibition of local vintages accompanied by tastings; this is an excellent way to sample the products of the many wineries in the hills surrounding Asti and nearby Alba. On the second Sunday of September, surrounding villages mount feasts (almost always accompanied by a communal meal) known collectively as the **Pjasan.**

As the agricultural center that it is, Asti has two **food markets.** The larger is held Wednesdays and Saturdays from 7:30am to 1pm in the **Campo del Palio,** with stalls selling every foodstuff imaginable—seeds, herbs, flowers, farm implements, and no end of other merchandise spilling over to two adjoining piazzas, the Piazza della Liberta and Piazza Alfieri. Meanwhile, Asti's covered food market, the **Mercato Coperto,** is also located in this vicinity, on Piazza della Liberta, and is open Monday through Wednesday and Friday from 8am to 1pm and 3:30 to 7:30pm, Thursday from 8:30am to 1pm, and Saturday from 8am to 7:30pm. There's also a small **antiques fair** on the fourth Sunday of every month except August.

Exploring the Town

If you take the train to Asti, you will step right into the heart of the action—the town's lively clothing-and-food **markets** occupy three adjoining piazzas just to the north of the station (Campo del Palio, Piazza Liberta, and Piazza Alfieri). If you're driving into Asti, you're most likely to find parking in one of the lots in this area as well.

Walk through the piazzas to **Corso Alfieri;** the town's Renaissance palaces are located on or just off this major thoroughfare, usually closed to traffic. This street and Asti's grandest piazza are named for the town's most famous native son, the 18th-century poet Vittorio Alfieri. His home, on the Corso at 375, houses a small, memento-filled museum.

Second to none in Asti is San Secondo, the town's patron saint. He was imprisoned at the western end of Corso Alfieri in the **Torre Rossa**—much of which dates to the 1st century (probably part of a Roman gate) with two levels tacked on in the 11th century— then beheaded on the spot just south of Corso Alfieri where the church erected in his honor, the **Collegiata di San Secondo** (✆ **0141-530-066**), now stands. Not only does this Romanesque-Gothic structure have the honor of housing the saint's remains in its eerie crypt, but it is also the permanent home of the coveted Palio Astigiano, the banner awarded to the horseman who wins the town's annual Palio (see the "Horses & Donkeys" box, above; Secondo is the patron saint of this event). The church is open daily from 10:45am to noon and 3:30 to 5:30pm (Sun morning for Mass only).

Asti's "other" church is its 14th-century, redbrick **Cattedrale** (© **0141-592-924**), which you can reach by walking through Piazza Cairoli, at the western end of Corso Alfieri, into the nearby Piazza Cattedrale. Every inch of this brick church's cavernous interior is festooned with frescoes by late-18th-century artists, including Gandolfino d'Asti; trompe l'oeil vines climb many of the columns. The cathedral is open daily from 8:30am to noon and 3 to 5:30pm.

The most notable feature of the church of **San Pietro in Consavia** (© **0141-353-072**), at the eastern end of Corso Alfieri, is its round, 10th-century baptistery; the 15th-century interior and adjoining cloisters house a one-room paleontology collection (open Tues–Sun 10am–12:30pm and 3–7pm).

Where to Stay

Hotel Rainero ★ (**Kids**) Occupying a centuries-old house, the Rainero enjoys a wonderful location near the Campo del Palio and San Secondo. Not only is this setting convenient, but since many of the surrounding streets are closed to traffic, the neighborhood is quiet. Room nos. 301 to 303 have terraces (views only of surrounding modern buildings), and nos. 153 and 155 have balconies looking onto a cobbled street; there's also a large roof terrace. Despite the provenance of the structure, renovations are tasteful but lean toward a clean, modern look. As a result, the rooms are perfectly comfortable, though a little bland. The modular furnishings vary and seem to represent each decade since the 1960s; the best have bent-tube bedsteads and granite-topped sinks with brass-plated fixtures. Room nos. 157 and 158 (which families can connect) open off a hanging walkway over a pretty pair of tiny courtyards and red-tile roofs; no. 158 is large enough to be a quad and has a table and chairs on the walkway out front. Large room no. 161 gets one of those plant-filled courtyards all to itself.

Via Cavour 85, 14100 Asti. © **0141-353-866.** Fax 0141-594-985. www.hotelrainero.com. 55 units. 85€–110€ double; 140€–150€ suite. Breakfast 8€. AE, DC, MC, V. Parking 10€. Closed 1st week of Jan. **Amenities:** Bar; room service. *In room:* A/C, TV, hair dryer, minibar.

Hotel Reale ★ This has been an inn on Asti's main piazza since 1793, with good-size rooms, modern furnishings, double sinks, and, from some, views over the piazza. The floors are wood panel, the beds comfy, some rooms have couches that double as cots for kids, and the location can't be beat. Just don't come in August, when it's closed for most of the month.

Piazza Alfieri 5, 14100 Asti. © **0141-530-240.** Fax 0141-34-357. www.hotelristorantereale.it. 23 units. 100€–130€ double; triple 145€. AE, DC, MC, V. Parking in nearby garage 10€. **Amenities:** Room service. *In room:* A/C, TV, hair dryer, minibar. Closed Aug.

Where to Dine

Campanarò ★ PIEMONTESE For years Duilio Moiso ran a popular restaurant in a medieval *palazzo* that stood at the city walls and was used as a prison from the 16th century through 1777, at which point it was converted into an inn. Though the inn closed, the restaurant survived until 2003, when Moiso's lease ran out and the owner forced him out. Undeterred, Moiso opened Campanarò on the other side of the center, and though the atmosphere doesn't compare to the former medieval setting, he is still offering the same fantastic Piemontese food. Delicious local dishes on the ever-changing menu may include *agnolotti* in ragù, *taglierini* with truffles, *cinghiale* (stewed wild boar), *stracotta alla Barbera* (strip beef cooked in red wine), or *coniglio al vino bianco* (rabbit cooked in white wine). The wine list is extensive and well priced.

Via Secondo Arò 30. ℭ **0141-33252.** Reservations recommended. Primi 8€–10€; secondi 10€–14€. AE, MC, V. Thurs–Tues noon–2pm and 7:30–10pm (closed Sat at lunch).

Il Convivio ★★ PIEMONTESE   The decor of this double-height, pastel-colored dining room is straightforward, with a clean, contemporary look. These no-nonsense surroundings reflect the fact that the main business here is to serve excellently prepared food and accompany it with the region's best, but not necessarily most expensive, wines (these are dispensed from an extensive cave that you are welcome to visit, and you can also purchase wine by the bottle or case on the premises). Only a few starters, pasta dishes, and main courses are prepared daily. They always include some wonderful fresh-made pastas such as the lightest gnocchi in a sweet-pepper sauce, a soup incorporating vegetables bought that morning from Asti's markets, and some serious meat dishes, such as a masterful *osso buco di vitello, brasato di cinghiale,* or *coniglio,* a rabbit that is often sautéed with olives and white wine. Desserts, including a heavenly *panna cotta al ciocco-lato,* are as memorable as the rest of the dining experience.

Via G. B. Giuliani 4–6. ℭ **0141-594-188.** Reservations recommended. Primi 6.50€–8€; secondi 8.50€–10€. AE, DC, MC, V. Mon–Sat noon–2:30pm and 8–10pm. Closed last 2 weeks of Aug.

ALBA

Lovely old Alba retains a medieval flavor that's as mellow as the wines it produces. It's a pleasure to walk along the Via Vittorio Emanuele and the narrow streets of the Old Town, visit the 14th-century Duomo, and peer into shop windows with lavish displays of Alba's wines; its other famous product, truffles; and its less noble, but enticing, *noc-ciola,* a decadent concoction of nuts and chocolate.

Essentials

GETTING THERE   By Train   Only one direct train (in the evening, after 6pm) runs between Turin and Alba (1 hr.); otherwise, there's one per hour requiring a change either in Brà or Cavallarmaggiore (1¼–2 hr.). There are 11 trains daily between Alba and Asti (30–60 min.).

By Bus   Alba's Autostazione bus terminal (ℭ **0175-478-811;** www.atibus.it) is on Piazza Medford. Hourly Satti (ℭ **800-019-152;** www.satti.it) buses make the trip between Alba and Turin in about 1½ hours. **Giachino** (ℭ **011-226-3190;** www.giachino.it) makes the hour-long trip to and from Asti, about once per hour.

By Car   The most direct way to reach Alba from Turin is to follow Autostrada A6 for 35km (22 miles) south to the exit near Brà, and from the autostrada exit S231, go east for 24km (15 miles) to Alba. If you want to work Alba into a trip to Asti, take A21 to Asti and, from there, follow S231 southwest for 30km (19 miles) to Alba.

VISITOR INFORMATION   Alba has two **tourist offices.** The downtown branch, half-way along Corso Vittorio Emanuele at no. 19 (ℭ/fax **0173-362-562;** www.comune.alba. cn.it), is open daily from 9am to 6:30pm (may close Sun in winter). A **regional info office,** at Piazza Medford 3, across from the bus station (ℭ **0173-35-833** or 0173-362-807; fax 0173-363-878; www.langheroero.it), is open Monday through Friday from 9am to 12:30pm and 2:30 to 6:30pm, Saturday from 9am to 12:30pm (afternoons, too, in Oct).

FESTIVALS & MARKETS   October is Alba's big month. Its annual **truffle festival** is held the first week, and this, in turn, climaxes in the **Palio degli Asini (Race of the Asses;** ℭ **0173-362-806**), a humble version of neighboring Asti's equine Palio (see "Horses & Donkeys" box, above). On Saturday and Sunday mornings from the second weekend in October through December, Alba hosts a **truffle market,** where you may well be tempted to part with your hard-earned cash for one of the fragrant specimens (which could cost as much as 770€ per lb.).

Exploring the Town

Alba's two major sights face the brick expanse of **Piazza Risorgimento,** at the northern end of its major thoroughfare, **Corso Vittorio Emanuele.** The 14th-century brick **Duomo** is flanked by a 13th-century bell tower. Most of the interior and paintings hail from the late 19th century, save the two late baroque lateral chapels and the **elaborately carved and inlaid choir stalls ★** from 1512.

The town's two art treasures hang in the council chamber of the **Palazzo Comunale** across the square (go through the door on the right and up to the top of the stairs)—an early-16th-century portrait of the Virgin by Alba's greatest painter, Macrino d'Alba, and *Concertino,* by Mattia Preti, a follower of Caravaggio. It's open only during city office hours, Tuesday through Friday from 8:15am to 12:15pm, Saturday from 8:15am to noon.

From here, stroll the shopping promenade **Corso Vittorio** a few blocks to enjoy the low-key pace in the traffic-free heart of the town.

Where to Stay

Hotel Savona ★   Renovations have added a slick, modern look to this old hotel facing a shady little piazza at the south edge of the Old Town. In fact, the premises have more or less been denuded of character, but the hotel offers solid comfort and many more amenities than you would expect for the price. Downstairs is a slick breakfast room and a bar that is also popular with patrons from the town. Upstairs, the guest rooms are pleasantly decorated in pastel shades and have contemporary furnishings and shiny new bathrooms, most with bathtubs and many with Jacuzzis. Many rooms open onto small terraces; the quietest face an interior courtyard. The TVs are interactive, allowing you to call up reams of information on Alba, its wines, and the surrounding area (or watch satellite channels and pay-per-view movies). The housekeeping staff seems to work overtime to keep the premises clean and running like clockwork.

Via Roma 1 (a block from Piazza Savona), 12051 Alba (CN). © **0173-440-440.** Fax 0173-364-312. www. hotelsavona.com. 99 units. 107€–127€ double; 250€ per week for a 1-bedroom apt. Rates include breakfast. AE, DC, MC, V. Parking 6€ in courtyard. **Amenities:** Restaurant (local cuisine); bar; concierge; room service. *In room:* A/C, TV w/pay movies, hair dryer, minibar, Wi-Fi (fee).

Villa La Meridiana/Az. Agrituristica Reine ★★★ (Finds   On a hillside outside Alba (about 2.5km/1½ miles from the center of town), this sprawling, ivy-covered villa, the home of the Pionzo family, is a pleasant and convenient retreat. Most of the public areas are outdoors and include a flower-filled patio, a covered terrace overlooking the town and countryside, a room with a billiards table and gym equipment, a patio with a barbecue and wood oven you can use, and (in summer) a swimming pool. A breakfast of homemade cakes and jams, accompanied by cheeses from local farms, is served in a brick-vaulted dining room. You'll find an array of accommodations in the main villa and its extension, formerly the stalls and peasant quarters. Some (nos. 3 and 4 or nos. 5 and 6) can be combined to create family suites, and the four mini apartments come with kitchenettes (and no. 1 has two rooms and a large terrace—great for families). All are decorated in a pleasant mix of old country furnishings that have been passed down through the family; no. 6 even has a working fireplace. All, save two cozy doubles (nos. 4 and 5, which have shady groves out the windows), provide airy views over the city and the surrounding hill towns with a snowy alpine backdrop, or of the family's Barbera vineyards, apricot orchard, and pine grove; some also have terraces.

Località Altavilla 9, 12051 Alba (CN). From the Piazza Grassi in Alba, follow signs to Barbaresco, into the hills on Via Nizza-Acqui; a sign to the villa is about 2.5km (1¹/₂ miles) outside Alba; turn left and follow the unpaved road to its end, where there is a gated drive onto the property. ℂ/fax **0173-440-112.** www. villalameridianaalba.it. 9 units. 90€ double; 95€ mini apts. Rates include breakfast. MC, V. Free parking. **Amenities:** Bikes; concierge; small exercise room; outdoor pool; room service. *In room:* TV, fridge (apts only), hair dryer, kitchenette (apts only).

Where to Dine

Enoclub ★ PIEMONTESE   The evocatively chic brick-vaulted basement here is devoted to fine wine coupled with solid, slightly refined Piemontese cooking. The nice variety of rich pasta dishes includes *tarajin* (Piedmont's answer to tagliatelle) topped with a rich lamb sauce, and *fettucine di farro* (noodles made from the barleylike grain emmer rather than wheat) tossed with pesto and served with potatoes and beans. The secondi are meaty: veal steak with aromatic herbs, rabbit cooked in red wine, and duck breast in a black-olive paste.

Up on the ground floor is the busy **Umberto Notte** bar (open evenings only), one of Alba's few late-night scenes, dispensing wines by the glass, from 2€. This is a fine place to sample the produce of the local vineyards as well as wines from all over the world.

Piazza Savona 4. ℂ **0173-33-994.** Reservations not necessary. Primi 8.50€–12€; secondi 10€–15€. AE, MC, V. Tues–Sun noon–2:30pm and 7:30pm–midnight. Closed Aug.

Lalibera ★★ PIEMONTESE   A careful eye to design permeates this stylish *osteria* in the center of town. The marble floors, blonde contemporary furnishings, and pale green walls provide a restful environment in which to enjoy the variations on traditional cuisine that the kitchen prepares: You can see it all happening there through a large window. An *antipasto misto* is a nice way to sample the daily specialties, which are often lighter than most of the regional cuisine—it might include *insalatina di tacchino* (a salad of fresh greens and roast turkey breast), *vitello tonato* (the traditionally warm-weather Venetian dish of veal and tuna sauce), *fiori di zucca* (zucchini flowers stuffed with a trout mousse), or another truffle season specialty, the *raviolone* (one giant ricotta- and spinach-filled ravioli cupped around an egg yolk and showered with *parmigiano* and truffle shavings). Pasta dishes are equally innovative, and many of them, such as *agnolotti* (pasta stuffed with cabbage and rice), often combine fresh vegetables, or else the famous Piemontese *tajarin*.

Via E. Pertinace 24a. ℂ **0173-293-155.** www.lalibera.com. Reservations recommended. Primi 9€–12€; secondi 12€–21€. AE, DC, MC, V. Tues–Sat noon–2pm; Mon–Sat 8–10pm. Closed 2 weeks in late Feb/early Mar and last 2 weeks of Aug.

VISITING THE WINE VILLAGES

Just to the south of Alba lie some of the region's, and Italy's, most enchanting wine villages. As you set out to explore the wine country, consider three words: **Rent a car.** While it's quite easy to reach some of the major towns by train or bus from Turin, setting out from those centers for smaller places can be difficult (there are some buses, but they tend to be very few and far between). In Turin, contact **Avis,** Via Lessona Michele 30 (ℂ **011-774-1962;** www.avis.com), or **Hertz,** at Corso Turati 37 (ℂ **011-502-080;** www.hertz. it). Before you head out on the labyrinth of small country roads, outfit yourself with a good map and a list of vineyards from the tourist office in Alba or Asti.

THE WINES   While the wines of Chianti and other Tuscan regions are on the top of the list for many oenologically minded travelers, the wines of Piedmont are often less heralded among non-Italians, and unjustifiably so. Most are of exceptional quality and usually made with grapes grown only in the Piedmont and often on tiny family plots, making the region a lovely patchwork of vineyards and small farms. Below are some wines you are likely to encounter repeatedly as you explore the area.

Barbaresco is refined, dry, and, with Barolo, one of the region's most exalted wines. **Barbera d'Alba** is smooth and rich, the product of many of the delightful villages south of Alba. **Barolo** is called the king of reds (and is considered one of Italy's top two wines), the richest and heartiest of the Piedmont wines, and the one most likely to accompany game or meat. **Dolcetto** is dry, fruity, and mellow (not sweet, as its name leads many to assume). **Nebbiolo d'Alba** is rich, full, and dry (the best Nebbiolo grapes are used to make Barbaresco and Barolo).

Spumanti is the sparkling wine that has put Asti on the map for many travelers, and **Moscato d'Asti** is a floral dessert wine. You can taste and purchase these wines at cantinas and *enoteche* in almost all towns and villages throughout the region; several are noted below.

THE REGION   The central road through the region and running between Alba and Asti is S231, a heavily trafficked and unattractive highway that links many of the region's towns and cities; turn off this road whenever possible to explore the region's more rustic backwaters.

One of the loveliest drives takes you south of Alba to a string of wine villages in what are known as the **Langhe hills** (from Corso Europa, a ring road that encircles the Old City in Alba, follow signs out of town for Barolo). After 8km (5 miles), you'll come to the turnoff for **Grinzane di Cavour,** a hilltop village built around a castle housing an *enoteca* (© 0173-262-159), open daily 9am to 7pm, where you can enjoy a fine sampling of local wines from their more than 300 labels.

Continuing south another 4km (2½ miles), you'll come to the turnoff to **La Morra,** another hilltop village that affords stunning views over the rolling, vineyard-clad countryside from its central Piazza Castello (with parking). It has places to eat (see below) and to taste the local wines. The **Cantina Comunale di La Morra** (© 0173-509-204), on the Piazza del Municipo, operates both as the local tourist office and as a representative for local growers, selling and offering tastings of Barolo, Nebbiolo, Barbara, and Dolcetto. You can also procure a map of hikes in the local countryside, many of which take you through the vineyards to the doors of local growers. It's open Wednesday to Monday 10am to 12:30pm and 2:30 to 6:30pm.

Barolo, a romantic-looking place dominated by its 12th-century castle (about 5km/3 miles from La Morra), is directly across the valley from La Morra and enticingly in view from miles around. Here, too, are a number of restaurants (see our top choice, La Cantinetta de Maurilio e Paolo, below) and shops selling the village's rich red wines. Among these outlets is the **Castello di Barolo ★** itself (© 0173-56-277; www.turismoinlanga. it), which houses a small wine bar, *enoteca* (where you can taste), and tourist office in its cavernous cellars. A tasting of three of Barolo's wines (all from the same year but different zones, so you can more accurately compare labels) costs 5€. It's open Friday to Wednesday 10am to 12:30pm and 3 to 6pm, and 10am-6:30pm from mid-September through November (closed Jan). The castle and its wine museum are undergoing renovations that were supposed to be completed in 2009 and are now slated to conclude mid-2010 (the wine bar will remain open throughout). The entrance fee before the renovations was 4.50€ for an obligatory guide in English (or 3.50€ for a guide in Italian.)

Tiny **Novello** is a hilltop village about 15km (9¼ miles) south of Alba and located about 3km (1¾ miles) away from Barolo on well-signposted roads. It crowns the adjoining hilltop, offering some pleasant accommodations and yet more stunning views.

Where to Stay

See "Visiting the Wine Villages," above, for information on how to get to the towns where the following hotels and restaurants are located.

Barbabuc ★   This charming and intimate hotel, which wraps around a garden, lies behind the centuries-old facade of a house near the village square and is managed by the same private tourism consortium that owns nearby Barolo castle. Walls of glass brick and open terraces fill the premises with air and light. Guest rooms are placed on different levels of a central staircase, ensuring privacy, and are simply furnished in a tasteful mix of contemporary Italian pieces and country antiques on terrazzo floors. A few even have third beds or hide-a-beds for families. Well-equipped bathrooms have corner stall showers. A roof terrace offers countryside views over the surrounding houses; downstairs you'll find a handsome bar area and sitting room that opens to the pretty garden, an *enoteca* where local wines can be tasted, and an intimate little dining room where a lavish buffet breakfast is served. The entire hotel is smoke-free.

Via Giordano 35, 12060 Novello. ✆/fax **0173-731-430**. www.barbabuc.it. 8 units. 85€–95€ double. Rates include buffet breakfast. AE, DC, MC, V. Free parking. Closed Jan. **Amenities:** Bar; bikes; concierge; golf courses nearby; room service, Wi-Fi. *In room:* T/V (in some), hair dryer.

La Cascina del Monastero ★★ (Finds)   The main business at this delightful farm complex, just minutes away from La Morra toward Barolo (4km/2½ miles), is bottling wine and harvesting fruit. But Giuseppe and Velda di Grasso have converted part of the oldest and most character-filled building into a bed-and-breakfast. Guests can relax on a large covered terrace, furnished with wicker couches and armchairs, or on the grassy shores of a pond. A sumptuous breakfast of fresh cakes, yogurt, cheese, and salami is served in a vast brick-walled reception hall. The guest rooms, reached by a series of exterior brick staircases, have been smartly done with exposed timbers, golden-hued tile floors, and attractive antique bureaus, armoires, and brass beds. Bathrooms are sparkling and quite luxurious, with state-of-the-art stall showers and luxuriously deep basins.

Cascina Luciani 112A, Fraz. Annunziata 12064 La Morra (CN). ✆/fax **0173-500-861**. www.cascinadel monastero.it. 10 units. 85€–100€ double; 90€–110€ apartment. Rates include breakfast. No credit cards. Free parking. Closed Jan–Feb. **Amenities:** Bike rental; small children's playground; small exercise room; small outdoor pool; room service; sauna. *In room:* Hair dryer, kitchenette, minibar, no phone.

Where to Dine

La Cantinetta de Maurilio e Paolo PIEMONTESE   Two brothers, Maurilio and Paolo Chiappetto, do a fine job of introducing guests to the pleasures of the Piemontese table in their cozy dining room grouped around an open hearth (in nice weather, book ahead for a table out on the tiny back terrace). A seemingly endless stream of servings, which change daily, emerges from the kitchen: a wonderful country pâté; *bagna cauda* (a cold-weather dish, translated as "hot dip"), in which raw vegetables are dipped into a heated preparation of oil, anchovies, and garlic; ravioli in a truffle sauce; risotto with wild mushrooms; that funky giant egg-stuffed *raviolo* also found at Lalibera in Alba (see above); a thick slab of roast veal; a tender cut of beef; and salad made with wild herbs.

The wonderful house wines come from the vines that run right up to the back door of this delightful restaurant (a bar/*enoteca* is located up front).

Via Roma 33, Barolo. ℂ **0173-56-198.** Reservations recommended. Primi 9€; secondi 12–14€; tasting menu 37€, not including wine. AE, DC, MC, V. Fri–Wed 12:15–3pm; Fri–Tues 7:30–11pm. Closed Feb.

L'Osteria del Vignaiolo PIEMONTESE   Halfway up the road to hilltop La Morra in the village of Santa Maria (which is part of the town of La Morra), this stylish countryside restaurant draws a clientele from many of the surrounding villages, as well as from Alba, about 13km (8 miles) away. Pale gold walls, richly hued tiled floors, and handsome furnishings achieve a sophisticated rustic ambience, and the kitchen adds flair to local favorites. Duck breast appears in a salad of fresh-picked greens; wild mushrooms are served in many variations, perhaps lightly fried or grilled (porcini) and served with polenta. The *tortelli di zucca* (pumpkin-stuffed pasta pillows in a sauce of toasted hazelnuts) is flavorful and light, but you are likely to find it only in the autumn, when the pumpkins are in season. Veal appears thinly sliced in tagliatelle or, more traditionally, infused with herbs and simply grilled. Wines, of course, are local, many from Barolo, the lights of which you can see twinkling across the valley (especially if you snag one of the wrought-iron tables out on the flagstone terrace next to a hillside of grapevines).

Santa Maria 12, La Morra. ℂ **0173-50-335.** Reservations recommended. Primi 7€; secondi 11€; tasting menu 30€, not including wine. AE, MC, V. Fri–Tues 12:30–2:15pm and 7:45–9:15pm. Closed mid-Jan to mid-Feb and Aug 15–31.

Ristorante Belvedere PIEMONTESE   The view from the baronial main room, built around a large brick hearth and perched high above vineyards that roll away in all directions, is in itself a pleasure and draws many diners here. When tour buses arrive to fill the back rooms and downstairs, service can turn brusque. But while the Belvedere is no longer the welcoming rustic retreat it once was, its moves toward refinement (classy table settings, complimentary Spumanti and *crostini* while you consider the menu, for example) have been pulled off well, and the kitchen maintains the high standards that have made it one of the region's most popular restaurants. A wonderful salad of truffles and Parmesan cheese, and homemade ravioli in a mushroom sauce, are among the house specialties, which include many other pastas and risottos. Main courses lean heavily to meat, including a rich *petto di anatra* (duck breast), *coniglio farcito alle erbe aromatiche* (deboned rabbit stuffed with herbs), and *straccotto di vitello al vino Barolo,* a shank of veal braised with the local wine. The wine list is 83 pages long and has a table of contents, and the prices are surprisingly decent (keep in mind that this area's wines are among Italy's most expensive).

Piazza Castello 5, La Morra. ℂ **0173-50-190.** www.belvederelamorra.it. Reservations recommended. Primi 12€; secondi 18€–25€; fixed-price menu 42€, not including wine. AE, DC, MC, V. Tues–Sun 12:30–2pm; Tues–Sat 7:30–9pm. Closed Jan–Feb.

Vineria San Giorgio WINE BAR   This friendly wine bar in the center of La Morra, at the corner of Piazza Castello, serves as the village social center, and the series of attractive rooms are filled with amiable chatter throughout the day and evening. Rough stone walls and vaulted brick ceilings provide just the right ambience in which to linger and enjoy the local wines and such regional fare as salamis and cheeses, accompanied by homemade bread. There are three or four special daily dishes, usually including delicious lasagna or another pasta dish.

Via Umberto I, 1, La Morra. ℂ **0173-509-594.** Primi 7€–10€. MC, V. Bar: Tues–Sun 11am–2am (daily in Oct); kitchen: Tues–Sun noon–4pm and 7–11pm.

3 AOSTA & THE VALLE D'AOSTA

Aosta: 113km (70 miles) NW of Turin, 184km (114 miles) NW of Milan; Courmayeur-Entrèves: 35km (22 miles) W of Aosta, 148km (92 miles) NW of Turin

Skiers, hikers, and fresh-air and scenery enthusiasts, eager to enjoy one of Italy's favorite Alpine playgrounds, flock to this tiny mountainous region 1 hour by car northwest of Turin (and 2 hr. by train). At its best, the **Valle d'Aosta** fulfills its promise: Snowcapped peaks, among them the Matterhorn (Monte Cervino in Italian) and Mont Blanc (Monte Bianco), rise above the valley's verdant pastures and forests; waterfalls cascade into mountain streams; romantic castles cling to wooded hillsides.

Also plentiful in the Valle d'Aosta are crowds—especially in August, when the region welcomes hordes of vacationing Italians, and January through March, the height of the winter ski season—and one too many overdeveloped tourist centers to accommodate them. You would be best off coming at one of the nonpeak times, when you can enjoy the valley's beauty in relative peace and quiet.

Whenever you happen to find yourself in the Valle d'Aosta, three must-sees are the town of **Aosta** itself, with its Roman and medieval monuments set dramatically against the backdrop of the Alps (and a fine place to begin a tour of the surrounding mountains and valleys), and the natural wonders of **Parco Nazionale del Gran Paradiso.** The third, more dramatic to-do is the thrilling cable-car ride from fashionable ski resort **Courmayeur-Entrèves** over the shoulder of **Mont Blanc** to France. While much of the Valle d'Aosta is accessible by train or bus, you'll probably want a car to ease your exploration of the quieter reaches of the region.

Of course, recreation, not sightseeing, is what draws many people to the Valle d'Aosta. Some of the best **downhill skiing,** accompanied by the best facilities, is on the runs at Courmayeur and Breuil-Cervinia (the Italian side and name of the Matterhorn). The Valle D'Aosta is also excellent for **cross-country skiing** and **hiking** (see the "Into the Great Outdoors" box, below).

AOSTA

GETTING THERE   By Train   Aosta is served by 13 trains a day to and from **Turin** (2 hr.); there are 11 trains a day to and from **Milan** (3 hr., with a change in Chivasso).

By Bus   Aosta's bus station, across the piazza and a bit to the right from the train station, handles about eight buses (only one or two direct; most change in Ivrea) to and from **Turin** daily; the trip takes 3 hours (2 hr. on the direct). Four to five daily buses also connect Aosta and **Milan** (2½–3½ hr.). Buses also connect Aosta with other popular spots in the valley, among them **Courmayeur,** where you can connect to the Palud cable car (see "Mont Blanc by Cable Car," later in this chapter) and **Cogne,** a major gateway to the Parco Nazionale del Gran Paradiso (see below). For information, call ℂ **0165-262-027.**

By Car   Autostrada A5 from Turin shoots up the length of the Valle d'Aosta en route to France and Switzerland via the Mont Blanc tunnel; there are numerous exits in the valley. The trip from Turin to Aosta normally takes about an hour, but traffic can be heavy in the busy tourist months—especially in August, and from January through March, the height of the ski season.

VISITOR INFORMATION   The **tourist office** in Aosta, Piazza Chanoux 2 (ℂ **0165-236-627;** www.regione.vda.it/turismo), dispenses a wealth of info on hotels, restaurants, and sights throughout the region, along with listings of campgrounds, maps of hiking trails, information about ski-lift tickets and special discounted ski packages, outlets for bike rentals, and rafting trips. It's open Monday through Saturday from 9am to 1pm and 2:30 to 8pm (closed Sun afternoons Oct–May).

FESTIVALS & MARKETS Aosta celebrates its patron saint and warm winter days and nights with the **Fiera Sant'Orso** on the last 2 days of January. The festival fills the streets and involves dancing, drinking vast quantities of mulled wine, and perusing the local crafts pieces, such as lovely woodcarvings and woven blankets, which vendors from throughout the Valle d'Aosta offer for sale. Aosta's other major event is the **Bataille des Reines (Battle of the Queens, who, in this case, are cows),** in which these mainstays of the local economy lock horns—the main event is held the third Sunday in October, and preliminary heats take place throughout the spring and summer. Aosta's **weekly market** day is Tuesday, when stalls selling food, clothes, crafts, and household items fill the Piazza Cavalieri di Vittorio Veneto.

Exploring the Town

This mountain town, surrounded by snowcapped peaks, not only is pleasant but has soul—the product of a history that goes back to Roman times. While you're not going to find much in the line of pristine Alpine quaintness here in the Valle d'Aosta's busy tourist and economic center, you can spend some enjoyable time strolling past Roman ruins and medieval bell towers while checking out the chic shops that sell everything from Armani suits to locally made fontina cheese.

The "Rome of the Alps" sits majestically within its preserved walls, and the monuments of the empire make it easy to envision the days when Aosta was one of Rome's most important trading and military outposts. Two Roman gates arch gracefully across the Via San Anselmo, Aosta's main thoroughfare: the **Porta Pretoria,** the western entrance to the Roman town, and the **Arco di Augusto** (sometimes called Arco Romano), the eastern entrance, built in A.D. 25 to commemorate a Roman victory over the Celts. A **Roman bridge** spans the River Buthier; just a few steps north of the Porta Pretoria, you'll find the facade of the **Teatro Romano (Roman Theater)** and the ruins of the **amphitheater,** which once accommodated 20,000 spectators; the ruins of the forum are in an adjacent park. The theater and forum are open daily, in summer from 9:30am to noon and 2:30 to 6:30pm, in winter from 9:30am to noon and 2 to 4:30pm; admission is free. Architectural fragments from these monuments and a sizable collection of vessels and other objects unearthed during excavations are displayed in Aosta's **Archaeological Museum,** at Piazza Roncas 12 (© **0165-238-680**); it's open daily from 9am to 7pm, and admission is free.

Behind the banal 19th-century facade of Aosta's **Duomo,** Piazza Giovanni XXIII (© **0165-40-251**), lie two remarkable treasures: an ivory diptych, from A.D. 406, that depicts the Roman emperor Honorius, which is housed along with other precious objects in the treasury; and 12th-century mosaics on the floor of the choir and before the altar. Heavy-handed restorations cloud the fact that the church actually dates from the 10th century. It's open Monday through Saturday from 8am to 12:30pm and 2:30 to 5:30pm (though I've noticed they often just stay open all day), Sunday from 12:30 to 5:30pm. Treasury hours are April to September Monday through Saturday from 8 to 11:30am and 3 to 5:30pm, and Sunday all year from 8 to 9:30am, 10:30 to 11:30am, and 3 to 5:30pm. Admission to the treasury is 2.50€ for adults and 1€ for children under 6.

The **Collegiata dei Santi Pietro e Orso,** at the eastern edge of the Old City off Via San Anselmo 9 (© **0165-262-026**), is a hodgepodge from the 6th through the 18th

Into the Great Outdoors

Recreation, of course, is what draws many people to the Valle d'Aosta. You'll find some of the best **downhill skiing** and facilities on the runs at **Courmayeur, Breuil-Cervinia,** and in the **Valle di Cogne.** Multiday passes, providing access to lifts and slopes of the entire valley, run 109€ for 3 days and 142€ for 4 days, with per-day rates sliding down a scale to 14 days at 388€. For more info, call (℃ **0165-238-871** or visit www.skivallee.it. Ski season starts in late November/early December and runs through April, if the snow holds out.

One money-saving option is to take one of the *settimane bianche* **(white-week) packages** that include room and board and unlimited skiing and are available at resorts throughout the Valle d'Aosta. You can expect to pay at least 450€ at Courmayeur, and slightly less at Cogne or one of the other less-fashionable resorts. Over the Christmas and New Year's vacation period, prices practically double and hotels often sell out well before Thanksgiving. A popular option is to rent a chalet in the area: The tourist board (www.regione.vda.it) is a good resource to start looking for availabilities (or for real estate agents who specialize in short-term lets) and more information on weeklong packages.

Cross-country skiing is superb around Cogne in the Parco Nazionale del Gran Paradiso, where there are more than 48km (30 miles) of trails. The Valle d'Aosta is also excellent **hiking** terrain, especially in July and August. For information about hiking in the Parco Nazionale del Gran Paradiso, ask at the tourist offices of Aosta and especially Cogne.

centuries. An 11th-century church was built over the original 6th-century church, and that, in turn, has been periodically enhanced with architectural embellishments representing every stylistic period from the Gothic through the baroque. In a room above the nave (the door on the left aisle marked AFFRESCHI OTTONIANI; search out sacristan or ring bell), the remains of an 11th-century fresco cycle recount the life of Christ and the Apostles on the bits of medieval church wall above the 15th-century vaults. The frescoes are open daily April to September from 8:30am to 6:30pm, October to March 8:30am to 4:30pm. The 12th-century cloisters are a fascinating display of Romanesque storytelling—40 columns are capped with carved capitals depicting scenes from the Bible and the life of Aosta's own Saint Orso.

Side Trips from Aosta

CASTELLO DI FENIS (CASTLE OF FENIS) Built by the Challants, viscounts of Aosta throughout much of the Middle Ages, this castle (℃ **0165-764-263**), near the town of Fenis, is the most impressive and best preserved of the many castles perched on the hillsides above the Valle d'Aosta. From it, you can enjoy some fine views of the Alps and the valley below. One of the most appealing parts of a visit to Fenis is catching a glimpse into everyday life in a medieval castle—you can climb up to wooden loggias overlooking the courtyard and visit the cavernous kitchens. Alas, you cannot scamper among the ramparts, turrets, towers, and dungeons, thanks to a new Italian safety law.

March through June and September, the castle is open daily from 9am to 6:30pm; July and August hours are daily from 9am to 7:30pm; October through February hours are Wednesday through Sunday from 10am to noon and 1:30-4:30pm (to 5:30pm Sun). Requisite half-hour guided tours (Italian only) leave every 30 minutes. Come early; tours tend to fill up quickly in summer, and you can't book them in advance. Admission is 5€ for adults and 3.50€ for students. The castle is 30km (19 miles) east of Aosta on route S26; there are 13 buses a day (only one, at 6:20am, on Sun from Aosta; the ride takes 30 min.).

BREUIL-CERVINIA & THE MATTERHORN   You don't come to Breuil-Cervinia to see the town, a banal collection of tourist facilities—the sight to see, and you can't miss it, is the **Matterhorn** (**Monte Cervino** in Italian) ★. Its distinctive profile looms majestically above the valley, beckoning year-round skiers and those who simply want to savor a refreshing Alpine experience by ascending to its glaciers via cable car to the Plateau Rosa (26€ round-trip; closed Sept 10 to mid-Oct). An excellent trail also ascends from **Breuil-Cervinia** up the flank of the mountain. After a moderately strenuous uphill trek of 90 minutes, you come to a gorgeous mountain lake, **Lac du Goillet** ★, and from there, it's another 90 minutes to the **Colle Superiore delle Cime Bianche** ★, a plateau with heart-stopping views.

The **tourist office,** Via Carrel 29 (© **0166-949-136;** www.montecervino.it, www. breuil-cervinia.net, or www.cervinia.it), can provide information on other hikes, ski packages, and serious ascents to the top of the Matterhorn. Breuil-Cervinia is 54km (33 miles) northeast of Aosta via routes A5 and S406. **From Aosta,** you can take one of the Turin-bound trains, get off at Chatillon (20 min.), and continue from there on one of the seven daily buses to Breuil-Cervinia (1 hr.).

PILA   It's well worth the trip up the winding road 16km (10 miles) south from Aosta to this resort, at 1,782m (5,845 ft.). The views are incredible. Aside from getting an eagle's-eye view of the valleys rolling away in all directions at your feet—and access to over a dozen trails around and to the tops of the surrounding mountains—you will glimpse the peaks of Europe's two most spectacular mountains, Mont Blanc on the far left and the Matterhorn peeking up to the far right. Directly in front of you, the Gran Combin rises over Aosta to 4,271m (14,009 ft.). The little information office in back of the Pila gondola station (© **0165-521-148;** fax 0165-521-437; www.pila.it) has a good hiking map and is open Monday through Friday from 8am to noon and 1 to 5pm.

A gondola runs to Pila in 20 minutes (5€ round-trip) from Aosta, June 27 through July 17 and August 24 to September 7 daily from 8am to 12:15pm and 2 to 5pm (to 6pm July 18–Aug 23). It leaves from a large parking lot southwest of the train station (shortcut: Take the *sottopassagio* passage under the tracks at the station to Via Paravera, turn right then take your first left). To drive, follow Via Ponte Suaz—next to the train station—south out of town.

PARCO NAZIONALE DEL GRAN PARADISO   The little town of Cogne is the most convenient gateway to one of Europe's finest parcels of unspoiled nature, the former hunting grounds of King Vittorio Emanuele that now make up this vast and lovely national park. The park encompasses five valleys and a total of 3,626 sq. km (1,414 sq. miles) of forests and pastureland where many Alpine beasts roam wild, including the ibex, a long-horned goat, and the chamois, a small antelope, both of which have hovered near extinction in recent years.

Humans can roam these wilds via a vast network of well-marked trails. Among the few places where the hand of man intrudes ever so gently on nature are a few scattered

High Mountain University

In the mountains that straddle Aosta's eastern border, you can take courses that prepare you to conquer the highest peaks in the world. At the base of Monte Rosa, the second-tallest massif in the Alps after Mont Blanc, Silvio Mondinelli, one of Italy's greatest living mountain climbers, will teach you all he has learned in 50 years of trekking. The school, **High Mountain University** (✆ **0163-922-970;** www.himu.eu), is based in Alagna Valsesia, a mountain hamlet just across the border in Piedmont. The first courses were held in the summer of 2009, and the cost for a day-long class is about 150€.

Mondinelli (who goes by "Gnaro," which means "baby" in the dialect of the town where he was born) is convinced that the lessons that are learned in the mountains can also benefit people in their everyday lives. "This is a school that, among other things, will teach people how to better confront life and function as part of a team," said Mondinelli, who is one of a dozen people to have scaled the world's 14 8,000m (26,247 ft.) peaks without supplemental oxygen.

hamlets within the park borders and in the **Giardino Alpino Paradiso** (✆ **0165-74-147**), a stunning collection of rare Alpine fauna near the village of Valnontey, just 1.5km (1 mile) south of Cogne. It's open mid-June through mid-September daily from 10am to 6:30pm (5:30pm June and Sept); admission is 3€ for adults and 1.50€ for ages 7 to 19 and those over 70.

Visitor Information   Cogne also offers some downhill skiing, but it is better regarded for its many cross-country skiing trails. The **tourist office** in Cogne, Via Bourgeois (✆ **0165-74-040;** www.cogne.org), provides a wealth of information on hiking and skiing trails and other outdoor activities in the park and elsewhere in the region; it's open Monday through Saturday from 9am to 12:30pm and daily from 3 to 6pm. You can also get info at www.pngp.it. Cogne is about 29km (18 miles) south of Aosta via S35 and S507; there are seven buses a day to and from Aosta.

Where to Stay

Many hotels in the Valle d'Aosta require that guests take their meals on the premises and stay 3 nights or more. However, outside of busy tourist times, hotels often have rooms to spare and are willing to be a little more flexible with their policies. Rates vary almost month by month; in general, expect to pay the most for a room in August and at Christmas and Easter, and the least for a room in the fall. For the best rates, check with the local tourist boards for information on *settimane bianche* (white week) packages, all-inclusive deals that include room, board, and ski passes.

Belle Epoque (Value)   The stucco exterior of this old building in a quiet corner of the historic center has a cozy Alpine look to it, but the same can't be said of the somewhat stark interior. What is appealing about this hotel is the family-run atmosphere, and the price is appreciated all the more in this often-expensive resort region. Though there's no elevator, rooms are large enough but spartan, with the bare minimum of modern pieces scattered about, but some have balconies and tidy little bathrooms. An equally service-able trattoria occupies most of the ground floor; you can arrange a half-pension deal.

Via d'Avise 18, 11100 Aosta. ℂ/fax **0165-262-276.** www.hotelbellepoqueaosta.it. 14 units, 11 with private bathroom. 46€–52€ double with shared bathroom; 50€–66€ double with private bathroom. Breakfast 6.50€. AE, MC, V. Free parking. **Amenities:** Restaurant; bar; babysitting; room service. *In room:* A/C.

Hotel Bus ★   One of the nicest things about this newer hotel is its location, on a pleasant side street just a short walk from the center of Aosta. The Roman ruins and other sights are within a 5-minute walk, yet this quiet neighborhood has an almost rural feel to it. Downstairs you'll find a contemporary-style bar, restaurant, and breakfast area. Upstairs, the smallish guest rooms are comfortably furnished in a somewhat somber modern style that includes many wood-veneer touches and thin, worn carpeting. The bathrooms are serviceable but suffer from the dreaded waffle towels. Since the hotel is taller than the neighboring houses, rooms on the upper floors overlook meadows and the surrounding mountains. Except at peak times, rooms are usually available without board. Fifteen rooms have air-conditioning; if you prefer the opposite sensation, check out the sauna downstairs.

Via Malherbes 18, 11100 Aosta. ℂ **0165-43-645.** Fax 0165-236-962. www.hotelbus.it. 39 units. 74€–116€ double; half-board 54€–74€ per person. Rates include breakfast. AE, DC, MC, V. Free parking. **Amenities:** Valdostana restaurant; bar; tiny exercise room; room service; sauna. *In room:* A/C (in some rooms), TV, hair dryer, minibar.

Milleluci ★★★ (Finds)   From its noticeably cooler perch on a hillside just above the town, this chaletlike hotel in a breezy garden offers pleasant views. Current owner Cristina's great-grandmother converted the family farm into a hotel 50 years ago, and it's been handed down from mother to daughter ever since. Downstairs, a large wood-beamed sitting area is grouped around an attractive hearth (always ablaze in winter) and woodsy bar. The spacious rooms (larger on the second floor; cozy on the first) sport some nice touches like traditional wood furnishings, beamed ceilings, canopied beds (in suites and in one double), rich fabrics, terrazzo floors, and handsome prints. The stupendous buffet breakfast alone would be reason to stay: all homemade cakes, freshly whipped cream, *frittata* wedges (eggs from their own chickens, veggies from the garden), Alpine cheeses, and more. In nice weather, you can take breakfast on the wraparound terrace overlooking the town.

In Roppoz (off Via Porossan 1km/¹/₂ mile northeast of Arco di Augusto), 11100 Aosta. ℂ **0165-23-5278.** Fax 0165-235-284. www.hotelmilleluci.com. 31 units. 140€ double without balcony; 150€–240€ double with balcony. Rates include breakfast. AE, DC, MC, V. Free parking. **Amenities:** Babysitting; children's playground; concierge; Jacuzzi; outdoor heated pool; room service; sauna; smoke-free rooms. *In room:* TV/VCR, hair dryer, minibar.

Roma   Tucked into a cul-de-sac near the Porta Pretoria and close to the center of town, the Roma is named for the monuments of the empire that surround it. The paneled lobby and adjoining bar are pleasant places to relax and, with their plaid carpet and furnishings, are a little cozier than the bright but crisply modern guest rooms upstairs.

Via Torino 7, 11100 Aosta. ℂ **0165-41-000.** Fax 0165-32-404. www.hotelroma-aosta.it. 38 units. 82€–90€ double; 111€–123€ triple. Rates include breakfast. AE, DC, MC, V. Limited free parking. **Amenities:** Bar; room service. *In room:* TV, hair dryer, Internet.

Where to Dine

This is the land of mountain food—hams and salamis are laced with herbs from Alpine meadows; creamy cornmeal polenta accompanies meals; a rich beef stew, *carbonada*, warms winter nights; and buttery fontina is the cheese of choice.

Caffè Nazionale CAFE   This lovely fixture on Aosta's main square dates from 1886, and little has changed since then. For an almost sacred experience, try taking your coffee and pastry in the frescoed room that was once a chapel of the dukes of Aosta.

Piazza Chanoux 9. ✆ **0165-362-130.** Pastries from 2€. AE, DC, MC, V. Tues–Sun 8am–2am.

Grotta Azzurra PIZZA/SOUTHERN ITALIAN   The best pizzeria in town also serves, as its name suggests, a bounty of fare from southern climes, along the likes of spaghetti with clam sauce. There is a wide selection of fresh fish, which makes this somewhat worn-looking trattoria popular with a local clientele. The pizzas emerge from a wood-burning oven and are often topped with fontina and other rich local cheeses and salamis.

Via Croix de Ville 97. ✆ **0165-262-474.** Primi 5€–11€; secondi 7€–14€; pizza 4.50€–8.50€. Thurs–Tues (daily in summer) 12:15–2:30pm and 6–10:30pm. Closed 3 weeks in July.

Osteria da Nando VALDOSTAN   The owners of "da Nando" recently moved their restaurant to this smaller location, which has room to seat 30 diners (down from 100). The new restaurant is still dedicated to Valdostan cuisine. The focus is on local cuisine: dishes such as *fonduta* (a creamy fondue of fontina, milk, and eggs served atop polenta), *crepes à la Valdostana* (filled and topped with melted cheese), and *carbonada con polenta* (beef stew dished over polenta). They are also known for an excellent selection of grilled meats, pizzas, salads, and *bruschette,* as well as a wine list that includes many choices from the Valle d'Aosta's limited but productive vineyards and from Piedmont.

Via Sant'Anselmo 99. ✆ **0165-44-455** or 349-432-0920. Reservations not accepted. Primi 7€–12€; secondi 9€–20€; pizza 4€–7€. AE, DC, MC, V. Tues–Sun noon–3pm and 7:15–10pm. Traditionally closes 15 days in late June/early July.

Trattoria Praetoria VALDOSTAN   This small, woody trattoria, one of the friendliest and best-priced in Aosta, takes its name from the nearby Roman gate and its menu from the surrounding countryside. This is the place to throw concerns about cholesterol to the wind and introduce your palate to Valdostan cuisine. Begin with *fonduta* (fondue) and follow it with *boudin* (spicy sausages served with potatoes) or *carbonada* (a hearty beef stew).

Via Sant'Anselmo 9. ✆ **0165-44-356.** Reservations recommended. Primi 7€–9.50€; secondi 7€–20€. MC, V. Fri–Tues 12:15–2:30pm and 7:15–9:30pm (Thurs closed in the evening). Closed 20 days in Oct.

COURMAYEUR-ENTREVES

The one-time mountain hamlet of **Courmayeur** is now the Valle d'Aosta's resort extraordinaire, a collection of traditional stone buildings, pseudo-Alpine chalets, and large hotels catering to a well-heeled international crowd of skiers. Even if you don't ski, you can happily while away the time sipping a grog while regarding the craggy bulk of Mont Blanc (Monte Bianco on this side of the border), which looms over this end of the Valle d'Aosta and forms the snowy barrier between Italy and France. The Mont Blanc tunnel—scene of a devastating fire in 1999—makes it possible to zip into France in just 20 minutes.

Entrèves, 3.2km (2 miles) north of Courmayeur, is the sort of place that the latter probably once was: a pleasant collection of stone houses and farm buildings surrounded by pastureland. Quaint as the village is in appearance, at its soul it is a worldly enclave with some nice hotels and restaurants catering to skiers and outdoor enthusiasts who prefer to spend time in the mountains in surroundings that are a little quieter than Courmayeur.

Mont Blanc by Cable Car

One of the Valle d'Aosta's best experiences is to ride the series of cable cars from La Palud, just above Entrèves, across Mont Blanc to several ski stations in Italy and France and down into Chamonix, France. You make the trip in stages—first past two intermediate stops to the last aerie on Italian soil, **Punta Helbronner** (20 min. each way; 38€ round-trip or 105€ for a family pass valid for two adults and two children ages 6–11). At 3,300m (10,824 ft.), this ice-clad lookout provides stunning views of the Mont Blanc glaciers and the Matterhorn and other peaks looming in the distance. In summer, you may want to hop off before you get to Punta Helbronner at **Pavillon Frety** and tour a pleasant botanic garden, Giardino Alpino Saussurea (✆ **333-446-2959;** www.saussurea.net), open daily June 24 to September 30; admission is 2.50€, or 1.50€ if you show your cable car ticket.

For sheer drama, continue from Punta Helbronner to **Aiguille du Midi** ★★★ in France in a tiny gondola to experience the dramatic sensation of dangling more than 2,300m (7,544 ft.) in midair as you cruise above the Géant Glacier and the Vallée Blanche (30 min. each way; tack on another 20€ round-trip). From Aiguille du Midi, you can descend over more glaciers and dramatic valleys on the French flank of Mont Blanc to the resort town of **Chamonix** (50 min. each way; 50€). If you go all the way to Chamonix, the best way to get back to Italy is to hop on a bus back through the tunnel, for a final 12€ per person. Buses back take 45 minutes and leave Chamonix at 8:45 and 10:10am, and at 1:30, 3, 4, and 5:45pm.

Hours for these cable cars vary wildly, and service can be sporadic, depending on weather conditions (winds often close the gondola between Helbronner and Aiguille du Midi; this is, after all, the tallest mountain in western Europe), but in general, they run every 20 minutes from 7:20am (8:20am in fall and spring) to 12:30pm and 2 to 5:30pm (all day long July 22–Aug 27; closed Nov 2–Dec 10). The last downward run is 5:30pm in summer and 4:30pm in winter. The Helbronner–Aiguille du Midi gondola is open only May through September. *Note:* Children up to the age of 6 travel free, while those ages 6 to 11 get 50% off the prices above, and seniors older than 65 get a 10% discount. Hourly buses make the 10-minute run from Courmayeur to the cable car terminus at La Palud. For more info, call ✆ **0165-89-925** (www.montebianco.com). For a report of weather at the top and on the other side, dial ✆ **0165-89-961.**

A cheaper but far less dramatic way to cross over just one flank of Mont Blanc (but missing out on that thrilling 2.5km/1½-mile dangle in the air while you cross a massive glacier field into France) is on the Courmayeur Monte Blanc Funivia, which leaves from a terminus in Entrèves and ascends to the Val Veny. The round-trip fare is 12€, with 20% off for those older than 65 and free for children shorter than 1.3m (4 ft., 4 in.). Cars depart every 20 minutes from 9am to 12:50pm and 2:15 to 5:40pm; closed from late August/early September to late December.

GETTING THERE **By Bus** Thirteen daily buses connect Courmayeur with Aosta (1 hr.). At least hourly buses (more in summer; ✆ **0165-841-305**) run between Courmayeur's Piazzale Monte Bianco and Entrèves and La Palud (10 min.), just above Entrèves.

By Car Autostrada A5 from Turin to the Mont Blanc tunnel passes Courmayeur; the trip from Aosta to Courmayeur on this much-used route takes less than half an hour (lots of time in tunnels; for scenery, take the parallel S26, about 1 hr.), and total travel time from Turin is less than 2 hours.

VISITOR INFORMATION The **tourist office** in Courmayeur, Piazzale Monte Bianco 8 (✆ **0165-842-060** or 0165-842-072; www.courmayeur.it or www.regione.vda.it/turismo), provides information on hiking, skiing, and other outdoor activities in the region, as well as hotel and restaurant listings. Office hours vary widely depending on the time of year; it's best to call ahead.

Where to Stay

Edelweiss ★ In winter, the pine-paneled salons and cozy rooms of this chalet-style hotel near the center of town attract a friendly international set of skiers, and in summer, many Italian families spend a month or two here at a time. The Roveyaz family extends a hearty welcome to all and provides modern mountain-style accommodations. Many rooms open onto terraces overlooking the mountains, and the nicest rooms are those on the top floor, tucked under the eaves. Basic, nonfussy meals are served in the cheerful main-floor dining room; you can arrange a half-board deal if you wish. The hotel also has a small exercise room.

Via Marconi 42, 11013 Courmayeur. ✆ **0165-841-590.** Fax 0165-841-618. www.albergoedelweiss.it. 30 units. Summer 80€–140€ double; winter 300€–410€ double per person, per week. Rates include breakfast. AE, DC, MC, V. Free parking. Closed Oct–Nov and May. **Amenities:** Aostan restaurant; bar; a few free bikes; exercise room; sauna; smoke-free rooms, Wi-Fi. In room: TV, hair dryer, Internet (fee).

La Grange ★★ What may well be the most charming hotel in the Valle d'Aosta occupies a converted barn in the bucolic village of Entrèves and is ably managed by Bruna Berthold. None of the rooms are the same, though all are decorated with a pleasing smattering of antiques and rustic furnishings; some have balconies overlooking Mont Blanc, which, quite literally, hovers over the property. The stucco-walled, stone-floor lobby is a fine place to relax, with couches built around a corner hearth and a little bar area. A lavish buffet breakfast is served in a prettily paneled room off the lobby, and the hotel also has an exercise room and a much-used sauna.

Loc. Entrèves. ✆ **0165-869-733** or 335-646-3533 in the off season. Fax 0165-869-744. www.lagrange-it. com. 22 units. 80€–150€ double; 100€–180€ triple; 150€–230€ suite; there are discounts of stays of 3-5 days that don't include a weekend. Rates include American breakfast. AE, DC, MC, V. Free parking. Closed May–June and Oct–Nov. **Amenities:** Bar; babysitting; bikes; concierge; exercise room; room service; sauna. In room: TV, hair dryer, minibar.

Pavillon ★ This first-class hotel offers a bit more warmth and personalized service than most large ski inns at Courmayeur. The modern lounges are decorated with wood sculptures and warmed by a copper-hooded fireplace, with sun terraces opening off the front. The rooms are all quite large; though larger ones do cost more, even the "standard"-size rooms are plenty, well, roomy. What you really should be concerned about is requesting one with a view of the Alps. They are all comfortably furnished with bland modern pieces and firm, genuine beds. The bathrooms are a bit cramped, however.

(Moments) Drinking with the Best of Them

The **Caffè della Posta,** at Via Roma 51, Courmayeur (© **0165-842-272**), is Courmayeur's most popular spot for an après-ski grog. Since it opened 90 years ago, it has been welcoming the famous and not-so-famous into its series of cozy rooms, one of which is situated around an open hearth.

Some suites are lofted with the bedroom upstairs. Oddly, the hotel's not well indicated. To find it, go into the heart of Courmayeur, veer right off the traffic circle, and then at the top of the brief hill, follow the signpost marked PUSSEY, to the right; the hotel's a short way down on the left.

Strada Regionale 62, 11013 Courmayeur. © **0165-846-120.** Fax 0165-846-122. www.pavillon.it. 50 units. 100€–155€ standard double; 115€–170€ superior double; 145€–220€ suite. Rates are per person for obligatory full pension. AE, DC, MC, V. Parking 10€ in garage. Closed May to mid-June and Oct–Nov. **Amenities:** 2 international restaurants; bar; babysitting; concierge; tiny exercise room; discount on nearby golf course; Jacuzzi; indoor heated pool; room service; sauna; 2 nearby tennis courts (indoor and outdoor); Wi-Fi. *In room:* TV, hair dryer, minibar.

Where to Dine

La Maison de Filippo ★★★ VALDOSTAN   The atmosphere at this popular and cheerful restaurant in Entrèves is delightfully country Alpine, and the offerings are so generous you may not be able to eat again for a week. Daily menus vary but often include an antipasto of mountain hams and salamis, a selection of pastas filled with wild mushrooms and topped with fontina and other local cheeses, and a sampling of fresh trout and game in season. Service is casual and friendly, and in summer you can choose between a table in the delightfully converted barnlike structure or one on the flowery terrace.

Loc. Entrèves. © **0165-869-797.** www.lamaison.com. Reservations required. Fixed-price menu 45€ not including wine. MC, V. Wed–Mon 12:30–2:30pm and 7:30–10:30pm. Closed June and Nov.

Ristorante La Palud SEAFOOD/VALDOSTAN   Come to this cozy restaurant, in the little cable-car settlement just outside Entrèves in the shadows of Mont Blanc, on Friday, so you can enjoy a wide selection of fresh fish brought up from Liguria. At any time, though, a table in front of the hearth is just the place to enjoy the specialties of the Valle d'Aosta: mountain hams, creamy *polenta concia* (with fontina cheese and butter folded in), and *cervo* (venison) in season. There is a selection of mountain cheeses for dessert, and the wine list borrows heavily from neighboring Piedmont but also includes some local vintages.

Strada la Palud 17, Courmayeur. © **0165-89-169.** www.lapalud.it. Reservations recommended. Primi 7€–10€; secondi 8:50€–21€; fixed-price menus 18€–25€, the more expensive one includes wine. AE, MC, V. Thurs–Tues noon–3:30pm and 7:30–10:30pm.

PIEDMONT & THE VALLE D'AOSTA

11

AOSTA & THE VALLE D'AOSTA

Liguria & the Italian Riviera

From the top of Tuscany to the French border, along the Ligurian and Mediterranean Seas, Italy follows a crescent-shape strip of seacoast and mountains that make up the region of **Liguria.** The pleasures of this region are no secret. Ever since the 19th century, world-weary travelers have been heading for Liguria's resorts to enjoy balmy weather (ensured by the protective barrier of the Alps) and turquoise seas. Beyond the beach, the stones and tiles of fishing villages, small resort towns, and proud old port cities bake in the sun, and hillsides are fragrant with the scent of bougainvillea and pines.

Liguria is really two coasts. First, the beachier stretch west of Genoa known as the **Riviera di Ponente (Setting Sun),** is studded with fashionable resorts, many of which, like San Remo, have seen their heydays fade but continue to entice visitors with palm-fringed promenades and gentle ways.

The rockier, more colorful fishing-village-filled stretch to the southeast of Genoa, known as the **Riviera di Levante (Rising Sun),** extends past the posh harbor of Portofino to the remote hamlets of the Cinque Terre.

The province's capital, Genoa, is Italy's busiest port, an ancient center of commerce, and one of history's great maritime powers. However, though it is one of Italy's most historic places, it is also one of the least-visited cities in all of Italy. But don't judge the area by its capital: Genoa's gritty feel and its brusque and clamorous elements are a world apart from the easygoing and charming seaside villages and resorts that populate the province

REGIONAL CUISINE Anywhere you travel in this region, you will never be far from the sea, though seafood is not as plentiful as you might assume here in the heavily fished north. What is plentiful are *acciughe* (**anchovies**)**,** and once you try them fresh and *marinate* (marinated in lemon) as part of an antipasto, you will never underestimate the culinary merits of this little fish again. More noticeable than fish are the many fresh vegetables that grow in patches clinging to the hillsides and find their way into tarts (the *torta pasqualina* is one of the most elaborate, with umpteen layers of pastry; some restaurants serve it year-round) and sauces, none more typical of Liguria than **pesto,** a simple and simply delicious concoction of basil, olive oil, pine nuts, and *parmigiano* ground together in a mortar and pestle (hence the name). It's often used to top *trenette:* a short, hand-rolled twist of pasta sort of like a 5cm-long (2-in.) extra-thick spaghetti. Ligurians are also adept at making fast food, and there's no better light lunch or snack than a piece of **focaccia,** flatbread that's often topped with herbs or olives, or a *farinata,* a chickpea crepe that's served in wedges. Both are sold in bakeries and at small stands, making it easy to grab a bite before heading out to enjoy the other delights of the region.

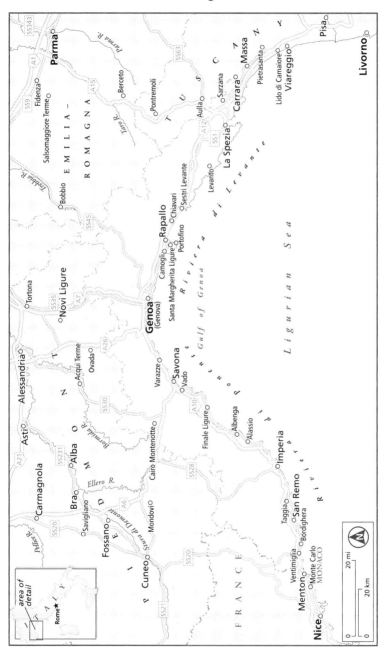

1 GENOA

142km (88 miles) S of Milan, 501km (311 miles) N of Rome, 194km (120 miles) E of Nice

With its dizzying mix of the old and the new, of sophistication and squalor, **Genoa** **(Genova)** is as multilayered as the hills it clings to. It was and is, first and foremost, a port city: an important maritime center for the Roman Empire, boyhood home of Christopher Columbus (whose much-restored house still stands near a section of the medieval walls), and, fueled by seafaring commerce that stretched all the way to the Middle East, one of the largest and wealthiest cities of Renaissance Europe.

Genoa began as a port of the ancient Ligurian people at least by the 6th century B.C., when it traded with the Greeks and Phoenicians. Genoa threw in its lot with Rome against Carthage and was destroyed for its loyalty in 205 B.C., but Rome rebuilt it. By the early Middle Ages, Genoa had become a formidable maritime power, conquering the surrounding coast and the mighty outlying islands of Corsica and Sardinia. Though all Mediterranean ports competed, the rivalry was particularly strident between neighbors Genoa and Pisa. After countless battles, Genoa soundly trounced its enemies at Meloria in 1284 (Pisa would never truly recover), after which Genoa's growth knew few bounds. She established colonies throughout North Africa and the Middle East, and made massive gains during the Crusades. With bigger success came new, bigger rivals, and Genoa locked commercial and military horns with Venice, which took the upper hand in 1380 with a naval victory at Chioggia. Though La Superba—"The Superb," a proud nickname given the city by Petrarch himself in 1358—nurtured its own powerful families, after Chioggia the city's power was broken, and Genoa was increasingly controlled by a series of French and Milanese kings and potentates.

In 1528, Genoese naval hero Andrea Doria led an insurrection that reestablished local control, but the self-made government quickly turned tyrannical. Genoa's days at the top of the heap were ending. The locus of sea trade was rapidly shifting to Spain and eventually to its American colonies, a trend exemplified by Genoa's most famous native son, Christopher Columbus, who had to travel to Spain to find the financial backing for his voyage of exploration across the Atlantic. By 1684, the French had reconquered the city, and soon after the Austrians took control until 1746, followed by Napoleon in 1767. Austria tried again and failed, and Genoa set up a Ligurian Republic in 1802, but it was quickly subsumed into Piedmont, which became a French province.

Genoa's new links with Piedmont made its future, though, as it was deeply embroiled from early on in the Risorgimento, the 19th-century Italian unification movement. In simplest terms, the Risorgimento was built on a four-sided foundation: a king (Vittorio

---

Tips **A Fading Scar**

Be prepared to deal with some seediness in the Old Quarter by the seaport. Though the city has almost completely cleaned up the legendary drug use in its historic center, and popular restaurants and wine bars have taken over previously shady piazzas, be aware that prostitutes and other unsavory characters still exist in the darker alleyways, all night *and* all day long.

ATTRACTIONS ●
Acquario di Genova **5**
Cattedrale San Lorenzo **16**
Galleria di Palazzo Bianco
(White Palace) **8**
Galleria di Palazzo Rosso
(Red Palace) **10**
Galleria Nazionale di
Palazzo Spinola **7**
Museo di Palazzo Reale
(Royal Palace) **2**
San Matteo **15**
Sant'Agostino–Museo
di Architettura
e Scultura Ligure **22**

ACCOMMODATIONS ▦
Agnello d'Oro **1**
Barone **20**
Best Western Hotel
Metropoli **12**
Bristol Palace **17**
Cairoli **4**
Fiume **19**
Ostello Per La Gioventù **3**

DINING ◆
Da Genio **21**
Da Guglie **18**
I Tre Merli
Antica Cantina **9**
La Berlocca **13**
Mario Rivaro **11**
Trattoria da Maria **14**
Trattoria Vegia Zena **6**

Emanuele II), a general (Giuseppe Garibaldi), a political leader (Camillo Cavour), and a political philosopher (Giuseppe Mazzini). Mazzini was Genoese born and bred, and in 1860, Garibaldi staged his single huge military push from this port city, the embarkation of the "Thousand" red-shirt soldiers who sailed to conquer and otherwise successfully bring all of the peninsula into the new Kingdom of Italy. In World War II, the Allies bombed the heck out of this major port, but Genoa responded by rebuilding and expanding rapidly in the following decades, becoming once again a major Mediterranean port.

It's easy to capture glimpses of these former glory days on the narrow lanes and dank alleys of Genoa's portside Old Town, where treasure-filled palaces and fine marble churches stand next to laundry-draped tenements and brothels. In fact, some of the life within the old medieval walls doesn't seem to have changed since the days when Genovese ships set sail to launch raids on the Venetians, crusaders embarked for the Holy Land, and Garibaldi shipped out to invade Sicily in the 19th-century struggle to unify Italy. The other Genoa, the modern city that stretches for miles along the coast and climbs the hills, is a city of international business, peaceful parks, and breezy belvederes from which you can enjoy fine views of this dingy yet colorful metropolis and the sea that continues to define its identity.

FESTIVALS & MARKETS   In June, an ancient tradition continues when Genoa takes to the sea in the **Regata delle Antiche Repubbliche Marinare** (not to be confused with Venice's very own **Regata Storica;** see p. 163), competing against crews from its ancient maritime rivals, Amalfi, Pisa, and Venice, who host the event in turn. Another spectacular—though more modern—regatta takes place here every April, the Millevele, or "thousand sails," when Genoa's bay is carpeted with the mainsails and spinnakers of nautical enthusiasts from around the world.

Genoa adds a touch of culture to the summer season with an **International Ballet Festival** that attracts a stellar list of performers from around the world. Performances are held in the beautiful gardens of Villa Gropallo in outlying Nervi, a late-19th-century resort with lush parks and a lively seaside promenade. Contact the tourist office in Genoa for schedules and ticket information, as well as for the summer concerts staged at different venues, many of them outdoors, around the city.

The **Mercato Orientale,** Genoa's sprawling indoor food market, evokes the days when ships brought back spices and other commodities from the ends of the earth. Still a boisterous affair and an excellent place to stock up on olives, herbs, fresh fruit, and other Ligurian products, it is held Monday through Saturday from 7am to 1pm and 3:30 to 7:30pm (closed Wed afternoons), with entrances on Via XX Settembre and Via Galata (about halfway btw. Piazza de Ferrari at the edge of the Old City and Stazione Brignole). The district just north of the market (especially Via San Vincenzo and Via Colombo) is a gourmand's dream, with many bakeries, *pasticcerie* (pastry shops), and stores selling pasta and cheese, wine, olive oil, and other foodstuffs.

ESSENTIALS

GETTING THERE   **By Plane**   Flights to and from most European capitals serve **Aeroporto Internazionale de Genova Cristoforo Colombo,** just 6.4km (4 miles) west of the city center (© **010-60-151** for the central line, 010-601-5410 for information; www.airport.genova.it). **Volabus no. 100** (© **010-558-2414**) connects the airport with Stazione Principe and Stazione Brignole, with buses running every half-hour from 6am to 10pm; buy tickets (2€) on the bus. The nearest airports handling overseas flights are at Nice, 187km (116 miles) west just over the border with France, and Milan, 137km (85 miles) to the north; both cities are well connected to Genoa by superhighways and train service.

By Train   An important thing train travelers should know about Genoa is that the city has two major train stations, **Stazione Principe** (designated on timetables as Genova P.P.), near the Old City on Piazza Acqua Verde, and **Stazione Brignole** (designated on timetables as Genova BR.), in the modern city on Piazza Verdi. Many trains, especially those on long-distance lines, service both stations; however, many trains stop only at one, making it essential that you know the station at which your train is scheduled to arrive and from which it will depart. Trains (free since they don't check tickets btw. the down- town stations) connect the two stations in just 5 minutes and run about every 15 minutes. The city buses nos. 40 and 37 also run between the two train stations, leaving from the front of each station about every 10 minutes; you must allow at least 20 minutes for the connection on Genoa's crowded streets.

Genoa is the hub for trains serving the Italian Riviera, with trains arriving and departing for Ventimiglia on the French border about every half-hour, and **La Spezia,** at the eastern edge of Liguria, even more frequently, as often as every 15 minutes during peak times between 7am and 7pm (regional: 1¾ hr.; high-speed: 1 hr.). Most of these trains make local stops at the coastal resorts (for towns covered in this chapter, see individual listings for connections with Genoa). Lots of trains connect Genoa with major Italian cities: **Milan** (one to three per hour; regional: 1¾ hr.; high-speed: 1½ hr.), **Rome** (hourly; 4½–5½ hr.), **Turin** (one to two per hour; regional: 1hr. 50 min.; high-speed: 1½ hr.), **Florence** (hourly but always with a change, usually at Pisa; 3 hr.), **Pisa** (hourly; regional: 3 hr.; high-speed: 1½–2 hr.).

By Bus An extensive bus network connects Genoa with other parts of Liguria, as well as with other Italian and European cities, from the main bus station next to Stazione Principe. While it is easiest to reach seaside resorts by the trains that run up and down the coast, buses link to many small towns in the region's hilly hinterlands. For tickets and information, contact **PESCI,** Piazza della Vittoria 94r (℡ 010-564-936).

By Car Genoa is linked to other parts of Italy and to France by a convenient network of superhighways. The A10/A12 follows the coast and passes through dozens of tunnels to link Genoa with France to the west (Nice is less than 2 hr. away) and Pisa, about 1½ hours to the southeast. The A7 links Genoa with Milan, a little over an hour to the north.

By Ferry Port that it is, Genoa is linked to several other Mediterranean ports by ferry service (www.traghettigenova.it). Most boats leave and depart from the Stazione Marittima (℡ 010-256-682), which is on a waterfront roadway, Via Marina D'Italia, about a 5-minute walk south of Stazione Principe. For service to and from the **Riviera Levante,** check with **Tigullio** (℡ 800-014-808; www.traghettiportofino.it); there's once-daily service early July to late September.

VISITOR INFORMATION The **main tourist office** is near the aquarium on Via al Porto Antico (℡ 010-253-0671 or 010-248-711; fax 010-246-7658; www.apt.genova. it), open daily 9am to 1pm and 2 to 6pm. The agency also has branches at **Stazione Principe** (℡ 010-246-2633), open Monday to Saturday 9:30am to 1pm and 2:30 to 6pm; **Cristoforo Colombo airport** (℡ 010-610-5247), open Monday to Saturday 9:30am to 12:30pm and 1:30 to 5:30pm; and a seasonal one at the cruise terminal (℡ 010-246-3686), whose hours vary year to year.

CITY LAYOUT Genoa extends for miles along the coast, with neighborhoods and suburbs tucked into valleys and climbing the city's many hills. Most sights of interest are in the **Old Town,** a fascinating jumble of old *palazzos,* laundry-festooned tenements, cramped squares, and tiny lanes and alleyways clustered on the eastern side of the old port. The city's two train stations are located on either side of the Old Town, known as **Caruggi;** as confusing as Genoa's topography is, wherever you are in the Old Town, you are only a short walk or bus or taxi ride from one of these two stations. **Stazione Principe** is the closest, just to the west; from **Piazza Aquaverde,** in front of the station, follow **Via**

Balbi through **Piazza della Nunziata** to **Via Cairoli,** which runs into Via Garibaldi (the walk will take about 15 min.). *Palazzo*-lined **Via Garibaldi** forms the northern flank of the Old Town and is the best place to begin your explorations. Many of the city's major museums and other major monuments are on and around this street, and from here you can descend into the warren of little lanes that lead through the cluttered heart of Caruggi down to the port.

From **Stazione Brignole,** walk straight across the broad, open, buildingless space to Piazza della Vittoria/Via Luigi Cadorna and turn right to follow broad **Via XX Settembre,** one of the city's major shopping avenues, due west for about 15 or 20 minutes to **Piazza de Ferrari,** which is on the eastern edge of the Old Town. From here, **Via San Lorenzo** will lead you past Genoa's cathedral and to the port, but if you want to use Via Garibaldi as your sightseeing base, continue north from the piazza on **Via XXV Aprile** to **Piazza delle Fontane Marose.** This busy square marks the eastern end of Via Garibaldi.

GETTING AROUND   Given Genoa's labyrinth of small streets (many of which cannot be negotiated by taxi or bus), the only easy way to get around much of the city is **on foot.** This, however, can be a navigational feat that requires a good map. You can get a basic one for free at the tourist office, but purchase a more detailed map—preferably one with a good street index and a section showing the old city in detail—at a newsstand. Genovese are usually happy to direct visitors, but given the geography with which they are dealing, their instructions can be complicated. You should also be aware of Genoa's unusual street numbering system, similar to that in Florence: Addresses in red (marked with an *r*) generally indicate a commercial establishment; those in black are offices or residences. So two buildings on the same street can have the same number, one in black, one in red.

By Bus   Bus tickets (1.20€) are available at newsstands and at ticket booths, *tabacchi* (tobacconists, marked by a brown and white T sign), and at the train stations; look for the symbol **AMT** (© **010-254-3431;** www.amt.genova.it). Otherwise, they cost 2€ on board. You must stamp your ticket when you board. Bus tickets can also be used on most of the funiculars and public elevators that climb the city's steep hills, which surround the ancient core of the town (Genoa's sprawl continues atop these hills and would probably continue right up them if they weren't so clifflike steep). Day tickets cost 3.50€. You can also buy a 10-pack or a three-person ticket for discounted rates.

By Taxi   Metered taxis, which you can find at cabstands, are an especially convenient and safe way to get around Genoa at night—or by day, for that matter, if you are tired of navigating mazelike streets or trying to decipher the city's elaborate bus system. For instance, you may well want to consider taking a taxi from a restaurant in the Old City to your hotel or to one of the train stations (especially Stazione Brignole, which is quite a bit farther). Cabstands at Piazza della Nunziata, Piazza Fontane Marose, and Piazza de Ferrari are especially convenient to the Old City, or call a **radio taxi** at © **010-5966.**

By Subway   The city's nascent subway system is still a work in progress, as there are still only seven stops on a single line between Piazza De Ferari and the aquarium. The tickets are the same ones used for the bus: They cost 1.20€ for a 90-minute pass, 3.50€ for a day pass.

(*Fast Facts*) **Genoa**

Bookstores Genoa's best source for English-language books and other media is **Feltrinelli,** Via Ceccardi, 16, near Piazza De Ferrari, just off of Via XX Settembre (© **010-573-331;** www.lafeltrinelli.it).

Drugstores Pharmacies keep extended hours on a rotating basis; dial © **192** to learn which ones are open late in a particular week. Several that are usually open overnight are **Pescetto,** Via Balbi 185r (© **010-246-2697**), across from Stazione Principe; **Ghersi,** Corte Lambruschini 16 (© **010-541-661**); and **Europa,** Corso Europa 676 (© **010-397-615**).

Emergencies The general emergency number is © **113.** If you require police assistance, call © **118.** If you have car trouble, call ACI, Soccorso Stradale © **116.** All of these are free calls.

Hospitals The **Ospedale San Martino,** Largo Rosanna Benzi 10 (© **010-5551**), offers a variety of medical services.

Internet **1PC4YOU,** Piazza Durazzo 12/N (© **010-868-8969**), has 30 computer stations, charges 5€ per hour, and stays open Monday afternoon to Saturday morning, from 9:30am to 12:30pm and 3:30 to 7:30pm.

Laundry There is a self-service laundromat called, simply, **Lavanderia Self-Service,** at Via Gramsci 181r (© **340-235-1492**), open from 9am to 6pm, closed Sunday and Wednesday. Small washing machines and driers are 3.50€ per load, large ones 6€.

Post Offices Genoa's main post office is at **Piazza Dante 4** (© **010-591-762**). This office, as well as those at the two train stations, the airport, and elsewhere around the city, is open Monday through Saturday 8:10am to 7:40pm.

Travel Services **CTS,** Via San Vincenzo 117/R (© **010-564-366** or 010-532-748), specializes in budget travel. It's open Monday to Friday 9am to 1pm and 2:30 to 6pm.

SEEING THE SIGHTS

Acquario di Genova (Aquarium of Genoa) ★★ (**Kids**) Europe's largest aquarium is one of Genoa's biggest draws and a must-see for travelers with children. The structure alone is remarkable, resembling a ship and built alongside a pier in the old harbor (the aquarium is about a 15-min. walk from Stazione Principe and about 10 min. from Via Garibaldi). Inside, more than 50 aquatic displays re-create Red Sea coral reefs, pools in the tropical rainforests of the Amazon River basin, and other marine ecosystems. These environments provide a pleasant home for sharks, seals, and just about every other known kind of sea creature, and the events it hosts are terrific: How about sending the kids to a **sleepover by the shark tank** ★ (70€; ages 7–13)? During the day, the playful seals and dolphins like to blow trick bubbles to entertain you, and there are small rays in a shallow pool that you can pet. All the descriptions are posted in English. There's also a 3-D film on ocean life (ask for a sheet with the narration in English).

Ponte Spinola. © **010-234-5678.** www.acquariodigenova.it. Admission 17€ adults, 11€ children 4–12. Mon–Fri 9:30am–7:30pm; Sat–Sun 9:30am–8:30pm. Bus: 1, 2, 3, 4, 5, 6, 7, 8, 12, 13, 14, or 15. Metro: Darsena.

Cattedrale San Lorenzo ★   The austerity of this black-and-white-striped 12th-century structure is enlivened ever so slightly by the fanciful French Gothic carvings around the portal and the presence of two stone lions. A later addition is the campanile, completed in the 16th century and containing at one corner a beloved Genoa artifact—a sundial known as L'Arrotino (the knife grinder) for its utilitarian appearance. In the frescoed interior, chapels house two of Genoa's most notable curiosities: Beyond the first pilaster on the right is a shell fired through the roof from a British ship offshore during World War II that never exploded, and in the Cappella di San Giovanni (left aisle), a 13th-century crypt contains what crusaders returning from the Holy Land claimed to be relics of John the Baptist. Fabled tableware of doubtful provenance appears to be a quirk of the adjoining treasury: the plate upon which Saint John's head was supposedly served to Salome, a bowl allegedly used at the Last Supper, and a bowl thought at one time to be the Holy Grail. The less fabled but nonetheless magnificent gold and bejeweled objects here reflect Genoa's medieval prominence as a maritime power. Entrance is only by guided tour; though the tours are in Italian, you should take one anyway to look at what's inside.

Piazza San Lorenzo. ✆ **010-254-1250.** Admission to cathedral free. Treasury: 5.50€ adults, 4.50€ seniors over 60 and students. Cathedral: Mon–Sat 9am–noon and 3–6pm. Treasury: By half-hour guided tour only (ask when you get there) Mon–Sat 9am–noon and 3–6pm. Bus: 1, 7, 8, 17, 18, 19, or 20.

Galleria di Palazzo Bianco (White Palace) ★★   One of Genoa's finest palaces, built of white stone by the powerful Grimaldi family in the 16th century and reopened to the public in 2004 after an extensive renovation, houses the city's most notable collection of art. The paintings reflect the fine eye of the duchess of Galliera, who donated the palace and her art to the city in 1884. Her preference for painters of the northern schools, whom the affluent Genovese imported to decorate their palaces and paint their portraits, becomes strikingly obvious. Van Dyck and Rubens, both of whom came to Genoa in the early 17th century, are represented here with one painting each, as they are in the city's other major collections; one of the museum's most notable holdings is *Portrait of a Lady,* by Lucas Cranach the Elder. The collection also includes works by other European and Italian masters (Filippino Lippi, Veronese, Palma il Giovanne, Caravaggio, Hans Memling, Jan Steen, Murillo, and Ribera), including several Genovese masters who were the catalyst for the city's flourishing art movements—an entire room is dedicated to the works of Bernardo Strozzi, whose early-17th-century school made Genoa an important force in the baroque movement. Its small rooftop terrace offers (for a fee) superb 360-degree views of the city.

Via Garibaldi 11. ✆ **010-557-2057** or 010-557-2013. Admission 7€ includes entrance to Palazzo Rosso and Palazzo Tursi. Admission to panoramic terrace 4€. Tues–Sat 9am–7pm; Sun 10am–7pm. Bus: 18, 19, 20, 30, 35, 37, 39, 40, 41, 42, or Volabus 100.

Galleria di Palazzo Rosso (Red Palace)   Another lavish 17th-century palace now houses a magnificent collection of art, as does its neighbor, the Galleria di Palazzo Bianco (see above). Many of the works—including many lavish frescoes—were commissioned or acquired by the Brignole-Sale, an aristocratic family who once lived in this red-stone palace. Van Dyck painted two members of the clan, Pauline and Anton Giulio Brignole-Sale, and their full-length portraits are among the masterpieces in the second-floor portrait galleries, whose ceilings were frescoed by Gregorio de Ferrari and Domenico Piola. *La Cuoca,* widely considered to be the finest work of Genovese master Bernardo Strozzi,

and works by many other Italian and European masters—Gudio Reni, Dürer, Titian,
Guercino, and Veronese among them—hang in the first-floor galleries.

Via Garibaldi 18. ℂ **010-247-6351.** Admission 7€ includes entrance to Palazzo Bianco and Palazzo Tursi. Tues–Fri 9am–7pm; Sat–Sun 10am–7pm. Bus: 18, 19, 20, 30, 35, 37, 39, 40, 41, 42, or Volabus 100.

Galleria Nazionale di Palazzo Spinola ★   Another prominent Genovese family, the Spinolas, donated their palace and magnificent art collection to the city only recently, in 1958. One of the pleasures of viewing these works is seeing them amid the frescoed splendor in which the city's merchant/banking families once lived. As in Genoa's other art collections, you will find masterworks that range far beyond native artists like Strozzi and De Ferrari. In fact, perhaps the most memorable painting here is *Ecce Homo,* by the Sicilian master Antonello da Messina. Guido Reni and Luca Giordano are also well represented, as are Van Dyck (including his fragmentary *Portrait of Ansaldo Pallavicino* and four of the *Evangelists*) and other painters of the Dutch and Flemish schools, whom Genoa's wealthy burghers were so fond of importing to paint their portraits.

Piazza Pellicceria 1. ℂ **010-270-5300.** www.palazzospinola.it. Admission 4€ adults, 2€ students 18–25; free for those under 18 or over 65, or pay 12€ for a Card Musei cumulative ticket (see box below). Tues–Sat 8:30am–7:30pm; Sun 1:30–7:30pm. Bus: 1, 3, 7, 8, 18, 20, or 34.

Museo di Palazzo Reale (Royal Palace)   The Royal Palace takes its name from its 19th- to early-20th-century tenants, the Royal House of Savoy, who greatly altered the 17th-century palace built for the Balbi family. The Savoys endowed the sumptuous surroundings with ostentatious frippery, covered with elaborate 17th- and 18th-century stuccowork and frescoes, most in evidence in the hall of mirrors, the ballroom, and the throne room. The rooms are filled with the dusty accouterments of the Italian royalty who once lived here (or at least used it as a home when they occasionally passed through) and a lot of paintings by relative nobodies interspersed with a few by Tintoretto, Luca Giordano (in the crushed velvet throne room), and Van Dyck. The English placards explaining each room will help you identify them.

Via Balbi 10. ℂ **010-271-0236.** www.palazzorealegenova.it. Admission 4€ adults, 2€ ages 18–25, free for those under 18 or over 65. Tues–Wed 9am–1:30pm; Thurs–Sun 9am–7pm. Bus: 20.

Sant'Agostino—Museo di Architettura e Scultura Ligure (St. Augustine Museum of Ligurian Architecture and Sculpture) ★   The cloisters of the 13th-century church and monastery of Sant'Agostino (most of which, save its two cloisters and a campanile, were destroyed in World War II bombings) are the evocative setting for an

---

Ⓣⓘⓟⓢ   **A Cumulative Ticket**

Admission to Genoa's major **palaces and art galleries** is grouped together on the **Card Musei** (12€ for 1 day, 16€ for 2), which includes entrance to the principal palaces, the Museo Sant'Agostino, San Lorenzo, the Galleria Nazionale di Palazzo Spinola, the Museo di Palazzo Reale, and a handful of other museums around town, plus a discount on admission to the aquarium and movie theaters. Pick one up at any city museum, the airport tourist office, and a handful of bookstores downtown (www.genova-turismo.it).

eclectic and fascinating collection of architectural fragments and sculpture. Roman columns, statuary, and architectural debris from Genoa's churches are scattered in what seems to be random fashion throughout the grassy monastery gardens and in a few bare interior spaces. The treasures here are the panels from Giovanni Pisano's crypt for Margherita of Brabant, wife of the German emperor Henry IV. She died in Genoa in 1312 while en route to Rome for her husband's coronation as Holy Roman Emperor.

Piazza Sarzanno 35r. (𝓒 **010-251-1263** or 010-557-2057. Admission 4€, or on the Card Musei cumulative ticket (see box below). Free for those younger than 18 or older than 60 and for all on Sun. Tues–Fri 9am–7pm; Sat–Sun 10am–7pm. Bus: 17, 18, 19, 20, 30, 32, 33, 35, 37, 40, 41, 100, 605, 606, or 607.

HISTORIC SQUARES & STREETS

PIAZZA DANTE   Though most of the square is made of 1930s office buildings, one end is bounded by the twin round towers of the reconstructed **Porta Soprana,** a town gate built in 1155. The main draw, though, is the small **house** (rebuilt in the 18th c.), still standing a bit incongruously in a tidy little park below the gate, said to have belonged to **Christopher Columbus's father,** who was a weaver and gatekeeper (whether young Christopher lived here is open to debate). Also in the tiny park are the reconstituted 12th-century **cloisters of Sant'Andrea,** a convent that was demolished nearby.

PIAZZA SAN MATTEO   This beautiful little square is the domain of the city's most acclaimed family, the seagoing Dorias, who ruled Genoa until the end of the 18th century. The church they built on the piazza in the 12th century, **San Matteo,** contains the crypt of the Dorias' most illustrious son, Andrea, and the cloisters are lined with centuries-old plaques heralding the family's many accomplishments, which included drawing up Genoa's constitution in 1529. The church is open Monday to Saturday 8am to noon and 4 to 5pm, and Sunday 4 to 5pm. The **Doria palaces** surround the church in a stunning array of loggias and black-and-white-striped marble facades denoting the homes of honored citizens—Andrea's at **no. 17,** Lamda's at **no. 15,** Branca's at **no. 14.** To get there, take bus no. 18, 19, 20, 30, 32, 33, 35, 37, 40, 41, 100, 605, 606, or 607.

VIA GARIBALDI ★★   Many of Genoa's museums and other sights are clustered on and around this street, one of the most beautiful in Italy, where Genoa's wealthy families built palaces in the 16th and 17th centuries. Aside from the art collections housed in the **Galleria di Palazzo Bianco** and **Galleria di Palazzo Rosso** (see above), the street contains a wealth of other treasures. The **Palazzo Podesta,** at no. 7, hides one of the city's most beautiful fountains in its courtyard, and the **Palazzo Tursi,** at no. 9, now housing municipal offices, proudly displays artifacts of famous Genoans: letters written by Christopher Columbus and the violin of Nicolo Paganini (which is still played on special occasions). Visitors are allowed free entry to the buildings when the offices are open: Monday through Friday 8:30am to noon and 1 to 4pm. To get there, take bus no. 19, 20, 30, 32, 33, 35, 36, 41, 42, 100, 605, or 606.

TOURS, VISTAS & WHALE-WATCHING

The Genoese for centuries have provided large boats to take passengers somewhere else. More recently, they have become proud purveyors of their own city's sights, both by land and by sea. A host of companies will take you out on the water to see the skyline and the whales, and through the seaside streets in an open-top bus.

The **Consorzio Liguria ViaMare** (𝓒 **010-265-712;** www.liguriaviamare.it or www.whalewatchliguria.it) offers a range of cruises that depart from the Porto Antico, near the aquarium, and go to Portofino, Camogli, and Alassio, as well as nighttime harbor cruises and whale-watching expeditions. For the whale watches, led by marine biologists from the World Wildlife Fund, you must check the schedule closely, as they run only most Saturdays in July, August, and September, plus an occasional midweek cruise. Tickets are 32€ per adult, 15€ for children, and last 6 to 7 hours. Reservations are required.

From April 1 to October 1, open-top tour buses leave every day on the half-hour (11am–5:30pm) from in front of the aquarium, and every 90 minutes in the off season. Tickets are 20€ per adult, 5€ for children 4 to 12. Commentary is available in English.

A quicker and cheaper way to see the entire city is from one of a number of vistas. One view-affording climb is the one on the **Granarolo** funicular, a cog railway that leaves from Piazza del Principe, just behind the railway station of the same name, and ascends 300m (984 ft.) to Porto Granarolo, one of the gates in the city's 17th-century walls; there's a parklike belvedere in front (1.20€ each way, or you can use a bus ticket; daily every 15 min. 6am–11:45pm).

An elevator lifts visitors to the top of **Il Bigo,** the modernistic, mastlike tower that is the new landmark of Genoa, built to commemorate the Columbus quincentennial celebrations in 1992. The observation platform provides an eagle's-eye view of one of Europe's busiest ports for 3.30€ for adults, 2€ for children ages 3 to 12. It's open Tuesday to Sunday 10am to 5pm (Mar–May and Sept open until 6pm; June–Aug until 8pm).

WHERE TO STAY

Despite the draw of the aquarium, Genoa is still geared more to business than to tourism, and as a result, decent inexpensive rooms are scarce. On the other hand, just about the only time the town is booked solid is during its annual boat show, the world's largest, in October. Except for the ones we include below, avoid hotels in the Old City, especially around the harbor—many are very dirty and prefer to accommodate guests by the hour.

Very Expensive

Bristol Palace   The majestic oval staircase and stained-glass dome of this historic late-19th-century *palazzo* set the tone for this oasis of comfort and calm in chaotic Genoa. It sits on the main shopping street one block off Genoa's main central piazza, halfway between the train station and the tangle of alleys that make up the center, but it is impressively quiet for the location. The rooms have been recently renovated and soundproofed, with modernized bathrooms, but the rooms still retain their period furnishings and classic air. A few choice ones along the front are larger, some with marvelous inlaid wood floors and Art Deco furnishings. The range for doubles below reflects a lower rate for the weekends.

Via XX Settembre 35, 16121 Genova. © **010-592-541.** Fax 010-561-756. www.hotelbristolpalace.com. 133 units. 166€–470€ double; 400€–670€ junior suite. Buffet breakfast included. AE, DC, MC, V. Parking in garage 22€. **Amenities:** Restaurant; bar; babysitting; bikes; concierge; room service; smoke-free rooms; Wi-Fi. *In room:* A/C, TV w/pay movies, hair dryer, minibar,

Expensive

Best Western Hotel Metropoli   Facing a lovely historic square, just around the corner from the Via Garibaldi, the recently restored Metropoli brings modern amenities combined with a gracious ambience to the Old City. No small part of the appeal of staying here is that many of the surrounding streets are open only to pedestrians, so you can step out of the hotel and avoid the onrush of traffic that plagues much of central Genoa. Guest rooms have somewhat banal and businesslike contemporary furnishings, but with double-pane windows and pleasing pastel fabrics, they provide an oasis of calm in this often unnerving city. Refurbished bathrooms are equipped with hair dryers, heated towel racks, and double sinks with lots of marble counter space.

Piazza delle Fontane Marose, 16123 Genova. ℂ **010-246-8888.** Fax 010-246-8686. www.bestwestern.it/ metropoli_ge. 48 units. 100€–240€ double; 120€–240€ triple. Lower rates during off season. Rates include buffet breakfast. AE, DC, MC, V. Parking 20€ in nearby garage. **Amenities:** Bar; bikes; room service; smoke-free rooms. *In room:* A/C, TV, hair dryer, minibar, free Wi-Fi.

Moderate

Agnello d'Oro   This converted, fairly simple convent enjoys a wonderful location—only a few short blocks from Stazione Principe, yet on the edge of the Old City, with a nice terrace overlooking it. A few of the lower-floor rooms retain the building's original 16th-century character, with high (rooms numbered in teens) or vaulted (rooms numbered under 10) ceilings. Those upstairs have been completely renovated in crisp modern style, with warm-hued tile floors and mostly modular furnishings; though many have only curtainless tubs with hand-held nozzles. Some top-floor rooms come with the added charm of balconies and views over the Old Town and harbor (best from no. 56). The friendly proprietor dispenses wine, sightseeing tips, and breakfast in the cozy little bar off the lobby.

Via Monachette 6 (off Via Balbi), 16126 Genova. ℂ **010-246-2084.** Fax 010-246-2327. www.hotelagnello doro.it. 20 units. 75€–120€ double; 85€–130€ triple. Ask about lower rates on weekends and Jan–Mar. Rates include breakfast. AE, DC, MC, V. Private parking 10€–25€. **Amenities:** Restaurant; bar; concierge; room service; smoke-free rooms. *In room:* A/C (5th floor only), TV, hair dryer (in some rooms), minibar.

Inexpensive

Barone   Near Stazione Brignole, this family-run *pensione* occupies the high-ceilinged large rooms of what was once a grand apartment. And it offers unusually pleasant accommodations at very reasonable rates—a rarity in Genoa. Marco, the young proprietor, gives a gracious welcome; self-service espresso is available around the clock. The rooms are indeed baronial in size (some can be set up with extra beds for families) and are reached by elegant halls hung with gilt mirrors and paintings. While the eclectic furnishings are a bit less grand, many retain lovely touches, like a stuccoed ceiling here (in most, actually) or a chandelier there. The beds are firm and comfortable, the linens are fresh, and the TVs are hooked up with Telepiù (Italy's equivalent of HBO, with movies often in English). The shared facilities are spotless. Two technically bathroomless accommodations have a shower in the room, but you must share the hall toilets.

Via XX Settembre 2 (3rd floor), 16121 Genova. ℂ/fax **010-587-578.** 12 units, 1 with private bathroom. 45€–75€ double with shared bathroom; 60€–90€ double with private bathroom; AE, DC, MC, V. Free parking in public lot nearby. Bus: 41. **Amenities:** Bar. *In room:* TV w/pay movies, hair dryer (on request).

Cairoli   Renovated in 2006, this pleasant family-run hotel on the third floor of an old building has an excellent location a little way south of Stazione Principe and near the port, the aquarium, Via Garibaldi, and the sights of the Old City. The small rooms are extremely pleasant, with tasteful modern furnishings and tidy little bathrooms; double-pane glass keeps street noise to a minimum. The friendly management gives it the homey feel of an upscale youth hostel, leaving a little basket of snacks in your room (cookies, crackers, and Pringles). In good weather, you can relax on a terrace covered with potted plants (compact no. 9 opens onto it). They also have added a small weight room, in case you feel the need to work off a few too many plates of *trofie*.

Via Cairoli 14, 16124 Genova. ℂ **010-246-1524.** Fax 010-246-7512. www.hotelcairoligenova.com. 12 units. 70€–150€ double. Breakfast 8€. AE, DC, MC, V. Parking 15€ in nearby garage. Bus: 18, 19, 20, 30, 34, 35, 37, 39, 40, 41, or 100. **Amenities:** Bar; concierge; small exercise room; room service; smoke-free rooms. *In room:* TV, hair dryer, minibar, Wi-Fi.

Fiume   This is not a memorable place to stay. Rather, the Fiume is a serviceable budget option: clean, safe, and close to Stazione Brignole, as well as to Genoa's intriguing Mercato Orientale food market and the profusion of food and wine shops around it. The desk staff in the brightly lit lobby can be brusquely efficient as they direct you to the rather run-down rooms, where the furnishings consist of little more than cotlike beds, tables, and functional chairs. Even so, everything—including shared facilities in the halls—is immaculate, and the travelers from around the world who stay here provide good company. This being a 19th-century *palazzo,* the second-floor rooms are more spacious, with higher ceilings than those on the first floor (no elevator).

Via Fiume 9r, 16121 Genova. ⓒ **010-591-691.** Fax 010-570-2833. 20 units, all but a few singles with shower, but only 4 with complete bathroom. 50€ double with shower; 55€ double with private bathroom. AE, MC, V. No parking. *In room:* TV, hair dryer.

Ostello per la Gioventù   This hostel is fairly new and attractive, and affords some marvelous views over the city from its hillside perch about a kilometer (½ mile) from the terminal of the Righi funicular (which you can take downtown to the tiny piazza of Largo Zecca, the place to which you take the funicular, every 15–20 min. 6:40am–midnight.) Families make out especially well here, in rooms with private bathrooms; other guests sleep four to eight in a room. There's a large terrace, a bar, a cheap cafeteria, a TV room, and a laundromat. Plus, though the hostel is in a safe area well above the hustle and bustle of the city, it's only about 20 minutes to Stazione Brignole on the no. 40 bus, which makes the run about every 10 minutes. (From Stazione Principe, take bus no. 35 to Via Napoli, where you can transfer to bus no. 40.)

Via Costanzi 120, 16136 Genova. ⓒ/fax **010-242-2457.** www.geocities.com/hostelge. 213 beds. 16€ per person. Rates include breakfast. No credit cards. Closed late Dec to Jan. Check-in 3:30pm–midnight. Curfew 12:30am. Bus: 40. **Amenities:** Restaurant; bar. *In room:* No phone.

WHERE TO DINE

Also don't miss out on the good food at the wine bar **I Tre Merli,** recommended under "Genoa After Dark," below.

Da Genio GENOVESE   One of Genoa's most beloved *trattorie,* handily situated near Piazza Dante in the Old Quarter, Da Genio is wonderfully animated. Local artists' works brighten the cozy dining rooms, which are almost always full of Genovese businesspeople and families who have been coming here for years. The assorted antipasti provide a nice introduction to local cuisine, with such specialties as stuffed sardines and *torte di verdure* (vegetable pie). While the menu usually includes a nice selection of fresh fish and some meat dishes (including delicious tripe or steak with porcini), you can also move on to some of the homey standbys the kitchen does so well, such as *spaghetti al sugo di pesce* (topped with a fish sauce) or an amazingly fresh *insalata di mare* (seafood salad)—though almost everyone starts off with Liguria's single most popular and famous traditional dish, *trenette al pesto* (linguine with pesto sauce). The wine list includes a nice selection from Ligurian vineyards.

Salita San Leonardo 61r. ⓒ **010-588-463.** Reservations recommended. Primi 7€–11€; secondi 8.50€–14€. AE, MC, V. Mon–Sat 12:30–3pm and 7:30–10pm. Closed Aug.

Da Guglie LIGURIAN   The busy kitchen here, with its open hearth, occupies a good part of this simple restaurant, which serves this neighborhood near Stazione Brignole with takeout fare from a counter and accommodates diners in a bare-bones little room off to one side. In fact, there's no attempt at all to provide a decorative ambience. The specials of the day (which often include octopus and other seafood) are displayed in the window; tell the cooks behind the counter what you want and they will bring it over to one of the oilcloth-covered tables when it's ready. Don't be shy about asking for a sampling of the reasonably priced dishes, because you could happily eat your way through all the greatest hits of Genovese cuisine here. *Farinata* (chickpea crepes), focaccia with many different toppings, gnocchi with pesto, *riso di carciofi* (rice with artichokes), and other dishes are accompanied by Ligurian wines served by the glass or carafe.

Via San Vincenzo 64r. ℂ **010-565-765.** Primi 5€–8€; secondi 5€–11€. No credit cards. Daily noon–10pm.

La Berlocca GENOVESE   Enrico Reboscio has turned this old pie and *farinata* shop into an oasis of good food in a somewhat seedy section of town. Service can be a bit slow in these two tiny rooms of small, sturdy wooden tables under stuccoed ceilings, but the seasonal Ligurian menu marrying sea and garden is delicious. I've enjoyed such dishes as *piccagge matte al pesto* (chestnut pasta with pesto), *taglierini neri con gamberi* (black pasta with crayfish and ginger), *stoccafisso accomodato alla genovese* (stockfish with potatoes, onions, pine nuts, and tomato sauce), and *filetto con mele, curry, e calvados* (a beef filet in a curry made with apples and Calvados liqueur). There's a good wine selection, too.

Via dei Macelli di Soziglia 45r. ℂ **010-247-4162.** Reservations not necessary. Primi 9€–13€; secondi 15€–20€. AE, DC, MC, V. Tues–Fri noon–3pm; Tues–Sun 7–11pm. Closed last week of July to 3rd week of Aug.

Mario Rivaro LIGURIAN/ITALIAN   Wonderfully located amid the Renaissance splendor of the nearby Via Garibaldi, this old institution does a brisk business with a loyal clientele from nearby banks and consulates, especially at lunch and in the early evening. The decor is pleasantly reminiscent of a ship's cabin, with inlaid wood panels and long wooden tables lit by brass lanterns. Many of the attentive, white-jacketed waiters have worked here their entire careers. Ligurian classics such as *trenette al pesto con patate e fagiolini* (pasta with pesto, potatoes, and beans) and a *zuppa da pesce* made with local fish emerge from the kitchen.

Via di Portello 16r. ℂ **010-277-0054.** Reservations recommended. Primi 8€–10€; secondi 10€–15€. AE, DC, MC, V. Mon–Sat noon–3:30pm and 6:30pm–12:30am.

Trattoria da Maria LIGURIAN ★ Ⓥⓐⓛⓤⓔ   Maria Mante, unfortunately, is no longer here, but her philosophy of good food at an honest price lives on, carried out by relatives young and old. The cooking and the close-knit ambience of the two-floor restaurant in the Old City near Piazza delle Fontane Marose draw a crowd of neighborhood residents, students, businesspeople, and tourists of all nationalities. This unlikely mix sits side by side at long tables covered with red- or blue-checked tablecloths and engages in animated conversation, while the staff hurries around them and shouts orders up and down the shaft of a dumbwaiter. The Genovese love a bargain, and the stupendously cheap menu—which often includes *minestrone alla Genovese, risotto buonissimo alla Genovese* (rice stirred with a sauce; they also feel secure labeling their creamy gelato *"buonissimo"*), *zuppe da pesce* (a rich fish soup you must try if it's available), and such simple main courses as a filet of fish sautéed in white wine or grilled sausages—is no frills, listed on sheets of paper on the shiny pale green walls. As befits a Genovese institution like this, the pasta with pesto sauce is especially delicious, as is *pansotti,* small ravioli covered with a walnut-cream sauce.

Vico Testadoro 14r (just off Via XX Aprile). ℂ **010-581-080.** Primi 3€–5€; secondi 4€–7€. MC, V. Sun and Tues–Fri 11:45am–2:15pm and 7–9:15pm; Mon 11:45am–2:45pm.

Fast Food, Genoa Style

Fast food is a Genovese specialty, and any number of storefronts all over the city disburse **focaccia,** the heavenly Ligurian flatbread often stuffed with cheese and topped with herbs, olives, onions, vegetables, or prosciutto. A favorite place for focaccia, and so close to Stazione Principe that you can stop in for a taste of this aromatic delicacy as soon as you step off the train, is **La Focacceria di Teobaldo** ★, Via Balbi 115r ((*C* **010-246-2294**), open daily 8am to 8pm; focaccia starts at .50€ a slice.

Another Genovese favorite is *farinata,* a cross between a ravioli and a crepe made from chickpea flour that is stuffed with spinach and ricotta, lightly fried, and often topped with a cream-and-walnut sauce. Locals say this delicious concoction gets no better than it is at the two outlets of **Antica Sciamada,** Via Ravecca 19r ((*C* **010-280-843**), and Via San Giorgio 14r, both open Monday through Saturday 9am to 7:30pm; prices from 3€.

Trattoria Vegia Zena GENOVESE In the *centro storico* (historic center) near the old port (on an alley across from the aquarium), this lively white-walled and wood-paneled room lives up to its name—dialect for Old Genoa—with expertly prepared Genovese dishes. Because the restaurant is very popular with Genovese and increasingly with the foreign crowd, you may well be asked to share one of the crowded tables with other diners. Pasta with pesto is excellent; follow it with a fine selection of fresh seafood.
Vico del Serriglio 15r. (*C* **010-251-3332.** Primi 6€–19€; secondi 7.50€–25€. MC, V. Mon–Sat noon–2:30pm; Tues–Sat 7:30–10pm.

Pastry & Gelato

Antica Pasticceria Gelateria Klainguti ★★, on Piazza Soziglia 98r–100r ((*C* **010-247-4552**), is considered to be Genoa's best bakery, as well as its oldest—it was founded in 1828 by a Swiss family. One satisfied customer was the composer Giuseppe Verdi, who said the house's Falstaff (a sweet brioche) was better than his. This and a stupefying assortment of other pastries and chocolates, as well as light snacks (including panini), are served in a pretty rococo-style room or in the piazza out front. It's open daily 8am to 7pm.

Add **Banarama,** at Via San Vincenzo 65r ((*C* **010-581-130**), to your explorations of the many food shops and markets in the neighborhood near Stazione Brignole. Is this the best gelato in Genoa? The jury is still out, but the creamy concoctions are indeed memorable. Just as good are the simple *granites,* shaved ice with fresh fruit flavorings. It's open Monday to Saturday until 7:30pm. Just off the waterfront and near the fairgrounds, the simple, no-frills **Cremeria Augusto,** at Via Nino Bixio 5 ((*C* **010-591-884**), is almost a mandatory stop when taking a stroll through this part of the city. The house makes dozens of flavors of rich, delicious gelato fresh daily, and it is marvelous, but the specialty is *crema,* a frozen egg custard. It's open Sunday to Friday to 10pm.

GENOA AFTER DARK

The Old City, some of which is sketchy in broad daylight, is especially unseemly at night. Confine late-hour prowls to the well-trafficked streets around Piazza Fontane Marose and Piazza delle Erbe, where many bars and clubs are located anyway.

LIGURIA & THE ITALIAN RIVIERA

12

GENOA

PERFORMING ARTS   Genoa has two major venues for culture: the restored **Teatro Carlo Felice,** Piazza de Ferrari (© 010-589-329; www.carlofelice.it), which is home to Genoa's opera company and also hosts visiting companies; and the modern **Teatro della Corte** (© 010-534-2200; www.teatro-di-genova.it), on Piazza Borgo Pila near Stazione Brignole, which hosts concerts, dance, and other cultural programs.

BARS & CLUBS   Open all day, **Brittania,** at Vico Casana (just off Piazza De Ferrari), serves pints to homesick travelers from morning to night, but caters to a largely Italian crowd at night (© 010-294-878).

New Yorkers will recognize the name and chic ambience from the branch of **I Tre Merli Antica Cantina,** at Vico Dietro il Coro della Maddalena 26r (© 010-247-4095; www.itremerli.it), which does a brisk business in Manhattan with a couple of restaurants. Here in Genoa, I Tre Merli operates a couple of *enoteche* (wine bars), and this one, with a location on a narrow street just off Via Garibaldi, is delightful, even if the surrounding alleyways are charmingly seedy. A dark stone floor and walls of brick and stone provide a cozy setting, augmented by "refined country"–style tables and chairs. You can sample the wide selection of wines from throughout Italy by the glass, and there is a full bar. The half-dozen each of primi and secondi are refined Ligurian and, along with the cheese and salami platters, make this a good spot for a late-night meal; it's open Tuesday to Sunday 7pm to 1am.

Le Courbusier, Via San Donato 36 (© 010-246-8652), opens early and closes late. This coffeehouse-cum-bar, in the Old Quarter just west of Piazza delle Erbe, is especially popular with students. The smoky room is perpetually busy, dispensing excellent coffee and sandwiches (from 3€), as well as wine and spirits.

QUICK ESCAPES

Two seaside retreats within the city limits are Boccadasse and, a little farther out, Nervi, both to the east of the city center and easily reached by public transportation. Take bus no. 41 from Stazione Principe or Piazza de Ferrari to Boccadasse (the trip takes 20–30 min., depending on traffic, and costs the same as a regular city bus ticket: 1€) and bus no. 17, or one of the frequent trains from Stazione Brignole to Nervi (the train trip takes only 15 min.).

Once a quaint fishing village, **Boccadasse** has long since given way to some urban development. Even so, this bustling seaside community is still a pleasant corner of the city. Fishing boats and nets litter the shore, and the rocky seaside is lined with tall, colorful Ligurian houses, whose bottom floors now accommodate gelaterias, focaccerias, and simple restaurants with outdoor terraces.

Nervi was a fashionable resort a century ago, and it's still easy to see why. A 1.6km-long (1-mile) seaside promenade affords stunning views of the sea, and elegant villas are surrounded by a lush profusion of flora. (As tempting as the waters are, you may want to refrain from a swim until you are a little farther away from Genoa, since the water is badly polluted—Italians don't go to the beach to swim, anyway, but to tan and socialize.) One of the most pleasant retreats in Genoa is Nervi's Parco Villa Grimaldi, where more than 2,000 varieties of roses bloom. Each July, Nervi hosts Genoa's International Ballet Festival (see "Festivals & Markets," earlier in this section).

2 THE RIVIERA DI PONENTE: SAN REMO, BORDIGHERA & MORE

San Remo: 140km (87 miles) W of Genoa, 59km (37 miles) E of Nice; Bordighera: 155km (96 miles) W of Genoa, 15km (9¼ miles) W of San Remo, 45km (28 miles) E of Nice

SAN REMO

Gone are the days when Tchaikovsky and the Russian empress Maria Alexandranova joined a well-heeled mix of titled Continental and British gentry in strolling along San Remo's palm-lined avenues. They left behind an onion-domed Orthodox church, a few grand hotels, and a casino, but **San Remo** is a different sort of town these days. It's still the most cosmopolitan stop on the Riviera di Ponente (Setting Sun), as the stretch of coast west of Genoa is called, catering mostly to sun-seeking Italian families in the summer and elderly Romans and Milanese who come to enjoy the balmy temperatures in the winter.

In addition to the gentle ambience of days gone by, San Remo offers its visitors a long stretch of beach and a hilltop Old Town known as La Pigna. For cosmopolitan pleasures, the casino attracts a well-attired clientele willing to try their luck.

San Remo is an excellent base from which to explore the rocky coast and Ligurian hills. So is Bordighera, a quieter resort just up the coast. With excellent train and bus connections, both are within easy reach of a full itinerary of fascinating stops, including Giardino Hanbury, one of Europe's most exquisite gardens; the fascinating prehistoric remains at Balzi Rossi; and Dolceacqua, perhaps the most enticing of all the inland Ligurian villages (for more information on these places, see later sections).

Essentials

GETTING THERE   By Train   There are trains almost hourly to and from **Genoa** (regional: 2½ hr.; high-speed: 1¾ hr.). Two to three trains per hour connect with **Bordighera** (13 min.). Trains from Genoa continue west for another 20 minutes to **Ventimiglia** on the French border. From Ventimiglia, you can continue across the border on one of the hourly trains to **Nice,** 40 minutes west.

By Bus   **Riviera Trasporti** buses (© 0184-592-706; www.rivieratrasporti.it) run every 15 minutes between San Remo and **Bordighera** (20 min.). Almost as many buses continue on to **Ventimiglia** (40 min. from San Remo).

By Car   The fastest driving route in and out of San Remo is Autostrada A10, which follows the coast from the French border (20 min. away) to Genoa (about 45 min. away). The slower coast road, S1, cuts right through the center of town.

VISITOR INFORMATION   The **APT tourist board** is at Largo Nuvoloni 1 (© 0184-571-571; fax 0184-567-649; www.sanremonet.com), at the corner with Corso Imperatrice/Corso Matteotti (cross the street from the old train station and go to the left a few hundred feet). It's open Monday to Saturday 8am to 7pm and Sunday 9am to 1pm. In addition to a wealth of information on San Remo, the office dispenses information on towns up and down the nearby coast, known as the Riviera dei Fiori.

FESTIVALS   August 15, the **Feast of the Assumption,** is celebrated with special flair in San Remo, with the festival of Nostra Signora della Costa (Our Lady of the Coast).

The Virgin Mary allegedly saved a local sailor from drowning, and she is honored with fireworks and a procession in medieval garb to her shrine on a hillside high above the town.

Since the 1950s, the **Sanremo Festival** (in late Feb or early Mar) has been Italy's—and one of Europe's—premier music fests. It's sort of an Italian version of the Grammy Awards, only spread out over several days with far more live performances—by Italian pop stars, international headliners, and plenty of up-and-coming singers, songwriters, and bands. "Volare" was Sanremo's first-ever Best Recording, and today if you peruse the CD collections of most Italian households, you'll find at least a few of the yearly compilation albums the festival puts out. The festival has spawned many other contestlike celebrations of film and music (international folk to *musica lirica*) throughout the year, but this is the big one, booking hotels up and down the coast months in advance. Call the tourist office if you want to try to score tickets.

Strolling Around Town

San Remo's new underground railway station, buried into the coastal hills much like its counterpart in nearby Monaco, is sleek and clean, but there are a few disadvantages. For one thing, the walk from the tracks to the exit is formidable (*Note:* Leave plenty of time to catch a train), and the walk from there to the center of town is also considerably longer than from the old station, which sits downtown, just by the coast. This leads to the final problem: Even today, a decade after the newer station was built, some locals might give you directions to a hotel, restaurant, and such, referring to the "train station," when, in fact, they mean the former station. Now home to the municipal library, the old station remains a primary point of reference.

To get downtown from the new train station, walk straight out of the exit, cross Corso Cavallotti, and continue downhill until you reach Corso Trento e Trieste. Take a right on that road, which hugs the shore and leads to the old port.

To the right of the old station are the beginnings of Corso Roma and Corso Giacomo, San Remo's two main thoroughfares. Corso Giacomo will lead you past the **casino** (see below) and into the heart of the lively business district. Continue on that until it becomes Via Matteotti, which, after a block, runs into Piazza Colombo and the flower market. If you turn left (north) on Via Feraldi about midway down Corso Giacomo, you will find yourself in the charming older precincts of town. Continue through the Piazza degli Eroi Sanremesi to Piazza Mercato, where Via Monta leads into the old medieval quarter, **La Pigna.** The hill on which this fascinating district is located resembles a pine cone in its

A Day at the Beach

Plunging into the Ligurian Sea in San Remo means spending some money. The pebbly beach below the Passeggiata dell'Imperatrice is lined with beach stations, where many visitors choose to spend their days: easy to do, since most provide showers, snack bars, and, of course, beach chairs, lounges, and umbrellas. Expect to spend up to 10€ for a basic lounge, but more like 15€ for a more elaborate sun-bed arrangement with umbrella. *Note:* As is standard at most European resort towns without "public" sections of beach (which are usually not very nice anyway), you cannot go onto the beach without paying for at least a lounge chair.

| Is Board Necessary?

Many hotels offer room-and-board rates that include breakfast, lunch, and dinner (full board or full pension), or breakfast and one of these other two meals (half-board or half-pension). Only in the busy late July and early August beach season do many require you to take these meals, however. If you can procure a room without the meal plan, do so—San Remo has many excellent restaurants, and this is not a place where you have to spend a lot for a good meal.

conical shape, hence the name. Aside from a few restaurants, La Pigna is today a residential quarter, with tall old houses that overshadow the narrow lanes that twist and turn up the hillside to the park-enclosed ruins of a **castle** at the top.

Visiting the Casino

Set intimidatingly atop a long flight of steps across from the old train station—Corso degli Inglesi swoops around it off Corso Matteotti—San Remo's white palace of a casino (© **0184-5951**) not only lords over the center of town, it's also the hub of the local nightlife scene. You can't step foot inside without being properly attired (jacket for gents Oct–June) and showing your passport. You must be 18 or older to enter. There are poker tables starting at 2€ games, but there are more serious tables that attract high rollers from the length of the Riviera. Gaming rooms are open daily 2:30pm to 3am (to 4am on weekends). Things are more relaxed in the rooms set aside for slot machines, where there is no dress code. It's open Sunday to Friday 10am to 3am.

Where to Stay
Very Expensive
Royal Hotel ★★★   San Remo's luxury inn of choice since 1872, the Bertolini family's Royal Hotel has been the preferred retreat of jet-setters passing through, as well as the first place rock stars call for a suite during the music festival. The terraces of palms and flowers of its 1.6-hectare (4-acre) park leading up to its edifice from the main road blend seamlessly with the verdant public gardens next door, and the stucco-ceilinged bars and salons, framed by granite ionic columns, promise a cushy, elegant stay. The rooms are exceedingly comfortable and restrained, with rugs on the polished parquet and a floral-print theme. Each has a small sitting area of chairs and love seats, real beds, and spacious new bathrooms. The shared door of neighboring corner rooms can be closed off to make family suites. The best accommodations, obviously, are those that enjoy the sea view from small terraces or small balconies; four floors have rooms facing all sides, and fifth-floor rooms all face the Ligurian Sea and distant Monaco. Of course, it wouldn't be "royal" if it didn't have a private beach across the road.

Corso Imperatrice 80, I-18038 San Remo. © **0184-5391.** Fax 0184-661-445. www.royalhotelsanremo. com. 136 units. 275€–450€ double; 350€–550€ junior suite. Add 35€ for half-pension. Rates include breakfast. AE, DC, MC, V. Parking 10€ or 18€ in garage. Closed Oct 6–Dec 17. **Amenities:** 3 Italian/international restaurants (elegant dining room, terrace dining in summer, poolside lunch restaurant Apr–Oct); 2 bars (1 at pool); babysitting; bikes; children's center (high season); concierge; nearby golf course; exercise room; minigolf; park; large outdoor heated saltwater pool; room service; outdoor tennis court; watersports equipment/rentals. *In room:* A/C, TV, hair dryer, minibar, Wi-Fi.

Miramare Continental Palace ★ (Value) The Miramare is a Liberty-style villa of sedate, faded elegance, and the only hotel on the shore side of the main road, but it is a 15-minute walk from the center. You really come for the setting, not the rooms, which are a bit small, with modular furnishings and sea views. The hotel is set in a 1-hectare (2½-acre) park of flower-fringed palms and a mighty baobab tree. A private pathway leads right onto the beach, and next door is an indoor lap swimming pool that's heated in winter and open to the public.

Corso Matuzia 9, 18038 San Remo. © **0184-667-601.** Fax 0184-667-655. www.miramaresanremo.it. 59 units. 130€–180€ double. For half-board, add 20€ per person; for full board in doubles, add 40€. Rates include breakfast. AE, DC, MC, V. Free parking. **Amenities:** Italian/international/regional restaurant; bar; babysitting; concierge; nearby golf course; indoor heated seawater pool; room service; smoke-free rooms. *In room:* TV, hair dryer, minibar.

Paradiso ★ Three generations of the Gaiani family have run this former villa, set in a pretty garden above the seaside promenade, as a hotel since 1926. Since then, the original villa has been topped off with several extra floors of very pleasant guest rooms, many of which have flower-filled balconies overlooking the sea (rooms with balconies cost slightly more). An understated elegance characterizes these relaxing surroundings. Guest rooms are extremely well maintained to retain the sort of old-fashioned comfort that brings a loyal clientele back year after year for their month by the sea. Furnishings are a homey collection of old armoires, armchairs, and upholstered headboards, and the tiled bathrooms, with large sinks and bathtubs, are luxuriously commodious. Cocktails are served in the evenings in the comfortable, elegantly furnished salon or in the nicely planted garden in good weather, and guests can take meals in an airy and newly renovated Liberty-style dining room.

Via Roccasterone 12, 18038 San Remo. © **0184-571-211.** Fax 0184-578-176. www.paradisohotel.it. 41 units. 120€–210€. Add 20€ for a room with balcony. Add 20€ per person for half-board, 35€ per person for full board. Rates include buffet breakfast. AE, DC, MC, V. Parking 8€ in hotel garage. **Amenities:** Restaurant (Italian cuisine); bar; babysitting; bikes; concierge; outdoor pool; room service. *In room:* A/C, TV, hair dryer, minibar.

Villa Maria ★★ It's fairly easy to imagine San Remo's late-19th-/early-20th-century heyday in this charming hotel incorporating three villas on a flowery hillside above the casino. The promenade is only a short walk downhill, yet the hubbub of the resort seems miles away from this leafy residential district. A series of elegant salons and dining rooms with parquet floors, richly paneled ceilings, and crystal chandeliers spread across the ground floor, and many of these public rooms open to a nicely planted terrace. The bedrooms, too, retain the grandeur of the original dwellings, with silk-covered armchairs and antique beds; many have balconies facing the sea. The bathrooms have old-fashioned details such as tubs with hand-held shower nozzles. Since rooms vary considerably in size and decor, ask to look around before you settle on one that strikes your fancy.

Corso Nuvoloni 30, 18038 San Remo. © **0184-531-422.** Fax 0184-531-425. www.villamariahotel.it. 38 units, 36 with private bathroom. 70€–130€ double. Rates include continental breakfast. Half-board (required Easter, Christmas, and Aug 1–15) 53€–89€ per person; full board 65€–105€ per person. AE, DC, MC, V. Free parking. **Amenities:** Restaurant (international cuisine); concierge; room service; smoke-free rooms. *In room:* TV, hair dryer.

Inexpensive

Al Dom This rambling, dark, old-fashioned *pensione* near the casino, city center, and harbor occupies the second floor of a grand 19th-century apartment house. The rooms, basically but nicely furnished with modern pieces and floral bedspreads, are carved out of former salons and tucked into the closed-off ends of ballroom-size hallways; no. 5 has a large balcony over the street. Tiny bathrooms (some of them modular units that resemble the public facilities you find in Paris and other cities) have been appended wherever they might fit. So be prepared for the unexpected: You may well find yourself staring up at an ornately plastered ceiling from a metal-frame bed crammed next to a marble fireplace. In short, the surroundings may not be stylish, but they are memorable, and the family that runs the *pensione* is friendly and always on hand to see that guests are comfortable.

Corso Mombello 13, 18038 San Remo. ✆ **0184-501-460.** 13 units. 50€–70€ double. Breakfast 5€. No credit cards. Parking 7€ in nearby garage. **Amenities:** Restaurant. *In room:* TV, no phone.

Riviera   While convenient to the beach and other attractions, this family-run *pensione,* on the ground floor of a rather dire cement-cube hillside apartment house, is close to the center but just far enough off the beaten path to enjoy peace and quiet. And it often has rooms available when other places in town fill up. Oriental runners and attractive slip-covered furniture lend an air of elegance to the public areas. The guest rooms, most of which overlook the sea and the Old Town, are spacious and modestly but attractively furnished in modern style with an eye to comfort—beds are firm, there are ample sur-faces on which to spread out belongings, and most of the bathrooms are up-to-date.

Corso degli Inglesi 86, 18038 San Remo. ✆ **0184-502-215.** Fax 0184-502-216. hotelriviera@ciaoweb.it. 14 units. 57€–83€ double; 75€–115€ suite. Breakfast 5€. For half-pension, add 45€–65€ per day. AE, DC, MC, V. Parking 2.50€ in hotel lot or 7€ in garage. Sometimes closed a few weeks in Nov and Mar. **Ameni-ties:** Restaurant; bar; room service; smoke-free rooms. *In room:* A/C, TV, hair dryer, minibar.

Sole Mare ★   Don't let the location on a drab side street near the train station put you off. This cheerful *pensione* on the upper floors of an apartment house is a delight and offers its guests a friendly welcome, along with some of the best-value lodgings in the resort area. A lounge, bar area, and dining room are airy and spacious and flooded with light, with gleaming white-tile floors, blond-wood furniture, and doors leading out to a wide terrace. The large guest rooms are also cheerful and are equipped with the trappings of much more expensive hotels—pleasant modern furnishings and soothing pastel fab-rics, TVs and minibars, small but modern and well-lit bathrooms—and almost all enjoy sea views, about half from wide balconies. Almost all the rooms have air-conditioning. It's best to check beforehand to make sure yours does, if you're arriving between May and September.

Via Carli 23, 18038 San Remo. ✆ **0184-577-105.** Fax 0184-532-778. www.solemarehotel.com. 21 units. 66€–140€ double. Room and half-board (required in Aug) 45€–73€ per person; room and full board 50€–78€ per person. Prices vary with length of stay. Breakfast included AE, DC, MC, V. Parking 7€ in nearby garage. **Amenities:** Restaurant (international cuisine); bar; babysitting; concierge; room service. *In room:* A/C, TV, hair dryer, minibar, Wi-Fi.

Where to Dine

Cantine Sanremese LIGURIAN   This cozy publike restaurant devoted to the local cuisine is firmly planted in the center of the modern town, as if to suggest that old San Remo traditions are not to be discarded. Patrons share tables as they enjoy the wide selec-tions of wine by the glass (from 1.50€) and sample the offerings that owner Renzo Morselli and his family prepare daily. The best way to dine here: Don't order a whole meal, but sample all the dishes that tempt you. These may include *sardemaira,* the local focaccia-like bread; *torta verde* (a quiche of fresh green vegetables); and many kinds of soups, including a minestrone thick with fresh vegetables and garnished with pesto.

Via Palazzo 7. ✆ **0184-572-063.** Reservations recommended. Primi and secondi 7€–12€. AE, MC, V. Tues–Sun 10am–3pm and 5–9:30pm. Closed last 10 days of June and all of Nov.

Il Mulattiere ★★ (Finds) LIGURIAN   Anyone who goes to San Remo should plan to visit this family-run trattoria in La Pigna, the oldest part of town. Whether you come for lunch or dinner or just to enjoy a glass of wine, you'll probably first want to stroll around the surrounding quarter, an amazing warren of steep lanes clinging to the side of a hill. This two-floor eatery is as rich in character as its surroundings—the tables, covered with red-checked cloths, are overhung with antique farm implements (*Il Mulattiere* means "mule driver") and other rural artifacts. The menu is simple, featuring Ligurian specialties that change daily and often include delicious *crostini all'acciughe* (toasted bread topped with fresh anchovies), *zuppa al pomodoro* (a spicy soup of fresh tomatoes) or minestrone, and many types of fresh pasta. For a light meal, you can choose from an antipasto table laden with fresh vegetables and olives, and accompany it with a bowl of pasta.

Via Palma 11. ✆ **0184-502-662.** Primi 4€–7.50€; secondi 6€–8€; *menù completo* 9.50€, including antipasto and a primo. No credit cards. Reservations recommended. Thurs–Tues noon–3pm and 7:30–10pm.

Nuovo Piccolo Mondo ★★ (Value) LIGURIAN   The attentive staff will make you feel at home the moment you step into the perpetually crowded rooms of this decades-old trattoria on a narrow side street near the waterfront in the commercial district. The clientele is local, and they come here in droves to enjoy the comfortable atmosphere (which includes the furnishings installed when the restaurant opened in the 1920s) and the distinctly Ligurian fare—*verdura ripiena* (fresh vegetables stuffed with rice and sea-food), fresh fish, and *polpo con patate* (octopus with potatoes). The menu changes daily to incorporate what is fresh in the markets, but includes excellent risottos, pasta dishes, and meat dishes that are standards. (The grilled veal chop topped with fresh mushrooms is delicious.)

Via Piave 7. ✆ **0184-509-012.** Reservations recommended. Primi 5.50€–8.50€; secondi 7€–15€. No credit cards. Tues–Sat 12:30–1:50pm and 7:30–9:30pm.

Ristorante da Giannino ★ LIGURIAN   With Anna in the kitchen and Giuseppe in the modern dining room, the Gasparini family runs one of the top (but also priciest) restaurants in town. In the summer months, it moves from its Corso Cavallotti address, near the train station, to an open space by a pool just a few dozen meters away on Via Anselmi. The menu is well balanced between surf and turf, and you can follow a *risotto* or *linguine ai frutti di mare* (rice or noodles richly studded with seafood) with *coniglio alle erbe* (rabbit roasted with fresh herbs), or catch of the day grilled or served under a cream sauce spiced with whole green peppercorns.

Corso Cavallotti 76 (in summer months, Via Anselmi 6). ✆ **0184-504-014.** Reservations recommended. Primi 18€–25€; secondi 22€–31€; tasting menu 55€, not including wine. AE, DC, MC, V. Tues–Sat noon–2pm; Mon–Sat 7:30–9:45pm.

Ristorante L'Airone ★ LIGURIAN/PIZZA   With its pale gold walls and green-hued tables and chairs, this delightful, friendly restaurant in a pedestrian-only section of the city center looks as though it's been transported over the border from Provence. The food, though, is definitely Ligurian, with a wide selection of fresh pastas, including gnocchi in pesto sauce, followed perhaps by a *grigliata mista* of fresh fish or grilled sole. For a more casual meal, light-crusted pizzas emerge from a tiled oven in the rear. In good weather, meals are served in a small garden out back covered by a reed-thatched tent—and there are some tables on the piazza outside (which, admittedly, is nothing special).

Piazza Eroi Sanremesi 12. (✆ **0184-531-469.** www.ristorantelairone.it. Primi 6€–14€; secondi 7€–17€; pizza 5€–9.50€; *menù turistico* 13€, not including wine; *menù degustazione* 31€, not including wine. DC, MC, V. Fri–Wed noon–2:30pm and 7:30–11:30pm.

The Cafe & Bar Scene

Agora Cafè, on Piazza San Siro (no phone), which faces San Remo's cathedral, makes no claim other than to be a comfortable watering hole, a function it performs very well. For footsore travelers, the terrace out front, facing the pretty stone piazza and cathedral of San Siro, is a welcome oasis. Sandwiches and other light fare are served late into the night, when an after-dinner crowd tends to make this one of the livelier spots in town. It's closed Monday.

Wanderings through the center of town should include a stop at Giovanni Fabris's handsome wine bar, **Enoteca Bacchus** ★★ (Via Roma 65; ✆ **0184-530-990**), open Monday to Saturday 10am to 9pm. This is where you can also stock up on olive oil and other Ligurian foodstuffs. Wine is served by the glass at a sit-down bar or at one of the small tables, and you can accompany your libations with fresh focaccia, cheeses, vegetable tarts, and even such substantial fare as *buridda,* a dish of salted cod, tomatoes, and other vegetables.

BORDIGHERA

Known throughout Italy for its palm trees, **Bordighera** lays claim to the legend that the seeds of date palms carried across the sea from Egypt first took root in European soil here. To this day, Bordighera has the honor of supplying its ubiquitous fronds to the Vatican for Palm Sunday services. The palm trees create a verdant canopy that extends up the hillside from the Mediterranean and the cluster of modern seaside development to the charming Old Town. Bordighera's other claim to fame is its enormous popularity with elderly Italian and British pensioners (its reputation as a getaway for retirees is similar to that of St. Petersburg in Florida). If you want glitter, you may be happier in San Remo; on the other hand, if you want to enjoy some peace and quiet and the same verdant vegetation that attracted Claude Monet, Bordighera may be just the stop for you.

Essentials

GETTING THERE **By Train** There are trains almost hourly to and from **Genoa** (regional: 2 hr., 20 min.; high-speed: 2 hr.), and two to three trains per hour connecting with **San Remo** (13 min.).

By Bus **Riviera Trasporti** buses (✆ **0184-592-706;** www.rivieratrasporti.it) run every 15 minutes between **San Remo** and Bordighera (20 min.). Buses also run between Bordighera and **Ventimiglia.**

By Car You can take Autostrada A10 between Bordighera and San Remo, but the coast road, S1, is almost as fast. In fact, there is such a contiguous line of development along the route that you won't know where one town ends and the other begins.

VISITOR INFORMATION The **tourist office** is at Via Vittorio Emanuele 172 (✆ **0184-262-322;** fax 0184-264-455). It's open Monday to Saturday 8am to 7pm and Sunday 9am to 1pm (closed Sun Oct–May).

It's a sign of the pleasant nature of this resort that one of the major annual events is a **humor festival,** held in late August/early September. Stand-up comics perform along the streets and seaside promenade, humorous films are shown, and general merriment is presented. **Thursday morning's market** fills the Lungomare Argentina (see below), with stalls selling a bit of everything.

Strolling Around Town

Lungomare Argentina is Bordighera's seaside promenade, and it extends for about a kilometer along a wide **beach;** the pebbly strand is public, so you can settle down anywhere you find a spot. If you want a more civilized beach experience, you can part with 5€ for a lounge at any number of beach stations. The promenade remains lively well past the height of the day, and it affords spectacular sunset views (since it faces west toward France's Côte d'Azur) that most of the town turns out to witness. The modern town, which in some parts is unattractively developed, clusters around the seafront, with many businesses lining coastal route S1.

You need only head inland, though, to discover how lovely Bordighera is, with palm-fringed streets and pastel-colored villas hidden behind the walls of verdant gardens. The fortified **Old Town** ★, a picturesque cluster of ocher-colored stucco and red tile, is several hundred meters up the hillside from the sea. Aside from a few restaurants and a charming hotel (see below), there aren't specific attractions that draw visitors to town; rather, it is the fusion of beauty of centuries-old architecture, charming ambience, and stunning views from the gardens that skirt the old walls. From here, you can also easily check out the sights surrounding nearby **Ventimiglia,** detailed in the next section.

Where to Stay

Del Capo   The only hotel in the Old Town is a delightful pinkish structure surrounded by palm trees and an inviting terrace where many guests choose to spend most of their time. The hilltop location affords stunning views over the lower town and sea, and there always seems to be a cooling breeze. Vaulted ceilings and colorful majolica-tile floors lend almost a Moorish look to the lobby, sitting rooms, and dining area, but once upstairs, the decor becomes utilitarian, though not unpleasing. Furnishings in the largish guest rooms are 1960s-style modern, but unobtrusive enough not to be offensive. Bathrooms have not been updated for a while and tend to be small but are certainly adequate. The best features in the rooms are the shuttered doors that open to balconies and afford dazzling views up and down the coast. The one drawback here? The owners aren't particularly friendly, but this is still a desirable place to stay.

Via Al Capo 3, 18012 Bordighera. ✆ **0184-261-558.** Fax 0184-262-463. 14 units. 80€ double. Breakfast 8€. AE, DC, MC, V. Free parking. Closed Nov and sometimes in Oct. **Amenities:** Restaurant; bar. *In room:* TV, hair dryer, minibar.

Piccolo Lido ★   This pink, sun-filled villa is at the end of the seafront promenade, with direct access to the pebble beach but far enough away from the main seafront avenue and the center of things to provide a great deal of peace and quiet. The public rooms are airy and bright, opening onto terraces like the one on the second floor scattered with deck chairs that let you soak in the sun and sounds of the surf. Upstairs, the newly renovated rooms are bright and attractive, with white-tile floors, pastel area rugs, and bright contemporary furnishings that include comfortable lounge chairs and some nice extras like round tables so you can dine in your room if you choose. Bathrooms are gleaming and modern and nicely equipped with hair dryers and heated towel racks. The best rooms, of course, are those that open onto terraces overlooking the sea. Service can be a little short.

Lungomare Argentina 2, 18012 Bordighera. ⓒ **0184-261-297.** Fax 0184-262-316. www.hotelpiccololido. it. 33 units. 89€–160€ double. Rates include buffet breakfast. AE, DC, MC, V. Parking 12€ in garage. Closed late Oct to late Dec. **Amenities:** Restaurant (Italian cuisine); bar; babysitting; children's center; concierge; Internet point; room service. *In room:* A/C, TV, hair dryer, minibar.

Where to Dine

Caffè Giglio CAFE   The most popular cafe in Bordighera seems to suit patrons of all stripes, whether they are British pensioners who sit on the terrace and sip tea, teenagers who stop on their way to the beach for a gelato (in 30 flavors, 2€ and up), or night owls looking for a place to enjoy a glass of wine (not easy to do in this sleepy town). As a result, this is almost a mandatory stop for visitors interested in checking out the local scene. The more substantial fare includes sandwiches, salads, and crepes, which, depending on the filling, are served either as a meal or as a dessert.

Via Vittorio Emanuele 158. ⓒ **0184-261-530.** Panini and snacks from 2€. Tues–Fri 11am–3pm and 7pm–1am; Sat 11am–1am; Sun 3pm–1am.

Chez Louis ★★ LIGURIAN   The chrome trim, New Age jazz music, and white tablecloths of this French-sounding restaurant conjure images of the nearby Côte d'Azur, and the proprietor's name is Jeanpierre, but both the menu and the ownership of Chez Louis are 100% Ligurian—and have been for half a century. Jeanpierre does, however, add a little foreign spice to his *tagliolini al pesto esotico con scampi:* saffron, to be exact. Or treat yourself to a grilled lobster and tuna filet with caviar, balsamic vinegar, and honey. Even the very French foie gras is seasoned with a very Italian *passito* dessert wine. They are all worth the price, as Chez Louis serves that rare combination of refined cuisine and sizeable portions.

Corso Italia 30 (just down the street from the train station). ⓒ **0184-261-603.** Reservations recommended for outdoor seating. Primi 10€–16€; secondi 12€–25€. AE, MC, V. Daily noon–2:30pm and 7–10pm.

Magiargé ★★ LIGURIAN   This attractive trattoria prepares only three or four pastas and main courses daily, announced on a blackboard. Starters often include a ratatouille-style fish, while pasta selections usually feature *trenette* or some other pasta with a rich pesto sauce. There is almost always a selection of fresh grilled fish and one or two meat courses, often including a game hen cooked with local olives and fresh vegetables, a house specialty, or maybe a rabbit casserole. If you liked the olive oil or wine served at lunch, go across the square to their newly opened wine shop, where local labels line the walls.

Piazza G. Viale. ⓒ **0184-262-946.** www.magiarge.it. Reservations recommended. Primi 10€; secondi 15€. AE, MC, V. Thurs–Tues noon–2:30pm and 8–10pm.

VENTIMIGLIA

Ventimiglia is a quiet and somewhat unremarkable Italian town 11km (6¾ miles) from the French border and only minutes from Bordighera and San Remo. Although the town holds little of particular interest, the surrounding coast and hills boast a few of the most interesting sights along this stretch of coastline.

GETTING THERE   By Train   There are one to three hourly trains from **Bordighera** and **San Remo** (7 min. on regional trains).

By Bus   Riviera Trasporti buses (© **0184-592-706;** www.rivieratrasporti.it) run every 15 minutes between **Bordighera** and Ventimiglia (10–30 min., depending on traffic).

By Car   Since traffic on the coastal S1 road can be extremely heavy approaching the French border, it's often faster to use the A10 Autostrada from Bordighera or San Remo.

VISITOR INFORMATION   The **tourist office** is at Via Cavour 61 (©/fax **0184-351-183**). It's open Monday to Saturday 8am to 7pm and Sunday 9am to 1pm (closed Sun Oct–May).

Festivals & Markets   July's **Battle of the Flowers** is fought by contestants vying to build the most elaborate float, three-dimensional sculptures whose surfaces are mosaics made up of thousands of flowers. **Friday morning's market** sells food, clothes, and all sorts of useful items in the park between Via Vittorio Veneto and the shoreline at Lungo Roia Girolamo Rossi and Passeggiata Oberdan.

Sights in Town

Sights in Ventimiglia are divided between the mostly modern, lower section of town, built after 1872 to service the new train station, and **Ventimiglia Alta,** a medieval town with a sweeping panorama from **Piazza Belvedere** ★, at the east end of Via Giuseppe Verdi. From here, turn up Via del Capo to reach the 11th- to 12th-century **Cattedrale dell'Assunta** and its octagonal **baptistery,** possibly built atop a temple to Juno. Via del Capo becomes *palazzo*-lined **Via Garibaldi.** At Piazza Fontana/Piazza del Canto, head to the back-right corner to continue up Via Piedmont to Piazza Colletta and the isolated **Church of San Michele** ★, the current version built around the 10th century using bits of ancient stones: The stoops and one of the crypt columns are Roman milestones, and two of the granite pillars in the crypt hail from a temple to Castor and Pollux.

Though today mostly modern, the more bustling **lower town** is actually built atop the remains of the ancient Roman border settlement of Albintimilium, which you can see a bit of at the far eastern end of main drag Corso Genova (the S1) in the splendidly preserved 2nd-century-A.D., 5,000-seat **Roman theater** ★, sandwiched between the road and the train tracks.

The Surrounding Sights

Giardino Hanbury (Hanbury Gardens), on the coast 6.5km (4 miles) east of Ventimiglia, is one of Europe's largest and most noted botanical collections. British merchant Sir Thomas Hanbury planted the gardens, which descend on terraces to the sea, in 1867, to nurture exotic species from five continents. As immensely important as the gardens were to the 19th-century study of botany, today they are a pleasure dome, a stunningly beautiful bower with heart-stopping views of the sea around every corner. The gardens (© **0184-229-507**) are open daily from the last Sunday in March through October (hours vary by season), and Thursday to Tuesday from November to the last Sunday in March 10am to 5pm (last entry 1 hr. before closing). Admission is 7.50€, or 20€ for a family ticket covering two parents and up to three children under 15.

At **Balzi Rossi (Red Rocks;** © **0184-38-113**), right on the French border 1.6km (1 mile) farther east along the coast from Giardino Hanbury, one of prehistoric Europe's most advanced Paleolithic cultures lived in cliff-side caves—first Neanderthals

(80,000–35,000 years ago) and later Homo Sapiens (35,000–10,000 years ago). Visitors may tour several of the caves, the most interesting of which is Grotto del Cavglione, named for a horse etched on one of the walls. Most of the finds—including weapons, fertility figures (copies; the originals are in France), simple stone tools, five human skeletons, and even a bit of Homo Erectus hip some 230,000 years old—are in the small Museo Preistorico split across two buildings. Many of the caves were damaged, and the only fossils once visible *in situ* destroyed, when the rail tunnels above were blown up during World War II. The caves and museum are open Tuesday to Sunday 9am to 7:30pm; admission is 2€, 1€ for ages 19 to 26, and free for those under 18 or over 65.

Another excursion from Ventimiglia takes you inland for 9.5km (6 miles) up the Val Nervia to **Dolceacqua,** a stone village that is as sweetly picturesque as its name implies it will be. The ruins of a 16th-century castle crown the collection of houses that climb from the banks of the river, spanned here by a single-arched medieval bridge. If you stumble into town at certain times of the year, you will find the locals engaged in strange revelries: On January 20 (St. Sebastian's Day), a man carrying a tree hung with communion hosts leads a procession through the streets; on August 15, costumed dancers celebrate Ferragosto.

From Ventimiglia, **Riviera Trasporti buses** (© **0184-592-706;** www.rivieratrasporti. it), which leave from Via Cavour near the train station, make but a handful of daily runs (currently at 9:05am, 11:05am, 1:25pm, and 2:25pm) that stop first at the **Hanbury Gardens** (15 min.) and then swing by the **Balzi Rossi** (30 min. from Ventimiglia) before returning to Ventimiglia. The stops aren't named after these sights, so be sure to let the driver know when you want to get off. To get back to Ventimiglia, hail the bus from the same stop where you got off.

There are also two direct buses (currently 7:05am and 12:05pm) from Ventimiglia to Balzi Rossi (15 min.), or you can stay on the **train** (usually only on local runs) past Ventimiglia to Menton-Garavan station (7 min. from Ventimiglia), from which Balzi Rossi is a 20- to 30-minute walk.

Ten buses a day leave Ventimiglia for **Dolceacqua** (20–30 min.).

Where to Stay & Dine

When you're in town, you might want to experience a dinner at **Marco Polo,** Passeggiata Felice Cavallotti 2 (© **0184-352-678**), with excellent Ligurian cooking, a good wine cellar, and outdoor tables right on the seaside promenade; meals average 45€ to 55€, not including wine.

Hotel Ristorante La Riserva di Castel d'Appio ★ There are plenty of narrow, switchback, two-lane roads in Italy, but the one up here may take the cake. The "castel" is actually a modern hotel, with modular furnishings and lurid chipped-stone floors, but fantastic coastal panoramas from the room balconies, most looking west over the French Riviera and Monte Carlo, some east over Italy. All superior doubles and suites have a large balcony overlooking the water. A few ground-floor standard doubles lack the sweeping views but open onto small lawns as compensation. The restaurant is on a panoramic terrace next to the pool and billiards, foosball, and Ping-Pong tables.

C.P. 108, 18039 Ventimiglia (IM). © **0184-229-533.** Fax 0184-229-712. www.lariserva.it. 23 units. 120€–170€ standard double; 135€–190€ superior double; 170€–280€ suite. (Prices are highest for the weekend of the Monaco Grand Prix in May.) Breakfast 8€. AE, DC, MC, V. Free parking. Closed Oct–Mar. **Amenities:** Italian/international restaurant; bar; babysitting; bikes; children's center; concierge; fitness center; outdoor pool; room service; smoke-free rooms. *In room:* A/C, TV, hair dryer, minibar, free Wi-Fi.

3 THE RIVIERA DI LEVANTE: CAMOGLI, SANTA MARGHERITA LIGURE, PORTOFINO & RAPALLO

Camogli: 26km (16 miles) E of Genoa; Santa Margherita Ligure: 31km (19 miles) E of Genoa; Portofino: 38km (24 miles) E of Genoa; Rapallo: 37km (23 miles) E of Genoa

The coast east of Genoa, the **Riviera di Levante (Shore of the Rising Sun),** is more ruggedly beautiful than the Riviera Ponente, less developed, and hugged by mountains that plunge into the sea. Four of the coast's most appealing towns are within a few kilometers of one another, clinging to the shores of the Monte Portofino Promontory just east of Genoa: Camogli, Santa Margherita Ligure, Rapallo, and little Portofino.

CAMOGLI

Camogli (abbreviated from "Casa dei Mogli"—House of the Wives) was named for the women who held down the fort while their husbands went to sea for years on end. The little town remains delightfully unspoiled, an authentic Ligurian fishing port with tall, ocher-painted houses fronting the harbor and a nice swath of beach. Given also its excellent accommodations and eateries, Camogli is a lovely place to base yourself while exploring the Riviera Levante. This is also a restful retreat from which you can explore Genoa, which is only about 30 minutes away.

Essentials

GETTING THERE   By Train   One to three trains per hour ply the coastline, connecting Camogli with **Genoa** (30–45 min.), **Santa Margherita** (5 min.), and **Monterosso** (50–60 min.) and other Cinque Terre towns.

By Bus   There is at least one Tigullio (© **0185-288-835;** www.tigulliotrasporti.it) bus an hour, often more, from **Santa Margherita;** since the bus must go around and not under the Monte Portofino Promontory, the trip takes quite a bit longer than the train—about half an hour.

By Boat   In summer, boats operated by Golfo Paradiso (© **0185-772-091;** www.golfo paradiso.it) sail from Camogli to **Portofino.**

By Car   The fastest route into the region is Autostrada A12 from Genoa; exit at Recco for Camogli (the trip takes less than half an hour). Route S1 along the coast from Genoa is much slower but more scenic.

VISITOR INFORMATION   The **tourist office** is across from the train station at Via XX Settembre 33 (©/fax **0185-771-066;** www.camogli.it or www.portofinocoast.it). It's open Monday to Saturday 9am to 12:30pm and 3:30 to 7pm (Mar–Oct it closes at noon and 6:30pm, respectively), Sunday 9am to 1pm.

FESTIVALS & MARKETS   Camogli throws a well-attended annual party, the **Sagra del Pesce ★★**, on the second Sunday of May, where the town fries up thousands of sardines in a 3.6m-diameter (12-ft.) pan and passes them around for free—a practice that is accompanied by an annual outcry in the press about health concerns and even accusations that frozen fish is used.

The first Sunday of August, Camogli stages the lovely **Festa della Stella Maris.** A procession of boats sails to Punta Chiappa, a point of land about 1.5km (1 mile) down the coast, and releases 10,000 burning candles. Meanwhile, the same number of candles **413** is set afloat from the Camogli beach. If currents are favorable, the burning candles will come together at sea, signifying a year of unity for couples who watch the spectacle.

Exploring the Town

Camogli is clustered around its delightful waterfront, from which the town ascends via steep, staircased lanes to Via XX Settembre, one of the few streets in the town proper to accommodate cars (this is where the train station, tourist office, and many shops and other businesses are located). Adding to the charm of this setting is the fact that the oldest part of Camogli juts into the harbor on a little point (once an island) where ancient houses cling to the little **Castello Dragone** (now closed to the public) and the 12th-century **Basilica di Santa Maria Assunta** (✆ **0185-770-130**), with an impressively overly baroque interior that's open daily 7:30am to noon and 3:30 to 7pm. Most visitors, though, seem drawn to the pleasant **seaside promenade** ★ that runs the length of the town. You can swim from the pebbly beach below, and should you feel your towel doesn't provide enough comfort, rent a lounge from one of the few beach stations for around 10€.

Where to Stay

Augusta (Value) This is an acceptable alternative if La Camogliese (below) is full, and, more than a fallback, it's pleasant and convenient, with a handy location a short walk up a steep staircase from the harbor. The couple and their son who run this *pensione* also operate the ground-floor trattoria, which serves as a sitting room for the hotel guests and makes it easy to enjoy a cup of coffee or glass of wine. The guest rooms are extremely plain, with functional furnishings and drab decor, but they are large and clean, and have good-size bathrooms. You also get 15 minutes of free Internet access (in the reception area) per day. Ask for a room in front—those in back face the train tracks.

Via Schiaffino 100, 16032 Camogli. ✆ **0185-770-592**. www.htlaugusta.com. 14 units. 62€–105€ double; 85€–135€ triple. Rates include breakfast. Show your Frommer's guide for a discount (especially during off season). AE, DC, MC, V. Parking 12€. **Amenities:** Restaurant (local cuisine); bar; room service. *In room:* A/C, TV, Internet.

Cenobio dei Dogi ★★ This Ligurian getaway sits just above the sea at one end of town and against the forested flank of Monte Portofino. The oldest part of the hotel incorporates an aristocratic villa dating from 1565; a chapel, still occasionally used as such, dates from the 17th century. Converted to a hotel in 1956, the premises now include several wings that wrap graciously around a garden on one side and a series of terraces facing the sea on the other. There's a pool and a private beach, and several airy salons, including a lovely bar and lounge area and a glass-enclosed breakfast room that hangs over the sea. The guest rooms vary considerably in size and shape, but all are furnished with a tasteful mix of reproduction writing desks, contemporary glass-top tables, and—especially in "standard"-category rooms—island-style furnishings (rattan, bent bamboo headboards, and the like). Many overlook the sea and have balconies, and a few have terraces that lead directly to the pool.

Via Cuneo 34, 16032 Camogli. ✆ **0185-7241**. Fax 0185-772-796. www.cenobio.it. 106 units. 160€–220€ standard double with garden view; 220€–320€ standard double with sea view; 190€–270€ superior double with garden view; 300€–430€ superior double with sea view. Rates include continental breakfast. AE, DC, MC, V. Free parking. **Amenities:** 2 Ligurian/international restaurants (1 at beach); 2 bars; babysitting; bikes; concierge; exercise room and sauna across the street; nearby golf course; 2 pools (indoor and outdoor saltwater pool); outdoor lighted tennis courts; watersports equipment/rentals. *In room:* A/C, TV, hair dryer, minibar, Wi-Fi.

La Camogliese ★★   A lot of Genovese come out to spend the weekend in this friendly, attractive little hotel near the waterfront, and they appreciate it for the same simple charms that will appeal to travelers from farther afield. (In fact, given the hotel's popularity, it's always a good idea to reserve, and it's essential on weekends.) Rooms are large, bright, and airy and decorated in modern furnishings that include comfortable beds. Some have balconies, and although the house isn't right on the waterfront, it faces a little river and is close enough to the beach that a slight twist of the head usually affords a view of the sea (best from corner room no. 16B). Bathrooms are small but adequate.

Via Garibaldi 55, 16032 Camogli. ✆ **0185-771-402.** Fax 0185-774-024. www.lacamogliese.it. 21 units. 70€–115€ double. Rates include breakfast. AE, DC, MC, V. Parking 15€. **Amenities:** Babysitting; concierge; exercise room; outdoor pool; room service. *In room:* TV, hair dryer, Internet.

Where to Dine

Bar Primula CAFE/LIGHT FARE   If you need a light meal (a pasta dish and seafood plate or two are usually available, along with sandwiches, salads, and omelets), this is the most convenient spot, but many regulars come in for a cup of the delicious house espresso and dessert, which presents a difficult choice between the delicious ice cream and pastries. If you're torn, try the sumptuous *camogliese* chocolate rum ball–like concoction.

Via Garibaldi 140. ✆ **0185-770-351.** Salads and other light fare 6€–10€. AE, MC, V. Fri–Wed 9am–2am.

Ristorante La Camogliese SEAFOOD   You probably won't be surprised to find that the menu at this bright seaside spot, perched over the beach on stilts, leans heavily to seafood. In fact, when the weather is pleasant and the windows that surround the dining room are open, you feel you are at sea. That's the real draw of this place, as the service here is shaky, and there are better dishes to be had on this coast. That said, the hearty fish soup for two is quite good, and you can never go wrong with a lightly fried swordfish steak.

Via Garibaldi 78. ✆ **0185-771-086.** Reservations recommended. Primi 11€–23€; secondi 18€–24€. AE, DC, MC, V. Oct–June Thurs–Tues 12:30–2:30pm and 7:30–10:30pm (daily July–Sept). Closed Nov.

A Hotel Between Camogli & Santa Margherita Ligure

Hotel Portofino Kulm ★★   This grand old hotel slung in a skyscraping hammock of greenery in the midst of the Tigullio's parkland halfway between Camogli and Rapallo/Santa Margherita Ligure was opened in 1908 but for decades stood derelict until Camogli's Cenobio dei Dogi overhauled it to reopen in 2000. The long vistas sweep across the forest down to the Riviera north of the promontory toward Genoa in one direction, and in the other south over Santa Margherita Ligure down the coast toward the Cinque Terre. Many balconies and rooftop terraces take full advantage of the panoramas. The modest-size, carpeted rooms come with wrought-iron bedsteads, stylish furnishings, marble bathrooms, and queen-size beds. The best ones come with those sea views from balconies. The hotel hosts lots of conventions during the week, turning to a tourism-based clientele on the weekends. Four rooms are in a separate structure a smidgen higher up the driveway, with even better views.

Viale Bernardo Gaggini 23 (6km/3¾ miles from Camogli on the over-mountain road to Santa Margherita Ligure), 16030 Ruta di Camogli, Portofino Vetta (GE). ✆ **0185-7361.** Fax 0185-776-622. www.portofino kulm.it. 77 units. 160€–200€ double with park view; 180€–240€ double with sea view; 220€–280€ double with sea view and terrace. Rates include breakfast. AE, DC, MC, V. Free parking. **Amenities:** International/Ligurian restaurant; bar; babysitting; bikes; concierge; tiny exercise room; Jacuzzi; indoor heated pool; room service; sauna. *In room:* A/C, TV, hair dryer, minibar, Wi-Fi.

SANTA MARGHERITA LIGURE

Santa Margherita had one brief moment in the spotlight, at the beginning of the 20th century when it was an internationally renowned retreat. Fortunately, the seaside town didn't let fame spoil its charm, and now that it's no longer as well known a destination as its glitzy neighbor Portofino, it might be the Mediterranean retreat of your dreams. A palm-lined harbor, a decent beach, and a friendly ambience make Santa Margherita a fine place to settle down for a few days of sun and relaxation.

Essentials

GETTING THERE **By Train** Two or three coastal trains per hour connect Santa Margherita with **Genoa** (regional: 35 min.; high-speed: 25 min.), **Camogli** (5 min.), Rapallo (3 min.), and **Monterosso** (regional: 55 min.; high-speed: 40 min.) of the Cinque Terre.

By Bus There is at least one Tigullio (© 0185-288-834; www.tigulliotrasporti.it) bus an hour to **Camogli** (30–35 min.) and to **Rapallo** (10 min.), leaving from Piazza Vittorio Veneto. Buses also ply the stunningly beautiful coast road to **Portofino,** leaving every 20 minutes from the train station and Piazza Vittorio Veneto (25 min.).

By Boat Tigullio ferries (© 0185-284-670; www.traghettiportofino.it) make hourly trips to **Portofino** (15 min.) and **Rapallo** (15 min.). In summer, there is a boat about 4 days a week to **Vernazza** in the Cinque Terre. Hours of service vary considerably with season; schedules are posted on the docks at Piazza Martiri della Liberta.

By Car The fastest route into the region is the A12 Autostrada from Genoa; the trip takes about half an hour. Route S1 along the coast from Genoa is much slower but more scenic.

VISITOR INFORMATION The **tourist office** is near the harbor at Via XXV Aprile 2B (© 0185-287-485; fax 0185-283-034; www.apttigullio.liguria.it). Summer hours are daily 9am to 12:30pm and 3 to 6pm; winter hours are Monday to Saturday 9am to 12:30pm and 2:30 to 5:30pm.

FESTIVALS & MARKETS Santa Margherita's winters are delightfully mild, but even so, the town rushes to usher in spring with a **Festa di Primavera,** held on moveable dates in February. Like the Sagra del Pesce in neighboring Camogli, this festival also features food—in this case, fritters are prepared on the beach and served around roaring bonfires. One of the more interesting daily spectacles in town is the **fish market** on Lungomare Marconi; this colorful event takes place from 8am to 12:30pm. On Friday, cars are banned from Corso Matteotti, Santa Margherita's major street for food shopping, turning the area into an open-air **food market.**

Exploring the Town

Life in Santa Margherita centers on its palm-fringed **waterfront,** a pleasant string of marinas, docks for pleasure and fishing boats, and pebbly beaches, in some spots with imported sand of passable quality. Landlubbers congregate in the cafes that spill out into the town's two seaside squares, Piazza Martiri della Liberta and Piazza Vittorio Veneto.

The train station is on a hill above the waterfront, and a staircase in front of the entrance will lead you down into the heart of town. Santa Margherita's one landmark of note is its namesake **Basilica di Santa Margherita,** just off the seafront on Piazza Caprera. The church is open daily from 8am to noon and 3 to 7pm and is well worth a visit to view the extravagant, gilded, chandeliered interior.

Annabella The nice proprietors manage to accommodate groups of just about any size in this old apartment that's been converted to an attractive *pensione,* with comfortable old modular furniture and whitewashed walls. Some of the rooms sleep up to four, and one family-style arrangement includes a large room with a double bed and a tiny room outfitted with bunk beds for children. None of the rooms have private bathrooms, but the four shared facilities are ample and hot water is plentiful.

Via Costasecca 10, 16038 Santa Margherita Ligure. (C) **0185-286-531.** 11 units, none with private bathroom. 60€–75€ double; 80€–93€ triple. Breakfast 4€. No credit cards. Free parking (call ahead to reserve a space). **Amenities:** Room service. *In room:* No phone.

Fasce ★★★ The Fasce family's hospitality includes the use of free bicycles, and if you stay 3 nights or longer, they'll give you a free Cinque Terre packet with train times and two free tickets to go all the way to Riomaggiore and back. The surroundings are lovely: A broad staircase leads into the flowery, courtyardlike entryway, off which there's a pleasant lobby and breakfast/bar area; a roof terrace affords lovely views of the sea and town. The guest rooms are large, bright, and modern in design, with cheerful white laminate furnishings and many thoughtful touches, such as copious amounts of storage space, shelves around the beds on which to place reading material, and in-room safes. Four rooms have balconies, and three accommodations (the triples and a quad) have folding beds, to make them perfect for families. With this many amenities at such reasonable prices, it's a good idea to reserve ahead.

Via Luigi Bozzo 3, 16038 Santa Margherita Ligure. (C) **0185-286-435.** Fax 0185-283-580. www.hotelfasce. it. 16 units. 118€ double; 140€ triple; 175€ family room. Rates include breakfast. AE, DC, MC, V. Parking 18€. Closed Dec 12–Mar 15. **Amenities:** Bar; free bikes; concierge; room service; smoke-free rooms. *In room:* TV, hair dryer, minibar, Wi-Fi.

Grand Hotel Miramare ★★ This was one of the first grand hotels on this coast, converted in 1903 from a massive private villa a 10-minute walk from the town center along the road to Portofino. Rooms are enlivened by some modest stucco decorations on the walls and ceilings, from which hang chandeliers over parquet floors scattered with Persian rugs and slightly funky walnut and veneer furnishings. The first-floor suite where Marconi stayed when conducting his radio experiments has been kept in 19th-century style, while fifth-floor suites are more modernized. A very steep, pretty park rises behind the hotel, from which a trail leads over the headland to Portofino (it also makes for a pleasant view, especially if you don't get a room with that preferred sea view). There's a small, private pebble beach/beach terrace across the busy road.

Via Milite Ignoto, 16038 Santa Margherita Ligure (GE). (C) **0185-287-013.** Fax 0185-284-651. www.grand hotelmiramare.it. 84 units. 255€–385€ double with park view; 285€–425€ double with sea view; AE, DC, MC, V. Free parking. **Amenities:** 2 restaurants (1 poolside lunch buffet; 1 international/regional); 2 bars (piano bar inside, pool bar); babysitting; concierge; nearby exercise room; nearby golf course; outdoor heated saltwater pool; room service; nearby sauna; nearby outdoor lighted tennis courts; watersports equipment/rentals. *In room:* A/C, TV, hair dryer, minibar, Wi-Fi.

Hotel Metropole ★★ (Kids) This popular hotel sits on the road into town, just above the port and a 5-minute stroll into the center. All rooms face the sea over a lovely shaded .6-hectare (1½-acre) garden blooming with flowers. Accommodations are split between the main, modern building and the far-preferable Villa Porticciolla, a dusty red Genoese villa right on the beach; the rooms are smaller in the latter, but they're graced with 19th-century stuccoes, and the sea laps practically right up against the building. Six rooms up on the far end of the garden (from where there are only glimpses of the sea through the palm fronds) have large terraces partly shaded by an arbor. All other guest rooms have large balconies. The fourth floor is made up of junior suites and one double with sloped ceilings. Two suites on the lower floor of the main building open onto small private gardens. The management enjoys working with families; several rooms can be joined to make family suites, and there's day care at the beach, with a separate area of sand just for the kiddies. The small private beach includes a curving sunbathing terrace and a private boat launch.

Via Pagana 2, 16038 Santa Margherita Ligure (GE). ℂ **0185-286-134.** Fax 0185-283-495. www.metropole. it. 59 units. 100€–238€ double; 136€–280€ double with half-board; 156€–300€ double with full board. Rates include buffet breakfast. AE, DC, MC, V. Parking 18€ in private garage; beach chair/bed 10€. **Amenities:** 2 restaurants (1 international/regional dining room; 1 beachside lunch restaurant); bar; babysitting; children's center (in summer); private beach; small exercise room; nearby golf course; swimming pool; sauna; watersports equipment/rentals; Wi-Fi. *In room:* A/C, TV, hair dryer, Internet, minibar.

Nuova Riviera ★ (Value) The Sabini family acts as if its sunny, early-20th-century Liberty-style villa in a quiet neighborhood behind the town center was a private home and guests were old friends. Every room is different, and though eclectically furnished with pieces that look like they may have passed through a couple of generations of the family, most rooms retain the high-ceilinged elegance of days gone by and have a great deal more character than you're used to finding in rooms at this end of the budget scale; the best have expansive bay windows. Modular furnishings are mixed with antiques, the beds are springy (very springy), and a few rooms get balconies. They also rent out apartments (65€–99€ for two people).

Via Belvedere 10–2, 16038 Santa Margherita Ligure. ℂ/fax **0185-287-403.** www.nuovariviera.com. 9 units. 85€–110€ double. Rates include breakfast. MC, V. **Amenities:** Restaurant (local cuisine, winter only); bar; smoke-free rooms. *In room:* TV, hair dryer, no phone.

Where to Dine

Ristorante Il Faro ★★ ITALIAN/LIGURIAN   This cozy trattoria is run by Roberto Fabbro, who opened Santa Margherita Ligure's first *rosticceria* more than 40 years ago. They give you a glass of Spumanti and a bit of pizza to help you digest the menu, which runs the gamut from *penne all'arrabbiata* (pasta quills in a spicy-hot tomato sauce) and a *fritto misto* (a mix of seafood deep-fried) to *minestrone alla Genovese* (thick vegetable soup), *trenette al pesto,* and *pesce alla piastra* (grilled bream or sea bass). The best seating is at a few tables under the arcade out back.

Via Maragliano 24A. ℂ **0185-286-867.** Reservations recommended. Primi 8€–12€; secondi 10€–12€. AE, DC, MC, V. Wed–Mon 12:15–2:30pm and 7–10pm. Closed Nov.

Trattoria Baicin ★ LIGURIAN   The husband-and-wife owners, Piero and Carmela, make everything fresh daily, from fish soup to gnocchi, and still manage to find time to greet diners at the door of their cheerful trattoria just a few steps off the harbor. You can get a glimpse of the sea if you choose to sit at one of the tables out front, and the owner/ cooks are most happy preparing fish, which they buy fresh every morning at the market just around the corner. The sole, simply grilled, is especially good here, and the *fritto misto di pesce* constitutes a memorable feast. You must begin a meal with one of the pastas made that morning, especially if *trofie alla Genovese* (a combination of gnocchi, potatoes, fresh vegetables, and pesto) is available. By ordering the tourist menu, you can get a nice sampling of the expertly prepared dishes served here.

Via Algeria 9. ℂ **0185-286-763.** Reservations recommended for outdoor seating. Primi 4€–7.50€; secondi 8.50€–17€; fixed-price menus 20€–22€. AE, DC, MC, V. Tues–Sun noon–3pm and 7–10:30pm. Closed Jan.

Trattoria da Pezzi (Value) GENOVESE/LIGURIAN The atmosphere in this cozy little restaurant in the center of town near the market is pleasantly casual. Two white-washed, tile-floored rooms are usually filled with local workers and businesspeople who invite newcomers to share a table when no other place is available. Service is minimal—the chef puts what he's prepared for the day on a table near the front door, you tell him what you want, and one of the staff brings it to the table when it's ready. Focaccia, *farinata,* and other Genovese specialties are usually on hand, as are at least one kind of soup (the minestrone is excellent), a chicken dish, and grilled fresh fish.

Via Cavour 21. (C) **0185-285-303.** Primi 5€–7.50€; secondi 5€–9€. MC, V. Sun–Fri 11:45am–2:15pm and 6–9:15pm. Closed Dec 20–Jan 20.

PORTOFINO

Portofino is almost too beautiful for its own good—in almost any season, you'll be rubbing elbows on Portofino's harborside quays with day-tripping mobs who join Italian industrialists, international celebrities, and a lot of rich-but-not-so-famous folks who consider this little town to be the epicenter of the good life. If you make an appearance in the late afternoon when the crowds have thinned out a bit, you are sure to experience what remains so appealing about this enchanting place—its untouchable beauty.

Essentials

GETTING THERE **By Train** Get off in Santa Margherita (see above) and catch the bus.

By Bus The **Tigullio** bus ((C) **0185-288-834;** www.tigulliotrasporti.it) leaves from the train station and Piazza Vittorio Veneto in **Santa Margherita** every 20 minutes and follows one of Italy's most beautiful coastal roads (25 min.). In Santa Margherita, you can change for a bus to **Rapallo** (another 15 min.).

By Boat The best way to arrive is to sail to Portofino on one of the Golfo Paradiso ferries ((C) **0185-772-091;** www.golfoparadiso.it) from **Camogli,** or on one of the Tigullio ferries ((C) **0185-284-670;** www.traghettiportofino.it) from **Santa Margherita** or **Rapallo.**

By Car On a summer visit, you may encounter crowds even before you get into town, since traffic on the shore-hugging corniche from Santa Margherita, just a few kilometers down the coast of the promontory, can move at a snail's pace. In fact, given limited parking space in Portofino ((C) **0185-267-475;** visitors must pay obscene rates—more than 5€ per hour—to use the town garage), you would do well to leave your car in Santa Margherita and take the bus or boat.

VISITOR INFORMATION Portofino's **tourist office** is at Via Roma 35 ((C)/fax **0185-269-024;** www.apttigullio.liguria.it). Summer hours are daily 10:30am to 1:30pm and 2 to 7:30pm; winter hours are Tuesday to Sunday 9:30am to 12:30pm and 2:30 to 5:30pm.

Exploring the Town and Sea

The one thing that's free in Portofino is its scenery, which you can enjoy on an amble around the town. Begin with a stroll around the **harbor,** which—lined with expensive boutiques and eateries—is stunningly beautiful, with colorful houses set along the quay and steep green hills rising behind them. One of the most scenic walks takes you uphill for about 10 minutes along a well-signposted path from the west side of town just behind the harbor to the **Chiesa di San Giorgio** ((C) **0185-269-337**), built on the site of a sanctuary Roman soldiers dedicated to the Persian god Mithras. It's open daily from 9am to 7pm.

An Excursion to San Fruttuoso

Much of the **Monte Portofino Promontory** can be approached only on foot or by boat (see below), making it a prime destination for hikers. If you want to combine some excellent exercise with the pleasure of glimpsing magnificent views of the sea through a lush forest, arm yourself with a map from the tourist offices in Camogli, Santa Margherita Ligure, Portofino, or Rapallo and set out for **Abbazia di San Fruttuoso** (© 0185-772-703). This medieval religious community, surrounded by a tiny six-house hamlet and two pebbly beaches, is about 2¹/₂ hours away from any of the above-mentioned towns (though Camogli and Portofino are closest, as they immediately flank the promontory on which Abbazia di San Fruttuoso sits) by a not-too-strenuous inland hike, or 3¹/₂ hours away by a cliff-hugging trail. En route, you can clamor down well-posted paths that descend from the main path to visit San Rocco, San Niccolo, and Punta Chiappa, a string of fishing hamlets hugging the shore of the promontory.

Once you reach San Fruttuoso, you may well want to relax on the pebbly beach and enjoy a beverage or meal at one of the seaside bars. You can tour the stark interior of the abbey for 6€. It is open June to September daily 10am to 5:45pm; in May Tuesday to Sunday 10am to 5:45pm; March, April, and October Tuesday to Sunday 10am to 3:30pm; and November to February Saturday and Sunday 10am to 3:30pm. Note, though, that despite these official hours, the abbey tends to close whenever the last boat leaves (see below). The abbey is just a plain, evocatively simple medieval monastic complex with a stellar setting on the coast. There's nothing really to "see" except how the monks lived. Should you happen to have your scuba or snorkeling gear along, you can take the plunge to visit Christ of the Depths, a statue of Jesus erected 15m (49 ft.) beneath the surface to honor sailors lost at sea.

You can also visit San Fruttuoso with one of the **boats** that run almost every hour during the summer months from Camogli. A round-trip costs 10€ (7€ one-way if you're headed southward from the abbey) and takes about 30 minutes each way. For more information, contact Golfo Paradiso (© 0185-772-091; www.golfoparadiso.it). *Note:* You can also reach it by hourly (in summer) Tigullio boats (© 0185-284-670; www.traghettiportofino.it) from Portofino (20 min.; 11€), Santa Margherita (35 min.; 15€), and Rapallo (50 min.; 15€). Bear in mind that the seas are often too choppy to take passengers to San Fruttuoso, since docking there can be tricky. In that case, there are private boats you can take—smaller, rubber crafts capable of bad-weather landings—though they are expensive: From Portofino, you will likely be charged 100€ for up to 12 people.

From there, you'll want to continue uphill for a few minutes more to Portofino's **Castello Brown** (© 0185-267-101 or 0185-269-046), built to ward off invading Turks. You can step inside the walls to enjoy a lush garden and the views of the town and harbor below. The castle is open daily from 10am to 7pm (until 10pm on Fri and Sat, and to 5pm in the winter). Admission is 6€. There are great views back over the town; for some lovely views on this stretch of coast and plenty of open sea before you, continue even higher up through lovely pine forests to the *faro* (lighthouse).

From Portofino, you can also set out for a longer hike on the paths that cross the **Monte Portofino Promontory** to the Abbazia di San Fruttuoso (see the box "An Excursion to San Fruttuoso," above), about a 2-hour walk from Portofino. The tourist office provides maps.

There's not much else to see in town, but most people are here to spend time on the water. If you're yachtless, one alternative is to take a dolphin-spotting cruise with **Delfini Metropolitani** (✆ **010-234-5666;** www.incomingliguria.it). A 2-day tour, hotel accommodations in Genoa included, costs about 120€ per person, or 40€ per child.

Where to Stay

Albergo Nazionale ★★ (Value) It may be set smack in the middle of Portofino's harborfront square, amid some of the priciest real estate in Italy, but the Nazionale costs only one-third to one-half the price of its pricier neighbors (which is why it gets the "value" icon). Decoration of the smallish to midsize rooms is minimal, but the pieces are a masterful mix of modern and antique, which adds to the relaxing elegance of the place. Several of the rooms are lofted suites with the bedroom upstairs. Only five rooms, all junior suites, enjoy views of the harbor.

Via Roma 8, 16034 Portofino (GE). ✆ **0185-269-575.** Fax 0185-269-138. www.nazionalehotel.com. 12 units. 200€–300€ double without sea view; 300€–400€ junior suite with sea view. Rates include breakfast. MC, V. Parking 18€. Closed mid-Dec to Mar. **Amenities:** Italian restaurant; bar; concierge; room service. *In room:* A/C, TV, hair dryer, minibar.

Hotel Eden ★ Osta Ferruccio runs this cozy, beachy-looking *pensione* in the heart of the tiny town, a long block up from the harbor. There are no views of the sea here, though those over the rooftops of the town itself are perfectly pleasant. The most sought-after room is no. 7, which comes with a small terrace. The rooms were recently renovated; the bathrooms are tight but well equipped. There's a lovely small garden where Ligurian dishes are served in summer. This is one of the area's few hotels that's open year-round.

Vico Dritto 18, 16034 Portofino (GE). ✆ **0185-269-091.** Fax 0185-269-047. www.hoteledenportofino. com. 12 units. 140€–280€ double. Rates include breakfast. AE, DC, MC, V. Parking 19€ in nearby lot. **Amenities:** Ligurian restaurant; bar; babysitting; concierge. *In room:* A/C, TV, hair dryer, high-speed Internet.

Hotel Splendido/Splendido Mare ★★ This 19th-century villa grafted onto the remains of a 16th-century monastery has been a hotel since 1901 and, since the early 1950s, one of those fabled retreats of the international rich and famous, of rock stars and Oscar winners. It's perched in a panoramic position atop the headland just before the last curve of the road into town (yes, it's a good 10-min. walk to Portofino harbor—and an uphill haul back—but there's a regular shuttle). Outrageous legends of romance abound here, such as the man who hired a helicopter to shower a deluge of rose petals on his sunbathing sweetheart. The spacious junior suites come with parquet floors, king-size beds, and antique-styled furnishings that hide the high-tech entertainment centers. Some come with a small terrace, and a few are set into the very private next-door building fronted by a grape arbor. A series of olive-lined, rosemary-scented paths wrap around the panoramic pool terrace and stretch along the hillside to various little lookouts. Though the Splendido closes down in winter, its sister, Splendido Mare (eight doubles and eight suites on Portofino's harborfront *piazzetta*), stays open year-round.

Salita Baratta 16, 16034 Portofino (GE). ℂ **800-237-1236** in the U.S., or 0185-267-801 in Italy. Fax 0185-267-806. www.hotelsplendido.com. 66 units. At Hotel Splendido (all rates include half-board): 965€–1,505€ double (separate rates for garden view, sea view, and balcony overlooking the sea); 1,515€–2,265€ junior suite; 2,115€–4,155€ suite. At Splendido Mare: 610€–730€ double with village view; 740€–930€ double with sea view. Half-board supplement at Splendido Mare 79€. Rates include full American breakfast. AE, DC, MC, V. Parking 21€ in garage. Closed Nov 12–Feb 28. **Amenities:** 2 restaurants (regional cuisine in an indoor/outdoor terrace dining room; poolside lunch buffet); bar (piano bar in the evening); babysitting; bikes; concierge; exercise room; nearby golf course; outdoor heated seawater pool; room service; sauna; spa; outdoor tennis courts; watersports equipment/rentals. *In room:* A/C, TV w/free movies, VCR, hair dryer, high-speed Internet, kitchenette (in a few junior suites and suites), minibar.

Where to Dine

Portofino's charms come at a steep price. Its few hotels are expensive enough to put them in the "trip of a lifetime" category, and the harborside restaurants can take a serious chunk out of a vacation budget as well. I suggest you enjoy a light snack at a bar or one of the many shops selling focaccia, and wait to dine in Santa Margherita or one of the other nearby towns.

La Gritta American Bar James Jones called this snug little room the "nicest waterfront bar this side of Hong Kong." We're not sure your praise will go that far, but it is very attractive, very friendly, and far enough along the harborside quay to be a little less hectic than other establishments. Most patrons stop in for a (pricey) cocktail, coffee, or other libation (the floating terrace out front is perfect for a drink at sunset), but light fare, such as omelets and salads of tomatoes and mozzarella, are also available to provide a light and relatively affordable meal.

Calata Marconi 20. ℂ **0185-269-126.** Salads and other light fare from about 7.50€. AE, MC, V. Fri–Wed noon–1am. Closed Nov.

Ristorante Puny ★★★ The gregarious owners make this a Portofino landmark, and also a difficult place to score a table in the summer. Right on the *piazzetta,* its tables enjoy views of the boats bobbing in the harbor and yachts having size contests beyond. Definitely book ahead to drink in those views and dig into *risotto al curry e gamberi* (curried rice embedded with tiny shrimp); *penne al puny* (pasta quills in a sauce of tomatoes, *pancetta* bacon, and mushrooms); fresh fish *al verde* (in a green sauce of parsley, lemon, and white wine) or *al sale* (baked under a thick salt crust); or *carne all'uccelleto* (diced veal sautéed in butter then cooked in white wine with bay leaves).

Piazza Martiri dell'Olivetta 5. ℂ **0185-269-037.** Reservations highly recommended. Primi 8.50€–15€; secondi 11€–22€; AE, MC, V. Wed–Fri noon–3pm and 7–11pm.

RAPALLO

When you step out of Rapallo's busy train station, you may be put off by the traffic, the blocks of banal apartment houses, and the runaway development that in some places has given the resort the look of any other busy town. Keep walking, though, because at its heart, Rapallo remains a gracious old seaside playground and port, and it's easy to see what drew the likes of Ezra Pound, Max Beerbohm, and D. H. Lawrence to take up residence here. Most of the town follows the sweep of a pretty harbor guarded by a medieval castle, and the gracious seafront promenade is cheerfully busy day and night, mostly with families.

GETTING THERE **By Train** More than 30 trains a day connect Rapallo and **Genoa** (regional: 40 min.; high-speed: 30 min.). The same trains connect Rapallo with **Camogli** (10 min.), **Santa Margherita** (3 min.), and **Monterosso** (regional: 50 min.; high-speed: 35 min.) at the north end of the Cinque Terre.

By Bus At least one bus an hour runs between Rapallo and **Santa Margherita** (about 15 min.).

By Boat **Tigullio** ferries (*©* **0185-284-670;** www.traghettiportofino.it) make hourly trips to **Portofino** (30 min.) via **Santa Margherita** (15 min.) from 9am to 4pm (hours of service vary considerably with season; schedules are posted on the docks).

By Car Autostrada A12 connects Rapallo with Genoa and takes about half an hour. Route S1 along the coast from Genoa is much slower but more scenic.

VISITOR INFORMATION The **tourist office** is at Lungomare Vittorio Veneto 7 (*©* **0185-230-346;** fax 0185-63-051; www.apttigullio.liguria.it) and is open Monday to Saturday 9:30am to 12:30pm and 2:30 to 5:30pm.

FESTIVALS & MARKETS Rapallo is at its most exuberant July 1 to July 3, when it celebrates the **Madonna di Montallegro,** whose hilltop sanctuary, the Santuario di Montallegro, crowns the town (see below). A famous icon of the Virgin is carried through the streets, and a huge fireworks display culminates in the burning of the castle (a mock event, of course). Piazza IV Novembre/Via Gramsci is the site of a lively outdoor **food market** on Thursday mornings.

Exploring the Town

From the train station, it's a walk of only about 5 minutes to the **waterfront** (follow Corso Italia to Piazza Canessa and the adjoining Piazza Cavour, and from there, Via Cairoli to the harborside Piazza IV Novembre). Dominating this perfect half-circle of a harbor is a **castle** built on a rocky outcropping reached by a causeway; it is open only for special exhibitions, but the boulders around its base are usually teeming with sunbathers. Nearby, two other buildings reflect the fact that Rapallo enjoyed a long and prosperous existence before it became known as a retreat for pleasure seekers. The **Cathedral of Santi Gervasio e Protasio,** on Via Mazzini, was founded in the 6th century, and the leper house of **San Lorenzo** across the street dates from the Middle Ages. You can go inside the church but not the leper house: It's just a medieval building to look at from the outside.

For striking views over the town and surrounding seacoast, make the ascent to the **Santuario di Montallegro** (*©* **0185-239-000**). You can take a bus from the train station (1€) or an aerial cableway *(funivia)* from Via Castagneto on the eastern side of town. The funivia (*©* **0185-273-444**) operates daily every 30 minutes from 8am to sunset; the trip takes 7 minutes and costs 5.50€ one-way or 7.75€ round-trip. Inside this 16th-century church are some interesting frescoes and a curious Byzantine icon of the Virgin that allegedly flew here on its own from Dalmatia. The views over the sea and surrounding valleys are the main reason to come up here, though, and they are even more grand from the summit of Monte Rosa, a short uphill hike away.

Where to Stay

La Vela This friendly, family-run *pensione,* about a block up from the seaside promenade and the center of town, is one of the better bargain choices in expensive Rapallo.

The old-fashioned, high-ceilinged rooms open off cozy, homey sitting rooms. Accommodations are extremely comfortable, and most are spacious. About half of the rooms have private bathrooms wedged into one corner; those that don't have sinks and bidets and share three facilities in the hallway. All bathrooms, though, could stand an overhaul. Many of the rooms face a garden in the rear of the building, ensuring a good night's sleep, and in some rooms you can enjoy this quiet retreat from a large balcony. They won't take reservations for 1 night only. The hotel is connected with the excellent Ristorante Elite downstairs (see below), where you may well want to take most of your meals.

Via Milite Ignoto 21/7, 16035 Rapallo. ✆/fax **0185-50-551.** www.eliteristorante.it. 13 units, 6 with private bathroom. 52€ double with shared bathroom; 57€ double with private bathroom. Breakfast 3€. AE, DC, MC, V. Free parking on the street. Closed Nov. **Amenities:** Restaurant (Italian cuisine); bar; bikes. *In room:* TV.

Riviera ★★ (**Value**) The Gambero family has run this small hotel, which occupies an old villa on the waterfront, since 1939, and it is now in the capable hands of Claudio and Silvana. The guest rooms have hardwood floors, with matching handsome wood desks and shelving units. Double-pane windows keep noise from the seaside avenue out front to a minimum, and bathrooms feature top-of-the-line fixtures. Many of the fine old touches remain, including small balconies off many of the rooms with vistas over the harbor. Three of the suites are perfect for families, consisting of two separate bedrooms and a shared bathroom off a hall, while the fourth is a single large corner room with three balconies, one off the double-sink bathroom. A sunny terrace overlooking the sea extends from the restaurant/breakfast room, where a generous buffet is served every morning and reasonable fixed-price menus (as well as a la carte) at mealtimes.

Piazza IV Novembre 2, 16035 Rapallo. ✆ **0185-50-248.** Fax 0185-65-668. www.hotelrivierarapallo.com. 20 units. 98€–145€ double; 132€–165€ double with sea view; 145€–183€ suite. Rates include breakfast. AE, MC, V. Free parking. Closed Nov–Dec 23. **Amenities:** Restaurant; bar; babysitting; bikes; concierge; nearby golf course; room service; tennis courts. *In room:* A/C, TV, hair dryer, minibar, Wi-Fi.

Rosa Bianca ★ (**Finds**) This small, lovely hotel is quiet, unassuming, and exceedingly personable, with friendly management and a perfect location right at the end of the main road at the port, with great views over the harbor and restaurant-lined promenade, all the way to the castle. Many of the smallish to midsize rooms are on corners with little semicircular balconies and are flooded with light. They're decorated with bentwood furnishings resting on somewhat tatty carpet, but the low beds lie on genuine box springs (a rarity in Italy). It's across and down a bit from the Riviera (see above), but enjoys better views.

Lungomare Vittorio Veneto 42, 16035 Rapallo (GE). ✆ **0185-50-390.** Fax 0185-65-035. www.hotelrosa bianca.it. 18 units. 120€–160€ double; 130€–200€ suite. Rates include buffet breakfast. AE, DC, MC, V. Parking 15€. **Amenities:** Bar; babysitting; concierge; room service; smoke-free rooms. *In room:* A/C, TV, hair dryer, Internet, minibar.

Where to Dine

La Goletta ★ SEAFOOD La Goletta is the ideal spot for couples, especially those who want to get away from the tourist crowds. Just 5 minutes from the seaside promenade, this place still proves the maxim that the farther you stray from a resort's main drag, the more honest the fare. Come for the simple but abundant *fritto misto,* or the catch of the day, and soak in the quiet atmosphere of Rapallo's seaside alleys at one of the dozen candlelit outdoor tables.

Via Magenta 28. ✆ **0185-230-636.** Reservations recommended in summer. Primi 9€–12€; secondi 14€–22€. AE, DC, MC, V. Thurs–Tues noon–2:30pm and 7:30–11pm.

O Bansin (Value) LIGURIAN   This colorful and boisterous restaurant has been a Rapallo institution since 1907, and even though the new young owners have moved it a few blocks away from the marketplace and spruced it up a bit, they've kept the original respect for simplicity, low prices, and traditional Ligurian cuisine. Minestrone, *pasta al pesto* or *al Bansin* (with tomatoes, pesto, and cream), *polpette in umido* (stewed meatballs served with peas), and *sardine alla piastra* (roast sardines) are served without pomp and circumstance at communal tables in a plain interior room or, whenever warm enough, on the covered, semi-open deck out back. The service is as warm and friendly as the environs.

Via Venezia 105. (*C*) **0185-231-119.** www.obansin.weebly.com. Reservations recommended in summer. Primi 7€–9€; secondi 8€–18€; fixed-price menu at lunch (Mon–Fri) 10€, including wine. AE, DC, MC, V. Sun 12:30–2:30pm; Mon–Sat noon–2:30pm; Tues–Fri 7:30–9:30pm (until 10pm on Sat). Closed Oct 8–20.

Ristorante Elite SEAFOOD   This popular seafood restaurant is just up a busy ave-nue from the harbor, and the pleasant room, hung with paintings of local scenes, is a little less formal (and less overpriced) than the many seafood restaurants on the water-front. The kitchen long ago won the approval of locals, who come here for the fresh fish of the day, which can follow such starters as seafood salad, a *risotto gamberetti e asparagi* (risotto with small prawns and fresh asparagus), or a *zuppe di pesce* (a hearty fish soup). Fresh fish can also be enjoyed on the fixed-price menus, veritable feasts that also include hot and cold seafood appetizers and a pasta course.

Via Milite Ignoto 19. (*C*) **0185-50-551.** www.eliteristorante.it. Reservations recommended in summer. Primi 5€–9€; secondi 8€–21€; fixed-price chef's menu 21€–32€, not including wine. AE, DC, MC, V. Thurs–Tues (daily in summer) noon–2:30pm and 7:30–10pm. Closed Nov.

4 THE CINQUE TERRE

Monterosso, the northernmost town of the Cinque Terre, 93km (58 miles) E of Genoa

Olive groves and vineyards clinging to hillsides, proud villages perched above the sea, hidden coves nestled at the foot of dramatic cliffs—the **Cinque Terre** is about as beauti-ful a coastline as you're likely to find in Europe. What's best about the Cinque Terre (named for the five neighboring towns of Monterosso, Vernazza, Corniglia, Manarola, and Riomaggiore) is what are *not* here—automobiles, large-scale development, or much else by way of 20th- and 21st-century interference. The pastimes in the Cinque Terre don't get much more elaborate than **walking** ★★★ from one lovely village to another along trails that afford spectacular vistas; plunging into the Mediterranean or basking in the sun on your own waterside boulder; and indulging in the tasty local food and wine.

Not too surprisingly, these charms have not gone unnoticed, and American tourists especially have been coming here in increasing numbers. In summer (weekends are worst), you are likely to find yourself in a long procession of like-minded, English-speaking trekkers making their way down the coast or elbow to elbow with day-trippers from an excursion boat. Even so, the Cinque Terre manages to escape the hubbub that afflicts so many coastlines, and even a short stay here is likely to reward you with one of the most memorable seaside visits of a lifetime.

ESSENTIALS

GETTING THERE   **By Train**   You often cannot coast directly into the Cinque Terre towns, as they are served only by the most local of train runs. You'll generally find that you must change trains in nearby **La Spezia** (one or two per hour; 8 min.) at the coast's

① 'Crinale' Footpath
② 'Azzurro' Footpath

SP1
Brugnato
A12
E80
0   2 mi
0   2 km
SP10
Beverino
San Cipriano
SP34
Montale
Pignone
SP1
SP10
To Pisa
Levanto
SP43
Sanctuary of Soviore
SP38
Pian di Barca
SP17
Ricco del Golfo di Spezia
M. Malpertuso ①
Monterosso
Sanctuary of Reggio
SP15
Buon Viaggio
Vernazza
Punta Mesca
San Bernardino
② M. Marvede
SP51
Corniglia
Sanctuary of Salute
Sanctuary of Montenero
La Spezia
Gulf of Genoa
Manarola
Volastra
Riomaggiore
Telegrafo
Biassa
Gulf of Spezia
Fezzano
Schiara
Cinque Terre
Ligurian Sea
area of detail
Rome ★
Portovenere
Isola Palmaria
I. del Tino

south tip, or in **Pisa** (about six daily; 1¼ hr.). This is true of the one or two trains per hour from **Rome** (total 4½–5 hr.) or the hourly ones from **Florence** (2½ hr.). There are one or two direct trains per hour from **Genoa** to La Spezia (1 hr., 40 min.); many more from Genoa require a change in Levanto or Sestri Levanto, both a bit farther north up the coast from Monterosso.

By Car   The fastest route is via Autostrada A12 from Genoa, exiting at the Corrodano exit for Monterosso. The trip from Genoa to Corrodano takes less than an hour, while the much shorter 15km (9¼-mile) trip from Corrodano to Monterosso (via Levanto) is made along a narrow road and can take about half that amount of time. Coming from the south or Florence, get off Autostrada A12 at La Spezia and follow CINQUE TERRE signs.

By Boat   Navagazione Golfo dei Poeti (© **0187-732-987** or 0187-730-336; www. navigazionegolfodeipoeti.it) runs erratic service from the **Riviera Levante towns,** as well as from **Genoa,** mid-June to mid-September, though these tend to be day cruises stopping for anywhere from 1 to 3 hours in Vernazza (see description below) before returning (though you can usually talk them into not picking you up again for a day or three).

By Foot The best way to see the Cinque Terre is to devote a whole day and hoof it along the trails. See "Exploring the Cinque Terre," below, for details.

By Train Local trains make frequent runs (two to three per hour) between the five towns; some stop only in Monterosso and Riomaggiore, so check the posted "Partenze" schedule at the station first to be sure you're catching a local. One-way tickets between any two towns are available, including one version that is good for 6 hours of travel in one direction, meaning you can use it to town-hop—or you can buy a day ticket good for unlimited trips.

By Car A narrow, one-lane coast road hugs the mountainside above the towns, but all the centers are closed to cars; parking is difficult and, where possible, expensive.

There are public **parking** facilities; Riomaggiore and Manarola both have small parking facilities just above their towns and minibuses to carry you and your luggage down. The cheapest option is the big open dirt lot right on the seafront in Monterosso. The priciest is the garage in Riomaggiore.

By Boat From the port in Monterosso, **Navagazione Golfo dei Poeti** (✆ **0187-732-987** or 0187-730-336; www.navigazionegolfodeipoeti.it) makes 8 to 10 trips a day between Manarola and Riomaggiore (a 25-min. trip), all stopping in Vernazza and half of them stopping in Manarola as well.

VISITOR INFORMATION The **tourist office** for the Cinque Terre is underneath the train station of Monterosso, Via Fegina 38 (✆ **0187-817-506;** fax 0187-817-825). It's open Easter to early November and again at Christmas daily 9:30 to 11:30am and 3:30 to 7:30pm. Even when it's closed or in the off season, posted outside the office is a rather handy display of phone numbers and other useful info, from hotels to ferries.

Useful websites for the region include www.cinqueterrenet.com, www.cinqueterre.it, www.aptcinqueterre.sp.it, and www.monterossonet.com.

EXPLORING THE CINQUE TERRE

Aside from swimming and soaking in the atmosphere of unspoiled fishing villages, the most popular activity in the Cinque Terre is **hiking from one village to the next** ★ along centuries-old goat paths. Trails plunge through vineyards and groves of olive and lemon trees and hug seaside cliffs, affording heart-stopping views of the coast and the romantic little villages looming ahead in the distance. The well-signposted walks from village to village range in difficulty and length, but as a loose rule, they get longer and steeper—and more rewarding—the farther north you go. Depending on your pace and how long you stop in each village for a fortifying glass of *sciacchetrà,* the local sweet wine, you can make the trip between Monterosso, at the northern end of the Cinque Terre, and Riomaggiore, at the southern end, in about 5 hours. You should decide whether you want to walk north to south or south to north. Walking south means tackling the worst trail first, which you may prefer, since you'll get it out of the way and things will get easier as the day goes on and you start to tire. Heading north, the trail gets progressively harder between each town, so perhaps you might like this if you want to walk just until you get tired and then hop the train.

The walk from **Monterosso to Vernazza** is the most arduous and takes 1½ hours, on a trail that makes several steep ascents and descents (on the portion outside Monterosso, you'll pass beneath funicular-like cars that transport grapes down the steep hillsides). The leg from **Vernazza to Corniglia** is also demanding and takes another 1½ hours, plunging into some dense forests and involving some lengthy ascents, but is among the prettiest and most rewarding stretches. Part of the path between **Corniglia and Manarola,** about 45 minutes apart, follows a level grade above a long stretch of beach, tempting you to break stride and take a dip. From **Manarola to Riomaggiore,** it's easy going for about half an hour along a partially paved path known as the Via dell'Amore, so named for its romantic vistas (great to do at sunset).

Since all the villages are linked by rail, you can hike as many portions of the itinerary as you wish and take the train to your next destination. Trails also cut through the forested, hilly terrain inland from the coast, much of which is protected as a nature preserve; the tourist office in Monterosso can provide maps.

BEACHES The only sandy beach in the Cinque Terre is the crowded strand in **Monterosso,** on much of which you will be asked to pay about 10€ to 15€ per day for two chairs and an umbrella.

Guvano Beach is a long, isolated, pebbly strand that stretches just north of Corniglia and is popular with nudists (almost entirely men, many of whom are happy it's almost entirely men). You can clamber down to it from the Vernazza-Corniglia path, but the drop is steep and treacherous. A weird alternative route takes you through an unused train tunnel that you enter near the north end of Corniglia's train station. You must ring the bell at the gated entrance and wait for a custodian to arrive to unburden you of 2.50€, good for passage through the dank, dimly lit 1.6km-long (1-mile) gallery that emerges onto the beach at the far end.

There's also a long, rocky beach to the south of **Corniglia,** and it is easily accessible by some quick downhill scrambles from the Corniglia to Manrola path. **Riomaggiore** has a tiny crescent-shaped pebble beach reached by a series of stone steps on the south side of the harbor. Everywhere else, you'll be swimming off piers or rocks.

MONTEROSSO

The Cinque Terre's largest village seems incredibly busy compared to its sleepier neighbors, but it's not without its charms. Monterosso is actually two towns—a bustling, character-filled Old Town built behind the harbor, as well as a relaxed resort that stretches along the Cinque Terre's only **sand beach** and is home to the train station and the tiny regional tourist office (upon exiting the station, turn left and head through the tunnel for the Old Town; turn right for the newer town and Il Gigante restaurant; see below).

The region's most famous art treasure is here: Housed in the **Convento dei Cappuccini,** perched on a hillock in the center of the Old Town, is a *crucifixion* by Anthony Van Dyck, the Flemish master who worked for a time in nearby Genoa (you can visit the convent daily 9am–noon and 4–7pm). While you will find the most conveniences in citified Monterosso, you'll have a more rustic experience if you stay in one of the other four villages.

Where to Stay

Aside from the traditional options below, you might try your luck at booking one of six spanking new rooms at **A Ca du Gigante** (Via IV Novembre; © **0187-817-401;** www. ilgigantecinqueterre.it; 160€ for a double). The theme of each room is based on famous rocks throughout Italian naval history, as the hotel itself is hosted by the promontory of the same name (Il Gigante).

Albergo Amici ★★ The aptly named Amici is unpretentious and extremely friendly, reached by a curving marble staircase lined with flowerpots and facing a delightful garden. Although the hotel is not on the seafront (which is only a few minutes away by foot), many of the rooms overlook the town and the sea beyond, and the location on a narrow street in the Old Town ensures quiet. The rooms are simply but tastefully furnished in blond-wood contemporary pieces and open to balconies through French doors. Like most hotels in Monterosso, the Amici requires, from June 15 to September 15, that guests choose either half- or full board. Meals, served in a cavernous dining room, are adequate, but you'd do well to opt for the half-board plan so you can sample other restaurants throughout the region. Once a week, the Amici offers a candlelit dinner—ask when booking.

Via Buranco 36, 19016 Monterosso al Mare (SP). ☎ 0187-817-544. Fax 0187-817-424. www.hotelamici.it. 40 units, 37 with private bathroom in room (3 singles each have a private bathroom in hall). 85€–135€ double with private bathroom; 130€–184€ double with half-board; 150€–205€ double with full-board. Buffet breakfast 10€. MC, V. Parking 9€ in nearby public lot. Closed Nov 3–Dec 22 and Jan 7 to around Feb 20. **Amenities:** Restaurant; bar; children's center (Ping-Pong and billiards in garden). *In room:* A/C, TV, hair dryer.

Hotel Pasquale ★★ (Value)   The Pasquale gives you spectacular views for the money, and the family who runs it will make you feel extremely welcome. It's built into a cliff face—some of which shows through the walls inside—right at the port of the Old Town, so all rooms overlook the beach and sea. The green tile floors support simple beds and basic, built-in units. Rooms are midsize, but bathrooms are cramped. Families will appreciate quad no. 3, with its two separate bedrooms. Note that it is also right next to the train tracks and the resulting noise, most of which is kept out by a closed window, but the view from the window makes it all worth it.

Via Fegina 4, 19016 Monterosso al Mare (SP). ☎ 0187-817-477. Fax 0187-817-056. www.pasini.com. 15 units. 150€–195€ double; 175€–220€ triple; 200€–260€ quad. Rates include breakfast. AE, MC, V. Parking 9€ in nearby public lot. Closed Dec 6–26. **Amenities:** Bar; concierge; room service. *In room:* A/C, TV, hair dryer, Internet, minibar.

Where to Dine

All the towns in the Cinque Terre have little shops like **Enoteca Internazionale ★★**, where you can taste and purchase the local wines by the bottle, or simply enjoy a glass of Cinque Terre DOC (starting at around 2€) or *sciacchetrà* (3€) on the premises. The selection here, in the bustling part of old Monterosso, also includes olive oil pressed just down the street and jars of homemade pesto.

Focaccerio Il Frontoio LIGHT FARE   Many patrons say this bustling shop, with a takeout counter and a few tables where you can dine on the premises, serves some of the best focaccia in Liguria. That's quite a claim, but suffice it to say that the freshly baked bread (especially when topped with fresh vegetables) is heavenly and provides one of the best fast meals around.

Via Gioberti 1 (off Via Roma). ☎ 0187-818-333. Pizza and focaccia from 1.50€. No credit cards. Fri–Wed 9am–2pm and 4–7pm. Closed Oct–Mar.

Ristorante Miky ★ (Kids) SEAFOOD   The first thing to strike you at this friendly and florid restaurant is a giant scallop shell, loaded with *trenette alla pescatrice* (homemade pasta with mixed shellfish) that waiters carry out to hungry patrons. The shells are actually made of dough, and in fact, all of the dishes are served in pottery or some other sort of creative presentation. Adding to the charm is the restaurant's position right on the beach, set in a blooming garden. The Defina family's specialty is *pesce al sale,* which is your choice of seafood covered in salt and slowly cooked in a wood-burning oven.

Via Fegina 104. ☎ 0187-817-608. Reservations recommended. Primi 6€–15€; secondi 7€–18€. AE, DC, MC, V. Daily noon–3pm and 7:30pm to late. Closed Tues in winter.

Monterosso's nightlife centers on the Old Town. Bookending the bocce ball court between the elevated railroad tracks and the beach are a **free outdoor disco** Saturday nights in summer and, at the far end, **Bar Il Casello,** Lungo Ferrovia 70 (no phone), with outdoor tables and beer on tap. Under the railroad tracks and in town itself, you'll find **Fast,** Via Roma 13 (no phone), a pub plastered with movie posters and serving the cheapest beer in town.

VERNAZZA

It's hard not to fall in love with this pretty village. Tall houses cluster around a natural harbor (where you can swim among the fishing boats) and beneath a **castle** built high atop a rocky promontory that juts into the sea (this castle—which is nothing special—is open Mar–Oct daily 10am–6:30pm; admission 1€). The center of town is waterside **Piazza Marconi,** itself a sea of cafe tables. The only Vernazza drawback is that too much good press has turned it into the Cinque Terre's ghetto of American tourists, in summer especially.

Where to Stay

Besides the Barbara (see below), you can rent one of **Trattoria Gianni Franzi**'s 23 rooms spread across two buildings; some come with a bathroom, some with excellent views up the coast, all with a steep climb up the stairlike streets of the town and then up the stairs within the building. No matter what room you get, it's worth the money. Rates are 65€ for a double with a shared bathroom, 80€ for a double with a shared bathroom and a sea view, 100€ for a double with a private bathroom and a sea view, and 140€ for a triple with all the luxuries. Call ✆ **0187-821-003** or fax 0187-812-228 to book, or when you arrive in town, stop by the trattoria's harborside bar at Piazza Marconi 5 (which is closed Wed except during the busy summer months). They're closed January 8 to March 8.

Albergo Barbara (Value) This is the sort of place threatened by overpopularity and subsequent development of former backwaters like Vernazza: an exceedingly basic but clean and cheap hotel in a stellar location, in the center of the tiny harbor piazza with views over the fishing boats and Mediterranean. This pleasant, bare-bones *pensione* on the two upper floors of a tall old house on the waterfront is at the top of four flights of broad stone steps (63 of 'em), and from there, many of the rooms are reached by an additional climb up a ladderlike spiral staircase. These efforts are rewarded by an eagle's-eye view of Vernazza's harbor from some rooms, and a partial view in others. Accommodations, though basic, are not without charm—there's a pleasant smattering of homey furniture, cool tile floors, and a sink. If no one answers the buzzer, step across the square to the **Taverna del Capitano** restaurant to ask about a room.

Piazza Marconi 30, 19018 Vernazza. ✆ **0187-812-398.** www.albergobarbara.it. 9 units. 50€ small double upstairs with shared bathroom; 60€ double with private bathroom down the corridor; 65€ double with private bathroom; 100€ large double with private bathroom and sea view. No breakfast. No credit cards. Closed late Nov to mid-Feb. *In room:* No phone.

Where to Dine

Al Castello LIGURIAN Operating as a bar all day and a restaurant at mealtimes, this establishment's reed-shaded terrace is set up against the medieval castle walls with pendulous fishing nets and stunning, vertiginous views over Vernazza's cove. The service can be chilly and the food is nothing special—the lasagne with pesto and the grilled fresh fish are fine—but the view is spectacular, especially in the summertime around 7:30 to 8pm, when you get to watch the sun set over the water. Book ahead, especially in summer, for the best views. The only drawback to the otherwise-idyllic setting: 10 minutes of endless stair climbing to get here.

Via Guidoni 56. ℂ **0187-812-296.** Reservations recommended. Primi 6€–10€; secondi 8€–13€. No credit cards. Thurs–Tues noon–2:30pm and 7 or 7:30–10pm. Closed Oct 26–Apr 24.

Gambero Rosso ★★ SEAFOOD/LIGURIAN It would be hard to find a more pleasant way to take in the scene on Vernazza's lively harborside square than to do so while enjoying the homemade pasta, fresh fish, and aromatic herbs on the terrace at this excellent restaurant. You will also be content ordering one or two choices from the a la carte menu—either way, you can explore some hard-to-find dishes such as *acciughe* (fresh, local anchovies) baked with onions and potatoes, *ravioli di pesci* (a delicate fish ravioli), and *muscoli ripieni* (*muscoli* is the Ligurian word for mussels, known as *cozze* elsewhere in Italy; here they are stuffed with fresh herbs). Another specialty, the *grigliata mista* of freshly caught fish, is excellent. Any meal should be followed by the house dessert, *sciacchetrà* (the local sweet wine), accompanied by homemade fried sweet milk. The stone-walled, stone-floored, timber-ceiling dining room is a pleasant alternative when the terrace is closed. Gambero Rosso's owners also rent out four apartments. (You can book them online at www.toninobasso.com.)

Piazza Marconi 7. ℂ **0187-812-265.** www.ristorantegamberorosso.net. Reservations recommended. Primi 7€–10€; secondi 11€–22€; AE, DC, MC, V. Tues–Sun 12:30–4pm and 7:15–10:30pm (sometimes open Mon in summer). Closed Dec 15–Mar 1.

CORNIGLIA

The quietest village in the Cinque Terre is isolated by its position midway down the coast, its hilltop location high above the open sea, and its little harbor. Whether you arrive by boat, train, or the trail from the south, you'll have to climb more than 300 steps to reach the village proper (arriving by trail from the north is the only way to avoid these stairs), which is an enticing maze of little walkways overshadowed by tall houses.

Once there, though, the views over the surrounding vineyards and up and down the coastline are stupendous—for the best outlook, walk to the end of the narrow main street to a belvedere that is perched between the sea and sky. More than these vistas, Corniglia is also the village most likely to offer you a glimpse into life in the Cinque Terre the way it was until a couple of decades ago.

Where to Stay

Da Cecio ★★ ⓕ Finds Elia and her son Carmelo rent out the second floor of their old stone house in the countryside just 2 minutes outside Corniglia (on the road to Vernazza) and offer what I consider one of the Cinque Terre's most pleasant inns. The rooms are big, bright, and stylish, with dark-wood veneer headboards and furnishings. Most feature great views over the sea, the olive groves, and the hilltop town (nos. 2 and 6 are on a corner with those vistas out both windows), and they all have smallish bathrooms. The sun-drenched rooftop deck or flowery terrace downstairs (which, at mealtimes, serves as an outdoor dining room for the excellent restaurant; see below) is the perfect place to idle away an afternoon. If a room is not available here, one of the proprietors will take you down to one of their four pleasant rooms in the village. The only drawback to the annex is that, as in most small Italian towns, the nearby churchbell can be loud.

Via Serra 58, 19010 Corniglia. ℂ **0187-812-043.** Fax 0187-812-138. www.cecio5terre.com. 12 units (4 are in a *dipendenza* nearby). 60€ double; 80€ triple. Breakfast 5€. MC, V. Closed Nov. **Amenities:** Ligurian restaurant (see review below); bar. *In room:* Hair dryer, no phone.

Osteria a Cantina de Mananan ★★ LIGURIAN   The pleasure of being in hilltop Corniglia is well worth the trek up to town, especially if the visit includes a meal at this tiny restaurant carved into the stone cellars of an ancient house. Agostino and Marianne, the husband-and-wife owners and chefs, draw on age-old local recipes and use only the freshest ingredients in their preparations; the results, posted on a blackboard in the one handsome vaulted room furnished with granite tables, are wonderful. Fresh vegetables from gardens just outside the village are grilled and mixed with herbs and smoked mozzarella as a simple appetizer, or there's the variety in *antipasto misto mare,* which can be followed by any of the hand-rolled pastas topped with homemade pesto or porcini. You can continue in this nonmeat direction with a plate of mussels, grilled fish, or fresh anchovies stuffed with herbs, but the few meat dishes on the daily menu are also excellent—especially the *coniglio nostrano,* rabbit roasted in a white sauce. Local wines accompany the meals.

Via Fieschi 117, Corniglia. (𝒞 **0187-821-166** or 0187-812-320. Reservations recommended. Primi 7.50€–8.50€; secondi 8.50€–13€. No credit cards. Wed–Mon 12:30–2:30pm and 7:30–9:30pm. Closed Nov.

Ristorante Cecio ★ LIGURIAN   Like the inn upstairs, the stone-walled, woodbeamed dining room and flower-filled terrace overlooking olive groves provide extremely pleasant surroundings. A nice selection of simple, homemade fare emerges from the family-run kitchen, including fresh pasta with a rich pesto or walnut sauce or *alla scogliera,* topped with fresh clams and mussels. Meat and fish are grilled over an open hearth. Outside of peak mealtimes, you can sit on the terrace and enjoy the view over a beer or glass of the house wine.

Via Serra 58, Corniglia. (𝒞 **0187-812-043.** www.cecio5terre.com. Primi 6€–15€; secondi 6€–18€. MC, V. Thurs–Tues (daily in summer) noon–3:30pm and 7–11pm. Closed Nov.

MANAROLA

Not as busy as nearby Riomaggiore or as quaint as its neighbor Corniglia, Manarola is a near-vertical cluster of tall houses that seems to rise piggyback up the hills on either side of the harbor. In fact, in a region with no shortage of heart-stopping views, one of the most amazing sights is the descent into the town of Manarola on the path from Corniglia: From this perspective, the hill-climbing houses seem to merge into one another to form a row of skyscrapers. Despite these urban associations, Manarola is a delightfully rural village where fishing and winemaking are big business. The region's major **wine cooperative,** Cooperativa Agricoltura di Riomaggiore, Manarola, Corniglia, Vernazza e Monterosso, made up of 300 local producers, is here; call (𝒞 **0187-920-435** for information about tours of its modern (est. 1982) facilities.

Where to Stay

Manarola's **Ostello 5 Terre** ((𝒞 **0187-920-215;** fax 0187-920-218; www.cinqueterre.net/ ostello) offers cheap accommodations: 20€ to 23€ for beds in six-bed dorm rooms or roughly the same price per bed in six-bed family rooms with private bathroom—but you gotta rent the whole room. Curfew is midnight in the off season, 1am in summer, though, frankly, Manarola shuts down well before then. The hostel offers services such as kayak, bike, and snorkel rental; Internet access; and cheap laundry. It's closed January 6 to February 15 and November 4 to December 6. Especially in high season, it is often necessary to book a week in advance.

Marina Piccola ★★ This cozy inn on the harbor in Manarola is a favorite with many travelers to the Cinque Terre, and it's easy to see why. Part of the premises, including the glass-enclosed seafood restaurant where you may be required to take half- or full board in the busy summer months, is right on the water, and many of the guest rooms in the tall house across the street have sea views as well. Decor is a cut above that of most inns in the region. The charming rooms have old prints, homey faded floor tiles, light pine-veneer furnishings, and a predominance of Santorini colors of white and pale. Rooms in the other building (the next one up the hill, containing the hotel lobby) are done in more of a country style, with nicer heavy wooden furnishings, flower-edged wallpaper, and fancy scrolled headboards. My only quibble with this otherwise pleasant hostelry is that the service can be somewhat scatterbrained and, occasionally, downright unfriendly.

Via Discovolo 38, 19010 Manarola. ② **0187-920-103.** Fax 0187-920-966. www.hotelmarinapiccola.com. 13 units. 115€ double. Half-board 90€ per person in double. Rates include breakfast. AE, DC, MC, V. Closed Nov. **Amenities:** Restaurant (local cuisine); bar. *In room:* A/C, TV.

Where to Dine

Aristide ★ LIGURIAN In this old house up the hill from the harbor (just below the train station), diners are accommodated on a couple of levels of small rooms, as well as on a covered terrace across the street. Many of Aristide's patrons live in the Cinque Terre or take the train here from nearby La Spezia, because this long-standing trattoria is known for its heaping platters of grilled fish, *gamberoni* (jumbo prawns), and *frittura di mare* (a selection of fried seafood). The *antipasta di mare* includes a nice selection of octopus, clams, sardines, and other local catches and serves well as a lighter meal. The house's white wine is from the hills above the town, and if the owner is in a good mood, he may come around after your dinner proffering a complimentary glass of *sciacchetrà,* the local dessert wine.

Via Discovolo 290. ② **0187-920-000.** Reservations recommended. Primi 6€–9€; secondi 8€–18€; fixed-price fish menu 36€ with wine. AE, DC, MC, V. Tues–Sun noon–2:30 and 7–9pm.

RIOMAGGIORE

Riomaggiore clings to the vestiges of the Cinque Terre's rustic ways while making some concessions to the modern world. The old fishing quarter has expanded in recent years, and Riomaggiore now has some sections of new houses and apartment blocks. This blend of the old and new works well—Riomaggiore is bustling and prosperous and makes the most of a lovely setting, with houses clinging to the hills that drop into the sea on either side of town. Many of the lanes end in seaside belvederes.

From the parking garage, follow the main drag down; from the train station, exit and turn right to head through the tunnel for the main part of town (or, from the station, take off left up the brick stairs to walk the Via dell'Amore to Manarola).

That tunnel and the main drag meet at the base of an elevated terrace that holds the train tracks. From here, a staircase leads down to a tiny fishing harbor, off the left of which heads a rambling path that, after a few hundred meters, leads to a pleasant little **beach** of large pebbles.

Where to Stay

Riomaggiore is a good bet for a room in a more genuine fishing-village Cinque Terre town (Monterosso is a bit more built up), especially in the off season, as both the town's inns remain open year-round, and Riomaggiore is home to two rental outfits that, between them, rent dozens of rooms and apartments across the village.

There are lots of folks renting out rooms illegally in the Cinque Terre (the rooms are fine—usually—and the price is right; it's just that they don't have the permits to do this and the properties are not inspected by the proper authorities). The people we've listed here, however, go to the trouble of filing the paperwork with the authorities and submitting themselves to oversight, which also means that, by going through them, you'll be assured a certain guarantee of quality.

Brothers Luciano and Roberto **Fazioli,** Via Colombo 94 (© **0187-920-822;** fax 0187-920-904; robertofazioli@libero.it), rent about two dozen rooms and apartments all over town, operating out of a pink stripe–awninged shop front halfway down the main street. (One of them is likely to come out and greet you if you walk past the office carrying a bag.) While the rooms vary considerably in size, views, and furnishings, most have newly installed bathrooms and cooking facilities. One of our favorite rooms, on the top of a house in the oldest part of town, opens onto a private rooftop terrace with views over Riomaggiore to the sea. Several choice apartments inhabit harborside houses, two on top floors with small terraces, and another on the ground floor with a chic new kitchen, bathroom, and a sitting area from which you can hear the waves lapping against the rocks below. Some apartments have satellite TV, some terraces, some sea views. Call ahead or come early to luck into the perfect one. The office is open daily from 9am to 8pm. Room rates vary from 20€ to 60€ per person, depending on size and style of room (the pricier ones have sea views or are on the water), number of people, and how long you stay—but if you tell them you're a Frommer's reader and show them this book, you can get a 5% discount in high season, 10% discount in low season.

Their friend Mario Franceschetti runs a hostel and above-board rental room business called **Mar Mar,** Via Colombo 25B (at the harbor end of town; ©/fax **0187-920-932;** www.5terre-marmar.com). A bed in a coed dorm costs 20€. Then there are eight apartments that sleep two to six people (65€–90€ for a double; 80€–120€ for the larger apartments; prices depend on how many are in the room), and six rooms in a nearby B&B (© **0187-920-773;** 60€–80€). Some of the rental units, and all the B&B rooms, come with TV and bathroom; some rental units have kitchenettes. Mar Mar's office is open daily from 8:30am to 12:30pm and 2:30 to 7pm.

Locanda Ca dei Duxi This is one of the more established outfits in the center, constantly expanding their little hospitality empire and offering more hotel-style amenities than most rental rooms around, spread across two *locandas* (the original six-room 18th-c. building and a five-room inn across the street, which opened in summer 2001), three rental rooms, and several apartments. All of the midsize rooms are simple, with new modular furnishings, tile floors, and firm wood-slat beds. On the top floor, room nos. 5 and 6 have exposed beams and a bit of castle view.

Via Colombo 36/Via Pecunia 19, 19017 Riomaggiore (SP). © **0187-920-036** or 338-841-8175. Fax 0187-920-036. www.duxi.it. 16 units, plus 3 in-house apts. 60€–130€. Rates include breakfast. AE, DC, MC, V. Parking 7€. **Amenities:** Room service. *In room:* A/C, TV, hair dryer (on request), minibar.

Villa Argentina The only full-fledged hotel in Riomaggiore is in the newer section of town, on a hillside about a 5-minute walk (up a lot of stairs) from the center. This location affords astonishing views, which you can enjoy from most of the guest rooms, and provides a nice retreat from the tourist-crowded main street and harbor. A breezy, arbor-shaded terrace and a bar area decorated by local artists off the lobby are the places to relax. And while the tile-floored rooms upstairs will not overwhelm you with their character, they are large and pleasant, if blandly furnished, with ceiling fans and (all except room nos. 4–6 and 10) balconies featuring views over the town to the sea. The hoteliers also offer apartments accommodating two to six people.

Via de Gaspari 187, 19017 Riomaggiore. ℂ/fax **0187-920-213.** www.hotelvillargentina.com. 15 units. 94€–140€ double; 45€–50€ per person in apts. Rates include breakfast. MC, V. Parking 10€. **Amenities:** Ligurian restaurant nearby; bar; concierge; room service; nearby sauna; watersports equipment/rentals. *In room:* TV, hair dryer, no phone.

Where to Dine

La Lanterna ★ SEAFOOD/LIGURIAN   From a table on the terrace here, perched only a few meters above Riomaggiore's snug harbor, you can hear the waves lap against the rocks and watch the local fishermen mend their nets. Seafood, of course, dominates the menu, with many unusual Ligurian-style dishes, such as *spaghetti al scoglio* (spaghetti with mussels and shrimp in a white-wine sauce) or *spaghetti ai ricci di mare* (with sea urchins). The antipasto of shrimp, smoked tuna, and grilled swordfish is excellent and can suffice as an entree; you should, however, make room for one of the house specialties, *chiche*—homemade gnocchi filled with seafood and topped with a spicy tomato sauce.

Riomaggiore. ℂ **0187-920-589.** Reservations recommended. Primi 6€–7.50€; secondi 9€–19€. AE, DC, MC, V. Daily 11am–midnight. Closed Nov.

Fast Facts

1 FAST FACTS: NORTHERN ITALY

AREA CODES The **country code** for Italy is **39. City codes** (for example, Milan's is 02, Venice's is 041) are incorporated into the numbers themselves. Therefore, you must dial the entire number, *including the initial zero,* when calling from *anywhere* outside or inside Italy and even within the same town. To call Milan from the States, you must dial **011-39-02,** then the local phone number. Phone numbers in Italy can range anywhere from 6 to 12 digits in length.

BUSINESS HOURS General open hours for **stores, offices,** and **churches** are from 9:30am to noon or 1pm and again from 3 or 3:30pm to 7:30pm. That early afternoon shutdown is the *riposo,* the Italian siesta. Most stores close all day Sunday and many also on Monday (morning only or all day). Some shops, especially grocery stores, also close Thursday afternoons. Some services and business offices are open to the public only in the morning. Traditionally, **museums** are closed Monday, and though some of the biggest stay open all day long, many close for *riposo* or are only open in the morning (9am–2pm is popular). Some churches open earlier in the morning, but the largest often stay open all day. **Banks** tend to be open Monday through Friday from 8:30am to 1:30pm and 2:30 to 3:30pm or 3 to 4pm.

DRINKING LAWS There is no legal drinking age in Italy, in the sense that a young person of any age can legally consume alcohol, but a person must be 16 years old in order to be served alcohol in a restaurant or a bar. Similarly, laws in other countries that exist in order to stamp out public drunkenness simply aren't quite as necessary in Italy, where binge-drinking is unusual. Noise is the primary concern to city officials, and so bars generally close at 2am at the latest, though alcohol is commonly served in clubs after that. Supermarkets generally carry beer, wine, and sometimes spirits.

DRIVING RULES See "Getting There and Getting Around," p. 58.

ELECTRICITY Italy operates on a 220 volts AC (50 cycles) system, as opposed to the United States' 110 volts AC (60 cycles) system. You'll need a simple adapter plug (to make the American flat pegs fit the Italian round holes) and, unless your appliance is dual-voltage (as some hair dryers, travel irons, and laptops are), an electrical currency converter. You can pick up the hardware at electronics stores, travel specialty stores, luggage shops, airports, and from Magellan's catalog (www.magellans.com).

EMBASSIES & CONSULATES The **Australian Embassy** is in Rome at Via Antonio Bosio 5 (© **06-8527-21;** www.italy.embassy.gov.au). Australia's consulate in Milan is at Via Borgogna 2 (3rd floor; © **02-777-041;** fax 02-7770-4242).

The **Canadian** Embassy is in Rome at Via Zara 30 (© **06-85444-3937;** www.canada.it). The Canadian consulate in Milan is at Via Vittor Pisani 19 (© **02-67581**), open Monday through Friday from 8:30am to 12:30pm and 1:30 to 4pm.

The **New Zealand Embassy** is in Rome at Via Clittuno 44 (☏ **06-853-7501**; www.nzembassy.com/italy). New Zealand's Milan consulate is at Via Terragio 17 (☏ **02-721-70001**; fax 02-4801-2577), open Monday through Friday from 8:30am to 12:45pm and 1:45 to 5pm.

The **U.K. Embassy** is in Rome at Via XX Settembre 80a (☏ **06-4220-0001**; fax 06-4220-2334; www.britain.it), open Monday through Friday from 9:15am to 1:30pm. The **U.K. consulate in Milan** is at Via San Paolo 7 (☏ **02-723-001**; fax 02-869-2405). It's open Monday to Friday 9:30am to 12:30pm and 2:30 to 4:30pm.

The **U.S. Embassy** is in Rome at Via Vittorio Veneto 119a (☏ **06-46-741**; fax 06-488-2672 or 06-4674-2217; www.usembassy.it). The **U.S. consulate in Milan**—for passport and consular services but *not* for visas—is at Via Principe Amadeo 2/10 (☏ **02-290-351**; fax 02-2900-1165), open to drop-ins Monday through Friday from 9am to 12:30pm. Afternoons 2 to 4:30pm, the consulate is open by appointment only; call ahead.

EMERGENCIES   Dial ☏ **113** for any emergency. You can also call ☏ **112** for the *carabinieri* (police), ☏ **118** for an ambulance, or ☏ **115** for the fire department. If your car breaks down, dial ☏ **116** for roadside aid courtesy of the Automotive Club of Italy.

GASOLINE (PETROL)   *Benzina* (gas or petrol) is even more expensive in Italy than in the rest of Europe. Even a small rental car guzzles 40€ to 60€ for a fill-up. Unleaded gas is *senza piombo.* An important thing to remember is that petrol stations in Italy rarely accept U.S. credit cards in the after-hour machines, which will usually take only cash and Italian ATM/debit cards. For that reason, it's always wise to stop and fill up if you see an open gas station. For more information, see "Gasoline" in chapter 3 (p. 61).

HOLIDAYS   Banks, government offices, post offices, and many stores, restaurants, and museums in Italy are closed on the following legal national holidays: January 1 (New Year's Day), January 6 (Epiphany), Easter Sunday and the following Monday (called *pasquetta,* or Little Easter), April 25 (Liberation Day), May 1 (Labor Day), August 15 (Feast of the Assumption), November 1 (All Saint's Day), December 8 (Immaculate Conception), and December 25 and December 26 (Santo Stefano).

For more information on holidays, see "Calendar of Events" in chapter 3.

HOSPITALS   In Milan, the **Ospedale Maggiore Policlinico** (☏ **02-5503-3103**; www.policlinico.mi.it) is centrally located a 5-minute walk southeast of the Duomo at Via Francesco Sforza 35 (Metro: Duomo or Missori). In Venice, the **Ospedale Civile Santi Goivanni e Paolo** (☏ **041-785111**), on Campo Santi Giovanni e Paolo, has English-speaking staff and provides emergency service 24 hours a day (*vaporetto:* San Toma).

INSURANCE   Italy may be one of the safer places you can travel in the world, but accidents and setbacks can and do happen, from lost luggage to car crashes. For information on traveler's insurance, trip cancelation insurance, and medical insurance while traveling, please visit www.frommers.com/planning.

INTERNET ACCESS   Cybercafes are in healthy supply in most Italian cities. In smaller towns, you may have a bit of trouble, but increasingly hotels are offering Wi-Fi throughout the rooms, although those in rural areas are not as likely to have a high-speed connection. In a pinch, hostels, local libraries, and often pubs will have some sort of terminal for access. For getting online in Milan and Venice, see their own "Fast Facts" sections.

LANGUAGE   Italians may not be quite as polished with their English as some of their European counterparts, but they've been hosting Anglophones for a long time now, and English is a regular part of any business day. In very rural parts, slow and clear speech, a little gesticulating, and a smile will go a long way. In Venice and other cities, you will probably be the 20th English-speaking tourist they've spoken with that day. In a pinch, please refer to "Useful Terms" (p. 441) for some vacation essentials.

LEGAL AID Your embassy or consulate can provide a list of foreign attorneys, should you encounter legal problems in Italy. In criminal cases, if you cannot afford an attorney, the local court will provide one for you.

MAIL At press time, the cost of sending a postcard or letter up to 20 grams, or a little less than an ounce, was 0.65€ to other European countries, 0.85€ to North America, and 1€ to Australia and New Zealand. Prices go up incrementally to 5.70€/8.70€/11.70€ for letters weighing up to 500 grams, or nearly 1 pound. For a full table, visit www.poste.it; there is an English version.

NEWSPAPERS & MAGAZINES The *International Herald Tribune* (published by the *New York Times* and with news catering to Americans abroad) and *USA Today* are available at just about every newsstand, even in smaller towns. You can find the *Wall Street Journal Europe,* European editions of *Time* and *Newsweek,* the *Economist,* and just about any major European newspaper or magazine at the larger kiosks. For events guides in English, see each individual city's "Visitor Information" listing.

PASSPORTS See www.frommers.com/planning for information on how to obtain a passport.

See "Embassies & Consulates," above, for whom to contact if you lose yours while traveling in Italy. For other information, please contact the following agencies:

For Residents of Australia Contact the **Australian Passport Information Service**

at ℂ **131-232,** or visit the government website at www.passports.gov.au.

For Residents of Canada Contact the central **Passport Office,** Department of Foreign Affairs and International Trade, Ottawa, ON K1A 0G3 (ℂ **800/567-6868;** www.ppt.gc.ca).

For Residents of Ireland Contact the **Passport Office,** Setanta Centre, Molesworth Street, Dublin 2 (ℂ **01/671-1633;** www.irlgov.ie/iveagh).

For Residents of New Zealand Contact the **Passports Office** at ℂ **0800/225-050** in New Zealand or 04/474-8100, or log on to www.passports.govt.nz.

For Residents of the United Kingdom Visit your nearest passport office, major post office, or travel agency, or contact the **United Kingdom Passport Service** at ℂ **0870/521-0410,** or search its website at www.ukpa.gov.uk.

For Residents of the United States To find your regional passport office, either check the U.S. State Department website or call the **National Passport Information Center** toll-free number (ℂ **877/487-2778**) for automated information.

POLICE For emergencies, call ℂ **113.** Italy has several different police forces, but there are only two you'll most likely ever need to deal with. The first is the urban *polizia,* whose city headquarters is called the *questura* and can help with lost and stolen property. The most useful branch—the cops to go to for serious problems and crimes—is the *carabinieri* (ℂ **112**), a national order-keeping, crime-fighting civilian police force.

SMOKING Smoking has been eradicated from all restaurants and bars in Italy, as well as most hotels. That said, there are still smokers in Italy, and they tend to take the outside tables. Be aware that if you are keen for an outdoor table, you are essentially choosing a seat in the smoking section, and requesting that your neighbor not smoke may not be politely received.

TAXES There's no sales tax added onto the price tag of your purchases, but there is a 19% value-added tax (in Italy: IVA) automatically included in just about everything. For major purchases, you can get this refunded. Some four- and five-star hotels don't include the 13% luxury tax in their quoted prices. Ask when making your reservation.

TIME All of Italy is in the same Western European time zone—that is, GMT plus 1 hour.

TIPPING In **hotels,** a service charge is usually included in your bill. In family-run operations, additional tips are unnecessary and sometimes considered rude. In fancier places with a hired staff, however, you may want to leave a .50€ daily tip for the maid, pay the bellhop or porter 1€ per bag, and tip a helpful concierge 2€ for his or her troubles. In **restaurants,** 10% to 15% is almost always included in the bill—to be sure, ask *"è incluso il servizio?"*—but you can leave up to an additional 10%, especially for good service. At **bars and cafes,** a generous gesture is to leave a 1€ coin per drink on the counter for the barman, though it is hardly expected; if you sit at a table, leave 10% to 15% only if the service is good. **Taxi** drivers expect 10% to 15%.

TOILETS Aside from train stations and petrol stations, where the typical donation to use the toilet is measured in .05€ pieces, public toilets are few and far between in northern Italy. Standard procedure is to enter a café, make sure the bathroom is not "out of order" *(fuori servizio),* and then order a cup of coffee before bolting to the WC. In Venice, the price of using a toilet is a little steeper: about 1€ in the major squares and parking garages, but they usually close at 8pm. It is advisable to always make use of the facilities in the hotel, restaurant, and bar before a long walk around the *calles.*

VISAS Travelers from Australia, Canada, New Zealand, the U.S., and the U.K. can visit Italy for up to 90 days without a visa, and can enter Italy with a valid passport. Visits of more than 90 days may require a visa, but the requirements vary depending on the purpose of your visit.

For more information on visas to visit or stay in Italy, go to the Foreign Ministry's English-language page at **www.esteri. it/visti/index_eng.asp**.

VISITOR INFORMATION In Milan, the main **Azienda di Promozione Turistica (APT) tourist office** is on the north side of Piazza del Duomo at the corner of Via Silvio Pellico (✆ **02-7740-4343;** www.visitamilano.it). Hours are Monday to Saturday from 8:45am to 1pm and 2 to 6pm, Sunday from 9am to 1pm and 2 to 5pm. There is also an office in **Stazione Centrale** (✆ **02-7740-4318**), open Monday to Saturday 9am to 6pm, and Sunday 9am to 1pm and 2 to 5pm.

In Venice, the main tourist office is **Venice Pavilion/Palazzina dei Santi** (✆ **041-529-8710** or 041-522-5150; www. turismovenezia.it), located near the San Marco *vaporetto* stop. Wedged between the Giardinetti Reali, a small green park on the Grand Canal, and the famous Harry's Bar, this tourist office is, frankly, often more interested in running its gift shop than in helping tourists; it's open daily from 10am to 6pm. There's also a small tourist office in Venice's train station.

See "Visitor Information" in each of the chapters for local websites and resources.

WATER Although most Italians take mineral water with their meals, tap water is safe everywhere. (Unsafe sources will be marked *"acqua non potabile."*) In fact, Venice is now urging its citizens to cut back on their plastic-wasting ways and turn back to the tap. If the water comes out cloudy, it's only the calcium or other minerals inherent in a water supply that often comes untreated from fresh springs. Also, the water from fountains in public parks is not only potable, it's often the best water you've ever tasted.

MAJOR AIRLINES THAT SERVICE MILAN'S MALPENSA AIRPORT

Aer Lingus
www.aerlingus.com

Air Canada
www.aircanada.com

Air China
www.airchina.com

Air France
www.airfrance.com

Alitalia
www.alitalia.com

American Airlines
www.aa.com

Austrian Airlines
www.austrianairlines.com

British Airways
www.british-airways.com

Continental Airlines
www.continental.com

Delta Air Lines
www.delta.com

EgyptAir
www.egyptair.com

El Al Airlines
www.el.co.il

Emirates Airlines
www.emirates.com

Finnair
www.finnair.com

Iberia Airlines
www.iberia.com

Japan Airlines
www.jal.co.jp

KLM
www.klm.com

Korean Air
www.koreanair.com

Lufthansa
www.lufthansa.com

Olympic Airlines
www.olympicairlines.com

Singapore Airlines
www.singaporeair.com

Swiss Air
www.swiss.com

Turkish Airlines
www.thy.com

United Airlines
www.united.com

US Airways
www.usairways.com

BUDGET AIRLINES

Aegean Airlines
www.aegeanairlines.com

Aer Lingus
www.aerlingus.com

BMI Baby
www.bmibaby.com

easyJet
www.easyjet.com

Germanwings
www.germanwings.com

Ryanair
www.ryanair.com

SkyEurope
www.skyeurope.com

Vueling
www.vueling.com

FAST FACTS

13

AIRLINE, HOTEL & CAR-RENTAL WEBSITES

Best Western International
www.bestwestern.com

Comfort Inns
www.choicehotels.com

Crowne Plaza Hotels
www.ichotelsgroup.com/crowneplaza

Doubletree Hotels
www.doubletree.com

Four Seasons
www.fourseasons.com

Hilton Hotels
www.hilton.com

Holiday Inn
www.holidayinn.com

Hyatt
www.hyatt.com

InterContinental Hotels & Resorts
www.ichotelsgroup.com

Marriott
www.marriott.com

Sheraton Hotels & Resorts
www.starwoodhotels.com/sheraton

Westin Hotels & Resorts
www.starwoodhotels.com/westin

CAR-RENTAL AGENCIES

Alamo
www.alamo.com

Auto Europe
www.autoeurope.com

Avis
www.avis.com

Budget
www.budget.com

Dollar
www.dollar.com

Enterprise
www.enterprise.com

Europe by Car
www.europebycar.com

Hertz
www.hertz.com

Kemwel (KHA)
www.kemwel.com

Maiellano
www.maiellano.com

National
www.nationalcar.com

Thrifty
www.thrifty.com

FAST FACTS

13

AIRLINE, HOTEL & CAR-RENTAL WEBSITES

Useful Terms

1 THE BASICS

USEFUL ENGLISH-ITALIAN PHRASES

English	Italian	Pronunciation
Thank you	**Grazie**	*graht*-tzee-yey
You're welcome	**Prego**	*prey*-go
Please	**Per favore**	*pehr* fah-*vohr*-eh
Yes	**Sì**	see
No	**No**	noh
Good morning or Good day	**Buongiorno**	bwohn-*djor*-noh
Good evening	**Buona sera**	*bwohn*-ah *say*-rah
Good night	**Buona notte**	*bwohn*-ah *noht*-tay
It's a pleasure to meet you.	**Piacere di conoscerla.**	pyah-*cheh*-reh dee *koh*-nohshehr-lah
My name is ____.	**Mi chiamo ____.**	mee *kyah*-moh
And yours?	**E lei?**	eh lay
Do you speak English?	**Parla inglese?**	*pahr*-lah een-*gleh*-seh
How are you?	**Come sta?**	*koh*-may *stah*
Very well	**Molto bene**	*mohl*-toh *behn*-ney
Goodbye	**Arrivederci**	ahr-ree-vah-*dehr*-chee
Excuse me (to get attention)	**Scusi**	*skoo*-zee
Excuse me (to get past someone)	**Permesso**	pehr-*mehs*-soh

GETTING AROUND

English	Italian	Pronunciation
Where is . . . ?	**Dovè . . . ?**	doh-*vey*
the station	**la stazione**	lah stat-tzee-*oh*-neh
a hotel	**un albergo**	oon ahl-*behr*-goh
a restaurant	**un ristorante**	oon reest-ohr-*ahnt*-eh
the bathroom	**il bagno**	eel *bahn*-nyoh

English   **Italian**   **Pronunciation**

English	Italian	Pronunciation
I am looking for . . .	**Cerco . . .**	*chehr*-koh
a porter	**un facchino**	oon fahk-*kee*-noh
the check-in counter	**il check-in**	eel check-in
the ticket counter	**la biglietteria**	lah beel-lyeht-teh-*ree*-ah
arrivals	**l'area arrivi**	*lah*-reh-ah ahr-*ree*-vee
departures	**l'area partenze**	*lah*-reh-ah pahr-*tehn*-tseh
gate number	**l'uscita numero**	loo-*shee*-tah *noo*-meh-roh
the waiting area	**l'area d'attesa**	*lah*-reh-ah daht-*teh*-zah
the men's restroom	**la toilette uomini**	lah twa-*leht woh*-mee-nee
the women's restroom	**la toilette donne**	lah twa-*leht dohn*-neh
the police station	**la stazione**	lah stah-*tsyoh*-neh
	di polizia	dee poh-lee-*tsee*-ah
a security guard	**una guardia**	*ooh*-nah *gwahr*-dyah dee
	di sicurezza	see-koo-*ret*-sah
the smoking area	**l'area fumatori**	*lah*-reh-ah foo-mah-*toh*-ree
the information booth	**l'ufficio**	loof-*fee*-choh
	informazioni	een-*fohr*-mah-*tsyoh*-nee
a public telephone	**un telefono pubblico**	oon teh-*leh*-foh-noh *poob*-blee-koh
an ATM/cashpoint	**un bancomat**	oon *bahn*-koh-maht
baggage claim	**il ritiro bagagli**	eel ree-*tee*-roh bah-*gahl*-lyee
a luggage cart	**un carrello**	oon kahr-*rehl*-loh
	portabagagli	*pohr*-tah-bah-*gahl*-lyee
a currency exchange	**un cambiavalute**	oon *kahm*-byah-vah-*loo*-teh
a cafe	**un caffè**	oon kahf-*feh*
a restaurant	**un ristorante**	oon ree-stoh-*rahn*-teh
a bar	**un bar**	oon bar
a bookstore	**una libreria**	*oo*-nah lee-breh-*ree*-ah
a duty-free shop	**un duty-free**	oon duty-free
To the left	**A sinistra**	ah see-*nees*-tra
To the right	**A destra**	ah *dehy*-stra
Straight ahead	**Avanti (***or* **sempre**	ahv-*vahn*-tee (*sehm*-pray
	diritto)	dee-*reet*-toh)

DINING

English	Italian	Pronunciation
Breakfast	**Prima colazione**	*pree*-mah coh-laht-tzee-*ohn*-ay
Lunch	**Pranzo**	*prahn*-zoh
Dinner	**Cena**	*chay*-nah
How much is it?	**Quanto costa?**	*kwan*-toh *coh*-sta
The check, please	**Il conto, per favore**	eel kon-toh *pehr* fah-*vohr*-eh

English	Italian	Pronunciation
When?	**Quando?**	*kwan*-doh
Yesterday	**Ieri**	ee-*yehr*-ree
Today	**Oggi**	*oh*-jee
Tomorrow	**Domani**	doh-*mah*-nee
What time is it?	**Che ore sono?**	kay *or*-ay *soh*-noh
It's one o'clock.	**È l'una.**	*eh loo*-nah
It's two o'clock.	**Sono le due.**	*soh*-noh leh *doo*-eh
It's two thirty.	**Sono le due e mezzo.**	*soh*-noh leh *doo*-eh eh *mehd*-dzoh
It's noon.	**È mezzogiorno.**	*eh* mehd-dzoh-*johr*-noh
It's midnight.	**È mezzanotte.**	*eh* mehd-dzah-*noht*-teh
It's early.	**È presto.**	*eh prehs*-toh
It's late.	**È tardi.**	*eh tahr*-dee
in the morning	**al mattino**	ahl maht-*tee*-noh
in the afternoon	**al pomeriggio**	ahl poh-meh-*reed*-joh
at night	**di notte**	dee *noht*-the

DAYS OF THE WEEK

English	Italian	Pronunciation
Monday	**Lunedì**	loo-nay-*dee*
Tuesday	**Martedì**	mart-ay-*dee*
Wednesday	**Mercoledì**	mehr-cohl-ay-*dee*
Thursday	**Giovedì**	joh-vay-*dee*
Friday	**Venerdì**	ven-nehr-*dee*
Saturday	**Sabato**	*sah*-bah-toh
Sunday	**Domenica**	doh-*mehn*-nee-kah

MONTHS & SEASONS

English	Italian	Pronunciation
January	**gennaio**	jehn-*nah*-yoh
February	**febbraio**	fehb-*brah*-yoh
March	**marzo**	*mahr*-tso
April	**aprile**	ah-*pree*-leh
May	**maggio**	*mahd*-joh
June	**giugno**	*jewn*-nyo
July	**luglio**	*lool*-lyo
August	**agosto**	ah-*gohs*-toh
September	**settembre**	seht-*tehm*-breh
October	**ottobre**	oht-*toh*-breh
November	**novembre**	noh-*vehm*-breh
December	**dicembre**	dee-*chehm*-breh

USEFUL TERMS

14

THE BASICS

English	Italian	Pronunciation
spring	**la primavera**	lah pree-mah-*veh*-rah
summer	**l'estate**	lehs-*tah*-teh
autumn	**l'autunno**	low-*toon*-noh
winter	**l'inverno**	leen-*vehr*-noh

NUMBERS

English	Italian	Pronunciation
1	**uno**	*oo*-noh
2	**due**	*doo*-ay
3	**tre**	tray
4	**quattro**	*kwah*-troh
5	**cinque**	*cheen*-kway
6	**sei**	say
7	**sette**	*set*-tay
8	**otto**	*oh*-toh
9	**nove**	*noh*-vay
10	**dieci**	dee-*ay*-chee
11	**undici**	*oon*-dee-chee
20	**venti**	*vehn*-tee
21	**ventuno**	vehn-*toon*-oh
22	**venti due**	*vehn*-tee *doo*-ay
30	**trenta**	*trayn*-tah
40	**quaranta**	kwah-*rahn*-tah
50	**cinquanta**	cheen-*kwan*-tah
60	**sessanta**	sehs-*sahn*-tah
70	**settanta**	seht-*tahn*-tah
80	**ottanta**	oht-*tahn*-tah
90	**novanta**	noh-*vahnt*-tah
100	**cento**	*chen*-toh
1,000	**mille**	*mee*-lay
5,000	**cinque milla**	*cheen*-kway *mee*-lah
10,000	**dieci milla**	dee-ay-chee mee-lah

2 A SHOPPER'S PHRASE FINDER

English	Italian	Pronunciation
Please tell me . . .	**Può dirmi per favore . . .**	*pwoh deer*-mee pehr fah-*voh*-reh
how to get to a mall	**come si arriva ad un centro commerciale**	*koh*-meh see ahr-*ree*-vah ahd oon *chehn*-troh kohm-mehr-*chah*-leh
the best place for shopping	**il posto migliore per fare compere**	eel *pohs*-toh meel-*lyoh*-reh pehr *fah*-reh *kohm*-peh-reh

English	Italian	Pronunciation
how to get	come si arriva	*koh*-meh see ahr-*ree*-vah
downtown	in centro	een *chehn*-troh
Where can I find a . . .	**Dove trovo . . .**	*doh*-veh *troh*-voh
antiques shop	**un negozio di antichità**	oon neh-*goh*-tsyoh dee ahn-tee-kee-*tah*
bookstore	**una libreria**	*oo*-nah lee-breh-*ree*-ah
cigar shop	**un tabaccaio**	oon tah-bahk-*kah*-yoh
clothing store for men/women/children	**un negozio di abbigliamento per uomo/donna/ bambini**	oon neh-*goh*-tsyoh dee ahb-beel-lyah-*mehn*-toh pehr *woh*-moh/*dohn*-nah/ bahm-*bee*-nee
designer fashion shop	**una boutique di moda fermata**	*oo*-nah boutique dee *moh*-dah feer-*mah*-tah
jewelry store	**una gioielleria**	*oo*-nah joh-yehl-leh-*ree*-ah
shoe store	**un negozio di scarpe**	oon neh-*goh*-tsyoh dee *skahr*-peh
souvenir shop	**un negozio di souvenir**	oon neh-*goh*-tsyoh dee souvenir
stationery store	**una cartoleria**	*oo*-nah kahr-toh-leh-*ree*-ah
toy store	**un negozio di giocattoli**	oon neh-*goh*-tsyoh dee joh-*kaht*-toh-lee
vintage clothing store	**un negozio di abiti usati**	oon neh-*goh*-tsyoh dee *ah*-bee-tee oo-*zah*-tee
flea market	**un mercatino delle pulci**	oon mehrkah-*tee*-noh *dehl*-leh *pool*-chee
I'm looking for a size . . .	**Cerco una taglia . . .**	*chehr*-koh *oo*-nah *tahl*-lyah
extra-small	**molto piccolo**	*mohl*-toh *peek*-koh-lah
small	**piccolo**	*peek*-koh-lah
medium	**media**	*meh*-dyah
large	**grande**	*grahn*-deh
extra-large	**molto grande**	*mohl*-toh *grahn*-deh
I'm looking for . . .	**Cerco . . .**	*chehr*-koh
cashmere	**qualcosa in cashmere**	kwahl-*koh*-zah een cashmere
a coat	**una giacca**	*oo*-nah *jahk*-kah
cotton pants	**dei pantaloni di cotone**	day pahn-tah-*loh*-nee dee koh-*toh*-neh
a hat	**un cappello/berretto**	oon kahp-*pehl*-loh/behr-*reht*-toh
a silk blouse	**una camicia di seta**	*oo*-nah kah-*mee*-chah dee *seh*-tah
socks	**dei calzini**	day kahl-*tsee*-nee
sunglasses	**degli occhiali da sole**	*dehl*-lyee ohk-*kyah*-lee dah *soh*-leh
sweaters	**delle maglie**	*dehl*-leh *mahl*-lyeh
a swimsuit	**un costume da bagno**	oon kohs-*too*-meh dah *bahn*-nyoh
underwear	**della biancheria intima**	*dehl*-lah byahn-keh-*ree*-ah *een*-tee-mah

English	Italian	Pronunciation
May I try it on?	**Posso provarlo?**	*pohs*-soh proh-*vahr*-loh
Where can I try this on?	**Dove posso provarlo?**	*doh*-veh *pohs*-soh proh-*vahr*-loh
This is . . .	**Questo è . . .**	*kwehs*-toh *eh*
too tight	**troppo stretto**	*trohp*-poh *streht*-toh
too loose	**troppo largo**	*trohp*-poh *lahr*-goh
too long	**troppo lungo**	*trohp*-poh *loon*-goh
too short	**troppo corto**	*trohp*-poh *kohr*-toh
This fits great!	**È perfetto!**	*eh* pehr-*feht*-toh
Thanks, I'll take it.	**Grazie, lo prendo.**	*grah*-tsyeh loh *prehn*-doh
Do you have that in . . .	**Ce l'ha in . . .**	cheh *lah* een
a smaller/larger size	**una taglia più piccola/grande**	*oo*-nah *tahl*-lya *pyoo* *peek*-koh-lah/*grahn*-deh
a different color	**un altro colore**	oon *ahl*-troh koh-*loh*-reh
How much is it?	**Quanto costa?**	*kwahn*-toh *kohs*-tah
Is there a craft/artisan market?	**C'è un mercato di artigianato?**	ch-*eh* oon mehr-*kah*-toh dee ahr-tee-jah-*nah*-toh
That's beautiful. May I look at it?	**Che bello. Posso vederlo?**	keh *behl*-loh *pohs*-soh veh-*dehr*-loh
When is the farmers' market open?	Quando apre il mercato di frutta e verdura?	*kwahn*-doh *ah*-preh eel mehr-*kah*-toh dee *froot*-tah eh vehr-*doo*-rah
Is that open every day of the week?	**È aperto tutti i giorni della settimana?**	*eh* ah-*pehr*-toh *toot*-tee ee *johr*-nee *dehl*-lah seht-tee-*mah*-nah
How much does that cost?	**Quanto costa?**	*kwahn*-toh *kohs*-tah
That's too expensive.	**È troppo caro.**	*eh* *trohp*-poh *kah*-roh
How much for two?	**Quanto per due?**	*kwahn*-toh pehr *doo*-eh
Do I get a discount if I buy two or more?	**Mi fa lo sconto se ne compro due o più?**	mee fah loh *skohn*-toh seh neh *kohm*-proh *doo*-eh oh *pyoo*
Do I get a discount if I pay in cash?	**Mi fa lo sconto se pago in contanti?**	mee fah loh *skohn*-toh she *pah*-goh een kohn-*tahn*-tee
No thanks. Maybe I'll come back.	**No grazie. Magari torno.**	noh *grah*-tsyeh mah-*gah*-ree *tohr*-noh
Would you take euros?	**Vanno bene euro?**	*vahn*-noh *beh*-neh *eh*-oo-roh
That's a deal!	**Affare fatto!**	ahf-*fah*-reh *faht*-toh
Do you have a less expensive one?	**Ne ha uno meno caro?**	neh *ah* oo-noh *meh*-no *kah*-roh

English	Italian	Pronunciation	447
Is there VAT tax?	**C'è l'IVA?**	ch-*eh lee*-vah	
May I have the	**Posso avere**	*pohs*-soh ah-*veh*-reh	
VAT forms?	**un modulo per**	oon *moh*-doo-loh pehr	
(Europe only)	**il rimborso dell'IVA?**	eel reem-*bohr*-soh dehl-*lee*-vah	
Is there a _____	**C'è _____**	ch-*eh* _____	
nearby?	**qui vicino?**	kwee vee-*chee*-noh	
bookstore	**una libreria**	*oo*-nah lee-breh-*ree*-ah	
newsstand	**un'edicola**	oon-eh-*dee*-koh-lah	
Do you have _____	**Avete _____**	ah-*veh*-teh _____	
in English?	**in inglese?**	een een-*gleh*-seh	
books	**libri**	*lee*-bree	
books about	**libri di storia**	*lee*-bree dee *stoh*-ryah	
local history	**locale**	loh-*kah*-leh	
magazines	**riviste**	ree-*vees*-teh	
maps	**cartine**	kahr-*tee*-neh	
newspapers	**giornali**	johr-*nah*-lee	
picture books	**libri illustrate**	*lee*-bree eel-loos-*trah*-tee	
travel guides	**guide turistiche**	*gwee*-deh too-*rees*-tee-keh	
Can I play this	**Funziona questo negli**	foon-*tsyoh*-nah *kwehs*-toh *nehl*-lyee	
in the U.S.?	**Stati Uniti?**	*stah*-tee oo-*nee*-tee	
Will this game work	**Questo gioco funziona**	*kwehs*-toh *joh*-koh foon-*tsyoh*-nah	
on my game console	**su una console**	soo *oo*-nah kohn-*sohl*	
in the U.S.?	**americana?**	ah-meh-ree-*kah*-nah	
Do you have this	**C'è questo in formato**	ch-*eh kwehs*-toh een fohr-*mah*-toh	
in a U.S. market	**americano?**	ah-meh-ree-*kah*-noh	
format?			
Can you convert	**Si può convertire**	see *pwoh* kohn-vehr-*tee*-reh	
this to a U.S.	**questo in formato**	*kwehs*-toh een fohr-*mah*-toh	
market format?	**americano?**	ah-meh-ree-*kah*-noh	
Will this work with	**Questo funziona con**	*kwehs*-toh foon-*tsyoh*-nah kohn	
a 110V AC adaptor?	**un adattatore**	oon ah-daht-tah-*toh*-reh	
	da 110 volts?	dah *chehn*-toh-*dyeh*-chee volts	
Do you have an	**Avete un adattatore**	Ah-*veh*-teh oon ah-daht-tah-*toh*-reh	
adaptor plug for	**da 110 a**	dah *chehn*-toh-*dyeh*-chee ah	
110 to 220 volts?	**220 volts?**	doo-eh-*chehn*-toh-*vehn*-tee volts	
Do you sell electronic	**Vendete adattatori**	vehn-*deh*-teh ah-daht-tah-*toh*-ree	
adaptors here?	**per sistemi**	pehr sees-*teh*-mee	
	elettronici?	eh-leht-*troh*-nee-chee	
Is it safe to use	**Posso usare il**	*pohs*-soh oo-*zah*-reh eel	
my laptop with	**computer portatile**	com puter pohr-*tah*-tee-leh	
this adaptor?	**con questo adattatore?**	kohn *kwehs*-toh ah-daht-tah-*toh*-reh	

English	Italian	Pronunciation
If it doesn't work, may I return it?	**Se non funziona, posso portarlo indietro?**	seh nohn foon-*tsyoh*-nah *pohs*-soh pohr-*tahr*-loh een-*dyeh*-troh
May I try it here in the store?	**Posso provarlo qui in negozio?**	*pohs*-soh proh-*vahr*-loh kwee een neh-*goh*-tsyoh

3 ARCHITECTURAL TERMS

Ambone   A pulpit, either serpentine or simple in form, erected in an Italian church.

Apse   The half-rounded extension behind the main altar of a church; Christian tradition dictates that it be placed at the eastern end of an Italian church, the side closest to Jerusalem.

Atrium   A courtyard, open to the sky, in an ancient Roman house; the term also applies to the courtyard nearest the entrance of an early Christian church.

Baldacchino (also ciborium)   A columned stone canopy, usually placed above the altar of a church; spelled in English *baldachin* or *baldaquin.*

Baptistery   A separate building or a separate area in a church where the rite of baptism is held.

Basilica   Any rectangular public building, usually divided into three aisles by rows of columns. In ancient Rome, this architectural form was frequently used for places of public assembly and law courts; later, Roman Christians adapted the form for many of their early churches.

Caldarium   The steam room of a Roman bath.

Campanile   A bell tower, often detached, of a church.

Capital   The top of a column, often carved and usually categorized into one of three orders: Doric, Ionic, or Corinthian.

Castrum   A carefully planned Roman military camp, whose rectangular form, straight streets, and systems of fortified gates became standardized throughout the empire; modern cities that began as Roman camps and still more or less maintain their original forms include Chester (England), Barcelona (Spain), and such Italian cities as Lucca, Aosta, Como, Brescia, Florence, and Ancona.

Cavea   The curved row of seats in a classical theater; the most prevalent shape was that of a semicircle.

Cella   The sanctuary, or most sacred interior section, of a Roman pagan temple.

Chancel   Section of a church containing the altar.

Cornice   The decorative flange defining the uppermost part of a classical or neoclassical facade.

Cortile   Courtyard or cloisters ringed with a gallery of arches or lintels set atop columns.

Crypt   A church's main burial place, usually below the choir.

Cupola   A dome.

Duomo   Cathedral.

Forum   The main square and principal gathering place of any Roman town, usually adorned with the city's most important temples and civic buildings.

Grotesques   Carved and painted faces, deliberately ugly, used by everyone from the Etruscans to the architects of the Renaissance; they're especially amusing when set into fountains.

Hypogeum   Subterranean burial chambers, usually of pre-Christian origins.

Loggia   Roofed balcony or gallery.

Lozenge   An elongated four-sided figure that, along with stripes, was one of the distinctive signs of the architecture of Pisa.

Narthex   The anteroom, or enclosed porch, of a Christian church.

Nave   The largest and longest section of a church, usually devoted to sheltering or seating worshipers and often divided by aisles.

Palazzo   A palace or other important building.

Piano Nobile   The main floor of a palazzo (sometimes the second floor).

Pietra Dura   Richly ornate assemblage of semiprecious stones mounted on a flat decorative surface, perfected during the 1600s in Florence.

Pieve   A parish church.

Portico   A porch, usually crafted from wood or stone.

Pulvin   A four-sided stone that serves as a substitute for the capital of a column, often decoratively carved, sometimes into biblical scenes.

Putti   Plaster cherubs whose chubby forms often decorate the interiors of baroque chapels and churches.

Stucco   Colored plaster composed of sand, powdered marble, water, and lime, either molded into statuary or applied in a thin concretelike layer to the exterior of a building.

Telamone   Structural column carved into a standing male form; female versions are called *caryatids.*

Thermae   Roman baths.

Transenna   Stone (usually marble) screen separating the altar area from the rest of an early Christian church.

Travertine   The stone from which ancient and Renaissance Rome was built, it's known for its hardness, light coloring, and tendency to be pitted or flecked with black.

Tympanum   The half-rounded space above the portal of a church, whose semicircular space usually showcases a sculpture.

USEFUL TERMS

14

ITALIAN MENU TERMS

4 ITALIAN MENU TERMS

Abbacchio   Roast haunch or shoulder of lamb baked and served in a casserole and sometimes flavored with anchovies.

Agnolotti   A crescent-shaped pasta shell stuffed with a mix of chopped meat, spices, vegetables, and cheese; when prepared in rectangular versions, the same combination of ingredients is identified as ravioli.

Amaretti   Crunchy, sweet almond-flavored macaroons.

Anguilla alla veneziana   Eel cooked in a sauce made from tuna and lemon.

Antipasti   Succulent tidbits served at the beginning of a meal (before the pasta), whose ingredients might include slices of cured meats, seafood (especially shellfish), and cooked and seasoned vegetables.

Aragosta   Lobster.

Arrosto   Roasted meat.

Baccalà   Dried and salted codfish.

Bagna cauda   Hot and well-seasoned sauce, heavily flavored with anchovies, designed for dipping raw vegetables; literally translated as "hot bath."

Bistecca alla fiorentina   Florentine-style steaks, coated before grilling with olive oil, pepper, lemon juice, salt, and parsley.

Bocconcini   Veal layered with ham and cheese, and then fried.

Bollito misto   Assorted boiled meats served on a single platter.

Braciola   Pork chop.

Bresaola   Air-dried spiced beef.

Bruschetta   Toasted bread, heavily slathered with olive oil and garlic and often topped with tomatoes.

Bucatini   Coarsely textured hollow spaghetti.

Busecca alla Milanese   Tripe (beef stomach) flavored with herbs and vegetables.

Cacciucco ali livornese   Seafood stew.

Calzone   Pizza dough rolled with the chef's choice of sausage, tomatoes, cheese, and so on, and then baked into a kind of savory turnover.

Cannelloni   Tubular dough stuffed with meat, cheese, or vegetables and then baked in a creamy white sauce.

Cappellacci alla ferrarese   Pasta stuffed with pumpkin.

Cappelletti   Small ravioli ("little hats") stuffed with meat or cheese.

Carciofi   Artichokes.

Do's & Don'ts

Italians measure foodstuffs by the kilogram or smaller 100g unit (**ettogrammo** abbreviated to *etto,* equivalent to just under 4 oz.). **Pizzerie al taglio** (pizza slice shops) generally run on this system, but hand gestures can suffice. A good server poises the knife, then asks for approval before cutting. **Più** *(pyoo)* is "more," **meno** *(meh*-noh) "less." **Basta** (*bahs*-tah) means "enough." To express "half" of something, say **mezzo** (*mehd*-zoh).

Carpaccio   Thin slices of raw cured beef, sometimes in a piquant sauce.

Cassatta alla siciliana   A richly caloric dessert that combines layers of sponge cake, sweetened ricotta cheese, and candied fruit, bound together with chocolate buttercream icing.

Cervello al burro nero   Brains in black-butter sauce.

Cima alla genovese   Baked filet of veal rolled into a tube-shaped package containing eggs, mushrooms, and sausage.

Coppa   Cured morsels of pork filet encased in sausage skins, served in slices.

Costoletta alla milanese   Veal cutlet dredged in bread crumbs, fried, and sometimes flavored with cheese.

Cozze   Mussels.

Fagioli   White beans.

Fave   Fava beans.

Fegato alla veneziana   Thinly sliced calves' liver fried with salt, pepper, and onions.

Focaccia   Ideally, concocted from potato-based dough left to rise slowly for several hours and then garnished with tomato sauce, garlic, basil, salt, and pepper and drizzled with olive oil; similar to a deep-dish pizza most popular in the deep south, especially Bari.

Fontina   Rich cow's-milk cheese.

Frittata   Italian omelet.

Fritto misto   A deep-fried medley of whatever small fish, shellfish, and squid are available in the marketplace that day.

Fusilli   Spiral-shaped pasta.

Gelato (produzione propria)   Ice cream (homemade).

Gnocchi   Dumplings usually made from potatoes *(gnocchi alla patate)* or from semolina *(gnocchi alla romana),* often stuffed with combinations of cheese, spinach, vegetables, or whatever combinations strike the chef's fancy.

Gorgonzola   One of the most famous blue-veined cheeses of Europe—strong, creamy, and aromatic.

Granità   Flavored ice, usually with lemon or coffee.

Insalata di frutti di mare   Seafood salad (usually including shrimp and squid) garnished with pickles, lemon, olives, and spices.

Involtini   Thinly sliced beef, veal, or pork, rolled, stuffed, and fried.

Minestrone   A rich and savory vegetable soup usually sprinkled with grated parmigiano and studded with noodles.

Mortadella   Mild pork sausage, fashioned into large cylinders and served sliced; the original lunchmeat bologna (because its most famous center of production is Bologna).

Mozzarella   A nonfermented cheese, made from the fresh milk of a buffalo (or, if unavailable, from a cow), boiled, and then kneaded into a rounded ball, served fresh.

Mozzarella con pomodori (also caprese)   Fresh tomatoes with fresh mozzarella, basil, pepper, and olive oil.

Nervetti   A northern Italian antipasto made from chewy pieces of calves' foot or shin.

Osso buco Beef or veal knuckle slowly braised until the cartilage is tender and then served with a highly flavored sauce.

Pancetta Herb-flavored pork belly, rolled into a cylinder and sliced—the Italian bacon.

Panettone Sweet yellow-colored bread baked in the form of a brioche.

Panna Heavy cream.

Pansotti Pasta stuffed with greens, herbs, and cheeses, usually served with a walnut sauce.

Pappardelle alle lepre Pasta with rabbit sauce.

Parmigiano Parmesan, a hard and salty yellow cheese usually grated over pastas and soups but also eaten alone; also known as *granna*. The best is Parmigiano-Reggiano.

Peperoni Green, yellow, or red sweet peppers (not to be confused with pepperoni).

Pesci al cartoccio Fish baked in a parchment envelope with onions, parsley, and herbs.

Pesto A flavorful green sauce made from basil leaves, cheese, garlic, marjoram, and (if available) pine nuts.

Piccata al Marsala Thin escalope of veal braised in a pungent sauce flavored with Marsala wine.

Piselli al prosciutto Peas with strips of ham.

Pizza Specific varieties include *capricciosa* (its ingredients can vary widely, depending on the chef's culinary vision and the ingredients at hand), *margherita* (with tomato sauce, cheese, fresh basil, and memories of the first queen of Italy, Marguerite di Savoia, in whose honor it was first made by a Neapolitan chef), *napoletana* (with ham, capers, tomatoes, oregano, cheese, and the distinctive taste of anchovies), *quattro stagione* (translated as "four seasons" because of the array of fresh vegetables in it; it also contains ham and bacon), and *siciliana* (with black olives, capers, and cheese).

Pizzaiola A process in which something (usually a beefsteak) is covered in a tomato-and-oregano sauce.

Polenta Thick porridge or mush made from cornmeal flour.

Polenta de uccelli Assorted small birds roasted on a spit and served with polenta.

Polenta e coniglio Rabbit stew served with polenta.

Polla alla cacciatore Chicken with tomatoes and mushrooms cooked in wine.

Pollo all diavola Highly spiced grilled chicken.

Ragù Meat sauce.

Ricotta A soft bland cheese made from cow's or sheep's milk.

Risotto Italian rice.

Risotto alla milanese Rice with saffron and wine.

Salsa verde "Green sauce," made from capers, anchovies, lemon juice and/or vinegar, and parsley.

Saltimbocca Veal scallop layered with prosciutto and sage; its name literally translates as "jump in your mouth," a reference to its tart and savory flavor.

Salvia Sage.

Scaloppina alla Valdostana Escalope of veal stuffed with cheese and ham.

Scaloppine Thin slices of veal coated in flour and sautéed in butter.

Semifreddo A frozen dessert; usually ice cream with sponge cake.

Seppia Cuttlefish (a kind of squid); its black ink is used for flavoring in certain sauces for pasta and also in risotto dishes.

Sogliola Sole.

Spaghetti A long, round, thin pasta, variously served: *alla bolognese* (with ground meat, mushrooms, peppers, and so on), *alla carbonara* (with bacon, black pepper, and eggs), *al pomodoro* (with tomato sauce), *al sugo/ragù* (with meat sauce), and *alle vongole* (with clam sauce).

Spiedini Pieces of meat grilled on a skewer over an open flame.

Strangolaprete Small nuggets of pasta, usually served with sauce; the name is literally translated as "priest-choker."

Stufato Beef braised in white wine with vegetables.

Tagliatelle Flat egg noodles.

Tonno Tuna.

Tortelli Pasta dumplings stuffed with ricotta and greens.

Tortellini Rings of dough stuffed with minced and seasoned meat, and served either in soups or as a full-fledged pasta covered with sauce.

Trenette Thin noodles served with pesto sauce and potatoes.

Trippe alla fiorentina Beef tripe (stomach).

Vermicelli Very thin spaghetti.

Vitello tonnato Cold sliced veal covered with tuna-fish sauce.

Zabaglione/zabaione Egg yolks whipped into the consistency of a custard, flavored with Marsala, and served warm as a dessert.

Zampone Pigs' feet stuffed with spicy seasoned port, boiled and sliced.

Zuccotto A liqueur-soaked sponge cake, molded into a dome and layered with chocolate, nuts, and whipped cream.

Zuppa inglese Sponge cake soaked in custard.

INDEX

See also Accommodations and Restaurant indexes, below.

RESTAURANTS